THE COMMUNIST
INTERNATIONAL
1919–1943
DOCUMENTS

VOLUME II

THE COMMUNIST INTERNATIONAL

1919–1943

DOCUMENTS

SELECTED AND EDITED BY

JANE DEGRAS

VOLUME II
1923–1928

Issued under the auspices of the
Royal Institute of International Affairs

OXFORD UNIVERSITY PRESS

LONDON NEW YORK TORONTO

1960

Oxford University Press, Amen House, London E.C.4

GLASGOW NEW YORK TORONTO MELBOURNE WELLINGTON
BOMBAY CALCUTTA MADRAS KARACHI KUALA LUMPUR
CAPE TOWN IBADANI NAIROB ACCRA

PRINTED IN GREAT BRITAIN
AT THE UNIVERSITY PRESS, OXFORD
BY VIVIAN RIDLER
PRINTER TO THE UNIVERSITY

PREFACE

THE period covered by this second volume opens with the entry of French troops into the Ruhr, an event which heightened Soviet interest in German affairs. The disturbances which followed, the importance of the German Communist Party, and the bitterness of the quarrels among its leaders, explain the relatively large number of documents included here dealing directly with German affairs, and the attention given to them in more general documents from which extracts have been made. For a number of reasons the documents concerning the British Communist Party are more numerous than would be warranted by its size and significance. In the first place, relations between the United Kingdom and the USSR went through a number of crises in the period covered, while the formation of the first Labour Government, the establishment of the Anglo-Soviet trade union committee, and the General Strike, all gave rise to acute controversies within the Comintern.

No justification is needed for the number of documents on China in the latter part of the volume. With the defeat of what was called the Chinese revolution of 1925–7, and the dissolution of the Anglo-Soviet trade union committee, the 'united front' period of Comintern history came to an end, to be replaced, in the year with which this volume closes, by a policy summarized in the slogan 'class against class', the parallel within the Third International of the policy of forced industrialization and collectivization within the USSR. What may be called the agrarian Soviet phase of the Chinese communist movement is not dealt with here, although its beginnings were apparent in 1927, since it properly belongs to the later years.

Interest in Italy and France declined after 1923 while Asia began to claim greater attention. Little is known about such communist movements as existed in the Middle East until after the period covered here. There are relatively more documents concerned with questions of organization than in the first volume; this corresponds with the greater output of organizational directives; only the most important have been selected for inclusion.

The influence of the disputes within the CPSU is clearly discernible throughout these years. Between the fourth Comintern congress at the end of 1922 and the sixth in the summer of 1928, the leading personnel of the Third International was almost entirely changed, largely as a result, direct or indirect, of the struggle within the CPSU.

The introductory notes are, on the whole, longer than they were in the first volume. The documents published by the Comintern were greater in number and length, and it seemed useful to mention and summarize some which, for reasons of space, could not be included. Secondly, I have made extensive use in them of the Trotsky archives and the papers of Jules Humbert-Droz concerned with his work for the ECCI before he was expelled in 1929.

I owed the opportunity to do so to the generosity of the Rockefeller Foundation, whose grant to the Royal Institute of International Affairs enabled me to spend some months in the United States, and I should like to express my thanks here. To the Librarian and staff of the Houghton Library at Harvard, which houses the Trotsky archives, to the Director and staff of the Harvard Russian Research Center, where I consulted the Humbert-Droz papers, to the Hoover Institute and Library of Stanford University, with its unrivalled collection of Russian materials, and to the Slavonic Division of the Library of Congress I also owe my thanks for their unfailing assistance and for the great friendliness with which I was received.

I should also like to thank Mr. Peter Berton, Mr. E. H. Carr, Mr. H. Dewar, Mr. Theodore Draper, Mr. Paul Langer, and Miss Ruth McVey, who gave me the advantage of their specialized knowledge. To Mr. R. C. North I owe the opportunity to read, in his typescript copy, Mr. S. Tagore's account of the Indian Communist Party; I learnt much from Mr. J. Rothschild's study of the Bulgarian Communist Party, which I read in manuscript, and Mr. Marshall Windmiller and Mr. G. Overstreet allowed me to make use of the material they had collected for their book, since published, on *Communism in India*. To all of them I am grateful.

As in the first volume, I have used mainly the German text of documents for these translations, comparing them when any doubt arose with the Russian. The only major discrepancy that came to my notice, however, occurs in the English version of the 'Bolshevization Theses' (pp. 199–200).

It has not been possible to establish the correct names of a number of persons mentioned in this volume, since the use of pseudonyms was a common practice in a number of communist parties. Footnotes reproduced from the original are shown with an asterisk; footnotes added by me are numbered.

J. D.

April 1959

CONTENTS

TABLE OF DOCUMENTS

1923

1927

January 1923   *Inprekorr*, iii, 2, p. 31, 6 *January* 1923

[In order to reconcile the CGTU, and to attract syndicalist organizations, the RILU, at its second congress at the end of 1922, replaced its earlier method of collaboration with the Comintern, effected by reciprocal representation, by the establishment of a joint committee, consisting of three representatives each of the ECCI and the RILU Executive, and one delegate from the Young Communist International (YCI). Its decisions, if unanimous, were binding on all organizations affiliated to the three bodies. *Ad hoc* committees were to be set up for special purposes; one of the earliest was the International Committee of Action against the War Danger and Fascism, of which Klara Zetkin and Henri Barbusse were joint secretaries.

Speaking at the June meeting of the ECCI later in the year, Zinoviev referred to the united front as a strategic manœuvre, necessary because the social-democratic leaders had more popular support than the Comintern had believed. 'What is this strategic manœuvre? It consists in our appealing constantly to people who, we know in advance, will not go along with us.']

A few days ago two international proletarian congresses were held in Moscow: the world congress of the Communist International and the world congress of the red revolutionary trade unions. More than sixty communist parties of all countries, revolutionary trade unions of the entire world, worked out a plan for future operations against the sharpening capitalist offensive. . . .

With unashamed cynicism the bourgeoisie are lengthening the working day, reducing wages, imposing new taxes, using lockouts against workers who take defensive action, and mobilizing their armed fascist bands against the working class. Instead of cutting down the enormous expenditure on the army and navy, on the maintenance of armed bands and a large police force, instead of pursuing a peace policy and using idle capital to support the ruined and exhausted working population, the unemployed disabled ex-servicemen, and the hungry children and proletarian mothers, instead of that the bourgeoisie are feverishly building new weapons and means of destruction, and holding the Damocles sword of new wars over the entire world. And at the same time they are draining the last living strength of the proletariat, snatching the last crust from the proletarian child. While in Russia, shattered by imperialist intervention, life is beginning to improve steadily, the situation in the capitalist countries is becoming more and more difficult and painful. In spite of the repeated disarmament proposals of the proletarian republic, the capitalist States are pushing militarism to the utmost. The situation will become more and more hopeless, unless the working class mobilizes all its forces.

Therefore, comrades, the two congresses call on you to form a united front against capital. . . .

Unless the working class is united in such a struggle, its separate groups and sections will be defeated one by one. That is why our congresses decided to fight, before everything else and at any cost, for the unity of the trade union movement. But the bourgeoisie have powerful supporters in the social-democrats and the trade union leaders. And precisely now, when it is more than ever essential to unite all forces, these gentlemen, who sell the proletariat to the Stinneses of this world and at the Hague ally themselves with bourgeois pacifists, are expelling communists from the trade unions. These expulsions are the fruit of a devilish conspiracy against the proletariat. Even the bourgeoisie could not have thought up anything better to disorganize the forces of the proletariat at a moment when a furious attack on the workers is being prepared.

We call on all honest workers, men and women, regardless of their party affiliation, to defend the unity of the trade unions. Do not let the agents of capital destroy the unity of the working class. Defend that unity with your hard proletarian fists!

The reformist socialist parties and the trade union leaders are acting on the direct instructions of the bourgeoisie, who are trying to beat the working class down section by section. At the same time they are trying by the most cunning tricks to deceive and mislead the working class. In Germany social-democracy pretends to be in opposition, while Ebert, the leader of that party, is President of the Stinnes Republic; in Italy the reformists ostensibly oppose the fascists, but in reality support them; in England the leaders of the Labour Party defend the government which keeps Ireland under by fire and sword. In reality the reformists are out to help the bourgeoisie at whatever cost to rebuild the capitalist world at the expense of the working class, and for this purpose they have to split the trade unions and the labour movement.

Our congresses brought the revolutionary trade union associations closer together than ever before. They instructed our executives to use every favourable opportunity to approach Amsterdam and the social-democrats with the demand for a common fight against capitalist attack. This is where your support, the support of the working masses, is required. Force your leaders towards a united front. And if they stand out stubbornly against it, bring about a united front over their heads, sweeping away all obstacles to united struggle.

The experience of working-class struggle has shown that capitalist governments are not prepared to renounce even a part of capitalist profits. They are not prepared to introduce a single reform, to make a single concession to the working class. Therefore:

Through united struggle to a workers' government.

You must fight for a government of workers' organizations. You must put the rudder of State into the hands of the delegates of the working class and push out the representatives of capital, of the banks, the stock exchange, the cartels. This is the goal that must light up your path of struggle. . . .

The oppressed people of the colonies and the young proletariat of Japan and China are uniting with us. Only the Communist International and the Red International of Labour Unions support the colonial movement against the London, Paris, and New York moneybags.

United front with the young workers! United front with the village poor! United front with the oppressed colonies! All forces against the Moloch of capital—that is our chief slogan.

Fight the disgrace of our time, the Versailles Treaty and the other so-called peace treaties. . . . This treaty harbours new wars in itself. Not for nothing are new battleships and aircraft and artillery being built. We must arm ourselves to ward off the coming devastating war.

On behalf of the Communist International we proposed at the Hague the creation of a united front against war. Our proposal was flatly rejected. The leaders of the Second International voted for a resolution calling for a general strike in the event of war. But this is open treachery, for they have not disavowed defence of the fatherland, they rejected the proposal to conduct propaganda among the soldiers, they solemnly declared that in the event of war they would do as they did in 1914. At the Hague conference they formed a bloc with the bourgeoisie and rejected a bloc with the revolutionary wing of the labour movement.

Comrades! Proletarians! Choose your road! Which unity will you fight for, unity with the bourgeoisie who are attacking you, strangling you, and stealing your last penny?

No! A thousand times no! You will fight for the unity of the working class!

LETTER FROM THE COMINTERN TO THE AMERICAN WORKERS' PARTY

January 1923 *Inprekorr*, iii, 8, p. 60, 11 *January* 1923

[The fourth congress of the Comintern in November 1922 had set up an American commission, which included *inter alia* Zinoviev, Bukharin, Radek, Kuusinen, and Lozovsky; it was chiefly concerned with the pros and cons of communist support for the Farmer-Labor Party, to which a strong group of American communists objected, and with the disputes between those who wished to concentrate on illegal activities and those who advocated a legal party. The commission recommended a legal party (with 'an illegal apparatus in reserve') and support for a Labour Party based, like the British Labour Party, on the trade unions. The second congress of the Workers' Party, which was held in New York at the end of December 1922, formally accepted the leadership of the Comintern, and applied for admission.]

The Communist International has decided to admit your party into its ranks only as a sympathizing party. That however does not in any way diminish the importance of the tasks confronting you.

The Communist International considers that the most important task of the American workers' movement is to unite the broadest possible masses of the workers under one common flag for a united mass fight against the capitalist offensive. Therefore your party must regard it as a primary task to close the proletarian ranks and to rally all those elements who really oppose capital not only on paper, but in action, not only with resolutions but with real struggles, and who are prepared to intensify that struggle. To win the masses, to liberate them from the influence of capital and of its hirelings, this is your primary task. This task, however, can be accomplished only if the party adapts itself to real life, intervenes in every conflict between capital and labour, supports the workers in every strike, carefully follows the daily life of the working masses, makes its press the mouthpiece of the daily needs and the daily struggle of the working class, generalizes these struggles and explains them from the standpoint of the principal basic ideas of the emancipation of the proletariat from the capitalist yoke.

The correct application of united front tactics is particularly important. The curse and the tragedy of the proletariat consists in this, that in the yellow reformist leaders of the trade unions and the socialist parties the bourgeoisie have at their disposal faithful servants and agents, who rely on the labour aristocracy. The curse and the tragedy of the workers' movement consists in this, that the bourgeoisie have been able to exploit the gulf between skilled and unskilled workers, between the workers of different nations and races. Your young party must learn at all costs to unite the masses, over the heads of the yellow leaders and in spite of the yellow leaders. These leaders now want to split the movement. That was predicted by Jack London in his novel *The Iron Heel*. That is why your party must systematically expose these traitors to the workers' cause, by proposing a common fight with them for the basic demands of the working class, and uniting behind this slogan ever wider circles of workers. The question of work in the trade unions is particularly important. It is necessary to win one position after another in the unions, constantly emphasizing our slogan of the unity of the movement. It will be a difficult, long, and stubborn struggle. But history will decide it in your favour, comrades, if you conduct an energetic struggle with the necessary enthusiasm and unity in your own ranks.

ECCI RESOLUTION ON THE RELATIONS BETWEEN THE CHINESE COM-
MUNIST PARTY AND THE KUOMINTANG

12 *January* 1923   *Strategiya i Taktika Kominterna*, p. 112

[In June 1920 Voitinsky was sent to China as Comintern delegate and established his headquarters in Shanghai. In July 1921 twelve Chinese communists
(including Mao Tse-tung), meeting in that city under the leadership of Chen
Tu-hsiu, founded the Chinese Communist Party. The majority at this first
meeting, which was attended on behalf of the CI by Maring (the Dutch Communist Sneevliet), were unwilling to support Sun Yat-sen and the Kuomintang
(KMT), and the first overtures were made at Moscow's instigation. (At about
the same time a Chinese communist group was being organized in France; it
included Chou En-lai and Li Li-san.) In May 1922, at the second CCP congress, attended by twenty delegates, the party decided to affiliate to the
Comintern, and to establish a united front with the KMT. The manifesto of the
second CCP congress stated that 'the proletariat's urgent task is to act jointly
with the democratic party to establish a united front of democratic revolution
to struggle for the overthrow of the military and for the organization of a real
democratic government'. But a few weeks later, again persuaded by Maring,
the central committee agreed reluctantly that members should join the KMT
as individuals. Maring argued that the KMT was not a bourgeois party, but a
coalition party of all classes. (This was later defined as a coalition of four
classes—bourgeoisie, petty bourgeoisie, peasantry, and proletariat.) Maring
convened a meeting of the CC in August 1922 and urged entry into the KMT in
order to transform it into a revolutionary force. Though the majority (including
Chen) were opposed to this, Maring invoked the authority of the Comintern, and
the proposal was agreed to. At the same time another Comintern representative,
Dalin, was discussing with Sun Yat-sen the possibility of a KMT–CCP alliance.
Sun Yat-sen, at first also reluctant, looked to Russia for practical aid. Arthur Ran-
some reported Sun Yat-sen as saying: 'The Republic is my child. It is in danger
of drowning. . . . I call for help to England and America. They stand on the
bank and jeer at me. Now there comes a Russian straw. Drowning, I clutch at
it. England and America on the bank shout to me on no account to clutch that
Russian straw. But do they help me? No. . . . I know that it is a straw, but it is
better than nothing.' The alliance between the two parties was given a formal
character after the joint statement issued on 26 January 1923 by Joffe, representing the Soviet Commissariat for Foreign Affairs, and Sun Yat-sen. Borodin
arrived in Canton as adviser to Sun Yat-sen from the Russian Communist
Party in the autumn of 1923. He drafted (in English) the constitution of the
KMT. According to Trotsky's own account, he was from the beginning opposed
to the communists entering the Kuomintang; it had been first discussed in the
political bureau of the Russian CP.]

1. The only serious national-revolutionary group in China is the
Kuomintang, which is based partly on the liberal-democratic bourgeoisie
and petty bourgeoisie, partly on the intelligentsia and workers.

2. Since the independent workers' movement in the country is still weak, and since the central task for China is the national revolution against the imperialists and their feudal agents within the country, and since, moreover, the working class is directly interested in the solution of this national-revolutionary problem, while still being insufficiently differentiated as a wholly independent social force, the ECCI considers it necessary that action between the Kuomintang and the young CCP should be co-ordinated.

3. Consequently in present conditions it is expedient for members of the CCP to remain in the Kuomintang.

4. But this should not be at the cost of obliterating the specific political features of the CCP. The party must maintain its independent organization with a strictly centralized apparatus. The most important specific tasks of the CCP are to organize and educate the working masses, to build trade unions and thus establish a basis for a powerful mass communist party. In this work the CCP should appear under its own colours, distinct from any other political group, while avoiding any conflict with the national-revolutionary movement.

5. In regard to foreign policy the CCP should oppose any overtures of the Kuomintang to the capitalist Powers and their agents, the Chinese warlords, and those hostile to proletarian Russia.

6. On the other hand the CCP should try to persuade the Kuomintang to unite its forces with those of Soviet Russia for a common struggle against European, American, and Japanese imperialism.

7. While supporting the Kuomintang in all campaigns on the national-revolutionary front, to the extent that it conducts an objectively correct policy, the CCP should not merge with it and should not during these campaigns haul down its own flag.

APPEAL OF THE COMINTERN AND PROFINTERN EXECUTIVES TO ALL WORKERS, PEASANTS, AND SOLDIERS ON THE ENTRY OF FRENCH TROOPS INTO THE RUHR

13 *January* 1923   *Inprekorr*, iii, 11, p. 75, 15 *January* 1923

[A few days before the entry of French troops into the Ruhr because of Germany's failure to carry out the terms of the reparations agreement, the French and German Communist Parties had called a conference at Essen, attended also by delegates of the British, Belgian, Italian, Czech, and Dutch Communist Parties, the Comintern, the Young Communist International, the RILU and CGTU. The theme of the conference was the fight against Versailles; Germany had become a colonial country, and only the KPD could lead the struggle for national independence. A Committee of Action was formed of representatives of the French and German Communist Parties and trade unions. On their return the French delegates to the conference were arrested by the French Government.

French troops occupied the Ruhr on 11 January 1923. A protest campaign was organized by the Comintern; and the Soviet Government, apprehensive of a move against its only important ally, protested officially on 13 January. The French Communist Party and the CGTU published protests denouncing the Versailles treaty and the occupation. Resolutions of denunciation were passed at meetings all over Russia, and the Soviet co-operatives sent 1,400 tons of grain to the Ruhr co-operatives. Radek contributed an article on the Russian offer of grain to Germany in 1918, and referred to the complementary nature of the Russian and German economies—'that explains Russia's great interest in the liberation of the German people'. Friendly feelings reflected their common interests. On 4 February 1923 the KPD organized at Essen a conference of factory committees in the coal and steel industry which passed resolutions calling for the withdrawal of Entente troops from Germany, for the formation of a workers' government, the arming of German workers, and an alliance with Russia, etc.]

Comrades, French capital is getting ready to commit a new and unprecedented crime. It is now hurling its battalions across the frontier in order to plunder Germany. Mankind is once more trembling on the brink of a new war, a prospect which means further tremendous sacrifices, greater famine, the annihilation of the proletariat, destruction, decline, and death. The victors in the world massacre, who brag so loudly of their culture and justice, are now themselves tearing off their hypocritical masks and appearing frankly as thieves. The German proletariat is being broken under the hatchet of Entente capitalism. To make sure of their victory, the bourgeoisie are putting the French proletarian fighters in chains, killing and robbing them in Italy, throwing them into prison in England, organizing pogroms in Czechoslovakia. The whole of central Europe will be given over to devastation unless the criminal policy of the financial barons is successfully countered.

Workers of France! Soldiers of the French army! It is your duty now to do everything you can to stop Poincaré's Government from starting a new conflagration that will lay Europe in ruins. You must not let the Paris usurers trample down your German working brothers under the gendarmerie's boots.

Your enemy is in your own country. The executioners of the working class must not be allowed to stain your proletarian honour. Do not let yourselves be degraded into wretched tools of Poincaré. Do not become robbers of the German people. Carry the living word of the living truth to the masses! Stop capital by strikes and demonstrations. Go to the limits of your power and strength.

Workers of Germany! What awaits you? A sea of suffering, a double oppression, starvation and decay. The bourgeoisie are not even able to assure you your daily bread. They are doing business with their French colleagues at your expense, at the expense of the working class. And this is what they will go on doing. Unite then in a single powerful proletarian front for the fight to win a workers' government. Through this workers' government organize a defensive struggle against the foreign robbers. Stretch out your hands to your French brothers, who are ready to fight shoulder to shoulder with you against the criminal French bourgeoisie. Carry among the masses the slogan of union with Soviet Russia. Only in that way shall we be able to hold down the enemy.

Workers of all countries! Working people of the countryside! You are all in danger of being dragged into a new massacre in the interests of capital. Against your governments put forward your will to defence, your will to struggle against capital, to struggle for your workers' power, for the European union of socialist republics. The bourgeoisie are ready to begin a new fight for the division of millions of profits, to do to death millions of the working masses, to tear them to pieces and cripple them. Unfurl the mighty banner of the universal war of all the exploited against the exploiters, the financial barons, the diplomats. Tear the hypocritical masks from the faces of those leaders who want to pacify you and reconcile you with the bourgeoisie. Organize mass actions, organize a mass on-slaught on the bourgeois governments.

LETTER FROM THE PRESIDIUM OF THE ECCI AND THE RILU BUREAU TO THE IFTU AND THE SECOND INTERNATIONAL PROPOSING JOINT MEASURES IN SUPPORT OF THE ITALIAN PROLETARIAT

15 *January* 1923   *Inprekorr*, iii, 17, p. 124, 26 *January* 1923

[This letter was followed three days later by an appeal 'to all workers and peasants' to support the 'International Fighting Fund against Fascism' that the two signatories had established. The world capitalist crisis, it was said, would bring fascism to power in all countries unless it was countered by working-class action. This and similar appeals were used as a pretext by the new Italian Government for the arrest early in February 1923 of communists, socialists, and anarchists. Their propaganda was declared to be directed against the security of the State.]

You are aware of the present tragic situation of the Italian proletariat. With fire and sword fascism is annihilating the workers' organizations, killing hundreds of Italy's proletariat. The Italian working class is being defeated in the struggle against the black reaction unloosed against it. If the international proletariat, regardless of political affiliation, does not get down to work and take energetic steps against the fascist monster, the Italian proletariat will be bled white. The Communist International and the Red International of Labour Unions propose a joint examination with your representatives of practical measures of struggle against the fascist bandits, and the working out of a series of practical steps to help our Italian brothers in their struggle against reaction. We ask you to form jointly with us an international committee of action which will appeal to all workers' organizations of all tendencies throughout the world to take part in the struggle against fascism. If the workers of all countries do not break the power of fascist reaction in Italy, they will themselves fall victims to the fascism of their own countries which is already raising its head everywhere. We are prepared to accept in advance all your proposals designed to fight Italian fascism and to help the Italian proletariat in its struggle for freedom from black reaction.

EXTRACTS FROM AN OPEN LETTER FROM THE COMINTERN AND PRO-FINTERN TO THE SECOND AND VIENNA INTERNATIONALS, AND THE INTERNATIONAL FEDERATION OF TRADE UNIONS ON THE OCCUPATION OF THE RUHR

16 *January* 1923   *Inprekorr*, iii, 12, p. 83, 16 *January* 1923

[The French move into the Ruhr was variously interpreted by communist writers, though all agreed that it would intensify nationalism, encourage fascism, and aggravate the danger of war. The entire post-war history of Europe was interpreted by some as part of a French plan to establish hegemony in Europe, for which France needed the heavy-industry resources of the Ruhr. Other writers analysed the occupation as a manœuvre of the French and German industrialists in combination to keep the workers of both countries in order. ('Loucheur, Stinnes, and Co.' was the title of an article by Sadoul.) Böttcher, on the other hand, referred to a state of latent war between France and Germany which might at any moment become active. This was the official attitude of the KPD, which called for a united front in France and Germany to establish workers' governments. Virtually all writers believed that the occupation would strengthen the KPD, and force Germany into still closer relations with Russia. Bukharin, in a speech to a conference of Russian newspaper workers, said that 'the confusion and acuteness of the situation is of advantage to the proletariat, because the re-establishment and consolidation of the capitalist order in Western Europe would for us be most dangerous of all. For if the situation of the working classes were improved they would become more passive, which would encourage reformism. There is now no longer any such prospect—the events in the Ruhr have been of extraordinarily great help to us.' Chicherin, on the other hand, in an article published at the end of February, said the Ruhr occupation was injurious to Russia, which needed stable economic relations with other countries. French industrialists wanted peaceful co-operation with German heavy industry, but they also wanted to penetrate it; the occupation might be an episode on the road to cartellization. But so long as the French

Government persisted in its action, and the German Government demanded evacuation before negotiation, the crisis from which all Europe was suffering would persist.

The IFTU, which in 1922 had considered calling a general strike in the event of French intervention in Germany, failed to agree on this step at a meeting held in February 1923, and appealed to the League of Nations to mediate between the two countries. Fimmen resigned from the secretaryship in protest, but became a member of its council the following year as representative of the Transport Workers' International Secretariat.]

On the 13th of this month the ECCI addressed an inquiry to you about the steps you intended to take to carry out the decision of the Hague congress on organizing a general strike in the event of the danger of war....

The Russian trade union delegation at the Hague strongly urged that an international protest strike should be organized on 2 January to demonstrate to the international bourgeoisie the determination of the proletariat to fight against the war danger. The Russian trade union delegation at the Hague conference predicted the occupation of the Ruhr in January. The majority of the delegates at the Hague ignored our warnings; they were content with platonic protests, convinced that bourgeois diplomacy would manage to find a way out. Capitalist diplomacy did not find a way out, just as it has been unable for four years to establish conditions for peaceful world development. The occupation of the Ruhr confronts the world with an acute danger of war.

The French Government's plan in seizing the German iron and coal industry of the Ruhr is to force the German capitalists to pay. But this presupposes that the French occupation authorities will be able to administer the Ruhr, to keep its industry going, and to exert pressure on German industry by releasing or withholding coal. This plan has been frustrated by the removal of the coal syndicate from Essen to Hamburg. The French occupation authorities are faced with the impossibility of keeping Ruhr industry going. The difficulty of paying the miners' wages will increase from day to day. It follows that they will strike out beyond the Ruhr, to turn the screw on the German people more tightly. Reports are already coming in of preparations for mobilization in Poland. France will set its vassals on the move against Germany. But even if that were not contemplated, there might at any moment be clashes between French troops and the closely packed population of the Ruhr which would drive nationalist feeling in Germany up to boiling-point. If the military elements in France exploit Poincaré's difficulties in the Ruhr to push him farther in his Rhineland policy, the policy of dismembering Germany, forces in Germany may easily be set in motion which will drive on to war in order to make use of nationalist fever to win power by a counter-revolution. The Governments on both sides of the Rhine do not know today what they will do tomorrow. The situation will become more acute on 31 January, for Germany will not be able to make the payment due on that date. The unilateral action of the French Government may then turn into general action by the Entente. And the German people may be called on to decide between complete subjugation and enslavement, or struggle.

The Hague conference resolved that the proletariat should use all means to ward off the danger of war; that should the danger arise, a general strike was to be organized. Now the danger is here. Only the blind can go on denying its existence. It is not only a danger of war between France and Germany. Such a war would set the entire east and south-east of Europe on the move. The Lithuanian attack on Memel and the events on the Rumanian-Hungarian frontier show how unstable is the balance of the last few years, how forces are already beginning to be set in motion whose development would turn any conflict in central Europe into a European conflict.

We do not doubt for a moment that the leaders of the Amsterdam Trade Union International, like those of the Vienna and London Internationals, regard the situation in the same light. We therefore call on them to give practical effect to the solemn declarations made at the Hague only a month ago and to prepare the rapid organization of a mass strike. We call on them to meet us immediately to determine the necessary measures. The parties of the Communist International and the working masses who support the RILU will do their duty, as our French comrades have already shown. We propose 31 January as the date for the beginning of the mass protest strike. The duration of the strike will have to be determined by the conference of representatives of the three political and the two trade union Internationals, which we suggest shall be called in Berlin for 21 January.

APPEAL FROM THE ECCI AND THE RILU TO ALL WORKERS AGAINST
DEATH SENTENCES PASSED IN INDIA

March 1923   *Inprekorr*, iii, 48, p. 378, 14 *March* 1923

[At this time no communist party had yet been established in India, although in May 1923 Evelyn Roy claimed that a communist party had been founded in October 1920 and had drawn up a programme two years later. The leading Indian communist was M. N. Roy, who had been brought to Russia from Mexico by Borodin. From February 1923 *Advance Guard* (formerly and subsequently *Vanguard*) was published as the 'Central Organ of the Communist Party of India'. It was published in Berlin, where Roy had his headquarters, and later in Switzerland and France. A number of young Indians had been trained in Russia, first at the military school in Tashkent, later at the University for Toilers of the East in Moscow. A number of those who returned to India to undertake revolutionary work were arrested, tried, and sentenced. In a letter to the Indian

National Congress at the end of December 1922 the ECCI wrote that 'British rule can and will be overthrown only by a violent revolution', and argued that the peaceful means advocated by Gandhi could not be successful. In *Inprekorr* in January 1923 Roy wrote that Gandhi and the Congress party represented the petty bourgeoisie, but the movement would eventually be captured by its radical minority, who wanted political action, not passive resistance. Gandhi's non-co-operation campaign was designed to get concessions for the petty bourgeoisie from the British Government.

At the meeting of the ECCI in June 1923 Lozovsky criticized the CPGB for not doing enough in India to counteract the activities of the Labour Party and the TUC. At this time Roy suggested a small illegal CP working through and controlling a mass workers' and peasants' party. The ECCI report to the fifth congress in 1924 said that their aim in India was to found a popular mass party as well as a proletarian class party. There were a number of small groups and study circles of a communist character, but attempts to unite them had so far failed. At the congress itself Manuilsky, reporting for the colonial commission, attacked Roy for his emphasis on the social as distinct from the nationalist movement; this, he said, was a reflection of Rosa Luxemburg's nihilist attitude on the national question.

The appeal refers to the trial of a number of Indians who, on 4 February 1922, had taken part in an attack on the Chauri-Chaura police station, in which all except two of the policemen were beaten to death. The condemned men appealed; thirty-eight were acquitted, nineteen death sentences were confirmed, and the remainder were sentenced to varying terms of imprisonment.]

Imperialist justice has condemned 172 men in India to death. A year ago 228 men, accused of taking part in the disturbances which led to the burning of the Chauri-Chaura police station and the murder of twenty-two policemen, were brought before the court. Now 172 men are to be executed in retaliation for the death of twenty-two policemen who fell in defence of 'law and order'. The ferocity of this judicial murder is unsurpassed even in the bloody history of British rule in India.

Since 1919 India has been the scene of mass murders and brutal repression. Beginning in Amritsar, British imperialism has freely made use everywhere of tanks, bombs, machine-guns, and bayonets to smother the rebellious people in streams of blood. More than 30,000 men and women are in prison under various sentences for having taken part in the nationalist movement. More than 6,600 poor peasants from Malabar are serving hard-labour sentences, 5 have been executed, and 70 hanged. In the Punjab 5,000 Sikh peasants are in prison, beaten and ill-treated there. This outrageous list is now to be extended by sending 172 men to the gallows.

The great majority of the condemned men are poor peasants, driven to revolt by the intolerable burden of war taxes and high prices. The revolt was directed against both the native landlords and the alien government, who together suck the peasants' blood. It took the form of a gigantic mass demonstration with nationalist slogans and under nationalist leadership. The demonstrations were peaceful, for the leaders of the nationalist movement are petty-bourgeois pacifists who believe in the victory of non-violence. But imperialism would not even allow a peaceful demonstration of the unarmed masses. The Chauri-Chaura police opened fire on a crowd of about 3,000 who were making their way to a nearby market where they wanted to put up posters against the sale of foreign goods. This provocative act angered the peaceful demonstrators, who attacked the police station, and all the inmates were killed. The number of casualties among the rebels was never established, but it is easy to imagine the effect of fire on a crowd of 3,000 persons. Indignation spread rapidly to neighbouring districts and grew into a dangerous agrarian uprising, which was suppressed by rapidly assembled military forces. The number of those who fell victim to the merciless hand of 'law and order' is not known. After the suppression of the revolt many arrests were made, and 228 persons were brought into court charged with murder and incendiarism. The case ended with 172 death sentences.

The international proletariat, which is waging a bitter struggle against capitalism throughout the world, must not allow this imperialist mass murder to take place without protest. The revolt of the working masses of the colonial countries is a powerful element in the revolutionary struggle for the overthrow of the bourgeois dictatorship, and the establishment of a new social order. Imperialism is trying to smother the revolt of the colonial masses in streams of blood. The proletariat of the imperialist countries cannot remain indifferent to this. Energetic action must be taken on behalf of our Indian comrades, who are waging a bloody struggle against the imperialist terror.

Men and women workers! Organize protest meetings and demonstrations which shall brand this act of imperialist mass murder and demand that the condemned men be set free. Call on the Second International and the Amsterdam Trade Union Federation to demand of their chief pillar, the British Labour Party, to save the lives of the 172 Indian peasants, whose only crime was their hunger, and who were in that state of unbearable hunger because they were forced to contribute too much to the waging of the 'war for democracy'. Call on the Two-and-a-half International to demand of its backbone, the Independent Labour Party, to give proof of its lofty avowal of pacifism.

Proletarians of Great Britain! It is your duty to take the lead in this affair. Demand that the Labour Party take action in parliament against this bloody deed of British imperialism. If the reformist leaders cannot be moved to action even by so flagrant a violation of every moral and juridical law which they recognize as authoritative for others, you must reject your leaders and take direct action yourselves in support of the right of subject peoples to rebel and in affirmation of the solidarity of the working masses in the fight against capitalism.

LETTER FROM THE ECCI TO THE FRANCO-GERMAN WORKERS' CONFERENCE AT FRANKFURT

16 *March* 1923   *Inprekorr*, iii, 49, p. 379, 16 *March* 1923

[The KPD and the French CP called a conference at Frankfurt on 17–18 March to discuss international action against the Ruhr occupation and to 'organize the fight against war and fascism'.

On 3 March the ECCI and the bureau of the RILU sent an open letter to all affiliated organizations urging support for the conference in its fight against 'the French bourgeoisie, the greedy and selfish policy of the German capitalist magnates, the covetous frenzy of the English industrial and financial sharks, the rapacity of the American moneybags and of their worthy partners in Japan', who were 'pushing the working masses of all countries into an abyss of mud and blood'. The conference was attended by 243 delegates (another report gives the figure of 232) including 10 from France, 9 from Holland, 6 from Russia, 3 each from Italy and Czechoslovakia, 2 from Britain, and 1 Indian. These were apparently all communists; of the Germans, 17 were USPD, 9 SPD, and 181 KPD. The ECCI instructions to communist delegates were 'to work out a genuine, joint, clear, firm, and concentrated programme of action for the most important sections concerned, and to work out a number of measures of an organizational and in part conspirative nature, and to put them into effect'. Kolarov spoke on behalf of the ECCI on the war danger, Lozovsky for the RILU on the united front, and Zetkin on fascism; Shatskin spoke for the YCI. Resolutions were passed on the Ruhr, the war danger, the united front, the capitalist offensive, etc.

A 'non-party international committee of action' was appointed to direct the work and convene a world congress.

The Second International, the Vienna Union, and the IFTU had been invited to attend the conference, but declined, the first two stating that representatives of the British, French, Italian, Belgian, and German socialist parties were to meet in Berlin to discuss the question of reparations and the Ruhr occupation.

On 3 May 1923 the committee of action invited the IFTU to co-operate; the IFTU replied that as a federation of affiliated organizations it could not itself decide on joint action. In any case, a united front implied mutual trust, and the communist parties had made it clear that they did not trust the IFTU.]

When the Executive of the Communist International received the invitation to the international conference at Frankfurt-am-Main sent by the Rhineland factory councils to all workers' organizations, it did not hesitate a moment in accepting. The Communist International places its entire influence at the service of that section of the German proletariat which is conscious of its international duty. A special delegation from the

Executive of the Communist International will make known to your conference our views on all the burning questions connected with the occupation of the Ruhr.

However, the Executive thinks it particularly important once more to
declare most solemnly to the entire organized working class of the whole
world that the Second and the Amsterdam Internationals have again
defaulted and openly neglected their elementary duty. All the resolutions
passed by the Second and Amsterdam Internationals at their recent
Hague peace conference have become scraps of paper. One of the best-
known leaders of the Amsterdam International, Edo Fimmen, stated
publicly that nobody dreams of carrying out these decisions. Edo Fimmen
tries to shift the responsibility for this on to the proletariat by declaring
that the international working class is split and helpless. This is the same
argument that was used by some disguised social-chauvinists when war
broke out in 1914. They too tried to shift responsibility for the vacillating
and treacherous attitude of the leaders on to the working class. It is true
that the Second and the Amsterdam Internationals are helpless, but that
is because they do not wish to do their duty. The working classes are helpless and split because the Second and the Amsterdam Internationals split
them and so made them helpless. If the leaders were ready to form and
operate a united front with the communists, the working class would have
stronger forces. Once more we propose to the leaders of the Second and the
Amsterdam Internationals a united front with the communists. We are
ready to negotiate with the social-democratic and trade union leaders,
although our opinion of them has been again confirmed, and most strikingly, by recent events. At the present moment the chief enemy is French
imperialism. The German working class can fight that imperialism successfully only if it defeats its own, the German bourgeoisie, forms a revolutionary
workers' government, and then allies itself closely with the international
working class, in the first place with Soviet Russia and the French proletariat.

The Communist International is ready to do everything to form a real
united front with the workers who belong to the Second and Amsterdam
Internationals. But if the leaders of the social-democratic organizations
succeed once again in blocking the united front, the Communist International will in any case march at the head of the militant sections of the
German and French working class.

Up to now only the communist parties and revolutionary trade unions
have done their duty. Only the German and French communist parties,
led by the Communist International, have determined on a common path
and begun the struggle together. Only the communists have carried out
their international duty in the struggle against French imperialism and
landed in Monsieur Poincaré's prisons because of their stand for the
interests of the international proletariat.

The mere fact that at such a critical moment two large communist parties, the German and the French, have acted together is a great political event for the working class of the entire world.

For us communists, international conferences are not parades, not empty demonstrations. What we desperately need is a real, serious merging of the day-to-day struggles of the various sections of the international working class. Politically, life is now internationalized to a very high degree. If bourgeois reaction is forced to make preparations on an international scale, the revolutionary proletarian movement is in even greater need of such action. The workers must learn not only to pass joint resolutions, but to act jointly, to co-ordinate their struggle, to prepare for universal struggle.

The Frankfurt conference is a signpost on the road of preparation for the victorious proletarian revolution. Stubbornly and relentlessly, with inexhaustible energy, the class-conscious workers of the various countries must work for the real unification of their struggles.

The Executive of the Communist International sends warmest fraternal greetings to the sorely tried workers of the Ruhr, to the militants in the French proletariat, and to the proletarian vanguard of the entire world.

EXTRACTS FROM AN ECCI RESOLUTION ON THE KPD

April 1923   *Bericht der Exekutive,* December 1922–May 1923, p. 67

[At the eighth KPD congress in Leipzig at the end of January 1923 (which claimed a membership of 218,500, and 13 deputies in the Reichstag) the main debate was not on the Ruhr, but on the united front and the SPD. Policies about the Ruhr appear to have been divided. (Ruth Fischer suggests that Radek— who appeared at the congress under the name of Arvid—and his supporters kept the Ruhr question off the agenda because the Foreign Affairs Commissariat in Moscow wished to have its hands free to pursue a flexible policy in Germany, and was unwilling to have the KPD committed to a specific policy.) Was the SPD the left wing of the bourgeoisie or the right wing of the working class? The right-wing majority in the KPD advanced the latter thesis, and were therefore in favour of united front tactics from above as well as below; that is, they favoured a coalition policy in the Saxon and Thuringian Governments—the elections of November 1922 for the Saxon Diet had given the SPD 40 seats, and the KPD 10, out of a total of 96—on a programme of social reform, control of production by factory committees, etc. The left wing argued that a workers' government could only follow the mass struggle, not precede it. The voting was 118 against 59. Although the minority abstained from voting for the central committee, three of its members were elected to that body. It was said at the time that this was on Zinoviev's advice, but Radek claimed later that it was he who had insisted on their inclusion.

The debate between the two wings was continued in the press. In an article published at the end of March 1923 Ruth Fischer attacked the belief of the majority that the KPD could gain influence among the masses by pandering to their democratic illusions. 'The masses are not with us, not because they believe in democracy, but because they are afraid of coming to grips with the bourgeoisie.' A genuine workers' government could not be based on parliamentary institutions, but only on the workers' mass organizations. The slogan introduced confusion and mistrust into the KPD, and weakened the belief in the revolutionary road. The idea of the SPD as the right wing of the working class, and not a counter-revolutionary party, was the beginning of liquidationism. A course of action based on democratic illusions would foster these illusions within the KPD. Brandler replied that it was not passivity and cowardice that kept the masses back from revolution, but their belief in the democratic road to political and economic power. Capitalist resistance to socialist measures introduced by a workers' government would lead to the extra-parliamentary mass struggle in the course of which democratic illusions would disappear.

With the continuation of the Ruhr occupation, the conflict between the left and right—between those who advocated militant action and those who rejected an insurrectionary policy—grew more acute. The ECCI supported the right wing, whose outstanding representatives were Brandler, Thalheimer, and Klara Zetkin. In March 1923 at a local KPD conference in Essen where the left were very strong, Klara Zetkin, in the name of the ECCI, said the KPD would not endorse any 'adventurist' action undertaken in the Ruhr.

The minority accused the majority of revisionism and liquidationism, and wanted the KPD to advance the slogan of 'occupy the factories'. They criticized collaboration with the left social-democratic government in Saxony, arguing that it arrested the disintegration of the SPD. (At the end of January the KPD votes had turned out the Lipinski Government in Saxony; after several weeks, a left SPD government was formed with KPD support.) An SPD-bourgeois coalition government was the lesser evil, because it would destroy democratic illusions among the masses. To avoid an open split in the KPD, the central committee in April called a conference with representatives of the opposition and a common platform was drawn up. Representatives of both wings were called to Moscow. Brandler and Böttcher appeared for the right wing, Fischer, Maslow, and Thaelmann for the left; Zinoviev, Trotsky, Bukharin, and Radek for the ECCI. The meetings of the commission lasted three days. The Leipzig congress resolution on the united front was rejected as opportunist, but the opposition charge of liquidationism was also rejected. It was agreed that no revolutionary action would be taken in the Ruhr unless and until it were justified by the situation in the rest of Germany and in France. Stalin made one of his earliest ventures into Comintern affairs at this time, writing to Zinoviev and Bukharin that the KPD should be curbed, not spurred on.

Four members of the left wing were added to the KPD central committee, including Fischer and Thaelmann. The central committee meeting at the end of May endorsed these decisions against two votes, with five abstentions. The central committee's report to the ninth KPD congress in the following year stated that it was at this 'conciliation conference' in Moscow that the question of arming the German proletariat was first brought up as a practical matter, although the question of seizing power was not directly raised.]

I

The Comintern Executive welcomes the convening by the KPD *Zentrale* of the conciliation conference which is to eliminate the obstacles that have for some time hampered united action by all members of the party. The Executive Committee observes that all communist workers in Germany are filled with the desire for party unity . . . and in this the EC sees a pledge that after the conference, after the decision of the Executive, and once the central committee has finally taken up its position, debates about former differences within the party will be reduced to a minimum and carried on calmly, objectively, and impersonally, so that they will promote and not hinder party work.

II

The differences within the party arise from the slow pace of revolutionary development in Germany and the objective difficulties this causes, producing both right and left deviations in the party. . . . It was the right deviation which the Executive and the fourth Comintern congress had in mind when they spoke of the dangers inherent in the application of united front tactics. These tactics were applied by the right-wing elements not as a method of detaching the working masses from reformist policy, but as a method of adapting the communist party to the reformist leaders.

The KPD *Zentrale*, whose policy has in general been correct, has not always managed to combat these dangers promptly. In some of its moves it lent support to right-wing tendencies by failing to note the danger, as for example when the *Zentrale*, in its resolution on the political situation and the immediate tasks of the proletariat submitted to the Leipzig congress, spoke of the need to use 'as a point of contact the illusions and prejudices and needs of the broadest masses of the social-democratic workers', or when, in the same resolution, it said the workers' government would 'carry on the fight with the instruments of power available in the bourgeois state'. These turns of phrase are certainly incorrect. . . . If the communist party fights against the dangers threatening the bourgeois State from the fascists, although it is the party of proletarian dictatorship and not of bourgeois democracy, this does not imply attaching ourselves to the democratic illusions of the social-democratic workers; it is in defence of the immediate interests of the working class, which cannot, it is true, be satisfied by democracy, but which would be in an even worse position under white-bourgeois rule than under bourgeois democracy. . . . When the workers' government begins to put its programme through, and has to defend its existence against the bourgeoisie, at that moment it must destroy the instruments of power of the bourgeois State and create proletarian instruments of power. . . . It is by the use of such phrases that the *Zentrale* has fed mistrust in circles within the party which tend towards left deviations.

In those circles, represented by the Berlin and Hamburg district committees, sound proletarian elements are dissatisfied because the CP is not yet able to conduct the struggle for the direct seizure of power. . . . They fear that, by fighting for the immediate and elementary interests of the working class, the party will become a reformist party. . . . The *Zentrale* was right in opposing these left deviations when, as in the Ruhr question, they might have led us into isolated struggles (e.g. the demand by the minority for the occupation of the factories in the Ruhr), in which the party would have suffered severe defeats; or when, as in Saxony, they would have isolated the KPD from the proletarian masses who were finding their way to us. But the struggle against left tendencies can be carried on successfully only if the KPD *Zentrale* eliminates, primarily by a struggle against the right-wing elements, the reasons for the revolutionary mistrust of the left.

The Executive notes that the representatives of the opposition, in the statement signed jointly with the *Zentrale* at the conference, recognize that 'the existing tactical differences are not so great as to hamper collaboration of the majority and minority in the party'. This is an admission that the charge that the policy of the *Zentrale* and the majority would lead to the liquidation of the communist party and of the communist theory of the State is unjustified. . . .

III

As to the practical questions of KPD policy in dispute, the Executive has the following to say:

(*a*) The Ruhr: the German proletariat in the Ruhr is between the upper and the nether millstone—the German and the French bourgeoisie. So long as there is no revolutionary movement in the unoccupied area and among the French working masses, so long as there are no signs of widespread disintegration among the French occupation troops, any attempt to occupy the factories would mean that the proletariat, dependent on the French occupation authorities, would have to supply them with the coal, and French imperialism, with this trump in its hand, could more easily reach agreement with German imperialism. The German bourgeoisie would then let loose on the communist workers all the scorpions of unleashed nationalism. . . .

(*b*) Saxony: By the correct application of united front tactics, the KPD has been successful in convincing the social-democratic working masses of the harmfulness of a coalition with the bourgeoisie. Unfortunately it failed from the first to conduct the struggle for a workers' government in Saxony as part of the struggle for a workers' government in the Reich. It was not strong enough to move the Saxon working class so far that from its revolutionary struggles a revolutionary coalition government of social-democratic and communist workers might have arisen worthy of the name of workers' government. Support of the social-democratic Government on the basis of concrete conditions marking a step forward was therefore the only means which (1) guaranteed our contact with the social-democratic masses, who were in a state of ferment, and (2) at the same time did not impose on us full responsibility for the social-democratic Government. . . . The Executive reminds the KPD that the question of a workers' government cannot be satisfactorily solved within the framework of the individual *Länder*; that on the contrary the danger exists that a solution within an individual *Land* may compromise the idea altogether. It is therefore of vital importance for the party to exploit the threat of using the Reich Executive against the social-democratic Saxon Government, and the danger of fascism, for a broad and energetic campaign throughout the Reich for a Reich workers' government. Only if the broadest working masses throughout the Reich rally for the struggle against the bourgeois Reich Government and for the formation of a workers' government, will they find the determination to ward off the blows of the counter-revolution against the positions already won by the workers in the *Länder*. . . .

The German bourgeoisie, defeated in war, are compelled to wage a struggle against victorious Entente capital, are compelled to strain again and again at the chains of the Versailles treaty. Concerned with maintaining their rule over the working class, and pursuing for this purpose a counter-revolutionary policy, they are nevertheless playing, in relation to Entente capital, a revolutionary disintegrating role. While prepared at all times to serve as the watch-dog of international capital, if the Entente bourgeoisie were inclined to grant German capital the conditions for its restoration, the German bourgeoisie are forced, because of the failure of their efforts to reach a compromise, to pursue the revolutionary policy we have indicated. In their struggle against the Entente they cannot rely on the popular masses; on the contrary, they are condemned by history to repulse those masses. The German bourgeoisie can no longer act as standard-bearers of the national struggle for liberation; they are incapable of fighting seriously and victoriously against the Entente, nor are they really prepared to do so. Therefore in the long run the national and nationalist sentiments which they have released will be turned against them. It is the task of the KPD to open the eyes of the broad petty-bourgeois and intellectual-nationalist masses to the fact that only the working class, once it is victorious, will be in a position to defend German soil, the treasures of German civilization, and the future of the German nation. Only the German working class, when it is in power, will be able to win the sympathy of the popular masses of other countries, and so make it more difficult for the imperialist Powers to carry through to the end their policy of annihilating the German nation. . . . Only the working class can by its victory bring about the closest relations with Soviet Russia, which is growing steadily stronger, and so create the basis for new advances by the German people.

IV

The decisions of the conciliation conference, with their careful consideration of the Executive's directives enumerated above, provide a basis for the united co-operation of all the party's forces. For this reason the Executive insists that no organs be established and no measures taken which might enlarge the differences that have not yet been completely eliminated.

The Executive therefore recommends the Berlin organization to refrain from asking approval for a special discussion organ, and it recommends the *Zentrale* to issue a discussion supplement to the *Rote Fahne*, to be published twice a month, in which questions newly arising for the entire party can be critically examined. The Executive takes for granted that the *Zentrale* will allow adequate space for dissenting opinions in this supplement, although of course it is the business of the *Zentrale* to decide whether or not a particular question should be discussed at any given time; it is obvious that when the *Zentrale*, after hearing all points of view, has decided on a particular tactical line, it cannot be criticized while the action in pursuit of that line is in progress. . . .

The Executive calls on the representatives of the Berlin and Hamburg organizations to desist from work in other districts. A unified party policy is impossible if two political party centres exist simultaneously. The differences within the party were examined in the various resolutions of the party congress; they are under discussion in the central committee. The party is aware of the differences and the local organizations are able to keep themselves informed about the questions in dispute without the intervention of the representatives of the Hamburg and Berlin districts.

While rejecting any step which might deepen the differences still existing, the Executive requests the *Zentrale*, in order to complete the work of the conciliation conference, to establish more intimate links with such important proletarian centres as Berlin, Hamburg, and Essen, by strengthening the representation of the opposition on the *Zentrale* by one representative from each of the said districts, to be nominated by the local organization. The three representatives of the opposition elected at the Leipzig congress to the *Zentrale* have shown by their work that they do not regard themselves as representatives of a separate group, but as

representatives of the entire party. . . . Stronger links with the oppositional districts will improve the party's striking power and help to crown
the work of the conference: to make the KPD a unified vigorous revolutionary communist party.

EXTRACTS FROM A MAY-DAY MANIFESTO OF THE COMMUNIST INTER-
NATIONAL

April 1923   *Inprekorr*, iii, 62, p. 497, 11 *April* 1923

. . . The bourgeoisie cannot restore the old 'normal' conditions of pre-
war capitalism, so they are making a desperate attempt to create a stronger
and more powerful capitalism. They speak of peace and work, but their
acts are acts of senseless destruction. They are organizing war and civil
war. The new millenial empire of capitalism is to be established by turning
the proletariat into a class of helots, a herd of draught animals. The
capitalist offensive is intended to depress the workers' standard of living
even below its pre-war level.

The reformist parties—openly and by concealed collaboration—have
done their part to help the bourgeoisie to attain this shameful goal. But
they were too weak, and so the bourgeoisie have dropped them and now
place their hopes on fascism. Fascism is only the continuation by other and
sharper methods of the policy of the social-patriots. What the social-
democratic leaders wanted but failed to obtain from the workers by
cunning and friendly persuasion is to be put through forcibly by fascism—
the subjection of the working class to conditions of life and labour without
parallel even in the history of capitalism. Fascism is capitalism preparing
for its final passage of arms with the proletariat; it reveals to the workers
the true features of that bourgeois democracy from which the reformists
expected salvation. . . . Every single worker must be summoned to the
fight against fascism. Against the united front of the exploiters—the united
front of the proletariat. . . .

The workers are no longer inclined to believe that they get on best when
they live 'in peace' with the bourgeoisie. That policy has brought them
nothing but wage reductions, higher prices, longer working hours, short
time, unemployment, degradation, and forcible suppression. To which has
now been added the growing danger of war. True, the bourgeoisie shout
for peace; not from feelings of humanity, nor from a pacifist naïveté, but
only because it is their job to make profits. But they cannot establish
peace. . . . Every day the contradictions between the imperialist Powers
are growing more acute, and new ones are arising. War has become the
normal state of affairs in bourgeois society, as we can see today from
the events in the Ruhr. . . .

The fight against fascism and war and for the united front is also the fight for Soviet Russia. Soviet Russia is a thorn in the flesh of bourgeois society, which rightly sees in the mere existence of the Bolshevik State the permanent threat of world revolution, and it therefore hates Soviet Russia with the same ardour that it loved the counter-revolutionary system of Tsarist Russia. . . . That is why it is the duty of all class-conscious workers to declare themselves unreservedly for Soviet Russia. In union with our Russian brothers they will defeat capitalism. . . .

The world revolution is approaching—in spite of everything. The insane rage of fascism, the descent on the Ruhr, the cynical treachery of the Second International—all that will not save the bourgeoisie.

REPLY FROM ZINOVIEV TO A LETTER FROM 'THE REPRESENTATIVES OF THE MESOPOTAMIAN PEOPLE' TO THE COMINTERN

April 1923   *Inprekorr*, iii, 16, p. 364, 21 *April* 1923

[The introductory note to this letter gives no indication of the names of those signing the letter to which it was the reply, nor of the organization to which they belonged. It states that they were deported by the British from Mesopotamia and were at the time in Persia. The letter to the Comintern is dated 21 December 1922, and asks whether the Comintern will 'consider the situation created in our country by this violation of the principles of the League of Nations [this refers to the Anglo-Iraqi agreement of 10 October 1922] and help us to liberate ourselves from the tyrannical yoke of the English, whose presence in Mesopotamia may be regarded as a constant threat to the general peace'. There was no communist party in Iraq before 1932.]

Dear friends,

I read your letter with the deepest interest. The tragic story of Mesopotamia's subjection reveals with the utmost clarity the hypocritical and treacherous policy of the English Government. And where has English imperialism behaved otherwise? In India, Egypt, South Africa—everywhere its policy is the same: lies, treachery, and pitiless cruelty. I have just read in the papers that as a result of the unceasing reprisals of the English in Mesopotamia a new and widespread revolt has occurred. The Communist International will follow the course of this heroic struggle with the greatest attention. The English hangmen will probably try not only to drown it in the blood of the Mesopotamian people, but also to break it down from within by tricks and cunning. There have been rumours that they are going to proclaim an amnesty for the arrested and deported leaders of the liberation movement and that they are even prepared to allow nationalist ministers to enter the cabinet of the treacherous Emir Feisal.

I am sure that past experience will lead you to reject these hypocritical concessions. Clearly Sir Percy Cox's intention is to get a favourable vote ratifying the treaty between England and Iraq, and to secure his blood-stained rule over Mesopotamia.

In your letter you observe that the regime established by English imperialism in your country violates the principles of the League of Nations. Obviously there is some misunderstanding here. The League of Nations was created after the war by the imperialist victors—England, France, etc.—so that they might more easily despoil the defeated. At the head of this predatory institution stands England itself. There is no difference between the 'principles' of the League of Nations and the 'lofty principles' which England is operating in Mesopotamia when it bombards the defenceless population from the air. In calling your attention to this misunderstanding may I ask you to explain it to your comrades, so that they may avoid the grave consequences that would inevitably follow from an incorrect idea of the true nature of the so-called League of Nations.

The emancipation of Mesopotamia will not be attained with the help and support of an imperialist State or of the League of Nations, but by the organized struggle of the broad masses of Iraq against the occupiers. To convince the masses that their material position will be made easier and better by driving out the English, to denounce with contempt all those treacherous Mesopotamians, with the Emir Feisal at their head, who would found their personal wealth on the oppression of their people, to win the confidence of neighbouring countries—if this were accomplished it would ensure the victorious outcome of your heroic struggle against English imperialism.

The Communist International, which unites millions of revolutionary workers and peasants in England, France, Germany, Russia, etc., assures you of its sympathy and support in your struggle for freedom.

If you, honoured friends, think it useful to come to Moscow, I look forward to our meeting.

If events make it impossible for you to come, I would ask you to collect and send documents, material, and photographs on the English regime in Mesopotamia.

If you think it possible to write a pamphlet on this question, it would be useful to have it published in European and Oriental languages.

With most cordial greetings,
The President of the Communist International,

EXTRACTS FROM ECCI INSTRUCTIONS TO THE THIRD CONGRESS OF THE
CHINESE COMMUNIST PARTY

May 1923   *Strategiya i Taktika Kominterna*, p. 114

[By the third congress, held in Canton in June 1923, most of the opposition to communist membership of the KMT (known as the 'block within') had been overcome. The revolution for which the party was to work was the bourgeois-democratic revolution, in which the peasant question was paramount. Maring was replaced by Voitinsky as Comintern representative. The organization, peasant, and propaganda departments of the KMT were in communist hands. In the summer of 1923 Chiang Kai-shek went to Russia, where he spent six months. On his return he was made director of the Whampoa military academy, established in May 1924 with Russian funds and staffed with Russian advisers, of whom Galen (Blücher) was the chief.

The third congress manifesto stated that 'the KMT should be the central force of the national revolution and should assume its leadership'.

The KMT held its first congress in January 1924; it agreed on a policy of alliance with the USSR and with the Chinese CP. Three communists were elected to its executive committee, and six (including Mao Tse-tung) to deputy membership.]

1. The national revolution in China and the creation of an anti-imperialist front will necessarily coincide with the agrarian revolution of the peasantry against the survivals of feudalism. The revolution will be successful only if the movement manages to attract the basic element in the Chinese population, the peasantry.

2. Thus the central question of all policy is the peasant question. To ignore this fundamental matter, on whatever pretext, implies a failure to understand the importance of the socio-economic foundations on which alone a victorious struggle can be waged against foreign imperialism and for the thorough extermination of feudalism in China.

3. Therefore the communist party, as the party of the working class, must attempt to establish a union of workers and peasants. This can be done only by unremitting propaganda and by realizing in fact the slogans of the agrarian revolution. . . .

4. Proceeding from these basic demands, it is essential to persuade the entire mass of poor peasants of the necessity of the fight against foreign imperialism, using as arguments the control by foreign capital of the customs, the salt monopoly, part of the finances, etc. . . .

5. It goes without saying that leadership must belong to the party of the working class. The latest events in the labour movement (the huge strikes) have clearly demonstrated the great importance of the workers' movement in China. To strengthen the CP, making it a mass party of the

proletariat, to assemble the forces of the working class in unions—this is the overriding obligation of communists. . . .

8. The CP must steadily push the Kuomintang on to the side of agrarian revolution. In the areas occupied by Sun Yat-sen's forces it is essential to get put through the confiscation of the land in favour of the poor peasantry, and a whole series of other revolutionary measures. . . .

9. On the other hand, we must fight by all means within the Kuomintang against any military agreement between Sun Yat-sen and the warlords, who are the agents of foreign capital and hostile to Soviet Russia, which is the ally both of the West European proletariat and of the oppressed peoples of the East. . . .

11. The boycott movement against Japan which is again beginning in China . . . must be fully exploited by the party. Our party must try to extend it into a general anti-imperialist movement of the Chinese democracy, aiming at the abrogation of treaties and obligations forced on China not only by England and America but also by other imperialist countries (extraterritoriality, the Boxer indemnity, etc.).

THE THIRD ENLARGED PLENUM OF THE ECCI

[The third plenary session of the ECCI was held from 12 to 23 June 1923. (It had originally been called for 20 May, but was postponed because of the crisis produced in Moscow by the 'Curzon ultimatum'. The ECCI telegram of 9 May postponing the meeting ran: 'In view of the ultimatum from England to Soviet Russia, which brings the danger of war into the immediate foreground, and to give our sections the opportunity to take the necessary organizational and agitational measures against it, the meeting of the enlarged Executive is postponed to 10 June.') It was attended by 75 delegates (including 21 members of the ECCI) representing 27 countries. Another source gives 69 delegates from 23 organizations; a third gives 'about 150'. Representatives of the 'fusionist' wing of the Italian Socialist Party were present; the Workers' Parties of the United States and Canada were included as 'sympathizing parties'. The report of the ECCI covered the period December 1922 to May 1923. The formation of an organization bureau (orgbureau) after the fourth congress had improved the work of the ECCI. An Eastern department, divided into three sections for the Near, Middle, and Far East respectively, had also been set up. Rapporteurs had been appointed for each country to provide material for the presidium.

A great deal of attention was given to the dispute between the Soviet Union and Britain, which Radek linked with the occupation of the Ruhr. Britain, he said, was neutral on this question, because it hoped that French hegemony in Europe would be broken by German resistance; the British Ambassador in Berlin had urged the German Government to resist France. When both France and Germany were weakened, Britain hoped with American support to capture control of the Franco-German iron and steel trust. When German resistance weakened, Britain asked Germany to pay reparations; Britain was risking the enmity of both Germany and Russia in order to win France for its anti-Soviet policy. In reply to Neurath (Czechoslovakia), Radek said that Poincaré's defeat was desirable because it would weaken the Versailles system.

The Scandinavian delegates were extremely critical of over-centralization in the Comintern. The ECCI practised absolute, not democratic, centralism. It should deal with and decide only international questions, and leave local ones to the national sections, which were allowed no room for independent action. The question had become acute in Norway. At the end of October 1922 a letter from Zinoviev and Bukharin to the central committee of the Norwegian Labour Party expressed the ECCI's astonishment at events in that party. It had not changed its name, or the name of its newspaper (*Social-Democrat*) which criticized Comintern policy towards the Italian Socialist Party and the activities of the party fraction in the Norwegian parliament, and had raised the question of fusion with the right-wing socialist party. The resolution of the fourth world congress on the Norwegian party was rejected by the Norwegian party congress in February 1923 and at the meeting of the central committee in May 1923 by narrow majorities.

Zinoviev reported to the plenum that the Executive had sent 'a whole series of our best comrades to Norway', including Bukharin, Radek, and Kolarov. The chief question in dispute was centralism versus federalism. He rejected the charge made by the Norwegian and Swedish parties that the Comintern was over-centralized. Höglund criticized the Executive's action. A split in the Norwegian party would sound the death-knell of the communist movement in Scandinavia. A Norwegian trade union leader had been expelled by the ECCI without a full knowledge of the facts, and without consulting the party centre. The ECCI had published in *Pravda* a letter to the Norwegian central committee before the CC knew of it; it had selected a member of the Norwegian minority to represent that party on the ECCI; and its open attacks on the party leaders, particularly Tranmael, had only made the conflict sharper. At the closing session Bukharin returned to the question. The Norwegian party, he said, wanted to control its internal and local affairs, to mandate its delegates, to choose its own ECCI delegates, and to be consulted about the choice of an ECCI delegate to Norway. This would give the International a federal character; it had made as many concessions as possible to the Norwegian party. In the commission Ström (Sweden) introduced an amendment that the Young Communist International should refrain from inciting the Norwegian Youth League against the party. He voted against the resolution which, in the plenary session, was passed against the votes of the Scandinavian delegates. Falk argued that the slogan of a workers' and peasants' government was inapplicable in Scandinavia, and reserved the right of the Norwegian party to propose at the fifth world congress amendments to the Comintern statutes. It had from the first been opposed to the 21 conditions of admission.

Influenced largely by the events in Bulgaria, the slogan of a 'workers' government' was changed to 'workers' and peasants' government'; and a resolution was passed explaining its meaning. This was to bring home the importance of the peasant question, which was vital for countries such as Poland. The Workers' Party in the United States had already issued the slogan of a 'workers' and farmers' government'. The resolution stated that 'the overwhelming majority of the CI sections had been deplorably passive about work in the countryside'. The peasants could not pursue an independent policy between the proletariat and the bourgeoisie, and had always been used by the bourgeoisie against the proletariat. They could not leave these rural positions to be monopolized by the enemy. If the peasants could not be won, they had to be neutralized. A workers' and peasants' government was the road to the proletarian dictatorship, not a denial of the dictatorship, but this did not mean parliamentary combinations with the representatives of peasant parties.

A special commission, to which ten additional delegates from Britain were invited, dealt with the situation in the CPGB. On their return H. Pollitt and R. P. Dutt took over the leadership, replacing those who had been the leaders of the small parties and groups which amalgamated to form the CPGB, and who represented 'federalist' tendencies. During the sessions of the ECCI the CPGB was criticized particularly severely for failing to pay enough attention to the national question. It had completely failed to conduct propaganda on the Irish and Indian questions, on which its attitude was reformist.

There was again a long debate on united front tactics. In his opening remarks Zinoviev recalled that the CI had always been in favour of good relations with social-democratic and non-party workers, but until 1921 they had not used united front tactics. The change came with the ebbing of the revolutionary wave. 'Formerly we wanted to attain this goal over the heads of the leaders. We see now that this cannot be done. We shall have to go on appealing to the leaders, until the masses at last understand that our ideas are right. Is that nothing but a strategic manœuvre? The answer depends on those leaders. If they really want a militant movement, it will not be a manœuvre. But I do not for a moment believe that . . . [they] want to fight alongside us.' Some comrades might ask whether this was morally permissible; he thought it was 'one way of organizing the working class'. 'Our class is numerically strong enough to win the fight, and it is only because of the strength of social-democratic influence among the proletariat that the working class has not yet triumphed.' Should they openly admit the nature of this strategic manœuvre? 'I am unconditionally in favour of any stratagem in the fight against an irreconcilable enemy, but only if it does not demoralize our own army.' He cited the French CP as an example of the confusion that could be caused by not openly admitting the nature of this strategic manœuvre. Treint had wanted to know whether united front tactics were compatible with the insulting language used about social-democracy.

The meeting also passed a resolution on the assassination, in April 1923, of Vorovsky, the Soviet delegate to the Lausanne Conference. In an earlier statement, issued by the CI and RILU on 14 May, this had been attributed to 'the Entente', angered by Russian support of Turkey at Lausanne; the object was to intimidate the Turks. The British plan for the Straits was a threat to the national independence movement in the East. 'The shot in Lausanne was directed not only against the liberty of the Asiatic peoples. It was aimed also at the revolutionary proletariat of Europe and the entire world.' At a memorial meeting in Moscow Chicherin said the French, Italian, and Swiss Governments were responsible. Turkey could win such inadequate concessions as it did at Lausanne only because of its diplomatic united front with Russia. The communist press had earlier attacked the Turkish Government which, 'to curry favour at Lausanne', had dissolved the Turkish Communist Party and arrested many of its members.

The report to the ECCI noted the difficulties created for the KPD by the Ruhr occupation; it had to fight the bourgeoisie, social-democracy, and nationalist fever, and still oppose French imperialism. Hence its slogan: 'Strike at Poincaré on the Ruhr and Cuno on the Spree.' In his opening speech Zinoviev said that one satisfactory feature was the collaboration between the French and German parties. The KPD had not had the courage to come out openly and say that it was hostile to the bourgeois fatherland but would defend a socialist fatherland; that, until it was strong enough to overthrow it, it would carry out the provisions of the Versailles treaty and continue to pay reparations by expropriating the bourgeoisie, while waiting for the workers of other countries to come to its aid. 'We German communists (and nobody else) defend the interests of the country, the people, the nation.' Those who believed in this policy had not the requisite energy and leadership to run a campaign on these lines, while the left opposition rejected the policy as opportunist. Radek said that in Germany emphasis on 'the nation' was a revolutionary act, as it was in the colonies. The German bourgeoisie were ready to capitulate to France if they were given a free hand with the German workers. They wanted to provoke a communist uprising in the Ruhr and thus be able to say that the communists had opened the door to the French. 'Thanks to the cool head of the KPD this plan failed.' Shortly after the ECCI meeting Radek wrote that the time for a general attack had not yet come, but was approaching. The KPD should accelerate it by expanding its organizational activities, making such compromises as were necessary with the proletarianized petty bourgeoisie.]

EXTRACTS FROM THE RESOLUTION OF THE THIRD ECCI PLENUM ON THE FUSION OF THE SECOND AND VIENNA INTERNATIONALS

June 1923   *Inprekorr*, iii, 128, p. 1120, 3 *August* 1923

[The fusion conference of the Second and Vienna Internationals convened at Hamburg on 21 May 1923. Fifty parties from thirty countries were represented. The International Committee against Fascism and War wrote to the conference suggesting negotiations for a united front; the proposal was rejected. In a statement published shortly before the opening of the conference, the ECCI wrote that 'nobody who looks at the facts soberly will be surprised at the Hamburg congress; he has long known that even in the intentions of its founders the Two-and-a-half was only a temporary refuge for the politically-homeless sham revolutionaries, and the entire history of that organization could therefore be nothing else than the history of its ordered retreat into the reformist camp. . . . How could it be otherwise? The attempt to reconcile the irreconcilable, to be both international and national, proletarian and bourgeois makes the centrist parties from the outset incapable of fighting, deprives them of determination, ruthlessness, and courage. . . . These elements, now urgently seeking their way back into the Second International, formed themselves, once their hopes of finding a home in the Third International and of infecting communism with reformism were disappointed by the 21 conditions, into the Two-and-a-half. But a formal reunion with the declared reformists did not yet seem advisable. . . . Now the Two-and-a-half is on its way home, and the Second will solemnly go and fetch it in Hamburg. The touching biblical idyll of the son that was lost and is found again is to be presented on the stage of world history. But the gentlemen are mistaken if they think that the proletariat will play with resignation its assigned part of sacrificial lamb.

'What is the meaning of the fusion of the two reformist Internationals? It means, above all, the liquidation of pseudo-radicalism. Reformists and centrists are distinguished from one another only by attaching a different value to revolutionary ideology . . . revolutionary-minded workers were in imagination to experience the satisfactions which in reality the centre was just as determined to refuse as the reformists. The centre thought this policy particularly necessary at a time when the economic dislocation caused by the war, the victory of the Russian revolution, and then the opening of the capitalist offensive threatened to rouse the proletarian masses to revolutionary struggle. They now think that that danger has passed. They think that capitalism has again become so strong that a revolutionary rising will seem hopeless to the masses, that there is therefore no longer any need to delude them with a revolutionary policy. . . . The united reformist front will stretch not only from Adler to Noske, but deep into the bourgeois camp. It will be a bourgeois-proletarian united front. That says enough. The moment a workers' party takes up the attitude that the workers of any country are more closely bound by interest to the bourgeoisie of that country than to the workers of other countries (and that is the basic idea of reformism), it deprives the proletarians who adhere to it of the possibility of having their own movement, of historically independent activity. The workers become politically an appendage of the bourgeoisie, an unquiet, troublesome, burdensome appendage it is true, but still an appendage. Their movement becomes as dependent on the movement of the bourgeoisie as that of the shadow on the body which casts it. . . . An international composed of such elements is dead even before it has really begun to live. We communists split the social-democratic parties led by traitors in order to unite the proletariat; the reformists will unite in Hamburg in order to split the proletariat again.

'Nevertheless, the Hamburg congress is a sign of progress. It creates clarity. The centre is finished; sham radicalism at an end. The proletariat is being mobilized into two great camps. The yawning gulf between revolution and reformism which seemed to be bridged by the centre is now visible to all. There is this side, and the other side, and only the two: and that creates the most favourable conditions for the fight for the proletarian united front.']

1. In August 1914 the Second International forfeited its life by the most disgraceful political and moral bankruptcy. By amalgamating with it the Two-and-a-half International has finally and formally put the seal on its own treachery. . . .

The Two-and-a-half International was a half-way house between the

Second and the Third Internationals. But its brief life has shown that without the methods of the Comintern, against the Comintern, it is impossible
to work for the revolution and the dictatorship, and that nationalization
without the proletarian dictatorship is self-deception or a swindle. That is
why the Two-and-a-half International was condemned to oscillate per-
petually between proletarian revolution and capitalist counter-revolution,
between its hopeless nationalization and capitalist reconstruction, until it
became ripe for capitalist reconstruction without extenuating phrases, for
government coalition with the capitalists, for unification with the Second
International.

The Two-and-a-half International was the expression of the radically-
minded section of the working class who stood for revolutionary class
struggle and the united front with communist workers in that struggle, but
were not yet ready for the proletarian revolution. But since it became more
and more obvious that their way of struggle, their promised nationalization, their progress were hopeless, and since the workers organized in their
ranks began to feel growing sympathy with the communist workers, the
leaders had no other choice, if they did not want to lose their followers
entirely, but to give the disappointed workers a new hope by pointing to
a new road, the road of unification with the great masses of workers supporting the leaders of the Second International. So the leaders of the new
International who have so often publicly asserted they were striving only
for the unification of all three Internationals and would not agree to
unification with the Second International only, have yielded unconditionally to that Second International.

2. . . . . The Second International was the child of the epoch that has
passed and died in the world war as a new epoch was coming into being
to whose new and great demands it was not equal.

The new Second International is stillborn. It will be buried at the first
international conflict, the first serious difference between capital and
labour.

That is the Comintern's latest rival in the labour movement, a rival
which is a guarantee of the Comintern's success.

3. The Hamburg International . . . will soon be recognized by the
workers still deceived by it as a bulwark of the bourgeoisie. Or it will fall
to pieces at the first shot, as its predecessor did in August 1914.

It is the task of the Comintern and its sections to accelerate this inevitable process. But this can and must be done only on the basis of the
struggle for the united front of the proletariat on a national and international scale. . . . The more tenaciously and sharply we wage that
struggle, the sooner will the great majority of the working and exploited
masses realize that only communism can liberate them from the horrors
of capitalism and build a better future.

RESOLUTION OF THE THIRD ECCI PLENUM ON THE PROGRAMME OF
THE COMMUNIST INTERNATIONAL

21 *June* 1923   *Inprekorr*, iii, 108, p. 934, 27 *June* 1923

[Bukharin reported on this question. There were three draft programmes—his own, Varga's, and one from the KPD. Drafts for the section on partial demands had also been received from the British and Japanese. There were some important theoretical differences; the German draft, for example, advanced Rosa Luxemburg's theory of the accumulation of capital as an explanation of capitalist decline. As he had done when reporting on the programme to the fourth world congress, Bukharin referred to the question of alliances between proletarian and bourgeois States. This was already a practical question, as was shown by Russian support for Turkey at Lausanne, or for the bourgeois government of Sun Yat-sen. The question of support for the revolutionary proletariat of one State by an already existing proletarian State was still theoretical, but would arise as a practical question in the future. This question would have to be included in the programme. The extension of socialism was not red imperialism—imperialism meant subjection to finance-capital. Tsarism had iron discipline in its army, and the Comintern had iron discipline in its ranks; Tsarism had the Okhrana, and Soviet Russia now had the GPU; it was not the formal aspect, but the class content of an institution or policy that determined its character. In a letter to Souvarine in January 1923 Bukharin had written that if Poland were to attack a revolutionary Germany, the Russians might have to advance against Poland, and had elaborated other hypothetical cases in which proletarian States might have to make agreements with an oppressed or threatened State to oppose the stronger State that was oppressing or threatening it. Zinoviev had referred to this question in his opening remarks. Most comrades had kept quiet about the social-democratic charge of 'red imperialism'; only Treint (France) had said: 'Well, why not?' This was carrying left infantilism too far. The use of force against the bourgeoisie was legitimate, but this was to establish the proletarian dictatorship, not red imperialism. Bukharin suggested that the programme should consist of a general theoretical statement valid for all parties, which, while outlining the maximum communist goals, would also explain why partial and transitional demands were necessary. Each party would then have in addition its own programme, adapted to local circumstances. The resolution was passed without discussion.]

The enlarged Executive thinks it necessary that a common general section should be included in the programme of all the parties. It also considers it desirable that the programme should deal with the following questions: *Weltanschauung* (Marxist materialism, attitude to religion, etc.), the national question, the strategy of proletarian States, the workers' and peasants' government.

Each party is to work up and forward to the Executive the following material: (1) an analysis of the situation of the country in the present epoch; (2) a list of partial demands; (3) material on the attitude to other workers' parties; (4) drafts for the national section of the programme; (5) opinions on the drafts for the general section already submitted, and further proposals for that section.

Each party shall appoint one comrade to take responsibility for this work. The enlarged Executive shall appoint a small commission to: (1) establish contact with the other parties; (2) initiate and conduct discussions on the question of the programme, work out a draft of the general section of the programme for the fifth congress on the basis of all the material so collected, and also examine the programmes of our national sections.

EXTRACTS FROM THE RESOLUTION OF THE THIRD ECCI PLENUM ON THE TRADE UNION QUESTION

23 *June* 1923   *Inprekorr*, iii, 113, p. 971, 5 *July* 1923

[Lozovsky reported on this question. Many comrades, he said, had interpreted the united front as an armistice with the reformists. It was nothing of the kind. Ideologically, there was no armistice at all, and as far as action was concerned, a truce could be maintained only so long and in so far as the reformists really served the proletarian cause. In May 1923 the International Transport Workers' Federation, of which Edo Fimmen was secretary, affiliated to the RILU. Lozovsky stated that they were ready to enter 'an honest coalition' with the left wing of the IFTU on the basis of the programme worked out with the Transport Workers. Gallacher spoke of the need for the communist party to exercise control over the work of the RILU bureau in the unions.]

I

In the last few months a great change has been taking place within the reformist wing of the labour movement, as shown by the formation within the Amsterdam International of a left wing anxious to form a united front with the Russian unions, and through them with the RILU and the organizations attached to it. . . .

II

The reasons for this change are:

1. The failure of the Amsterdam International's policy of class conciliation;

2. The growing tendency of the working masses to move to a revolutionary position as a result of our tactics of the united front and winning the unions. . . .

III

The new situation confronts all communist parties with the question of the further operation of the tactics laid down by the congresses of the Communist International. Mere propaganda for the united front is no longer enough; every worker must be made to understand the reasons for the united front, the forms it should take, and the methods of struggle. . . . The united front must be given an organizational basis by the creation of joint committees adapted to local special circumstances.

The most important task for the immediate future is to work out a concrete programme of action according to industry and area.

IV

Our struggle to re-establish the unity of the trade union movement must have its starting-point in the factories where the workers feel the need for that unity most clearly. It has become clear that the factory committees are the most suitable bodies for the united front, and therefore communists in those countries where there are no factory committees must fight among the broad masses for their establishment, and in the countries where they do exist must seek to revolutionize them and fight for an extension of their rights.

The transference of emphasis to work in the factories and the fight to establish factory committees do not by any means imply that the committees are to replace the unions organizationally. That would weaken the workers' movement and must be decisively rejected. It would make our struggle to win the unions and turn them into industrial unions more difficult, and surrender the unions to the present reformist leaders.

V

In countries where the workers are of various nationalities and races, communists must fight to get the workers of whatever nationality and race into the same union. But in this struggle to overcome national prejudices the communist party, which embraces the workers of the predominating nationalities, must fight vigorously against those elements in the labour movement who seek, behind an international banner, to hamper the free development of the oppressed nations. . . .

VI

Vigorous resistance must be offered to the continuing splitting policy of the reformist unions. If groups of workers or unions are expelled, those expelled should be kept together and every effort made to get them re-accepted. In no case should opposition elements who sympathize with the expelled be withdrawn from the old unions.

In those countries where two parallel trade union movements exist, one reformist and one revolutionary, the unions expelled by the reformist federation should join the revolutionary federation. But even in those countries individuals and groups who are expelled should fight for re-admission to the reformist unions so long as this seems to be in the interests of the revolutionary movement.

VII

The session of the enlarged CI Executive asks the entire party press to follow more attentively the life and struggles of the unions, to explain in detail the activities of the revolutionary unions and of the minority opposi-tions and fractions. . . . All communist parties must send regular reports on the activities of their trade union fractions to the Executive Committee, so that the experience of one country may be made the common property of the entire international movement.

VIII

Every member of the CI is obliged to join his appropriate trade union organization and to work actively in the communist fraction in that union or in the revolutionary opposition movement. Communist activities in the unions must be in accordance with the principles and decisions of the Red International of Labour Unions. The sections of the Communist International must make every effort to unite the trade unionists through-out the world under the banner of the RILU.

RESOLUTION OF THE THIRD ECCI PLENUM ON THE ANGLO-RUSSIAN CONFLICT

23 *June* 1923   *Inprekorr*, iii, 113, p. 988, 5 *July* 1923

[On 8 May a note from Lord Curzon, then British Foreign Secretary, com-plained of non-observance by the Soviet side of the provisions of the Anglo-Russian agreement of 1921. In particular, it referred to anti-British activities by Comintern and Soviet agents in the Middle East and India. The note con-cluded with a conditional threat to sever relations. In opening the debate at the enlarged Executive on the international situation, Radek said that the loss of the German market was a very serious blow to Britain, which now looked to its colonies more than before. This was the reason for the Curzon note to the Soviet Government; it explained British anxiety about the expansion of Russian trade with the Middle East. Britain hoped to weaken Russia by provoking a Russo-Polish war. This referred to Marshal Foch's visit to Poland early in May 1923, which was followed in a few days by a visit of the Chief of the Imperial General Staff. These visits reinforced the disquiet created in Moscow by the assassination of Vorovsky, which some communist writers described as 'the first result' of the Curzon note. Newbold (CPGB) at the plenum suggested that King George V was behind the note, as he had been left a great many shares in Persian and other Middle Eastern countries by his father, King Edward VII. Trotsky's speech implied that Curzon's policy was a continuation of traditional British policy towards Russia. Litvinov's reply of 11 May to the 'Curzon ultimatum' was conciliatory in tone.]

In the course taken by the Russian-English conflict, and in the manner in which it has just been settled, the enlarged Executive sees proof of English imperialism's readiness to utilize every opportunity to proceed against the first workers' and peasants' State with threats of armed struggle and armed attack, in order to liquidate the most important achievements of the first wave of the world revolution, just as it succeeded in destroying, in England itself, the conquests made by the working class in 1919.

The expansion of Soviet Russia's power, the beginning of its economic consolidation, the reappearance of Russia on world markets as an exporter of food and raw materials, the strengthening of ties between the Soviet Government and all sections of the working population, the steadily growing power and influence of the communist party—all these destroy English imperialism's hopes of exploiting Russia's economic needs to overthrow the Soviet Government, of defeating it on the economic field, and bringing it into subjection to world capital. Since the strengthening of Soviet Russia is also bound to exercise an encouraging influence on the awakening peoples of the East, the English imperialist Government is trying to force Russia to its knees and so make of it an English vassal, or at the least to provoke it into fighting. English imperialism indulged the hope that the universal hatred of capitalist governments for the Russian revolution would induce other Powers to join in the struggle against the Soviet Government and so bring about general intervention. The enlarged Executive congratulates the Soviet Government on not allowing itself to be provoked by English imperialism, but instead, by a clear and decisive policy which involved certain sacrifices, on having avoided the rupture which England's ruling classes wished to precipitate. The enlarged Executive expresses its sincere pleasure at the firm and conscious resolution with which the Russian working masses rallied protectively behind the Soviet Government immediately the English ultimatum became known. It sees in this a pledge that, should the imperialist governments again one day unleash a new struggle against the Soviet Government, they would encounter not only the resistance of the international working class to such a criminal attack on the achievements of the Russian revolution, but would break their own teeth on the granite-hard will of the heroic revolutionary people of Russia.

The enlarged Executive notes that the Second International found it possible, while protesting at its Hamburg congress against Lord Curzon's assault on the Russian revolution and thus on the peace of the nations, to announce their solidarity with the Russian pace-makers of the Entente counter-revolution, the mensheviks and SRs. In denouncing this support given to world imperialism, the enlarged Executive calls on the workers of all countries to come out still more vigorously in defence of Soviet Russia. The English Government has rejected all the Soviet Government's proposals for an effective settlement of the questions in dispute. Any day may see the danger of a rupture of Anglo-Russian relations, even the danger of a new war. This sense of danger must be kept permanently alive among the proletarian masses of the entire world, so that they may be ready at any time to oppose the policy of attacks on the Russian revolution. The enlarged Executive calls on the working masses of the East to rally under the banner of Soviet Russia, which parries the blows aimed at the Eastern peoples fighting for their emancipation.

RESOLUTION OF THE THIRD ECCI PLENUM ON THE COMMUNIST ATTITUDE TO RELIGION

23 *June* 1923   *Inprekorr*, iii, 113, p. 988, 5 *July* 1923

[The discussion on this question arose in connexion with the Swedish CP whose leader, Höglund, had written that religion was a private matter in relation to the party as well as to the State. He said it was not an important question in the Swedish party, but Zinoviev had made it central. An explicit anti-religious campaign would repel many workers who were finding their way to communism. If their religious opinions were not in conflict with the party's political programme and activities, they should be ignored. Britain as well as the Scandinavian countries was opposed to direct anti-religious propaganda, except as part of party education. Falk added that anti-religious propaganda would in particular antagonize the peasants. Bukharin said that in Eastern countries religion might play a revolutionary part, as the fight of religious fanatics in Asia against British imperialism showed. Zinoviev said: 'In our party we exclude members, even those who fought five years against the whites, if they marry in church.' To make religion a private matter in relation to the bourgeois State was a political question—it was intended to deprive the bourgeoisie of one of their means of oppressing the working class, the church. The dispute about religion was aggravated by differences on other matters. Höglund had supported the Norwegians in criticizing the exaggerated centralism of the Comintern.

Humbert-Droz, in Paris, wrote to Zinoviev that the ECCI resolution had offended some good Protestant militants associated with the French CP, and greatly embarrassed the politbureau.]

In view of the fact that erroneous statements have been made in the Swedish communist press, which might cause confusion among communists, the plenary session of the Comintern Executive declares:

Communists demand that religion shall remain a private matter in relation to the bourgeois State; in no circumstances, however, can communists declare that religion is a private matter in relation to the communist party also. Communists demand that the bourgeois State as such shall have no relations with religion and that religious associations shall not be connected in any way with the bourgeois State authorities. Communists demand that every citizen shall be free to acknowledge any religion he chooses or no religion, that is, to be an atheist, which normally every conscious communist is. Communists demand that in regard to the rights of citizens the State shall make no distinction which is based on religious affiliation. They demand that in official documents no mention should be made of the religious adherence of the citizen. They would deprive the bourgeois State of any power of granting any material or other support to ecclesiastical or religious bodies. Taken all together, this amounts to the demand that, in relation to the State, religion shall be declared a private matter.

But in no case can the communist party remain indifferent to the fact that some of its members devote themselves, even as 'private persons', to religious propaganda. The communist party is an association, voluntarily formed, of conscious and advanced fighters for the emancipation of the working class. The communist vanguard of the working class cannot and must not remain indifferent to ignorance, unenlightenment, and religious obscurantism. The communist party is obliged to train its members not only in the devoted pursuit of a particular political programme and economic demands and party statutes; they must also have implanted in them the clear-cut and homogeneous world outlook of Marxism, of which atheism is an essential part.

It is obvious that anti-religious propaganda must be conducted with particular caution and after careful consideration, according to the kind of groups among whom it is being conducted. Communist anti-religious propaganda, particularly among young people, must be carried out according to a carefully elaborated programme which takes any special circumstances into consideration.

Occasionally members are to be found in a mass communist party who have not entirely discarded religious sentiments and prejudices. The party as a whole, on the other hand, and in particular its leading sections, must combat religious prejudices and carry on propaganda for atheism in an expedient manner. Active religious propaganda by leading comrades, especially intellectuals, is absolutely inadmissible, however up to date the form it takes.

Communists are in favour of all workers, whatever their religious opinions, joining the trade unions which have a class character. Since, in many countries, there are still millions of workers of a religious turn of mind, communists must draw them into the general economic and political struggle; in no circumstances should they be rejected because of their religious prejudices. In their agitation for a workers' government or a workers' and peasants' government, communists should in particular always emphasize that they are proposing a fraternal alliance with all workers, whether believers or atheists.

EXTRACTS FROM A RESOLUTION OF THE THIRD ECCI PLENUM ON FASCISM

23 *June* 1923   *Inprekorr*, iii, 113, p. 989, 5 *July* 1923

[Klara Zetkin, moving the resolution, referred to fascism as 'the strongest, most concentrated, and classical expression of the general offensive of the world bourgeoisie'. Historically, it was a punishment for the proletariat not having carried farther the revolution begun in Russia. It was a result of the breakdown of capitalist society and a symptom of the dissolution of the bourgeois State. It was recruited from the middle classes impoverished and proletarianized by the war, from ex-officers now unemployed, and from all those disappointed in reformist socialism who, instead of turning left, had lost hope in socialism. It had attracted thousands of disappointed proletarians who hoped that the will to build a new and better world would rise above class contradictions and find its embodiment in the nation. The Italian CP had seen in fascism only a militarist terrorist movement, not a mass movement with a broad social basis which had already won a political and ideological victory over the working class before it came to power in Italy. The communist parties must make the utmost efforts, politically and ideologically, to rescue those who had gone over to fascism, including the bourgeois intelligentsia. Against fascist force and terror the working class must organize for self-defence.

Radek was the next speaker, and it was on this occasion that he made his famous 'Schlageter speech'. Schlageter, a German nationalist, had been executed by the French on 26 May 1923 for sabotage in the Ruhr. 'I could not follow Klara Zetkin's speech all through', Radek said, 'because all the time I had before my eyes the corpse of the German fascist, our class enemy, condemned and shot by . . . French imperialism. . . . The fate of this German nationalist martyr should not be passed over by us in silence, or with a contemptuous phrase. . . . Schlageter, the courageous soldier of the counter-revolution, deserves honest and manly esteem from us, soldiers of the revolution. . . . Against whom do the German nationalists want to fight? Against Entente capital or the Russian people? With whom do they wish to ally themselves? With the Russian workers and peasants, together to shake off the yoke of Entente capital, or with Entente capital to enslave the German and Russian peoples? Schlageter is dead and cannot answer this question. At his grave his comrades vowed to carry on his work. They must answer: Against whom? On whose side? If German patriotic circles do not decide to make the cause of this [workers'] majority their own, and so establish a front against Entente and German capital, then Schlageter's road was a road into the void, and Germany, faced by foreign invasion and by constant danger from the victors, will become the field of bloody internal battles, and it will be easy for the enemy to destroy and dismember it.' Shortly after the ECCI meeting Radek wrote that fascism was the reaction of the petty bourgeoisie to the situation created by the war, which the big bourgeoisie would use to restore their power wherever it was shaken or endangered. The conference at Frankfurt in March had described it as 'preventive counter-revolution', differing from ordinary counter-revolution by making a direct appeal to the masses with pseudo-radical slogans.

Tentative moves to detach working-class followers of the nationalist parties had been made by the KPD before, and Radek's speech was greeted with applause, but Neurath attacked the KPD for competing with the German nationalists instead of fighting internationally. The majority spokesmen replied that to win the masses to their side they must take their national ideology as the starting-point; the nationalism created by the occupation of the Ruhr was a revolutionary factor which the KPD must exploit. The ECCI approved the tactics of the KPD in regard to the Ruhr. Neurath was correct in arguing that to fight the French bourgeoisie the German working class had to fight and defeat its own bourgeoisie, but the KPD were taking into account the 'objectively revolutionary role' of the German bourgeoisie at this juncture. The bourgeoisie would fail, and it was for the KPD to prove that it alone represented the true interests of the German nation. In July 1923 a pamphlet appeared under the title *Schlageter: eine Auseinandersetzung*, with contributions from Radek and Frölich, and from two prominent German nationalists, Graf von Reventlow and Moeller van der Bruck. The reviewer, 'L.B.', in *Inprekorr* (1 August 1923) suggested that anyone who was surprised by its appearance, or by Radek's speech, had a confused idea of fascism. 'Fascism is not a bourgeois movement. It is primarily a movement of broad popular masses whose basic economic interests are hostile to the exploiting and impoverishing policy of the bourgeoisie'. The movement was exploited by the bourgeoisie but it had its own political and economic aims. Fascism was the political enemy of the revolutionary working class 'not because of historically irreconcilable class contradictions' but because of the treachery of the social-democrats, who had driven those masses into the enemy camp and now taunted the communists with trying to win them back. Nationalist and communist speakers appeared on the same platform in Germany until this was stopped, from the nationalist side, in August 1923. This was interpreted in *Inprekorr* as a sign of the success of communist tactics.

At the fifth Comintern congress in 1924 one German delegate attacked Radek's 'Schlageter policy'. Radek replied that the 'Schlageter declaration' in the *Rote Fahne*, though written by him, had been signed by Thaelmann, Fischer, and Maslow, and his speech at the ECCI had been approved by that body, and specifically by Zinoviev. In September 1923 Humbert-Droz reported to Moscow that KPD policy towards the German nationalists was creating uneasiness in the French party. Was it out to win the support of the nationalist German petty bourgeoisie and lose the support of the French working class for the German revolution? 'They understand defence of the revolutionary fatherland after the conquest of power by the proletariat, but the defence of the revolutionary fatherland by anticipation, while Germany is still the "patrie de Stinnes" ruled by the bourgeoisie, is too subtle for them.']

Fascism is a characteristic phenomenon of decay, a reflection of the progressive dissolution of capitalist economy and of the disintegration of the bourgeois State.

Its strongest root is the fact that the imperialist war and the disruption of the capitalist economy which the war intensified and accelerated meant, for broad strata of the petty and middle bourgeoisie, small peasants, and the 'intelligentsia', in contrast to the hopes they cherished, the destruction of their former condition of life and especially their former security. The vague expectations which many in these social strata had of a radical social improvement, to be brought about by reformist socialism, have also been disappointed. The betrayal of the revolution by the reformist party and trade union leaders . . . has led them to despair of socialism itself. The weakness of will, the fear of struggle shown by the way in which the overwhelming majority of the proletariat outside Soviet Russia tolerates this treachery, and under capitalist whips drudges to consolidate its own exploitation and enslavement, has robbed these small and middle bourgeois, as well as the intellectuals, brought into a state of ferment, of their belief in the working class as the mighty agent of a radical social transformation. They have been joined by many proletarian elements who, looking for and demanding action, feel dissatisfied with the behaviour of all political parties. Fascism also attracts the disappointed and declassed, the rootless in every social stratum, particularly ex-officers who have lost their occupation since the end of the war. This is particularly true of the defeated Central Powers, where in consequence fascism has taken on a marked anti-republican character. . . .

In the period of revolutionary ferment and proletarian risings, fascism to some extent sympathized or at least flirted with proletarian revolutionary demands. The masses which followed fascism vacillated between the two camps in the great and universal class contradictions and class struggles. But with the consolidation of capitalist rule and the general bourgeois offensive they threw themselves definitely on to the side of the bourgeoisie, where their leaders had stood from the beginning. The bourgeoisie immediately took fascism into paid service in their fight to defeat and enslave the proletariat. . . . The old, allegedly non-political apparatus of the bourgeois State no longer guarantees the bourgeoisie adequate security. They have set about creating special class-struggle troops against the proletariat. Fascism provides these troops. Although fascism by its origin and its exponents also includes revolutionary tendencies, which might turn against capitalism and its State, it is nevertheless becoming a dangerous counter-revolutionary force. That has been shown where it triumphed, in Italy. . . . In Italy the door to fascism was opened by the passivity of the socialist party and the reformist trade union leaders; its revolutionary phraseology won over many proletarian elements, which made its victory possible. . . . The triumph of fascism in Italy spurs the bourgeoisie of other countries to take the same course in defeating the proletariat. The working classes of the entire world are threatened with the fate of their Italian brothers. . . .

It is the task of the conscious revolutionary vanguard of the working class to take up the struggle against victorious fascism in Italy and in the rest of the world where it is organizing. Fascism must be disarmed and defeated politically, and the workers organized strongly for self-defence against fascist violence. To accomplish this it is necessary to take the following steps:

I

In every workers' party and workers' organization, of whatever tendency, a special body must be set up to conduct the struggle against fascism and its foreign representatives. This body shall:

1. collect information about the fascist movement in its country;
2. systematically enlighten the working class about the hostile class character of the fascist movement by articles in the press, pamphlets, posters, meetings, etc.;
3. systematically enlighten the recently proletarianized masses, and those threatened with proletarianization, about the nature of fascism and its functions in the service of large-scale capitalism;
4. organize the defensive struggles of the workers by setting up and arming special detachments. Since the fascists are particularly active in their propaganda to young people, young workers must be drawn into the united front, and those over seventeen should be included in the factory self-defence detachments. Workers' co-ordinating committees should be set up to prevent the transport of fascist gangs and their weapons. Any fascist attempt to terrorize the workers and hamper them to be ruthlessly defeated;
5. draw workers of whatever opinion into this struggle. Call on all workers' parties, unions, and proletarian mass organizations for joint defence against fascism;
6. fight against fascism in parliament and all public bodies; emphasize its imperialist and arch-chauvinist character, which increases the danger of new international wars.

II

The fascist forces are being organized on an international scale, and it is consequently necessary to organize the workers' struggle against fascism internationally. For this purpose an international workers' committee must be set up which, besides exchanging experiences, shall organize international actions, in the first place against Italian fascism. This committee shall consider:

1. an international educational campaign, through the press, pamphlets, photographs, mass meetings, on the anti-labour character of the Italian fascist regime and its destruction of all workers' organizations and institutions;
2. the organization of mass meetings and demonstrations against fascism, and against the representatives of the fascist Italian State abroad;
3. the parliamentary struggle: getting parliaments, the workers' representatives in parliament, and international workers' organizations to send commissions to Italy to investigate the situation of the working class;
4. the struggle for the immediate liberation of communist, socialist, and non-party workers imprisoned or under arrest;
5. the preparation of an international anti-Italian boycott: the refusal to despatch coal to Italy, the refusal of all transport workers to load and forward goods destined for Italy. International committees of miners, merchant seamen, railwaymen, transport workers, etc., to be set up for this purpose;
6. material and moral support for the persecuted Italian workers by the collection of funds, hospitality for refugees, support for their work abroad, etc. The International Red Aid shall be used for this work, and the co-operatives should be drawn into it.

The workers must be made aware that they will share the fate of the Italian workers if they do not engage in energetic revolutionary struggle against the ruling class and prevent the less class-conscious elements from joining the fascists.

EXTRACTS FROM THE RESOLUTION OF THE THIRD ECCI PLENUM ON
THE ITALIAN QUESTION

23 *June* 1923   *Inprekorr*, iii, 113, p. 994, 5 *July* 1923

[After the fourth Comintern congress Jules Humbert-Droz, the Executive's representative in Italy, reported that he found more hostility to the united front in Rome than the Italian delegation had shown in Moscow. The ECCI in January 1923 had suggested that the 'fusionists' in the Italian Socialist Party should call for a party congress; if the request were refused, they were to declare their fraction the party, loyal to the earlier resolution on amalgamation with the communists. At the congress of the Italian Socialist Party in Milan in

April 1923 the majority was opposed to fusion. Comintern supporters were told to stay in the socialist party, avoid giving pretexts for expulsion, and work to secure a majority at the next congress. 'Nenni made a very bad impression on me. He is a *jeune arriviste* who has exploited the traditions of the Socialist Party to get control of *Avanti*', Humbert-Droz wrote, adding that the central committee of the Italian Communist Party was trying to get rid of those who supported fusion by posting them abroad. Fusion could not be forced by the ECCI. Moreover, it might be better, under fascism, to have the socialist banner, with a reputation and prestige among the masses which the communist party had not yet won. He reported that the disagreements between the two other ECCI representatives in Italy at that time, Manuilsky and Rakosi, had made the situation much more difficult.

The ECCI report stated that the preparatory commission to effect the merger between the Italian Socialist and Communist parties had stayed too long in Moscow and moved too slowly. Meanwhile the opposition in the communist party and the anti-fusionists in the socialist party had exploited the reluctance of the communists to merge and campaigned against fusion. When the commission returned to Italy, most of its members were arrested.

In his opening report, Zinoviev observed that the Italian central committee, led by Bordiga, still believed that Serrati, and not Mussolini, was the enemy. It had agreed to the merger as a matter of discipline, but the negotiations had been dragged out until it was too late. The vote of the Italian Socialist Party against fusion was not the last word but merely an episode. He proposed that the socialist party should be admitted to the Comintern as a sympathizing party, and that the CPI and SPI should establish a united front with the moral support of the Comintern. The spokesman for the socialist party said that the conditions put forward by the communists were an insult to the fusionists in the SPI. Urbani, speaking for the Italian CP, said that unification could not be effected in Moscow. The CPI had made mistakes, but it was not solely responsible. The socialists had sabotaged the negotiations, and the representatives sent by the Comintern did not agree among themselves. Giacomo referred to the difficulties created by Mussolini's victory, which had taken the CPI by surprise. When the resolution was put forward, Lunacharsky read a letter from the Italian Socialist Party, dated 10 June, containing the resolution of the Milan congress of that party which stated that the delegates to the fourth Comintern congress had exceeded their mandate. The SPI wanted to renounce neither its name, nor its banner, nor its autonomy. The Comintern should be more flexible about the conditions put to parties in different countries with widely varying positions. It should accept the SPI as it was, without further discussion, otherwise the SPI would have to take action against those members whose entire activity in it consisted of getting it to adhere to the CI, and a united front would be impossible.

Lunacharsky, reporting for the commission, recommended that two members of the minority in the Italian Communist Party should be added to the central committee. The representatives of the majority stated that they would vote for the resolution, but wished it placed on record that they had done everything they could to implement the instructions of the fourth congress. 'Since the discussion in the plenum and in the commission has revealed deep differences between the methods of the central committee elected by the party majority, and now to be replaced, and the International, the passage in the resolution which states that the composition of the central committee must be such as to guarantee the execution of CI decisions can be interpreted only as meaning the elimination from the central committee of the tendency which up to now has been predominant in the party leadership.' The resolution was passed unanimously. Meanwhile, in Italy, the socialist party split on the question of collaboration with the Italian CP; the majority found the terms unacceptable and expelled Serrati and many of his supporters. In a letter to the socialist party in October 1923 the ECCI accused Nenni and the majority of sabotaging the united front; they were strike-breakers who, objectively, were carrying out Mussolini's orders. It called on the members to reject these leaders and join the communists.

In January 1924 Humbert-Droz reported that Bordiga's extremist policy was receiving less support; the proposal to form an electoral bloc with other proletarian parties had been accepted. The CP and the fusionists were to issue a daily paper. The socialist party, he reported a few days later, had fortunately refused to join the bloc; if it had agreed the (clandestine) communist fraction in the socialist party would have lost the advantage. 'But we prevented this, when we realized the danger, by a letter from the fraction which suggested that acceptance of the proposal for an electoral bloc would mean the eventual capitulation of the socialist party.' Serrati was a problem, for, depressed and defeatist as he was, he could not be used in a responsible post and was difficult to use in a subordinate one. The Italian CP was opposed to putting him forward as a parliamentary candidate because it would increase his importance. It wanted the ECCI to find him a job outside Italy. 'But', wrote Humbert-Droz, 'Serrati is a leader despite us, and he has been a leader against us.' He was of interest to them only as a leader, and if they could not use his popularity they need not use him at all. He was useful in so far as he could bring back those he had earlier alienated from the Comintern.

Humbert-Droz asked to be sent copies of the letters from the ECCI to the Italian CP and the fusionists, otherwise he could not do his job properly. He wanted to know why Bordiga, who had been dropped from the ECCI in June 1923, had been reappointed. He complained on several occasions of the changes in Moscow on the question of amalgamation between the Italian CP and the fusionists—a question, he said, of which the fusionists were tired and by which the communists were hypnotized. The fusionists were angry because, although a communist attended the meetings of their executive, they were not allowed to send a representative, even for consultation, to the communist meetings. Their anger grew, he wrote to Zinoviev on 15 March 1924, when *Avanti* published a CP circular on the aims of communists in the socialist party; they accused the CPI of duplicity and sabotage. Togliatti had told them that Humbert-Droz had seen and approved the circular, but this was not true. 'The atmosphere of distrust in which the party lives is due to repeated manifestations of this absence of loyalty.' Writing to Zinoviev again shortly before the fifth congress, he referred to the 'frequently shabby and underhand manœuvres' of the communists in operating the electoral alliance. The communist editor of the joint communist-socialist paper had refused to publish a fusionist resolution which referred to the CP circular as 'unfortunate', and the fusionists now refused to admit a communist to the meetings of their executive. The alliance gained 19 seats, of which 13 went to the communists, 6 to the fusionists.]

The resolution of the fourth world congress on the Italian question stipulated the fusion of the CPI with the majority of the SPI who at the Rome congress had voted for the Third International, and called for the utmost unity of all revolutionary workers against the threat of fascism. Events have shown that this resolution was and remains correct. While reaffirming it, the enlarged Executive notes with deep regret that the wishes of the fourth congress have not yet been realized.

The chief reasons for this failure are:

1. The fascist white terror, the persecution of the working class, the unpunished murder of revolutionary workers, the countless arrests have temporarily driven the workers' movement into illegality and caused some degree of demoralization. Since the heaviest blows have fallen on communists, it is understandable that at the moment the more irresolute socialists are reluctant to amalgamate with the communists. . . .

2. The right wing of the SPI . . . conducted a systematic campaign against amalgamation with the communists, exploiting the unfavourable conditions in which the advocates of fusion found themselves.

To some extent the failure was due also to the incorrect tactics of the majority of the CC of the CPI. Hypnotized by the previous struggle against Serrati's group, and suffering from extreme dogmatism, the CC majority failed completely to take into account that the situation in the labour movement had changed radically. . . . Not only did they not campaign for fusion with the SPI; they actually frustrated the execution of the fourth world congress decision.

The enlarged Executive decides:

A. In regard to the CP:

1. The International demands of the CC of the CPI, not merely formal acknowledgement, but practical execution of this decision. . . .

3. The CP must use united front tactics adapted to Italian conditions, i.e. it must make proposals to the SP leaders in a form consistent with CI decisions.

4. The composition of the Executive of the CP must be such as to guarantee the carrying out of these measures.

B. In regard to the SP:

1. The enlarged Executive notes that the present SP leadership relies

on the votes of a doubtful majority. The Milan congress was convened during the white terror which reduced the membership from 32,000 to 9,000. Nevertheless more than 40 per cent. were in favour of amalgamation with the communists. . . .

4. The Executive notes that at a moment when there is a crisis in the Amsterdam International and the most class-conscious left among the workers are drawing nearer to the RILU, the CC of the SPI found it appropriate to rejoin the Amsterdam International.

5. The Executive must conclude from the above that up to now the SP leadership has acted in a fashion hostile to the CI.

6. The Executive regards the Milan congress and the present situation in the SP as a temporary episode. . . .

7. The Executive wishes to leave nothing undone which can accelerate the coming together of all revolutionary forces in Italy, and believes it is meeting the wishes of the majority of workers in the SP by welcoming the desire to draw closer to the CI expressed in the letter of 10 June, despite the hostile actions referred to above.

8. To give practical form to this rapprochement, the Executive proposes that the CC of the SP form a working alliance with the CP. . . .

9. In proof of its solidarity with the SP workers . . . the Executive requests the Executive of the SP to send a delegation to Moscow to effect adherence to the Comintern.

ECCI APPEAL TO THE WORKERS AND PEASANTS OF BULGARIA TO
OPPOSE THE NEW BULGARIAN GOVERNMENT

23 *June* 1923   *Inprekorr*, iii, 113, p. 985, 5 *July* 1923

[On 8 June 1923 the Government of Stambuliski and his Peasant Union was overthrown, and Tsankov became the Prime Minister of the 'constitutional bloc' which had engineered the coup. In the elections of April 1923 the Peasant Union had won 212 out of a total of 245 seats, the communists 16, and the socialists 2. The 'constitutional bloc', consisting of the bourgeois parties which had been virtually outlawed by Stambuliski, also got 16 seats. The Bulgarian CP had from the first been unwilling to accept the slogan of 'a workers' and peasants' government' for Bulgaria, arguing that they could detach the peasants from Stambuliski, and that the slogan was applicable only to countries where the workers and peasants were confronted by strong bourgeois parties. Relations between the peasant and communist parties were very bad, and at the time of Professor Tsankov's coup d'etat the central committee advised neutrality as between 'two wings of the bourgeoisie', and called off resistance where it did occur. At a meeting of the central committee of the Bulgarian party held on 11 June it was agreed that the battle between the new and the deposed Governments was one between two wings of the capitalist class, in which the party and the masses had no part. At the ECCI meeting which opened a few days later,

Zinoviev urged the necessity of joining forces with the Peasant Union against the new Government. The Bulgarian party's attitude was a great blunder; if it entered the struggle, this might lead to the formation of a workers' and peasants' government; if it did not, the Tsankov Government would remain in power and the party would be threatened; if, while the party remained passive, the masses took action, it would lead to a serious split in the party. Kabakchiev defended the Bulgarian party's policy; Stambuliski had no support in the towns, and only scattered support in the villages (Stambuliski himself was killed in the fighting); he had alienated the masses, and a communist call for an uprising would not have received their support. (In the debate on the report of the ECCI at the fifth Comintern congress in 1924, Kolarov said the Bulgarian party was mistaken in thinking that the Peasant Government had lost the confidence of the peasant masses and become a government of the rural bourgeoisie. The party had been wrong not to apply united front tactics from above as well as from below. The united front from above was initiated only after June 1923.) Radek was instructed to examine the situation, and reported on the last day of the Executive meeting. He bitterly attacked the passivity of the CPB. It had been caused not by the strength of the enemy, but by the absence of any will to fight; the party had even failed to understand that it *was* a defeat. It had neither allied itself with the Peasant Union, nor split it. It might have allied itself with the Macedonian nationalists to exert pressure on Stambuliski, but had ignored them. The ECCI had to bear responsibility, not for the incorrect Bulgarian policy, but for having failed to intervene earlier. This was a more serious defeat than the one suffered by the Italian party, which had been young and inexperienced. Stambuliski should have been supported as the only 'alien body' in bourgeois domination of the Balkans; he had the support of the great majority of peasants. 'To quote the third volume of *Capital* and say that the peasantry is also a part of the bourgeoisie is to fail in revolutionary duty.' Radek linked the Bulgarian events to his favourite thesis of Anglo-French rivalry. The Tsankov coup was part of the struggle between the two Western Powers for hegemony in Europe, and its success fortified England's policy of encircling Russia. The Little Entente, clients of France, had supported Stambuliski's policy of fulfilling the provisions of the Neuilly treaty A week later the Bulgarian party met and endorsed the neutrality policy by a vote of 42 to 2. Kolarov, who had been sent from Moscow to attend the conference, was arrested and did not reach Sofia until August. On 9 July Zinoviev wrote in *Inprekorr* of the errors of the Bulgarian party. A peasant government that was both anti-proletarian and anti-bourgeois could not survive, but Kabakchiev's argument that the urban workers were indifferent to its fate was merely a pretext to make the working class responsible for the party's inactivity. The bolsheviks had co-operated for a time with Kerensky against Kornilov, although Kerensky was no friend of the working class. On 10 July the Bulgarian CP published a resolution again approving the central committee's policy. The ECCI, it said, had not been well informed about the situation. The resolution was publicly criticized by Rakosi on behalf of the ECCI. Some local communists who had resisted the coup were arrested and tried; the CC of the Bulgarian CP disavowed them; four were sentenced to death.]

Comrades! In Bulgaria a small clique of bankrupt bureaucrats, un-employed officers, and speculators have captured the Government by a military coup d'état. The same men who drove the Bulgarian people into the world war, who have 200,000 dead on their conscience, who were three times rejected by the Bulgarian people in democratic elections—this same clique has dared to seize power by a putsch. They are setting up a regime of furious terror against the great majority of the population, against the workers and peasants. The prisons of Bulgaria are being filled with workers and peasants, the villages are being subdued to the will of reactionary adventurers by punitive expeditions. They are shooting the leaders of the peasantry, but have not the courage to take responsibility for their actions. Tomorrow they will begin to massacre the leaders of the working class also.

The white coup d'état of the Bulgarian bureaucrats, generals, and speculators took place with the consent and assistance of the social-democratic party, which is a section of the Second International. This party, which shares responsibility for the crimes of the Bulgarian war Government, a party from which all workers have turned away so that it has shrunk to nothing, allowed itself to be used as a fig-leaf for the counter-revolutionary revolt. It has thus shown itself worthy of Noske and Turati, who smoothed the way for the white revolt in Germany and Italy.

The revolt was accomplished with the help of the scum of the European counter-revolution, officers of Wrangel's army, and with the support of Horthy's hangmen and Rumanian boyars. Capitalist Europe, which is hypocritically trying to incite the so-called civilized world against the red terror, is hastening to recognize these murderous and dangerous adven-turers. The English Government, the Government of the English landlords and manufacturers, is supporting them, because it hopes to make Bulgaria a bulwark against Soviet Russia. The Italian Government supports them because it sees in the military adventurers of Sofia helpers in the struggle against Yugoslavia. The whole capitalist world has approved the white coup d'état in Bulgaria. The fascist gangs in all countries see in it a proof that it is easy to trample the working people under foot. We, the Com-munist International, the union of all militant workers in East and West, call on the Bulgarian workers and peasants, on the international working class, to fight against the Bulgarian putschists.

Peasants of Bulgaria! The victory of the white gangs is a lesson you must understand if you want to free yourselves from the yoke which is being laid on you. Stambuliski's peasant Government was overthrown because it did not understand the need of uniting with the urban workers. The interests of the great majority of the Bulgarian peasants, who are poor, are at one with the interests of the urban workers and artisans. Stambuliski perse-cuted the working class and so lost the one support which he could have had in the towns against the clique of bureaucrats and officers who have for forty years exploited and enslaved the Bulgarian people and want to go on doing so. Stambuliski has paid for his policy with his life. But the Bulgarian peasants are still living, and they must fight if they do not want to go on being treated as cattle. We call on them to unite with the workers in the towns, and to begin the fight with the slogan of establishing a government of urban and rural workers.

Workers of Bulgaria! Stambuliski's Government persecuted the labour movement in the interests of the village bourgeoisie and the village usurers; it sacrificed the interests of the working people in the towns and of the poor peasants. But if Stambuliski's Government persecuted the workers, Tsankov's Government, the Government of bureaucrats and generals, wants to annihilate them. Whoever mistakenly thinks that the struggle of the now triumphant white clique against Stambuliski is a struggle between two bourgeois cliques in which the working class can be neutral, will now be taught better by the bloody persecution of the workers' organizations. The putschists are now *the* enemy, and must be defeated. Unite for the fight against the white revolt not only with the broad masses of the peasantry, but with the leaders of the peasant party who are still alive. Show them what the split between workers and peasants has led to, and summon them to a common struggle for a workers' and peasants' government.

Peasants of Macedonia! Macedonian revolutionaries! You have let yourselves be misused by the Bulgarian counter-revolution for a coup d'état, although, as your past shows, your interests and your destiny are closely bound up with the interests of the working people, the interests of the revolution in the Balkans and throughout the world. Stambuliski's Government surrendered Macedonia to the Serbian bourgeoisie in order to get their support. It persecuted you bloodily. But do not think that the counter-revolutionary Government is in a position to liberate the Macedonian people. It will fight against the Bulgarian workers and peasants, against your brothers, but not for the liberation of the Macedonian peasants. In order to secure its rule, it will betray Macedonia a thousand times and oppress you, because it cannot tolerate a revolutionary peasant movement in Macedonia. Only a peasants' and workers' government in Bulgaria will arouse the sympathies of the peasants and workers of Rumania, Yugoslavia, and Greece. That alone will clear the path for the establishment of a Balkan federation of workers' and peasants' governments, which can alone free you without Macedonia again becoming the scene of bloody struggles in which your cottages will be burnt down, your fields laid waste. Macedonian peasants and Macedonian revolutionaries! However great your resentment of the Bulgarian Peasant Union and its leaders may be, none of you should give the slightest support to the white-terror Government in Bulgaria. On the contrary, for the sake of your national liberation you must unite with the militant Bulgarian workers and peasants.

Workers and peasants of Yugoslavia, Rumania, and Greece! Resolutely oppose all those in the Balkans who support Tsankov's Government, surround the ambassadors of these Governments with your hatred, surround white Bulgaria with the wall of your resistance, take advantage of every opportunity to help the peasants and workers of Bulgaria, the brave Bulgarian working people who are beginning the fight against the white Government. Workers of Czechoslovakia, Austria, and Germany! The victory of the fascist group in Bulgaria will encourage the fascist adventurers in your countries. Be on your guard, be vigilant, do not let yourselves be intimidated or taken unawares. Fight energetically against any help being given to white Bulgaria and learn the lesson of Bulgarian reaction and the mistakes of the Bulgarian peasants and workers. Exert all your efforts to create an alliance between the poor peasants and the workers against the attacks of the mercenaries of capital and of the military cliques, and learn to dare severe battles in the hour of danger, if you do not want to pay for your faintheartedness with the lives of the best among you.

Proletarians of all countries! We appeal to you to watch the development of events in Bulgaria most carefully. We appeal to you to let the broad masses know of all the outrages committed by the victorious clique of Bulgarian fascists against the working people of Bulgaria, helped by the capitalist Governments of all countries; we appeal to you to mobilize these masses against the Government of murderers in Sofia. The warning given by Sofia is as clear as the warning from Rome. The working classes of all countries are in danger. Prepare to defend yourselves.

OPEN LETTER FROM THE ECCI AND THE RILU TO THE SECOND INTERNATIONAL AND THE IFTU PROPOSING A JOINT CONFERENCE ON GERMAN PROBLEMS

25 *August* 1923   *Inprekorr*, iii, 140, p. 1220, 31 *August* 1923

[The German Government replied to the French occupation of the Ruhr by a policy of 'passive resistance', endorsed by the Reichstag by 284 votes to 12 (the KPD voting against) and 16 abstentions. Radek wrote that the German bourgeoisie supported passive resistance because inflation was one way of reducing wages; in another article he argued that the German bourgeoisie would capitulate to France as the only way of bringing inflation to an end. Unrest and discontent mounted steadily in Germany throughout the spring and summer of 1923, and inflation made the lot of wage-earners and others highly precarious. The June meeting of the ECCI (at which Radek made his Schlageter speech) referred to the situation in Germany in general terms only, not as immediately revolutionary. The Cuno Government resigned on 11 August, amid a mounting wave of strikes, food riots, etc. This was attributed (by a writer in *Inprekorr*) to the 'massive pressure of the KPD'; on the following day Stresemann formed a Government which included four members of the SPD, described by the KPD as 'the last reserve of the counter-revolution against the rising tide of the approaching proletarian revolution', and opened negotiations for settling the Ruhr dispute, thus ruling out the possibility of Germany's seeking Russian support for continued opposition to the Entente.

On 27 August the ECCI and RILU published an appeal 'to support the German proletariat' who were 'in the greatest danger'.

'Conditions in Germany are becoming more and more acute; unless all signs are deceptive, they are making for revolution.

'In these struggles the German proletariat will be opposed not only by the armed forces of the German bourgeoisie; there is the danger that, at the moment when the German proletariat, attacked by the German bourgeoisie, will be engaged in decisive struggles, the Entente bourgeoisie and their vassals will forget their hostility to the German bourgeoisie and hasten to their support. There is a danger that France, Poland, and Czechoslovakia will attempt the military occupation of Germany in order to subjugate the working class, in order to come to a final agreement with the German bourgeoisie at the expense of the German proletariat. There is a danger that English imperialism, by a naval blockade, and the vassals of the Entente in Eastern Europe, by a land blockade, will try to stop the import of food into Germany.' Radek wrote that Stresemann was preparing to sell out to the Entente, whereas Germany's only reliable ally was Russia. Some days later he wrote that German capitulation to the Entente would endanger Russia, for the West would then seek to overthrow the Russian Government and restore the old regime.]

Events in Germany confront the international labour movement with an extremely important historical task. Twenty million German proletarians, the solid core of the international proletariat, are moving into the fight against the German capitalists and the imperialists of the Entente. The coming struggles will be the central events of the entire political history of the immediate future. Their outcome will decide the fate of the international labour movement for many years. The course of all political developments, and especially the course of the labour movement throughout the world, will turn on the outcome of the approaching German crisis.

What happens in Germany is quite clearly of tremendous importance for other countries. In no country can the workers be indifferent to German events. Every honest proletarian whose heart beats for his class must hasten to the help of the German proletariat fighting under the red flag. The cause of the German workers is the cause of workers everywhere.

We suggest that we examine jointly with you the practical measures which can and must be taken by all international organizations of the proletariat in support of the revolutionary German proletariat. Such support can be given in many ways:

1. Fascism is raising its head in Germany. The international organizations of the proletariat must help the German revolutionary workers to repulse fascism.

2. German capitalists are throwing tens of thousands of revolutionary workers on to the streets. These workers have nothing to eat. It is the duty of international labour organizations to rush help to these proletarian victims of the class struggle.

The French and Polish bourgeoisie may perhaps try to give open help to the German capitalists in their attempt to defeat by arms the German workers' movement. The international labour organizations must be ready to nullify all such attempts. The struggle for peace is the chief duty of all to whom the welfare and the life of the worker is dear.

The international proletarian organizations must be on guard. At your Hague congress you issued the watchword, fight against war and for the safeguarding of peace. Now the danger is indisputably here.

Bearing all this in mind, we propose that you convene with us a joint international conference, to be devoted to the following questions: (1) organization of comprehensive support for the German workers by the international proletariat; (2) prompt fighting measures for peace.

We suggest that the conference be called for not later than 10 September.

The crisis is ripening so quickly that every day counts. We suggest that the conference be held in Moscow, but we are ready to have the discussions in any other city.

ECCI STATEMENT ON TSANKOV'S ACTION AGAINST THE BULGARIAN COMMUNIST PARTY

September 1923   *Inprekorr*, iii, 149, p. 1285, 21 *September* 1923

[Although reluctant to abandon its earlier policy, the central committee of the Bulgarian CP, urged forward by Kabakchiev and Dimitrov, committed its party to the September rising 'to establish a government of workers and peasants'. (The central committee report to the Bulgarian Communist Party in December 1948, reviewing the past, stated that 'in August 1923 the sound nucleus of Marxists, aided by the Comintern, gained the upper hand in the leadership of the party'. The position had worsened since June, but 'even in September victory was still objectively possible'.) The rising had been planned for late October, but was called earlier because information about the plans had reached the Government. On 12 September about 2,000 communists were arrested, and their newspapers and offices closed down. The central committee met to decide whether the rising was still possible, and set up a small revolutionary committee, which included Kolarov and Dimitrov. The night of 22–23 September was chosen, but again the Government was warned in time, and no rising occurred in any major city. In a few small towns the rebels held out for a number of days. The revolutionary committee had directed the rising from a town near the border of Yugoslavia, into which it fled on 28 September, with a number of its followers. In the following month the Bulgarian CP moved its headquarters to Vienna. It denied Tsankov's charge that the CPB had been preparing a revolt; it had only been preparing for the elections, and had risen only after the Government's attack to stand at the head of a popular insurrection. This was the explanation given in the ECCI report to the fifth CI congress in 1924. Local spontaneous insurrections had been provoked by Government action; they were premature and ill-prepared and were therefore defeated.

The brutal reprisals taken by the Government won sympathy in the country for the communists who, standing with the peasant bloc in the elections of November 1923, received 218,000 votes, representing 31 seats for the Peasant Union and 8 for the communists. In the Bulgarian parliament, Sakarov, one of the eight, on 24 December 1923, disavowed the rising and asserted that it had been forced on them by the Russians acting through Kolarov and Dimitrov. He and six others (the eighth deputy, Kabakchiev, was in gaol) then pledged themselves to legal activity only, and were expelled by the Vienna committee of the Bulgarian Communist Party. At a secret conference of the party held in the following year the critics of the rising were defeated (and subsequently expelled) by the followers of Kolarov and Dimitrov, whose leadership had been approved in Moscow in February 1924, and who were appointed the 'foreign bureau' of the Bulgarian CP. In May 1924 Bukharin reported to the RCP conference that 'the Comintern had had to interfere drastically' in affairs in Bulgaria, where united front tactics referred to the peasants, not to the weak social-democratic party. The Bulgarian CP's neutrality in June had been followed by an easy bourgeois victory, and when it did organize a rising the time was past and it was defeated. The Bulgarian comrades, he said, now admitted that the ECCI had been right.]

Events in Bulgaria have happened just as the Comintern predicted the day after the white insurrection of 9 [8] June. The waiting attitude incorrectly adopted by the leaders of the Bulgarian Communist Party was utilized by the bandits who have rallied round Tsankov to consolidate their positions before passing to the offensive. On 12 September, on the pretext that the communists were allegedly planning a coup d'état, Tsankov's gang arrested thousands of communists, including nearly all the responsible officials of the party. All communist newspapers were suppressed, all party trade union institutions destroyed.

Tsankov's Government is spreading the lying report that compromising correspondence with Moscow was found on comrade Kabakchiev and other leading party officials who were arrested, as well as letters from Comintern officials.

The arrested leaders were declared to be hostages, who would be shot should any revolutionary movement break out.

The Executive of the Comintern declares that all the reports about the letters, about a conspiracy, and the rest are a malicious provocation.

Tsankov's Government, which is losing ground every day, is forced to take this slippery path; it is doomed to destruction, and this new provocation against the communists will only accelerate its decline. Tsankov's gang is looking for an excuse to take proceedings against the leaders of the Bulgarian proletariat. Let Tsankov and all his ministers and his eminent lackeys remember that they will have to answer to the Bulgarian workers and peasants and to the international proletariat for all their misdeeds. Let Tsankov and his ministers and the gang leaders who support his party bear in mind that they will have to answer to the Bulgarian workers for the lives of the leaders of the Bulgarian proletarian movement. Not a drop of the blood they shed will be forgiven them when the day of reckoning comes. Bulgarian reaction may rage, but its days are numbered. The yellow Bulgarian social-democrats, some of whom tried especially hard to prove by example that there is no baseness of which the parties of the Second International are not capable, may creep whimpering in the dust before the Bulgarian fascists—the alliance of the working class and the peasantry in a country like Bulgaria will, the moment it is formed, be unconquerable. The tactics of the present criminal Government will help to bring this alliance about quickly.

The Comintern sends fraternal greetings to the workers and peasants of Bulgaria in their hour of severe affliction. They must answer Tsankov's provocative policy by closing their ranks, by organizing illegal groups throughout the country, by mass agitation among thousands and millions of workers, and, when the moment comes, by forming a workers' and peasants' government.

EXTRACTS FROM A LETTER FROM THE ECCI TO THE FRENCH COMMUNIST PARTY

September 1923   *Inprekorr*, iii, 149, p. 1290, 21 *September* 1923

[In April 1923 Humbert-Droz reported to Moscow on the unsatisfactory state of affairs in the French party. The central committee was overloaded with work, *L'Humanité* was losing readers, there was open hostility between Souvarine and other members. The party's greatest weaknesses, he wrote later, were its 'complete absence of political perspective' and the lack of any bolshevik discipline among the leaders. It had not, for example, discussed the agenda of the ECCI plenum of June 1923, and correspondence between Moscow and the KPD about the Ruhr had not been put before the central committee. The French working class was losing interest in the Ruhr, since it was clear that war would not break out. (Radek complained later that the French party had not even staged a demonstration against the shootings in the Ruhr, and had none of its members working there illegally.) Quarrels between the editors of *L'Humanité* and the political bureau were frequent. Sellier and Treint, who were joint secretaries, disliked each other and invaded each other's work, and this had a bad influence on the party's activity. The visit to Moscow by these two and Cachin in an attempt to settle their differences had brought no improvement. At the end of 1923 Humbert-Droz asked the ECCI to send a delegate to the congress of the French CP to work with Rakosi (whose methods he distrusted). After the congress, held at Strasbourg, he reported to Zinoviev that the arrangements were 'scandalous'. Even the politbureau did not know what the congress ought to do. He and Rakosi were going to try to settle the differences between Treint, Souvarine, and Rosmer, and hoped to persuade Treint to resign as secretary.

At the elections in May 1924 the communists increased their representation from 13 to 29; the parties in the *cartel des gauches* from 170 to 309.]

The Executive of the Communist International notes with satisfaction that the decisions of the fourth world congress on the French party have been carried out by the joint efforts of the best comrades of the three fractions which previously existed. It may be stated with certainty that it was only by the exclusion of those elements which were alien to the proletarian revolution that the vanguard of the French proletariat were able to break in fact and finally with the bourgeoisie and to ensure for themselves for the future complete freedom of political action. Co-operation with the revolutionary trade unions is proceeding satisfactorily. The struggle for the united front, which was possible once the unity of the party itself was secured, has already proved its revolutionary importance. It can be said with certainty that the continuation of this struggle in one form or another will lead to the re-establishment of trade union unity, to the recruiting of thousands and millions of workers into the trade unions, and to the party's winning the confidence of an ever-growing section of the proletariat.

Our action in this field must be taken in such a way as to deprive the socialist and syndicalist saboteurs of any opportunity of saying to the workers that our proposals for unity have only a demonstrative character or that they are only a trap. Our proposals, in keeping with our real intentions, must be formulated quite concretely. But we must miss no opportunity of exposing pitilessly the hesitations, the sabotage, and the treachery of the official reformist leaders. The necessary balance between these two elements of our tactics can and will be established in practice. . . .

The parliamentary elections to be held next year will be the decisive factor in the French internal situation, and also for the progress of the communist party. Their significance extends far beyond the scope of the usual parliamentary mechanism. This time, under the false forms of so-called democratic parliamentarianism, a thorough regrouping of forces and a change in the orientation of the various classes will occur.

The present Chamber was the result of the political torpidity of the war years. Financiers, industrialists, landowners, the new rich and the old, military and parliamentary cliques—in short, all the elements that the war brought to the top—created after the victory a parliament to their own liking, the Chamber of the national bloc, of the embodiment of un-fettered greed, of crude violence and vulgarity. On the other hand, this Chamber is the most gross and reactionary embodiment of the illusions which the war planted among the masses. The chief element in these illusions was the conviction that Germany would pay. The emptiness of that hope is obvious today.

The occupation of the Ruhr, like French policy towards Germany as a whole, is aimed at ruining Germany and making it for many years incapable of fighting—an aim more or less successfully pursued. But the impossibility of getting payments from Germany only becomes more obvious. Hence it follows that French political life depends on the budget question. By clever political and financial manœuvres the French bour-geoisie have up to now been able to postpone collapse. But it is becoming ever clearer that the crisis is unavoidable. All the problems of French domestic policy, and to a great extent also the problems of French foreign policy, are connected with the approaching financial crisis. At the present time the political struggle consists in fact of the efforts of every class of bourgeois society to throw the financial burden on to the class below it.

The bourgeoisie as a whole . . . are determined to put the tax burden on to the workers and peasants. This makes it impossible for the present reactionary bloc of militarists and plutocrats to remain in power, for the bourgeoisie can only hope to avoid the financial crisis by plundering the working class in town and country, if the execution of this policy is en-trusted to their radical and socialist hacks. That is the meaning of the left bloc which will follow the national bloc. The illusions of victory have faded. The radical bloc will try to use the illusions of pacifism and demo-cracy for the same reactionary purposes.

The problems to be solved are too refractory, and the new orientation of the bourgeoisie too difficult for this to be carried on behind the scenes. The elections will offer the spectacle of a great fight of classes and parties, while in reality the balance of the war and of victory will be struck. There are a number of circumstances which are highly favourable to independent action by the communist party. The bourgeoisie want to make the workers and peasants bear the costs of the war. The communist party comes forward as their defender against all groups and parties of the bourgeoisie. It opposes to the national bloc and the left bloc the bloc of the working classes in town and country. The best elements in town and country must by tireless work explain the meaning of the struggle going on within the bourgeoisie between the national bloc and the left bloc. They must show the necessity of the working class itself first uniting and then acting to-gether with the peasants to defend the vital interests of the people which are acutely endangered by the financial crisis. . . .

During the election campaign the communist party must have nothing whatever to do with any form of parliamentary reformism and of place-hunting, even if it is clothed in revolutionary phrases. The party should put forward as candidates only those people who are able to fling in the face of bourgeois society the accusations and demands of the workers which derive from their daily life, that is, in the first place, people from the factory and the field. . . . The slightest attempt to build a bridge between the party and the left bloc must be punished in the sight of the entire working class by expulsion, but at the same time we must show the utmost initiative and activity in uniting the various sections of the working class on a purely proletarian basis. Only such a broad and vigorous policy can give confidence to the passive elements of the working class who are at present inclined to give their votes to the reformists, not because they have confidence in them, but because the reformists are less hated than the nationalists. Only the rallying of the workers on a united basis will give the poor peasants too the incentive to seek their salvation in an alliance with the proletariat.

It is certain that the policy of our French party before and during the elections will also be of the greatest importance for the still large number of revolutionary workers who have not yet discarded their distrust of political parties as such. If these comrades see that for us the elections are only a means of carrying out the revolutionary work of rallying the masses, and that the communist party does not for a moment turn into an ordinary parliamentary party, but always remains the revolutionary force which shakes the foundation of the present system, then the ice of syndicalist mistrust will melt and our party will be strengthened by the addition of thousands of revolutionary workers steeled in the class struggle. Their confidence will be a far more important gain than the winning of a dozen seats in parliament.

EXTRACTS FROM A LETTER FROM THE ECCI TO ALL MEMBERS OF THE NORWEGIAN LABOUR PARTY

October 1923   *Inprekorr*, iii, 167, p. 1425, 29 *October* 1923

[The central committee of the NLP called a special congress on 2–5 November 1923 to discuss differences with the CI. The majority was opposed to trade union affiliation to the RILU and to the slogan of a workers' and peasants' government, considered that religion should be the private concern of the individual member, and deplored the lack of democracy in the Comintern. Bull, Falk, and Tranmael, who led the opposition to the CI, were followed out of the congress by 169 delegates; the remaining 110 constituted themselves into a congress of the Norwegian Communist Party. At the thirteenth congress of the RCP in 1924 Bukharin attributed the split in part to the dispute within the Russian party; Tranmael and his followers supported the opposition. The resolution of the fifth Comintern congress urged the ECCI to do all in its power to win over to the Comintern the proletarian elements in the NLP.]

The present leaders of the majority of your central committee have, without consulting the Comintern, called an extraordinary party congress for 2 November 1923 to discuss the differences of opinion between these leaders and the Communist International. Everything points to the conclusion that some of these leaders are aiming to split your party and to break with the Communist International. Anyone who knows the early history of the present internal struggles cannot escape this impression. None of you should forget that the present leaders of the majority, with Bull and Falk at the head, put through a resolution even before the last Christiania congress which meant a break with the Communist International, and it was only the pressure of the Norwegian workers which compelled these leaders to abandon at that time their open splitting policy. From being open they became disguised splitters. Now they think the time has come to push things to a break.

Bull, Falk, and unfortunately comrade Tranmael also maintain that the Communist International has made mistakes on these points: (1) the question of a workers' and peasants' government; (2) the religious question; and (3) the question of the Red International of Labour Unions.

1. A WORKERS' AND PEASANTS' GOVERNMENT

The Communist International decided to issue the slogan of a workers' and peasants' government. All the parties adhering to the CI (fifty-six in all) welcomed this slogan and can already point to certain political successes in this field. All the social-democratic parties of the Second International gnashed their teeth because they realized that this slogan would open a road for the communists to the broadest masses of the workers and peasants. Now Falk and Bull (and unfortunately comrade Tranmael also) come out with the statement that this slogan may be all right for the rest of the world, but at the present time it is unacceptable for Sweden [Norway]. Not satisfied with that, they declare that the acceptance of this slogan in Norway indicates a social-democratic overvaluation of parliament and may lead to ordinary ministerial socialism.

Comrades, why should this slogan not be suitable for a country like Norway? The Norwegian party has about 60,000 members only. The small and middle peasants and the fishermen represent a very large part of the population. Anyone who really wants to defeat the bourgeoisie and fight for the power of the proletariat must seek to win these sections of the population for the proletarian cause. Only those who want a narrow craft party, who are not really interested in overthrowing the bourgeoisie and putting power into the hands of the proletariat, can be indifferent to the task of winning the peasants and fishermen. Of course, only the industrial workers can and must act as the chief factor in the socialist revolution, in Norway as elsewhere, and in the formation of a proletarian government. But they can only do that if they understand how to carry the great mass of the small peasantry and the fishermen with them in the fight against the right, against the exploiters, against the bourgeoisie.

If the Communist International is accused of a social-democratic over-estimation of parliamentarianism, we must point out that when the slogan of a workers' and peasants' government was first formulated at the meeting of the enlarged Executive, the President of the CI stated, amid general agreement, that anyone who interpreted this slogan in a parliamentary sense would be in conflict with the spirit of the Comintern.

The most important task of the Communist International is for communists to go to the villages with the slogan of a workers' and peasants' government, to conduct communist propaganda as widely as possible among the small peasants, and to stir them up for a common struggle under the leadership of the revolutionary proletariat. Only those elements who do not hesitate to use any means to split their own party and to discredit the Communist International could distort this slogan in the way some leaders of the present majority in Norway have done.

2. THE RELIGIOUS QUESTION

The same is true of the religious question. How has this come about? Before the enlarged Executive the Swedish comrade Höglund published an article which aroused general antagonism in the Comintern. Unanimously—apart from a few Swedish and Norwegian comrades—the Communist International passed a resolution which drew attention to the ABC of communism. There was no mention of our wanting to repulse religious or semi-religious workers. Communists must win the entire working class, including those workers who are still organized in the Christian trade unions. But it is axiomatic that the class-conscious section of the working class, and above all the leading ranks of our party, must fight against religious prejudices and the priesthood, and it is a disgrace that it should be necessary to have to argue this thesis.

Unfortunately, we had to remind leading comrades in the Swedish and Norwegian parties of this axiom. Their attempt to refer back to Marx on this question is more than peculiar. Every Marxist knows the phrase that religion is the opium of the world. We communists demand from the bourgeois State freedom for all religions, non-interference by the authorities in religious affairs. But that does not mean that within our party we will allow the workers to be stupefied by the fog of religion. Comrades, read the resolution of the enlarged Executive of the Comintern, and you will see for yourselves the methods which the Bulls and the Falks use to fight against the international organization of the world proletariat.

3. THE RED INTERNATIONAL OF LABOUR UNIONS

The great majority of the workers in your country who are organized in trade unions are hostile to the yellow treacherous Amsterdam International and are body and soul for the Red International of Labour Unions, the Profintern. But the Bulls and Falks, who are helped by Lian and Tranmael, are using every possible and impossible means to keep the Norwegian trade unions from joining the RILU. At a time when even the left wing of the Amsterdam unions is working for adherence to the RILU, at a time when new unions in the countries most important for the labour movement are daily joining the RILU, you have leaders calling themselves communists who work against it.

What is the Red International of Labour Unions? It is the international association of all the sections of the proletariat organized in trade unions who really believe in the class struggle and are prepared to wage the fight against the bourgeoisie to the end. What reasons can honest revolutionaries have to remain outside such an international organization? Nothing but petty diplomacy explains this policy, diplomacy which represents treachery to the idea of the international association of the militant working class. . . .

People who have been active in the labour movement at the most for a couple of years, who have done nothing to prove their fidelity to the proletariat, dare to run an old and tried workers' party which they have already brought to the brink of a split. We all know and value comrade Tranmael as an old fighter. We were prepared to make all possible personal concessions to him, but the Communist International has only the sharpest mistrust of such ambiguous elements as Falk and Hakon Meyer. Things have already gone so far that openly alien elements not only have rights in the Norwegian workers' party but actually claim the leadership. Will the class-conscious Norwegian working class go on tolerating such a degradation of its party? . . .

Tranmael's group asserts that there is too little democracy and a too rigid centralism in the Communist International. The statutes of the CI were, however, unanimously ratified by all the communist parties. The leadership of the International reports on its activities twice a year to all sections, and our parties have up to now unanimously approved this policy.

But what do the Falks, the Bulls, and unfortunately the Tranmaels also do? It was enough for an old and tried comrade to write a sharp article against Tranmael for him to be immediately and in a dictatorial fashion excluded from the party, without being given the chance of justifying his position. This does not preserve the unity of a party; it destroys it. Only those people can act in such a way for whom any method is justified if it helps to break up the party. At the last congress in Christiania the majority fraction won by two votes only. That was enough for them to use force against the minority and in practice to sabotage the decision to carry out all the decisions of the Communist International.

Comrades, the decisive hour has come. Now is the time to prove your loyalty to the Communist International and to the idea of the unity of your own party. Call the splitters to order! Call to order those who do not submit to international proletarian discipline and who want to introduce among you the customs of the treacherous Second International. You must procure such a defeat for Falk and Bull, you must see that they remain in such a dwindling minority, that they will lose all desire to break up the Workers' Party. Get rid of the opportunist elements in your party and concentrate your attention on the questions which are today the most important for every thinking honest revolutionary worker in the world, above all on the German proletarian revolution. At a moment when one of the most important parties in the Communist International, our brother German party, is waging a life and death struggle, the leaders of the present majority in your party attack the Communist International from the rear. The yellow social-democrats are rubbing their hands in joy. The bourgeois parties are heaping praise on comrade Tranmael; the great mistakes he has lately made have misled him into conducting an anti-communist policy.

Unity of the party at any cost! Real loyalty to the Communist International! All-out support for the German proletarian revolution!

Down with the splitters and opportunists. That should be the slogan of your congress.

Choose as delegates only those comrades who agree to abide by this slogan. Take in your own hands the fate of your party, which was created by great efforts and great sacrifices, which up to now has enjoyed great affection and respect in the Communist International, and which the splitters are now trying to destroy.

EXTRACT FROM A LETTER FROM THE ECCI TO THE GERMAN COM-
MUNIST PARTY ON THE SAXON COALITION GOVERNMENT

December [?] 1923   *Inprekorr*, iv, 16, p. 169, 4 *February* 1924

[According to Thalheimer, the question of direct revolutionary struggle arose when preparations were being made in Moscow to hold an 'anti-fascist day' in Germany on 29 July. The KPD manifesto issued on that day declared that civil war was inevitable. The KPD leaders were called to Moscow. The politbureau of the RCP met on 23 August, decided that the time for revolution in Germany was ripe, and appointed a committee consisting of Radek, Piatakov, Unshlikht, and Shmidt to supervise policy in Germany. In September the situation was discussed at great length with the Germans and representatives of some other European parties in Moscow, and, according to the report to the ninth KPD congress, 'the great plan of struggle was examined in detail and decided upon'. It was agreed to make preparations for insurrection, although no definite date was fixed, and a small revolutionary committee of German and Russian officers, directed by Skoblevsky, was appointed to direct the rising, which was to start in Saxony, where the presence of KPD ministers in the Government (they did not actually enter the Government until 10 October) would, it was hoped, give them access to arms.

In Saxony the SPD had formed a Government under Zeigner in March 1923 which relied on the KPD for its majority; the SPD Government in Thuringia also relied on KPD support. (Some of the German delegates to the fourth Comintern congress at the end of 1922 had suggested collaboration with the SPD to form a Saxon Government, but this had been dismissed by the Russian delegation as 'pure opportunism'.) Some Red Army leaders were said to favour an offensive against Poland if Poland, at French instigation, intervened in Germany. A Soviet emissary, Kopp, was sent to Poland in October to negotiate about freedom of communication between Russia and Germany in the event of a German uprising. Throughout the Ruhr occupation the Soviet press took a strongly anti-French line, and warned Poland that any threat to Germany, taking advantage of the difficulties created in the Ruhr, would be interpreted as a threat to Russia. In a speech on the Comintern programme five years later, Stalin said that in the autumn of 1923 'the proletarian dictatorship was getting ready to render direct assistance to the German revolution'.

While these discussions were going on, passive resistance in Germany was ended on 26 September. On the following day a general strike in the Ruhr was the prelude to the proclamation of a state of emergency throughout the Reich. On the same day the KPD issued a manifesto to the workers of Germany on the 'Stresemann–Hilferding surrender to Poincaré'. Germany would become a French colony; it would be dismembered, and its working class enslaved. The united front of capitalists, generals, and fascists was led by the right-wing SPD.

An ECCI telegram to the KPD, dated 1 October, on the decision to enter the two Governments, also instructed the KPD to 'ignore Müller'—this being the Reichswehr General who, acting on the orders of the Reich Government, demanded the dissolution of the 'red hundreds' in Saxony. The 'government of proletarian defence' was formed in Saxony on 10 October, followed on the 16th by a similar coalition Government in Thuringia. Zinoviev wrote of the 'classic proletarian character of the approaching revolution', and drew an analogy between Russia in the period 1905 to 1917 and Germany in 1918 to 1923. 'It cannot be too early, historically speaking, for the German proletariat to seize power.' In action the KPD would win the majority of the German working class.

Brandler arrived in Germany on 8 October; the ECCI delegation, consisting of Radek, Piatakov, Skoblevsky, Guralsky, and Shmidt, also travelled to Germany later in October. The theses of the central committee of the Russian

Communist Party issued in October 1923 for the forthcoming celebration of the sixth anniversary of the Russian revolution stated that 'the development of the revolutionary movement in Germany opens up the prospect of a further consolidation of the economic and political power of Soviet Russia. . . . Alliance with a revolutionary Germany will also strengthen Soviet Russia's international position.'

Zeigner's Government rejected the demand for the dissolution of the red hundreds, and Seeckt ordered the Reichswehr to depose the Saxon and Thuringian Governments. On 20 October the KPD *Zentrale* decided unanimously to call a general strike and launch an armed struggle, although it disposed of only 11,000 rifles as against the half million planned for. It was, however, decided to consult the conference of factory committees then meeting in Chemnitz before taking action. The refusal of the SPD to endorse the KPD proposals, and their rejection by the Chemnitz conference, led to the reversal of the decision on insurrection. The earlier instructions were cancelled, but the cancellation did not reach Hamburg in time; there, after two days of small-scale fighting, in which no organized body of workers joined the communists, the revolt was easily suppressed.

The Reichswehr intervened on 21 October; General Müller marched his forces into Saxony, entered Dresden on the 23rd, and deposed the Government after Zeigner had refused to resign. Similar action was taken in Thuringia; in both States Reich commissioners were appointed in the place of the Government. The SPD members of the Reich Government then resigned. In November the KPD was declared illegal and its offices were closed by the police, but it continued to work more or less openly under a number of disguises. The prohibition lasted until 1 March 1924.

Although the 'October defeat' bedevilled Comintern and KPD affairs for years, the entire episode was at first treated fairly lightly; Zinoviev wrote: 'Events have shown that our calculations were exaggerated. . . . The KPD revealed many weaknesses and made a number of serious mistakes during those critical weeks, but we do not consider it mistaken in not bringing out the proletariat into a general struggle in October. . . . The retreat should have been less passive. But the abstention from fighting a decisive battle was in the circumstances inevitable.' The central committee of the KPD, meeting on 3 November, charged the SPD leaders with full responsibility for the defeat (as Zinoviev had done); the struggle against them was a question of life and death. The resolution on 'the end of the November republic' said fascism had triumphed over bourgeois democracy; the fight against the fascist dictatorship, which would lead to the establishment of the proletarian dictatorship, might break out any day. It was drafted by Brandler and Radek, and carried by 40 votes to 13.

The decision of the KPD to call off the insurrection had been unanimous, and there is no evidence that any of the Comintern delegates disagreed. By the end of the year, however, the fiasco of the 'German October' led to one of the most severe crises in the history of the KPD—in Bukharin's opinion, the most severe—which was aggravated when it merged, inside the Comintern, with the struggle going on within the RCP to settle the question of the succession to Lenin.

Within the KPD three groups disputed the leadership. The right wing, represented by Brandler and Thalheimer, argued that the decision to call off the rising had been correct because its prospects were hopeless; the left, which included Ruth Fischer and Thaelmann, maintained that the situation had been objectively revolutionary and that the defeat was due to timid and opportunist leaders who had never genuinely believed in the rising. The centre, which included Remmele, Pieck, and Koenen, believed that a retreat had been necessary, but it should have been 'a fighting retreat', not a passive surrender.

The theses drafted by the right-wing majority of the central committee, dated 1 December 1923, opened with the words: 'The October retreat was unavoidable and correct.' The working class, though not prepared to fight for Weimar, was not yet ready to fight for the proletarian dictatorship. The theses of the left wing argued that between August and October conditions were ripe for the seizure of power in Germany; failure was due to strategic and tactical errors. Some years after his expulsion from the KPD, Rosenberg, a left-wing member of the central committee, wrote: 'There has never been a period in recent German history which would have been so favourable for a socialist revolution as the summer of 1923.'

The date of the letter given here is uncertain. The extract was quoted by Zinoviev at the thirteenth conference of the RCP in January 1924. He introduced it with the words: 'As soon as we saw what course events were taking, we sent a confidential letter to the KPD *Zentrale*, to which the ECCI, including Trotsky, agreed.']

The political error was a necessary consequence of your over-estimation of the degree of political and technical preparation. We here in Moscow, as you must be well aware, regarded the entry of communists into the Saxon Government only as a military-strategic manœuvre. You turned it into a political bloc with the 'left' social-democrats, which tied your hands. We thought of your entry into the Saxon Government as a way of winning a jumping-off ground from which to deploy the forces of our armies. You turned participation in the Saxon cabinet into a banal parliamentary coalition with the social-democrats. The result was our political defeat. And what was still worse, there was an element of comedy in the business. We can stand a defeat in battle, but when a revolutionary party on the eve of revolt gets into a ridiculous position, that is worse than a defeat. In the Reich the party did not pursue a policy which could be and had to be the overture to decisive struggle. Not a single decisive revolutionary step. Not one even partially clear communist speech. Not a single serious measure to expedite the arming of the Saxon workers, not a single practical measure to create Soviets in Saxony. Instead of that, a 'gesture' by Böttcher; who declared that he would not leave the government building until he was ejected by force. No, comrades, that is not the way to prepare a revolution.

EXTRACTS FROM INSTRUCTIONS FOR COMMUNIST FRACTIONS IN WORKERS' ORGANIZATIONS AND BODIES OUTSIDE THE PARTY

January 1924[1]   *Inprekorr*, iv, 24, p. 263, 21 *February* 1924

INTRODUCTION

The question of communist fractions in non-party organizations is closely connected with the need for communist parties to establish their influence over the broad non-party masses. In order to do this, every communist party must make use of agencies pursuing a communist policy in non-party surroundings. Communist fractions are such agencies. The correct carrying-out of party directives depends on the correct organization of these fractions; it is these directives which ensure that the communists express a single will, pursue uniform tactics, and act in harmony; without this, correct activity for a communist party is unthinkable.

The existence of communist fractions raises the question of their relations with the party organs. There can be no satisfactory outcome to the work of the fractions if these relations are not defined, in harmony with the interests of the party as a whole. Communist fractions are not autarkic plenipotentiary organizations entitled to settle all questions of party life. They are subordinate to those party organs which are in charge of party activities in the given sphere and locality where the fraction has to work. In each factory, for example, the factory-committee fraction is subordinate to the party cell; the fraction in a co-operative, town council, or trade union is subordinate to the town party organization in the person of its committee, while the fraction in any national organization or in parliament is subordinate to the central committee. . . .

It is in the interests of the entire party that fractions should strictly carry out the directives of the relevant party organs and work under their constant supervision. In their capacity as party members the members of the fraction discuss and decide all party questions in their cell, in the aggregate district meetings, or in their local group. At these meetings they may complain about incorrect conduct of and instructions to the fraction.

The activities of communists at national congresses and in parliament are the responsibility of the entire party. From this it follows that the central committee must exercise special care in selecting communist candidates for parliament, or the fraction members for trade union national committees, or for the central factory-committee organization. Careful selection will ensure that the party will not be compromised by the behaviour of communists in these fractions and that the party line will be carried out in full. Great care in selecting parliamentary candidates minimizes the chance that they will fail to follow party decisions, for it

[1] The correct date is 4 February.

must be remembered that the more important the role of a communist fraction in a national body (parliament, national trade union committee, etc.), the stronger the tendency may be to display independence in relation to the party.

All efforts to create a strict organization, suitable for establishing contact with the broad masses and leading them in a victorious struggle against capitalism, will be fruitless if the communist parties fail to give sufficient attention to the formation of communist fractions in all non-party organizations or to establish the correct mutual relations between the fractions and the party organizations. While proceeding to organize fractions, it remains a condition of all party organizational activity that the centre of gravity is to be shifted to the establishment of factory cells and to making them the foundation of the entire party organization.

INSTRUCTIONS FOR COMMUNIST FRACTIONS IN WORKERS' ORGANIZATIONS AND BODIES OUTSIDE THE PARTY

1. In all organizations and bodies of workers and peasants (trade unions, co-operatives, cultural and educational societies, sports clubs, factory councils, committees of the unemployed, congresses and conferences, municipal councils, parliaments, etc.), where there are at least three communists, communist fractions must be formed to increase the influence of the party and to carry through its policy in the non-party environment.

2. Communist fractions, regardless of their importance, must be subordinate to the corresponding party organization—the party cell (its bureau), the district or area committee in large towns, the town committee, the regional committee, or the central committee, according to whether the organization or body in which the fraction is working is of local or national significance. It is from these that the communist fractions receive the necessary directives. . . . Their decisions must be strictly and precisely obeyed by the fractions.

3. When the party leadership discusses questions concerning a particular fraction, thorough preparations must be made and for this purpose representatives of the fraction should be called in for previous consultation. . . .

4. Communist fractions shall elect, in agreement with the relevant party committee, a bureau or presidium which is responsible to the relevant party body for the activity of the fraction.

5. Between congresses (conferences) the fraction in the central trade union or co-operative committee is the body which covers and guides all the communists belonging to the union or co-operative. . . .

6. The relevant party committee has the right to send members to the fraction and to recall any member of the fraction, which shall be informed of the reasons for such actions.

7. Candidates from the communist fraction for trade union national committees and for the governing committees of other organizations or bodies may be nominated only in agreement with the appropriate party organ. The same applies to the recall and replacement of communists.

8. In internal matters and current work the fraction is autonomous. The party authorities should not interfere in the daily work of the fraction. . . . Should the fraction and the party leadership disagree fundamentally on any question within the competence of the fraction, the question must be reconsidered by the leadership and the representatives of the fraction, with the object of reaching a final decision, which must then be operated by the fraction.

9. When questions of political importance are discussed by the fraction, representatives of the relevant party committee must be present. The committee is obliged to send representatives at the request of the fraction.

10. All questions pending in the organization in which the fraction is operating must be discussed in advance by the fraction or its bureau.

11. The fraction must report on its work to the relevant party organization . . . which lays down the tactics and the political line for the future activity of the fraction.

12. On every question about which a decision has been reached in the fraction, all fraction members must speak and vote in accordance therewith at the meetings of the organization in which the fraction is operating. Anyone breaking this rule will be subject to disciplinary measures by the appropriate party bodies.

EXTRACTS FROM AN ECCI STATEMENT ON THE EVENTS IN GERMANY IN OCTOBER 1923

19 *January* 1924   *Die Lehren der deutschen Ereignisse*, p. 95

[As the dispute between the various factions in the KPD grew more bitter, and the quarrel within the RCP found its echo in other communist parties, the ECCI intervened in the debate within the KPD. Although the KPD centre and left disagreed in their interpretation of the 1923 events, they were brought together to defeat Brandler, and to act with Zinoviev and Stalin in the fight against Trotsky; Brandler's chief defender in the ECCI was Radek, Trotsky's avowed supporter. The politbureau of the RCP met on 27 December 1923. It condemned Radek's support of the right wing in the KPD; he was trying to start a fractional struggle between the left and centre. He had refused to obey the instructions of the RCP central committee, saying he was appointed by the ECCI, not the RCP. 'Formally he is right, but it is obvious that we must represent our party in the ECCI.' Trotsky, Radek, and Piatakov had sent their own theses to the KPD without submitting them beforehand to the RCP central committee. Radek rejected the charge of opportunism; it was at his insistence that the left had been represented in the German *Zentrale*; those now being attacked by the Russian politbureau (Brandler, Thalheimer, Zetkin) were founders and staunch pillars of the German Communist Party. In replying Zinoviev remarked that Radek was always in favour of making concessions to the West, as shown by his vote in favour of the Urquhart concession.

The criticism of Radek was endorsed by the central committee of the RCP, which met on 14–15 January 1924, and by the thirteenth conference, which opened a day later.

In December 1923 representatives of the KPD were summoned to Moscow, and on 11 January 1924 the Comintern presidium discussed 'the lessons of October'. In addition to the members of the presidium, there were present other ECCI members then in Moscow, representatives of the Polish and Bulgarian parties, and representatives of the three wings of the German party. Five draft resolutions were considered, one drawn up by Zinoviev, one by Radek and Trotsky, one each from the German left and the German centre, and the last a composite one embodying parts of Zinoviev's draft and parts of the German centre draft. Radek, as ECCI representative in Germany, spoke first: the four members of the ECCI delegation in Germany at the time had been in agreement throughout the events of October, although they had not been present at the Chemnitz conference. The operation had failed because the Saxon Government had been unable to arm the workers, and because the SPD would not support the KPD plan. He had proposed the calling of a general strike, of a defensive character, but the KPD had rejected this on the ground that it would lead to an armed uprising, for which the prospects were hopeless. A great historical opportunity had been missed because of lack of revolutionary experience. The fight should have started earlier, in May, but the ECCI did not take the situation seriously until August. The June plenum should have had only one item on the agenda—preparation for the German insurrection. It was a mistake to have set the date for the insurrection in Moscow—it could only have been decided in Germany itself. Brandler had returned to Germany on 8 October, and had entered the Saxon Government on the 12th. Radek himself arrived on 22 October, i.e. after the Chemnitz conference. Brandler accepted full responsibility for the decision to cancel the orders for an insurrection. He insisted that the objective circumstances were wholly unfavourable. Zinoviev, concerned with the dispute in his own party, had withdrawn his support from the KPD central committee, and made Radek and Brandler the chief scapegoats. (They were known to have Trotsky's support, although Trotsky disagreed with them in his interpretation of the October events; he wrote later that the defeat arose from tactical errors, and was not inherent in the German situation.) Radek had accused him, Zinoviev, of destroying the German *Zentrale*; the *Zentrale* had destroyed itself by its irresolution, its lack of the will to power.

A drafting commission was appointed consisting of two supporters of the left, two of the centre, one of the right, and Kuusinen for the ECCI. Zetkin proposed the addition of Radek and Brandler, but was outvoted. The commission's draft resolution was presented on 17 January, and on the 19th it was endorsed by the presidium against the votes of Radek and Zetkin; Brandler, Walcher, and Pieck abstained. Pieck's proposal that a paragraph should be added to the resolution explaining that, in the circumstances, and given the errors that had been made, it was right for the KPD to call off the insurrection was rejected by 18 votes to 11. At the final session on 21 January Zetkin said she would vote for the resolution, as unity was essential, although it did not clear up the position, but rather drew a veil over ideas and facts on which clarity was essential in the forthcoming debates in the KPD and the Comintern. Radek also announced his willingness to vote for the resolution because 'as an Executive we have always appeared united to the outside world'. Zetkin, Pieck, and their supporters added a 'minority declaration' which contended that unity must be based on an absolutely clear analysis, which was lacking in the resolution; this gave an incomplete and partly incorrect analysis of the causes of the October defeat, did not state clearly whether the retreat was necessary, or criticize clearly enough the errors of the left opposition; further disputes were therefore unavoidable. Prukhniak, for the Polish delegation, also made a declaration. The resolution attributed responsibility incorrectly; part rested on the ECCI, which had been too optimistic. Zetkin, Brandler, and Thalheimer were the best and most devoted party leaders, and to discredit them would be a severe blow to the KPD. He objected to the charge of opportunism against Radek. This was both groundless, and damaging to the Comintern's authority. Differences of opinion in the past had not led to such charges. The resolution was published with a statement from Zinoviev that the right wing now had only 2 of the 27 votes of the *Zentrale*. The centre had 17, the left 8.

At the thirteenth conference of the Russian Communist Party (16–18 January 1924), Zinoviev reported on the international situation and the Comintern. The opposition in the party, and Radek particularly, he said, had accused the ECCI of bringing ruin on the KPD. 'For our views, particularly on the German question, the entire central committee and the entire politbureau bear responsibility. The question is of the most direct interest to Russia. For that reason alone the representatives of the RCP in the CI were compelled to bring every question before the politbureau, and that was necessary in any case because of the situation in our party.'

Bukharin attributed the German defeat to the opportunism of Brandler and his colleagues; Brandler had misunderstood the united front tactics as applied to Saxony; he had thought it meant co-operation with the social-democrats, whereas it should have been used as a manœuvre to break social-democratic influence. 'In October we were mistaken in our assessment of the tempo of development, but as to the lines along which development was proceeding, these were wholly correctly formulated by the CI.' Radek asserted that there was a revolutionary situation, but the KPD had been unable to exploit it. It had no arms; not only could it not engage the enemy, it could not defend itself. The June 1923 meeting of the ECCI had not even raised the question of power in Germany. The decision was taken in September, but both the right and the left wing in the KPD continued to act as before, although from August it had been clear that either the communists would seize power, or the fascists would. The fascists took the offensive first. They were better organized and showed more political initiative, and the KPD was shown to be not only without arms, but also without the masses. Radek challenged Bukharin's assertion that the mistakes were due to Brandler's opportunist leadership. How, he asked, could they charge with opportunism a group that from the very first had advocated the split with social-democracy, had borne the entire burden of the illegal struggle against the 1914–18 war, had gone in to attack in March 1921? Brandler and Thalheimer were the victims of the party's weakness, which resulted not from their tactics, but despite them. Bukharin was exploiting the conference's ignorance of the facts; Brandler had from the first been doubtful about entering the Saxon Government. If Brandler was opportunist, why did not the ECCI disavow him before October? 'When the ECCI representatives reached Dresden the night after the Reichswehr occupied the town, comrade Brandler stated that he had given the order to retreat, and if the ECCI representatives thought it wrong (the couriers had not yet been sent out) he would submit without dispute. When the ECCI representatives . . . approved the decision, Brandler said: "If you agree to the retreat, then you must sacrifice me, otherwise you will share with me the responsibility for the defeat."'

Radek asked what the ECCI had been doing while Brandler was making his mistakes. 'Or do you want to accept responsibility only for victories, not for defeats?' He, Radek, attributed the defeat to the inadequate experience of the KPD. On 7 December, with a full knowledge of the facts, Zinoviev had said that no other central committee was possible for the KPD. The resolution of the ECCI in January 1924 had precisely the same contents as the resolution of the KPD central committee of 3 November, except that it added 'Down with Brandler' to 'Down with the social-democrats and fascists'.

In his *Lessons of October*, published in 1924, Trotsky wrote that Germany in 1923 was a classic example of how a revolutionary opportunity could be missed, but admitted that it would have been fatal to start an armed rising in October itself. In his critique of the Comintern programme (published in German in 1929), he wrote, in connexion with October 1923, that he was opposed to the 'intolerable system which tried to demonstrate the infallibility of the central leadership by periodic dismissals of national leaders'.

After his expulsion from the KPD, Thalheimer wrote that the change in the ECCI line about October 1923 in Germany came only in December of that year, and was a direct outcome of the dispute within the Russian party. On 13 December Radek had delivered a speech in Moscow in which he said that if the majority of the Russian central committee turned against Trotsky, not only he— the speaker—but also the leaders of the Polish and German parties would turn against the CC majority. It was some days after this speech that Zinoviev—at that time working with Stalin to prevent the assumption of leadership in Russia by Trotsky—sent a letter to the KPD containing violent attacks on the policy of its leaders. Zinoviev and Stalin had taken Radek's threat seriously, although Thalheimer did not support Trotsky. Trotsky in his *Lessons of October* had said that the situation in Germany in the autumn of 1923 was the classical revolutionary situation, not because he agreed with Zinoviev's change of tune, but to attack Zinoviev, who was the head of the Comintern when the fiasco occurred. Brandler had not wished to enter the Saxon Government, but had agreed as a matter of discipline, and the entire KPD delegation in Moscow, which included Ruth Fischer, had agreed. Stalin had written to Zinoviev and Bukharin early in

August 1923 that it would be a disaster if the KPD were to attempt to seize power without the SPD. The entire plan had been based on the assumption that events in Germany would develop as they had done in Petrograd in 1917, with factory committees taking the place of Soviets. Far from that being the case, the German Government had consolidated its position by calling off passive resistance, stabilizing the currency, and reaching agreement with France.

The bracketing of Poland with Bulgaria and Germany in the statement referred to the insurrection which broke out in Cracow in October 1923, in the midst of a wave of strikes; it lasted a few days and was suppressed. It does not appear to have been communist in origin.]

The events in Germany, Poland, and Bulgaria between May and November 1923 represent the beginning of a new chapter in the history of the international movement.

In Germany, in connexion with the development of the Ruhr crisis, the proletarian class struggle entered on a new phase, passing from that of the gradual mobilization of revolutionary forces into one concerned with the struggle for power. In view of the far-reaching importance of the German revolutionary movement, the historical change which occurred in August–September and the events of the autumn are of the greatest significance for the Communist International. The lessons and consequences of those events must therefore be thoroughly evaluated by the entire International. . . .

I. UNITED FRONT TACTICS

. . . It is necessary for communists in all countries to get clearly into their minds what the united front tactics are, and what they are not; they are tactics of revolution, not evolution. Just as the workers' (and peasants') government cannot, for us, be a fixed democratic transitional stage, so united front tactics are not a democratic coalition, an alliance with social-democracy. They are only a method of revolutionary agitation and mobilization. We reject all other interpretations as opportunist.

We must keep firmly in mind that united front tactics have a meaning for the CI only if they promote the object of winning the bulk of the proletariat for the revolutionary struggle for power. . . .

The time will come when entire social-democratic parties, now still strong, will collapse or, if they continue their treachery, burst as soap-bubbles do, when entire strata of social-democratic workers will complete the turn to our side. United front tactics promote and accelerate this process.

II. THE REVOLUTIONARY CRISIS IN GERMANY

Shortly after the occupation of the Ruhr by French troops, the Executive of the International directed the attention of all sections to the approaching revolutionary crisis. The international conferences at Essen and Frankfurt were also devoted to these questions. . . .

In the months up to the winter of 1923 class forces in Germany moved steadily in favour of the proletarian revolution. From the beginning of the Ruhr movement the 18 to 20 million proletarians were free of any national-ist sentiment. A profound ferment was at work among the 6 to 7 million petty bourgeois of the towns and the 4 to 5 million smallholders and tenant farmers.

The democratic coalition policy was obviously bankrupt. The social-democrats, who had shared the government with the bourgeois parties, had to decide whether they would make a firm alliance with the repre-sentatives of heavy industry and the reactionary army groups; and that is in fact what they did.

It was and still is the task of the KPD to exploit the period of inter-national complications following on the Ruhr crisis, the period of intense crisis within German capitalism, and the liquidation of the Ruhr crisis to overthrow the bourgeoisie and establish the proletarian dictatorship. For this purpose it should have mobilized the industrial proletariat for the fight against German heavy industry and against French imperialism, and at least neutralized the urban and rural middle classes, bringing them wherever possible under its leadership.

The first task could have been accomplished only if the majority of the proletarian masses were liberated from any kind of social-democratic influence, and so organized that they were ready for the fight against the capitalist positions. This task was only in part accomplished; the reasons will be discussed below. . . .

In the camp of the bourgeoisie disintegration increased from week to week; confidence in the KPD grew steadily greater. This confidence should have been given an organized form, and all forces prepared for the decisive blow.

The KPD and the Executive of the Comintern, in discussions held in September with representatives of the five largest parties, came to the conclusion that the revolutionary situation in Germany had reached such a pitch that the decisive struggle was a question of the next few weeks.

From that moment the party mobilized all the forces at its disposal and armed for the decisive struggle. The party worked feverishly to stir up every member and equip him to meet the demands of the struggle. In order to enrol the entire proletariat in the revolutionary fighting front, the party initiated and supported the formation of local action committees everywhere. Intensive work was done among railwaymen, electrical workers, and public employees.

The Executive of the CI focused the attention of the entire Inter-national, particularly the sections in the countries bordering on Germany and in Soviet Russia, on the approaching German revolution, and settled with each section its tasks.

III. THE OCTOBER RETREAT AND ITS CAUSES

Despite all weaknesses, the KPD was in October consciously aiming at the revolutionary struggle for power. If, in spite of the revolutionary situation and the efforts of the KPD and the CI, there was neither a decisive revolutionary struggle nor a political mass struggle, that was due to a series of errors and defects which were partly of opportunist origin.

Defective Evaluation of Revolutionary Development

The party was too late in recognizing the stage of maturity reached by the revolutionary situation in Germany. Nor did the Executive of the CI direct attention energetically enough to the approaching decision, so that the most important measures were taken in hand too late. At the close of the preceding period (Cuno Government, entry into Ruhr), the question of power should have been brought up and technical preparatory work begun. The party was slow in recognizing the significance of the mass struggles in the Ruhr and in Upper Silesia as signs of growing consciousness of strength and of increasing political activity of the working masses; it began to make the necessary changes only after the Cuno strike.

Tactical Errors

The task of stepping up and expanding the numerous separate actions from July to September and giving them a political direction was not carried out. . . . One of the most serious mistakes was the failure to transform the instinctive rebellion of the masses into conscious revolutionary militancy by directing it to political goals.

The party failed to conduct energetic and lively agitation on behalf of the political workers' councils, and to connect transitional demands and partial struggles with the final goal of the proletarian dictatorship. The neglect of the factory-council movement also made it impossible for the factory councils to take over for a time the functions of workers' councils, so that in the decisive days there was no authoritative centre around which the vacillating working masses who had shaken off the influence of the SPD could rally.

Since other united front organs (action committees, control committees, fighting committees) were not systematically used either to make political preparations for the struggle, that struggle became almost exclusively a party affair, and not a united proletarian struggle.

Political-Organizational Weaknesses and Defects

The party developed in only a minor degree the capacity to consolidate organizationally its growing influence in proletarian mass organizations,

Even less was it able to concentrate its forces over a long period on a particular fighting task. Technical preparations, the re-focusing of the apparatus for the struggle for power, the arming and internal consolidation of the red hundreds were carried out to a minimal degree. . . .

Mistaken Estimate of the Relation of Forces

The over-hasty technical preparations in the decisive weeks, the emphasis on the action as a party struggle and on the 'decisive blow' alone, without previous partial actions and mass movements, made it impossible to test the real relation of forces or to set the right date. Consequently there was no reality or certainty in the calculation whether the majority of the working class at the decisive points was following the leadership of the KPD. What could be ascertained was only that the party was on the road to winning over the majority, without actually having its leadership. . . .

The party also mistook the character and role of the left SPD leaders; even within the party the illusion grew that we could by mass pressure force those leaders to take up the fight together with us.

The Incorrect Political-Strategic Attitude in Saxony

The stubborn insistence on using the defence of the central German positions as the starting-point of the decisive struggle was wrong. It led to the neglect of other important industrial and fighting areas, and, after the passive surrender of the Saxon positions, to a marked disorientation. It was a fatal mistake for the party to stake everything exclusively on the Saxon card, without providing a line of retreat should it fail, or having other plans for attack.

As a result of all these mistakes and deficiencies in the party, and of the weakness of the working class, the decisive struggle for power was at the last moment avoided. In Bulgaria, where the party had never undertaken armed struggle, defeat may still become the basis of future victories; but in Germany, after the defeats of 1919 and March 1921, we were in a situation in which the communists should have been able to lead the masses to victory. . . .

IV. THE SAXON EXPERIMENT AND THE HAMBURG STRUGGLES

As class contradictions in Germany came to a head, with the economic crisis becoming more acute, and the party turning towards decisive struggles, the Executive of the CI and the KPD initiated the experiment of the entry of communists into the Government of Saxony. The purpose of this step, in the mind of the Executive, was specifically military and political, and was defined in the following instructions:

Since, in our view, the decisive moment will come not later than in four, five, or six weeks, we think it essential to occupy immediately every position that can be of direct use. On the basis of the situation we believe we must take a practical attitude towards the question of our entry into the Saxon Government. Provided that the Zeigner people are really ready to defend Saxony against Bavaria and the fascists, we must enter, immediately arm 50,000 to 60,000 men, ignoring General Müller. The same in Thuringia.

On the assumptions originally made, this step was in accordance with the decisions of the fourth congress. The unleashing of revolutionary struggles, the fusing together of the working masses should have been the pre-conditions of entry into the Saxon Government. The entry should have been supported by mass movements. Even if the direct military task had to be postponed because of the slowing down of the revolutionary process, communists should and could still have engaged in really revolutionary activity. . . .

Above all, they should have boldly raised the question of arming the workers; in the very first hours of their participation in the workers' government the communists should have insisted, as their primary task, on the arming of the proletariat. . . .

They should likewise from the outset have exposed and condemned before the broadest masses Zeigner's two-faced attitude, his concealed negotiations with the military dictators, and the entire counter-revolutionary role of the left SPD leaders. . . .

Only if the entire party had worked in correct revolutionary fashion could the Chemnitz conference have turned out successfully for the party. The party let itself be taken by surprise by the enemy's blow, although intervention by the Reich had been expected. It was a still greater error that, although a general strike should have been proposed, nothing was done to get the conference from its opening to concentrate exclusively on defence against the Reich Executive. That mistake was undoubtedly facilitated by the treacherous game of the left SPD leaders.

The Hamburg rising was the complete antithesis of Saxony. There it was shown that by sudden and bold attack by resolute forces the enemy could be militarily overwhelmed. At the same time it was shown that such an armed struggle, even if, as in Hamburg, it is regarded by the population not without sympathy and is supported by a mass movement, is doomed to failure if it remains isolated and cannot rely locally on a workers'-council movement, the absence of which in Hamburg was felt particularly keenly.

The struggle itself was hampered by contradictory instructions from the party centre, and even the strikes in progress in Hamburg were called off because of the absence of reports of any struggle in the rest of the Reich and the news of the outcome of the Chemnitz conference.

Nevertheless the Hamburg struggle was called off with exemplary discipline. Its lessons are valuable for the party and the Comintern. Particularly noteworthy was the scoundrelly behaviour of the Hamburg SPD leaders. . . .

V. THE ROLE OF SOCIAL-DEMOCRACY AND THE CHANGE IN UNITED FRONT TACTICS IN GERMANY

The leading strata of German social-democracy are at the present moment nothing but a fraction of German fascism wearing a socialist mask. They handed State power over to the representatives of the capitalist dictatorship in order to save capitalism from the proletarian revolution. . . .

It is not just now that these leaders of German social-democracy have gone over to the side of capital. At bottom they have always been on the side of the class enemies of the proletariat, but it is only now that this has been revealed to the masses in a glaring light, by their completing the transition from capitalist democracy to capitalist dictatorship.

This circumstance induces us to modify the united front tactics in Germany.

There can be no dealings with the mercenaries of the white dictatorship. This must be clearly grasped by all German communists and solemnly and loudly announced to the entire German proletariat.

Even more dangerous than the right-wing SPD leaders are the left— the last illusion of the deceived workers, the last fig-leaves for the filthy counter-revolutionary policy of Severing, Noske, and Ebert. The KPD rejects not only any dealings with the SPD centre, but also with the 'left' leaders until they shall have shown at least enough manliness to break openly with the counter-revolutionary gang in the SPD presidium.

The slogan of the united front tactic in Germany is now: Unity from below! . . .

The KPD must learn how to put this slogan of the united front from below into operation. There is a greater ferment than ever before among the workers still belonging to the SPD. They see that their leaders are bankrupt and are seeking new roads. There is therefore no reason for us to reject local negotiations and agreements with SPD workers, when they are honest proletarians ready to prove their devotion to the revolution.

The united front bodies, factory councils, action committees, and control committees, must be interlocked and woven into a dense network, so that they can finally become the centrally-directed apparatus for the proletarian struggle for power.

VI. IMMEDIATE TASKS OF THE PARTY

The basic appraisal of the German situation given by the Comintern Executive last September remains in essentials unchanged. The character of the phase in the struggle and the chief tasks of the party are the same. The KPD must not strike from the agenda the question of insurrection and seizure of power. . . . However great the partial victories of the German counter-revolution, they do not solve any of the critical problems of capitalist Germany.

The KPD is therefore confronted with a number of immediate tasks, arising from the experience gained in the last few months.

The party must organize the proletarian struggle against the abolition of the eight-hour day and of workers' rights. It must bring the unemployed movement into organizational and political association with the movement of employed workers, and so ward off the danger of the working class being split into hungry unemployed and workers who still have a crust of bread. The party will be able to do this work best if it prepares in advance for the forthcoming economic struggles in such a way that they are directed not only against wage reductions, but with a political purpose, under the slogan: Work for the unemployed.

The party's agitation must bring home to the broadest masses that only the proletarian dictatorship can bring them salvation. This task must be linked to the goal of the political annihilation of the Social-Democratic Party; it requires the organization of united front organs and a clear objective in all partial struggles. . . .

The KPD must be good not only in agitation; it must also be a good fighting party. The arming of the workers and the technical preparations for the decisive struggle must be doggedly continued. Proletarian hundreds must be set up, not only on paper but in reality, relying on the sympathy of the broad working masses, won over by the active leadership of the KPD in all the day-to-day struggles and actions of the proletariat. . . .

The communist party is the only revolutionary party; it is strong enough to prepare for and achieve the victory of the proletarian masses against all other parties; this must become the firm conviction of every party member. . . .

The maintenance of party unity is imperatively demanded by the Communist International. The Executive calls on the entire KPD membership to do everything possible to see that at the party congress the entire party unanimously and resolutely liquidates all fractional struggles and achieves full capacity for action.

The Executive of the Comintern reminds all members of the KPD and all other Comintern sections of the gigantic tasks arising from the present revolutionary crisis. It is firmly convinced that the experiences of the last few months have not been in vain and will, if seriously examined and evaluated, bring the victory of the proletariat nearer.

EXTRACTS FROM A RESOLUTION OF THE ECCI ON THE ORGANIZATION
OF FACTORY CELLS

21 *January* 1924   *Inprekorr*, iv, 24, p. 261, 21 *February* 1924

[The reorganization of communist parties on the basis of factory cells was part of the attempt to 'bolshevize' them. The theses of the central committee of the RCP adopted to mark the twenty-fifth anniversary of the foundation of that party stated that: 'The experience of the RCP is the most valuable possession of world communism . . . its history, victories, and defeats provide a source from which not only the Russian but the entire world proletariat can draw lessons and guidance on all questions of the theory and practice of the class struggle.' In an article published together with the resolution, it was asserted that German experience had shown that 'the organizational principles of the Russian party are completely valid for the West European parties also', but whereas some of these principles could be applied in Russia only after the revolution, in western Europe they had to be in operation before. Organization on an area basis was a survival of social-democratic practice, concerned only with the counting of votes. The resolution was passed unanimously, with the reservation that modifications might have to be made, in the light of experience, according to varying circumstances in the sections. At the same time special instructions were issued by the presidium for the organization of factory cells in Germany. It was laid down that a majority of the members of district and local committees must be members of factory cells. Unlike other sections, the KPD had to work out a time-table for reorganization, and report progress periodically to the ECCI. The fifth Comintern congress later in the year endorsed the resolution, and declared that since January it had become apparent that reorganization required, not a superficial tactical change, but basic reconstruction of the parties on bolshevik lines. The parties themselves had not yet recognized this. Where factory cells existed, there was a tendency to limit their work to that of trade union fractions. They were, on the contrary, the primary party organization, recruiting members and sympathizers, collecting dues, etc. The social composition of the parties had to be improved; industrial workers should form the majority. When this had been done, street cells could be dropped entirely, and non-industrial members attached to factory cells. The ECCI was asked to draw up instructions for all sections on local and central organization.]

The organization of the party must be adapted to the conditions and purposes of its activity. . . .

The final goal of our party is the overthrow of bourgeois rule, the conquest of power by the working class, the attainment of communism. Its immediate task is to win over the majority of the working class by active participation in the daily struggle of the working masses and the leadership of that struggle. This can be accomplished only by the closest association of our party organization with the working masses in the factories.

With this in mind, the third world congress of the CI decided that factory cells were to be the foundation of the CP. This change has not yet been carried out in the majority of CI sections; in many sections the question of organizing factory cells has not even been raised in a practical form. The experience of the German revolution (end of 1923) has, however, shown most clearly that, in the absence of cells based on the factories and of close connexions with the working masses, the latter cannot be drawn into the struggle and led, their moods cannot be rightly appraised, the moment most favourable to us cannot be exploited, nor victory won over the bourgeoisie.

BASIC FORMS OF LOCAL PARTY ORGANIZATION

1. The basis of party organization is the party cell in the factory. All communists who work in a particular factory must belong to that factory cell. *Note*: In factories with only one or two party members, these will be attached to the nearest factory cell, which must extend its work to cover all the factories in the area which have no cells.

2. Communists who do not work in factories, workshops, stores, etc. (housewives, domestic servants, porters, etc.) shall be in street cells organized according to locality. *Note*: All members of factory cells who live in other districts must be registered with the district bureau of the district in which they live. The district bureau shall make use of them in the street cells. Members of cells in other districts who are assigned to a street cell by the district bureau may not vote in those street cells on questions on which they have already voted in their factory cells (questions of party principle, elections of party delegates, etc.).

3. The unemployed remain members of the cell of the factory where they were previously employed. In cases of prolonged unemployment they may, with the permission of the district committee, be detached from that cell and transferred to a cell in the area where they live.

4. In small industrial centres, towns, and villages, where workers live close to their place of employment in factory or farm, homogeneous cells should be formed wherever possible around the factory or farm.

5. Factory cells and street cells shall elect a bureau or presidium of from three to not more than five members, who shall distribute the work among themselves. . . .

7. In large towns with many factory and street cells, these shall be organized into districts, and districts into areas. The areas together make up the town organization. . . . In small towns and villages cells are organized into local groups. . . . *Note*: The districts and local groups shall hold regular meetings of all members of all cells in their area.

8. At the head of every district and local group there shall be a bureau of three to five members elected by the general meeting of all cell members, or by delegate meetings, according to local circumstances. . . .

10. The leadership of town party organizations shall be elected at town conferences consisting of delegates from all districts in the town in proportion to their membership.

11. In order to strengthen the influence of the factory cells, more than half the members of the district bureau and the area committee must be members of factory cells. . . .

12. In conditions of illegality, the higher party bodies have the right, in exceptional circumstances such as the arrest of the area committee, to appoint a new area committee, provided that a delegate meeting is held at the first opportunity to confirm the appointment or elect a new committee. . . . Area committees working in illegal conditions should be kept as small as possible.

TASKS OF THE FACTORY CELLS

Emphasis in the party's political organization work must be shifted to the factory cells.

By taking the lead in the struggle of the working masses for their daily needs, the factory cell should guide them forward to the struggle for the proletarian dictatorship. . . .

In addition to general party matters, the tasks of the factory cell are the following:

1. To conduct communist agitation and propaganda among the non-party working masses, and systematic work with individual workers in order to draw them into the CP. To distribute political literature in the factory, and even issue a special factory paper. . . .

2. To work persistently and tenaciously to capture all official posts in the factory (trade union), co-operative society, factory council, control committee, etc.

3. To intervene in all industrial disputes and demands of the working masses; the cell should extend and deepen the movement, explain to the workers the political consequences of the struggle, and move them on to the path of broader struggle (not only industrial but political), and create a united workers' front against the bourgeoisie and fascism.

4. The cell must fight persistently in the factories against the followers and members of other parties, including the socialist and other 'labour' parties, using for this purpose material about the activities of these parties which is comprehensible even to the backward strata of the working class.

5. To establish contact between the employed and the unemployed, in order to prevent conflict between them.

6. When conditions are ripe, to fight for workers' control of production, banks, estates, transport. . . .

B 8173   G

7. To work among the women and young persons in the factory and draw them into the struggle. . . .

8. Every cell member must take active part in all party work in the factory, assigned to him by the cell bureau or presidium.

Apart from these special tasks in the factories, the factory cells also have territorial tasks. . . .

The most important of these are:

1. Political and organizational party work in the area where the members live; carrying through of election, housing, and cost-of-living campaigns. . . .

2. Distribution of party literature, recruiting of new readers and new party members, agitation, propaganda, and individual recruiting in local organizations (clubs, etc.); drawing sympathizers into demonstrations. . . .

3. House-to-house agitation in the area, reporting on the party affiliation of local residents, on political work in the area, on fascist activity; observation of arms-stores, etc.

EXTRACTS FROM AN ECCI RESOLUTION ON THE BRITISH LABOUR GOVERNMENT AND THE COMMUNIST PARTY OF GREAT BRITAIN

6 *February* 1924   *Inprekorr*, iv, 21, p. 235, 16 *February* 1924

[The British Labour Government, which took office on 23 January 1924, established *de jure* diplomatic relations with the USSR on 1 February 1924, a step which was welcomed by the second Soviet congress, meeting at the time, as 'historic'. After the special conference in Moscow with CPGB representatives, called to discuss the reasons why the British party was developing so slowly, it had concentrated on work in the trade unions. The ECCI report to the fifth congress in 1924 noted progress in this field, but complained that on the colonial question it had done 'as good as nothing'. MacManus, speaking on the ECCI report to the congress, said that the object of the CPGB in working for affiliation to the Labour Party (which had been rejected by the Labour Party conference in 1923 by 2,880,000 to 366,000 votes) was to have the opportunity 'to organize the workers against the Labour Government and against the Labour Party'.]

The entry into office of the English Labour Party is an event of the greatest significance: it reflects the awakening to class consciousness of more and more working masses, and their realization that both bourgeois parties merely represent the class interests of the possessing and exploiting minority. At the same time the policy of the Labour Government in England provides the test for the broadest working masses of the entire world, as well as for the peoples of the East, whether the ideas of the Second International about the road to socialism are correct. Consequently the attitude of the Communist International and the Communist Party of England to the Labour Government's policy is of decisive importance for the development of the communist movement. This attitude will be determined by the following basic facts:

I. The formation of a Labour Government is the result of England's economic and political decline following the burdens and shocks inflicted by the war. The 4 million votes for the Labour Party in the election were not the result of its own stubborn, vigorous, and consistent work. . . . It has taken over the government as a minority party, partly with the approval of the bourgeois parties, partly because of the disunity in the ranks of the bourgeoisie and their inability to overcome this disunity because of the tremendous tasks and difficulties left behind by the war.

II. The entire Communist International knows that the working class cannot free itself from economic slavery and political subjection unless the bourgeoisie are defeated in revolutionary struggle. . . . But the majority of English workers have democratic illusions, instilled into them in particular by the Labour Party leaders. Now the Labour Government will give the English working class the experience which will test the value of bourgeois democracy.

The Labour Government is not a government of proletarian class struggle; on the contrary, it aspires to strengthen the bourgeois State system by reforms and by class peace. . . . If, contrary to our expectations, the Labour Government were to be driven by proletarian class movements into a struggle with capital, that would sharply aggravate England's internal crisis. But if, as we expect, the Labour Government betrays the interests of the proletariat, it will give the proletariat an object lesson on how to be cured of the illusions of capitalist democracy, and so immensely accelerate the movement of the working class towards a revolutionary position. . . .

It is for the Communist Party to do all in its power to carry out the following tasks:

(a) To mobilize the broadest masses of the English proletariat to exert pressure on the Labour Government and the Labour Party to engage in serious struggle against the capitalist classes.

(b) Every effort must be made to help the workers to be convinced from their own experience of the utter unfitness of the Labour Party leaders, their petty-bourgeois and treacherous character, the inevitability of their bankruptcy.

For this purpose the immediate tasks of the English Communist Party are:

1. To launch a broad campaign at once concerning the promises made by the Labour Party leaders, as well as for other slogans designed to

mobilize the class-conscious section of the working masses for joint action. . . . In particular, disregarding the possibility that the Liberals and Conservatives may unite to overthrow the Government, the demand must be made that the Labour Government come out in favour of the following measures:

(*a*) To deal with unemployment by effective taxation of the capitalists, and by taking over, under State and workers' control, enterprises shut down by the capitalists.

(*b*) To take the initiative in nationalizing the railways and mines; these to be administered in conjunction with the workers' organizations.

(*c*) The Government must take energetic steps to liberate the peasants and workers of Ireland, India, and Egypt from the yoke of English imperialism.

(*d*) It must be active in fighting the war danger in Europe and conclude an alliance with the Union of Soviet Republics. . . .

(2) The Communist Party must preserve its ideological, tactical, and organizational independence. . . . It must appeal to all groups and organizations of the working class who demand of the Labour Government a resolute struggle against the bourgeoisie. . . .

The Communist Party of England must realize that the objective prerequisites are now being created for its development into an influential revolutionary mass party. It must therefore do everything possible to plant its organization deep among the revolutionary working masses, above all at their place of work.

EXTRACTS FROM A LETTER FROM THE ECCI TO THE NINTH CONGRESS
OF THE KPD

26 *March* 1924 *Inprekorr*, iv, 48, p. 562, 24 *April* 1924

[At the ECCI presidium meeting in January 1924 Ruth Fischer declared that at the time of the Leipzig congress (1923) the KPD was on the verge of a split; this had been prevented only by the last-minute intervention of the ECCI. Between Leipzig and October, every action showed the disharmony between the mood of the workers on one side, and that of the KPD *Zentrale* on the other. Unless the leadership were changed, the KPD would split and its members would go over to the KAPD and the SPD. Zinoviev advocated a left-centre *Zentrale*, in which proletarians like Thaelmann and Remmele would have a majority. Fischer and Maslow had made mistakes, but patience must be shown towards them. It would be necessary to convene a special congress to elect a new central committee. Neither the ECCI nor the RCP could take responsibility for nominating new leaders. There was good material for a new *Zentrale*; if the KPD did not make the necessary changes, the ECCI would, however reluctantly, have to intervene. New fractional struggles in the KPD would only revive the dying

SPD. 'The civil war in the KPD must cease.' The January resolution of the
ECCI on the events of October was endorsed by the central committee of the
KPD at its meeting on 19 February, thus reversing the decision of its meeting in
November 1923. The new *Zentrale* consisted of five representatives of the centre
and two of the left. In March the reorganized central committee passed by a
large majority a resolution condemning the opposition in the RCP. All factions
in that party were anxious to get the support of the KPD. Zinoviev and Stalin
each sent personal letters to Maslow and Ruth Fischer, leaders of the left wing
which carried the day at the Frankfurt (ninth) congress of the KPD in April
1924. There were 118 delegates, of whom only 11 were avowed supporters of
Brandler. Membership had fallen from 267,000 in September 1923 to 121,400
in April.

The ECCI sent two letters to the congress, dated 24 and 26 March. The
first dealt with trade union policy, and deplored the strong movement in the
KPD to leave the unions and found new revolutionary unions. The left opposition in the German trade union federation had called a conference at Weimar
in Autumn 1923, which was attended by 273 delegates, of whom two-thirds
were communists. The decision to stay within the ADGB was carried against a
large minority. New unions were formed of those expelled by the ADGB and
some break-away groups; the communist group which opposed the policy of
attempting to get those expelled back into the ADGB—its chief exponent was
Schumacher—was expelled from the KPD. The letter of 24 March admitted
that there were circumstances in which it was necessary to split the unions, and
that the KPD should not tie its hands; but the general rule was to stay in and
fight the union leaders, and try to capture the unions. The prime weapon in the
fight against the union leaders was factory committees, on which the KPD should
concentrate; they must not be allowed to fall under the control of the unions.
The proposal to hold a conference in May of the trade union opposition was to
be dropped in order to avoid giving the social-democrats a pretext for expelling
them. Under pressure from the ECCI delegation, the congress adopted trade
union theses which laid down that no communist could leave his trade union
without the permission of the central committee.

The chief ECCI delegate at the congress, Manuilsky, was strongly opposed to
the draft theses on the political situation put forward by Maslow, on the ground
that they were mistaken about the Ruhr, the British Labour Government, and
the position of the German nationalists. Moreover, they criticized Comintern
inactivity over the Ruhr crisis, alleging that since its third congress in 1921
its policy had been directed to the most backward sections of the working
class. This charge, he urged, was groundless. The elastic tactics of the
Comintern were the outcome of firm principles, and for the KPD to accept
Maslow's theses would be tantamount to a declaration of war on the International.

Klara Zetkin, who was not present at the congress, wrote a letter saying that
if it was to be able to do its work in the future, the KPD must destroy the legend
that the October defeat was the outcome of the errors of the leaders, especially
Brandler, and not one forced on them by circumstances, including the political
incapacity, organizational weakness, and inexperience of the party. Answering

the charge of opportunism, she wrote: 'I do not attach much value to an amnesty from a party that finds no place in its leadership for men like Brandler, Thalheimer, Walcher, and Pieck.' The letter was described later by one of the majority spokesmen as 'a provocation'.

The political resolution put forward by Brandler's supporters received no votes. The one adopted stated that 'the defeat of the German proletariat was more severe than in 1919, 1920, or 1921, because victory had never been so near'. The resolution on tactics, drafted by the left majority and the ECCI delegates, said that 'the party must now eradicate the last remnants of Brandlerism'. The theory of the right wing was revisionist, and was bound to lead to the liquidation of the KPD.

The proposals of the Comintern delegation for the composition of the new *Zentrale* were rejected by the congress. Manuilsky expressed his misgivings, and announced that the question would be submitted to the ECCI and the fifth CI congress. The 15 members elected to the *Zentrale* included 11 of the left majority, and 4 of the centre, among them Zetkin and Pieck.

The ECCI also criticized those who had argued that Russian State interests were in conflict with revolutionary policies, and who urged that the CI move its headquarters from Moscow and the sections should renounce Russian financial help. The disappointment felt after October must not lead to any revision of basic bolshevik principles. All fractions should be dissolved, and attacks on members who loyally carried out party decisions must end.

At the thirteenth congress of the RCP Bukharin said that the ECCI had for a long time supported the right wing in the KPD against the left; but when it became clear that the right wing was infected by social-democratic opportunism, which was responsible for many of the 'negative aspects' of the events of October 1923, the ECCI realized that there would have to be a change; as then constituted, the KPD was unable to attract the revolutionary working class elements among the left.

Immediately after the congress, Zinoviev wrote that the left wing in the KPD consisted of good and devoted revolutionary workers, and also of a group of intellectuals, some of whom were immature, without Marxist training or serious revolutionary traditions; these might do the KPD great harm.

Two years later, at the sixth enlarged plenum of the ECCI, Zinoviev revealed that three members of the Russian central committee had been sent to the KPD at the time of the Frankfurt congress. Thaelmann had supported the ECCI, but the majority on the CC had wished the ECCI to withdraw its letters, and Stöcker had been sent to Moscow to ask the ECCI not to insist on the application of its trade union policy to Germany. Only the threat of an open breach between the Comintern and the KPD had got the trade union resolution through the congress. Lozovsky recalled that the ECCI had sent six delegates to the congress (of whom he was one). They had held a twelve-hour session with the central committee; he had said that the acceptance of Maslow's resolution would be tantamount to a declaration of war on the CI, and some of the worst passages had been deleted. Even so, the KPD had not wished to publish the ECCI's letter on the trade union question; the ECCI itself had then published it in Germany.]

Never before has a congress of the KPD been faced with such immense responsibilities. It is no exaggeration to say that your congress will determine for many years the fate of the KPD and therewith of the German revolution.

I. THE INTERNATIONAL SITUATION

. . . The German bourgeoisie have won an apparent respite. What is now happening may be described as the shadow of an improvement in the international position of the German bourgeoisie. But it is only a shadow. The sword is still suspended over Germany. Either Germany will become a colony of victorious imperialism or it will accomplish the proletarian revolution—these are the alternatives confronting it.

II. PROSPECTS OF THE GERMAN REVOLUTION

The proletarian revolution in Germany is inevitable. The mistakes in estimating the tempo of events committed in October 1923 created many difficulties for the party. They are nevertheless merely an episode. The basic estimate remains unchanged. The revolution is approaching. . . .

We understand the passion with which the German comrades are discussing whether in October–November 1923 we should have taken up arms or whether the retreat was unavoidable. . . . But the party must now in spite of everything look forward, not back. The party is not destroyed; it has kept its most important cadres. It has emerged from the period of illegality with honour and with its ranks unbroken. It must now put before the German working class, more sharply than ever before, the most important of all tasks—the preparation for the direct struggle for power, for the proletarian dictatorship.

III. WINNING THE MAJORITY

It is still a fundamental task of the party to win the majority of the proletariat and to draw over to its side as broad strata as possible of the fellow travellers of the proletariat from among the urban petty bourgeoisie and the peasantry. We should not underestimate the first successes of the fascists among the workers. They are extremely dangerous symptoms, to which the party must direct the most serious attention. If we fail to consider the national question as bolsheviks should, we shall not win over the little man from the fascists, and to fail in that means to surrender hegemony in the revolutionary movement. . . .

IV. PARTY WORK AMONG THE NON-PROLETARIAN POPULATION

The party which claims the hegemony of the revolutionary movement, which intends to win power in the State and transform the bourgeois republic into a soviet republic must also carry on its preparatory work among the non-proletarian strata of the population. The working class and its party will be able to establish the proletarian dictatorship only if they are able to neutralize one part of the small and middle bourgeoisie in town and country, and to win the rest over to their side. . . .

V. UNITED FRONT TACTICS AND TRANSITIONAL SLOGANS

The ECCI has already laid down its views on this question in the theses adopted at the January session in Moscow. . . . In our opinion there is no reason to change what was then said. . . .

In Germany it is essential for us to use the united front tactic only *from below*, that is to say, we will have no dealings with the official social-democratic leaders. The tactics of the united front from below must, however, be pursued honestly, consistently, and to the end. No fractional diplomacy can be permitted in this question. . . .

VI. ORGANIZATIONAL QUESTIONS

We are compelled to note that up to now the KPD has not organized itself on the basis of communist factory cells. . . . But we cannot even talk of creating a serious revolutionary proletarian party, able to seize power from the hands of the bourgeoisie, unless the foundations of the party are communist cells in the factories. The CI thinks it high time to proceed from words to action in this matter. The party congress must set a date by which time the entire party shall have been reorganized on these lines. . . .

The congress should resolve to maintain and improve the illegal party apparatus. We should in no circumstances rely on the continuation for any length of time of the present state of legality. . . .

VII. ARMING THE WORKERS: THE RED HUNDREDS

To arm the workers remains the party's most important task. . . . What has so far been done in this respect is no more than a drop in the ocean. The German workers want to be armed and it must be one of the most important tasks of the party to satisfy this desire. . . .

The party must work to strengthen the red hundreds, both those composed exclusively of party members, and those in which other revolutionary workers also take part. . . . The German workers must be made to realize that the red hundreds are required in the daily struggle. Only when we accustom the red hundreds to the idea that they are to protect workers' demonstrations from attacks by the Reichswehr, guard leading militants from arrest, undertake a raid in order to procure arms for the workers, etc., will the red hundreds strike deep roots among the workers. They must be anchored deep among the working masses, in the factories. If they are, even the bourgeois authorities will be unable to touch them.

VIII. THE SITUATION WITHIN THE PARTY

. . . The triumph of the left wing of the KPD is of tremendous significance for the fate of the German revolution. It undoubtedly reflects the
profound processes at work within the working class or at any rate within
its vanguard. It testifies to the growing readiness for struggle . . . to the
radicalization of important sections of the proletariat. But woe to us if we
overestimate these symptoms, if we take what is desired as what is present,
if we assume that the majority of the German proletariat is now ready to
take up the fight under the leadership of the KPD left wing. That is not
yet the case; it is the main task of the party to reach this goal.

The severe crisis which the KPD is now living through can become the
starting-point of the rebirth and strengthening of the party. The party
can now march forward along the broad road of revolution. It can at last
rid itself of opportunist errors and take up a firm communist position
towards the right and the 'left' leaders of German social-democracy. . . .

The chief task of the party is to put an end to fractional struggles within
the party. . . . The victorious majority should take intelligent political and
organizational measures which will enable it to create a new regime in
the party, to use all the party's valuable forces, whatever wing they belonged to previously, and lead the party to the fulfilment of the great
historical tasks which confront it.

EXTRACTS FROM A CIRCULAR LETTER FROM ZINOVIEV ON THE CON-
VENING OF THE FIFTH WORLD CONGRESS OF THE COMINTERN

April 1924   *Inprekorr*, iv, 46, p. 535, 18 *April* 1924

Programme. The fifth congress will finally have to confirm the programme
of the CI. The first drafts were published in connexion with the fourth
congress. In the five years of its existence the CI has issued a number of
fundamental documents . . . which will serve as the chief component parts
of the programme. . . .

The same congress will have to confirm the programmes of the largest
individual sections of the CI; these must hasten to complete their preparatory work.

Future tactics. This question will be discussed in association with another
item on the agenda, the world economic situation. The fifth congress will
have to draw up a balance sheet of the application of united front tactics
in the last few years. It is already quite clear that these tactics will again
be subjected to sharp criticism. We should not hide from ourselves that in
practice these tactics have repeatedly been used in a way tending towards
opportunism; nevertheless the balance-sheet will show a profit. United
front tactics remain correct for an entire epoch. It is merely necessary to

take stronger precautionary measures against their distortion. . . . Opportunist dangers from the right remain, now as before, the chief dangers for the CI. . . . The CI is passing through a period between two waves of the revolution. One wave has passed, the other has not yet mounted. . . .

Important questions in dispute in the sections. . . . The Executive Committee of the CI has this time placed the problems of four of its largest sections on the agenda.

Russia. The congress will learn of the present economic situation in the USSR, and draw up the balance sheet of the New Economic Policy. It will deal with the outcome of the recent discussions in the RCP and utter its decisive word on the discussion.

Germany. The congress will give a final appraisal of the conflicts within the KPD connected with the October retreat of the German proletariat. The congress will undoubtedly take the same view of the opportunist tendencies in the KPD as the ECCI did at the time, and it will at the same time come out decisively against the 'ultra-left', but in fact non-bolshevik, attitude growing up in the KPD, and condemn the tactical excesses from which the new KPD majority is not free.

Italy. The congress will undoubtedly agree on the immediate amalgamation of the communists with the third internationalists (fusionists) in the Italian Socialist Party, and help the Italian CP to institute a still more decisive struggle against fascism and social-democracy.

Bulgaria. The congress will determine its attitude to the very important events through which the Bulgarian CP has lived. The mistakes made by the Bulgarian CP majority in June 1923 are now admitted by that majority itself. . . .

England. For the first time in the history of the English labour movement the conditions are now being created for the establishment of a mass communist party. In this sense what is now happening in the English labour movement is more important than the events in Germany. . . .

United States. The American Workers' Party is becoming a mass party. It has to decide its attitude to the petty-bourgeois 'third' party which is being formed, and to the farmers. . . .

Japan. The Japanese workers' movement is only in the first stages of its development. The furious persecution to which Japanese communists are exposed has so far prevented the formation of a mass Japanese Communist Party. With communist participation a mass workers' and peasants' party is being started in Japan. . . .

The trade union question will again claim an important part of the congress's time. The more the influence of communists in the unions grows, the more furiously do the social-democratic leaders try to accelerate splits in the unions. The provocative policy of the social-democratic leaders has had important consequences in many places. Among the German left a completely false and most dangerous attitude is growing on the question of further work in reactionary unions. With all the force of its authority, with the utmost vigour and decision, the fifth congress must come out against leaving the unions. . . .

No less important will be the discussion of the national question. The theoretical basis for solving this question has been laid down at previous congresses. . . . The fifth congress will have to give more concrete form to Comintern national policy in individual countries, particularly the countries of the East and the colonies. . . . Without a solution of the national question and the agrarian question in a Leninist spirit the CI cannot win a majority of the workers, and unless that is done no decisive victory can be gained.

The question of the attitude to the peasantry will be raised on the report of the formation of the Peasant International. . . . The European communist parties have so far not done the hundredth part of what should be done to bring over to their side the sections of the peasantry which can be won over to the working class. . . .

A new question on the agenda of the fifth congress is the attitude of communists to intellectuals (using the word in its broad sense, to include also the technical intelligentsia). Because of the general economic situation the intellectuals in a number of countries are opposed, more or less sharply, to the existing regime. . . . The CI must seize the initiative in this field, too, and show how living revolutionary Marxism differs from the traditional and lifeless formulation of the problem of the intellectuals. . . .

'Without Lenin in the spirit of Leninism' is the slogan of the fifth congress. The great leader of the CI is dead but his work lives, and above all in the Comintern. The fifth congress will settle all the problems confronting it in the spirit of true Leninism. Lenin's teaching will remain the guiding star for all sections of the CI.

EXTRACTS FROM AN ECCI MANIFESTO TO THE WORKERS AND PEASANTS
OF JAPAN

5 *May* 1924   *Inprekorr*, iv, 61, p. 735, 3 *June* 1924

[The Japanese Communist Party was founded secretly in July 1922 in Tokyo, by some Japanese who had earlier in the year attended the 'Congress of Toilers of the Far East' in Moscow. It consisted of about forty left-wing intellectuals; it gave its support to the General Labour Federation (Sodomei), and was represented at the fourth Comintern congress at the end of the year. Its programme, drafted in 1922 under the supervision, it is believed, of Bukharin, included abolition of the monarchy, confiscation of large estates and of the property of religious bodies, withdrawal of Japanese troops from China, Korea, Sakhalin, and Formosa, and diplomatic recognition of Russia. Arahata, chairman of the central committee, went to Moscow in the spring of 1923, and appeared at the June ECCI plenum under the name of Aoki. He did not believe that it was possible to establish a legal party in Japan, but Zinoviev argued in favour of doing so; it could not be assumed that the attempt would fail. In the same month the Japanese police arrested a large proportion of the party membership, and further arrests were made after the September earthquake and an attempt on the life of the Prince Regent. The few leaders still at liberty advised dissolution, and this was carried out early in 1924. In June the ECCI set up a commission to study the Japanese situation; Katayama, speaking at the fifth CI congress in June, referred to the steady growth of the Japanese Communist Party. The ECCI report welcomed the formation of a legal Japanese Workers' and Peasants' Party.]

Your country is in the power of a ruling class of militarists, landowners, bureaucrats, and monopoly capitalists who deny you every right, who pitilessly exploit you and suppress you with cruel violence. . . . The class which rules over you is completely incapable of solving the economic crisis with which your country is permanently saddled, or of accomplishing the great task of reconstruction. . . .

At the same time the country is falling into the power of American finance-capital, which will add to the evils you already suffer the burden of exploitation by foreign capitalists and turn your Government into an instrument of foreign imperialism. . . .

Your ruling class also tries to employ cunning tricks to enslave you. They offer you apparent recognition of your labour unions if you agree to ensure the regime of your exploiters by sending delegates to the capitalist conference of the so-called International Labour Organization of the League of Nations in Geneva. They offer you the 'protection of the law' in the form of a trade union Bill which will in fact cripple the activities of your organizations. They are trying to corrupt your leaders by offering them high official positions. They offer to establish rural courts to settle, in the interests of the large landowners, disputes about rents and mortgages. They talk of universal suffrage, but have no intention of giving you the vote. They use every swindle to keep you in slavery.

It is significant that before the 1905 revolution the tyrannical Tsarist Government of Russia employed the same mixture of force and cunning. . . .

The Government has dissolved the old parliament and 'appealed to the country'. But you have no voice in the election of a new Government. If you think that a change of Government will bring any serious improvement of your position you will be disappointed. . . . You yourselves must take up the fight for your emancipation. You alone can put an end to reaction and open the road to the future development of your country.

You have shown a good fighting spirit. . . . But that is not enough. You must storm the citadel of reaction. Organize your forces for the fight for your civil liberties. Hasten the formation of your workers' and peasants' parties, which alone will enable you to carry on your fight for freedom. Your party must be independent of the 'radical' bourgeoisie.

Carry on an untiring struggle for your programme until you have put it through. Demand a democratic government, universal franchise, the right to form unions and to strike and to make collective agreements, freedom of political opinion, and the right of assembly. . . .

Workers and peasants of Japan!

The vicious verdict on your worker comrades in Nagoya shows that the Government is preparing the same fate for your comrades now awaiting trial in Tokyo. . . .

You must protest. Begin your campaign for political freedom with the demand for the setting free of all those who have been persecuted for their political opinions.

EXTRACTS FROM AN ECCI MANIFESTO AGAINST FRENCH IMPERIALISM IN SYRIA

11 *May* 1924   *Inprekorr*, iv, 57, p. 692, 23 *May* 1924

[The Communist Party of Syria and Lebanon was founded in 1924, and admitted to the Comintern in 1928, but did not appear openly until 1930; a few individual communists in Beirut appear to have had influence in a Lebanese People's Party in existence in 1924–5, which organized opposition to the French Mandate. No large-scale risings against the French occurred before 1925.]

French imperialism has a long and sad history; it was French imperialism which, by laying hands on Morocco twenty years ago, opened the era of rivalry and brutal greed in Europe from which the world war with its 10 million victims arose.

The Versailles treaty which heaped it with spoils could not satisfy its greedy appetites. In virtue of this robber treaty, whose black wickedness can never be sufficiently condemned, French imperialism got a foothold in Asia Minor; and though fear of Turkey has forced it to renounce Cilicia, it continues to keep Syria under military occupation. . . .

At the present time the French State, at the end of its resources, is trying to cover part of its expenditure by taxing the Syrian population. The Syrians cannot accept this without resistance. The payment of taxes to the invaders would be a recognition of the yoke forced on them. Refusals to pay have been reported from many districts. The expeditionary corps, scattered over a large area, is in a serious situation. In the last few weeks more than 200 young soldiers have fallen as innocent victims to the blows of the rebels. . . .

The Communist International does not confine itself to condemning the actions of French imperialism in Syria as a violation of the right to national self-determination. It calls on the French proletariat to wage an energetic struggle against the instigator of the war, imperialism. It calls on the French peasants to join with the workers in this struggle against French industry's costly delusions of grandeur. The peasants have nothing to gain from French capital's conquest of Syria, except perhaps a greater burden of taxes because of higher military expenditure and the further prospect of seeing the blood of their children flow again.

Decades ago the Second Empire flinched before the insuperable difficulty of conquering Syria, although at that time it did not have to deal with a Syrian people conscious of its strength, or an Arab nationalism awakened from its lethargy, supported as on unshakeable pillars by the enthusiastic nationalism of an awakened Turkey and of the entire Near East, which is determined to fight for its independence and to repel by arms subjugation by an alien capitalism.

The Communist International, including its French section, stands by the Syrians . . . in everything they may do to avoid the hated yoke of the guiltiest imperialism in the world today, the imperialism of Poincaré, Millerand, the Comité des Forges, and French finance.

The struggle of the Syrian rebels is joined to the struggles now being waged in France by the mining, textile, and engineering workers. . . . Syrian peasants and French workers form, perhaps unconsciously, an anti-imperialist united front. It will be the task of the Communist International and its French section to make everyone aware of the unity of this front.

THE FIFTH CONGRESS OF THE COMMUNIST INTERNATIONAL

[The fifth congress met from 17 June to 8 July 1924; one report gives the number of those in attendance as 406, of whom 324 had voting rights (of these 117 were Russian), representing 40 parties; the mandates commission reported a total of 504 delegates, of whom 336 had voting rights, representing 41 countries; a third source gives a total of 510 delegates (346 voting), representing 49 countries; 10 countries had only consultative voice: they included Australia, Hungary, Indonesia, Korea, and Mongolia. Another report gives the total of parties represented (both with full rights and consultative voice) as 52. The membership of the larger parties was given as 310,000 for Russia, 350,000 for Germany, 130,000 for Czechoslovakia, 50,000 for France, 16,000 for Norway, 12,000 each for Italy and Sweden, and 27,000 for the American Workers' Party (which was present as a sympathizing party only); Java, 2,000; China, 800. Efforts to unite the scattered groups of communists in Korea into a party had so far been unsuccessful.

It was reported that a communist party had been established in Turkey after the fourth congress; it had been dissolved, re-established, and again dissolved.

In Persia there was communist activity in a few of the larger towns, where the trade union movement, though small and weak, was under communist control. In Palestine a party had been established at the end of 1923 and admitted as a section to the International. Its programme supported the Arabs against the Anglo-Zionist occupation. In 1923 the Egyptian socialist party had renamed itself communist party and accepted the 21 conditions. It had about 700 members but the arrest of its leaders had virtually put a stop to its activities. The Eastern department of the ECCI, which had a sub-department in Irkutsk, was in constant communication with communist organizations in the Far East and the Middle East. It had no direct contact with the French colonies in North Africa, in which the French Communist Party had been very inactive. Representatives of the parties covered by the department had come to Moscow and settled important questions of policy with the presidium.

The information and statistics department of the ECCI complained that the majority of parties did not reply to its letters and failed to complete the questionnaires sent to them; the press department reported that many sections had not yet appointed regular correspondents for *Inprekorr*. Between the fourth and the fifth congress the ECCI had sent thirty-one delegations to the sections with a total membership of sixty-five.

The events of October 1923 in Germany and the dispute within the KPD dominated the discussions. Bukharin had dealt with their repercussions on the RCP at its thirteenth congress in May: the right wing in the Comintern supported the opposition in the RCP; in the ECCI the majority of the RCP delegation had been attacked by some KPD delegates for bringing that party to the verge of ruin. He denied that the ECCI had fixed a date for the rising in Germany; it had only suggested a 'certain time limit to guide the party' but had left the actual date to be determined on the spot. He accused Radek of mobilizing opportunist elements in other parties against the new KPD leadership. The ECCI had for too long supported Brandler's leadership, although this had no support in the KPD, precisely because it had thought so highly of him.

The RCP congress resolution approved the work of its delegates to the ECCI, condemned the right deviations defended by Radek, and in particular approved the ECCI line with regard to Germany, France, and the United Kingdom. The central committee was instructed to send 'more highly qualified workers to the ECCI' in view of the importance of its work.

The ECCI report to the fifth congress dwelt on the importance to Russia of events in Germany; if an imperialist attack on Germany succeeded, it would then be Russia's turn. In October 1923 the Russian party had explained to the Russian masses that a proletarian victory in Germany would improve Russia's difficult economic situation. 'At the same time Soviet diplomats held conversations with the countries between Soviet Russia and Germany about non-interference in German affairs and maintaining neutrality.' Zinoviev opened the attack on Radek and Brandler early in his report. Their theory that fascism had triumphed over social-democracy was false. The social-democrats had become the third bourgeois party; they had no intention of fighting fascism, or they would have drawn closer to the communists. They had in fact become a wing of fascism. Radek had distorted the idea of a workers' and peasants' government.

What had happened in Saxony showed how strong were the vestiges of social-democracy in the KPD. Ruth Fischer also attributed the failure of the previous autumn to right deviations in the KPD, resulting from Radek's policy. Brandler should never have entered the Saxon Government. 'Communists enter top-level negotiations in order to detach the social-democratic masses from their leaders, not to conclude long-term alliances, which would be a rope round our necks.' The farther they got from October, the more they were convinced that the struggle for power had been possible and necessary. Neither Radek nor Brandler believed in a German or a European revolution, but only in an alliance with reformism to protect the workers' interests within the framework of the bourgeois State. Radek was responsible for the rejection of the proposal, made by the left KPD leaders, to convene a congress of factory committees; he preferred the united front from above. The party could not fight in October because it was crippled by opportunist leadership. But the hatred between the different factions of the KPD was now a thing of the past. If the ECCI had not intervened in January in favour of getting rid of Brandler and Co., the Berlin and Hamburg organizations would have left the party.

Brandler and Klara Zetkin replied to Zinoviev and Ruth Fischer. Brandler said he was watching history being rewritten at the congress. A legend had already grown up around October, and even those who witnessed the events were coming to believe it, because of their disappointed hopes; he and his colleagues were really being accused of carrying out the decisions of the third and fourth Comintern congresses. October was a failure because they had set themselves a false task and misjudged the relations of forces; they had led the workers into battle without sufficient preparation. That policy had been worked out in September, when the KPD leaders spent four weeks in Moscow discussing their plans with the ECCI. As Zinoviev had admitted in his opening speech, representatives of all the important communist parties were there, and none of them had challenged the proposal to prepare for and start a rising in Germany. They did not realize that they had lost the initiative; they had missed the opportunity at the time of the Cuno strike, and when the vote was taken at Chemnitz he had no alternative but to call off the entire action. Klara Zetkin came to Radek's defence, as she had three years before to Paul Levi's: until recently he had been regarded as one of the staunchest supporters of the German left. If the Radek–Brandler policy was wrong, the ECCI must share the responsibility. Why had the left not criticized the ECCI before the October fiasco? The situation then was objectively revolutionary, but the party did not know how to exploit it, how to make the masses understand that civil war was their only road, how to utilize every local struggle and every partial demand for that purpose. The Saxon Government would have been the right thing if it had been the achievement of a mass movement, supported by extra-parliamentary political organs of the proletariat. A workers' government could not be the starting-point. Even in Hamburg there had been no widespread will to fight—if there had been, no orders from the party centre could have stopped it. Neither the masses nor the party were ready for the fight.

The German delegation, which did not include Brandler and his supporters, though they attended the congress, put in a statement criticizing Radek's and

Brandler's conduct and leadership. The right wing represented nobody but themselves, as they had received no votes at the Frankfurt congress of the KPD.

The left-wing Italian delegates attributed the October defeat not to the actions of the German leaders, but to the mistaken decisions of the fourth congress on the united front and to the policy of the ECCI. (In December 1923 Humbert-Droz had written to Zinoviev that nobody in France could understand the thoughtlessness (légèreté) with which the German action had been prepared.)

In replying to the debate on the ECCI report, Zinoviev deplored Klara Zetkin's support of Radek. Her loyalty to friends was a political error. He enumerated ten occasions on which the ECCI had had differences of opinion with Radek, but the ECCI could not have disavowed his actions 'for reasons which you will well understand'.

Klara Zetkin spoke on the crisis among intellectuals, a sign that bourgeois society was shaken and no longer able to carry out its mission. As part of the capitalist crisis, the question of the intellectuals became part of the question of the proletariat, whose mission it was to promote all the forces of production and of civilization. The brain worker was exploited just as much as the proletarian. Intellectuals felt themselves bound to bourgeois society, which needed them for its ideological superstructure. The crisis had brought the intellectuals into politics. They now expected change not from the application of reason and intellect, but from the pressure of the political struggle. Some were turning to fascism, others to democratic pacifism.

The congress approved the idea of a Balkan Federation of equal and independent workers' and peasants' republics, and passed resolutions on party reconstruction on a factory-cell basis, on national questions in Central Europe and the Balkans, on Norway, Poland, Sweden, and Iceland, and on the publication of the complete works of Marx and Engels.

The drafting of a resolution on the Negro question was referred to the ECCI. Jackson (USA) argued that the Negro problem in the United States was psychological as well as economic, and covered all classes of Negroes. It was a waste of time to use the same literature for Negro as for white workers. He reported on the congress of Negro organizations held in Chicago in February 1924, at which ten communists had been present. The congress was dominated by the ecclesiastical and petty-bourgeois Negroes. 'Nevertheless we were successful in the last two days of the congress in provoking a split.'

In his criticism of the draft programme of the Comintern four years later, Trotsky wrote that what the fifth congress should have done was to call the October defeat a defeat and expose its roots. Its announcement of a rising revolutionary wave was a refusal to face the implications of the 1923 defeat and the facts of capitalist stabilization. It should have noted that a new epoch was opening in which the masses would be inactive while the social-democrats would advance, and it should have made preparations for this. Zinoviev had said that he had expected the revolution, but it did not happen; in fact it had happened, but the Comintern was late for the appointment. The decisions of the congress were bureaucratic whitewashing; they were a drag on the sections.

Closing the congress, Zinoviev listed its achievements. After a year and a half of severe reaction, the Comintern found itself with strengthened forces; it had cleared up the confusion about united front tactics and eradicated opportunist deviations; it was now recognized that 'workers' and peasants' government' was a synonym, in simpler terms, for the dictatorship of the proletariat, excluding coalitions with other parties. Its course was now set for the phase of democratic pacifism which capitalism had reached, and its work would be guided by the watchwords 'bolshevize the parties' and 'to the masses'.]

EXTRACTS FROM THE RESOLUTION OF THE FIFTH COMINTERN CONGRESS ON THE REPORT OF THE ECCI

26 *June* 1924   *Inprekorr,* iv, 91, p. 1154, 17 *July* 1924

[Zinoviev's tone in opening the congress and reporting for the ECCI was not optimistic. 'After five years of the International we have to state that the movement has not developed as quickly as we expected. We can all remember the time when Lenin thought . . . that the victory of the proletarian revolution in all countries was a matter of months.' They had mistaken the elemental discontent of the masses for a solid communist force. Half a dozen monarchies had fallen, and one-sixth of the earth was communist; the movement in Asia was advancing, while in the West the labour aristocracy had become part of the bourgeois State—in itself an index of the weakened position of the bourgeoisie. The democratic-pacifist phase through which they were now passing marked the trough between two waves of the revolution, but the objective situation was still revolutionary. That was the key to their tactics, although the immediate future might bring more intense counter-revolutionary activity by the bourgeoisie. In the discussion which followed, and in which most speakers dealt with the situation in their own countries, Bordiga complained that there was no real analysis of the ECCI's report, whereas its work should be carefully examined. The congress did not sit in judgement on the Executive, but the ECCI sat in judgement on the sections, and each national speaker dealt only with that part of the report which concerned his own country. Nothing of a genuinely international nature was said. Bordiga also challenged the overriding authority of the Russian party. Its position at the head of the International was no guarantee that it would always be right. They must remember the special conditions of the Russian revolution. The International was trusted because it represented the revolutionary proletariat of the entire world. On this question of differences between Russia and the developed capitalist countries, Zinoviev admitted that methods of agitation might differ, but asserted that, on cardinal questions like the proletarian dictatorship, conditions were the same for Russia, Germany, America, etc. Togliatti (Ercoli) spoke against Bordiga's views; it was a choice, he said, between Bordiga and the International. Radek, like Bordiga, attacked the practice of promoting artificial unanimity. 'If in the Comintern we rely only on official discipline, we shall become an official skeleton, but not a living International.'

Discussion of the ECCI report, which occupied eleven sessions of the congress, reviewed again the events in Germany leading up to the fiasco of October 1923. The meeting of the German central committee in November, attended by ECCI representatives, had, according to the report, given an incorrect analysis of the situation and failed to criticize past errors. When the ECCI intervened, the majority in the committee split, and the greater part admitted that the ECCI was correct; this was followed by the exclusion of the right wing from the central committee at the meeting in Moscow of January 1924. The Frankfurt congress of the KPD in April endorsed the change. The crisis in the German party had become so deep, Zinoviev said, that unless the ECCI had disavowed the old leaders, there would have been a split. He warned the KPD not to reopen the question of leaving the trade unions, and said the ECCI would continue to fight ultra-left tendencies in the KPD. Radek (who, since his views had been condemned by the thirteenth RCP congress, had to get the permission of that party's delegation to the Comintern congress to explain his attitude) made a long and witty speech, continually interrupted by the German delegation. He referred to Zinoviev's approval of KPD tactics in the Saxon Government, written immediately after October. The two chief lessons of October were that such attempts must not be made without proper preparation, and that, without a united front from below, there must be no united front from above. Brandler, speaking 'not as a member of the KPD delegation but as the accused, or rather the condemned', recounted the 1923 events and his part in them, maintaining that he had throughout been applying the tactics advocated by the third and fourth Comintern congresses, and the policy proposed at the ECCI before October. Thalheimer condemned the way in which the ECCI intervened organizationally in other parties, not the intervention itself; obliquely, he criticized the dominant position of the Russian party, which hampered the less experienced parties in their development towards maturity. Klara Zetkin said the account of October given by the KPD majority was a caricature; if the present central committee accused its predecessors of having pursued an opportunist and liquidationist policy since 1921, the same charge would have to be made against the ECCI for not having corrected that policy. The entire party, and particularly the central committee, was to blame for not having grasped at an earlier stage the revolutionary possibilities of the German situation, and for not organizing mass discontent into the struggle for power. The KPD delegation put in a statement objecting to the amount of time allowed by the congress to representatives of the 'Radek–Brandler' tendency who represented nobody but themselves; they trusted that the decisions of the congress would eradicate right-wing tendencies in the CI so effectively that their advocates would never again be represented at its congresses. In his reply Zinoviev recounted the story of Radek's disagreements with the ECCI since 1920, ten in all. Lenin had condemned Radek's attitude at the 1922 conference of the three Internationals; Radek's agreement with Tranmael in Norway was a rotten compromise; he had opposed the slogan of Soviets in Germany at the September 1923 meeting in Moscow. Zinoviev described him as 'a good journalist'.

The Polish party, in which the majority supported the Russian opposition as well as the Brandler group in the KPD, came in for severe criticism. The attack on the Warski–Kostrzewa–Walecki majority was led by Stalin in the Polish commission (since the Polish party was illegal, most of its leaders lived in the Soviet Union); they were accused of having misled the Polish party about Comintern policy and the debate in the RCP, of having worked for the Russian opposition, and of having excluded from leadership those who really represented the Comintern line. A special commission was appointed to run the Polish CP and to convene a conference which would adopt a more correct line and elect a new central committee.

The report of the ECCI noted that the failure of the Italian central committee to act energetically enough on the question of fusion with the left-wing socialists had made it necessary to change its composition and to put in members who would work for fusion not merely from discipline but from conviction. In the 1924 elections, when the electoral law had been changed to favour the fascist candidates, the two parties, in alliance, had won 19 seats, of which 15 were held by communists. (How serious the quarrels in the Italian party were is revealed in the papers of Humbert-Droz. In February 1924 he had written to Zinoviev that Bordiga was 'creating a delicate situation'. The party had wished to put him up as a candidate in the elections, but, being an abstentionist on principle, he had refused, saying he had never known a communist parliamentarian. 'I am in disagreement with the party, and cannot therefore defend its policies in parliament.' A few days later Humbert-Droz again reported on Bordiga's indiscipline. Bordiga had said that if the Comintern line kept on changing, discipline was purely arbitrary: 'They can choose another gramophone'; he would not play the part of a marionette. The central committee could either ignore Bordiga or discipline him, but its position was weak because it was often reproached, directly and indirectly, with the fact that it had not been elected by the party and therefore had no authority over it. To ignore him would open the door to indiscipline and amount, in fact, to a renunciation of leadership, while disciplinary action against him, when the majority of the party were unaware that the Comintern no longer considered him the leader, would provoke a crisis. Tasca (Rossi), a member of the minority on the CC, had proposed that the central committee should resign to bring home to the ECCI the impossible position in which it had been placed since the last plenum.) Manuilsky reported on the Italian question. The commission had agreed unanimously on a programme of action for the Italian party, but this had not been accepted by the Italian left. The commission recommended that as the 'third-internationalists' had been excluded from the socialist party, they should amalgamate with the Italian CP. The left wing, under Bordiga, refused to enter the central committee, and it was proposed that a letter be sent by the ECCI to the members of the Italian party on the ideological struggle waged by the Italian left for many years against the CI and its decisions, while keeping within the bounds of formal discipline.

Togliatti spoke at the congress on behalf of the Italian CP centre (formerly he had supported the left wing), objecting to the admission of the Italian socialists as a sympathizing party.

The programme of action for the CPI said that fascism was undergoing a crisis because it could not unite all sections of the bourgeoisie, and in its decay the communists might be confronted with the question of seizing power. The masses could be won from the reformist leadership by a united front in the factories. The Italian question was referred to the ECCI, which met immediately after the congress. Manuilsky said: 'The proposals of the commission on the composition of the leading organs of the CPI mark a serious intervention in the internal life of the party. But it had to be made, because all the fractions of the CPI demanded a settlement of the question. The commission had to take a decision on the resignation of the four comrades of the left who belonged to the CC. Under our statutes and the decisions of the world congresses such resignations are wholly impermissible. But since the left comrades declared that they would collaborate in disciplined fashion in carrying out the decisions of the congress, the commission thought it could dispense with the strict application of statutory regulations. It took note of the resignations, or rather, no member of the left was included on the new list for the CC, which, on the proposal of the commission, is to be composed of 9 members of the centre, 4 members of the so-called right, and 4 third-internationalists. That is by no means an ideal solution, but in face of the attitude of the left, it had to be adopted.' All the Italian fractions had agreed to support these decisions at the next Italian CP congress, which was to be convened by the new central committee. Bordiga had agreed that, in the circumstances, this was the most expedient course, and undertook to persuade the left-wing to support the ECCI.

The appeal to the Italian workers by the ECCI, dated 23 July 1924, on the amalgamation of the CPI and the fusionist wing of the Italian socialists, made a strong attack on Nenni, who had led the SPI in its betrayal of the Rome congress resolution on fusion (1922). Amalgamation added an estimated 3,500 members, and the CPI now claimed a membership of 25,000. Humbert-Droz reported in October 1924 that Bordiga refused for the time being to go to Moscow to take up his ECCI post. If Terracini returned from Moscow and Togliatti took his place, the secretariat would be completely in the hands of Bordiga and his supporters. In the districts the CC representatives who opposed the decision of the fifth congress were gradually being replaced. (At one district party congress Bordiga and Gramsci had debated for fourteen hours the decisions of the fifth congress.) Humbert-Droz was recalled to Moscow at the end of 1924 at his own request, as the Italian police were getting suspicious. He urged the ECCI not to appoint Rakosi as his successor. 'He would be very badly received.'

Kolarov introduced the debate on the agrarian question; for peasant parties, the sections were to use united front from below tactics, although they could occasionally also be used from above, as in Bulgaria. In July 1923 the ECCI had urged the sections to promote the establishment of peasant parties and to organize strong communist fractions within them. 'If we do not ourselves create such parties, they will arise of themselves but will work under the leadership of our enemies.' The proposal to set up a 'Peasant International' (Krestintern), attached to the CI, had been accepted. This body had been formally set up in October 1923 at a conference of 'revolutionary unions of landworkers' and revolutionary minorities in other unions; it was held in Moscow to coincide with the opening of the Russian agricultural exhibition, and was attended by 122 visitors representing, it was claimed, forty countries. The council elected there included A. P. Smirnov, President of the RSFSR, Dombal, of the Polish CP, Ho Chi Minh, and Katayama. The Krestintern had a secretariat, but no other organized existence. The sections were to try to get peasant and agricultural-labour organizations to affiliate.

Several speakers at the fifth congress emphasized the importance of the agrarian question in colonial countries. Varga attacked the ultra-lefts who argued against supporting the peasants' claim to land, because once they got land they would cease to be revolutionary. He agreed that the ideal would be for the peasants to receive their land from the proletarian dictatorship, but communists could not cut themselves off from the peasants by refusing to support their claims. The congress endorsed the Krestintern statement that the peasantry could not win State power independently of the proletariat. Where peasant parties existed, the communist parties must work to give them a class character, and rid them of landowners and rich peasants, even if this meant splitting the peasant parties. Their slogan must be expropriation without compensation.

Criticizing the CI programme four years later, Trotsky derided the claims made for the Krestintern, and condemned the policies to which it had given cover, such as the overtures to Radic in Croatia, and La Follette in the United States.

The assertion that what had happened in Bulgaria, Germany, and Poland testified to the ripening of new revolutionary events echoed Zinoviev's statement in December 1923 that 'taken as a whole, they signified the beginning of the second wave of the international proletarian revolution', and his remark in reporting for the ECCI that the KPD was not far from winning the majority of the decisive sections of the German working class. In his speech winding up the debate he spoke more cautiously. The time factor was most important. It was true that capitalism would break down, but there was a possibility that they were entering a relatively prolonged period of democratic pacifism in which capitalism would vegetate. It was also possible that capitalism would disintegrate rapidly—these were 'the two perspectives'.

Ruth Fischer reported for the political commission which put forward the resolution on the Executive's report. Bordiga had put forward an alternative resolution which, she said, amounted to an attack on the Comintern and the ECCI; it had received only his vote. Radek and Bordiga in the commission voted against the resolution, which was put forward by the Russian, German, French, and British parties. In congress it was passed against eight votes—those of the Italian left and of Macchi, a member of the French delegation in charge of work among the Italian communist émigrés in the French Communist Party.]

The fifth congress of the Comintern fully endorses the activities of the Executive since the fourth congress, and observes that correct and firm leadership by the Executive made an essential contribution to the emergence of the Communist International practically everywhere with greater strength from this period of savage attack by capital fighting for its dictatorship. . . .

The communist movement withstood this violent attack not without severe losses, and not without serious blunders and deviations. But in no country was the capitalist power able to destroy the organization of the communist vanguard or cut it off from the proletarian masses. . . .

During these great class struggles the Executive Committee took a number of most important measures of decisive importance for the correct leadership of the sections of the CI. The congress notes in particular the following cases:

1. At the international conferences in Essen and Frankfurt in the spring of 1923 the Executive indicated correctly the practical tasks of intensified revolutionary preparation arising from the occupation of the Ruhr for the European proletariat, above all for the communist parties of Germany and France.

2. When in August the expansion of the revolutionary mass movement presaged a situation favourable to the decisive struggle for power in Germany, the Executive immediately called on the party to direct its work towards the immediate seizure of power, assured the KPD of the utmost help in this work, and mobilized several other sections to give powerful support to the German revolution.

3. After the October surrender in Germany, effected practically without fighting, and attributable to the treachery of the social-democratic leaders and the failure of the communist party leadership, it was wholly correct and necessary for the Executive, made aware of the strong left tendency in the German party, and with the support of the left, to condemn the opportunist attitude of the German *Zentrale*, and particularly the distortion of the united front tactic in the Saxon Government experiment, and to decide to draw the political and organizational consequences by a more vigorous and unrelenting struggle against opportunism.

4. Even earlier the Executive, in line with the ideas of the left, had not only criticized the opportunist deviations of the Leipzig congress of the KPD, but on two occasions before October added representatives of the left opposition to the *Zentrale* elected at Leipzig. Now, in collaboration with the Executive, a fighting bloc against the right wing has been formed by the union of the left and centre, and it has taken over the leadership of the party, confident that the mass of the membership would approve and ratify the expulsion of the politically bankrupt right wing, as in fact happened.

This determined solution by the Executive both helped the KPD and eliminated the dangers of a split threatened by the unbridgeable internal contradictions, and of the crisis in the German party developing into a crisis of the entire Comintern as a result of the feelings of panic which could be discerned here and there among the more uncertain elements. Credit is due not only to the German party, but also to the German working class, which vigorously demanded the ruthless eradication of right deviations, and which, supported by the International, found within itself the strength to come through such a severe crisis undiscouraged and with forces unimpaired.

5. Confronted by the danger of right deviations, which turned out to

be far greater in the execution of the united front tactics than could have been foreseen, the Executive vigorously rejected all opportunist interpretations of these tactics, as well as every attempt to build them up into anything more than a revolutionary method of agitation and of mobilizing the masses, or of using the slogan of a workers' and peasants' government not for agitation for the proletarian dictatorship, but as a means towards coalition with bourgeois democracy. Similarly, in contrast to the opportunist outlook, the Executive emphasized the true character of social-democracy as the left wing of the bourgeoisie.

6. Relying on the lessons of the events in Germany for the development of party organization, the Executive initiated vigorous measures in Germany and elsewhere for the formation of factory cells as the basis of party organization. In a few countries a noteworthy beginning has already been made in establishing the factory-cell system.

7. In opposition to the short-sighted opportunist passivity displayed by the Bulgarian party leadership in the June coup d'état, the Executive immediately sought by open and emphatic criticism to urge the party towards serious preparations for struggle against the expected counter-revolutionary offensive. We were not at the time successful in getting the party leadership to share the Executive's opinion. But with the experience of defeat the Executive's attitude was adopted as the party platform, on which the CP of Bulgaria reformed its ranks and got rid of the decaying right wing.

8. Similarly, with the collaboration of the Executive and the support of the central committee majority, the French party was freed of the greater part of its opportunist ballast, and thus the party was consolidated. Very great difficulties were experienced in Norway, where the communists, a badly organized minority in the opportunist 'Labour Party', had to wage a severe fractional struggle and were constantly exposed to the danger of being cut off by the ruthless anti-communist leadership. When the boundless presumption of the opportunist leaders of the NLP in regard to Comintern decisions developed into open and systematic sabotage, and, after the October defeat in Germany, turned into cowardly desertion, it was impossible to allow such behaviour to continue under communist colours. Although it was realized that in a break between the leaders of the NLP and the CI a number of good proletarian members would for a time go with their anti-communist leaders, the Executive was compelled to demand of the NLP congress a clear decision for or against loyal co-operation with the International. That led to a split in the party and to the foundation of the independent Norwegian Communist Party. In six months it has won, particularly by its influential participation in big labour disputes, the authority of a revolutionary mass party. . . .

9. At its second congress in 1923 the Polish party, with the active colla-

boration of the Comintern Executive, adopted decisions which gave it a bolshevik foundation for the expansion and consolidation of party influence. But in its practical work, particularly in the period of mass struggle in October, the party leadership did not follow a correct revolutionary line. In the Russian and German questions the Polish central committee supported the right wing and tried to suppress any left-wing criticism in their own ranks. . . .

12. Right-wing deviations were also apparent on the question of the united front in England and America, and on the attitude of the CP to the Labour Party leaders (in America, the so-called third party). The Executive was able to convince the English and American comrades of the necessity to revise their ideas; the new and peculiar problems of the revolutionary movement in the Anglo-Saxon countries were considered in great detail by the Executive many times, and the parties there will need much greater attention in future from the international leadership.

13. The Executive also had to help overcome ultra-left deviations. In the Italian party there are still tendencies towards an un-Marxist dogmatism, which refuses on principle to apply the implications of a given tactic to the concrete situation and so restricts the party's ability to manœuvre. The Italian Communist Party must now stand firmly and without reservation on the tactical ground of the Communist International, if it wishes to solve the problem of becoming a mass party. The amalgamation of the third-internationalists with the CPI eliminates one question which caused differences between the CPI and the Comintern. But even after this amalgamation the CPI must deal energetically with the question of winning over those masses who still adhere to the Italian Socialist Party.

13 [sic]. In several countries (particularly France) progress was made in trade union work, giving it greater intensity and uniformity, and important successes registered (for example in England). In Germany last winter communists and sympathizers left the unions in large numbers because of anti-trade union sentiments for which the trade union bureaucracy was responsible. Since the KPD failed to oppose this dangerous deviation with vigour, the Executive intervened energetically, until the decision of the Frankfurt congress, with the emphatic support of the Executive, called a halt to this catastrophic behaviour and effected a complete reversal in favour of revolutionary work in the unions.

14. Propaganda among the semi-proletarian and petty-bourgeois middle classes was frequently recommended to the sections as a means of combating fascism. In Germany the CP has had considerable success in this respect; in Italy, on the other hand, practically none.

15. The Executive has emphatically directed all sections to carry out constant and active agitation to win the masses of the poor peasantry to

support of the proletarian revolution. With this aim in view the slogan of a 'workers' government' was expanded to 'workers' and peasants' government'. The foundation of the Peasant International, which has turned out to be a most important step, was carried through with the active co-operation of the Executive. The elaboration of an independent communist agrarian policy will in the immediate future be one of the most important tasks of practically all sections.

16. On the nationality question the Executive had ample cause to remind many sections, for which this question is of the utmost importance, of their inadequate execution of the decisions of the second congress. One of the basic principles of Leninism, requiring the resolute and constant advocacy by communists of the right of national self-determination (secession and the formation of an independent State), has not yet been applied by all sections of the CI as it should be.

17. In addition to winning the support of the peasant masses and of the oppressed national minorities, the Comintern has to win the revolutionary movements of liberation, among the colonial peoples and all Eastern peoples, as allies of the revolutionary proletariat of the capitalist countries. This requires not only the further development of direct links between the Executive and the national liberation movements of the East, but also closer contacts between the sections in the imperialist countries and the colonies of those countries, and above all an unceasing and relentless struggle in every country against the imperialist colonial policy of the bourgeoisie. In this respect communist work everywhere is still very weak.

As to work inside the army, the Executive together with the Executive of the Youth International made excellent practical preparations (Ruhr). Nevertheless the sections which have the strongest imperialist Powers to fight have all too often neglected Lenin's teachings about the fight against war and the Executive has had to call them to order. . . .

The CI still falls far short of being a real world party. The congress reminds the sections of their duty to collaborate collectively in the further development of CI work by participating more actively than hitherto in the solution of international questions by regular reports and correspondence, as well as through their members on the Executive.

Experience has shown that it is often impossible to convene the national party congresses after the world congress. Consequently congress repeals the decision on this question. No national party congress (regular or extraordinary) may, however, be convened without the agreement of the Executive.

Congress instructs the Executive to demand more emphatically than before iron discipline from all sections and all party leaders. Congress notes that in some cases the Executive, in order to spare the reputation of deserving comrades, did not proceed energetically enough against breaches of discipline. Congress empowers the Executive to act far more decisively when necessary and not to shrink from the most extreme measures.

EXTRACTS FROM A MANIFESTO OF THE FIFTH COMINTERN CONGRESS ON THE TENTH ANNIVERSARY OF THE OUTBREAK OF WAR

July 1924   *Inprekorr*, iv, 89, p. 1118, 16 *July* 1924

[The manifesto was written by Trotsky.]

I

Workers and peasants! Remember what your rulers said and promised in the very first days of the war. You were told that the war would give a secure existence to the people. You were promised that after the war there would be no more military burdens to bear. You were assured that it would be the last war. . . . Now, ten years later, you can draw up the balance-sheet. You can see how your confidence was abused. Even the victor States are incomparably poorer than they were before the war. If the bourgeoisie have swindled you, that was only to be expected. The bourgeoisie are our irreconcilable and pitiless enemy. But you were also swindled by those whom you looked on as your leaders. The social-democrats, who won the confidence of the workers by their speeches against the bourgeoisie, moved to their side on 1 August 1914 and lent all their authority and weight to help them carry on the slaughter to the end. . . .

The social-democrats promised as the outcome of the war a just, democratic, and honest peace between the peoples. They lied. Their deception was conscious and calculating. They knew that the peace would be dictated by the victorious imperialists. A dishonourable war conducted by the bourgeoisie with the dishonourable support of the social-democrats could only end in a dishonourable peace. . . . Germany and its allies were crushed and dismembered.

To justify the enslavement of the German people, an enslavement no less despicable than the war itself, the socialists in all victorious countries repeated, with their bourgeoisie: Germany is being punished because it wanted and provoked war. What hypocrisy, and what stupidity. Even if it were true that the Hohenzollerns and Habsburgs were alone responsible for the war, should a people be punished for the misdeeds of the dynasty by which it was oppressed? Should the German proletariat be throttled for the crimes of its bourgeoisie? . . . . But can any honest man with a clear head believe even for a moment that responsibility for the war rests exclusively on Germany and Austria-Hungary? Do we not know the insatiable imperialism of the English bourgeoisie, the oppressor of the colonial peoples? Do we not know the repulsive greed of the French stock exchange? Did not Tsarist Russia in alliance with France and England plan to seize Constantinople and the Straits? The imperialist war resulted from the clash of the unleashed desires of both parties. . . . The ruling classes of both camps are responsible for the war, for its four-year duration, for its victims and destruction, for its insane outcome in Versailles. No less responsibility rests on the social-democratic politicians, the patriotic trade unionists, the accomplices of the bourgeoisie, the voluntary agents of imperialism, the socialist lawyers of the Versailles peace. . . . The same people, the same politicians, the same traitors who for four years helped the bloodstained Hohenzollern gang to wipe out the German people restrained the workers at the end of 1918 from getting rid of their exploiters. If after the war the power of capital survived in a Europe shaken to its foundations, that is due solely and entirely to the Second International, the watch-dogs guarding the gates of the bourgeoisie.

II

There is not a single healthy spot in Europe. Economically, Germany has been thrown back for decades. The fragments of the Austro-Hungarian Empire are separated from each other by barriers of barbed wire. Even worse is the situation in the Balkans. France is collapsing under the weight of war debts and the burdens of militarism. Italy is weakened and cannot recover from the convulsions which shake it. England cannot even dream of regaining its pre-war strength. . . .

The occupation of the Ruhr by French troops in January of last year meant a direct continuation of the imperialist war: the victors dealt the last blow to the vanquished. . . . But how could it happen that the working masses of France and of all Europe did not prevent this new robber attack? If you think about it, workers, you will see that it was only Socialist support for the French and German bourgeoisie which made the occupation possible, involving as it did the further ruin of Europe. We repeat: if the working masses of France and Germany had decided to make the sacrifice involved in a revolutionary rising which the Ruhr occupation itself required of them, the bourgeoisie would have been overthrown, militarism destroyed, and peace and labour would celebrate their triumph in Europe. But it is precisely at such critical moments, moments of life and death for the bourgeoisie, when the future of the workers is at stake, that the social-democrats maliciously destroy the united front of the proletariat, bring irresolution into the workers' ranks, promote discouragement, isolate the communist party, and become the pace-makers of capitalist reaction. . . .

Once the bourgeoisie are convinced that the revolutionary surge has been beaten back by the united efforts of fascism and social-democracy, they think it expedient to restore a less bloody, less exacting, more normal regime, one clothed in the rags of legality. Only yesterday the fascists occupied the foreground, flourishing revolver and dagger, while the social-democrats acted as assistants behind the scenes. Today, when the immediate danger seems to be past, the bourgeoisie hurry the fascists off the stage, lead out from behind the curtain the radicals, reformists, and mensheviks, the apostles of legality, democracy, and peace, and advance them to the front. . . .

Conservatives, radicals, fascists, and mensheviks come and go, but militarism remains, piling up stocks, improving weapons, drafting new plans, waiting until the worst memories of the last war have faded, until the social-democrats have succeeded in reconciling the workers once again to the idea of the impregnability of the bourgeois State. Then it will again openly take the road of universal plunder. Then the hour of the new imperialist war will strike.

III

The causes and occasions of a new war follow with iron necessity from the last war and the Versailles peace. The ruling classes of France feel more and more strongly that the regime of terror they have established in Europe cannot endure much longer. The French bourgeoisie, the reactionary as well as the radical, fear German revenge, but at the same time provoke it. On their side the German bourgeoisie, who are ready to come to an agreement at the cost of the people, are waiting impatiently for the hour of revenge to strike. The antagonism between England and France in Europe and the colonies is growing more and more acute. . . . The military programmes of the two allies, particularly in aircraft and chemical warfare, are designed with reference to the approaching Anglo-French war. While Herriot coos pacifically, the General Staff in Paris is drawing up plans for a future air offensive against London, and the British Staff is busy planning return visits. . . .

The strongest antagonism is that developing along the line where the interests of the British Empire collide with those of the United States. In the last two years it has seemed that a lasting agreement had been reached between these two giants. But the appearance will persist only as long as the economic boom in North America, based largely on the home market, and this is now unmistakably nearing its end. . . . America's productive forces must seek broader outlets on the world market. America's foreign trade can expand primarily at the expense of British foreign trade, and the American merchant marine and navy at the expense of the British. The period of Anglo-American understanding must be succeeded by one of steadily growing conflict, which in its turn involves the danger of war on an unparalleled scale.

The antagonism between Japan and the United States retains its full force. . . . The prohibition on the immigration of yellow people gives the imperialist struggle in the Pacific the character of a racial struggle. If the United States and Great Britain clash, the role of Japanese militarism will be an incomparably more active one than it was in the last war. . . .

The growth of the revolutionary movement in the East in these last ten years gives the colonial rule of the imperialist Powers the character of open military violence. The constitutional illusions and hopes of reconciliation among the enslaved masses of India are fading. The parties of national liberalism and petty-bourgeois Utopias are melting into the void. The revolutionary movement is penetrating deeper and reaching wider and wider masses. A strong, centralized, revolutionary party is required to take control of this movement and deal British imperialism its death-blow.

In dismembered China the imperialist Powers have introduced a regime of masked military occupation, using paid Chinese troops. . . . Here, as in India, a revolutionary organization is being created, whose mission it is to free China from its foreign and native rulers. . . .

IV

In a concealed form, war rules mankind even today. For what is the new solution of the reparations question, the Experts' report, but the application of methods of war to the solution of economic problems? America, whose pockets are bulging with European money, relies on France's military strength and prescribes a particular economic regime for Germany as a punishment for having lost the war. Only downright charlatans can assert that the report offers a peaceful, democratic solution of the question. In fact the Entente is dictating its decision with its guns in position. . . .

The German bourgeoisie have agreed to this because they hope, with the help of foreign capital, and if necessary foreign troops, to settle accounts with the German proletariat. The workers are being forced into a heavier yoke, deprived of all the achievements of the revolution, their working day lengthened and its intensity stepped up. By these means the German bourgeoisie hope to make the workers bear once again all the burdens, deprivations, and sufferings of the period of primitive accumulation. The weakening and degrading of the German proletariat will help the European bourgeoisie to make the working class in other countries afraid of German competition. Finally, American capital is preparing, with the help of its experts, to 'control' Europe, that is, to rule it. . . .

This monstrous plan to enslave the European working masses by Anglo-Saxon capital with the help of French militarism has been accepted and approved by the parties of the Second International. In doing so the Entente socialists have found a hypocritical, pacifist cloak to cover the robber policy of their bourgeoisie, with which they are in full accord. The German social-democrats look to the re-establishment of a strong capitalist regime to give them victory over the communist danger.... Amid an outcry about communist plots and an 'international Cheka' there is unfolding before our eyes a vast conspiracy of capital against the workers of Europe and the entire world. The organizer of the conspiracy is finance-capital, with its headquarters in New York and its branch in London. The most important executive work is assigned to the French stock exchange. The interpreter, defender, and advocate of the conspiracy is social-democracy and the Amsterdam trade unions. The experts in treachery come to the aid of the experts in capital.

V

Again we ask: What is it that prevents the workers and peasants from rising as one against militarism, which is destroying them? The answer is: international social-democracy, the mensheviks, the Second International, the Amsterdam trade union bureaucracy. That is the chief lesson of the imperialist war. That is the basic conclusion to be drawn from the past decade....

We want our words to reach the ear of every working man and woman in town and country. We want to awaken revolutionary discontent in the hearts of the oppressed. The bourgeoisie are preparing a new war and social-democracy is corrupting your minds so that it can the more easily betray you and sell you out....

The chief occupation of the pacifists today is their fight against the revolution and especially against the Red Army. They are opposed to the revolutionary use of force, to rebellion, to the civil war. But the bourgeoisie are armed, the workers unarmed. By opposing the arming of the workers, the pacifists are supporting capitalist militarism and so clearing the road for a future war, which makes their appeals to humanity and civilization the more repellent. And if you prove to them that they are supporting the militarism of their bourgeoisie, they always reply with a reference to the Red Army, implying that the existence of the Red Army, which was created by the Russian workers in defence against the imperialists, justifies the arming of capitalist States to plunder the world and suppress the revolution. . . . But it would be the greatest stupidity to believe that there is no longer any danger of war on the workers' and peasants' State. The growth of communist parties consolidates the international position of the Soviet Union, while it troubles and angers the imperialists. When the direct danger of revolution rises again, the imperialists may once more turn to large-scale military intervention. . . . Between the capitalist world and the Soviet Republic agreements are possible, but not reconciliation. Just as the Governments of MacDonald and Herriot will at a certain moment have to give way once more to more open and more resolute reaction, so at a certain moment different interests may and will cut across the agreements of capitalist countries with the Soviet Union. That is why the Red Army and the Red Navy are necessary. . . .

VI

. . . The fight against militarism cannot be postponed until war itself breaks out, for then it would be too late. The fight must be waged now, day in, day out. The first step in this fight is to refuse the capitalist State the budgetary means to arm, to give it no confidence or support . . . . The inhuman sufferings of their fathers and elder brothers must be tirelessly recalled to the working and peasant youth, and transformed into burning hatred of those responsible for the war. Young men should join capitalist armies with the determination to turn their weapons not against their proletarian brothers, but against the class enemy, the bourgeoisie. The artificial barriers between the army and the working class must be torn down, and contacts maintained with the barracks. The conscious soldiers should be organized in small groups. Revolutionary organizations for the railways should be formed of the best and most courageous proletarian fighters. Particular attention should be paid to armaments and ordnance factories. In each of these there should be a solid militant cell, able when the decisive moment comes to carry all the workers along with it. The bourgeoisie are not afraid of pacifist sermons or of the social-democrats' threat of a general strike, but they tremble with hate and fear at any report of a small illegal cell in the railways, in the munitions factories, and especially in the army and navy. . . .

The revolutionary education of the colonial peoples is becoming a vital question for the proletariat. If the bourgeoisie are seeking by oppressing the colonies to maintain and perpetuate the oppression of the proletariat, we on our side must look to colonial revolts to help the revolt of the proletariat.

National and race prejudices are a product of slavery and nourish slavery. An avowed or masked chauvinist mentality is the best support of militarism and a certain means to prepare new wars. A relentless struggle must be carried out against national prejudices and racial arrogance. Not only open hostility, disdainful behaviour, an ironical attitude, but even the patronizing, condescending tone of the whites towards yellow or black people must be sharply condemned by working-class public opinion as a repulsive violation of solidarity, malicious strike-breaking. . . . The workers in the colonies must be taught to regard white workers as their brothers, and to do that the white proletariat must learn to act as brothers to the coloured population of the colonies.

Proletarians of Europe! Pay more attention to the colonial question, devote more of your forces to revolutionary work in the colonies. There, where the bourgeoisie would wish to find their most reliable supporters, they must instead be dealt a damaging blow.

Workers of the colonies! Slaves of imperialism! Brothers! Awake to struggle and independence! The Communist International is on your side!

At the present moment our first and most urgent task in the struggle against war is to fight the capitalist conspiracy which goes by the innocent name of Experts' report. In this, as in everything else, the first blow must be directed against social-democracy. Social-democracy is frightening the workers with America's tremendous power; it requires subjection and obedience of them. It predicts decline for Europe and before all for Germany, if it refuses obedience to American capital. But we communists say to the workers of Europe: your salvation lies in irreconcilable war against the Experts' report, against those who defend it and carry it out. Social-democracy must be cleared out of the way, and the bourgeoisie overthrown; we have to seize power and guide it along socialist channels. If Soviet Russia was able over a number of years to stand out against capitalist Europe and America together, the victory of the European proletariat will be the more certain when, after capturing power, the States of Europe come together in a Soviet Federation, the United Workers' and Peasants' States of Europe. . . .

The revolutionary movement in America would then receive a tremendous impulse. The European Socialist Federation will in this way become the corner-stone of the Socialist World Republic. . . . This is the mission of the Communist International, a stupendous mission, but it can be accomplished.

EXTRACTS FROM THE THESES ON THE WORLD ECONOMIC SITUATION ADOPTED BY THE FIFTH COMINTERN CONGRESS

July 1924   *Inprekorr*, iv, 119, p. 1565, 16 *September* 1924

[Varga reported on this subject. There was an upward curve in world economy within the general trend downwards that marked the crisis. Capitalist world economy had ceased to operate as a comprehensive system; the situation was bound to deteriorate, and create favourable objective possibilities for successful proletarian struggle. The earlier sections of the theses dealt with the capitalist offensive, which had brought some temporary gains to the bourgeoisie, but the world market and the world investment market had not been re-established. The agrarian crisis, the growth of autarky, the widespread series of currency crises, the difficulties of inter-allied debts, etc., still dominated the scene. The theses were adopted unanimously, as they had been in the commission. The report of the commission was given by Pepper.

In the late autumn of 1923, at the suggestion of the American President, a committee was set up to examine the reparations question; it was presided over by General Dawes, and met first on 7 December 1923. Its report, which recommended a sliding scale of reparation payments based on the earnings of the German economy, was accepted by the SPD and the German unions. The

Comintern launched a large-scale campaign against the Dawes report, treating it as a further move towards rapprochement between Germany and the West, and consequently as inimical to Russia.]

VI. REPARATIONS AND INTERNATIONAL CONTRADICTIONS: THE POSITION OF SOVIET RUSSIA

The question of reparations is still unsolved. The attempt to squeeze reparations out of Germany in foreign currency . . . shattered the German currency and the entire capitalist economic order in Germany. This brought class contradictions in Germany to such a pitch that the danger of social revolution or of a nationalist-chauvinist coup became immediate and acute.

22. Until recently, political contradictions among the imperialist great Powers, France, England, the United States, as well as the acute contradictions among the various social classes within each State, prevented any attempt at combined action on the reparations question.

23. The plans of the militarist and heavy-industry circles in France were to attach the left bank of the Rhine and the Ruhr to France, politically and economically. . . . This would in fact have made Germany into a French colony. France's military superiority to England in decisive arms (submarines, aircraft) would be finally consolidated by the incorporation of the Ruhr and the large chemical plants. The violent and predatory occupation of the Ruhr was an attempt to realize this imperialist programme.

24. France's momentary military superiority made it impossible for England to oppose French plans by force. It contented itself with supporting German passive resistance openly and secretly in the hope that the two opponents would so weaken themselves economically that they would have to submit to England's demands.

25. England feared German economic revival as much as French military superiority. . . . Consequently its policy was directed not to liberating Germany from the burden of reparations, but to its economic enslavement, while preventing its incorporation in the French imperialist system.

26. Because of the boom, the American bourgeoisie had no inducement to intervene directly in European affairs. Those in favour of participation in solving the reparations problem, that is, in exploiting the German proletariat, were part of the industrial bourgeoisie . . . banking capital, particularly the Morgan concern, which would like to make large loans and at the same time get control of the German iron industry; and finally the farmers, who hope for a rise in food prices. . . . With the end of the boom and the need to find new sales outlets for goods not taken up on the home market, interest in Europe is increasing and participation in

the exploitation of Germany appears more desirable to the American bourgeoisie.

27. The Ruhr war ended with Germany's surrender, after the German bourgeoisie, instead of making sacrifices, exploited passive resistance to enrich themselves and to rob the Treasury. . . . But France proved too weak to seize its victory. The rapid fall of the franc in the spring of 1924 forced France to seek the aid of English and American banking capital. It had to abandon the 'French solution' of the reparations problem, the dismemberment of Germany, and agree to a new solution in accordance with English and American interests. . . .

28. The Experts' report is an attempt by the bourgeoisie of the imperialist Powers to solve the problem in common. The report expels Germany from the ranks of independent States, and brings it financially and economically under the supervision of the Entente bourgeoisie. The system of reparations payments it envisages is designed to guard the mark against a new collapse and so to guard Europe against the danger of proletarian revolution. The French iron and steel industry is to get the necessary fuel. Control of taxation, finance, and transport is, on the other hand, to protect the West European industrial countries from serious German competition in the world market if Germany reaches its pre-war productivity.

The reparations problem is insoluble. Entente capitalism is incapable of finding a way of squeezing reparations out of Germany without exposing its own economy to the most serious dangers. . . .

29. The economic and political position of the USSR has grown much stronger in the last few years. The chronic sales crisis in the European industrial countries gives the Russian market particular importance. . . . The hope of transforming the Soviet Republics into a capitalist colony of the Entente was shattered by the vigorous resistance of the Soviet Government. Therefore, despite bourgeois interest in the Russian market, a further intervention against Soviet Russia is by no means excluded. . . .

30. But the capitalist crisis may become so acute that the Entente bourgeoisie see no other prospect of suppressing the revolutionary movement than a new war, either against Soviet Russia or among the Entente Powers. . . . Imperialist war or proletarian revolution remain the sole alternatives.

VII. THE SHARPENING OF CLASS CONTRADICTIONS

31. The process of concentration and cartellization, of the formation of cartels and trusts, is proceeding more rapidly in the present period of capitalist decline. . . . The gulf between the small group of capitalists controlling these concerns and the medium and petty bourgeoisie is growing steadily deeper. . . .

32. In countries where the currency has depreciated inflation has wiped out the property of the petty bourgeoisie.... The *rentier* has disappeared.... The income of the members of the free professions, of public servants and employees, has sunk below the pre-war level. ... Some have thrown themselves into the fascist movement; other have swelled the ranks of the revolutionary proletariat.

33. The agrarian crisis is ruining millions of farmers and peasants. ... The blind adherence of the peasantry to capitalist society is weakening. ...

35. The restrictions on immigration into America have closed the safety valve which emigration always represented for European capitalism, and so deepen the revolutionary ferment in the European proletariat.

VIII. PROSPECTS AND TASKS

36. ... In the immediate future we must reckon on a phase of crisis in the United States, which has already opened with great violence. The creeping crisis in the European industrial countries is bound to turn, if any serious attempt is made to operate the Experts' report, into a new phase of acute crisis which will spread simultaneously to all European countries. ...

The opinion of the social-democratic theoreticians (Hilferding) that capitalism has surmounted the post-war crisis and is entering a boom is unfounded. This idea only serves the interests of the bourgeoisie; it is designed to hold back those workers who are still hesitating to join the communist revolutionary movement.

37. The immediate future will witness further serious struggles between the proletariat, which wishes not only to repel new capitalist attacks but also to regain at least its former position, and capital, which is objectively incapable of meeting the requirements of the proletariat. ... The political disintegration of the middle classes, their vacillation between bourgeoisie and proletariat, give the proletarian struggle great chances of success if the communist party succeeds in sharpening the economic struggle and turning it into political struggle.

38. Whether the present phase in the period of capitalist decline leads to the overthrow of the bourgeoisie, or to a new and prolonged relative stabilization of its class rule, depends to a large extent on the ability of the communist parties to exploit, organizationally and politically, the objectively revolutionary situations which will develop. Class rule will never break down automatically, without a resolute, persistent, selfless offensive by the revolutionary proletariat. Great mass movements of the proletariat are inevitable in the immediate future. If the communist parties succeed in finally breaking the hold of the social-democratic and nationalist-fascist parties over the proletariat, mobilizing the majority of the decisive

strata of the proletariat under their leadership . . . these struggles will lead
to successful struggles for power.

STATUTES OF THE COMMUNIST INTERNATIONAL ADOPTED AT ITS FIFTH
CONGRESS

July 1924   *Inprekorr*, iv, 119, p. 1569, 16 *September* 1924

[The ECCI had been instructed by the fourth congress to amend the statutes
adopted at the second congress in 1920 in accordance with subsequent decisions.
Piatnitsky reported for the commission which had examined the statute drafted
by the orgbureau of the ECCI and published on 3 June. Of the earlier statutes,
only three paragraphs remained (2, 3, 10). The Italians in the commission had
proposed a number of amendments, including the deletion of para. 17 on
sympathizing parties, but none had been accepted. They had therefore abstained
from voting in the commission, and no votes had been cast against the draft.
Rossi (Tasca) proposed that the statutes should explicitly forbid fractions
within a party; this was rejected on the ground that it would prevent the ECCI
from itself organizing fractions in cases where this was considered expedient.
Rossi and Terracini were equally opposed to fraction-formation from above,
describing it as a very effective method of disorganization. Piatnitsky explained
that there was no question of the ECCI forming fractions, but 'it might find it
necessary to support one tendency in a party against another'. The statutes were
adopted unanimously.]

I. PRINCIPLES

1. The new international association of workers is a union of the communist parties of the various countries in a world party, which fights as
the leader and organizer of the revolutionary movement of the proletariat
of all countries to win the majority of the working class and broad strata
of poor peasants for the principles and aims of communism, for the establishment of the proletarian dictatorship, for the foundation of a world
union of Socialist Soviet Republics, and for the complete abolition of
classes and the realization of socialism, the first stage of communist society.

2. The new international association of workers is called the Communist International.

3. All parties belonging to the Communist International bear the name
'Communist Party of such and such a country (section of the CI)'. In each
country there shall be only one communist party belonging to the CI.

4. Whoever acknowledges the programme and statutes of the CP of the
country in which he lives, and of the CI, may be a member of the CP and
the CI. Members of a primary party organization are those who take an
active part in its work, obey all decisions of the party and the CI, and pay
their dues regularly.

5. The basis of party organization, its foundation, is the factory cell (in factory, mine, workshop, office, shop, farm, etc.), to which all party members working in that place must belong.

6. The CI and the communist parties are built up on the basis of democratic centralism. Its fundamental principles are:

(*a*) the election of both lower and upper party bodies at aggregate meetings of the party membership, at conferences and congresses;

(*b*) periodical reporting by the elected bodies to their electors;

(*c*) obligatory recognition of the decisions of superior party bodies by the lower bodies, strict party discipline, and prompt and precise execution of decisions of the ECCI and leading party organs. Party questions may be discussed by party members and organizations only until they have been decided by the relevant party organ. Once a decision has been reached at a CI congress, a party congress, or by the leading party body, it must be carried out unconditionally, even if part of the membership or some of the local organizations do not agree with the decision.

In conditions of illegality it is permissible for the lower party bodies to be constituted by higher ones, and for members to be co-opted if approved by the higher body.

II. THE WORLD CONGRESS OF THE CI

7. The supreme organ of the CI is the world congress of all the parties (sections) and organizations affiliated to it.

The world congress discusses and decides the most important programmatic, tactical, and organizational questions connected with the activity of the CI as a whole as well as of its individual sections. The world congress alone has the right to change the programme and statutes of the CI.

Ordinary world congresses of the CI shall be held at least once in two years. The date of meeting shall be determined by the ECCI. All sections send delegates, whose number is determined by the ECCI.

The number of votes accorded each section shall be determined each time by a separate congress decision, which shall take account of the size of the membership of the party and the political importance of the country in which it operates. Binding mandates are not allowed and shall be declared invalid in advance.

8. An extraordinary world congress of the CI may be convened at the request of the parties which, at the preceding CI congress, together accounted for at least one-half of the total voting strength.

9. The world congress elects the President of the CI, the Executive Committee of the CI, and the International Control Commission (ICC).

10. The seat of the ECCI is determined by each world congress.

III. THE EXECUTIVE COMMITTEE AND ITS APPARATUS

11. The ECCI is the leading organ of the CI in the period between world congresses. It issues binding directives to all parties and organizations affiliated to the CI and supervises their activities.

The ECCI publishes the central organ of the CI in not fewer than four languages.

12. Decisions of the ECCI are binding on all sections and must be carried out by them without delay. Sections are entitled to submit appeals against ECCI decisions to the congress. But until such decisions are repealed by the congress, sections are not freed from the obligation to carry them out.

13. The central organs of the sections affiliated to the CI are responsible to their congresses and to the ECCI. The ECCI has the right to annul or to amend decisions of both the central organs and the congresses of the sections, and to take decisions which the central organs are obliged to carry out (see para. 12).

14. The ECCI has the right to expel from the CI parties, groups, or individual members who act contrary to the programme, the statutes, the decisions of the world congress, or the ECCI. Such parties and individuals have the right to appeal to the world congress and to the enlarged Executive.

15. The ECCI ratifies the programme of every section of the CI. Should it not ratify the programme, the section has the right of appeal to the world congress.

16. It is advisable to publish decisions and official documents of the ECCI in all party newspapers of the CI sections; publication in the central organ is obligatory.

17. The ECCI is entitled to admit to the CI, with consultative voice, organizations and parties which sympathize with communism or stand close to the CI.

18. The ECCI elects from among its members a presidium, which is a permanently functioning body, conducting the entire work in the periods between meetings of the ECCI. The presidium reports on its activities to the ECCI. The President of the Communist International is President of the ECCI and of the presidium.

19. The ECCI elects an orgbureau, which shall discuss and decide all organizational and financial questions of the ECCI. Appeals against decisions of the orgbureau may be made to the presidium, but such decisions remain in force until annulled or amended by the presidium. The ECCI determines the composition of the orgbureau. The secretariat of the ECCI is attached to the orgbureau.

20. The ECCI elects a secretariat, which acts as the executive body of the ECCI, the presidium, and the orgbureau.

21. The ECCI elects an editorial board for the monthly organ of the CI, as well as the editors of other CI publications.

22. The ECCI appoints an international secretariat for the communist women's movement, and in collaboration with it takes all decisions, whether political or organizational in nature, necessary for the international women's movement.

23. The ECCI organizes departments for information and statistics, for agitation, propaganda, and for organization, and an Eastern department. The ECCI is entitled if necessary to set up other departments, and in general to shape the working machinery as expedient.

24. The ECCI and the presidium of the ECCI are entitled to send plenipotentiary delegates to the individual sections. The delegates receive instructions from the ECCI and are responsible to it for their actions. These delegates must be admitted to all meetings and sessions of the central organs and the local organizations of the sections to which they are sent by the ECCI. The ECCI delegates carry out their mission in closest contact with the central committee of the section concerned. Nevertheless they may, in the interests of the consistent execution of ECCI directives, put forward opinions differing from those of the central committee of the section concerned at congresses, conferences, or meetings called by the committee. It is the special duty of the ECCI delegates to supervise the execution by the sections of the decisions of the ECCI and the CI congresses.

25. The ECCI shall meet at least once a month. One-half of the membership of the ECCI constitutes a quorum.

IV. THE ENLARGED EXECUTIVE

26. To deal with particularly important questions which do not need to be settled immediately, the ECCI shall convene, at least twice a year, in the period between world congresses, a session of the enlarged Executive.

In addition to the members of the ECCI, the attendance at the enlarged Executive shall include representatives of all sections of the CI. The number of such representatives from each section is determined by the CI congress.

There shall be a meeting of the enlarged Executive immediately before the world congress.

V. THE INTERNATIONAL CONTROL COMMISSION

27. The tasks of the International Control Commission elected at the world congress are:

(*a*) To examine complaints by individual members or entire organizations against disciplinary measures taken against them by their sections, and to make proposals thereon to the ECCI, which shall then reach a decision.

(*b*) To audit the finances of the ECCI.

(*c*) To audit the finances of the individual sections if requested to do so by the ECCI, the presidium, or the orgbureau.

The Control Commission does not intervene in political and organizational conflicts within the sections of the CI.

The seat of the ICC is agreed upon between the ECCI and ICC.

VI. RELATIONS BETWEEN THE CI SECTIONS AND THE ECCI

28. The central committees of all sections of the CI and of all organizations admitted to the CI as sympathizing organizations are obliged to send the ECCI minutes of their meetings and reports on their activities.

29. Resignation from office, whether by individual members of the central committee of any of the sections, or by groups, shall be regarded as an act disorganizing the communist movement. Every leading post in a communist party belongs to the CI and not to the holder of the office. The members of the central committee of each section may resign office only with the consent of the ECCI. Resignations endorsed by the central committee of the party without the agreement of the ECCI are invalid.

30. Sections of the CI, particularly sections in neighbouring countries, should establish the closest connexions with each other in matters concerning organization and information. These connexions may take the form of reciprocal representation at conferences and congresses, as well as of the exchange of leading personnel, if agreed by the CI.

Copies of reports made by these representatives to their sections are to be sent to the CI.

Two or more sections of the CI which (as in the Balkans or Scandinavia) are in special relations with each other because of the political similarities in their struggle may, with the agreement of the ECCI, form a federation in order to co-ordinate their action; such federations are under the control and direction of the ECCI.

31. Sections of the CI must pay regular contributions to the ECCI, the amount to be determined by the ECCI.

32. All national congresses, ordinary and extraordinary, may be convened by the sections of the Comintern only with the consent of the ECCI.

If no congress has been held before the world congress, the section must (before the selection of delegates to the world congress) convene a party conference or plenary session of the central committee to deal with questions concerning the world congress.

33. The Young Communist International is a full member of the CI and subordinate to the ECCI.

34. Communist parties must be prepared to carry on their work

illegally. The ECCI is obliged to support them in their preparations for illegal work and to see that the work is carried out.

35. Members of the CI may move from one country to another only with the consent of the central committee of the section concerned. Communists who have changed their domicile are obliged to join the section of the country in which they reside. Communists who move to another country without the consent of the CC of their section may not be accepted as members of another section of the CI.

EXTRACTS FROM THE THESES OF THE FIFTH COMINTERN CONGRESS
ON THE PROPAGANDA ACTIVITIES OF THE CI AND ITS SECTIONS

July 1924   *Inprekorr*, iv, 119, p. 1572, 16 *September* 1924

[The report of the Executive to the congress noted that the ECCI propaganda department had not been working satisfactorily, and was in process of reorganization. The theses foreshadowed the establishment of what came to be known as the Lenin School in Moscow.]

I. THE AIMS AND OBJECTS OF COMMUNIST PROPAGANDA

1. Struggles within the CI are at the same time ideological crises within the individual parties. Right and left political deviations, deviations from Marxism–Leninism, are connected with the class ideology of the proletariat.

Manifestations of crisis at the second world congress and after were precipitated by 'left infantile sicknesses', which were ideologically a deviation from Marxism–Leninism towards syndicalism. . . . The present internal struggles in some communist parties, the beginning of which coincided in time with the October defeat in Germany, are ideological repercussions of the survivals of traditional social-democratic ideas in the communist parties. The way to overcome them is by *the bolshevization of the communist parties*. Bolshevization in this context means the final ideological victory of Marxism–Leninism (or in other words Marxism in the period of imperialism and the epoch of the proletarian revolution) over the 'Marxism' of the Second International and the syndicalist remnants.

2. The bolshevization of communist parties . . . does not mean the mechanical adoption of measures taken by the RCP, but the concrete application of bolshevik methods to the concrete conditions of each country in the given historical epoch. Only if the communist parties acquire theoretical understanding of revolutionary practice can they become real leaders of the masses, conscious of their aims . . . reduce the possibility of mistakes to a minimum, and accomplish the emancipation of the working class. 'Without revolutionary theory no revolutionary

movement is possible . . . the role of vanguard can be filled only by a party which is guided by a vanguard theory' (Lenin). It is therefore one of the primary tasks of the CI and its sections to make Marxism–Leninism the common property of all members. . . . For this purpose cadres must be created who are in full possession of these theoretical weapons, and who can in turn equip the broadest circles of the party membership with them. . . .

Before propaganda work can be built up every communist party must recognize the importance of theoretical mastery of Marxism–Leninism. They must all realize that revolutionary activity by no means implies indifference to the theoretical problems of the emancipation of the working class and to the requirements of a theoretical struggle. On the contrary: practical successes in the revolutionary struggle can be won only by clear theoretical understanding, widespread theoretical clarity within the communist parties.

3. . . . Theoretical work in the spirit of Marx, Engels, and Lenin is practically at a standstill in almost all sections of the CI. That is the more dangerous since theoretical work makes the analysis of concrete conditions possible. The discovery of the concrete forces which make for revolution, of the conditions and prospects of revolutionary change, makes it possible to determine more precisely party policy, organization, and agitation. Theoretical work of this kind gives the political work of the parties greater certainty.

It is only the indifference of some of the leading comrades to theoretical questions that explains the emergence within the Communist International of 'theories' which are completely incompatible with Marxism–Leninism. The first consequence of these 'theories' is confusion among the leading cadres or party masses . . . but then they enter the field of policy and tactics in the form of 'left' or right deviations. . . .

Even the propagandist training of the party masses leaves much to be desired. That is a natural result of the failure of leading party circles to grasp the necessity of this propaganda work. The overwhelming majority of the party masses came to the party because they became convinced of the treacherous character of opportunism and reformism, and of the purely proletarian class character of the communist parties; they reached this conclusion almost entirely by empirical means, in the midst of the daily economic and political struggle. This is an immense advantage to the parties and to the CI in comparison with the Second International, but it also means that the party proletarian masses may themselves be burdened with survivals of social-democratic ideology. This social-democratic heritage cannot be eliminated in a mechanical way; it must be tackled by systematic propaganda of the ideas of Marxism–Leninism, by implanting in them at least its basic principles and methods. . . .

4. In the person of Lenin . . . the CI and all communist parties had a sure guide in the domain of theory and political practice. Only Leninism, which Lenin and his collaborators, the old bolshevik guard, created as the theory of the proletarian revolution, can replace him. Lenin's death must give as great an impulse to the propaganda of the theory of Marxism–Leninism in all sections of the CI, as it has done in the RCP. Because of the ideological state of the parties, and particularly because of the shortage of capable leading cadres, this task falls to the CI. . . .

II. GENERAL ORGANIZATIONAL MEASURES CONCERNING PROPAGANDA

5. What is most characteristic of the present state of propaganda is the fact that until now neither the CI nor the individual parties have set up any special organs for propaganda work, or have only quite inadequate ones. . . .

6. A further serious obstacle to the propaganda of Marxism–Leninism is the inadequate distribution of Marxist–Leninist literature, both the original sources and popular studies and readers which would facilitate the conduct and popularization of propaganda work. In many western countries the classical works of Marxist literature rank as bibliographical rarities. As for new works, they appear very seldom. . . .

7. Another serious obstacle is the inadequate contact among Marxist theoreticians. Among the Marxists in the various CI sections who are active or interested in matters of theory, there are no contacts which would enable them to organize a division of labour, an exchange of experience, and hence to do more fruitful work.

8. The immediate concrete tasks of the CI in regard to the central direction and promotion of propaganda activity are:

(*a*) To organize and expand the agitation and propaganda department, to staff it with trained Marxist–Leninists well versed in organizing propaganda work. Systematic survey of the propaganda work of the sections, evaluation and exchange of experiences, helping the parties to work out concrete methods and forms of party training.

(*b*) To reorganize and expand the publishing work of the CI, with the object of supplying the parties with theoretical and propagandist literature. . . .

(*c*) Publication of a propagandist journal for the instruction of party officials, particularly propagandists. The aim of the journal will be to facilitate the exchange of experiences, work out questions of the training programme, guide and systematize party training. . . . The journal is to be published in German, French, and English.

(*d*) In order to be able to meet the requirements of at least the most important parties for theoretically trained workers, the CI will summon to Moscow for a prolonged period a number of party workers from the German, English, American, Czech, Italian, French, and Eastern sections, and if possible others, who will devote themselves exclusively to the study of Marxist–Leninist theory and practice. . . .

(e) To convene and arrange a conference of those in charge of propaganda work in the most important sections, and of heads of party schools, to work out the most important concrete tasks of party education. . . .

(f) To give effective support to the Youth International in the education of young communists.

III. ORGANIZATIONAL TASKS OF THE SECTIONS IN PROPAGANDA WORK

9. Wherever possible, but at least in all the most developed mass communist parties, agitation and propaganda activities are to be treated as a special branch of the party apparatus. . . .

12. The obligation of all party members, and particularly of elected officials, to study must be raised to the level of a party decision. . . . All party members must be asked to acquire a minimum of political and theoretical knowledge, at least enough to enable them to answer questions by non-communist workers about the programme, objects, and tactical principles of the communist party, and to rebut the most obvious forms of petty-bourgeois and social-democratic prejudice of the workers in their factories. . . .

IV. THE SYSTEM OF MARXIST PROPAGANDA

15. Varying propaganda systems and methods must be used according to the varied conditions and stages of development of the sections. The following instructions may be regarded as applying to all countries and parties:

(a) The system of party training must cover all party members in one form or another. An effort must be made to see that every member acquires at least an elementary knowledge of Marxism–Leninism.

(b) Every part of the system of communist training and propaganda must be directed to practical and definite ends and wherever possible cover homogeneous groups. . . .

(c) Every part of the system must be a self-contained whole and cover clearly defined independent work. It should not be considered merely as preparation for a higher stage of training.

16. To cover as high a proportion of the party membership as possible, despite the shortage of intellectual and material resources, the system of propaganda institutions must be organized on two lines: party schools and self-education.

17. Every party must try to set up . . . (a) a central party school; (b) elementary party courses (evening classes, lecture series, one-day Sunday schools, etc.).

18. The central party school will serve advanced party workers who have already mastered the principles of Marxism–Leninism. . . . It will systematize, extend, and deepen their knowledge, and so train new cadres of propagandists. . . .

19. The object of the elementary courses is to provide a foundation of elementary political knowledge . . . to train the party membership for active party work and for individual propaganda among the working masses.

20. Between these two extremes various other forms of party training may be organized according to the special circumstances of the country and the party. . . .

21. Communist parties should not neglect those schools which, under the cloak of impartiality, are concerned with workers' education (workers' universities, labour colleges, trade union schools, etc.). The parties must try to combat the dangers to a proletarian class ideology in these schools, get as much influence in them as possible, and get them under their control in order to make them of use for communist training.

22. Since resources are inadequate for a comprehensive system of schools . . . and the school system by itself cannot lead to the complete and thorough acquisition of Marxist–Leninist theory, the interest of party members in self-education must be aroused and self-education organized on the widest possible scale. . . .

24. The Executive of the CI must see that within the next year a model school and a few model evening classes are set up at least for all the important parties. . . .

26. The parties must direct their attention to the further training of communist students and other communist intellectuals. Communist students must not be isolated and cut off from the party. Existing communist student fractions or cells are usually closed and unsystematic self-education study circles, usually of little use to the workers' movement; they must be turned into useful propaganda instruments by giving them the guidance of well trained members with experience in the practical workers' movement. The members of these student groups, without exception, must also take part in practical party work. . . .

V. THE SYLLABUS AND METHODS OF PROPAGANDA

28. The direct political object of the propaganda of Marxism–Leninism: To promote the bolshevization of the party, training everywhere must be connected with the current political problems, the tactical and organizational tasks of the CI and the various communist parties. The

syllabus and methods of propaganda work must adhere to this principle. . . .

29. Any mechanical separation which suggests that Marxism is the theory and Leninism the practice of the revolutionary workers' movement should be avoided. Both Marxism and Leninism contain the theory and the practice of the working-class struggle for emancipation; they signify the unity of revolutionary theory and practice, in contrast to the Marxism of the epigones, the Marxism of the Second International, which even in its so-called orthodox form separated theory and practice, and rejected revolutionary action even when it was recognized in theory. 'Leninism is Marxism in the epoch of imperialism and the proletarian revolution. More precisely: Leninism is the theory and tactics of proletarian revolution in general, and of the proletarian dictatorship in particular' (Stalin). . . .

30. At the higher stages of communist training Marxist–Leninist economic theory and theory of the State must be included in the syllabus. . . . Comprehensive and thorough-going propaganda of the theoretical and tactical problems of armed insurrection and civil war is very important. So are the Leninist principles concerning the national and colonial question in the countries where this subject is relevant.

31. At no stage of communist party training should the philosophic aspects of Marxism–Leninism be ignored. Marx and Engels and Lenin were all militant materialists. . . .

VI. THE ORGANIZATION OF MARXIST RESEARCH AND WRITING

33. Leninism implies not merely the renaissance of revolutionary Marxism, but also an extension of its theoretical and practical content. . . .

34. We have international centres for theoretical work in the sense of scientific research in the field of Marxism–Leninism in the Marx–Engels Institute, the Lenin Institute, and the Communist Academy. It is the task of the CI to make the results of research at these scientific institutes the common property of the international communist movement.

EXTRACTS FROM THE THESES ON TACTICS IN THE TRADE UNIONS ADOPTED BY THE FIFTH COMINTERN CONGRESS

July 1924   *Inprekorr, iv, 119, p. 1577, 16 September 1924*

[In January 1924 the presidium had published a resolution sharply criticizing the tendency in a number of Comintern sections, particularly the KPD, to leave the reformist trade unions, and making suggestions for organizing trade unionists expelled from their unions, as well as those who were not in any union. It recommended the application of 'united front from below' tactics to all parties. In opening the fifth congress, Zinoviev said that withdrawal from the unions would mean that in a period of illegality the party would be no more than a sect. Lozovsky, introducing the theses, said the unions were the natural channel between the party and the working class; only Soviets were more comprehensive in character. But the links between the ruling classes and the trade union leaders were growing stronger; the IFTU supported the occupation of the Ruhr and the Dawes report; in protest against the IFTU's role as strike-breaker, unionists were turning more and more to the communist party. Consequently the re-formists, who were a tool of fascist reaction, hated the Comintern and Profintern more than ever. This had reinforced the belief among many communists that the unions could not be won. On the contrary, the fight for unity gave com-munists their best opportunity to win over the masses in the unions. Where the unions were already split, the communist parties must work for a joint congress to re-establish unity. This did not mean that occasions might not arise when it would be necessary to found 'parallel organizations' of those who had been expelled from the unions or who had left, but their purpose must be to keep together the forces working for unity. Communists in trade unions must re-member that they were in the first place communists; they could not have an independent policy; they must redouble their efforts against Amsterdam's policy of splitting the unions and make more careful preparations for trade union con-gresses. 'For the reformists—and in this they are quite right—the Comintern, the Russian revolution, and the RILU are one.' The factory, the factory com-mittee, and the trade union were the natural field for united front tactics. This emphasized the importance of the greatest defect in all their work, and the root of all their weaknesses—that they had not yet established factory cells.

Lozovsky went on to enumerate fifteen 'immediate tasks', covering fraction work, the formation of factory committees and their co-ordination on a regional basis, the organization of the opposition to the reformist leaders under com-munist control, propaganda for unity where there were parallel organizations, opposition to the anarchist idea of the autonomy of the trade union movement. Special attention should be given to industries of crucial importance in the class struggle, such as transport, public utilities, etc., and to establishing and main-taining contact with trade unionists doing national service—legally if possible, illegally if necessary. A practical platform must be worked out for each union: 'Our parties have usually spread their work equally over all sections of the workers, whatever their occupation. But it is essential to select, from the entire mass of the proletariat, a few branches of industry to which quite special atten-tion must be paid in virtue of their role in the forthcoming class struggles. . . . The success of the work of communist parties must be measured by the success of their activities among the workers of the most important branches of the national economy.' The reformists were beginning to take an interest in the trade union movement in the colonies, but they were doing so as agents of imperialism; this had to be exposed and denounced. Revolutionary trade union propaganda in the colonies should receive greater attention from the parties concerned.

Schumacher, of the KPD, said it was impossible to continue to work in the old trade unions; he pleaded for a return to the earlier policy of forming new unions, because wherever communists acted as communists in the unions they would be expelled. Schumacher, who was disavowed by the German delegation and subsequently expelled, was the subject of a special congress resolution which declared his attitude to be 'inconsistent with the decisions of the world congresses of the Comintern' and called on all who had left the unions to return. In the debate Heckert referred to his presence at the December 1921 conference of French trade unions 'where the unfortunate split occurred', and where the CP, despite a warning telegram from Lozovsky, did nothing to stop it. 'We always thought that this split was a mistake.' Treint reported that they were trying to re-establish trade union unity by means of a conference of all unions. They were often met by the argument that, if they wanted unity, they would first have to establish it internationally. MacManus asserted that the CPGB was organizing the Minority Movement in such a way that it would be a constant threat to the reformist leaders of every trade union.

The question whether the Comintern should seek and promote the amalgamation of the two trade union Internationals aroused heated controversy. Early in 1923 the IFTU notified the RILU that it would no longer maintain communications, but would deal only with the Russian unions when this appeared useful. At the Vienna congress of the IFTU in May 1924 a resolution was adopted, on the initiative of the British delegates, 'regretting the continued absence of the Russian trade union organizations from the International Federation due to their refusal to accept its rules and constitution', and recommending the IFTU bureau 'to continue consultations . . . with the object of securing the inclusion of Russia in the international trade union movement'.

In his opening report to the congress Zinoviev said that the attitude of the British unions at Vienna showed that there was a crisis in the IFTU, but this should not be exaggerated. The British stand had been partly demonstrative, because of the negotiations then proceeding for an Anglo-Soviet treaty. The RILU, he said, was 'founded at a moment when it seemed that we would be able to break through the enemy's front by a frontal attack and quickly capture the unions. . . . You know, comrades, that the movement later subsided, that the whole problem, all the tactical difficulties of the CI in these five years, have arisen precisely because the development was much slower than we thought. Social-democracy has partially consolidated its position, in the trade unions too. Now we must fight it by roundabout means.' Lozovsky said the IFTU leaders had become instruments of fascist reaction. The IFTU had instructed its bureau to enter into negotiations with the Russian unions, with the object of affiliation on the basis of the IFTU statutes. They could reject this out of hand, or they could agree and dissolve the RILU, or they could propose instead a world unity congress with proportional representation. Bordiga attacked the suggestion that the RILU should be liquidated. If it were, the Comintern would become a sect concerned with ideological propaganda and unable to intervene directly in mass industrial struggles. Schumacher urged that the negotiations with the IFTU should be dropped. To liquidate the RILU would in the end involve the liquidation of the Comintern. Heckert (KPD), like the majority of his delegation, was critical of the 'rapprochement' between the Russian and British unions. Zinoviev assured him that no diplomatic considerations were involved; the repercussions in Britain would be all to the good. A KPD memorandum on the negotiations between the Russian unions and the IFTU suggested that this would hinder mobilization of the masses against the Dawes report. This, said Zinoviev, was not true. The IFTU feared rapprochement with the Russian unions, which would make it their first condition that no support should be given to the Dawes proposals. Heckert argued that the KPD had fought bitterly against united front from above tactics, and now they were suddenly confronted with these 'from above' negotiations. Their effect on the masses would be deplorable, as no preparatory explanations had been given. Lozovsky, replying to the debate, said 'we are for unity because it gives us the opportunity of expanding the field of our communist activity'. On a resolution submitted by the Russian, French, Polish, British, American, and Balkan parties the theses were approved and referred to a commission for final drafting. The section on the attitude to the IFTU was to be discussed by the ECCI. The KPD, while urging that the proposed steps were untimely, 'condemned and rejected any attempt to exploit this statement as a difference of principle between the Russian and German parties on the trade union question'. When the ECCI met after the congress Zinoviev admitted that there was some point in the KPD criticism. Top-level negotiations must be accompanied by work among the masses. The Russian unions would not act independently of the Profintern, but the opportunity to negotiate with Amsterdam must be used. The Executive, with Bordiga dissenting, agreed on 12 July to the following formula:

'1. The enlarged Executive is in principle in favour of the amalgamation of the two trade union Internationals on certain conditions.

2. The amalgamation of the two Internationals will be possible only if this question is made the central point in the attention of the working masses, i.e. if we are successful in initiating a serious movement from below.

3. Therefore it is necessary to begin a far-reaching international campaign, primarily in the name of the Comintern and the Profintern, for the idea of unity of the trade union movement on a world scale. For this purpose the Comintern–Profintern manifesto can be used.'

Section IV of the theses adopted by the congress was rejected as inexpedient; it was omitted from later texts.

After the congress the KPD *Zentrale* passed a resolution repeating the grave misgivings of its delegation about the proposed moves towards unification. This could be accepted only if the RILU programme were adopted as the basis of the united organization. The third congress of the RILU, held in July 1924, proposed a joint IFTU–RILU conference with proportional representation. A joint Comintern–Profintern manifesto issued in July 1924 accused 'social-democracy and Amsterdam' of splitting the unions, and called on the working class to rid the unions of the splitters. In September 1924 Manuilsky wrote: 'When a few years ago we organized our red trade union International, we were confronted with a rising revolutionary wave in Europe. . . . We were convinced that by direct pressure we would be able in a short while to wrest the trade union movement from the reformists. We have had tremendous success in three years, and can without exaggeration say that at the present time our strength and influence in the trade union movement equal those of Amsterdam. But just recently we have noticed that this relation of forces shows a tendency to "set". . . . For the Amsterdam leaders, who represent the dying tendencies in the movement, this standstill is exceptionally favourable . . . but for the young communist sections in whose hands lies the future of the movement such a state of affairs can be highly injurious.' They had made no conditions for calling an IFTU–RILU congress, knowing that these would be rejected. What they wanted in a unified movement was a broader field of activity.]

II. THE STRUGGLE FOR UNITY

. . . By fighting inside the unions for unity, communists extend the sphere of influence of the communist parties and the Communist International, without for a moment losing contact with the masses. The fight for the unity of the trade union movement is the best way of winning the masses. . . . The old Comintern slogans of winning, not destroying the unions, of opposing flight from the unions, of fighting for the re-entry of those who have left, of fighting for unity—these slogans remain in force and must be carried through with resolution and energy. . . .

III. THE AMSTERDAM INTERNATIONAL AND ITS LEFT WING

Our attitude to the Amsterdam International as defined by previous congresses remains in force. In its top ranks the Amsterdam International is a bulwark of international imperialism, an organization expressing particularly blatantly the conservatism, backwardness, national narrowmindedness, bourgeois-imperialist sentiments of the workers most corrupted by the bourgeoisie. The fight against the Amsterdam International remains the most important task of the Comintern and its sections. . . . In our fight there are two things we must remember: (a) that there are millions of workers in the Amsterdam unions; (b) that a left wing has arisen there, still formless and politically vacillating. . . . These workers will be emancipated from reformist illusions to the extent that communists manage to take the lead in the industrial struggles of the working class. Industrial disputes are particularly favourable occasions for the application of united front tactics and for exposing the fascist strike-breaking role of the leaders. The left wing of the Amsterdam International has no clear programme and tactics. . . . A beginning has been made on the question of the attitude to the Russian unions, but on the fundamental political questions (reparations, Dawes plan, colonial policy, coalitions with the bourgeoisie, etc.), the left wing does not yet differ in essentials from the right. The fundamental and cardinal defect of this left wing is that it wishes to 'reconcile' reformism and communism, and cherishes the hope that it can find a middle way between these two deadly enemies. . . . The Comintern and the communist parties support the left wing in so far as it really fights against the programme and tactics of the Amsterdam International. To overestimate the left wing, to ignore its timidity and inconsistency would be a grave error. Communists and the trade union organizations they control must propose to the left wing of the Amsterdam

International the formation of joint committees of action. . . . Communists must demand of the left wing in the Amsterdam International, who say that an understanding with the revolutionary unions is desirable, that they put these proposals into action in every country in the daily struggle. . . .

IV. THE STRUGGLE FOR THE UNITY OF THE WORLD TRADE UNION MOVEMENT

The four years' work of the RILU has brought together and united all revolutionary elements in the world trade union movement into a single world organization. The Amsterdam International has long lost its monopoly. It is the task of the Comintern and its parties to fight energetically for the further unification of the revolutionary unions, for their organization in the RILU, and for the extension of communist influence and communist leadership in the red unions of all countries. These tasks can be accomplished only if the fight for the unity of the trade union movement is carried through with all consistency. . . . Unity could be re-established by convening an international unity congress at which all unions affiliated to Amsterdam and the RILU are represented on a proportional basis. Such an international unity congress, at which all unions throughout the world would have to be represented, could lay the foundations for a new united trade union international. . . . The creation of a united international on the basis of freedom of agitation and the strictest discipline in all actions against the bourgeoisie would naturally lead to the dissolution of the existing parallel Internationals (RILU and IFTU). But so long as we do not succeed in re-establishing the international unity of the trade union movement, the Communist International and the communist parties must continue to give support and assistance to the RILU and all organizations affiliated to it.

V. THE WEAKNESSES IN OUR WORK

. . . The weaknesses in our trade union work are in general the following:

1. In many countries there are no communist fractions; where they exist they have been created from above.

2. The failure to form fractions in organizations led by communists or communist sympathizers.

3. The failure to form fractions in reformist unions when there are parallel revolutionary unions (France).

4. Inadequate discipline applied to party members who follow their own line, leading to flight from the unions and the pursuit of their own independent trade union policy, regardless of the decisions of the parties and the Comintern (Germany).

5. The parties pay too little attention to the revolutionary unions which have been formed alongside the reformist unions (America, Belgium,

Holland); they should systematically guide these revolutionary workers and train them in the use of communist tactics.

6. Propaganda in the unions is too abstract. . . .

7. With few exceptions (Germany), work in the factory committees lacks care and thoroughness; inability to exploit mass industrial struggles to build up factory committees.

8. Craft traditions and prejudices, still deeply rooted even among revolutionary workers, are not combated strongly enough.

9. Preparations for trade union and trade union federation congresses and conferences are extremely bad from the political and party angles; speeches by communists at such meetings are quite casual.

10. Excessive nervousness in regard to reformist splitting measures, inadequate exploitation of individual and particularly mass expulsions from the unions.

11. Underestimation of the fact that the factory, the factory committee, and the trade union are the natural field for organizing the workers' united front.

12. Underestimation of the importance of trade union work. . . .

All these weaknesses exist in different degrees in almost all countries. The basic defect, and the origin of all weaknesses in our trade union work, is the absence of party cells in the factories. . . .

VI. OUR IMMEDIATE TASKS

1. The central task of all communist parties is to build fighting fractions, beginning with the factory . . . and to strengthen the control of party organizations over the activities of individual members and particularly over trade union fractions.

2. Work must be concentrated on the masses and the factories. Hence the necessity of forming factory committees where they do not yet exist, and of revolutionizing and intensifying the work of those already in existence. . . .

4. All independent revolutionary unions, and unions of those expelled by the reformists, must be united in every country and brought together with the opposition in the reformist unions through committees of action. . . .

6. Where the trade union movement is split, systematic work must be carried on among the masses for the re-establishment of unity by the calling of a unity congress on the basis of proportional representation and freedom of the ideological struggle. . . .

7. . . . Unrelenting struggle must be waged against communists leaving the unions. The slogan must be 'Back to the unions'. . . .

9. Particular attention must be paid to the organization of workers in those industries which may play a decisive part in the working-class

struggle for power (transport, mining, engineering, chemicals, electrical power stations, and gas-works). The success of communist party work in the unions will be measured by its success in uniting and organizing these most important branches of the national economy.

10. A start must be made on the formation of mixed committees (French–German, German–Polish, German–Czech, English–Russian, Russian–Polish, etc.) to organize joint parallel action on both sides of the frontier. . . .

11. The communist parties in countries where the bourgeoisie exploit colonial and semi-colonial peoples must pay particular attention to the growing trade union movement in the colonies. . . .

13. It is a condition of success in the struggle that we should know our enemies. Therefore the communist parties and the unions must make a thorough study of employers' organizations, their structure, their agencies, and the means they use to corrupt and disintegrate the workers' organizations. . . .

14. All communist parties must establish close contacts between the unions and the members of the unions doing military service. . . . In particular we must try to establish close contact between merchant seamen's organizations and sailors in the navy.

VII. CONCLUSION

The fifth Comintern congress endorses all decisions of previous congresses on the tasks of communists in the trade union movement, and directs the attention of all communist parties to the extreme importance of this work. . . . This is a question of life or death for the social revolution. That is why the fifth congress summons all its sections not to depart by one hair's-breadth from the decisions, and to carry through to the end the winning of the unions, that is, the winning of the masses.

EXTRACTS FROM THE RESOLUTION OF THE FIFTH COMINTERN CONGRESS ON THE BRITISH LABOUR GOVERNMENT

July 1924   *Inprekorr*, iv, 119, p. 1580, 16 *September* 1924

[Bukharin, reporting to the thirteenth RCP congress, said that the Russian model which in 1919 they thought would, by and large, be reproduced in other countries was now shown to be inadequate; it did not cover such developments as the left bloc in France or the Labour Government in Britain; at first the British Communist Party had given too much support to MacDonald, and its policy had had to be corrected by the ECCI. In his opening report to the Comintern congress Zinoviev said that, politically, the CPGB was its most important section. It had only between 3,000 and 4,000 members, and conditions were ripe for it to become a mass party; this would bring them half-way to victory in Europe. MacDonald was bound to fall, but the CPGB should not wait for that; it should attack the Labour Government from the start, so that the masses, when they lost their faith in the Labour Party, would realize that the communists had been right. In the debate Murphy (CPGB) said: 'The Labour Party is the organized working class of England, and those who suggest that we leave the Labour Party are suggesting that we should also leave the unions, that we should draw away from the working class.' The only way of making the CPGB a mass party was through the united front. Larkin argued that if the communists put up candidates against the Labour Party in elections this would automatically make any work inside the Labour Party impossible.

MacManus, for the British delegation, put in a memorandum describing the Labour Government as 'quite simply a capitalist and imperialist government'. The CPGB would try, through mass campaigns, to get its candidates adopted, but was too weak to put up its own candidates if they were not adopted by the local labour parties. Roy said the British party's tasks extended beyond Britain, as the enemy it was fighting did. Britain's strength was in its colonies, and the CPGB had to organize the working class throughout the Empire. The resolution was moved by Ruth Fischer and passed unanimously. Zinoviev, winding up the debate, recalled Lenin's advice that the communists should support a Labour Government in England as the rope supports a hanged man. MacDonald's Government was objectively counter-revolutionary, but it might unintentionally make the position of the bourgeoisie worse. In his report to the seventh congress of the CPGB in 1925 Campbell said that it was now clear that the Labour Government was not a victory for the working class, but a capitalist experiment which had caused confusion in working-class ranks.]

The Labour Government in England is a bourgeois-imperialist government and not a government of the working class. It is a faithful servant of His Majesty the King of the empire of capitalists, divorced from socialism, divorced from the labour movement, and bound only to the ruling classes. As manager for the bourgeoisie, it is continuing the policy of imperialist oppression and exploitation of the masses in India, Egypt, Africa, etc., and defends the policy designed to protect capitalism, strengthen English imperialism, and carry out the economic and financial colonization of the countries defeated in the war. . . .

The formation of a Labour Government is not a specifically English phenomenon. It is a product of the period of capitalist decay, in which the old forms of capitalist rule prove incapable of solving the problems, national and international, social, political, and economic, created by capitalism. In this period the capitalist class resorts to the most varied means of defence, from the use of labour parties (ministerial socialism) with their social pacifism, to fascism in all its forms, according to the degree of acuteness reached by class contradictions and the class distribution of power. Labour governments and fascist governments are the two extreme methods used by the bourgeoisie to maintain their dictatorship. . . .

Behind a screen of trivial concessions, the Labour Government pursues a bourgeois-imperialist policy as energetically as and certainly more successfully than its predecessors. . . . It has made no attempt to break the power of the aristocratic officer class over the armed forces, or to weaken in any other way this powerful weapon of English capitalism in its anti-working-class activities.

Under a cloak of pacifist promises it has gone to the limit in the construction of cruisers and air forces, and has energetically set about improving armaments. Under a cloak of pacifism this Labour Government is preparing a new slaughter which in its horror will surpass the mass murder of the so-called great war.

The fight of the working class against the Labour Government has therefore become a fight to safeguard humanity from mass annihilation.

As guardian of English imperialism the Labour Government refuses the Indian workers the elementary rights of political organization, allows them to be persecuted and starved, and supports with its authority the bombings, shootings, and terrorism against the masses in India, Egypt, and Mesopotamia. Ireland remains in the clutches of English imperialism and hundreds of workers in Ireland remain in prison with the consent of the Labour Government. The Labour Government has become the administrator of the Versailles treaty and allies itself openly with English and French imperialism and the German bourgeoisie to carry through the Dawes plan and to enslave the German workers completely. Even in its relations with the USSR it showed, by its shameful support of the bondholders and bankers against workers' and peasants' Russia, the falseness of its assertion that it guards the workers' interests. . . .

It is the task of the Communist International and its sections, of the English Communist Party, to rescue the labour movement from its reactionary leadership, to destroy the illusions in the minds of the masses that their emancipation can be a gradual process of parliamentary reform, and to make clear to the workers that they can free themselves from capitalist exploitation only by ruthless class struggle and by destroying the power of the bourgeoisie. For this purpose, and only for this purpose, the English Communist Party must continue its fight for affiliation to the Labour Party. . . .

The movement to the left has now become noticeable even in the leading circles of English trade unionism. It has no clear programme; it is timorous and vacillating. Nevertheless it reflects the growing discontent of the workers with the old leadership. Instead of a formless left movement organized minority movements are appearing. They have a clear programme, they consist of revolutionary and disciplined workers, and are spreading from district to district, popularizing the policy of the RILU. Although derided and condemned by the trade union bureaucracy, they are taking the first steps to organize the workers' rejection of the treacherous leadership; they are a pledge that the revolutionary spirit of the masses is growing and, led by the communist party, will save the labour movement from catastrophe. To win the victory, the English Communist Party must

(*a*) Support the left in all their actions against the trade union bureaucracy, in strikes and in propaganda; it must fight against all hesitation in their ranks and also against the weaknesses and inconsistencies in this movement;

(*b*) reinforce the solidarity of the Minority Movement and mobilize it on a national scale around a programme based on the platform of the RILU;

(*c*) strengthen the Minority Movement by the struggle for the creation of factory cells and so lay the foundations for industrial unions with the factory cells as the basic union organization;

(*d*) fight for the active participation of the English trade union movement in the international struggles of the proletariat.

EXTRACTS FROM THE RESOLUTION ON FASCISM ADOPTED BY THE FIFTH COMINTERN CONGRESS

July 1924   *Inprekorr*, iv, 119, p. 1581, 16 *September* 1924

[Bordiga opened the debate on fascism. He had referred to it earlier in the proceedings, arguing that, like social-democracy, it was basically a bourgeois party seeking mass support. It differed from the traditional party of reaction and terror by being more up to date, more cunning, and more experienced. They could expect a joint fascist-social-democratic offensive against the revolutionary movement, and must avoid the danger of being moved in self-defence to enter into coalitions with socialist and non-fascist bourgeois parties. In his main speech Bordiga said that although at first sight fascism might appear to be a movement of the middle class, the organized expression of their discontent, it was in fact initiated and led by the conservative big bourgeoisie with the help of the State machine. It had no new programme or aims; its purpose was to defend the existing bourgeois order. What was new about it was its political and military organization, unknown to the traditional bourgeois parties, which had never sought to win over the proletarian masses. From the outside, its goal seemed to be the elimination of all economic and social conflicts, but in fact it was anxious to eliminate them only among the bourgeoisie. Its assumption of power in Italy marked not a revolutionary change, but a change in the management of the forces of the bourgeoisie, effected with the silent complicity of the State apparatus. The maintenance of the old policy of equality before the law did not mean that the proletariat was not being persecuted. The workers' press was not forbidden by law, but their premises were broken up and their papers burnt; the old unions were not officially dissolved, but workers were being forced into fascist unions. In the elections the fascists had not completely excluded the opposition 'because they realized that if they had done so the elections would have lost all political significance'. The reformist socialists had won 22 seats, the left socialists 22, and the communists 19.

Referring to Italian recognition of the USSR, which had taken place earlier that year, Bordiga reported that many Italian comrades thought the Russian declaration of friendship went too far; it sounded as though approval were being extended to official fascist Italy, and should, they thought, have been omitted. (This reproach put the case very mildly; the unpublished papers of Humbert-Droz reveal how strong the feeling was, particularly during the Matteotti crisis in July. Later in the year, on 14 October, he wrote from Rome to the Comintern presidium about the Italian situation, reporting the growing hostility to Mussolini. 'It is in this atmosphere of political isolation and of scandal that our Soviet Ambassador here intends to invite Mussolini to a banquet on the 7 November anniversary. . . . It would scandalize the Italian proletariat. On 7 November the workers who try to demonstrate will be beaten up and arrested in the streets, and on the same day Mussolini will be the guest of the Russian Ambassador.' He suggested that Yurenev, the Ambassador, should be replaced by a communist who did not pay court to fascism. A week later Humbert-Droz wrote that the social-democratic idea that the communist party was, *au fond*, philo-fascist, was unfortunately nourished by the policy of Soviet diplomacy, the interviews and speeches in which Mussolini was referred to as a 'great man'. The Russian party should show far more reserve; its policy was strengthening Mussolini's position at home. The central committee of the Italian CP had written in the same vein.)

A German delegate, appearing under the name of Freimuth, reported that at the Frankfurt congress of the KPD it had been decided to oppose fascist demonstrations by force. 'We began a truly revolutionary small-scale war.' This had encouraged the party, and had exposed the 'arm-chair communists', the social-democrats in official positions who had tried to give the fascists protection, and the fascists themselves, who, despite their programme, sought the protection of the bourgeois republic. In the elections the fascists had obtained large votes in a number of strongly industrial areas where the communist vote was also large. To fight fascism they would have to fight the reformists. 'In this fight against the social-democrats we shall win back from fascism, for the proletarian class struggle, all those elements and groups which are the foundation of the fascist mass movement.' He proposed to answer fascist terror with terror, to organize armed defence corps against armed fascism, to drive known fascists out of the factories, etc. There was no discussion of the Bordiga and Freimuth speeches. Reporting for the Russian delegation to the ECCI at the thirteenth RCP congress earlier in the year, Bukharin argued that fascism and 'labourism' were both manifestations of the bourgeois united front; it took the form of fascism in countries which had lost much in the war, and where the class struggle was acute.]

I

Fascism is one of the classic forms of counter-revolution in the epoch when capitalist society is decaying, the epoch of proletarian revolution, particularly where the proletariat has taken up the struggle for power, but where, for lack of revolutionary experience, and in the absence of a leading revolutionary class party, it has been unable to organize the proletarian revolution and to intensify the insurrection of the masses to the point of establishing the proletarian dictatorship.

Fascism is the bourgeoisie's instrument for fighting the proletariat, for whose defeat the legal means at the disposal of the State no longer suffice ... but in its social structure fascism is a petty-bourgeois movement; it has its roots in the middle classes doomed to decay as a result of the capitalist crisis, and in the elements (such as ex-officers) declassed as a result of the war, and partly also in the embittered proletarian elements whose revolutionary hopes were disappointed.

As bourgeois society continues to decay, all bourgeois parties, particularly social-democracy, take on a more or less fascist character. . . . Fascism and social-democracy are the two sides of the same instrument of capitalist dictatorship. In the fight against fascism, therefore, social-democracy can never be a reliable ally of the fighting proletariat.

Because of its internal contradictions fascism, after its victory, becomes politically bankrupt, and this leads to its disintegration (Italy). . . . Where, without having won formal victory, it is forced openly to support and defend the bourgeois regime (as in Germany), it gets into a similar state of crisis.

II

The communist fight against fascism must be waged with the means and methods to secure both its political defeat and the defence of the revolutionary proletariat against its armed attacks. . . . These are, *inter alia*:

A. IN THE POLITICAL SPHERE

1. Genuinely revolutionary strategy and tactics, which give the proletarian, petty-bourgeois, and peasant masses confidence in the communist movement. . . .

2. Educating the working class to understand the counter-revolutionary and anti-working-class character of fascism.

3. Explaining to the petty-bourgeois and peasant masses . . . the functions of fascism in the service of capitalism.

4. An active foreign policy. Fight against the imperialist peace treaties, reparations, League of Nations swindle. . . .

5. Fight for revolutionary unity with the Union of Soviet Republics. An active Leninist policy in the national question. Fight for the right of self-determination and secession of all oppressed nations.

6. . . . Fight for the international united front under Comintern leadership. . . .

B. IN THE ORGANIZATIONAL AND MILITARY SPHERES

1. Formation of armed defence detachments against armed fascism.

2. Disarming of the fascists. . . .

3. Fascist demonstrations to be answered by counter-demonstrations of workers with armed protection.

4. Terrorist fascist actions (destruction of trade union offices, printing works, etc.; attempts on workers and workers' leaders, etc.) to be answered by general strikes, the use of working-class mass terror by reprisals against the fascists, their leaders, their printing works and other undertakings.

5. Stopping railway transport when the fascists organize marches, meetings, and demonstrations.

6. Driving the fascists out of the factories; sabotage; passive resistance; strikes in factories where fascists are employed or are used to supervise and to split the workers.

EXTRACTS FROM THE RESOLUTION OF THE FIFTH COMINTERN CONGRESS ON THE RUSSIAN QUESTION

July 1924   *Inprekorr*, iv, 125, p. 1665, 25 *September* 1924

[By the end of 1923 the dispute within the central committee of the Russian party had come out into the open, and had widespread repercussions in the Comintern. On 8 October 1923 Trotsky had written to the central committee of the RCP about the 'incorrect and unhealthy regime in the party', demanding 'party democracy' in the place of 'secretarial bureaucratism'. A week later the 'platform of the 46' was sent as a secret document to the political bureau. It echoed Trotsky's criticisms; the signatories included some members of the central committee. Radek wrote separately, appealing for reconciliation. Stalin's first open attack on Trotsky was published on 15 December, and at the same time Zinoviev attacked him at a meeting in Petrograd at which the term 'Trotskyism' was first used to denote a deviation from and opposition to 'Leninism'. Although at first Trotsky acted independently of other critics of the central-committee majority, he was everywhere regarded as the leader of the opposition. In the Polish CP in particular, there was at the end of 1923 very strong support for Trotsky, whose name, it was said in a letter from the Polish central committee to the RCP, 'was indissolubly bound up with the victorious October revolution, with the Red Army, with communism and the world revolution'. The Polish central committee had asked for an open statement from the Russian CC that there was no intention of removing Trotsky from his party and government posts. A statement signed by Prukhniak, 21 January 1924, for the Polish delegation at the ECCI, ran in part: 'Since Lenin, the greatest and most authoritative leader of the revolutionary world proletariat, no longer takes part in guiding the CI, and since the authority of Trotsky, a leader recognized by the revolutionary world proletariat, has been put in question by the Russian CC, there is a danger that the authority of the CI leadership will be shaken.' At the thirteenth conference of the RCP in January 1924 Trotsky was accused of failing to obey the decision of the October 1923 meeting of the central committee and of continuing his campaign against that body. The October meeting had condemned his 'profound political error', which threatened the unity of the party and encouraged the formation of fractions.

Reporting on the work of the Comintern at the thirteenth RCP congress in May 1924, Bukharin said that there had been many members in the sections, and in some cases entire central committees, which leaned towards the Russian opposition; but now that they had seen how rapid progress was in Russia, they had all come to agree with the Russian majority. The crisis in the Russian party, he said, was one link in the chain of crises within the International. Communism had suffered defeats in Germany, Poland, and Bulgaria, and a number of parties had made serious mistakes, which the ECCI had had to correct. Trotsky was invited to speak at the Comintern congress (his appearance at the opening session was greeted with applause), but declined to do so, explaining in a letter that, as nobody had disputed the resolution passed at the thirteenth congress of the RCP, a statement by him on the platform of the opposition would create unnecessary difficulties. At the meeting of the ECCI which immediately preceded the opening of the congress Trotsky had been nominated, together with Stalin and Bukharin, to represent the Russian party in the congress presidium.

Rykov reported fairly briefly on the discussion in the RCP at the end of a long report on the economic situation in the USSR. Forces hostile to the RCP, both inside and outside Russia, he said, were attracted to the opposition and rested their hopes on them, whether the opposition wanted this or not; every attack on the party apparatus, which was no more than the organizing agency of the party, weakened discipline and unity. There was no discussion in the plenary sessions, and none when Kolarov reported for the Russian commission. The resolution was carried unanimously.

A declaration put forward by the German, French, British, and American delegations, said that they spoke 'on behalf of parties which from the beginning followed the Russian party discussion with the greatest attention and with considerable concern, and which give whole-hearted support to the central committee of the Russian Communist Party. They are actuated by the conviction that the proposals of the opposition will imperil the dictatorship of the proletariat and the unity of the Russian Communist Party. Therefore, they maintain that the action of the Russian Communist Party opposition was directed not only against the central committee of the Russian Communist Party, but objectively (irrespective of its subjective intentions) against the interests of the entire Communist International. For, by imperilling the dictatorship of the proletariat in the Union of Soviet Republics, and by weakening the Russian Communist Party, which alone is capable of maintaining this dictatorship, it attacked the legacy of Lenin which is dear to every communist throughout the world. Therefore, the Communist International must insist on the unequivocal rejection by all members of the International and by all its sections, of such un-Leninist conceptions, which are contrary to the interests of the world revolution, and which bring into contempt the authority of the Bolshevik old guard, which is the leader not only of the Soviet State, but also of the Comintern.']

The RCP was the essential force in the foundation of the Comintern, and still remains one of the chief factors determining the success of the international communist movement. The successes of the RCP, as well as its failures, and even more the formation in its midst of fractions and groups, are therefore of the most serious consequence for the revolutionary movement in other countries. . . .

The debate in the RCP in the autumn of last year and the formation in its ranks of an opposition to the majority of the central committee made it necessary for the congress to study this question attentively, although the RCP itself at its thirteenth congress unanimously condemned the opposition as the outgrowth of petty-bourgeois influences, and emerged from the discussion stronger and firmer. Although the Communist International asked the representatives of the RCP opposition to put their point of view to the congress, and although the RCP delegation gave their consent, they declined on a formal pretext to appear.

On the other hand the congress has seen no evidence that the opposition has understood its errors and has fully adopted the views of the thirteenth RCP congress. In these circumstances there is a danger that the discussion in the RCP will be revived. The congress also observes that the opposition in the RCP was supported by groups in other parties, in the Polish, German, and French parties, etc.; this, like the RCP opposition, is a manifestation of a right (opportunist) deviation in these parties and was condemned as such by the fifth congress of the Communist International.

Having heard a special report on the situation in the Soviet Union and in the RCP, and having examined the material relating to these questions, the congress resolves . . . to endorse the resolutions of the thirteenth conference and the thirteenth congress of the RCP, which condemned the platform of the opposition as petty-bourgeois, and its conduct as a threat to the unity of the party and consequently to the proletarian dictatorship in the Soviet Union.

EXTRACTS FROM THE THESES ON TACTICS ADOPTED BY THE FIFTH
COMINTERN CONGRESS

July 1924   *K.I. v dokumentakh*, p. 397

[The 'Saxon experiment' made the 'workers' government' slogan a focus of controversy, and united front tactics continued to cause confusion and discord. (Humbert-Droz had reported earlier from Paris that at bottom the disputes in the central committee of the French party were concerned with the nature of the united front proposals. Were they really seeking a united front or were they to make proposals only in order that they should be rejected?) At first, Zinoviev said, these tactics had expressed the realization that the communist party did not have on its side the majority of the working class, that the reformists were still strong and the communists on the defensive. But they were not evolutionary tactics, an attempt to form an alliance with social-democracy. They were a strategic manœuvre designed to mobilize the masses in a period when the revolution was temporarily halted. It was never right to have a united front from above alone, and it was nearly always right to have it from below. The use of these tactics from above and below was correct in a country such as England. But they had to revise the exaggerated, imprudent, and incorrect formulation of the tactics introduced by Radek at the fourth congress. Radek replied that no objection had been raised at the time to his speech at the fourth congress. He had said then that it might mean temporary coalitions with social-democrats. If the tactics were meant merely to 'unmask' them, on the assumption that they would not and could not fight, it was a misleading trick. They *did* want a united front, and were prepared to go along with the social-democrats as long as they were willing to fight. That was the idea behind the conference of the three Internationals in the spring of 1922. They had no confidence in the social-democratic leaders, but the struggle of the working class demanded unity of action. Saxony was a tragi-comedy for the party because it had not been prepared for. It was a united front from above only, with nothing below. A number of speakers admitted that they were confused on these questions. Bordiga was opposed to a united front with organizations that could not be won for communism. He asked for 'a third-class funeral' for these tactics and the workers-government slogan, which had become a synonym, not for the proletarian dictatorship, but for vulgar parliamentarism. He was also opposed to the admission of 'sympathizing parties' into the Comintern (the left wing of the Italian Socialist Party had been admitted in this capacity).

Zinoviev replied that these tactics had proved their worth in the case of the USPD and the Labour Party. Klara Zetkin suggested that if the communist party were strong, centralized, and disciplined, neither tied to another party nor lost in the masses, it did not matter whether the united front—assuming that the unity was based on unity of principles and tactics—was from above or below; in the end it was always from below, because it was a response to mass pressure. Nor was the slogan of a workers' and peasants' government free from ambiguity. According to Zinoviev it was a 'pseudonym for the dictatorship of the proletariat'. She disagreed; it was taken from the history of the Russian revolution, where it had proved to be the most attractive, accessible, and popular way of winning the masses for the proletarian dictatorship; this was not true of developed capitalist countries; there it would come about as the result of a revolutionary mass movement, when the bourgeoisie could not maintain power, but the proletariat was not mature and united enough to seize power, still believing that the old State forms could be utilized; such a government could not last long; it would have to take the road to the proletarian dictatorship. Rossi said that if a workers' government was just the proletarian dictatorship in simple language, they had to realize that it could result only from a direct frontal attack for the seizure of power.

Radek also contended that the slogan of a workers' government was not a synonym for the proletarian dictatorship, but a possible stage on the road to it. It was part of genuine united front tactics. He pleaded for a return to the position of the fourth congress on these questions.

Thaelmann reported for the commission; it had had two sets of theses to consider, one drafted by Zinoviev and submitted by the Russian delegation, and the other by Bordiga; the two coincided in many respects, but Bordiga's rejected the slogan of a workers' and peasants' government even for agitational purposes. Bordiga announced that the Italian left would vote for the theses, since they approximated more nearly to their position than the theses of the fourth congress. The theses were adopted unanimously.]

I. THE INTERNATIONAL SITUATION

1. *The Democratic-Pacifist Phase*

What is new in the present international political situation is the opening of a certain democratic-pacifist phase. A change of this kind in the world policy of the bourgeoisie was predicted by the fourth Comintern congress, which met at a time when bourgeois world reaction had reached its climax. The shift in policy now apparent is indicated by the following signs:

In England the so-called Labour Government, with the leaders of the Second International at its head, is in power. In France the so-called left bloc won an electoral victory as a result of which the French Socialist Party, one of the chief parties of the Second International, has virtually become a part of the present French Government. In Germany there is also a tendency, connected with propaganda for the Dawes report, for democratic-pacifist illusions to grow stronger, together with social-democracy, which embodies this policy; at the same time there is a marked trend in the opposite direction, because in order to operate the Dawes plan the ruling class with the help of the SPD must proceed more openly and brutally than before to suppress the revolutionary movement. . . . In America that wing of imperialism which condescends to interfere in European affairs, and is ready to support the so-called Experts' report, has triumphed. The growing movement to found a 'third' (petty-bourgeois) party in America also represents a certain shift towards a 'democratic-pacifist' phase in American politics. In Japan the 'democratic' bourgeoisie are approaching power and getting ready to take over the government from the feudal party. . . .

2. *The Real Significance of the Present Stage in International Politics*

What is now happening is in reality not the beginning of the stabilization of the capitalist 'order' on the basis of 'democracy' and peace, but merely the concealment of its rule while bourgeois world reaction is intensified and the people betrayed.

The 'democratic-pacifist' era has not brought any reduction in armaments and cannot do so. . . . Every democracy is arming more or less openly for the irreconcilable imperialist conflict with other democracies.

The fundamental antagonism between American and Japanese imperialism has not been eliminated, but continues automatically to work, and must inevitably lead to a new imperialist war.

The conflict of interests between the imperialist cliques of England and France has not been eliminated or mitigated by the victory of 'democracy' in the two countries. The form, not the substance, of their competitive struggle has changed.

The looting of the colonies and semi-colonial countries continues as a natural pre-condition of 'progress' and 'civilization'.

3. *The Experts' report*

The gospel of present-day pacifism and modern democracy is the so-called Experts' report. In reality their plan is intended to plunder the German working masses. It is furthermore an attempt by the imperialists of the countries which only yesterday were at war with each other to improve their business at the expense of the workers. . . . The Experts' report, which has now received the approval of the entire international counter-revolutionary social-democracy, is in fact the most disgraceful document of the present age. It will become a halter round the neck not only of the German workers, but also of the working masses of a number of other countries. Social-democratic support of the Dawes report is as much a betrayal of the cause of the working people as support of the imperialist war, for it is nothing but the continuation of that war by other means. . . .

4. *The International Position of the Soviet Union*

The one country which is consistently pursuing a policy of peace is the Soviet Union. . . . The USSR has recently had considerable success in consolidating its international position. The improvement in welfare at home, the support which the country received from all honest and conscious elements in the international working class, the intelligent policy of the Soviet Government led to *de jure* recognition of the Soviet Union by some of the largest States. Nevertheless it is by no means impossible that it is precisely this 'democratic-pacifist' era which will create new difficulties for the first proletarian State. There is no doubt that the most treacherous part of 'democracy' is now working to build an international united front against the Soviet Union, in order to force the victorious proletarian revolution to its knees and compel it to repay the old debts. . . . The nearer capitalism draws to its end, the more difficult and contradictory the situation of the international bourgeoisie, the more probable becomes the instigation of outright war against the Soviet Union. The participation of social-democrats in present-day 'democratic' governments only increases the danger of such a military adventure. . . .

5. *The International Policy of Social-Democracy*

. . . In all countries where social-democracy represents a substantial force it continues as before to support its own imperialists, but conceals this treacherous policy behind talk about democracy and pacifism. There is no doubt that it is the social-democratic leaders who display the greatest zeal in carrying out the policy of the Experts' report, in preparations to isolate the Soviet Union, and even in preparations for a military campaign. To lull the vigilance of the masses, the counter-revolutionary social-democratic leaders indulge in hypocritical talk about fighting war by means of a general strike. . . .

II. THE PROBLEM OF POWER

1. *The Dissolution of the Bourgeois Order*

Although the first imperialist world war towards its end released a violent outbreak of spontaneous mass discontent, bourgeois society has managed to prolong its existence for a certain time. The forces of the international proletariat turned out to be not well enough organized, the parties of international proletarian revolution not strong enough, and so at the end of the war the proletarian revolution could not triumph. Nevertheless the war provoked deep upheavals. Its consequences will continue to be felt for a number of years. . . .

At times symptoms of failing capitalist stability are to be observed even more clearly in the political than in the economic field. The constant and rapid changes of government in a number of countries put the problem of power on the order of the day, in a form unknown before the imperialist war.

2. *Two Trends in the Policy of the World Bourgeoisie*

In the last few years, and to some extent even before the war, two trends in the policy of the world bourgeoisie have become clearly apparent, one openly reactionary, and the other democratic-reformist. . . . The first aims at crushing and defeating the revolutionary forces in open and furious struggle before they have ripened, while the other, more far-sighted, aims at changing the relations of power in favour of the bourgeoisie by small concessions, by bribing the top men in the working class, in short, by the methods of 'democracy', pacifism, and reformism.

3. *Between Social-Democracy and Fascism*

The bourgeoisie can no longer rule by the old methods. That is one of the symptoms of the slow but certain growth of the proletarian revolution.

The bourgeoisie make use at one time of fascism, at another of social-democracy. In both cases they are concerned to screen the capitalist character of their rule. . . .

4. *Social-Democracy as the 'Third' Party of the Bourgeoisie*

In America a great fuss is being made about the foundation of a 'third' party of the bourgeoisie (the petty bourgeoisie). In Europe social-democracy has already become, in a certain sense, the 'third' bourgeois party. This is particularly obvious in England where, in addition to the two classical bourgeois parties which took it in turn to rule, the so-called Labour Party has now become a governing party, a Labour Party which in fact pursues a policy close to that of one of the two wings of the bourgeoisie. . . .

For a number of years social-democracy has been caught up in a process of change; from being the right wing of the labour movement it is becoming one wing of the bourgeoisie, in places even a wing of fascism. That is why it is historically incorrect to talk of 'a victory of fascism over social-democracy'. So far as their leading strata are concerned, fascism and social-democracy are the right and left hands of modern capitalism. . . .

6. *Between White Terror and 'Labour Governments'*

Despite the apparent consolidation of the bourgeois order, its power is in fact being more and more undermined. The situation as a whole is extremely unstable. Parliamentarism is approaching its end. Day by day it becomes more difficult for the bourgeoisie to establish even a moderately safe position on the ruins of the old parliamentarism. . . . The bourgeoisie will have to turn now to one side, now to the other, resorting to open white terror or attempting to find support in a so-called labour government.

It is not unlikely that in the next few years we shall see so-called labour governments in a number of countries. These 'labour governments' are a function of the struggle of the revolutionary proletariat for power and of the vacillations within the bourgeoisie which are unavoidable in the present epoch. Objectively these so-called labour governments signify an advance in so far as they testify to the progressive decline of the bourgeois regime, to irresolution in the policy of the ruling classes. In this sense even the counter-revolutionary MacDonald Government (in reality a liberal government) represents historical progress. But the job of true adherents of the proletarian revolution is naturally not to praise such 'labour governments' but to mobilize the proletarian army for irreconcilable revolutionary struggle, and to work for the quickest possible transition from so-called labour governments to the proletarian dictatorship.

III. THE BUILDING OF MASS COMMUNIST PARTIES AS THE CARDINAL TASK OF THE COMINTERN

1. *The Crisis of Capitalism and the Subjective Factor*

At the end of the imperialist war the world bourgeoisie were not defeated primarily because there were in the decisive countries no communist mass parties able to organize the revolution and to lead into struggle the masses who rose spontaneously against the war criminals. Consequently capitalism obtained a respite.

In a situation in which capitalism can no longer rule without the support of the social-democrats, in which the capitalist crisis becomes steadily, if slowly, more hopeless, the 'subjective factor', that is, the degree of organization of the proletarian masses and their communist vanguard, is the cardinal question of the entire historical epoch.

2. *The Slogan: To the Masses*

The slogan: To the masses, put out by the third world congress of the Comintern, remains in force, unchanged. The successes which the Comintern has had in the preceding period are only initial achievements. The successes of the individual sections have not yet been consolidated. If we make no progress in winning the masses, a retrograde movement may easily set in.

3. *Winning the Majority*

. . . The fifth world congress of the Comintern confirms in full the formulations of the third and fourth congresses. It decisively rejects as incorrect those right-wing tendencies which insist on the winning of a statistical majority of the working masses as a preliminary, and believe that there can be no serious revolutionary struggles unless the communists have already won if possible 99 per cent. of all the workers. It equally rejects the errors of the 'ultra-left', who have still not grasped the decisive world-historical importance of the slogan: To the masses, and who even occasionally go so far as to maintain that communist parties may be parties of a 'terrorist minority'; that is, they believe that, without having become mass parties, communist parties can at any moment lead the masses into struggle.

IV. THE BASIC CONDITIONS FOR THE FORMATION OF MASS COMMUNIST PARTIES

These conditions are:

1. *The Methodical Building up of the Party on a Factory-Cell Basis*

The great majority of European communist parties still adhere to the organizational principle of party structure taken over from the social-democrats. That is a survival from the times when the party was still regarded as an electoral machine. There can be no talk of building a serious internally-solid mass communist party so long as it is not based on party cells in the factories themselves. . . . This is not merely an organizational, but a serious political question. No communist party will be in a position to lead the decisive masses of the proletariat to struggle and to defeat the bourgeoisie until it has this solid foundation in the factories, until every large factory has become a citadel of the communist party.

2. *Correct Communist Work inside the Trade Unions*

Further basic pre-conditions for the building of solid mass communist parties are the creation of a network of communist fractions in the trade unions (legal where possible, illegal if necessary), not merely on paper but in fact, and a systematic, unyielding, prolonged struggle to capture the unions, a struggle which replies to splitting and to provocations by the social-democratic leaders, designed to drive communists out of the unions, with more intensive activity for unity in the unions.

3. *Launching a Factory-Committee Movement*

Factory committees are a new form of proletarian organization, which will gradually give rise to new and genuinely revolutionary unions, and which in favourable circumstances may form the kernel for councils of workers' deputies. A communist party which has not yet succeeded in establishing a serious factory-committee movement in its country, or in securing for itself strong influence within an already existing factory-committee movement, cannot be regarded as a serious mass communist party. . . .

4. *The Correct Attitude to the Peasantry*

. . . The proletariat cannot triumph and establish the Soviet regime unless it steadily pursues a policy of neutralizing one section of the peasantry and winning over other sections to its cause. . . . Communist parties which have not learnt to do revolutionary work among the peasantry cannot claim to be mass communist parties dealing seriously with the question of capturing power. Obviously our sections must remain Marxist workers' parties, and not be transformed into 'workers' and peasants' parties'.

5. *Correct Policy on the National Question*

In a number of countries, as a result of the re-division of the world after the first imperialist war, there is greater national oppression and dismemberment. In a number of European countries, and still more in colonial and semi-colonial countries, a mass of inflammable material has been heaped up which may blow bourgeois rule sky-high. Correct communist policy on the national question, which was thoroughly analysed in the theses of the second world congress, forms one of the most important constituents in the policy of winning the masses and preparing a victorious revolution. Nihilism and opportunist deviations in the national question, which still prevail in a number of communist parties, are the weakest side of these parties, which will never be able to accomplish their historical mission if they do not overcome these weaknesses.

V. BETWEEN TWO WAVES OF THE PROLETARIAN REVOLUTION

Signs have been apparent in the last year of the rise of a new revolutionary wave. The beginning of the revolutionary struggle in Germany, the risings in Bulgaria and Poland, the big industrial strikes in a number of countries bear witness to the ripening of new revolutionary events.

It is precisely the period between two revolutions, or two rising revolutionary waves, that encourages both opportunist right deviations and 'ultra-left' tendencies towards passivity, menshevism upside down, clothing itself in radical phrases.

VI. RUTHLESS STRUGGLE AGAINST RIGHT-OPPORTUNIST TENDENCIES

The period between the fourth and fifth Comintern congresses showed that opportunist tendencies in the communist movement are stronger than was to be expected. . . .

At the fifth congress it has become unmistakably clear that in some countries, of the utmost importance for the workers' movement, the representatives of the right-wing tendency tried to distort completely the tactics of the united front and of the workers' and peasants' government, interpreting them as meaning a narrow political alliance, an organic coalition of 'all workers' parties', that is, a political alliance of communists with social-democracy. While for the Comintern the main purpose of the united front tactics consists in the struggle *against* the leaders of counter-revolutionary social-democracy and in emancipating social-democratic workers from their influence, the representatives of the right-wing tendency tend to interpret the united front as a political alliance with social-democracy. . . .

VII. CLEARING UP 'ULTRA-LEFT' TENDENCIES

Bolshevism, as the movement of the Russian revolutionary proletariat, developed in relentless struggle not only against menshevism and centrism, but also against 'ultra-left' tendencies. From the first day of its existence the Comintern, as the international organization of bolshevism, has waged a relentless struggle not only against right opportunism but also against the 'ultra-left', which is often only the reverse side of opportunism. In the period between the fourth and fifth congresses 'ultra-left' tendencies took on a peculiarly threatening character in regard to work in reactionary trade unions. The movement in favour of communists leaving the unions is extremely dangerous for communism. If the Comintern fails to reject decisively these tendencies, which can profit only the counter-revolutionary social-democratic leaders who want to get rid of communists in the unions, we shall never be able to create genuine bolshevik parties. 'Ultra-left' tendencies were also apparent in the rejection 'on principle' of the tactics of manœuvre as such, particularly in the failure to understand the united front tactics, the refusal to operate them in practice. . . .

VIII. THE UNITED FRONT TACTICS

Despite serious opportunist errors and the distortion of united front tactics by the right—which in many cases might have meant the outright ruin of the communist parties—the application of united front tactics between the fourth and fifth congresses was, by and large, of undoubted use to us, and furthered the development of a number of Comintern sections into mass parties.

In a period when the communist parties in a number of the most important countries are still in a minority, when social-democracy for a number of historical reasons is still supported by large proletarian masses, when the capitalist offensive is continuing in various forms and the working class cannot summon up sufficient energy to wage serious defensive struggles, united front tactics were and are correct and necessary. . . .

United front tactics are only a method of agitation and of revolutionary mobilization of the masses over a period. . . .

1. The tactics of the united front *from below* are necessary always and everywhere, with the possible exception of rare moments during decisive struggles when revolutionary communist workers will be compelled to turn their weapons against even groups of the proletariat who out of deficient class consciousness are on the enemy's side. . . .

2. Unity *from below* and at the same time negotiations with leaders. This method must frequently be employed in countries where social-democracy is still a significant force. . . .

It is understood that in such cases the communist parties maintain their complete and absolute independence, and retain their communist character at every stage of the negotiations and in all circumstances. Therefore all negotiations with the social-democratic leaders must be conducted publicly, and communists must do their utmost to get the working masses to take a lively interest in the negotiations.

3. United front only *from above*. This method is categorically rejected by the Communist International.

The tactics of the united front from below are the most important, that is, a united front under communist party leadership covering communist, social-democratic, and non-party workers in factory, factory council, trade union, and extending to an entire industrial centre or area or industry. . . .

United front tactics were and remain a method of revolution, not of peaceful evolution. They are the tactics of a revolutionary strategic manœuvre of the communist vanguard, surrounded by enemies, in its struggle against the treacherous leaders of counter-revolutionary social-democracy. . . . United front tactics were and are a means of gradually drawing over to our side the social-democratic and the best non-party workers; they should in no circumstances be degraded to the tactics of lowering our ideals to the level of understanding reached by these workers.

IX. THE WORKERS' AND PEASANTS' GOVERNMENT

The slogan of a workers' and peasants' government was and is formulated by the Comintern as a deduction from the united front tactics as defined above. Opportunist elements in the Comintern tried to distort this slogan too by interpreting it as a 'government within the bourgeois-democratic framework' and as a political alliance with social-democracy. The fifth world congress emphatically rejects this interpretation. For the Comintern the slogan of a workers' and peasants' government is the slogan of the proletarian dictatorship translated into popular language, into the language of revolution. The formula workers' and peasants' government, derived from the experience of the Russian revolution, was and can be nothing but a method of agitation and mobilization of the masses for the revolutionary overthrow of the bourgeoisie and the establishment of Soviet power. . . . The overthrow of the bourgeoisie, making them harmless, overcoming their resistance, and creating the conditions for a true workers' and peasants' government can only be accomplished by an armed uprising of the proletariat supported by the best part of the peasantry, only by the workers in civil war. . . .

For communists the slogan of a workers' and peasants' government never means the tactics of parliamentary agreements and coalitions with social-democracy. On the contrary; communist parliamentary activity must be directed to exposing the counter-revolutionary role of social-democracy and to making clear to the working masses the treacherous nature and sham character of so-called labour governments which owe their existence to the bourgeoisie and are in fact liberal, bourgeois governments.

X. PARTIAL DEMANDS

. . . Whereas reformist partial demands are designed to *replace* the proletarian revolution, partial demands put forward by communists are designed for the exactly opposite purpose of preparing the proletarian revolution more successfully. Communist agitation for partial demands links each of them to the programme of revolutionary overthrow. This is particularly valid for those countries where the crisis of the bourgeois system has begun. . . .

XII. THE WEST AND THE EAST

The Communist International is an organization for world revolution. But as a result of a number of special circumstances the attention of the Comintern has been claimed in far too great a degree by the West. Far greater attention than before must be paid to work in the East, using that word in its broadest sense. In India, Japan, China, and Turkey the seeds of a communist movement have taken root. In all these countries a widespread economic struggle is opening, to which the Comintern must give the utmost attention. It must also give all-round support to the anti-imperialist movement of all oppressed nationalities in the spirit of the third world congress resolution, bearing in mind that this movement is one of the most important elements in the universal movement for emancipation. . . .

XIII. TWO PERSPECTIVES

The era of international revolution has opened. But the tempo of its development, particularly of its development in one continent or another, cannot be predicted with certainty. The situation as a whole is such that two prospects are possible:

1. The possibility of slow and postponed development of the proletarian revolution; or
2. Since capitalism is already seriously undermined and its internal contradictions are in general growing rapidly more acute, the catastrophe may occur very shortly in one country or another.

Comintern tactics must reckon with both these possibilities. The Comintern must develop its capacity to manœuvre and to adapt itself to changes in the tempo of development. . . .

XIV. BOLSHEVIZING THE PARTIES AND FORMING A UNIFIED WORLD COMMUNIST PARTY

In the present period the most important task of the CI is the bolshevization of its sections. This slogan should not be interpreted as the mechanical transference of the entire experience of the Russian Bolshevik Party to all other parties. The basic features of a genuine bolshevik party are:

1. The party must be a real mass party, that is, it must be able, both when legal and illegal, to maintain the closest and strongest contacts with the working masses and express their needs and aspirations.

2. It must be capable of manœuvre, that is, its tactics should not be sectarian or dogmatic. . . .

3. It must be revolutionary, Marxist in nature, working undeviatingly towards its goal. . . .

4. It must be a centralized party, permitting no fractions, tendencies, or groups; it must be fused in one mould.

5. It must carry out systematic and persistent propaganda and organization in bourgeois armies.

Bolshevization of the parties means that our sections take over for themselves everything in Russian bolshevism that has international significance.

Only to the extent that the decisive sections of the CI really become bolshevik parties will the Comintern become, not in words but in fact, a homogeneous bolshevik world party permeated with the ideas of Leninism.

XV. CONCRETE TASKS OF THE MOST IMPORTANT SECTIONS OF THE CI

The tasks of these sections are in essentials as follows:

1. *England*

Because of the present world situation England, with its possessions, is in general playing the premier part in all international questions. It follows that the CPGB also acquires greater importance. To train the CPGB to fulfil its tasks is one of the most important CI tasks. In its attitude to the Labour Government the CPGB displayed some ideological and tactical deviations. In the forthcoming period the CPGB must concentrate its forces on the following questions:

(*a*) Inside the Labour Party, to support and drive forward its left wing so that it becomes a genuinely revolutionary wing, and to carry on most intensive work in the trade union Minority Movement;

(*b*) to combat MacDonald's so-called Labour Government among the masses, openly and unambiguously, by exposing its bourgeois anti-working-class character;

(*c*) at all by-elections and in the next election campaign to follow a clear, decisive, unambiguous communist line;

(*d*) to wage industrial struggles in such a way that the main emphasis is laid on the formation of united front bodies built from below (strike committees), factory committees . . .;

(e) the CPGB must conduct an active campaign to set up committees of action in the factories and unions, to exert pressure on the so-called Labour Government to carry out that part of its programme which it has dropped, namely the nationalization of the railways and mines, higher unemployment benefits, more workers' housing, etc. Only if the CPGB exposes the treachery of the Labour Government in relation to the workers' daily needs will it be able to destroy their illusions about the so-called Labour Government . . .;

(f) particular attention must be given to contacts with the colonies, to supporting the national-revolutionary movements in the colonies, to militarism, disarmament, England's relations with the Soviet Union and imperialist France, and to the Dawes plan;

(g) the CPGB must also begin serious work to influence the unemployed. . . .

2. *France*

Congress notes with satisfaction the substantial successes of the French party . . . but at the same time points to the necessity of carrying out the following tasks without delay:

(a) the building of a real party apparatus, without which a proletarian party cannot exist . . .;

(h) the party must do its utmost to get rid of the survivals of right-wing attitudes, bring the entire organization together under the Comintern banner, and set up a really capable, solid nucleus at the centre. Friction between the left and the former centre must be eliminated . . .;

(i) the international contacts of the French CP must be improved. Above all, permanent and unbroken relations with the KPD must be maintained;

(j) French heavy industry is becoming of steadily greater importance in imperialist conflicts and inter-imperialist relations. The CPF must wage a struggle against the growing influence of French heavy industry, particularly in connexion with the Experts' report, and in closest fighting collaboration with the KPD;

(k) the recruitment of class-conscious communist elements in the CGTU must be accelerated . . .;

(l) the CGTU leaders must adopt a clear position in the struggle against anarchism and vulgar syndicalism of the old type. In this struggle no concessions must be made to the false theory of 'neutrality'. . . .

3. *Germany*

The prospects for the German revolution, as outlined by the ECCI in the autumn of 1923, remain unchanged. It is not impossible that the victory of 'democratic-pacifism' in England and in France will give a temporary access of strength to the German bourgeoisie and German social-democracy. . . . All this complicates the political situation in Germany and may mean a slowing down of development. Nevertheless, by its very nature the international position of the German bourgeoisie and social-democracy remains hopeless. . . . The internal crisis may come to a head very quickly. . . .

The party crisis has been surmounted. But to ensure that no trace of it survives and to avoid new dangers, the present *Zentrale* of the party must:

(*a*) Vigorously oppose any inclination to leave the social-democratic unions; oblige all party members without exception to carry out the decisions of the CI and the Frankfurt congress on the trade union question; reorganize the party on the basis of factory cells, which will be a tremendous advantage to the party when it becomes illegal. . . .

The ECCI and all fraternal sections must give unreserved support to the present KPD *Zentrale*. Then the KPD will be able to overcome easily the right-wing tendencies which caused it such tremendous harm and which might here and there again arise.

EXTRACTS FROM A MANIFESTO TO THE PEOPLES OF THE EAST ISSUED
BY THE FIFTH COMINTERN CONGRESS

July 1924   *Protokoll*, v, p. 1048

[In the debate on the ECCI report Nguyen Ai Quoc (Ho Chi Minh) complained that this question was neglected, and Katayama echoed his complaint. Semaoen (Java) said the Dutch party had done very little to encourage the Indonesian party. Manuilsky reported on the national and colonial question (his speech, for the first time at a Comintern congress, linked Stalin's name with Lenin's as a source of revolutionary theory). The question was being brought up again because many parties had made mistakes, and because the formation of the USSR showed how the national question could be solved under the proletarian dictatorship. The new problem they had to consider was the attitude of the CP to parties like the Kuomintang and peasant parties. The Comintern had allowed the Chinese CP to join the KMT, and the Indonesian party to join the Java workers' and peasants' party. Where such parties did not exist, should the CP take the initiative in founding them? The leadership of the national-revolutionary movement must not be left to the nationalist elements. The ECCI report to the congress stated that the KMT was moving to the left and waging a genuine revolutionary struggle against imperialism. It reviewed the differences between the ECCI and the central committee of the Chinese CP on the correct attitude towards the KMT. Manuilsky also dealt with this question; in the discussion a Chinese delegate whose name is given as Chin Wha (Chieh Hua?) stated that by joining the KMT the communists hoped to correct its false attitude and to get the leadership into their hands. They accounted for 20 per cent. of the delegates to the first KMT congress, and had helped to draft its programme and resolutions. When (in March 1924) China had refused to ratify the Sino-Soviet treaty, they had persuaded the KMT to organize a protest demonstration.

Irredentist movements raised particular problems. If there were a revolution in Germany, what should their attitude be to the Germans in the Sudetenland? It was a mistake to think that the national question could not be solved until after the proletarian revolution; this would mean passivity in regard to a question of burning importance; or that it could be settled by constitutional changes, as the Austrian social-democrats had believed before the war. Not enough anti-colonial propaganda was done by the parties in the metropolitan countries, not enough attention paid to the common interests of bourgeoisie and proletariat in the national struggle. When, a year earlier, they had issued a summons to the colonial slaves to rise against their masters, a French communist group in Algiers had protested that France was bringing civilization to its colonies. The French party did nothing to organize colonial workers in France; it had put up seven candidates in the colonies, but all were French. The British party was also passive.

In the discussion Roy suggested that the metropolitan parties had failed to work well in this respect because they were confused. There was not one comprehensive formula covering all cases. Colonies could be divided into the patriarchal-feudal, the semi-colonial, which were nominally independent but actually under outside financial and military control, and the colonies which were under the political, economic, and military rule of an imperialist Power, and even these categories had to be subdivided. The national bourgeoisie were forced to fight imperialism because it hampered the development of the country's productive forces; communists should organize the masses to support that fight so long as it was genuinely conducted. But imperialism needed allies inside; sometimes it relied on the feudalists, sometimes on the intellectuals. With the growth of internal class contradictions, imperialism tried to split and weaken the national movement by making concessions to the bourgeoisie, who, when they came to power, would be hostile to the proletariat. They could not therefore be given unconditional support.

Some nationalist demands supported by the Comintern caused dismay in the sections concerned. In Central Europe and the Balkans, the communist parties were to support the demand for a federation of national republics, and to organize their fractions within the organizations of the national movement and try to gain control of them. Manuilsky reported that the manifesto in favour of Macedonian independence published by the Balkan Federation had provoked a strong protest to the ECCI from the Greek Communist Party, which refused to publish the manifesto. On 15 October 1924 an ECCI presidium statement reported strong opposition from the Czech party to the Comintern policy on the national question, which, applied to Czechoslovakia, would imply the break-up of the State.

Speaking at the ECCI plenum a year earlier, in June 1923, Zinoviev had said:

'What we ask is that those of our parties in countries where the national question is important should learn how to make use of the nationalist element against the bourgeois regime. Our parties must try to set in movement against the government those elements which are naturally discontented'—as the Russian party had stirred up Ukrainian nationalists against Kerensky. 'Of course we did not admit Ukrainian nationalists into our party; there was no question of that. But we did exploit their discontent for the good of the proletarian revolution.' They had been told that after the revolution they would be independent, not that Karl Marx had said that the proletariat had no fatherland.

Manuilsky reported for the commission; they had agreed on five resolutions, covering the colonies, the Far East, the Middle East, Central Europe and the Balkans, and Negroes. He proposed referring them to the enlarged Executive. At the meeting of the enlarged Executive on 12 July he proposed that they be referred to the presidium. The proposal was accepted.]

The Communist International and the entire world proletariat are following with tense and steady attention your heroic struggle for national independence, for liberation from the crushing pressure of international capital.

In their *Drang nach Osten* to capture new markets the international bourgeoisie are accustomed to thinking of the Eastern countries as the object of pitiless and rapacious exploitation, as the source of their colonial power. In your millions, you, the masses who inhabit the vast spaces of the Near, Middle, and Far East, are in the eyes of the bourgeoisie their inalienable slaves, born for the sole purpose of creating wealth for the ruling class of Western Europe and America.

During the world war the capitalists of all countries were generous in high-sounding declarations and promised the colonies they rule autonomy, home rule, virtual independence. That was a cunning diplomatic manœuvre of the exploiting bourgeoisie, designed at a critical moment to keep their colonies obedient and to secure fresh reinforcements for their depleted armies from this rich human reservoir.

But once the blood-bath was over the imperialist world bourgeoisie cynically forgot their promises and turned with fresh and unexampled force to the throttling of India, the robbing of China, the division of Turkey, and the enslaving of Persia.

In reply you, the oppressed peoples of the East, have risen as one in the struggle for your national freedom.

Remember that in this selfless struggle you are not alone.

On your side you have the unbounded sympathy of the most advanced proletarians of all countries. The same rapacious bourgeoisie who oppress and exploit you in the colonial and semi-colonial countries of the East oppress and torment equally ruthlessly the working class of Western Europe and America.

Our roads, which lead to the overthrow of capitalist forced labour and imperialist oppression, coincide exactly. For you, as for the working class of the West, true and final liberation is possible only in close alliance and common struggle against world imperialism. . . .

The fifth congress of the Communist International extends a brotherly hand to you for mutual help and support in the common struggle. It sends greetings to you, young communist parties of the East, working and fighting in conditions of extreme difficulty, economic backwardness, feudal survivals, and barbaric torture.

In unceasing struggle against the imperialists and native feudalists, the communist parties of the East will now as before support every honest expression of the movement for national liberation directed against the exploiting yoke of foreign capital, thus confronting the rapacious international bourgeoisie with the anti-imperialist united front.

The fifth congress of the Communist International welcomes you, too, peoples of Turkey and Afghanistan, who have thrown off the vassal's yoke and repelled all the attacks of the imperialist bandits. At the same time the congress sends fraternal greetings to the Chinese Kuomintang party and the People's Revolutionary Party of Mongolia, who are forging a great and bright future for their peoples.

DECISION OF THE SOUVARINE COMMISSION OF THE FIFTH COMINTERN CONGRESS

July 1924   *Thesen und Resolutionen*, v, p. 187

[Souvarine was an outspoken follower of Trotsky from the outset of the dispute in the Russian Communist Party, and the first prominent foreign communist to be expelled for Trotskyism. Trotsky's *New Course*, which Souvarine published in French 'with a wholly tendentious preface', was a collection of articles that had appeared in the Russian press criticizing bureaucracy in the party, and the excessive power of the party apparatus, urging a greater measure of inner-party democracy, etc.; it was published in Russia early in 1924. It was in a letter to a party meeting, included in this collection, that Trotsky referred to the pressure of the bureaucracy on young members, the basis for the subsequent charge against him that he had attempted to turn the younger generation against 'the old guard'. In November 1923 Humbert-Droz had written to Moscow from Paris deploring Souvarine's return to France. There had been many painful incidents since his arrival; he quarrelled with Treint, who was still at loggerheads with Sellier. At the thirteenth congress of the RCP Manuilsky accused the opposition of carrying the debate within that party into the Comintern. It was no accident that in the French party the right wing, led by Souvarine, supported the opposition in the RCP and the Brandler group in Germany, and favoured communist support for the British Labour Government. Souvarine spoke at the congress and denied Manuilsky's charges. Like many others in the French party, he said, he had been shocked by the bitterness of the Russian dispute. Trotsky was an international figure; for the world proletariat his name was a synonym for the revolution, and the tone of the attacks on him was unworthy. By 22 votes to 2 the French central committee had asked its representative on the ECCI to intervene, not in support of the opposition, but to put an end to the polemics which reflected on the entire Russian party and the Comintern. There was no question of principle involved. The lies spread about Trotsky had impelled him, Souvarine, to come to his defence. He knew the central committee would carry the day at the congress, but he thought it his duty to maintain his position.

The congress of the French CP at Lyons in January 1924 had passed a resolution put forward by Souvarine and his followers complaining of over-centralism and mechanical discipline in the party. It was directed against Treint, known to be a supporter of Zinoviev. Treint replied in *Bulletin Communiste*, but Souvarine was not allowed to reply to Treint, although he was at the time editor of that periodical. He published a statement in the *Bulletin* explaining that he obeyed from discipline, but would appeal to the party. A meeting of the political bureau summoned by Treint agreed to ask the ECCI to remove Souvarine from the editorship and from the post of French representative in Moscow. This was endorsed by the French central committee.

The ECCI report to the Comintern congress stated that, after a vote in the French central committee which gave a majority of 22 against 3 on the position in the Russian party and on the communist attitude to the Labour Government, Souvarine, in the minority, had resigned from the politbureau, and Rosmer from his post as general manager of *L'Humanité*. A conference of district secretaries in April, and of the National Council in May, had given overwhelming support to the majority. At the ECCI meeting preceding the congress the French delegation disavowed Souvarine (who was present as a member of the ECCI) as a member of the French delegation and proposed that he should be accorded only a consultative voice. He had published the *Cours Nouveau* on his own responsibility. Souvarine in reply criticized the prevailing desire for 100 per cent. unanimity. As to the letter from the CPF congratulating the Labour Government (which had not in fact been sent), it was drafted at the request of the CPGB and had been approved by the French central committee against one vote.

It was decided to set up a commission to inquire into Souvarine's conduct. The question was referred by the congress to the session of the ECCI which met immediately afterwards. Souvarine had been asked to attend, but had not done so. The Italian delegates, Ercoli and Bordiga, pleaded mitigating circumstances in his favour. Discipline in general in the French party was lax, and personal policies were being pursued at the time. Nor would the French workers understand his expulsion, since in the past he had been considered the strongest advocate of adherence to the Comintern line. Sellier insisted that Souvarine had misused his authority. The five Italian votes were cast against the resolution.]

In the course of its work the Souvarine commission has come to the conclusion that communist discipline in the French Communist Party is still far from being completely and unconditionally applied. The commission is of the opinion that it is absolutely essential for the enlarged

Executive of the CI to intervene energetically by means of an open letter to the party membership, to remind them of the real meaning of party discipline, and to demand of them to ensure its strictest application, with severe penalties for every serious breach of discipline and all personal policy, from whatever member of the party it may proceed.

After hearing several comrades of the French delegation and comrade Boris Souvarine, and after a careful examination of all the material concerning the breaches of discipline with which comrade Souvarine is charged, the commission is unanimously of the opinion:

1. that Souvarine has committed breaches of discipline of the gravest kind, by

(a) his statement in the *Bulletin Communiste*;
(b) his letters to the subscribers to the *Bulletin Communiste* containing attacks on the party central committee;
(c) his publication, without the knowledge of the customary party authorities, of comrade Trotsky's pamphlet *The New Course*, with an introduction hostile to the party and the CI;

2. that these actions show that Souvarine's conduct is governed by a petty-bourgeois spirit which places personal feelings above party interests;

3. that this attitude on the part of a particularly responsible party comrade has brought confusion into the ranks of the CPF, and has indeed endangered party discipline as such;

4. that the explanations given by comrade Souvarine do not mitigate the gravity of his breaches of discipline, which were repeated over many months; and that they bear witness to the same petty-bourgeois cast of mind which characterized his entire attitude during the events which aroused such excitement in the party.

The commission therefore recommends to the ECCI:

1. To agree to the request put forward by the CPF delegation to the fifth congress to expel comrade Souvarine;

2. to grant the French section of the CI the right to propose Souvarine's readmission at the sixth world congress of the CI if, during the interval, he shows a loyal attitude to the party and the CI.

RESOLUTION OF THE FIFTH COMINTERN CONGRESS ON THE PROGRAMME OF THE COMMUNIST INTERNATIONAL

8 *July* 1924   *Protokoll*, v, p. 1008

[Bukharin reported on this question. He asked the congress to accept a draft for discussion by the sections. The programme was needed to train the party ideologically, to determine the Comintern's goal and the road to it, and to demonstrate and promote its international unity. A number of parties were showing signs of old Hegelianism, Lassallism, idealistic voluntarism. The revolutionary philosophy of Marxism must be clearly stated in the programme. A German comrade had asserted that it was nonsense to talk of a labour aristocracy and surplus profits for German imperialism; high wages were paid because the workers had fought for them and increasing productivity made them possible. But if they discarded the theory of surplus profits and the corruption of the labour aristocracy, they would lose the theoretical basis for the fight against imperialism and the labour aristocracy. The programme must also answer one of the commonest charges of the social-democrats, that revolution interrupted the continuity of production and exposed the workers to suffering and starvation. Revolution, like war, had its overhead costs, and one of them was the temporary destruction of productive forces. Bukharin and Thalheimer, who also reported on the programme, discussed the value of war communism and the New Economic Policy introduced in Russia in 1921. War communism was a political measure, designed to break bourgeois resistance; NEP ensured the growth of productive forces. Maturity for revolution and maturity for socialism after the revolution were two different things. It was incorrect to think that NEP was something to be excused on the grounds of political expediency, a concession to the petty bourgeoisie. On the contrary, it was clear that NEP was the only policy which ensured the growth of the productive forces; war communism had been a necessary corrective required for the purposes of the direct struggle against the bourgeoisie. There was never a clear-cut case of only proletariat and only bourgeoisie; there were various intermediate stages and subordinate classes and forms of economy. In this mixture the proletariat must retain hegemony, and socialized industry must keep hegemony in economic life. Socialism could not be established at one stroke because of the existence of these intermediate forces; the transition period, in which they were gradually eliminated and replaced, was NEP. War communism represented the rational consumption of stocks in hand to guarantee victory in the civil war. Thalheimer referred to the need to reformulate their position on the role of the party; as given in the *Communist Manifesto* it was out of date. He also suggested that bourgeois projects for agrarian reform should not be opposed or passively accepted, but pushed forward in a revolutionary direction; for example, to bourgeois proposals for breaking up large estates they should add 'without compensation'. In reporting back from the commission later in the congress, Bukharin stated that they had 'deleted the entire passage about the right to Red intervention, etc., but not on theoretical grounds'.]

1. The congress accepts the draft worked out by the programme commission as a basis for discussion in the sections.

2. An editorial commission shall undertake the final editing of the draft in accordance with the decisions of the commission.

3. The congress instructs the Executive to appoint a standing programme commission, which shall as soon as possible publish the draft together with the necessary explanatory material, take charge of its discussion within the International, and evaluate the results.

4. The final decision on the programme shall be taken at the next congress.

THE FOURTH ENLARGED PLENUM OF THE ECCI

[The enlarged Executive met for one day (12 June 1924) before the fifth Comintern congress opened, and for two days after it had ended, on 12 and 13 July. On 12 July the Executive dealt with the work referred to it by the congress. Manuilsky reported for the Italian commission. MacManus reported that the Japanese commission had been unable to work 'owing to a number of incidents', and the Japanese question was referred to the presidium; the resolution submitted on behalf of the Bulgarian commission was adopted unanimously, but does not appear to have been published. The resolution on Poland, adopted unanimously, confirmed the charge of right-wing deviations among the Polish communist leaders as shown in their attitude to the Russian opposition, to the disputes in the KPD, and to internal Polish affairs; they had systematically obstructed the Polish minority which truly reflected Comintern policy. An extraordinary conference of the Polish party was to be called to correct the line and choose a new central committee. In the meantime the Executive was to appoint a committee of five to take charge. The resolution on the question of the intellectuals was referred to the Executive.

The report of the Swedish commission was given by Thaelmann. Höglund held the ECCI responsible for the split in the Norwegian party and resigned from that body, but in December 1923, after a conference between representatives of the ECCI and the Swedish party, he withdrew his resignation. The plenum adopted the resolution of the Swedish commission against the two votes of Höglund and his followers, who described it as a catastrophe. Höglund, contrary to Comintern statutes, had called a congress of the Swedish party without consulting the ECCI. Asked if he would co-operate in its executive, Höglund said that if the Swedish central committee thought it possible to continue on the lines of the resolution he would co-operate. The resolution amounted to a vote of no confidence in the Swedish party leaders; Samuelson, for the Swedish minority, and Bukharin said that the central committee majority had always been anti-Comintern. Zinoviev suggested that, to avoid humiliating Höglund, the discussion and the resolution need not be published, but only circularized to the parties, if they were assured that the decision would be carried out. They did not wish to change the composition of the central committee, but to send an ECCI representative to see that Comintern decisions were carried out. The resolution was published. An ECCI resolution of 11 August 1924 'warned Höglund for the last time'. He had referred to the resolutions of the fifth congress as a 'Jesuit comedy'. At the end of August he and his followers were condemned by the ECCI as 'renegades and enemies of communism'. Although he carried with him a majority of the Swedish central committee (the opposing faction was led by Kilbom and Samuelson) Höglund took only a minority of the party with him when the split came.

The plenum approved the formation in January 1924 of the Scandinavian communist federation, consisting of the Norwegian, Swedish, Danish, and Finnish communist parties, with headquarters in Oslo. It was agreed to set up a standing Negro commission, with representatives of the British, French, and Belgian parties, to organize propaganda among Negroes.]

EXTRACTS FROM AN ECCI MANIFESTO ON THE DAWES REPORT

July 1924   *Inprekorr*, iv, 99, p. 1267, 1 *August* 1924

[On 1 May 1924 the ECCI called a conference in Berlin of representatives of the German, French, Belgian, and Italian parties (the British were invited but did not attend) to discuss the Dawes report and draw up a provisional programme of action to fight the 'second and more cynical Versailles'. The conference issued an appeal to the European proletariat to oppose the report, which meant the colonization of Germany and the enslavement of its working class. On 24 June 1924 a conference was held in Cologne of representatives of the French and German communist parties and revolutionary unions; the Dawes plan, said the resolution adopted at the conference, was a scheme to organize world capitalism for the fight against the proletariat and against Russia; German capitalists would act as the slave-drivers. It was agreed that the communist parliamentary fractions in both countries would oppose the report.

On 9 October 1924, after the adoption of the Dawes report, communist deputies from France, Germany, Britain, Belgium, Holland, Switzerland, Italy, and Czechoslovakia met in Cologne to co-ordinate action; the resolution adopted, which dealt with hours, wages, unemployment, etc., described the plan as an attack on working-class standards. A manifesto issued by the Comintern said that this attack could be met effectively only if the trade union movement were united; it was therefore essential to clear the reformist splitters out of the unions.]

TO THE PROLETARIANS OF ALL COUNTRIES

After four years of war and six years of fruitless conferences on the division of the spoils, the victorious imperialist robbers are planning to squeeze out of the German proletariat the profits of their robbery. American capital is once again joining the old European robber band. . . . After four years of a fruitless reparations war, America, the most frightful and furious of the belligerents, is again entering the European scene. Once again the working millions are to be mowed down by the tanks of hunger and the poison gas of pacifist illusions. This is the 'new method' of reparations policy.

The old fascist war method, which culminated in the occupation of the Ruhr as a solution of the reparations problem and as a means of strengthening capitalism, did not stand the test. It frightened the invader with the spectre of communism in Germany, brought down the franc, furthered the decline of world capitalism and the destruction of the European market, and so brought about an economic and to some extent even a political crisis in America.

The world war ended with the 'peaceful war' of the Versailles treaty, which was followed by the Ruhr war. After the Ruhr war, the 'peaceful war' has begun again, this time in the form of a systematic, elaborate, considered squeezing of the German proletariat according to the Morgan-group plan which goes by the name of the Experts' report. Anglo-American capital needs Europe as a market, as a colony; with this in mind finance-capital thrusts the Labour Government forward as a screen and turns to 'civilized' and 'peaceful' methods, recommended by the best experts, of throttling the proletariat.

International social-democracy, the trusted servant of the hangmen, comes to their aid. Ten years ago it voted the war credits; everywhere it supported its national bourgeoisie; it supports the Versailles treaty, dictated to the defeated peoples, and set its signature to it; in all countries it promotes efforts to restore capitalism at the expense of the proletariat; only on the surface did it fight against the Versailles treaty, against its robberies, against the Ruhr occupation. And now it is the first to sing the praises of the Morgan-group plan. . . . This is being done in order to bind the revolution in the chains of pacifist-democratic illusions. In every treachery to the working class the Amsterdam International was a loyal ally of the Second International. Even its left wing did not utter a single word at the Vienna congress about the need to liquidate Versailles. The Dawes plan was subjected to formal criticism, but at the joint conference of the two Internationals it was stated to be 'the only possible solution'.

What is French imperialism after? It wishes to establish the political and military hegemony of France on the European continent for ever. It wants to perpetuate the Versailles treaty; it wants to perpetuate the enslavement of the German proletariat; it wants to arm for a new war. It wants to squeeze the blood out of the veins of the German proletariat, and the marrow out of its bones, to ensure the payment of reparations. . . .

What is English imperialism after? It wants to frustrate and break French hegemony in its own interests. MacDonald is carrying out the programme worked out by the Conservative Baldwin for the construction of an air force, and reduces the old military budget by a few miserable pence. The allies, France and England, can neither get on together nor part. For the present they are avoiding war, because neither has its armaments ready, and above all because America has not yet decided which of the two hostile imperialist groups it will support. . . .

Germany is to be turned into an international colony, a field of exploitation for the robbers of all countries. All the bourgeois German parties are wholly in favour of the Experts' report. . . . The London conference imposes crushing taxes on German industry, but these are to be shunted to the last penny on to the German proletariat, the urban middle classes, and the working peasantry. That is why all the German bourgeois parties are in favour of the report and only seem to be carrying on a struggle against Entente capital. The social-democrats and trade union bureau-crats—traitors by profession—have again offered their services to world capital and are helping to establish the dictatorship of American imperialism throughout Europe.

The London conference means for the German proletariat a twelve-hour day, the dismissal of half the railwaymen, a steep reduction in the number of public employees, work to the point of exhaustion, insane taxation, higher tariffs, higher fares and prices. The German workers will become the white slaves of democracy, coolies of pacifism, involuntary strike-breakers for the whole world. . . .

The London conference may lead to a new attempt to build an imperialist united front to exploit Soviet Russia and to introduce imperialist supervision of Germany's trade with Russia. . . .

Down with the international stock exchange and its branch, the Second International!

Down with the Versailles treaty!

STATUTES OF THE AGITATION AND PROPAGANDA DEPARTMENT OF THE ECCI

August 1924   *Inprekorr*, iv, 107, p. 1381, 15 *August* 1924

[The statutes were published over the signature of Bela Kun.]

1. The agitation and propaganda department is an organ of the Executive of the Comintern. Through this department the Executive Committee and its organs organize, unify, and guide the entire agitation and propaganda activities of the Comintern and its sections.

2. Task of the department: To organize the agitation and propaganda activity of the Comintern, to guide the corresponding activity of its sections, to bring uniformity into the activity of the sections by studying, systematizing, and generalizing the experiences of the sections.

I. STRUCTURE OF THE DEPARTMENT

1. The general management of the department, in accordance with the instructions of the Executive Committee of the Comintern, is in the hands of the head of the department or his deputy. At least once a fortnight, if necessary more often, the head of the department shall convene a meeting of the collegium, consisting of (i) the heads of the sub-departments; (ii) the heads of the agitation and propaganda department and the press section of the CC of the RCP, or their representatives; (iii) the head of the organization department of the CI Executive, as well as the head of the

agitation and propaganda department of the Executive of the YCI, and a representative of the international women's secretariat. If necessary, representatives of other departments of the secretariat, members of the Executive, and the rapporteurs for individual countries or groups of countries may be called in.

2. Important questions of agitation and propaganda work shall be discussed twice a year at meetings of the enlarged collegium, which shall consist, in addition to those enumerated above, of representatives of all departments of the Comintern secretariat and the heads of the agitation and propaganda departments of the German, French, Czechoslovakian, Italian, and English sections, and possibly others.

3. The work of the department shall be divided among the following sub-departments:

(*a*) sub-department for agitation;
(*b*) sub-department for propaganda;
(*c*) sub-department for press and publications;
(*d*) sub-department to collate the experiences of the sections.

4. Other sub-departments and commissions may be set up if necessary, with the agreement of the Executive.

II. SUB-DEPARTMENT FOR AGITATION

The tasks of the sub-department for agitation are the following:

(*a*) to work over and carry out the political-agitation tasks set by the Executive Committee; to popularize the idea and the slogans of the Comintern;
(*b*) to determine the general direction of the agitation work of the sections; to work out general directives; to take charge of and distribute material for particularly urgent political campaigns;
(*c*) to work out and communicate the methods, forms, and techniques of mass agitation.

For this purpose the sub-department draws up circulars and periodical instructions in close collaboration with the sub-department for press and publications.

III. SUB-DEPARTMENT FOR PROPAGANDA

1. The tasks of the sub-department for propaganda are the following:

(*a*) to make uniform, to systematize, and to guide party education work (propaganda of Marxism–Leninism);
(*b*) to work out the forms and methods of education work within the party;

(*c*) to help draw up the material for education, curricula for party schools, lecture courses, Marxist reading circles;

(*d*) to work on questions concerning the school policy of communist parties and to give them political direction;

(*e*) to guide and supervise the cultural societies connected with the communist parties.

2. The sub-department for propaganda pays special attention to the party life of the Comintern sections, devises measures to organize the theoretical forces of the communist parties, attends to the development of their theoretical and literary activity.

3. The sub-department for propaganda shall promote the organization of party schools in the Comintern sections by working out programmes and teaching plans.

The sub-department shall set up a methodology commission to examine and work out the methods for the propaganda of Marxism–Leninism.

The sub-department shall maintain the closest relations with the Marx–Engels Institute, the Lenin Institute, and the Communist Academy, as well as the Institute of Red Professors in Moscow, and shall utilize the results of the research of these Institutes for the propaganda activities of the communist parties.

IV. SUB-DEPARTMENT FOR PRESS AND PUBLICATIONS

1. The tasks of the press sub-department are:

(*a*) to guide and supervise the communist party press and publications, and to issue instructions for them;

(*b*) to guide the periodical and information organs of the Executive Committee of the Comintern (with the exception of those in the direct charge of the presidium);

(*c*) to assign tasks to the periodical press of the sections in matters concerning agitation and propaganda; to inform the workers' press about the Soviet Union, and the Russian party press about the activities of the Comintern and its sections.

2. The sub-department for press and publications shall work out plans and material for agitation campaigns in conjunction with the sub-department for agitation.

3. Arrangements for non-periodical publications shall be dealt with by the press and publications sub-department in conjunction with the sub-department for propaganda.

4. The press and publications sub-department shall use for translation work the general machinery of the Comintern secretariat.

V. GENERAL REGULATIONS

1. All circulars of the agitation and propaganda department shall be approved by the secretariat or the Executive before being issued. The most important documents, as well as documents on special questions which have general political significance, must also be signed by one of the secretaries.

2. The agitation and propaganda department takes part through its representatives in all the agitation and propaganda work of the Profintern, the International Peasants' Council, the women's secretariat of the Comintern, the Youth International, the Co-operative International, etc.

3. The agitation and propaganda department shall take steps to enlarge the Comintern secretariat library.

ECCI MANIFESTO ON CHINA

4 September 1924   *Inprekorr*, iv, 117, p. 1538, 9 *September* 1924

[In the summer of 1924 a body called the Merchants' Volunteers, armed and financed by the local compradores in association with British commercial under-takings, challenged KMT control of Canton. On 10 August a boatload of arms destined for the Volunteers was seized by the KMT authorities. On 26 August the British Consul-General threatened naval intervention if the Volunteers were attacked. Protests from Sun Yat-sen to the League of Nations and to Ramsay MacDonald remained unanswered. In October the KMT forces disarmed the Volunteers; the British took no action. The ECCI in collaboration with the RILU bureau started a 'Hands off China' society in the summer of 1924, with branches in a number of countries.]

The British Government, which is a Labour Party Government with a leader of the Second International at its head, is preparing armed inter-vention in South China with the object of overthrowing the Government of the Chinese national-revolutionary Kuomintang Party. The consul of the British Labour Government has transmitted a Note to the Chinese National Government, according to imperialist custom. The Note threatens the Chinese population with shooting if the Chinese National Government defends itself against the revolt of the merchants, who were aided and provided with munitions from the British port of Hong Kong. The leader of the revolt is a Chinese merchant, an agent of the Shanghai–Hong Kong Bank, which belongs to British shipping interests.

Before the eyes of the entire world, of the international revolutionary workers' movement, the MacDonald Government is destroying the basis of the national liberation movement of the long-suffering Chinese people. Sun Yat-sen, the tried leader of China's revolutionary party, who over-threw the despotic Manchu dynasty in 1911 and is now head of the

Government of South China, has stated with full justice that the imperialists have assumed the role of the fallen feudal despotism. The imperialism of the pacifist-democratic MacDonald does not serve Chinese interests, but only those of the English financial system and the Chinese feudal counter-revolution which has tormented China for more than a century.

Comrades! American imperialism is taking the offensive against North China, while English imperialism advances against South China. Herriot's French Government is sending warships from Saigon to Tientsin and Shanghai. The lesser imperialists are attaching themselves to these stronger Powers. Thus world imperialism has organized a conspiracy against the Chinese liberation movement, against the working masses of China, which is being put into operation by the MacDonald Government.

The ink has not yet dried on the MacDonald–Herriot declaration at the London conference which proclaimed the opening of an era of peace and disarmament, and already these Governments are sending warships to massacre the working millions of China.

Workers of England! You cannot allow British imperialists to shoot down, in your name, Chinese revolutionaries, as they did in the summer in Hankow and Yangtse-kiang, when English hangmen shot the leaders of the railwaymen's union and the dockworkers. You cannot allow a Government which calls itself a Labour Government to encourage feudal reaction in order that British banks and British colonizers can get their profits more easily.

Comrades! English workers! You must make the Trade Union Congress now meeting in Hull intervene to stop the blood-bath in China. You must raise a mighty protest against armed intervention in South China and stay the hand of the imperialists who are training their guns on the centre of the Chinese national-revolutionary movement.

Long live the Chinese national-revolutionary movement!

Down with the imperialism of MacDonald and Herriot.

INSTRUCTIONS FROM THE ECCI TO THE CPGB ON THE CONDUCT OF THE CPGB IN THE BRITISH GENERAL ELECTION OF OCTOBER 1924

10 *October* 1924   Cmd. 2682, p. 48

[The instructions were accompanied by the following letter from Kuusinen, of the ECCI secretariat:

'Herewith a copy of the instructions adopted by the Executive to-day which have already been sent you by cable. We are also sending you the speeches of Comrades Zinoviev and Bukharin at to-day's session of the Presidium. The instructions given in these speeches should also be considered as instructions from the Executive to your Party.

'We expect that you will energetically carry through the election campaign already begun. In particular we want to emphasise the importance of immediately issuing your weekly paper as a daily newspaper. It is the opinion of the Secretariat that your Party should take advantage of the election campaign in order to transform the "Workers' Weekly" into a *permanent* daily. We know that this demands the greatest efforts on the part of the British Communist Party and great self-sacrifice on the part of the sympathetic working-class masses; but it is not impossible.

'Conscious of the great historical importance of your fight we wish you every luck and for our part will of course give you our help.'

The 1924 conference of the Labour Party had voted by 4 million against 200,000 not to accept communist party affiliation, and by a smaller majority that no communist was to be endorsed as a Labour Party candidate in elections. It also voted that members of the communist party were not eligible for individual membership of the Labour Party.]

TO THE CENTRAL COMMITTEE OF THE COMMUNIST PARTY OF GREAT BRITAIN

The Executive sends the following instructions for the election:

Sharp criticism in principle of the conduct of the MacDonald Government.

The imperialist character of the Government should be unmasked.

A bitter fight should be carried on against MacDonald's policy in China, India and Egypt.

Against the League of Nations.

Against the danger of war and naval policy.

Against the economic exploitation and national oppression of the Irish working-class by the English bourgeoisie.

A sharp fight should be conducted for the acceptance of the Communist Party of Great Britain into the Labour Party.

The adoption of bourgeois politicians as labour candidates and the rejection of old working-class leaders should be criticised.

Active agitation should be conducted against the I.L.P.

In general, we support Labour candidates.

Certain candidates should be put forward where this will not help the bourgeois candidates.

The appeals for support of the Labour candidates should contain a sharp fundamental criticism.

Slogans for the election campaign:—

For the Anglo-Russian Treaty.

Not His Majesty's Labour Government but a real workers' government.

Down with the Dawes Report.

Put the workers' charter into effect.

Four pounds per week for every unemployed worker.

A six-hour day.

For international trade union unity.

The fraternisation of soldiers and workers.

Soldiers should not shoot upon workers on strike.

Votes for soldiers and sailors.

Instructions for conducting the campaign:—

Every candidate should distribute and sign Campbell's appeal.

Campbell should issue another manifesto to the soldiers and sailors.

Roy should be put forward as candidate.

If possible, he should be brought into the election campaign.

Send him a telegram.

During the elections the "Workers' Weekly" should come out daily.

Further instructions follow. Representatives of the German, French and Chinese workers will take part in the election campaign. Invitations have been sent from here. The Georgian trade unions will send an appeal to the British trade unions. A manifesto from the German, French and British Parties to the British proletariat follows by the next post.

EXTRACTS FROM THE MODEL STATUTES FOR A COMMUNIST PARTY DRAFTED BY THE ORGANIZATION DEPARTMENT OF THE ECCI

January 1925   *Inprekorr*, v, 17, p. 212, 29 *January* 1925

[This draft was discussed and accepted unanimously at the organization conference called by the orgbureau of the ECCI which met at the same time as the fifth enlarged plenum; the resolutions of the organization conference were ratified by the ECCI in April and published in May. The ECCI report to the sixth Comintern congress stated that from the middle of 1925 the sections had begun to revise their statutes under the guidance of the organization department. A great deal of resistance had been encountered, but for most European countries the work had been completed. In the colonial and Latin American countries it had only just begun.]

I. THE NAME OF THE PARTY

1. The Communist Party is a section of the Communist International and is called: Communist Party of ———, section of the Communist International.

II. PARTY MEMBERSHIP

2. Membership is open to those who accept the programme and statutes of the Communist International and the Communist Party. The membership of a primary unit of the party consists of those who take an active part in its work, submit to all decisions of the Comintern and the party, and pay their membership dues regularly.

3. Acceptance of new members is effected through the party cell, and must be confirmed by the area or district committee. . . .

III. PARTY STRUCTURE

6. Like all sections of the Comintern, the ——— Communist Party is built up on the basis of democratic centralism. Its chief principles are:

(a) Party organs, both lower and higher, are elected at aggregate meetings of the party membership, at conferences, and at congresses.

(b) Periodical reporting by party organs to their electors.

(c) Binding recognition of the decisions of higher party organs by lower; strict party discipline, and prompt and precise execution of decisions of the ECCI and leading party organs. . . . Party questions shall be discussed by the membership only until the question is decided by the appropriate party organ. When a decision has been taken by a Comintern congress, a party congress, or a leading party organ, it must be unconditionally carried out, even when part of the membership or some local organizations do not agree with the decision.

7. In conditions of illegality it is permissible for higher party organs to decide the composition of the lower, as well as to co-opt members, subject to ratification by higher organs.

8. On local questions party organizations are autonomous, within the framework of Comintern and party decisions.

9. The highest instance of any party organization is the aggregate-membership meeting of that organization, the conference, or the congress.

10. The aggregate meeting, conference, or congress elects the leadership, which serves as the leading organ between such meetings and carries out the current work of the organization.

11. The outline structure of the party is as follows:

(a) For the entire national territory: party congress—central committee.

(b) For the territory of a district: district conference—district committee.

(c) For the territory of a sub-district: sub-district conference—sub-district committee.

(d) For the territory of part of a town: area conference—area committee.

(e) For a small town, village, etc.: local-cell conference (village-cell conference) or local aggregate (village aggregate)—local committee.

(f) For individual factories, offices, shops, estates, streets, etc.: cell meeting—cell committee.

12. To carry out special party tasks, party committees set up special departments, e.g. for organization, agitation, propaganda, trade unions,

women, etc. These departments are subordinate to the party committee and work on its instructions. . . .

IV. THE CELL

13. The primary organization of the party, its foundation, is the factory cell (in factory, mine, workshop, office, etc.), to which all party members working at that place must belong. . . . It must have at least three members.

14. In factories in which there are only one or two party members, they shall be attached to the nearest factory cell. . . . *Note*: Party members who do not work in a factory, etc. shall, as a rule, be attached to factory cells in their neighbourhood; otherwise they form street cells.

15. The cell is the organization which connects the party with the workers and small peasants. The functions of the cell are to carry out party work among the non-party working masses by means of systematic communist agitation and propaganda: to recruit new members, distribute party literature, issue a factory newspaper, conduct cultural and educational work among the party members and workers in the factory, to work persistently and uninterruptedly to win all official positions in the factory, to intervene in all industrial conflicts and demands by the employees, to explain them from the standpoint of the revolutionary class struggle, to win the leadership in all struggles of the employees by persistent and unflagging work.

16. To conduct its current work the cell elects a committee, consisting of three to five members. . . . The committee is responsible for the work of the cell.

V. THE LOCAL GROUP

17. The local group consists of the cells in a given area. . . .

18. . . . At least half of the local committee must be members of factory cells. The committee elects a responsible secretary or chairman. The committee is responsible for the work of the group. It is in charge of fraction work in the area.

19. As a rule a local aggregate-membership meeting is held once a month.

VI. AREA ORGANIZATION

20. The highest party instance within the town area is the area committee, elected by the area conference. The basis of representation at the area conference is decided by the district committee.

21. The area committee carries out the decisions of higher party bodies and guides the entire party work of the area. It convenes an area conference at least once a quarter. The area committee chooses an area secretary in consultation with the district committee.

22. The area conference is attended by delegates from the cells. It receives and approves the reports of the area committee, and elects the area committee.

23. The area committee is in charge of fraction work in the area.

VII. THE SUB-DISTRICT ORGANIZATION

24. The sub-district committee . . . is elected by the sub-district conference; the basis of representation at the conference is determined by the district committee.

25. The sub-district committee . . . guides all party work in its area. It convenes a sub-district conference at least twice a year. The secretary is selected in consultation with the district committee.

26. Cell delegates attend the sub-district conference, which receives and approves the reports of the sub-district committee, and elects the sub-district committee.

27. In the town in which the sub-district committee has its seat, party work is conducted by the committee.

28. Fraction work in the sub-district is in the charge of the sub-district committee.

VIII. DISTRICT ORGANIZATION

29. The highest party instance in a district is the district conference, which meets twice a year. Extraordinary conferences may be convened by the district committee at the request of half the party organizations in the district or of the central committee. The district conference receives reports from the district committee and the district audit commission, and elects the district committee and the district audit commission.

30. The district committee is the highest party organ in the district in the period between district conferences. It must consist in part of factory workers, and include representatives from the chief towns of the district and other important centres. It determines how often it shall meet in plenary session, but this shall be at least once a month. The district committee elects a bureau to conduct current work. The number of members on the committee and the bureau is determined by the party centre. The district committee also elects a district secretary, subject to confirmation by the centre. The secretary must have been a party member for at least three years. Exceptions can be made with the consent of the centre.

31. The district conference elects an audit commission, whose function it is to check the entire administration and finances of the district, and any district party enterprises.

32. The district committee carries out the decisions of the central committee and is obliged to set up special bodies to deal with various tasks

(organization, agitation, propaganda, trade unions, work among peasants, women, etc.). These bodies shall as a rule be in the charge of a member of the district committee, and shall carry out their work under the direction of the district committee. The district committee, in agreement with the CC, appoints the editorial board of the district party paper. The district committee is in charge of all party work within the district. It is responsible for its work to the district conference and the CC, to which it is obliged to send written reports about its work every month.

33. The town in which the district committee has its seat has no party committee of its own. The work is done by the district committee. . . .

IX. THE PARTY CONFERENCE

34. The party conference meets as a rule twice a year. The basis of representation and the composition of the conference are decided by the centre. The district representatives are chosen by the district committee. The centre may call in individual party workers to the conference meetings, with consultative voice.

35. Decisions of party conference enter into force after ratification by the CC.

36. The party conference may elect the delegation to world congresses of the Comintern if it is held immediately before the world congress.

X. THE PARTY CONGRESS

37. The party congress is the highest party instance and is as a rule convened once a year by the central committee in agreement with the Executive Committee of the Comintern. Extraordinary congresses may be convened by the CC either on its own initiative or on the initiative of the ECCI, or at the request of at least one-half of the total membership represented at the previous congress. An extraordinary congress cannot, however, be held without the consent of the ECCI. The convening of the congress, as well as its agenda, must be notified to the members at least one month in advance. The congress will be entitled to take decisions if at least one-half of the total membership is represented.

The basis of representation at the congress is decided either by the central committee or by the party conference held before the congress.

38. The party congress

(a) receives the report of the CC and the central audit commission;
(b) decides questions of the party programme;
(c) takes decisions on all political, tactical, and organizational questions;
(d) elects the CC and the central audit commission, etc.

39. The party congress is composed of delegates, who must be elected by the district conferences. In conditions of illegality the election of dele-

gates may as an emergency measure be replaced, with the consent of the ECCI, by the appointment of delegates by the district committee. The congress may also with the consent of the ECCI be replaced by a party conference.

XI. THE CENTRAL COMMITTEE

40. The CC is the highest party organ between party congresses. It represents the party *vis-à-vis* other party institutions, sets up various party organs, guides the entire political and organizational work, appoints the editorial board of the central organ, which works under its guidance and control, organizes and directs those undertakings which are of importance to the party as a whole, distributes the forces of the party, and manages the party's finances.

The CC is in charge of the work of fractions within those organizations which have a national character.

41. The number of members in the central committee is determined by the party congress.

42. The CC elects from among its members a political bureau to take charge of political work, an organization bureau to conduct the organizational work, and a secretariat (or secretary) for current work. The CC further appoints the heads of the different departments; these should if possible be members of the CC. (*Note*: para. 42 applies only to the larger parties; in smaller parties it is enough for the CC to choose a presidium.) . . .

XII. THE CENTRAL AUDIT COMMISSION

45. The party congress elects a central audit commission to take charge of the party's finances, keep its books, and supervise all the party's business affairs.

XIII. PARTY DISCIPLINE

46. The strictest party discipline is the highest duty of all party members and all party organizations.

Decisions of the CI, the party congress, the party centre, and all the higher party bodies must be carried out promptly and precisely. All questions which provoke differences of opinion may be freely discussed so long as no decision has been reached on them.

47. A breach of party discipline involves punitive measures by the relevant party body. In regard to organizations the following punitive measures may be employed: reprimand; dismissal, and appointment of a provisional committee to exercise the functions of the dismissed body until a conference is convened; dissolution of the organization and re-registration of its members. In regard to individual members the following

measures will be taken: party reprimand, public reprimand, dismissal from post, expulsion for a stated period, final expulsion. . . .

49. The question of the expulsion of a member from the party is proposed by a meeting of the party organization concerned (cell) to the party committee above it. The decision on exclusion enters into force when ratified by the district committee. Appeals may be made up to the highest party instance. While confirmation of expulsion is pending, the member concerned must be withdrawn from party work.

Expulsions are as a rule to be published in the party press. . . .

XIV. PARTY FINANCES

50. The funds of a party organization are derived from members' dues, special collections, returns on party enterprises, contributions from higher party bodies, etc.

51. Membership dues should account for not less than — per cent. of party income. The rate of dues is decided by the party congress or party centre. . . .

52. Those members of the party who, without sufficient cause, fail to pay their dues for three months are to be regarded as expelled from the party; the meeting of the cell concerned is to be informed.

XV. FRACTIONS

53. In all non-party organizations of workers and peasants (trade unions, co-operatives, educational associations, sports leagues, factory committees, committees of the unemployed, municipal councils, parliaments, congresses, conferences, etc.) in which there are at least two communists, a communist fraction must be organized to increase the influence of the party, and to put communist policy into effect in the non-party environment.

54. Fractions are the organs of the party in non-party organizations. They are not independent bodies, but are subordinate to the appropriate party committee.

In regard to its internal affairs and to its current work, the fraction is autonomous. Should differences arise between the fraction and the committee, the committee is obliged to discuss the question afresh with representatives of the fraction, and to reach a conclusion which must be unconditionally obeyed by the fraction. On appeal by the fraction, the question is finally decided by the next higher committee. Pending the appeal, the fraction must carry out the decision of the committee.

55. When discussing questions referring to the work of a fraction, the committee must invite a representative of the fraction to take part, with consultative voice.

56. Communist fractions elect their leadership; the choice must be ratified by the relevant party committee. Fraction leaders are responsible to the committee for the work of the fraction.

The committee is entitled to attach members to the fraction leadership. . . .

57. For all important posts in the organizations in which fractions are active, candidates will be put forward by the fraction in agreement with the appropriate party committee. The transfer of individual comrades from one fraction to another is effected in the same way.

58. Every question to be decided by the body in which the fraction is working must be discussed in advance by the fraction as a whole or by its leadership.

On every question about which the fraction has taken a decision, the members of the fraction must, in the meeting of the organization concerned, speak and vote as one. Disciplinary measures will be taken against any fraction member who infringes this rule.

EXTRACTS FROM THE DRAFT RULES FOR THE ORGANIZATION OF AGITATION AND PROPAGANDA WORK BY THE SECTIONS OF THE COMINTERN, SUBMITTED BY THE AGITPROP DEPARTMENT OF THE ECCI

March 1925   *Inprekorr*, v, 34, p. 514, 12 *March* 1925

[In endorsing these rules at its meeting on 3 April, the ECCI emphasized the need for ideological training of the party membership; its resolution said, in part:

'The enlarged Executive, while directing the attention of all sections to the decisions of the agitprop conference held in connexion with the Executive meeting, underlines the following current tasks in this field:

'1. An end must be put to the passive attitude of sections hitherto towards the question of the party training of the entire party membership. . . .

'2. For the theoretical training of the basic party cadres, every party centre must establish a central party school, with a two to nine months course, according to the practical possibilities. . . . The agitprop department of the ECCI must promote and support these schools in every way.

'3. The enlarged Executive approves the plan to organize international party courses in Moscow, and instructs the presidium to see that work begins in this school in the autumn of the present year. . . .

'6. The steadily growing interest of the broad working masses in the economic and cultural life of the Soviet Union, and the continuing campaign of calumny in the bourgeois and reformist press, make it necessary to devote special attention to supplying correct and comprehensive information about conditions in the Soviet Union. . . . All sections are obliged to maintain the closest contact through their agitprop departments with the agitprop department of the ECCI.'

Speaking at the agitprop conference, Bukharin underlined the importance of theoretical training for future practical activities, and the need to raise the theoretical level of the party press; the English party press was best at dealing with its own local problems; he could not say that the British or American party press showed deviations, because there was no theory at all in their journals. At the same meeting on 3 April a resolution was passed on the tasks of the communist press, which should carry party propaganda into the factories. The press was to be intelligible to the broadest masses. Information about the USSR was a powerful propaganda weapon and should receive special attention. Lies in the bourgeois and reformist press were to be answered promptly. Since the experience of one country could be useful, both as warning and as lesson, to other countries, sections were to report regularly on their propaganda work, and assign members to collect and study reports.]

A. CENTRAL COMMITTEE

1. For the unified conduct of party agitation and propaganda work in all its forms, verbal as well as printed, every section of the Comintern, regardless of the party's influence or the political conditions in which it works, must have an agitprop department attached to its central committee.

2. Instructed by the CC of the party, the agitprop department works out the entire plan of party agitation and propaganda in their various branches, and supervises the execution by all local party organizations of congress and CC decisions concerned with these questions.

3. The CC appoints one of its members to take charge of the work of this department.

4. The head of the department works with an agitprop commission, consisting of four to eight members appointed by the CC, the head acting as chairman. The commission carries out all preliminary work on general agitprop questions, drafts the plan of work for the department. . . . The commission meets regularly, at least once a week.

5. In order to maintain contact with other departments of the CC, and with organizations related to the communist party, and to bring uniformity into their work, representatives of the organization department of the CC, of the women's secretariat, of the young communist league, of the red sports organization, the International Red Aid, and others will be attached to the commission. Care should be taken in appointing the commission to see that comrades concerned with educational work in the trade unions and co-operatives are included. . . .

6. In allocating functions within the agitprop commission the department should bear in mind the following three chief spheres of work: (a) agitation work among the masses; (b) work concerned with propaganda or party education; (c) the political periodical press. The commission may set up special sub-commissions to co-ordinate the work in these three fields. Their composition, and the choice of a responsible head of each

sub-commission, is determined by the agitprop commission and must be ratified by the CC of the party. They may include comrades who are not members of the agitprop commission.

7. . . . In sections which have not yet developed very far, it is enough to form a small agitprop department, consisting of a head of department and a commission of three (including the head), without any sub-commissions. A sub-commission for the press should be set up only where the party press is already well developed or where good opportunities are open for our comrades in the trade union press. . . .

8. . . . It is desirable that two or three leading party members should receive regular pay for this work, so that they can devote all their time to it.

9. The entire work of the agitprop department of the CC must be carried out on the basis of a thorough study of the working experience of all local party organizations. If it issues a circular or directives, the department must see that the instructions really are carried out. . . .

10. About twice a year the CC should call a meeting to discuss general questions of the agitprop department (or its sub-sections), to be attended by members of the department and the agitprop leaders of the most important district and local committees, as well as the agitprop organizers of the three to five largest factory cells. . . . .

B. DISTRICT COMMITTEES

11. Agitprop departments shall also be attached to the district committees, on the same lines as the CC department, but on a smaller scale. . . .

C. LOCAL COMMITTEES

12. One member of the presidium or bureau of the local committee must be appointed to take charge of the entire agitation and propaganda work of the area, for which he is responsible to the local committee. . . .

[13.] For all the preparatory work there will be an agitprop department consisting of the leader mentioned in para. 12 and a commission of five to seven members. One of these must be a member well versed in the theory of Marxism–Leninism, who will be in charge of all propaganda (party education) work in the area. . . . At the meetings of this commission the cell agitprop organizers shall report on their work and take part in discussing and deciding general questions of the commission's work. . . .

15. All decisions of the agitprop commission which have a general character must be endorsed by the presidium or bureau of the local committee. . . .

17. At least once every two months the committee shall call a meeting of the secretaries and agitprop organizers of the factory cells and area party committees, to hear the report of the department and discuss agitprop work.

18. The agitprop department of the local committee must send regular reports to the central party agitprop department. . . .

E. FACTORY CELLS

22. From the very beginning of the work to organize factory cells it is necessary to give great attention to the agitation and propaganda work of the cell among the working masses of the factory. . . . One member of the cell shall be appointed agitprop organizer to take charge of the work and supervise the execution of all decisions.

23. It is the job of the agitprop organizer to:

(*a*) draw up a list of members of the group suitable for agitprop work;
(*b*) organize a group to study the party programme and party tactics;
(*c*) organize individual agitation among non-party workers, in the first place those who sympathize with the party;
(*d*) organize agitation meetings;
(*e*) organize party participation at meetings called by trade unions and other bodies;
(*f*) organize the distribution of party literature, etc.

TELEGRAM FROM ZINOVIEV TO THE KUOMINTANG ON THE DEATH OF SUN YAT-SEN

14 *March* 1925   *Inprekorr*, v, 36, p. 543, 17 *March* 1925

[Zinoviev's telegram was in reply to one from the Kuomintang announcing Sun Yat-sen's death and ending: 'We are convinced that you, as true pupils of Lenin, will fight together with us, the heirs of Sun Yat-sen.' An article by Zinoviev on the dead Chinese leader said that, though not a communist, he was a great revolutionary leader. His watchwords of nationalism, democracy, and socialism (the usual rendering of the 'three principles' is nationalism, people's rights, and people's livelihood), reflected the backward social conditions of his country. Unlike Gandhi, whose policy was tantamount to a surrender to imperialist oppression, Sun Yat-sen hated the imperialists who had subdued his country. 'The Russian revolution can be proud of the great influence it has exercised on the national liberation movement of the Eastern peoples.' At the same time the ECCI published a manifesto to the masses of China calling on them to rally more closely around the Kuomintang and the communist party, and to fight all those who would compromise with the imperialists. In the autumn of 1925 the Sun Yat-sen University was opened in Moscow; it was directed first by Radek, then by Pavel Mif. Of its 147 Chinese students, about 20 per cent. were members of the communist party, the rest of the Kuomintang. It was more predominantly Chinese in character than the Communist University of Toilers of the East, of which Vasiliev, in an article celebrating the tenth anniversary of the Russian revolution, wrote: 'The whole world knows of the existence in Moscow of the

Communist University of Toilers of the East. Its students occupied and occupy many of the responsible posts of the Chinese revolution. . . . There are many such "Moscow agents" now in the capitalist and colonial countries.']

The news of Sun Yat-sen's death will be received with sorrow by thoughtful workers throughout the world.

Sun Yat-sen died at the moment when his life's work was beginning to bear fruit. Slowly but surely the movement of the revolutionary proletariat is growing stronger, and is uniting with the national emancipation movements of the oppressed peoples against imperialism, which will only be successful if they develop hand in hand with the international proletariat fighting against imperialism.

The national emancipation movement of the Chinese people is of the greatest world-historical importance. With the utmost attention the Communist International follows the struggle of the Chinese people: it knows that the Chinese working class, which has only just begun to tread the path of history, has a great future before it.

Faithful to Lenin's legacy, the Communist International teaches the workers of all countries to support all the forces of the national-revolutionary movement of the Eastern peoples, particularly in China. The Executive of the Communist International will do everything in its power to explain to the broad working masses of all countries the significance of Sun Yat-sen's work. It is convinced that all sections of the Communist International will give support to the Kuomintang party, which will carry Sun Yat-sen's cause to a successful end, and it does not doubt that the communist party in China, too, which is co-operating with the Kuomintang party, will be equal to the great historical tasks confronting it.

The independence and freedom of the Chinese people will be secured, despite all the efforts of imperialism.

To the eternal memory of Sun Yat-sen!

Long live the workers and peasants of China!

THE FIFTH ENLARGED PLENUM OF THE ECCI

[Two articles published at the time the session opened, one by Stalin and one by Zinoviev, suggested that while the situation in Germany and Europe had achieved a certain stability, the situation in the world as a whole, and particularly in the East, was objectively revolutionary. Stalin wrote that the revolutionary movements of the Western proletariat and the colonial peoples had to be brought closer together, and the working class and peasantry drawn in to support the Soviet Union, because 'to preserve and strengthen the Soviet Union is to accelerate the victory of the working class over the world bourgeoisie'.

The session met from 21 March to 6 April 1925; there were 244 delegates representing 34 sections, and including 32 members and 5 candidate members of the ECCI. Of the total, 104 had voting powers. The affairs of most of the parties came up for discussion. The resolution approving the ECCI report was passed unanimously; it stated that events had confirmed the correctness of the analysis made at the fifth congress, called for a more vigorous campaign for trade union unity, which 'undermines the influence of the trade union leaders', and recommended the 'bolshevization' of all sections. Zinoviev, reporting on the international situation, said the centre of gravity of the Second International had shifted from Germany to Britain, and perhaps the central revolutionary focus too, as a result of Britain's loss of power to America, the revolts in the colonies, and the militancy of the British working class. In an article on the opening of the plenum he had said that the British party was now progressing on the right lines: 'The time is not far off when it will be clear to everybody that this fact alone gives the Comintern tremendous strength.' He criticized sharply those (Trotsky and Radek) who over-emphasized the significance and durability of the Anglo-American rapprochement and thus hinted at the possibility that Anglo-American super-imperialism would eliminate contradictions in Europe. England's deteriorating economic position was destroying the basis of the old labour aristocracy. 'Our entire trade union campaign arose historically in con-nexion with the conditions which developed in the English labour movement.' The consolidation of the trade union left wing, and the influence of the Minority Movement had led to Anglo-Russian trade union co-operation. Lozovsky also spoke on this question. Since the fifth congress, he said, there had been the TUC delegation's visit to Russia (long extracts from its report were reproduced in a special number of *Inprekorr*), and the negotiations between the British and Russian unions and the IFTU. He repeated Zinoviev's warning against treating the unity campaign as a mere manœuvre, or alternatively of advocating it at any price, which would be prejudicial to their fight against reformism and encourage the tendency towards liquidating the revolutionary unions and even the RILU. There was no question of unconditional unity; the reformist demand to dissolve the RILU was unacceptable; that could happen only after unity had been achieved.

Purcell, Bramley, and Tillett, of the TUC General Council, attended the sixth congress of Russian trade unions in October 1924, while Russian delegates had attended the British trade union congress in Hull in September; it was at these meetings that the decision to form an Anglo-Russian trade union unity com-mittee was taken, and endorsed by the TUC and the ARCCTU (All-Russian Central Committee of Trade Unions) in April of the following year. Manuilsky wrote at the time that this presented the CPGB with wonderful opportunities. The resolution on trade union unity passed by the plenum on 1 April 1925 contained the following passage: 'The enlarged session of the ECCI attaches immense importance to the rapprochement between the English and Soviet trade unions, in which it sees a pledge that the international unity of the trade union movement is beginning to assume practical shape. The enlarged Executive welcomes the activities of the Anglo-Russian trade union conference and calls on workers of all countries, without distinction of political belief, to support resolutely and energetically the formation of the Anglo-Soviet trade union bloc, and to fight untiringly for the re-establishment of unity in the international trade union movement.' The IFTU council had in February 1925 rejected by 13 to 6 a British proposal for an unconditional conference between the IFTU and the Russian unions, and by 14 to 5 agreed to invite the Russian unions once more to affiliate to the IFTU.

On united front tactics, Kuusinen said they had 'to consider the possibility that for a time the social-democratic leaders will go along with us, but in our united front tactics we must always fight them, expose them, and defeat them'. On a workers' and peasants' government he said: 'For us of course this slogan is a pseudonym for the proletarian dictatorship and nothing else. But for the masses, the backward masses who stand aside, it is not that. They are not mature enough to fight for the proletarian dictatorship, and that is why we need this slogan.' He referred to the charge made by Thalheimer and Kreibich (Czechoslovakia) that the Russian leaders of the Comintern wanted to get rid of the independent people in the leadership of the Western parties in order to be able to control those parties directly from Moscow, and that the decision as to who was to be left in the leadership and who got rid of was determined by their attitude towards Trotsky at the fifth congress. These 'independent communists', said Kuusinen, were opportunists who were really fighting the Comintern, and what they called 'Russian' was really 'revolutionary'. Kreibich was also attacked by Zinoviev as 'Radek's deputy' for asserting that there was a regime of terror in the party. He had nearly split the Czechoslovak party.

The affairs of the Balkan parties also came up for discussion. In July 1924 the Balkan Communist Federation (Bulgaria, Yugoslavia, Rumania, Greece) had moved its headquarters to Moscow. Disputes within the Federation, which were at times very bitter, reflected the preoccupations of Soviet foreign policy. Greece was a tool of Britain, Yugoslavia and Rumania tools of France; Rumania moreover had seized part of Russian territory. Bulgaria was not a client of the Entente and had no territorial disputes with Russia; the Bulgarian leaders, furthermore, had been closely associated with the Russian revolutionary movement in the past, and it was therefore on all grounds natural for them to be given the leadership of the Balkan Federation. To strengthen their position Bulgarian revisionist claims (against Greece, Rumania, and Yugoslavia) were endorsed by the Comintern. The other parties in the Federation resented Bulgarian domination; one section of the Greek party broke away in protest against the endorsement of Bulgarian claims to Macedonia and Thrace, and at the enlarged plenum the Yugoslavs, who had unsuccessfully contested Comintern and Bulgarian communist policy (which implied the virtual dissolution of the Yugoslav State) at the fifth congress, were vigorously attacked by Kolarov and Stalin. They had openly criticized Bulgarian CP policy at the time of the Tsankov coup, and their opposition at the enlarged Executive was followed by a severe 'purge' of the party's ranks.

Bordiga's position in the Italian party had created difficulties. He had been invited to attend the plenum but had refused. Scoccimarro said he had great influence in the party and the working class, but he refused to change his ideas in accordance with a changing situation—they were absolute. He thus deprived the Italian party, by his abstract schematism, of any possibility of manœuvre and condemned it to passivity. He and his followers had refused to work in the central committee, and their attitude could be interpreted only as a belief in the political degeneration of the party and the Comintern.

The resolution on the Italian Communist Party was largely an attack on Bordiga for his failure to support the programme of action approved by the fifth congress, and for his support of Trotsky. It claimed progress for the Italian party, and attributed this to the abandonment of Bordiga's policy. The writings of Graziadei (a professor of economics who, with Lukacs, had been attacked at the fifth congress for 'revisionism') were said to represent the right-wing danger in the Italian party, but this danger was less than the danger from the ultra-lefts.

The report on the French Communist Party was given by Treint, who said that membership had increased from 50,000 to 75,000; the parliamentary fraction and the central press had now been brought under the leadership of the central committee; their links with the revolutionary movements in the colonies were still weak. Semard asked whether Trotsky had authorized Rosmer and Monatte to quote him in their struggle against the party, and whether he sympathized with them; in a letter to the central committee of the Russian party Trotsky wrote that the struggle in the French party arose partly from the re-actions in France to the discussion in the Russian party. Rosmer's and Monatte's expulsion had been ratified by the fifth Comintern congress; had he taken part in the congress discussion, he would have opposed their expulsion. When, later, he read their journal *Révolution Prolétarienne*, he concluded that their expulsion was justified. He rejected their defence of his position; though excluded, they should have behaved like good soldiers of the revolution, and thus found their way, sooner or later, back to their place in the CPF.

The American delegation was, as usual, sharply divided. The majority of the central committee, led by Foster and Cannon, disappointed by their failure to make headway in LaFollette's Farmer-Labor Party, argued that the policy of trying to form a labour party on the British model was opportunist, and wanted to concentrate on capturing the unions. The minority, led by Ruthenberg and Lovestone, disagreed, and were supported by the ECCI. The Workers' Party, said the resolution, drafted by a commission composed of Bukharin, Zetkin, and Kuusinen, should not proceed immediately to the formation of a labour party, but should try to get support for the idea among the unions. The United States had temporarily overcome the economic crisis, at the expense of the workers and small farmers. The working class, though not revolutionary, was becoming more class conscious; the politically inexperienced masses followed the La Follette party, which acted as a capitalist safety valve. The party's organization by language groups (of which there were thirteen), each tending to concentrate on special interests, was incompatible with bolshevik principles of organization. The party was urged to double its membership, and quadruple its American (i.e. not foreign-born) membership, and develop the Trade Union Educational League into an active left-wing trade union opposition. The differences dividing the party, which had led to the formation in many cities of two separate local party organizations, were to be settled by a commission, to meet before its next, fourth, congress, with equal representation for both sides and a neutral chair-man. The new central committee should give 13 seats to the majority, 8 to the minority. Both sides agreed to the resolution.

The congress, held at the end of August 1925, was attended by Gusev (appearing under the name of P. Green) for the ECCI. He replaced Pepper, whose conduct appears to have antagonized many of the American CP leaders. The majority had 40 delegates, the minority 21; a telegram from the ECCI during the congress recommended equal representation on the central committee, since the Lovestone group was more loyal to Comintern decisions. The majority split between the followers of Foster and Cannon, the latter joining the Ruthenberg group, which then obtained a majority on the central committee and the political bureau. The post of chairman, held by Foster, was abolished, and Ruthenberg was made party secretary. On 14 September 1925 the orgbureau discussed the Negro congress to be held the following month in Chicago, organized by the American CP. It was attended by forty delegates and set up a national committee to convene a world congress of Negroes.

The Executive adopted unanimously a series of resolutions put forward by the colonial commission on India, Java, Egypt, and other dependent countries. (These do not appear to have been published.) In a speech shortly after the meeting, Stalin referred to the differentiation that was proceeding in the colonies, which made it necessary to distinguish between that part of the native bourgeoisie which was prepared to compromise with imperialism, and that part which was still revolutionary. In certain countries such as China and Egypt alliance with the revolutionary petty bourgeoisie could take the form of a single party, provided the communists were not in any way restricted in their agitation and propaganda.

In articles published shortly after the ECCI meeting, Zionism was described as an imperialist instrument designed to direct the movement for national independence among oppressed Jews into safe channels, and to direct the movement among Arabs on to an anti-Jewish instead of an anti-imperialist line. The agreement between Zionist organizations and the Polish Government concerning Jewish emigration from Poland was an anti-Soviet move instigated by the British. Zionism being a British tool, the agreement strengthened Britain's position in Poland and hence 'automatically destroyed the rapprochement with Russia' contemplated in Poland.

Reporting on the ECCI meeting to the RCP conference at the end of April 1925, Zinoviev noted that turning-points in the Comintern almost always coincided with turning-points in the Russian party, just as the Second International followed the ups and downs of the bourgeoisie. The conference resolution on Zinoviev's report stated that while continuing to support revolutionary movements in other countries—as the international proletariat would support the USSR—the Soviet Union, by developing its own socialist economy, must increase its weight as a factor in the world revolution. Even without the world revolution, the Soviet Union could maintain itself for a long time. 'By and large the victory of socialism (not in the sense of its *final* victory) is certainly possible in one country alone.']

EXTRACTS FROM THE THESES ON THE BOLSHEVIZATION OF COMMUNIST
PARTIES ADOPTED AT THE FIFTH ECCI PLENUM

April 1925   *Inprekorr*, v, 77 [80], p. 1017 [1069], 11 *May* 1925

[In an article in January 1925 on the forthcoming plenary session of the ECCI,
Zinoviev wrote that 'bolshevization' was the slogan of the 'third period', the
period of relative capitalist stabilization and the ebbing of the revolutionary
wave (the first was the period of revolutionary upheavals from the Russian
revolution to 1921, the second was the period of the capitalist offensive, when
genuine communist parties were being built up). The bourgeoisie were helping
to bolshevize by repression and reaction, proving that there was no peaceful
road to socialism. The theses were passed unanimously in both the political
commission and the plenary session.

In the introduction to the German edition of the theses, the KPD *Zentrale*
urged the membership 'to grasp the necessity of manœuvres and compromises
made for the purpose of exposing the social-democratic and petty-bourgeois
deceivers, and of winning the masses of workers, middle classes, and peasants'.

Later in the year, at the fourteenth Russian party congress (when the name
was changed from Russian Communist Party to Communist Party of the Soviet
Union—CPSU), Zinoviev said: 'Bolshevization of the Comintern parties means
utilizing the experience of the bolshevik party in the three Russian revolutions
(and the experience of the best Comintern sections) in its application to the
concrete situation of the given country.' In the period of comparative quiet
through which they were passing—though the revolutionary wave would soon
rise again—the important question was who would gain the confidence of the
masses and so secure the leadership at the critical moment, the communists or
the reformists. Bolshevization would give leadership to the communists.]

PART ONE

FORMULATION OF THE QUESTION

I. *The Resolution of the Second World Congress on the Role of the Party*

The resolution of the second world congress of the Comintern on the
role of the party in the proletarian revolution . . . retains its full significance
today. It was drafted at a time when the Comintern was being established
. . . and outlined the role of the party in the proletarian revolution in
general.

Now, when the Communist International has taken definite shape . . .
and mass communist parties have arisen in a number of countries, it has
become necessary to formulate the ideas of the Communist International
not only about the role of the communist party in general in the proletarian revolution, but also about what must be done if our parties are to
become bolshevik parties, in the fullest sense of the word, in the shortest
possible time.

It should not be forgotten that in 1919–20 we had parties in Germany and Italy which were part of the Comintern, but they were not equal to the demands which history made on them, despite the tremendous spontaneous surge of the mass movement, precisely because they were not out-and-out bolshevik parties.

II. *The Slowing Down of World Revolution and the Slogan of Bolshevization*

Already at the time of the third world congress of the Comintern it was becoming clear that we were approaching a slowing-down phase in the development of the world revolution. . . . This gives the slogan of bolshevization not less, but more importance.

A bolshevik is not one who joins the party at the height of the revolutionary flood, but one who knows how to go on for years, if necessary for decades, building up the party even when the tide is ebbing and revolutionary development slows down. . . . A bolshevik party does not come into existence by itself when the revolutionary wave reaches its climax. It takes part in every struggle and builds itself up over the years in the course of these struggles. . . .

The communist party must be elastic enough to be able to make the transition to illegality in good order, should circumstances require it, without getting into a panic; legality should not be lightly surrendered, however, and legal must be combined with illegal work, and every legal foothold utilized by the party to break through the constraints of illegality and place itself at the head of open mass movements to prepare the revolution. . . .

III. *Right-Wing Dangers and Ultra-Left Deviations*

The slogan of bolshevization arose in the struggle against the right danger. . . . The correct slogan of the third world congress, 'To the masses', was so wrongly applied in a number of countries over the past two years that there was a real danger of independent communist tactics being replaced by a policy of communist 'coalition' with the counter-revolutionary social-democracy. . . .

But bolshevization is impossible without a simultaneous struggle against ultra-left tendencies, which are frequently only the obverse of opportunism. . . . The mistakes of the ultra-left, for example in regard to communist participation in reformist and reactionary unions, could destroy communist parties for years to come. . . .

IV. *Communist Parties and Bolshevik Parties*

In themselves communism, Marxism, and bolshevism are one and the same. 'Communist party' and 'bolshevik party' are, in themselves, identical concepts. In practice, however, they are not always one and the same. Some important sections of the Comintern still have to complete the development from left social-democracy (and in some cases from anarcho-syndicalist ideology) to genuine communism. . . .

V. *Bolshevization and the Conditions of Struggle*

It should not be thought that there is one panacea which can be applied uniformly in the bolshevization of all Comintern parties. True bolshevization requires careful consideration of the concrete circumstances of time and place. . . .

Bolshevization of the Comintern sections means studying and applying in practice the experience of the RCP in the three Russian revolutions, and of course the experience of other sections which have serious struggles behind them. . . . But it would be the greatest mistake to transfer Russia's experience mechanically to other countries, a mistake against which Lenin uttered a warning. There is much in the experience of the Russian revolution which Lenin considered of general significance for other countries. . . .

Bolshevization is the application of the general principles of Leninism to the concrete situation of the given country. . . . It is a permanent and continuing process which has only just started in the best European parties of the Comintern. The work still to be done in this direction is tremendous, and will require a number of years to accomplish.

PART TWO

MARXISM AND LENINISM

VI. *Marxism and Leninism*

In the present epoch the sections of the Comintern can become really communist parties only if they rally under the banner of Leninism.

It goes without saying that Leninism cannot be in any way opposed to Marxism. . . . There is no Leninism without Marxism. But Leninism has enriched Marxism with the experiences of the three Russian revolutions and with the experience of a number of other revolutionary movements. . . . Above all, Leninism has enriched the general theory of Marxism by mastering the following problems:

1. The theory of imperialism and the proletarian revolution;
2. The conditions and forms of realizing the dictatorship of the proletariat;
3. The interrelationships between proletariat and peasantry;
4. The significance of the national question in general;

5. The special significance of national movements in colonial and semi-colonial countries for the proletarian world revolution;
6. The role of the party;
7. The tactics of the proletariat in the epoch of imperialist wars;
8. The role of the proletarian State in the transition period;
9. The Soviet regime as the concrete type of the proletarian State in this period;
10. The problem of social stratification within the proletariat as a source of the division in the workers' movement into opportunist and revolutionary tendencies;
11. The struggle against right-wing social-democratic tendencies and also against left deviations in the communist movement. . . .

The idea that Marxism is only theory, and Leninism only practice, is false. Leninism is the theory and practice of Marxism in the period of imperialism, of imperialist wars and proletarian revolutions ushered in by the proletarian dictatorship in Russia. . . .

VII. *Bolshevization and Revolutionary Traditions*

Bolshevization does not mean abandoning the legacy of previous generations of revolutionaries. The study of the history of the revolutionary struggles of their own and other countries is absolutely essential for all bolshevik parties. . . .

VIII. *Bolshevization and some Theoretical Mistakes in the Communist Camp (particularly the Mistakes of the Luxemburgians)*

Mastery of Leninism and its practical application in building communist parties is impossible unless attention is paid to the errors of some prominent Marxists who tried, but not quite successfully, to apply Marxism to the conditions of the new epoch.

These include the errors of the 'left' communists in Russia, the group of Dutch Marxists (Gorter and Pannekoek), and also the errors of Rosa Luxemburg. The closer these political leaders stand to Leninism, the more dangerous are their views in those respects in which they do not coincide with Leninism. . . . Among the most important mistakes of the Luxemburgians of practical significance today are:

(*a*) the unbolshevik treatment of the question of 'spontaneity' and 'consciousness', of 'organization' and 'the masses'. Their false ideas on this question . . . prevented them from appraising correctly the role of the party in the revolution;

(*b*) underestimation of the technical factor in preparing insurrections was, and is in part today, an obstacle to the correct treatment of the question of 'organizing' the revolution;

(*c*) mistakes in regard to the attitude to the peasantry. . . .

A 'tolerant' attitude towards theoretical deviations, etc., makes genuine bolshevization impossible. . . . Mastery of the theory of Leninism is essential to successful bolshevization.

Trotskyism is a particularly dangerous deviation from Leninism; it is a variety of menshevism combining 'European' opportunism with 'left-radical' phrases which frequently conceal its politically passive character. Trotskyism is not an isolated deviation towards menshevism, but a year-long system of struggle against Leninism. Nor is Trotskyism a purely Russian phenomenon; it is international in character. To achieve Leninism in the Comintern means to expose Trotskyism in all parties and to liquidate it as a tendency.

PART THREE

BOLSHEVIZATION AND WINNING THE MAJORITY OF THE WORKING CLASS

IX. *Bolshevization and the Slogan: 'To the Masses'*

. . . A bolshevik is, above all, a man of the masses. The slogan of the third world congress, 'To the masses', remains in full force. Far from removing this slogan from the order of the day, the fifth world congress gave it a deeper and broader meaning.

X. *Bolshevization and Trade Union Work*

Deviations in communist trade union work involve the greatest dangers for the cause of true bolshevization of the parties. Throughout the capitalist world trade unions are the most important form of the mass organization of the proletariat. . . . Work in the existing social-democratic and other (yellow, national-socialist, confessional, and fascist) trade unions is a most important and integral part of bolshevization, to which a hundred times more attention than before must be devoted.

Only in this way can the monopoly of the reformist leaders (the labour aristocracy) in the unions be broken. Only in this way can the unions be liberated from the disintegrating influence of reformism, which seeks to undermine the unions as a reliable instrument of the class struggle. The same, of course, applies to factory committees where they exist. . . .

Communists will increase their influence and gain authority among the working masses by backing all immediate demands for higher wages and the eight-hour day, by conducting a fight against unemployment, by placing themselves courageously at the head of all conflicts with the employers. . . .

XI. *Bolshevization and Correct United Front Tactics*

Bolshevization of the parties of the Comintern presupposes the application of united front tactics. . . . United front tactics were and remain nothing other than a method of revolutionary agitation and organization of the masses, that is, the correct communist approach to the broad working masses in the given stage of development, when in a number of countries social-democracy is still supported by the majority of workers. . . .

The struggle for the unity of the international trade union movement supported by the Comintern will fill the next few years. . . . The time is not far off when this question will become the most burning one for every union in every country. . . .

XII. *Bolshevization and Partial Demands*

. . . Bolsheviks make use of every partial demand to explain to the masses the necessity of revolution, to show the masses, by the concrete facts of the case, the impossibility of even a moderately serious and lasting, let alone fundamental, improvement in their position so long as the power of capital is maintained.

At the same time the communists demonstrate to the masses in the light of experience that it is precisely the reformists who sabotage every serious struggle for partial demands, while it is the communist party which is alone able to lead a consistent struggle for the day-to-day interests of the working masses and ward off attacks on their standard of living.

Bolsheviks place every concrete demand to which the workers rally in the perspective of the fight for the revolution. . . .

XIII. *Work among Those Belonging to the Second and the Amsterdam Internationals*

In the majority of countries the Second and the Amsterdam Internationals still unite in their ranks, in one way or another, considerable strata of workers. The bolshevization of our own parties involves the imperative task of constant work among those proletarians who still belong to these hostile organizations. . . .

XIV. *Bolshevization and the Youth Movement*

Communist parties still do not pay enough attention to work among young people. Even in the largest communist parties there are dozens of organizations which have not formed local communist youth groups.

One of the tasks of bolshevization is to win over the youth of the entire world without exception. . . .

XV. *Bolshevization and Work among Women*

. . . The enlarged Executive of the Comintern notes that our work in this field is extremely unsatisfactory. Drawing proletarian women into active work and struggle is a precondition of winning over to our side the majority of the working class. . . .

XVI. *Work among Unemployed*

Communist parties throughout the world must devote the most serious attention to work among the unemployed. With the attitude of the bourgeoisie and social-democracy to the millions of unemployed what it is . . . we can win decisive influence among this stratum of the proletariat.

XVII. *Bolshevization and our Press*

We cannot tolerate a situation in which, as in Berlin, Paris, and Milan, for example, we have a relatively large number of communist voters and a relatively small number of constant readers of our press. . . . Bolshevization requires that our press should become a popular press in the best sense of the word; that is, it should be found in every worker's home and read by everyone who sympathizes with us. . . .

PART FOUR

BOLSHEVIZATION AND THE QUESTION OF THE ALLIES OF THE PROLETARIAT IN THE REVOLUTION

XVIII. *The Allies of the Proletariat in the Revolution*

The principles underlying the attitude of communists to the petty bourgeoisie as a possible ally of the proletariat in the revolution have been explained with exhaustive clarity in the classical works of Marx, Engels, and Lenin. . . .

It is a basic task of Leninism to provide a precise and concrete answer to the question, what intermediate strata at any given stage of revolutionary development are capable of becoming allies of the proletariat, what are the demands which in the given situation will unite them with the proletariat.

Precisely because Leninism puts the question of the proletarian dictatorship as a practical item on the agenda of history, it places the question of potential allies of the working class in the revolution in the foreground as one of the most important tactical problems of the day.

By and large Leninism divides the petty bourgeoisie into three groups: certain strata of the petty bourgeoisie can and must be won as direct allies, if only temporarily; other strata we must manage to neutralize; a third group (the upper ranks of the urban and rural petty bourgeoisie) will inevitably have to be fought outright. . . .

XIX. *Bolshevization and Proletarian Policy towards the Peasantry*

The bolshevik party is an industrial-workers' party. The doctrine of the proletarian dictatorship is the basic tenet of bolshevism. Nevertheless the question of the peasantry as the class closest to the working class and the most important of the potential allies of the proletariat in the revolution is of cardinal importance for bolshevism, both before and after the seizure of political power by the proletariat. . . .

XX. *Bolshevization and Proletarian Policy on the National Question*

The national question in colonial and semi-colonial countries—and not only in these—is very largely a peasant question, since the majority of the population there are peasants. . . .

The experience of the last few years has shown that in different countries, in different situations, communists have again and again made the mistake of underestimating the national question, a mistake which deprives them of the opportunity of winning over substantial, at times decisive, strata of the population. . . .

PART FIVE

THE CONCRETE TASKS OF THE VARIOUS PARTIES

XXI. *The Immediate Practical Tasks of the Various Parties*

A. For the Soviet Union: here the task of bolshevization at the present time consists primarily in the following:

1. The final liquidation of Trotskyism as a tendency within the party....

2. To take all measures to carry out the wholly correct . . . policy of the party in the peasant question, to develop systematically (with the help of the dictatorship) the elements of socialist economy, and so strengthen the economic basis of the proletarian dictatorship and the transformation of Russia from a country of the 'new economic policy' into a socialist country.

B. For the English communist party, which is now having its first considerable successes in its development into a mass party, the central task of bolshevization consists in:

1. Work in the trade unions. Particular attention for the Minority Movement. . . .

2. Agitation against the imperialist sentiments of the English labour aristocracy. . . .

3. The creation of a firmly centralized party organization and liquidation of dilettante methods of work.

4. Systematic application of united front tactics.

C. In France at the present time bolshevization consists in:

1. The campaign for trade union unity. . . .

3. Closest contact between the party and the CGTU at any cost on the basis of the principles and tactics laid down by the CI.

4. Despite all earlier French traditions, the creation of a firmly organized mass communist party. . . .
8. Anti-militarist propaganda. . . .
10. Energetic work in the colonies.

D. Germany: Here bolshevization consists in the first place of the following tasks:

1. Liquidation of 'left' errors in regard to trade unions. . . .
3. Application of united front tactics. . . .
4. Greater attention to winning the masses organizationally. . . .
7. Propagation of the slogan 'workers' and peasants' government' as interpreted by the fifth congress, that is, in its revolutionary sense. . . .
8. To take all steps to secure the normal and healthy internal development of the party, and to eradicate the effects of the previous fractional struggle, to guard party unity from any new fractionalism. . . .

F. Italy:

1. To increase still further the organizational influence of the party on the broadest strata of the workers, breaking through the restrictions of illegality imposed on the party by fascism. . . .
4. To begin systematic work to create, consolidate, and capture the factory committees.
5. To penetrate the countryside more deeply. . . .
6. To pay greater attention to Marxist ideology.
7. To fight against all ideological deviations, against Bordiga's theoretical and tactical ideas, and against Graziadei's revision of Marxist economic theory. . . .

XXII. *Bolshevization and Anti-Monarchist Agitation*

It is incorrect to refrain from anti-monarchist agitation on the ground that even under a monarchy it is the bourgeoisie who rule. Communists must put forward the slogan 'Down with the Monarchy' in England, Italy, the Balkans, etc. In Germany, too, communists must know how to combine their anti-monarchist agitation with the day-to-day political and economic struggle. . . .

XXIII. *The Numerical Growth of a Number of Parties: Illegal Parties*

In a number of countries—France, Germany, England, Czechoslovakia, Italy, Sweden, Norway, Holland, and America—communist parties are today working in conditions in which the size of their membership could be and must be considerably increased. . . .

Those parties which are forced to work illegally must use every means to extend their organized influence over the broadest strata of workers and peasants by carefully exploiting every legal opportunity. . . . Illegal parties must take advantage of every opportunity, even a passing one, to unite sympathizing workers in organizations, however loose, and so secure for the party legal channels for propaganda and agitation activities.

PART SIX

BOLSHEVIZATION AND QUESTIONS OF ORGANIZATION

XXIV. *Bolshevization and Questions of Organization*

. . . The basic form of organization of every bolshevik party is the party cell in the factory. . . .

Besides the factory cell, and work in such organizations as trade unions, factory committees, consumers' co-operatives, etc., steps should be taken to establish a whole series of non-party subsidiary organizations—tenants' leagues, unemployed committees, ex-service men's associations, etc. (with communist cells working in them). Bolshevization requires our parties to use every opportunity to make this organizational network as dense and closely woven as possible. . . .

The initiative in creating such organizations must be taken by the party leadership through the party members, who must then take the management of these organizations into their own hands. Communists must form fractions in these organizations, receiving instructions from the party leadership. . . .

XXV. *Bolshevization and Comintern Resolutions on Organizational Questions*

The third world congress resolution on questions of organization is far from having been carried out. One of its most important points dealt with the necessity for every member being given a definite party job to do. . . . The enlarged Executive is of the opinion that the practical carrying-through of this point is essential to bolshevization.

The enlarged Executive directs the attention of all parties to the fifth world congress resolution on questions of organization. It also ratifies the resolutions adopted by the organization conference of the CI sections and recommends their execution in their entirety.

XXVI. *Bolshevization and the Problem of Party Cadres*

To create a bolshevik party it is necessary over the years to forge strong party cadres. Such cadres are not formed by means of formal elections, but rather by selection in the course of practical work. The process of selection is necessarily slow; from the party cell up to the party centre it occurs in the course of the struggle which tests the members. . . .

The communist cadres of organizers must be trained in the sense that their work in preparing the revolution should not be a spare-time job; all their time must be given to the revolutionary struggle; they must be wholly and completely at the disposal of the party. The communist organizer and cadre worker . . . must live and work among the masses in the factory, the shop or mine, always ready to be sent elsewhere by the party in the interests of the cause. . . .

XXVII. *Bolshevization, Party Democracy, and Discipline*

. . . The forms of internal party organization are subordinate to the overriding interests of the struggle for the proletarian dictatorship. But in all circumstances the communist party must preserve a certain freedom of criticism within the party, a spirit of equality among the party members. . . . This is in accordance with the interests of stimulating the entire party mass, securing the co-operation of all the lower party bodies and the cells in the political and organizational life of the party, and arousing the initiative of the workers in the party.

Iron proletarian discipline is one of the most important pre-conditions of bolshevization. Parties which carry on their banner 'Dictatorship of the Proletariat' must realize that there can be no talk of a victorious proletarian dictatorship without iron party discipline, acquired in the course of years and decades. Bolsheviks . . . must realize that the civil war cannot be fought, political power conquered, or the proletarian dictatorship maintained and strengthened, without the strictest internal discipline founded on ideological unanimity; without this the civil war is doomed in advance to failure.

XXVIII. *Bolshevization and the Party Apparatus*

A centralized, firmly welded, and strictly organized bolshevik party is impossible without an appropriate party apparatus.

At present a few Comintern sections have a thoroughly unwieldy, disproportionately large, and hence frequently bureaucratic party apparatus. Other sections have practically none at all.

The enlarged Executive of the CI instructs the presidium to work out, with the orgbureau and the representatives of the parties concerned, a series of measures which will enable the parties to establish an apparatus in harmony with the interests of their work.

XXIX. *Bolshevization and Self-Criticism*

The struggle against what comrade Lenin called 'communist boasting', against self-satisfaction and conceit, is a most important pre-condition of bolshevization. . . .

XXX. *Planned Work and Checking its Execution*

In all countries in which communist parties carry on their work in comparatively normal conditions it is necessary to draw up a general plan of work for six months, a year, etc., in order to learn how to concentrate the party's forces. . . . There must be a check by all organizations on the carrying out of any decisions taken. Better have fewer decisions, but see that they are at all costs carried out in practice. . . .

PART SEVEN

BOLSHEVIZATION AND THE INTERNATIONAL LEADERSHIP

. . . Bolshevization is incompatible with separatist and federalist tendencies. The world party of Leninism must be strongly fused, not by mechanical discipline, but by unity of will and action. . . . Every party must give its best forces to the international leadership. It must be brought home to the broadest masses that in the present epoch serious economic and political battles of the working class can be won only if they are led from one centre and on an international scale.[1]

No Communist Party should recoil from illegal work. Illegality is a condition in which many Communist Parties must now work and which in the epoch of the increased intensification of the social struggles might extend to many Parties of the Comintern which to-day are still legal.

Every Communist Party must reckon with illegality as a possible and probable condition, and must be prepared to transfer to illegal work. Whenever the political situation becomes seriously acute, it must take the proper measures which will enable it to continue its work illegally after its organization has been prohibited; it must keep its whole technical apparatus for illegality in readiness. But all unnecessary playing with illegality must be avoided and the Party must defend its legality to the bitter end.

On the other hand the Parties which are compelled to work illegally must take advantage of every passing opportunity of conducting legal activity and for the extension of such opportunities.

The Party should not allow any form of legal activity to be taken from it (election campaigns, parliamentary activity, the legal press, factory councils, trade unions, educational societies, co-operatives, sick benefit societies, etc.). The masses of workers and peasants must become accustomed to protect the legal opportunities of their Party, and to meet every attack of the bourgeoisie and the social traitors against these opportunities with mass demonstrations (strikes, demonstrations, etc.).

[1] The German text as given in *Inprekorr* ends here, as does the Russian text in the official collection of documents edited by Bela Kun; the following section is taken from the theses as given in *Bolshevizing the Communist International* (London, CPGB, 1925), p. 167.

The principal basis of the activity of an illegal Party is strict Party discipline which must be much more strict than that of the legal Parties. But this discipline should not be confounded with bureaucratization. Even under the most extreme illegality, there is still the possibility of Party democracy, freedom of discussion, and of election of all Party representatives. Any unnecessary limitation to this democracy would cause the separation of the Party from the masses, would make it pedantic and transform it into a group of conspirators. But once the Party officials have been elected, they must be able to count in all their activities on the iron discipline of the Party membership, and Party discussion may be carried on only until the Party comes into action.

Party discipline in an illegal Party also includes the strictest methods of conspiracy. The composition of the Party organs, the internal Party affairs and such like, must be kept strictly secret from the Party members. Any breach of conspiracy must be ruthlessly punished, by the dismissal of the responsible Party officials, Party trial and expulsion from the Party.

In the illegal Parties, more care must be exercised in the acceptance of new members. The moral value of the new Party members, their strength of character, etc., must be very carefully investigated. The behaviour of Communists under arrest, cross-examination and in prison is extremely important; such situations serve as the fiery ordeal for the firmness of a Communist and his devotion to the Party, and are of extreme importance for the authority of the whole Party. Especially during cross-examination a revolutionary must be doubly careful in his demeanour; every word carelessly dropped might endanger both the Party and the Communist movement.

One of the most important tasks of illegal Parties is the fight against spying and provocation. The most important weapon in the fight against provocation is to mobilize the opinion of the working class against it and to train the workers to react to all acts of provocation and denunciation with the most determined methods. In factories we must continually be on the watch to discover and drive out police informers.

EXTRACTS FROM THE THESES OF THE FIFTH ECCI PLENUM ON THE PEASANT QUESTION

April 1925   *Inprekorr*, v, 77 [80], p. 1026 [1078], 11 *May* 1925

[The theses were drafted and introduced by Bukharin. The discussion was brief and uncontroversial. The voting is not recorded.]

INTRODUCTION

1. The general communist line towards the peasantry was laid down in the agrarian theses drafted by Lenin for the second CI congress. The

fourth congress endorsed these theses and supplemented them with considerations drawn from the subsequent experience of various communist parties. The second congress theses still remain the basic principles on this question, to which all parties affiliated to the CI are committed.

2. . . . Since the overwhelming majority of the world's population are peasants, the struggle for the peasantry becomes a vital political question, from the point of view of the proletarian struggle for power, the consolidation of that power, and the economic prerequisites of that consolidation. The colonial question is at bottom nothing but the question of the relations between town and country on a world scale, in which the countryside suffers under the threefold pressure of feudal landownership, capitalist exploitation, and national inequality.

3. As a result of the instability of capitalist relations the question of the peasantry has also become extremely acute for the ruling classes too, for the bourgeoisie and the large agrarians. . . . The ruling classes are trying to extend their influence along the entire peasant front, to win it for the fight against the revolutionary proletarian front. . . .

6. The peasantry, which in the past was the basic class in feudal society, is not a class at all, in the real sense of the word, in capitalist society. . . . But in so far as we are dealing with a society which is passing from feudal relations to the relations of capitalist production, the peasantry as a whole is in a contradictory situation: in relation to the large landowners it is a class, but in so far as capitalist relations have invaded and disintegrated the peasantry, it ceases to be a class. In countries with strong feudal agrarian survivals, the peasantry, whose interests are sharply opposed to those of the landowners, may therefore at a certain phase of the revolution become as a whole allies of the proletariat. This applies above all to the colonial and semi-colonial countries. . . .

8. The essential factor dividing the proletariat and the large peasants is the interests of capitalist property, that is, the contradiction between the buyer and seller of labour power. . . . In the proletarian revolution which destroys capitalist property the large peasants therefore become a reserve of the anti-proletarian forces. But in those countries where the agrarian revolution against feudal landownership is still to come, even the large peasants may revolt against the landowners.

[9.] The essential factor which divides the interests of the middle peasantry from those of the working class is the interests of private commodity economy. . . . The interests of grain sellers (peasants) and grain buyers (workers) are in this respect in conflict. But a number of other factors connected with the entanglement of the medium peasants in the process of capitalist exploitation (money-lending, the high-price policy of industrial trusts, taxation, the pressure of the imperialist State machine, wars, etc.) may far outweigh those which divide the medium peasants from the proletariat. Therefore these strata can be neutralized. . . .

10. The factors dividing the small peasantry also derive from the character of private commodity interests. But the proportion between dividing and unifying factors is quite different in this case. The small-holder often has to buy grain, and often has to hire himself out as a wage labourer. . . . The small peasants can therefore be won over as allies of the proletariat. . . .

12. Agricultural labourers are a part of the proletariat. But there are special features in their situation which often make their fight against capitalist society difficult. These arise from their geographical dispersal in the labour process, and from the strongly 'patriarchal' character of rural conditions . . . which make the agricultural proletariat a 'backward' stratum of the working class. It is obviously the job of proletarian parties to win this stratum over first of all. . . .

III. THE AGRARIAN PROBLEM OF THE PEASANTRY IMMEDIATELY BEFORE THE SEIZURE OF POWER BY THE WORKING CLASS

20. The period of proletarian revolution creates a situation . . . in which absolutely everything must be subordinated to the task of seizing power and establishing the proletarian dictatorship. . . .

21. In countries with large-scale capitalist production the proletariat must aim at transforming large landholdings into State undertakings farmed by wage labour. But the principle of the technical superiority, economically, of large-scale agricultural production should not stop communists from dividing part of the large estates among the small, and in some cases even the medium, peasants. . . . In the great majority of countries the proletarian dictatorship cannot be established without the direct help of the small peasants and the neutralization of the middle peasants. The negative experience of the Hungarian, Italian, and Polish movements, and the positive experience of the Russian, show that mistakes on this question are absolutely fatal. . . .

23. . . . Since the proletarian dictatorship in the most important industrial countries creates conditions enabling development in countries of a colonial type to take another course, the basic task in these latter is not the struggle against anti-capitalist, pre-capitalist, and other ideas; it is to criticize irresolution and timidity in the fight against foreign capital and feudal landownership, and to give the movement greater scope and impetus.

IV. THE PROBLEM AFTER THE SEIZURE OF POWER

24. With the seizure of power by the working class, with the expropriation of the capitalists and landlords . . . there is a radical change in the

conditions of economic life in general, and the life of the rural population in particular. . . .

25. These new conditions make possible a non-capitalist evolution of peasant farming, which . . . can pass through co-operation to socialism. . . .

26. It is obvious that this process of 'evolution' will occur only as the result of the struggle of various economic forms which reflect the struggle of classes. The proletarian State . . . must so regulate the capitalist relations which are bound to arise that in the final result the victory of socialism is ensured. . . .

27. It will equally be possible for the colonial countries to by-pass the stage of capitalist development if the developing proletarian revolution gives the proletariat mastery of the important industrial centres. . . . This does not mean that there will be no capitalist development at all in these countries. The entire process will occur in contradictory forms . . . but there will be a powerful socialist tendency which will determine the character of the process as a whole.

28. The most important guide for the ruling proletarian party must be: to reach agreement with the peasantry. It must be clearly recognized that this problem cannot be avoided, for the peasantry form the majority of the world's population. . . . But agreement can be reached only if the proletarian State's economic policy takes account of the inclination of small producers towards private economy and, taking this as its starting-point, gradually guides the small producer to combine and to engage in more and more comprehensive forms of collective economy. . . .

31. . . . The partnership with the peasantry does not by any means imply a sharing of power. But to the extent that the peasantry is really drawn into socialist construction and in the process subjected to socialist re-education, its most advanced elements will naturally have to be drawn into co-operation with the State apparatus. . . . The Soviet form of the proletarian dictatorship, as the experience of the revolution has shown, ensures the proletarian class character of the State organization and enables the peasantry to be drawn to a growing extent into the process of constructing socialism. . . .

33. The final goal of the movement is the organization of collective large-scale agricultural production, the elimination of contradictions between town and country, and an end to the backwardness of agriculture which is inherent in the laws of capitalist development. . . .

VI. THE PEASANT MOVEMENT AND THE COMMUNIST PARTIES

41. The most fundamental task to be accomplished by the communist parties is to study the agrarian problem in their own country and 'their' colonies. Very little has so far been done in this respect. . . .

42. The chief object of communist party work is to emancipate the

relevant strata of the peasantry from the influence of the bourgeoisie and the landowners. In agrarian countries with strong feudal survivals the agrarian question must be given first place. . . .

43. In most countries of developed capitalism the emphasis in our propaganda and agitation must be placed on questions of taxation, the high monopoly prices of industrial products, the pressure of the imperialist State machine, and future wars. . . .

48. In the colonies all these questions appear in a more acute form: the pressure of feudal landownership and land-hunger, high prices, excessive taxation and dues, and the threat of war. All this is further complicated by the addition of exploitation by foreign capital and national oppression. It is therefore the task of communist parties to expand the struggle in all these directions. . . .

VII. WORK AMONG THE PEASANTRY AND THE ATTITUDE TO PEASANT ORGANIZATIONS

50. Where various strata of the peasantry are united in a common organization led by the landowners and the capitalist large peasants, communist parties must aim at detaching the small peasants (and, as far as possible, the medium peasants also). If it is impossible to capture such organizations, i.e. to get rid of the landlord leaders (as in the majority of cases), then efforts should be made to detach and form separate organizations of the small peasantry. . . . For this it is necessary to adopt the tactics of a bloc between the communist party and associations of small peasants.

51. In those capitalist countries where the small peasants are badly organized or not organized at all, efforts should be made to organize them into peasant unions, peasant committees, etc., in which the party should wield influence through party fractions. The formation of separate political *peasant parties* by the communists is inadvisable and cannot be recommended. By peasant unions, irrespective of the names they bear, should be understood broader organizations than political parties in the specific sense of the term. These unions have no definitely defined programmes, discipline, or strict organizational forms. For that reason they can embrace a larger section of the masses, and also permit the existence in their ranks of various political tendencies and shades.

52. Where the peasantry is organized in political parties, heterogeneous in class composition, the communist party must support the small-peasant left wing and, at the necessary moment, promote its organization as a separate organization.

53. Communist parties form a bloc with small-peasant parties, and aim at bringing them under their ideological influence; they propagate the idea of the necessity of an alliance of workers and peasants as the

indispensable prerequisite for the victorious struggle of the working people against the exploiters. . . .

57. All parties must try to get peasant organizations to affiliate to the International Peasant Council; they are obliged to support this international body. . . .

58. . . . Communists must make it clear to the peasantry everywhere that the peasants have always been defeated and betrayed when they have tried to act as an independent third power, without allying themselves with the proletariat and without its leadership. The experience of so-called peasant governments (Stambuliski) has also shown that the peasantry are not able to maintain power. Therefore it is only the dictatorship of the proletariat, supported by the peasantry, which can really ensure victory in the struggle of both classes against the exploiters.

EXTRACTS FROM THE RESOLUTION OF THE FIFTH ECCI PLENUM ON THE DISCUSSION IN THE RUSSIAN COMMUNIST PARTY

April 1925   *Inprekorr*, v, 77 [80], p. 1033 [1085], 11 *May* 1925

[The central committee of the RCP, together with the CCC, met from 17 to 20 January 1925 and passed, against the votes of Piatakov and Rakovsky, and one abstention, a resolution on Trotsky's 'attacks on bolshevism', which were said to be interpreted as cracks in the proletarian dictatorship by the bourgeoisie and the social-democrats, who drew practical conclusions therefrom for their policy. Inside the country they were regarded by all hostile elements as a signal to rally against the party's policy. The resolution traced differences with Trotsky (after his entry into the communist party) back to the Brest-Litovsk treaty of 1918. It removed Trotsky from his post as Commissar for War and warned him that if he continued to violate party discipline he would be expelled from the politbureau. Trotsky himself was absent from the meeting because of ill-health.

Bukharin reported to the ECCI on this question. Examination, he said, had revealed the existence of a bloc within the Comintern formed by the members of the Russian opposition and the right wing, as exemplified by Kreibich in the Czech party, as well as the ultra-left, as shown by Bordiga's support of Trotsky. The question of the Russian opposition had thus become an international question. Moreover, many who had left the communist party, for example Höglund, Tranmael, Balabanova, Rosmer, Monatte, expressed their solidarity with Trotsky and also supported the right deviationists Brandler, Thalheimer, and Radek. Support also came from the bourgeois press, although nobody believed that Trotsky personally was connected with these elements. The chief elements in Trotskyism were his underestimation of the peasantry and an over-estimation of the role of the State apparatus and the possibilities of centralization and planning at that time. His introduction to the *Lessons of October* repeated his incorrect theory of the permanent revolution. Subjectively Trotsky was an absolutely honest party comrade, but objectively he had a disruptive effect. That was why hostile elements in the USSR supported the opposition, and why

the central committee had removed him from his post as commissar and condemned him politically. Some comrades had asked whether differences of
opinion about industry, currency, etc., had to have organizational consequences.
They had to because this was not a literary but a practical question. None of the
speakers at the plenum supported Trotsky, and the resolution received a
unanimous vote.]

The enlarged plenum of the ECCI observes that comrade Trotsky's
behaviour, which has provoked a new discussion within the RCP, represents an attempt to revise Leninism and to change the leadership in the
RCP.

The enlarged plenum observes that this behaviour is supported by all
the forces hostile to bolshevism. Within the CI it is supported by the
right-wing elements in the parties, that is, by those whose tactics have
been repeatedly condemned by the international congresses as semi-
socialist. Outside the CI it is supported by various people expelled from
the communist ranks (Levi, Rosmer, Monatte, Balabanova, Höglund,
etc.).

Finally, the social-democratic and bourgeois press has also tried to
exploit this behaviour.

It is thus objectively not merely an attempt to disorganize the ranks
of the RCP; it has also done the greatest damage to the entire CI.

The enlarged plenum of the ECCI declares that it fully and completely
approves the resolution of the plenum of the CC of the RCP.

EXTRACTS FROM THE DECISION OF THE CENTRAL CONTROL COM-
MISSION OF THE RUSSIAN COMMUNIST PARTY AND THE INTERNATIONAL
CONTROL COMMISSION OF THE COMINTERN REGARDING BRANDLER,
THALHEIMER, RADEK, AND OTHERS

4 *April* 1925   *Inprekorr*, v, 53, p. 743, 10 *April* 1925

[The KPD *Zentrale* had asked the central committee of the RCP to examine
the case of Brandler and Thalheimer (who were living in Moscow and were
members of the RCP), of Radek, and of others accused of fraction work in the
KPD. The question was referred to a joint meeting of the control commission
of the RCP, the ICC, and the ECCI, which came to the conclusion that their
views were fractional, anti-bolshevik, semi-Trotskyist, and in opposition to the
resolutions of the fifth Comintern congress. The fraction work had been designed
to change the political line of the KPD *Zentrale* and restore Brandler and Thalheimer to their old posts. Fraction meetings had been held in Moscow, and
friends in Berlin had been used to get reports about the situation in the KPD.
Radek had given money to expelled right-wing members of the KPD (he admitted this, but denied that it was for fractional purposes; it had been given
only to help them in their difficult material situation). Although they deserved

expulsion, the commission proposed that they should only be severely reprimanded and warned. If Brandler and Thalheimer engaged in any activities in
connexion with the KPD they would be expelled. None of them was to work in
the Comintern. In a statement on 23 March 1925 the three accused replied that
their differences with the fifth congress resolution on a workers' government
were of historical importance only. The situation had now changed and they
agreed that, because of capitalist stabilization, the slogan now could only be an
agitational one. This statement, said Manuilsky for the Russian delegation, was
unsatisfactory. The three bore the greatest responsibility for the social-democratic distortions of KPD policy which had been so harmful in 1923. Their
expressions of solidarity with the Comintern line could not be taken seriously.
Radek had supported Trotskyism, and Brandler's and Thalheimer's attitude was
ambiguous.

The KPD delegation endorsed these views although they would have preferred more severe measures against the three. Ruth Fischer urged the need to
continue the fight against Brandlerism and Radekism, and to go even further
back, to Luxemburgism. The KPD had been criticized by the agitprop department of the ECCI for allowing favourable reviews of Trotsky's *October* to appear
in the communist press. (Trotsky's *Lessons of October* was published in November
1924 as an introduction to a volume of his collected writings.) Not every deviation could be called Trotskyism, Ruth Fischer explained. There were thousands
of members in the KPD who agreed with the argument in that pamphlet that
the defeat of October 1923 was due to the mistakes of the leaders. There were
no groups or fractions in the KPD, but in practice there were several right
deviations on such questions as municipal policy and the trade unions. Klara
Zetkin objected strongly to Ruth Fischer's tirade against 'the so-called right'
who had spent their lives in the forefront of the German working-class struggle.
(In a letter to a member of the central committee of the KPD, Stalin wrote
that 'Brandler and Thalheimer belong to the category of the old type of leaders
who have outlived their time and are being pushed into the background'.)
The new leaders had few successes to show. Since October 1923 the communist
fraction had fallen from 400 to 42 in the metalworkers union, from 100 to 6 in
the transport union, and from 2,700 to 200 in the unions as a whole. The resolution was endorsed by the politbureau and the central committee of the RCP and
approved unanimously by the ECCI at its fifth plenum 'amid stormy applause'.]

. . . The CCC considers that organized fractions do exist in the KPD;
and there exists a fraction to which a few groups within the party belong,
as well as a group of members of the RCP (Brandler, Thalheimer, Radek,
and others), and which carries on fractional work on the basis of a political
platform formulated in a series of articles and documents. The CCC is of
the opinion that the German *Zentrale*, proceeding from the facts cited
above, was quite right to demand the expulsion of Brandler and Thalheimer from the RCP, for they had deserved expulsion. . . .

Nevertheless, prompted by the desire to liquidate the fractional groups
in the KPD as painlessly as possible, and to give comrades Brandler,

Thalheimer, Radek, and others the opportunity of proving in action the sincerity of the declaration they made at the CCC meeting that they will not carry on any fraction work, the CCC thinks it possible to restrict itself to the following measures:

1. To issue a sharp reprimand and a warning to comrades Brandler, Thalheimer, Radek, Felix Wolf, Heinz Möller, and Edda Baum about their systematic fraction work and grave breaches of party discipline.

2. To forbid these comrades to intervene in any way in the work of the KPD.

3. The CCC warns these comrades that any further fraction work on their part, or any interference in the affairs of the KPD, will inevitably place them outside the ranks of the RCP.

4. Comrades Brandler, Thalheimer, and Radek shall not be permitted to take part in the work of the Comintern.

5. The CCC considers that the KPD *Zentrale* should carry out a broad campaign within the party to explain the political significance of this decision to all party members.

RESOLUTION OF THE INFORMATION CONFERENCE OF THE ECCI ON THE WORK OF INFORMATION DEPARTMENTS

6 *April* 1925   *Inprekorr*, v, 69, p. 934, 27 *April* 1925

[The information conference was held on 6 April 1925, attended by 25 representatives of 17 countries. The report on the work of the ECCI information department was given by Pepper: the department had been set up in the previous December to keep the ECCI and its agencies informed about the national sections, to keep the sections informed about the ECCI and each other, to report to the ECCI on problems arising, and to make proposals. It drew up daily and special reports and distributed information letters to the sections on special subjects. Questionnaires had been sent to all sections, but communication between the ECCI and the sections was still faulty and incomplete. The conference had been called to put that right. Sections were to send in monthly or bi-monthly reports. The failure to defeat social-democracy was due in part to lack of information. The collection of information about the reformists was to be assigned to a responsible member in each party. In the discussion Bell (CPGB) reported that they already had an information centre in London, the Labour Research Department. This was not formally a party institution, but it was completely under communist control.]

The information conference notes that detailed information about the work of the sections, about the economic and political situation in the different countries, and about the enemy is essential to the successful work of the Executive and its sections.

The conference notes further that the work of the information department of the ECCI, still in its early stages, has been satisfactory, but emphasizes the urgent need to expand that work both in the ECCI apparatus and in the individual sections.

It therefore proposes:

1. That the central committee of every section appoint an information officer, preferably a member of the central committee, to maintain regular contact with the information department of the ECCI and provide it with material.

2. Further, those parties which are in a position to do so should set up special information departments as part of the central apparatus. These departments should create an information network from the factory cell up to the centre, and should be adapted to the special circumstances of each section. The information department of the ECCI should co-ordinate and centralize their work by suggestions, advice, and proposals for action.

3. The information department of the ECCI shall expand its activities by issuing monthly bulletins on the world situation, the work of the ECCI, and the activities of the sections, for the central committees of all the sections.

4. A special section of the ECCI information department shall be set up to fight social-democracy. Its job will be to collect, in close co-operation with the sections, all material exposing the treacherous role of social-democracy, and, in collaboration with the agitprop department of the ECCI, to work up this material for the use of the entire CI.

These new tasks of the information department and the work it has done hitherto require the utmost attention and support from all sections of the CI.

EXTRACTS FROM A LETTER FROM THE ORGANIZATION DEPARTMENT OF THE ECCI TO THE ORGANIZATION BUREAU OF THE CC OF THE CPGB

22 *April* 1925   Cmd. 2682, p. 5

The Party Congress of the C.P. of Great Britain, which is to be held in a few weeks time, will no doubt turn its attention to a number of organisational questions which are awaiting solution. The thesis elaborated by the C.C. of the C.P. of Great Britain deals with several important points, namely:—

(1) Utilisation of the experiences of the reorganisation of the Party on a factory nucleus basis.

(2) Strengthening and consolidation of the local leading Party organs.

(3) Recruiting of new members.

(4) The work of the fractions.

The question of making secure by organisational measures the great amount of sympathy which the C.P.G.B. has gained, has assumed enormous importance. Therefore, the Party should pay special attention to making its position secure among the masses, in order to make the fullest possible use of the present favourable veering to the left of the masses. If the C.P.G.B. is to gain political influence over the proletariat it must concentrate on the question of reorganisation. Therefore, the Party should not only make the most of the experiences of the already existing nuclei, but must also take the necessary measures to break down the resistance which still exists with respect to the formation of factory nuclei. The main obstacle in the way of the formation of factory nuclei is the workers' fear of dismissals. To remove this obstacle a systematic ideological campaign is essential. In this campaign it should be made perfectly clear that the nuclei are not to work openly. As to the factory nuclei themselves, we would like to point out that the unemployed too should be given an opportunity to join them. Wherever no factory nuclei exist, the unemployed connected with the factories should endeavour to form nuclei from outside. Party officials (trade union officials), including members of the Central Committee, must also join factory nuclei. Party organs, and above all, local committees, should do their utmost not only to form more nuclei, but also to develop the already existing factory nuclei. The decision of the C.C. concerning the appointment of an instructor is most welcome. Of course the appointment of an instructor is not everything. We would like to propose to the C.P.G.B. to introduce the system of instructors in general. This system has been tried with great success in other parties of the C.I. These instructors (of the C.C., the districts, etc.) need not become Party officials.

The reorganisation of the Party is not a mechanical measure, but should always be connected with the campaigns of the Party. With respect to this, recruiting campaigns are of particular importance. We draw the particular attention of the C.P.G.B. to the importance of recruiting Party members in the nuclei and in the factories. This does not of course mean that we are against the other forms of recruiting (through the Minority Movement, Trade Union fractions, etc.). . . . .

The question of factory newspapers is closely connected with the factory nuclei. We have hitherto received four copies of your factory newspapers. We must say that one cannot see by their outward appearance that they are organs of Communist Party nuclei. This must be remedied in future, for our aim is that the factory nuclei should use factory newspapers as one of the means by which they will be able to control the masses. Moreover, another object of factory newspapers is the activisation of the nucleus itself. We must, therefore, reiterate that factory newspapers must be produced at the cost of the nucleus and must be written and made up by the nucleus itself. At the same time the corresponding party committee must exercise its control over the factory paper. . . . But we must draw your attention to the following point: factory newspapers should also have in view the connection of the factory with the main Party organ and should look upon themselves as a means to arouse the interest of the indifferent masses in our Party newspaper.

Another important Org. question is that of the Party apparatus. The further development of the C.P.G.B. makes it incumbent on the latter to consider the question of the formation of new Party organs. Hitherto, there was a direct connection between the different local[s] of the same town and the district Party organisations. In such towns the various local branches were only loosely connected through a co-ordination committee. Such a state of affairs impedes the activity of the Party, and therefore the question of the formation of town committees endowed with all the rights of a leading Party organ, has become very acute. . . .

The question of the apparatus is also closely connected with the question of the Central Committee. Closer collaboration between the Pol. and the Org. Bureaux should be established. With respect to this we would like to suggest that two members of the Pol. Bureau be also members of the Org. Bureau. The departments of the C.C. which functioned hitherto as departments of the Pol. and Org. Bureaux should be converted into departments of the C.C. as a whole and co-ordinated through the Secretariat. The Pol. and Org. Bureaux should carry out their decisions through the Secretariat. Concerning the construction of the Party apparatus there are also special decisions of the Org. Conference to go upon. As Org. questions grow in importance it will become necessary to form a special Org. Department in the Central Committee. We want to draw your special attention to this point.

The development of the Minority Movement and the campaign which is already proceeding for the formation of factory committees makes it incumbent upon the Party to form strongly welded together fractions, which should be entirely under the control of the Party. Otherwise, there would be the risk of the strongly developed Minority Movement slipping out of our hands. . . .

The reorganisation of the Party on factory nuclei basis and the other alterations in the structure of the Party, made it incumbent on the Central Committee to elaborate new Party statutes and to place them before the Party Congress (or it should obtain from the Party Congress a mandate for their elaboration). The model statutes elaborated by the Org. Conference should be used as a basis for the new statutes.

STATEMENT BY THE ECCI ON THE SOFIA CATHEDRAL EXPLOSION

23 *April* 1925   *Inprekorr*, v, 66, p. 891, 24 *April* 1925

[On 16 April 1925 a bomb exploded in Sofia Cathedral where a funeral service was being held, attended by members of the Government. There were a number of casualties. The Bulgarian Government attributed the explosion to a communist plot, the prelude to a planned rising of which it had knowledge. On 3 March 1925 the Prime Minister, Tsankov, had published what he claimed to be the text of an ECCI resolution instructing the Bulgarian Communist Party to start an insurrection on 15 April. The ECCI immediately denied the authenticity of the resolution, and declared that the fabrication was designed to justify the murders and executions, past and to come, carried out by the Bulgarian Government. The foreign bureau of the Bulgarian Communist Party, in a statement signed by Kolarov and Dimitrov published on 7 May, denied any plan for an uprising and any complicity in the explosion. Like other terrorist acts, the statement went on, it was an inevitable retort to government terror. The ECCI also issued a denial of the Bulgarian Government's charges, as did Chicherin on behalf of the Soviet Government. Their statements, as well as a number of articles in the Russian and other communist papers, attributed the incident to public indignation against the Bulgarian Government's policy of judicial and extra-judicial murder. To justify that policy, Tsankov had forged documents about a planned rising and a plot to assassinate the King.

The Bulgarian communists continued to deny the charges until 1948 when Dimitrov, in his report to the fifth congress of the Bulgarian CP, described the explosion as 'an ultra-left deviation . . . an act of desperation perpetrated by the leadership of the military organization of the party'. About 1,500 arrests were made in the few days after the explosion, and many communists, socialists, and Peasant Union members were executed.]

Forgeries and deceptions are being more and more frequently used by enemies of the Communist International. Month after month, and recently week after week, cruder and cruder forgeries are published, now in one country, now in another, of alleged letters, instructions, decisions, and other documents attributed to the ECCI. The fascist Tsankov Government has broken the record. Following the explosion in the Sofia Cathedral this fascist Government published some hastily fabricated documents designed to prove the complicity of the Communist International in that act of terrorism. It is superfluous to explain that neither the Communist International nor any of its sections could, if only because of their opposition on principle to acts of individual terror, have had any connexion whatever with the Sofia explosion.

The Executive of the International declares emphatically that all the documents attributed to it concerning this event, as well as the alleged fixing of a date for a Bulgarian insurrection, are forgeries from beginning to end. The frenzied enemies of the Communist International who are conducting a 'holy war' against communists are growing more insolent every day.

The ECCI calls on the workers of all countries to get ready to defend themselves, and to condemn the treachery of the fascist Tsankov Government as it deserves. No white terror will stop the fight of the workers and peasants for their emancipation. The sympathies of progressive workers everywhere are wholly on the side of the workers and peasants of Bulgaria and their vanguard, who do not shrink from the struggle even in the face of death.

EXTRACTS FROM AN ECCI STATEMENT ON THE ELECTION OF HINDENBURG AS GERMAN PRESIDENT

27 *April* 1925   *Inprekorr*, v, 72, p. 961, 1 *May* 1925

[In the presidential election in Germany at the end of March 1925 the KPD vote dropped by 800,000, while the SPD remained unchanged. This continued the decline in the KPD vote shown in 1924, when it had fallen by more than a million between May and December, with the loss of 17 seats, while the SPD vote had increased by nearly 2 million, with a gain of 31 seats. At the first ballot for President, the KPD polled 1·9 million votes, the SPD 8 million. When the size of the nationalist vote in the first round became known in Moscow, Zinoviev advised the KPD to support Braun, the SPD candidate. The majority of the central committee were opposed to this, and made the offer only after the SPD had committed itself to support Marx, the Centre Party candidate, in an attempt to defeat Hindenburg. (Radek said later that the ECCI gave no guidance on the election, and its advice after the first round arrived too late to prevent Thaelmann standing again.) KPD policy was sharply criticized by the ECCI and French Communist Party representatives who attended the meeting of the German central committee in May, and by the Polish central committee. When reporting on the fifth plenum to the fourteenth conference of the RCP, Zinoviev cited the election of Hindenburg as proof of the relative stabilization of capitalism and the reduced tempo of the revolution. This could not, however, improve Germany's relations with France and Poland; on the contrary, it would make them worse. It might also mean a change in German policy towards Russia. According to Ruth Fischer, Moscow was shocked by the results of the election, and feared an Anglo-German bloc against Russia which would be supported by the SPD.]

The 'peaceful, democratic, bloodless tactics of evolution' have set Hindenburg on the throne. Noske and Ebert bring forth Hindenburg, predecessor of the new Hohenzollerns. . . . Among those responsible for the belief in Hindenburg as national hero among the more backward sections of the population the SPD is not the last.

The Entente imperialists contributed in no small degree to this result. Fourteen-and-a-half million votes were given for Hindenburg. A part of these votes was not so much for Hindenburg as against the Entente, for the idea of revenge on those who made the Versailles peace. In the hands of the Hindenburg clique these votes will become instruments of social reaction, of white terror, of monarchism.

There are two ways of struggle against monarchy. The first was taken by the Russian workers in 1917 and 1918. The other road, the evolutionary democratic road, is the one the Second International, embodied in German social-democracy, wanted to demonstrate. The social-democrats did not want to overthrow Wilhelm, but they were the first to come out for the overthrow of the German Soviets. They beheaded the Soviets in 1918. 'Noske is for democracy against any dictatorship', the German social-democrats maintained. Now even the blind can see that Noske and the SPD are not against all dictatorships but against the proletarian dictatorship and in favour of the bourgeois dictatorship. . . .

The Communist International suggested that the KPD support the social-democratic candidate in the second round if the SPD put its candidate forward again. But, faithful watch-dogs of the bourgeoisie that they are, the social-democrats withdrew their candidate in favour of the bourgeois candidate Marx. . . . Once more the SPD leaders showed the world that they are as dubious republicans as they are bad socialists. There is not the slightest doubt that the SPD leaders and the Second International will try to place responsibility on the German communists. They will throw sand in the eyes of the masses. Once again they will take up the campaign against the vanguard of the German proletariat. . . .

The class-conscious workers of Germany and the whole world must reflect on the political significance of Hindenburg's election. The workers who still sympathize with social-democracy must realize clearly that social-democratic tactics lead inevitably to the triumph of bourgeois reaction.

There is a monarchist danger in Germany. The workers and the communists must see this clearly. Communists cannot take up the position that the choice between monarchy and bourgeois republic is a matter of indifference. . . . They again propose a united front with social-democratic workers for the revolutionary struggle against the monarchist danger.

The black shade of reaction is covering more and more of the political map of Europe. In a number of countries reaction is growing stronger. Throughout the world the communists lead the struggle for trade union unity. The Second International is making wild attacks against unity, and again demonstrating that it is the most faithful pillar of the bourgeoisie; the same social-democrats who are responsible for Hindenburg's victory are the most deadly enemy, among all parties of the Second International, of trade union unity. . . .

The Communist International summons you to close your ranks, to establish the unity of workers of all countries, under the banner of class struggle, for the common fight against the monarchist danger. Remember that Hindenburg's election does not improve the prospects for peace, but conjures up the danger of new wars. Bear in mind that only the iron unity of the international proletariat can ward off this danger. . . . If the working masses do not turn away from the social-democratic leaders they will themselves be preparing new imperialist blood-baths. . . .

The 15 million German proletarians could free their country from the capitalist yoke and establish a soviet republic if they were not split, if they would recognize and reject the counter-revolutionary tactics of the SPD.

EXTRACTS FROM THE RULES ON THE ORGANIZATIONAL STRUCTURE OF COMMUNIST PARTIES APPROVED BY THE ORGBUREAU OF THE ECCI

4 *May* 1925   *Inprekorr*, v, 83, p. 1132, 15 *May* 1925

[The organization conference called by the ECCI met on 15 March 1925 and held seven sessions under the chairmanship of Piatnitsky. The two chief subjects were progress in the formation of factory cells and the organization of fractions in non-communist organizations. At the beginning of the year there were said to be 1,000 cells in Germany, 600 in France, and 30 in Britain. By March the total in 22 parties was 8,800, not all of them working well. In an article on fraction work, published while the Executive was meeting, Piatnitsky explained that the members of a fraction must vote according to party instructions, whether they agreed or not. The votes given to communist candidates in national or local elections were given not to the individual but to the party, and the mandate therefore belonged to the party in the person of its central committee. In trade unions fractions must be formed whether the union was reformist or revolutionary, and various organizational schemes were outlined to suit different unions. Fractions in factory committees were of the utmost importance; the committees covered the widest field, trade union and non-trade union, reformist and revolutionary. The fractions, working under the control of the factory cell, must capture the committees.]

THE IMPORTANCE OF PARTY ORGANIZATION

Correct party organization has an important part to play. The party can accomplish its mission only if its policy is communist, that is, a class policy. But however excellent the policy, it can only be realized if the party organization is so constructed that the policy can really be carried out among the broad strata of the working class. . . .

The party organization and its leadership must organize communist fractions in all mass organizations of workers and peasants. These fractions are the agents of the party in those organizations. Party campaigns should be so organized that all party bodies, wherever they are operating, act on uniform lines and with complete unanimity. It is therefore necessary for the party leadership to issue clear directions and precise instructions about the campaigns. . . .

Only an organization with such a structure is in a position to strengthen the influence of the communist party on the working masses. . . .

DEMOCRATIC CENTRALISM AND PARTY DISCIPLINE

. . . The communist party is a living party of action. Consequently differences of opinion are bound to arise among the members in discussions of programme and tactics; frequently a majority and minority opinion is to be found. In these cases the minority must obey the majority, and conscientiously carry out all decisions. . . .

THE FACTORY CELL

The basis of the communist party is the working class. The communist party is only the most class-conscious, most active, and most revolutionary part of the working class. To exert influence over the working class . . . to lead it in the struggle, is possible only where the workers are gathered together, that is, at their place of work.

In the factory communists must . . . intervene actively in all disputes between workers and employers, formulate the workers' demands, and show how the struggle is to be conducted. Economic struggles must be linked up with the party's political demands. The factory cell has the opportunity of drawing the best elements in the factory or other place of work into the factory cell. . . .

LOCAL PARTY ORGANIZATION

1. All members of factory, street, and other cells hold regular aggregate meetings to discuss and decide on all party questions; after these have been dealt with in all cells and the cells have agreed about their attitude, they elect representatives to the district conference and elect the local committee. . . .

2. The local committee guides the entire party work of the locality, issues directives to the cells, organizes and leads all party campaigns. It organizes cells in factories, workshops, etc., where they do not exist, and may direct party members to such factories, etc. in order to carry out this work there. It organizes all communists in trade unions, municipal councils, co-operatives . . . and all other organizations into communist fractions, instructs them and guides their work. . . .

THE DISTRICT

3. The district conference discusses all party questions, receives reports from the party centre and the district committee, elects delegates to the party congress, and elects the district committee. . . .

5. The district committee elects a presidium and a secretary, who is a full-time party worker, and sets up various bodies for party work in the district, such as organization, agitprop, and trade union departments, which maintain contact with the corresponding party organizations at a lower level exclusively through the district secretary. . . .

THE CENTRE

1. The central committee of the larger legal parties may consist of twenty-five or more members, and a few candidates. . . .

2. The central committee of the larger parties elects a politbureau and an orgbureau. . . .

3. The central committee meets in plenary session at least once a month. . . .

5. The politbureau and orgbureau deal with all current work at the centre.

6. The politbureau consists of three to seven members of the central committee and meets at least once a week. . . . its decisions can be revoked only by a plenary meeting of the central committee.

7. The orgbureau consists of three to seven members. . . . Appeals against decisions of the orgbureau can be made to the politbureau, which can reverse these decisions.

8. The plenary meeting of the central committee appoints a secretariat of two or three comrades (who must be central-committee members), who carry out decisions of the plenum, the politbureau, and the orgbureau, and prepare material for the meetings of these three bodies. . . .

10. At least one of the secretaries must be a member of the politbureau, and all are members of the orgbureau. . . .

COMMUNIST FRACTIONS

To exert influence on the broad working and peasant masses outside the party, the communist party must have agencies pursuing a communist policy in non-communist surroundings. Among these agencies are the communist fractions. . . .

2. As soon as a fraction is formed, it elects a leader or, if the fraction is large enough, a presidium.

3. Fractions are subordinate to the local, district, or central committee of the party, according to the scope of the organization in which they are working. . . .

4. The leader or presidium must be endorsed by the relevant party committee, as well as the fraction's choice of candidates for election in the trade union, co-operative, etc. For parliamentary and local elections the party committee or conference decides in advance on the choice of party members as candidates. . . .

7. The centre maintains contact with all fractions operating on a national scale. . . .

9. Communist fractions in the national committees of trade unions maintain direct contact with the communist fraction in the central body of the trade union federation and work according to its instructions. . . .

13. Where there is no communist fraction in the central body of the trade union federation, the trade union department of the party centre must set up a body to take the place of such a fraction, consisting of representatives of the fractions in the national committees of the individual trade unions.

EXTRACTS FROM A MANIFESTO OF THE ECCI, RILU, AND YCI AGAINST
IMPERIALIST ATROCITIES IN CHINA

8 *June* 1925   *Inprekorr*, v, 93, p. 1260, 12 *June* 1925

[Large-scale strikes and student unrest in Shanghai culminated in a demonstration on 30 May 1925, when thirteen demonstrators were killed by the concession police commanded by a British sergeant. This was followed by a general strike in Shanghai, and anti-British and anti-Japanese demonstrations throughout the country. The influence of the Chinese Communist Party, already strong among students (who had their own communist newspaper) and among industrial workers because of its active promotion of trade unionism, increased greatly, membership rising from roughly 900 to 20,000. The second conference of Chinese labour unions, held in Canton in May 1925, decided to affiliate to the RILU, and a Russian trade union delegation visited Shanghai in July–August 1925. From the middle of 1925 onwards, affairs in China began to occupy a more and more prominent place in the communist press, where they were compared with events in Russia in 1905, and *Inprekorr* ran a regular 'Hands off China' section. The central committee of the CCP issued a manifesto in June 1925 explaining that the bloody events in Shanghai were a result of imperialist policy; the movement started by 30 May had to be turned into a permanent movement to abolish foreign rule in China, and all classes in China must be drawn into it. The lead had to be taken by the working class.

The strike movement spread from Shanghai, and was particularly powerful in Canton, where the Kuomintang established its Government on 1 July 1925. Hu Han-min, a member of that Government and commander of the Canton army, arrived in Moscow at the end of 1925 to study the structure of the Red Army. In a speech at the end of 1925 Zinoviev said: 'Canton is already very like Moscow.' At the fourteenth CPSU congress he placed China at the centre of the world revolutionary movement. 'The events of the present year in Shanghai, in my opinion, may boldly be described without any exaggeration as the most important events of the year in world history. Now the Chinese movement has sunk in, has gone deep; the experience of the whole movement is being digested by the masses. There was a time when the Chinese CP . . . faced the question: Whither to lead the revolutionary masses? The Chinese party received a directive proposing to put on the brakes to a certain extent. . . . There was a tendency which spoke in favour of dying nobly, of carrying the movement to an acute phase, even to armed insurrection. The Comintern gave a directive against these moods.' If they waited they would have not thousands but millions of followers. The congress sent greetings to the second Kuomintang congress (which met in Canton in January 1926), and compared its role to that of the communist party in Russia—to destroy the bulwark of imperialism in Asia. This could be accomplished only if the KMT created a fighting alliance of the workers and peasantry, guided its actions by their interests, and supported every movement genuinely opposed to imperialism.]

World imperialism, which oppresses and exploits the Chinese workers and peasants, and grows ever more insolent, has with a savage cynicism worthy of the Russian tsars allowed fire to be opened on a peaceful crowd of striking textile workers in Tsingtao, whose only fault was that they dared to raise their voice for an alleviation of their bitter lot. . . .

For a long time the Chinese working class endured in silence this prison of international capitalist oppression; now their patience is at an end. In March the Chinese workers in the Japanese cotton mills of Shanghai decided to put an end to their unbearable sufferings and went on strike for an improvement of their economic position. In April the strike was supported by the Chinese workers in the Japanese factories of Tsingtao in the province of Shantung. . . . The Japanese industrialists were forced to yield to the pressure of the working masses. This struggle ended on 9 May with victory for the workers.

Meanwhile orders came from Japan to withdraw the concessions made. Encouraged by this support, the Japanese exploiters in Tsingtao, taking advantage of the weakness of the Chinese Government, sent their gendarmes and spies into the factories on strike. The Chinese workers did everything to preserve the peaceful character of their movement. . . . But on 29 May the warlike clique of Japanese militarists organized a bloodbath among the workers of Tsingtao . . . . which shook the millions of Chinese workers and awakened the slumbering but mighty revolutionary forces of this people to action.

A mighty wave of indignation swept over China. On the very next day, on 30 May, many thousands of people, including the revolutionary students, led by the communist party and the Kuomintang party, demonstrated their indignation and uttered a flaming protest against the insolence of the imperialists. . . .

As though by agreement the English and American police in Shanghai, while the Japanese gendarmerie were shooting unarmed workers in Tsingtao, took over the job of shooting demonstrators who expressed their sympathy with the Tsingtao workers and protested against Japanese militarism. . . .

These acts of atrocious violence were the foreign capitalists' revenge for their recent defeat; the blood of workers and students compensated them for their unsuccessful attempt to break the resistance of the trade unions and destroy the trade union movement. . . .

A detachment of 2,000 English, American, and Italian soldiers has been landed in Shanghai. . . . Warships are being concentrated in the harbour and further troop disembarkations prepared. This means the beginning of a new war, open armed intervention. While French imperialism wages war in Morocco the English, American, and Italian imperialists are beginning war with China. . . .

This united front of aggressive imperialism must be opposed by the unbreakable iron front of the European and American workers and peasants with the oppressed workers of the East.

The recent events in China bear eloquent witness to the uninterrupted growth of the national emancipation movement and the dominating role of the working class in this movement. . . . The greater the pressure exercised by the workers in the West on world capital, the better the prospects for the movement of the oppressed millions of the East, who from their end are undermining the rule of capitalism, which with equal ruthlessness oppresses the working masses of East and West.

EXTRACTS FROM A MANIFESTO OF THE EASTERN BUREAU OF THE ECCI AGAINST THE WAR IN MOROCCO

8 *June* 1925   *Inprekorr*, v, 93, p. 1264, 12 *June* 1925

[Fighting between the French in Morocco and Abd el Krim's Rif forces followed hostilities in 1924 between the Rifis and Spain in Spanish Morocco, in which Abd el Krim had been very successful. On 10 September 1924 Semard and Doriot, on behalf of the French CP, sent congratulations to Abd el Krim and urged him 'to fight all imperialisms, French imperialism included', until Morocco was free. The frontier between French and Spanish Morocco was undefined and uncertain, and the Rif forces opened an attack on the French on 13 April 1925. A French CP manifesto in May 1925 demanded the evacuation by the French of their zone in Morocco and the recognition of a Rif republic. (Abd el Krim surrendered to a combined Franco-Spanish offensive in May 1926.) The CPGB endeavoured to organize a campaign against the war in Morocco in the Middle East and India. The communist parties in Syria, Palestine, and Egypt were asked to organize a joint conference and to set up a committee of action, and some Indian socialists visiting London were persuaded to write to India in similar terms. 'Due to lack of finance, our party is absolutely unable to send anyone to either India or Egypt to develop the connexions made.'

An Algerian delegate at the sixth Comintern congress in 1928 said that during the demonstrations and strikes in France against the Moroccan war, the North African workers in France had made no response at all, the communist party organizations in the areas where they lived having done no work among them. This failure was followed by the appointment of a colonial organizer, and in 1926 the French CP set up a colonial bureau.]

The Painlevé–Briand–Caillaux Government has launched a war in Morocco that Herriot had for months been preparing, in agreement with the Resident General Marshal Lyautey. The imperialism of the left bloc, concealed behind symbolic gestures of peace, is now seen to be as dangerous as the imperialism of the national bloc. . . . The proposals for negotiations made by Abd el Krim were systematically rejected by Lyautey and Herriot, who organized a blockade of the Rifis. . . .

Events in Morocco in 1907–11 and the stroke at Agadir were the forerunners of the great battles of 1914–18. The robber campaign now being conducted by France against the Rif again threatens to provoke serious international complications. Italy and England, as well as France and Spain, are interested in plundering Morocco. France is waiting for Spain's defeat to annex the Rif area. . . . England and Italy are awaiting a suitable moment to claim their share of the booty for the sake of their national prestige. . . .

The socialist leaders, who belong to the left bloc and support the Government, are equally guilty with Herriot of preparing the war, and with Painlevé of launching it and carrying it on. They are the same as they were in 1914, giving an ideological cover to the imperialist adventure of the left bloc . . . . and helping to spread lies about the peaceful and legitimate character of the events in Morocco. . . .

If the democrats and social-democrats of the left bloc do not demand the complete destruction of the Rif Kabyles as openly as do the reactionary imperialist clique of the national bloc, that is only for tactical reasons and with the object of the better deceiving the broad masses of peasants and workers, who are opposed to the war. . . .

The war in Morocco will be long and murderous, and will provoke new conflicts and new international complications between the rival imperialists. England will resist to the utmost the establishment of a French Gibraltar on the conquered Rif shores, and is intriguing in Spain to prevent an understanding between the two countries. . . . Italian imperialism is exploiting these events to demand Tunis; it is condemning French ambitions in order to mask its own desire for colonial expansion and to conceal the preparations it is making to this end in Tripoli. . . .

The horrors of the last war will be as nothing in comparison with what may now be unleashed on the world by murderous imperialism and militarism. . . .

Comrades! Workers and peasants! The Communist International warns you of the danger and summons you to call it to a halt. On you alone does it depend to put an end to this slaughter. Unite and organize, and raise such a protest that your criminal governments will retreat and hasten to conclude peace with the Rif Kabyles.

EXTRACTS FROM A RESOLUTION OF THE ORGBUREAU OF THE ECCI ON IMMEDIATE ORGANIZATIONAL TASKS

14 *July* 1925   *Inprekorr*, v, 117, p. 1627, 4 *August* 1925

[Introducing the resolution, Piatnitsky said the department was concentrating on organizing factory cells and trade union fractions. It had issued instructions to all parties and circulated reports received from the sections. Some parties had organized instruction courses on factory cell and fraction work. The department offered advice on how to start factory news sheets, and issued a number of special booklets.]

Having heard the report of the orgdepartment on its activities since the meeting of the enlarged Executive, and on the position of organization work in the CI sections, the orgbureau declares that cell work in the communist parties still leaves much to be desired. Consequently the orgbureau decides:

1. The orgdepartment is instructed to issue ideological and organizational directives for giving a more political character to existing cells and for the formation of new cells. The leadership in the parties should aim at getting the factory cells to deal in particular . . . with the following questions:

The campaign for trade union unity on a national and international scale;

The war in Morocco;

Intervention in China;

The campaign and conspiracies against Soviet Russia.

The leadership should energetically promote factory-cell work by directives, instructions, publications, supplying speakers, etc. . . . .

2. The orgdepartment should aim at getting the cells to discuss all party questions. That is the only way of . . . reducing passivity. The state of affairs at present, in which a small circle of officials do the work for the entire membership and make the decisions, must be liquidated as quickly as possible. Every party member must be assigned party work. . . . .

3. . . . Because of the difficulties of communist factory-cell work (employer-terrorism, danger of dismissal, denunciation by social-democratic officials, etc.) the party leadership and members in countries with deeply rooted social-democratic traditions still neglect factory-cell work, for their work in the area where they live is easier and makes fewer demands on

the members. . . . These tendencies are an obstacle to the political activity of communist parties and their development into mass parties. . . .

4. Some hostile parties (social-democrats and fascists) have recognized the importance of winning the factory workers. . . . It must be clear to every communist that the fight against those hostile parties which still have workers in their ranks . . . can only be won by the systematic and untiring work of the communist factory cells. Many workers organized in trade unions and social-democratic parties do not read our press or attend our meetings. Planned cell work, and personal contact in the factory, helped by the factory-cell newspapers, are the best method of winning the workers and weakening the influence of hostile parties. . . .

7. Communist parties must try by steady and assiduous recruiting work to get sympathizers to join the communist party. . . . Where the parties are legal, the admission of factory workers as members should not be made difficult by a candidate system, trial period, or other formality.

8. The orgdepartment should as before vigorously direct the attention of sections to the formation of fractions in all non-party organizations, in the first place the trade unions. . . .

9. The orgdepartment of the ECCI should work closely with the Eastern department, in order to promote organizational and particularly cell work in Eastern countries. . . .

11. It is necessary for the orgdepartment to do more than it has done hitherto to instruct the sections of the CI on organization work by sending out instructors, and to keep under review the execution of the organizational decisions of the CI.

EXTRACTS FROM A LETTER FROM THE ECCI TO ALL ORGANIZATIONS
AND MEMBERS OF THE GERMAN COMMUNIST PARTY

20 *August* 1925   *Inprekorr*, v, 128, p. 1863, *4 September* 1925

[The Russian party was becoming more and more uneasy about the position of the KPD, and distrustful of the Maslow–Fischer leadership. It had taken to sending its own delegations, independently of the ECCI, to other parties, including the British, French, and Polish, and was suspected of a 'westward orientation'. The KPD had lost support at elections, and its influence on the trade unions was at a low ebb; moreover, its distrust of the moves towards a rapprochement with the IFTU endangered that policy. The fifth ECCI plenum, which admitted the 'temporary stabilization of capitalism', had urged the KPD to be more conciliatory to social-democratic workers. The weakness of the KPD was explained primarily in terms of the October 1923 fiasco. In an article published in June 1925 Manuilsky wrote that the Dawes plan, the partial stabilization of capitalism, American dictatorship in Europe, the transformation of the German proletariat into colonial slaves, the new offensive against the

Soviet Union, and the growth of fascism all over the world were 'interlocking links in the chain of events which started with the defeat of the German revolution'. At the tenth KPD congress, which met from 12 to 17 July 1925, the ECCI delegates made a sharp attack on the ultra-left wing of the party, led by Rosenberg and Scholem. They were attacked as 'part of the international fraction against bolshevism'. The ultra-left, in their turn, accused the majority of the central committee of centrism. Zinoviev sent a letter in the name of the ECCI to the congress, urging it to recognize as a fact the temporary stabilization of capitalism in Germany. It was this that in part explained the strength of the SPD, which the workers believed was useful in getting reforms. To apply the tactics required for this situation the 'ultra-left fever' must be eradicated. The new central committee should have more working-class members, and more members engaged in trade union work. The party should not hesitate to give responsible posts to former right-wing members if they really followed the party line. The letter urged greater freedom of discussion in the party, and a careful review of all expulsions. Manuilsky, who appeared at the congress under the name of Samuely, again advocated a more conciliatory attitude to the SPD rank and file 'against their leaders'. The political theses of the congress, carried by 166 votes to 4, made the 'destruction of the counter-revolutionary influence of the SPD among the masses' the chief task of the party. Another resolution referred to the ECCI resolution of March 1925 which said that Brandler and Thalheimer 'deserved expulsion', and added that the KPD 'expects this decision to be executed without delay if this group in defiance of the International's decisions should continue its anti-party fraction work'. Manuilsky asked for Rosenberg's and Scholem's names to be removed from the list of candidates for election to the central committee, but the congress in closed session refused this request, and they were elected. Added to this and other acts of insubordination, Maslow (in prison in Germany) had been extremely critical of the situation in Russia, where, he said, the pressure of the kulaks was forcing the Russian party and the Comintern to the right. The ECCI presidium, meeting on 29 July 1925, approved the action of its delegates to the tenth KPD congress, and decided to intervene again in the German party against the 'ultra-left danger'. The KPD was invited to send a delegation to Moscow; it consisted of nine members, including Thaelmann and Fischer; according to Borkenau, they were given the choice of abandoning Maslow and Fischer, or breaking with Moscow. With Thaelmann taking the lead in support of the ECCI, the 'open letter' was then sent to the KPD. Ruth Fischer, who voted against the letter at the meeting, was induced to sign it as a matter of discipline. At the end of September 1925 she was again called to Moscow, and temporarily prohibited from returning to Germany. At the meeting in August Bukharin urged the pressing need for more democracy in the party and more conciliatory language to the SPD. The fate of the KPD was at stake. Some weeks later an article in *Inprekorr* elaborated these arguments: 'It is a question of developing the greatest possible recruiting strength to expand and reinforce the eastward orientation of the proletarian red front against the western orientation, against the black united front of the bourgeoisie.' From the outside the KPD congress had appeared virtually unanimous, but it was not bolshevik unanimity based on agreement with the

Comintern and the KPD membership. It reflected a system that was estranging the party officials from the membership, and the party itself from the masses. Affairs in the central committee were moving towards a personal dictatorship, to a policy independent of the CI, to the revision of Leninism in a 'West European' direction, and to passive resistance to the Comintern's trade union policy.

The open letter was signed by all members of the ECCI and by the KPD delegation, and was published in the *Rote Fahne* on 1 September. On the same day the central committee of the KPD passed, against one vote and one abstention, a resolution approving without reservation the report of the negotiations of its delegation with the ECCI, and endorsed the ECCI's criticism of the KPD leaders. A conference of party secretaries and editors passed a similar resolution against seven votes and two abstentions. It agreed that the German bourgeoisie were turning West, but the working class, oppressed by the Dawes regime, was turning to the Soviet Union. The resolution enjoined 'a new language, a new tone, and new forms of agitation towards social-democratic workers', and persuasion rather than dictatorial methods towards KPD members; there must be no hesitation or reservation in working as one with the Comintern.

At a meeting of the central committee of the RCP on 10 October 1925 Zinoviev said that the ECCI had from the first been dubious about the Maslow–Fischer group, but it had had no choice because of the extreme disappointment in those who had led the KPD at the time of the October defeat. The Comintern trade union line had been put through at the Frankfurt congress 'only thanks to an ultimatum from the ECCI'. The wall between the KPD and the social-democratic masses was growing higher. The rank-and-file members of the KPD had been unaware of the dispute between the ECCI and Maslow–Fischer before the open letter, and that was why the ECCI had been compelled to put Thaelmann's 'workers group' at the head of the German central committee.

At a conference called by the KPD on 30 October to discuss the open letter, the ECCI delegate spoke of the serious crisis in the KPD. Although it took the form of a dispute between the ECCI and the Fischer–Maslow group, it was at bottom an internal KPD question, concerned with the relation of the leaders to the rank and file, of the party to the masses, and of the present leaders to the Comintern. They were trying to establish their own dictatorship by discrediting the International. The KPD needed left leadership, but there was a difference between the proletarian and intellectual left. The party needed at its head not literary bohemians, but left-wing workers, who could inspire confidence in the non-party masses.

At the conclusion of the conference a resolution was adopted by 217 to 30 votes, with one abstention, which condemned the sectarianism of the Fischer–Maslow group, their neglect of trade union work, their underhand fight against the Comintern, their theoretical deviations, and their suppression of party democracy.]

During the last session of the enlarged Executive in March–April 1925, and shortly afterwards, we discussed fully with the representatives of the KPD the questions on which, in our opinion, party work showed the greatest defects. The most important question—the question of the German party—was then and is now the problem of increasing the recruiting strength of our party, the problem of winning the masses, and particularly the social-democratic masses. . . . It was from this standpoint also that we considered other questions, such as . . . work in the trade unions, convincing the social-democratic workers, normalization of party life . . . (which is itself a prerequisite for the correct attitude to the non-party masses), the liquidation of the concealed struggle against the International (liquidation of the practice of sending so-called independent emissaries to other parties). . . .

Before the [tenth KPD] congress the representatives of the Executive discussed matters once more with the German delegation . . . the three most important subjects were:

First: the Executive pointed out that the leading Ruth Fischer–Maslow group showed some right-wing deviations, too great an emphasis on parliament, etc.

Second: it was decided to make a real change in the trade union question, and, to advertise this, to elect at the congress a strong and capable trade union department, or to instruct the new party centre to do so.

Third: the representatives of the Executive insisted that fresh and capable personnel should be elected to the central committee, particularly comrades familiar with trade union work, including some oppositional comrades. . . .

Subsequently the Executive was consulted three times about the composition of the central committee, and three times gave its advice.

At the congress these decisions were for the most part not carried out. Comrade Ruth Fischer's group not merely sabotaged the decisions, but instigated such treatment of the Executive's delegates that they were compelled to make a statement on it. At the close of the congress an offer of alliance with the Scholem–Rosenberg group against the Executive was silently accepted. . . .

This caused a severe crisis. The first delegation which came to us with the instruction to ask the Executive to disavow its delegates was forced to admit, after a vigorous discussion, that the Executive was right. The entire delegation declared that it considered the ECCI's criticism correct, and the speeches of the ECCI delegation correct. . . .

The second delegation was divided. Comrade Ruth Fischer at first fought against the ECCI's criticism, but after long discussion in the ECCI commission, at which representatives of all the important parties were present, she too made a statement recognizing the correctness of the ECCI's criticism. . . .

1. THE GENERAL SITUATION

The world political situation can be described as very critical. Despite the relative stabilization in central Europe, the most important contradictions of present-day capitalism show a high degree of tension. The rapid growth of the Soviet Union and the decline in England, the successes of the international red united front . . . and the unprecedented accentuation of the colonial and semi-colonial liberation struggles . . . the concentration of imperialist forces against the Soviet Union . . . all these are signs that the situation is becoming more acute.

A most important phenomenon is Germany's new orientation to the West. This gives rise to a change in popular attitudes, and is to some extent reflected among the least class-conscious sections of the proletariat.

Two processes can be observed among the German working class: first, a new wave of sympathy for the Soviet Union; social-democratic workers are beginning to move towards communism, although not directly towards the communist party. . . .

Secondly, there are growing among corrupted sections of the working class so-called 'anti-Muscovite' tendencies, which reflect the new orientation of the bourgeoisie. This process is in fact to be found also in the KPD. The so-called ultra-left tendency is often only a cover for social-democratic . . . sentiments which threaten to turn into direct treachery to the international working class. Both these processes are international in character and therefore particularly important. . . .

The Ruth Fischer–Maslow group did not understand the need to fight energetically against the 'ultra-left' but actually anti-communist tendencies, and even supported them by playing a highly ambiguous part on international questions.

2. TRADE UNION WORK, THE COMINTERN, AND THE LEADING PARTY-CENTRE GROUP

These defects of leadership were most obvious in the trade union question. As early as the Frankfurt congress in 1924 . . . marked differences arose between the Executive and the new German party leadership on this question. . . . The failure to understand the importance of trade union work meant that for months on end the decisions of the Comintern were inadequately carried out by the Maslow–Fischer group. A confidential telegram from the Executive [central committee] after the Frankfurt congress was circularized to all district secretaries in order to incite them to protest against the Executive; not enough was done before the fifth world congress to combat anti-trade union propaganda in the party.

The fifth world congress put the slogan of international trade union unity on the order of the day for the first time. It considered this the basic element of our entire bolshevik strategy. . . . At the fifth congress the German delegation led by Ruth Fischer at first opposed the Executive's proposal. Their attack concealed the charge that the struggle for trade union unity was only a 'move in Russian foreign policy', an attempt to establish better relations with MacDonald's social-democratic Government.

Long negotiations were necessary to convince the delegation of the baselessness of their policy. The charge that the fight for trade union unity was part of a diplomatic game being played by Russian foreign policy can be explained only by the basically anti-bolshevik, social-democratic mentality of the leading group. The same charge was made by MacDonald himself and all English and international social-traitors to discredit the struggle for trade union unity. . . .

Thus the severe losses which our party has suffered in recent years in all spheres of trade union work were multiplied. At the ADGB congress in 1922 the opposition had 88 delegates; this year there were only two. We have lost a number of trade union branches and local union posts. Our ideological influence on the 80 per cent. and more of the members of the free German unions not organized in political parties has dropped steeply. . . .

We have already mentioned that comrade Ruth Fischer's group frivolously dissolved the former trade union department of our party centre. The explicit promise of the representatives of the centre to propose, at the tenth party congress, the formation of a new and strong trade union department, was not kept. . . .

3. THE ATTITUDE TO THE COMMUNIST INTERNATIONAL

Broad political tendencies within the working class are not without their influence on the party of the proletarian revolutionary vanguard. . . . The vacillations and treacheries of certain groups of workers influenced by the bourgeois campaign against Moscow are reflected in 'anti-Muscovite' tendencies within our party, that is, tendencies directed against the Soviet Union, against the RCP, and against the Comintern.

This danger is greater in the KPD because all the present tendencies and shades within it are still without exception strongly influenced by social-democratic, 'West-European' traditions.

Every deviation in communist policy in Germany has begun with an attack on Soviet Russia, the RCP, and the Comintern. The seven-years' experience of the German revolution has made it clear that all such deviations, whether masked as left or right, lead straight towards social-democracy or to an alliance with it. . . .

The change in the political situation, the final turn of the German bourgeoisie towards the West, the social-democrats' intense anti-Russian campaign, make the present danger of anti-bolshevik deviations in the KPD greater and more acute than ever before.

The ultra-left group of Scholem, Rosenberg, Katz, who accuse the Comintern and its most important parties of opportunism, have not only nothing in common with Leninism; in their attitude to the Comintern and to the problems of the German revolution, they have an explicitly anti-bolshevik character. Dangerous social-democratic deviations . . . are also to be found among the leading members of the Fischer–Maslow group. . . .

Comrade Maslow's ideology is not only in tactical contradiction to Leninism; the contradiction is also one of principle. It is one of the roots of the resistance within the KPD to Comintern tactics. It is one of the roots of the failure of the leading group of the German *Zentrale* over many years to understand trade union work, the core of our policy. . . .

Since the third world congress the attitude of comrade Maslow's group to the Comintern has been incorrect, unbolshevik. At the Jena congress this group opposed the views of Lenin and the Executive . . . they expressed every possible misgiving and reservation about the Comintern's united front tactics and the slogan of a workers' and peasants' government. . . . During the past year comrade Ruth Fischer, despite the protest of the Executive, sent emissaries to several sections of the Comintern, whose 'mission' it was to change the Executive's tactics by fractional means. The result of these journeys was to discredit and alienate the German party among the fraternal sections of the Comintern. . . .

The entire German party, and above all the best comrades of the German left in all party organizations and districts, are in duty bound to do their utmost to break the unbolshevik system of the party's attitude to the Comintern encouraged by the Maslow–Ruth Fischer group. . . .

Events since the Frankfurt congress have shown that in all disputed questions the Comintern was completely right as against the Maslow–Ruth Fischer group. It was right about united front tactics and the trade union question. It was also right on the question of the presidential elections. . . .

We are firmly convinced that the communist workers of Germany will quickly recognize that the Comintern is absolutely right in the present struggle about the inner-party line of the KPD, about its attitude to the Comintern and to the German working masses, about its attitude to Leninist theory, while the Maslow–Ruth Fischer group are absolutely wrong on all these questions.

4. THE INNER-PARTY LINE

The leading group in the party *Zentrale* were incapable of devising measures which gave them access to the masses. And they could not do so because their internal party policy was incorrect.

As already mentioned, questions of inner party life were discussed fully

with representatives of the German *Zentrale* at the meeting of the enlarged
Executive. The Executive representatives pointed out that ultra-centralism,
mechanical pressure, administrative methods, the absence of propaganda
and of methods of persuasion in general, fear of new forces, etc., were
bound to have damaging effects. At that discussion it was decided to
strengthen inner-party democracy. . . . We believe that without these
internal reforms the party will be unable to pursue a correct policy among
the masses. Consequently the Executive demanded these reforms to
'normalize party life'. At the Executive the German delegation, with
comrade Ruth Fischer at their head, accepted these proposals. . . .

But the German party congress was organized and conducted in such a
way that despite all the promises made the exact opposite was achieved.
Although there are strong groups on the wings of the party (ultra-left and
right), this fact found no reflection whatever at the congress. There was
no political discussion, since the delegates had decided beforehand what
they were going to say; freedom of discussion was annulled at the congress
itself, the highest party instance. . . .

What is lacking in the party is control from below, that is, from the
party membership. At the same time the leading group continue to fight
against control from above, that is, by the Comintern Executive. This has
created a situation in which all sense of responsibility is lost, which has
had a number of intolerable results.

With such a structure it is impossible for the party to develop its recruiting powers. With such a system the party itself is being ruined. The system
must be broken, in order to avoid a still greater crisis, which would have
really catastrophic results.

5. THE DANGER OF LACK OF PRINCIPLE

Practical bolshevism consists, *inter alia*, in acting on theoretically valid
and honestly-thought-out political lines. Among the Maslow–Fischer
group, however, innate convictions and subjective appraisal of the situation
are in glaring conflict with the accepted line. They are at bottom profoundly pessimistic: there are no revolutionary perspectives; on the contrary, the masses are completely passive, they flee from the daily reality
and play at being soldiers, etc. It is impossible to win them over. The
Comintern, however, 'demands' that the masses be won over. Hence the
ambiguity in the actions of this leading group. Pessimism is connected with
flirting with the ultra-left. The demands of the International are met by
recognition on paper, and by the attempt to fulfil them without any belief
in the possibility of their fulfilment. Hence the vacillating position and
political instability of this group, accompanied by the worst kind of diplomatic attitudes in their relations with the Comintern. . . .

6. THE TASKS OF THE PARTY

Criticism of the mistakes of the group who have up to now led the party will be of real and lasting use only if it leads to a better and more resolute fulfilment of the party's positive tasks in winning the masses.

At the present time the most important task of the party is to respond promptly and actively to the political regrouping which is beginning to take place within the German working class. The most significant phenomenon in recent months has been the beginning of resistance among broad working masses to the 'westward orientation', that is, to the going-over of the bourgeoisie to the side of the Entente imperialists, resistance to the leadership of the Second International; these working masses are turning to the Soviet Union and—although by roundabout ways—to the proletarian revolution. Without exaggerating the importance or speed of this development, the party must place these new phenomena at the centre of its attention, carefully follow their development, and pay due regard to them in all its practical political activities.

What it all comes down to is that the party must greatly improve its recruiting work. . . .

The way to reach the best part of the German social-democratic workers is to take up the fight against those excesses which had their origin in the time when the struggle was being waged with arms in hand. Great harm is done to the working-class cause, for example, when communists and social-democrats come to blows; this still happens, and the communists are not without blame, as well as the social-democrats. These fights are grist to the mill of the counter-revolutionary leaders of German social-democracy, who of course deliberately stir them up. Communists must take the initiative in putting an end to these fights, and this naturally requires the good will of the social-democratic workers. . . .

The drive towards trade union unity must be embodied, as rapidly as possible, in a trade union left wing, as it is in England. That is the next step forward which the German party must take. . . . The serious intention of the party leadership to make this the basic task of the party must be demonstrated in the formation of a strong trade union department at the KPD centre.

What is the significance for the communist party, in a country like Germany, of winning influence in the trade unions? It means, above all, winning influence over the organized workers in factory, mine, workshop, and railway, in all industrial undertakings. Only those communist workers can have substantial influence in the German unions to-day who have influence in the factory. But it is precisely in the factories that communist influence has recently grown weaker, and we should not conceal this fact. We must grasp the simple truth that in the long run the struggle between communism and social-democracy for influence over the masses will be decided at factory level. . . .

Of the greatest importance, in addition to reform of the internal party line and reorganization on the basis of factory cells, is the rapid building up of a system of truly bolshevik party fractions, working with initiative, in all workers' organizations without exception, wherever there are communists. . . .

7. WHY MUST THE PARTY BE REORGANIZED NOW, AND QUICKLY?

Many comrades will ask why a change in the KPD leadership has become essential 'so suddenly'; in fact there is nothing 'sudden' about the differences which have arisen between the Executive and the Ruth Fischer group. These differences have been apparent throughout the last eighteen months, and have grown steadily more acute until they have reached the present stage, which is intolerable for the party and the International. The Executive warned the leading group more than once against persisting in their deviations. . . . The Berlin congress, and the events immediately following, finally made it clear that the Executive's hopes of settling the differences by the usual forms of co-operation were unfounded. The attacks by comrades Fischer and Maslow make it urgently necessary to place the German party question openly before the entire membership. . . .

We repeat that it is not the German left which is bankrupt, but a few of its leaders. With all its mistakes in the past and the present, the German left is not merely a group of individuals. It has a great historical mission to perform. It drew the lessons of October 1923, defeated Brandlerism; it united the torn party at the hour of its most severe crisis. . . .

The chief defects are to be sought not in the healthy proletarian party membership; it is those at the very top who have failed. Great new tasks confront the party. The situation is developing not against us, but for us. In the last few months the class struggle in Germany has been moving on an ascending line.

Only if the entire party recognizes the signs of the times, becomes aware of itself and its own strength, of the Communist International and the invincible might of the German working class, can it surmount the crisis and lead the German proletariat to victory. But if it does so, victory is certain.

[The letter was signed by members of the ECCI, the nine members of the KPD delegation in Moscow, and the central committee of the KPD.]

LETTER FROM THE ORGANIZATION DEPARTMENT OF THE ECCI TO THE
CENTRAL COMMITTEE OF THE CPGB

26 *September* 1925   Cmd. 2682, p. 18

[This letter was followed on 30 October 1925 by one from E. Brown, CPGB
representative on the ECCI, explaining its origin. '. . . At a recent meeting oi
the Org. Bureau I was called upon to give a report on the progress of organisational work in England. Of course the whole interest of the Comintern is now
centred upon England and everybody rolled up to hear the report. When it was
finished, and after a discussion, a mass of suggestions were made as to the best
ways of tightening up the organisation of the Party in England.

'In a small Commission which subsequently met I had all my work put out to
prevent the new enthusiasts from sending a 20-page letter of instructions which
had been prepared by Comrade Fried who is the man in charge of British
organisational matters in the Org. Bureau. Finally, the letter which you have
received was drafted by myself and accepted by the Commission. On the first
point, dealing with the question of extending our work in the textile and seamen's Union, I know you will agree with. From past minutes of the Political
and Org. Bureaux I know that much attention has already been given to this
work.

'On the second point I feel that the Comintern are right and that to direct
the purely organisational work of the Party in addition to the Org. Bureau it
is necessary to have a responsible department. It is quite obvious that there is
a mass of detailed material coming in from the districts which is not being given
the detailed attention it merits. Neither is the centre here being provided with
the organisational material in the same manner, and to the same extent, which
characterises the reports of the purely political work of the Party. On the face
of it, and judged from Moscow, the proposition seems reasonable. However,
if there is good reason why the step should not be taken the whole matter can
be reviewed when the Delegation is here at the Plenum.

'On the third point, I agreed to it being inserted in the letter because of the
unity of the opposition. They are of the opinion that a party nucleus in a trade
union local branch is quite clear that its only responsibility is to the Party, but
on the question of a Party fraction, elected by workers to serve in a representative capacity on some committee or other, they are not quite clear that our
members recognise only Party obligations. They assume that in addition to
responsibility to the Party these comrades have responsibility also to the workers
who have elected them, and, further, that this dual responsibility leads to
divided allegiance. Support is lent to their viewpoint by the definitions on this
question which is contained in the organisational part of our Party training
syllabus. Anyway, a note from the Org. Bureau stating that in whatever capacity
our Party members are serving in the general working-class movement their
party allegiance must supersede all other responsibilities will be sufficient I
think. This is the way to dispose of this latter question.'

Both letters were included in the White Paper published by the Home Office
in June 1926, containing a selection of the papers seized during a police raid

on communist premises in London in October 1925, when twelve members of the CPGB central committee were arrested and brought to trial.]

The organisation Department of the E.C.C.I. at a recent session, discussed the position of organisation in the C.P.G.B. and was pleased to record that the influence of the Party is making rapid headway amongst the masses of workers. Particularly was this shown during the recent industrial crisis and in the strikes and lockouts of the last few months. The growing influence of the Party was also reflected, to a satisfactory extent, in the discussion and decision of the Scarborough Trade Union Congress.

At the same time, however, it is distinctly noticeable, and our information confirms this, that the fundament organisation of the Party is inadequate. This fact may be primarily attributed to the numerical weakness of this Party. The first task is of course to transform our gains into actual party membership. This is the way to the mass Party—the most important task of the CPGB. We note with pleasure your arrangements for Red recruiting week and hope that all sections of the Party will rally round your slogan of 'Double the Factory nuclei' and 'Double the Party membership'.

But we believe that even with the united and limited membership further organisational progress can be made. Great tasks await the Party. The class struggle in Britain threatens to spread as a result of the decay of capitalism and the British Empire on one hand and the rise of the revolutionary spirit amongst the masses on the other. If the Party is to fulfil its historic mission its apparatus must be constructed in accordance with the demands. We consider that the greatest drawback to proper organisational work in the C.P.G.B. is the lack of an Organisation Department.

The lack of this department, with a full time paid officer in charge, makes it very difficult for the C.P.G.B. to carry on systematic work. The absence of such a Department leaves the task of assisting the Districts in their day to day organisational work more to chance than definite plan. The absence of an Organisation Department is perhaps responsible for the non-return of Questionnaire we sent to you.

In our opinion it is essential that the Central Executive Committee should form an Organisational Department with a paid chief. The Organisation Department should have control over a number of instructors whose duty it would be to instruct lower Party organs and exercise control of same.

Further the first task of the Organisation Department should be to set up corresponding organs working under its direction and control in every District Committee of the Party. These should instruct and direct the work of the local organs and control same reporting regularly to the Central Committee.

In the past the Party has rightly concentrated its Party fraction and Minority Movement work upon Metal, Mining and Transport Unions. The time has now come for a further development and recent events have proved that we must spread out our work to cover the Textile and Seamen's industry. We welcome the initial attempts in both these industries and would urge you to give even greater attention than at present.

Another matter which should take your attention is the practice of differentiating between Trade Union nuclei and Trade Union fractions. Some British comrades explain that the two terms are necessary because a nucleus is a number of INDIVIDUAL members organised in another working-class organisation whilst a fraction is a number of REPRESENTATIVE members who, in addition to their Party obligations, have a FORMAL responsibility to the workers who elected them.

We see no reason for calling Communist comrades organised within a local trade union section a trade union NUCLEUS, whilst the Communist comrades in district or national trade union executives are called trade union FRACTIONS. For Party reasons Communists in all trade unions (and other non-Party organisations) must be organised into fractions. In their organisations they carry out the decisions of the Party and are responsible to the latter for this. Communist comrades with a seat in the Executive of a non-Party organisation are at the same time members of their fraction. They are responsible for their work solely to the Party.

The fact of the confusion between these two terms necessitates certain explanation being made. This will be the task of the Organisation Department and the Industrial Department of the Party.

EXTRACTS FROM THE ECCI AGITPROP DEPARTMENT'S THESES FOR PROPAGANDISTS ON THE SECOND ANNIVERSARY OF LENIN'S DEATH

January 1926   *Inprekorr*, vi, 10, p. 125, 14 *January* 1926

[A parallel set of 'theses for agitators', issued a few days earlier, stated that 'indications of a future fascist dictatorship are quite clearly visible even in such "democratic" countries as England and France', and that 'one of Lenin's greatest strokes of genius was his assertion of the possibility of building socialism in a single country. This idea has been corroborated by the economic and cultural successes of the Soviet Union which have occurred in the two years since his death.' The theses also came out strongly against Locarno: 'The praise for Locarno as an instrument of peace, the agitation of the bourgeois and socialist press which emphasize the "love of peace" embodied in Locarno in contrast to the "imperialism" of the USSR, are nothing but ideological armaments for new wars.'

As part of the campaign against the Locarno pact, initialed on 16 October 1925 and signed in London on 1 December, the ECCI had called a conference of representatives of the central committees and parliamentary fractions of several European communist parties; it was held in Brussels on 10–12 October 1925, and was attended by delegates from the French, German, British, Polish, Belgian, Dutch, and other communist parties. It agreed that in their respective parliaments communist deputies would make a declaration against the pact, which was designed to provide security for American investments in Europe, to replace French by British hegemony on the continent, and to draw Germany into an anti-Soviet bloc. The conference also called for a plebiscite in Alsace-Lorraine, to determine whether it should be French, German, or independent, and passed resolutions on the eight-hour day, tariff policy, and Syria. On 13 October *Inprekorr* wrote that Chicherin's arrival in Berlin on the eve of the departure of the German delegation to the Locarno conference was a last warning to the Reich Government. 'Chicherin's appearance in Berlin opens up the debate on the western or eastern orientation of Germany today.' The proposal for a guarantee pact was an English imperialist plot to organize a military front against the Soviet Union. 'That is the reason why the entire international working class opposes the plan', which would deprive Germany of the last shreds of its independence and reinforce the fetters of Versailles. It was the political and military counterpart of the Dawes plan, designed to suppress the proletarian revolution in Germany, and it brought the danger of war nearer. Another article explained that Locarno was Britain's method of exploiting Franco-German difficulties to its own advantage. Germany agreed because it hoped to have British support (by restraining France) for a German attack on Poland, under cover of which Britain would start war against Russia. Locarno was thus one link in the British plan to isolate Russia. Radek wrote that it was a stage in the liquidation of Versailles and an attempt by England, caught in an economic crisis, to restore the European economy; French control of the continent was weakened: it was now dependent politically on Britain, and economically on the United States. Germany turned towards the countries that could give credits because of its need of working capital. Its subordination to the League of Nations under the Locarno agreements was a step towards the creation of a European Concert of Powers directed against the USSR. Locarno represented 'a new coalition of forces, led by the United States and Britain'. Rakovsky, referring to the conflict revealed by Locarno between Europe and America, wrote both that the agreements gave the USSR a certain freedom of action and that they were a grave danger to the USSR. Zinoviev at the CPSU congress at the end of 1925 gave roughly the same analysis as Radek, and added that to some extent Locarno represented a rapprochement among European States for self-defence against future threats from America. At the sixth ECCI plenum in March 1926 Pepper took up this point, stating that it gave a certain parallelism to European and Soviet interests; on the other hand, since Britain was the leader of the anti-Soviet campaign, Anglo-American rivalry gave a certain parallelism also to Soviet and American interests.

A certain parallelism in Soviet and American interests was suggested by Radek in another article. Britain feared the development and independence of the East because of the effect on India; but the United States looked forward to the development of bourgeois-democratic States with which it could do business. In this respect the United States had reason to oppose Britain, but not Russia. The coupling of Estonia with Germany and Bulgaria in the theses refers to the rising which took place in Reval on 1 December 1924; no more than a few hundred communists were involved; it lasted only a few hours. Throughout 1924 the Estonian Government had made a series of arrests of suspected revolutionaries, one of whom was executed in November. The rising was generally regarded as a desperate attempt at self-defence, rather than an action to exploit a revolutionary situation. Trotsky later attributed the decision (which was made with the ECCI's consent) to the incorrect appraisal of the forthcoming period as a revolutionary one by the fifth Comintern congress. The Estonian Government declared a state of emergency and made many further arrests.]

THE WORLD ECONOMIC AND POLITICAL SITUATION

1. The fifth world congress of the CI noted an improvement in the position of world capitalism. . . . With this in mind the enlarged Executive issued the necessary directives for changing the strategy and tactics of the communist parties in the present epoch, which must be concentrated on one item, the creation of the revolutionary proletarian united front. For, now as before, the basic Leninist appraisal of the essential character of the present historical epoch remains valid—that of the progressive decay and dying away of capitalist world economy and of the actuality of the world revolution. There has been no change in the operation of those forces which are driving the contradictions within the imperialist camp to a state of greater and greater acuteness, and forcing the antagonism to the first proletarian State, the Soviet Union, to a decision. . . .

2. The analysis of the present stage must therefore be concerned with the two recent phenomena which the social-democratic ideologues of the bourgeoisie interpret as proof that capitalism has been restored and its contradictions overcome: that is, the Dawes plan and the Locarno pact. . . .

3. Even a superficial examination of the present state of world economy shows that the idea of the possibility of the restoration of a unified world economy on a purely capitalist basis is false. As regards both its present position, and the tendencies towards its future development, world economy is split by the existence of the Soviet Union into two parts—a capitalist economy and a socialist economy. . . .

4. The new factors in economic development introduced by American attempts to restore the capitalist world market and the international credit system do not change the situation. The United States, which changed its former debtor position in regard to Europe into an uncontested financial and economic hegemony and which emerged from the world war as the strongest imperialist State, had to abandon its isolationist attitude towards Europe. The limitations of the home market, the need to find markets to absorb the output of the tremendously expanded

production apparatus and to export capital forced this change on America. With the London conference of 1924 which adopted the Dawes plan, America began to bring Europe under its economic and political control. The external occasion for putting the plan into operation was provided by the failure of the French adventure in the Ruhr. The occupation of the Ruhr represented the last attempt of French imperialism to establish its hegemony on the Continent. The attempt was frustrated by the opposition of the United States and England. . . . The imposition of the Dawes plan on Germany, as well as the 'Dawes-ation' of the rest of Europe, makes the restoration of an orderly economy possible only by still greater exploitation of the masses. . . .

6. The Anglo-Saxon Powers emerged as the strongest imperialist group from the war and the immediate post-war years. The United States and England have won the economic hegemony of the capitalist world, but the rivalry between them for sole supremacy reflects and comprehends all the inner contradictions of imperialism. The rivalry can be summarized in a simple formula—America is trying to break up the English world empire from within, by bringing the Dominions, particularly Canada and Australia, under its financial and hence its political sway. . . . To this should be added that in the Far East too (China), America is pursuing the opposite policy to England's, for it is to a certain extent interested in the industrialization of China, in order to find markets for the output of its engineering industry, whereas England wants to keep China as a market for its manufactured goods and as a source of raw materials.

This basic antagonism is supplemented and modified by lesser contradictions among the other imperialist States, those, for example, between America and Japan, England and France, France and Germany. . . . Thus the characteristic feature of the present stabilization phase of world capitalism remains sharper competition, the struggle for world markets, and the economic re-division and recasting of the world. . . .

8. In only one respect can we speak of the relative solidarity and internationalizing of capitalist interests; in regard to the Soviet Union, the capitalist States are able to form a united front. The Locarno pact, praised by the social-democrats as the 'no-more-war pact', reflects the fact—admitted with cynical candour by the imperialist Powers themselves—that despite the contradictions they are uniting to fight the fundamental and epoch-making war against the Soviet Union.

9. The Locarno pact is the general political formula for the reorganization of Europe under the control and hegemony of the United States and England. It complements the Dawes plan. . . . It signifies the complete defeat of France and of French imperialism's attempt to establish its hegemony on the continent of Europe. England appears in the role of arbitrator between France and Germany, and will henceforth use Germany as an

instrument to counter French offensive aims. America is preparing to impose a Dawes regime on France. Germany is condemned to a dual slavery. On the one hand it must enter the League of Nations, in order to be in a position to serve as a jumping-off ground for the imperialist attack on the Soviet Union; on the other hand it is forced into obedience to the will of Anglo-Saxon imperialism, now by slight ameliorations of its economic and political situation, now by a turn of the reparations screw.

But the primary significance of Locarno is the attempt to build up the united front of the capitalist world by pushing aside its internal contradictions in order to establish an imperialist anti-Soviet bloc. Caught between the pincers of victorious and expanding American capitalism, and of the rebellious colonies, hemmed in on all fronts where it might advance by the existence of Soviet Russia, Great Britain is the chief instigator of the policy of a decision by arms between capitalism and socialism and is trying to form a Holy Alliance against the Union of Soviet Republics. The United States, on the other hand, favours a more peaceful policy, being concerned with drawing its profits from Europe and hoping to introduce a Dawes regime in Soviet Russia and China. . . .

THE PERSPECTIVES OF WORLD REVOLUTION

1. By 'perspectives of world revolution' we do not mean precise or approximate prediction of the date when the revolution will break out in one country or another, or even in the world. When, in the years from 1918 to 1920, the communists counted on an early outbreak of the revolution in the most important European countries, they were influenced by two facts—the imperialist robber war and the Russian proletarian revolution. . . .

These hopes were not fulfilled, as we know, not because the conditions of a socialist revolution in the West were not present, but primarily because of the treachery of one section of the proletariat (the labour aristocracy) and their party, social-democracy. They helped capitalism and the bourgeoisie economically (by restoring production) and politically (by bourgeois democracy) to maintain their political and economic power. The directly revolutionary situation which did exist thus passed without the proletariat managing to gain power in the important countries of Europe. . . .

3. Since then for every communist it is part of the ABC of Marxism–Leninism that the world revolution will occupy an entire epoch of world history, prolonged and painful, and that the continuation of the world revolution in West Europe will be incomparably more difficult than its beginning was in Russia. We understand by . . . 'perspectives of world revolution':

(a) the demonstration that the basic forces making for world revolution, that is, the trends of development, remain unchanged, . . . (*b*) the exact analysis of the stage in which we now find ourselves; (*c*) the balancing of the relation of forces operating in favour of and against the further development of the revolution.

4. As to the first, it was shown in the first part of these theses that the world economic and political situation reveals unchanged those contradictions and rivalries which make the 'normal' functioning of capitalism impossible. The basic thesis of Leninist theory, that 'imperialism is the epoch of dying capitalism', remains unshaken.

As to the analysis of the immediate situation, it is to be noted that we are again in a period when the revolutionary movement is on the upgrade, that large parts of the world are indeed in a directly revolutionary situation.

In the first place there is the revolution in China. The significance of the events in China is immeasurable. . . . The national revolution in China is irresistible; it will be a tremendously powerful factor in revolutionizing the entire East. In the proletarian revolutionary movement the Chinese revolution will play a threefold part: (*a*) it will intensify the difficulties and contradictions among the imperialist Powers; (*b*) it will revolutionize the European proletariat, and at the same time (*c*) it will stand as an ally of the proletariat against the common enemy and support its struggle.

The Chinese revolution is a link in the chain of world revolution, and hence large parts of the world are in an immediately revolutionary situation. This is a sign of the actuality of world revolution.

5. In Europe the situation is not directly revolutionary; that is to say, the revolutionary upheavals which took the form of outright civil war during the demobilization period and in some degree up to 1923 have yielded to less stormy but no less significant events which bear witness everywhere to a state of profound crisis. . . .

6. Crisis and signs of crisis everywhere. But the workers' movement which, after the defeats in Bulgaria, Germany, and Estonia, after the victory of the Conservative Government in England, the election of Hindenburg in Germany, etc., seemed for a moment to have yielded to reaction, is again showing an upward curve. The main indications are:

(*a*) The united front movement and the Anglo-Russian rapprochement. The antagonism between capitalist England and proletarian Russia was never so sharp as it is with the present Conservative Government, but the English working masses have never been so close to the Russian workers as since the Scarborough congress. . . . The English working class is beginning to shake off its reformist leaders. Not only in England, but everywhere, the working class is beginning to turn to Russia. . . . The workers' delegations which visit Russia and tear down the web of lies fabricated by the bourgeoisie and social-democracy are the best sign and one of the best methods of the revolutionizing of the European working class.

(*b*) The electoral victories of the communists in Germany and Czechoslovakia, and of the Labour Party in England. . . .

(*c*) The most important sections of the Comintern have surmounted their crisis, and the parties are beginning to operate, organizationally and ideologically (factory cells, party training) on bolshevik foundations. The further this process goes, the more it shows results, the more will it contribute to revolutionizing the situation, for the absence of a well-organized well-trained disciplined revolutionary party was the chief reason why the genuinely revolutionary situation of 1918–23 was not exploited.

THE SOVIET UNION

1. The existence of the Soviet Union is in itself a sign of the revolutionary situation and an important factor in the revolutionary perspective. Two hostile economic and social systems confront each other, capitalism and socialism. The strengthening of one means the weakening of the other, and vice versa. . . .

4. The growing power of Soviet Russia is a support for the world revolution; it is not only an ideological, but a material factor of the first importance for all the oppressed (classes, peoples) everywhere. And Soviet Russia's economic power will grow from year to year. . . .

5. This does not mean that the capitalist Powers will yield to the inevitable and make no attempt to stay this triumphant advance. On the contrary, they will try to exploit the inner contradictions associated with the tremendous economic development of a peasant country like the Soviet Union . . . and create difficulties for the proletarian State, by methods including blockade and war. The CPSU and the Russian proletariat will deal with internal contradictions. The international proletariat must see to it that the aggressive intentions of the reactionary imperialist great Powers are brought to nothing.

6. The tactical tasks which follow from the present stage of the world revolution, and which are common to all communist parties, are:

(*a*) To strengthen the organizational structure of the party (factory cells).

(*b*) To strengthen educational work among the members. . . .

(*c*) United front. As we have seen, we are in a period of rising revolution. The proletarian masses are again becoming revolutionary-minded. To win them and keep them is the most urgent of our tasks. At the same time trade union work must be strengthened.

(*d*) To organize workers' delegations to Russia. The living example of Soviet Russia is the best means of agitation.

(*e*) To expose the tactics of the bourgeoisie and of social-democracy, who describe Soviet policy as red imperialism. The Soviet Union signifies the practical realization of socialism, and as such it must live in the consciousness of all workers.

(*f*) To pay greater attention to the peasantry. . . .

(*g*) At every government crisis to increase agitation for a workers' and peasants' government.

(*h*) To increase agitation against imperialism and the coming world war.

(*i*) To increase agitation against government plans to attack the Soviet Union. . . .

THE SPLIT IN THE WORKING CLASS AND UNITED FRONT TACTICS

1. The fight for the united front, which has for four years been the basic tactic of the CI, has its theoretical roots in the old principle of the necessity for working-class unity. . . .

The outbreak of the world war and the attitude of the social-democratic leaders in favour of civil peace meant in fact the liquidation of working-class unity, the rupture of working-class international relations; proletarians of various countries shot at each other. The bankruptcy of the Second International had become a fact.

3. The split in the working class was thus provoked by the spontaneous forces of imperialist development; the working class was split horizontally, along lines of hostile countries. The cause of the international workers' movement could be saved only by changing this horizontal split into a vertical split, that it to say, by a definite organizational separation of the revolutionary from the opportunist elements. This process . . . was embodied organizationally in the foundation in 1919 of the Communist International. . . .

4. In these circumstances the split was an unavoidable necessity, but it was not an end in itself. The split, that is, the destruction of proletarian unity on an opportunist basis, was necessary in order to erect proletarian unity on a higher basis, the basis of revolutionary class struggle for the overthrow of capitalism and the establishment of the proletarian dictatorship.

So long as the revolutionary wave was advancing there was a basis for establishing this unity of the masses in the midst of the direct struggle for the seizure of power. In the period of revolutionary storms it was the only method of establishing unity. But when, because of the treachery of international social-democracy, the revolutionary wave ebbed . . . other methods of establishing unity had to be found.

5. The third world congress of the CI noted this change in the world situation and coined the slogan: 'To the masses'. This raised the problem of united front tactics, which since then has been and still is the basis of all tactical movements in the CI. . . .

6. Politically, the most important factor in the Comintern struggle for the united proletarian front is without doubt the struggle to establish international trade union unity. . . . The RILU and its organs were created as a result of the furious persecution of the revolutionary elements in the reformist trade unions by the bureaucratic leadership, in order to keep the excluded together and organize resistance to the capitalist offensive. Although the revolutionary unions in some countries (France, Czecho-slovakia) have many successes to their credit, the elimination of the split in the trade union movement is still a necessary condition for success in the approaching struggles. The crystallization of the left wing in the Amsterdam International, the extremely significant leftward movement of the English proletariat, the formation of the Anglo-Russian unity com-mittee, etc., mark the first great successes in the movement for trade union unity. . . .

8. But the fight for unity cannot be limited to the unions. It must take advantage of every factor and every organizational opening to get closer to the non-party and social-democratic masses, and to convince them that the communist party is the only party which fights resolutely, consistently, and to the end for the interests of the proletariat. Sports organizations, peace associations, every mass organization of the proletariat must be intensively cultivated by our parties for this purpose. The sending of workers' delegations to the Soviet Union—the majority should consist of social-democratic factory workers—has proved brilliantly successful and must be continued with the utmost energy.

CIRCULAR LETTER FROM THE ECCI PRESIDIUM TO ALL SECTIONS ACCOMPANYING A CIRCULAR LETTER FROM THE CENTRAL COMMITTEE OF THE CPSU TO ALL COMMUNIST PARTIES

15 *January* 1926   *Inprekorr*, vi, 12, p. 147, 19 *January* 1926

[The report of the ECCI to the sixth plenum, which covered the year 1925, did not contain a section on the Russian party. In the final paragraph of a volume of more than 360 pages, it was stated that the secretariat considered a report on the CPSU unnecessary, since the proceedings of its fourteenth con-gress, held in December 1925, had been reported in the communist press. At that congress Zinoviev and Kamenev, who were strongly critical of the party's policy of conciliation towards the more prosperous peasantry, and of its neglect of industry, were heavily outvoted. Many of their supporters in the party had been removed and intimidated by administrative and police measures before the congress, where they were supported by Krupskaya, Lenin's widow, and Sokolnikov, the Commissar for Finance. On 4 September 1925 Kamenev, Zinoviev, Krupskaya, and Sokolnikov had put forward a statement of their views which became known as 'the platform of the four'. Kamenev and

Sokolnikov were deprived of their government posts (Kamenev was vice-chairman of the Council of Commissars).

Zinoviev's report on the work of the Russian delegation to the ECCI attributed the crisis in the Russian party to the delay in the world revolution, to the difficulties of building socialism in a backward country and of establishing a collective leadership after Lenin's death. Since the report to the thirteenth congress there had been a period of decline in the CI and voices of doubt and disbelief had been heard. 'From all sides has come the question, where are our victories?' He compared the period, outwardly unsuccessful, to the period between 1907 and 1917 in Russia, when the preparatory work for decisive victories was being carried out. Manuilsky, in the debate, said Zinoviev had been given the 'friendly advice' not to report on the ECCI, since it would drag the Comintern into the quarrels in the CPSU; such reticence was no longer possible; the German left wing was already using them to attack the CC of the KPD. Three weeks earlier, at the direction of the ECCI, he, Manuilsky, had written to the most important CI sections announcing that the forthcoming CPSU congress would be a brilliant demonstration of party unity and discipline. Difficulties would be created in the CI because, after Zinoviev's report, it would be impossible for the CPSU delegation to the ECCI to act as one, as they had done in the past even on questions on which they disagreed. The rift which had now opened between the Comintern leadership and the CPSU might mean that policies would be put forward in the CI which were incompatible with CPSU policy. The discussion would also revitalize the ultra-lefts, encouraged by the ultra-leftism of the Leningrad delegation. The right wing would also raise its head again, suspecting that anarchy prevailed in the CI (Radek: 'So it does'). The social-democrats would attempt to detach the masses from the communist party by pointing to the opposition's charges of the restoration of capitalism in the USSR. In the sections sides would be taken for and against the opposition, the collective leadership recently established would break down, and the authority of the CPSU would decline. Lominadze followed with an attack on Zinoviev for not dissociating himself clearly enough from Maslow–Fischer. Skrypnik said that the CPSU, and in particular the politbureau, did not take enough interest in the work of the ECCI; the ECCI itself did not really work, but only the presidium and the enlarged plenum. Shmidt thought the CI had not done enough to promote unity, and a number of very good comrades were leaving the sections. The parties were not independent enough, but waited for the ECCI to give them instructions and advice. The Russian delegation had done too little to correct these tendencies. Riazanov said that the CI parties were going through their worst period so far, the CPSU most of all. The KPD was virtually impotent. What was happening about the Comintern programme? What was the most important section of the CI doing about this? The theoretical level in the CPSU had fallen very low.

In his reply to the discussion Zinoviev said that the crisis in the Russian party had become a matter of international interest before the congress—he had done nothing whatever to carry it over into the CI. He had never discussed the CPSU with a single foreign comrade. It was the Russian press which had carried the discussion to every party. The resolution approving 'by and large' the Russian delegation's work at the ECCI was passed by 424 votes, with 101 abstentions. Riazanov's amendment instructing the CPSU delegation to insist on a new programme commission was rejected. The resolution instructed the CPSU delegation to work to strengthen the Comintern apparatus, *inter alia* by helping to increase the influence of foreign parties in its leadership. The letter from the CC of the CPSU to all fraternal parties on the disputes in the Russian party circulated by the ECCI analysed their causes, and maintained that on questions of foreign policy and the policy towards other communist parties there were no essential differences. The delay in the international revolution and the relative stabilization of capitalism had generated a sense of depression which found its ideological embodiment in the opposition. Internal questions had been settled by the decisions of the party congress, and party unity was now assured. 'The CC of the CPSU is completely unanimous in the belief that it is undesirable to carry the discussion of the Russian question into the ranks of the Comintern.']

Dear Comrades,

The CC of the CP of the Soviet Union sent the enclosed letter to the presidium of the ECCI, with the request to send it on to all fraternal parties. The presidium of the ECCI is therefore forwarding the said letter, and endorses the attitude of the CC of the CP of the Soviet Union that it is undesirable for the discussion in the CP of the Soviet Union to be carried over into the Comintern.

The Presidium of the ECCI

THE SIXTH ENLARGED PLENUM OF THE ECCI

[The plenum met from 17 February to 15 March 1926. There were 77 voting delegates, of whom 28 were ECCI members, and 53 non-voting delegates. Thirty-two parties were represented. Hu Han-min, a member of the Kuomintang, attended for that party, which had been admitted to the Comintern as a sympathizing party; in the meeting of the CPSU political bureau in March 1926 the decision to admit the KMT was carried against the vote of Trotsky. The report of the ECCI for April 1925 to January 1926 dealt (in addition to the questions considered in the following pages) with the unsatisfactory state of affairs in the Italian party, in particular Bordiga's policy of abstentionism and opposition to trade union united front tactics in Italy; Bordiga's fraction endangered party unity, and the presidium had intervened by sending a representative to Italy. Bordiga made a long and bitterly critical speech. The entire position in the Comintern was unsatisfactory. After the October 1923 defeat it had demoted a few people, instead of holding the entire CI responsible. At every congress and ECCI plenum the situation was described as satisfactory, but new analyses had to be introduced to explain the failure of the proletarian revolution, and new slogans advanced to correct errors. As to fractions and differences of opinion, these were a sign that the party had not yet reached its goal, real singleness of outlook. Discipline was the result, not the starting-point, of party unity. A regime of terror had grown up in the Comintern, a kind of sport consisting of intervening, punishing, annihilating, and this with an air of satisfaction, as though it were the ideal of party life and a demonstration of party vitality. Sanctions should be used in rare cases only, not as the normal process of settling differences. He did not object to parties acting without consulting the membership in emergencies, but he did object to a show of democracy when in reality the party centre had entire control of the apparatus and the press. Opposition entered the party not in the form of fractions, but in the guise of sham unity. Fractions were a tribute not to the party in which they appeared, but to the comrades who formed them, for example Lenin. They should be opposed only when they came under bourgeois influence or were built up for personal reasons. Fractions were a sign that something was wrong, and it was this that should be examined. The relapse of Rosmer and Monatte into their previous syndicalist position was a mistake which reflected not on them, but on the French CP and the Comintern. Many comrades believed that the Russian party, with its experience and authority, should be allowed to determine disputed questions in other parties, but what if, as now, the Russians themselves disagreed? Ercoli (Togliatti) asked the plenum to condemn Bordiga's deviations, derived from his undifferentiated attitude to the bourgeoisie, which would make it impossible for the party to utilize differences and contradictions in the bourgeois camp. The Italian central committee had to be composed of members who accepted the Comintern line without reservation. Bukharin answered Bordiga in a conciliatory tone, while disagreeing with his views. In a further speech, Bordiga again urged the Comintern to cease the practice of humiliating and terrorizing members. 'This mania to destroy ourselves must cease if we are really to make good our claim to lead the revolutionary struggle of the proletariat.' The scenes he had witnessed at the plenum opened gloomy prospects. He denied that he was opposed to trade union unity at the national level; but internationally it was a mistake. The IFTU was not a proletarian mass organization but an organ of the bourgeoisie, connected with the ILO and the League of Nations; it could never be won by the proletariat.

At one stage in the proceedings Bordiga expressed his lack of sympathy with the German ultra-lefts, who approved the political analysis of the resolutions but were dissatisfied with what was said about themselves. They were now being treated as they had themselves earlier treated their opponents. One kind of language was used in the official resolutions, and another behind the scenes. The Italian representatives who had attended the KPD congress in 1925 had reported that the CC of the KPD had the overwhelming support of the party, and was an example to the Italian CP. Two weeks later had come the open letter of the ECCI condemning the German CC. At the fifth congress in 1924 everything that was wrong in the KPD was Brandler's fault; now it was Ruth Fischer's. In both cases the Comintern should accept responsibility for the mistakes made.

For the Eastern countries, the ECCI report stated (over-optimistically) that there were more or less well organized parties in China, Japan, Korea, Indonesia, Turkey, Syria, Palestine, Persia, Algeria, Tunis, Egypt, India, and South Africa. In all cases the party apparatus was still weak. Since 1924 the Eastern division of the women's secretariat had a special representative for work among Chinese women; there were fifteen women students at the Communist University for the

East and forty-one at the Sun Yat-sen University. The British party had set up a colonial commission which had established close contact with the parties in India, Egypt, Syria, and Palestine; it had so far failed to set up a party in Ireland. After the ECCI meeting in April 1925 the Eastern department had been strengthened; it was run by a collegium which had its own organization and propaganda sub-departments. Twenty-four comrades from eight Eastern countries were now working in the department, and it was hoped to increase this number. So far only the first steps had been taken to draw the European parties into the work. One of the department's chief activities was to establish contact with non-communist revolutionary organizations and help them to work out their programme and tactics. Only in China and India was the proletariat strong enough for the question of proletarian hegemony in the revolutionary movement to be a practical one, but the problems involved had not yet been seriously examined. In most Eastern countries there was an ultra-left tendency in the parties which underestimated the importance of the peasantry and the national movement. This was the reason why the Chinese party had been reluctant to enter the KMT. In Egypt, Persia, and Turkey the party was illegal, and had to contend with great difficulties. In Syria and North Africa the French communist groups had at last begun to include the natives in their organization. In Algeria they accounted for 300 out of a total of 1,200.

In his opening speech Zinoviev said that the fusing of the national-revolutionary and proletarian movements was the pledge of their victory. If they succeeded in winning the colonies for socialism before a strong native bourgeoisie had grown up, these countries could skip the capitalist stage of development.

It was reported that in March 1925 the Japanese trade union federation had split into the Japanese Council of Labour Unions, inclined towards the RILU, and the Japanese Federation of Labour, which was sympathetic to the IFTU. Sometime in 1924 a group of Chinese, Indians, Annamites, and Koreans had formed an 'anti-imperialist committee of action' to set up an 'international association of oppressed peoples'. The first conference of this body was held in the summer of 1925 in Canton; the second accepted affiliation from the Kuomintang, some Chinese trade unions and Kwantung peasant unions. Statutes were adopted which described the aims of the association as to rally all the forces of the oppressed nations for the national revolution. It issued an appeal to 'our oppressed brothers throughout the world' calling for unity with the Western proletariat, and considered plans to bring in like-minded organizations in Japan, the Philippines, and Java, and Negro organizations in the United States and Africa.

Domski (who had on the recommendation of the ECCI replaced Warski as leader of the Polish CP after the fifth Comintern congress, but had been removed from the central committee following an ECCI resolution of 28 July 1925 condemning Polish support of the ultra-lefts in Germany and France) attended the plenum, though not as a delegate. There, while admitting the ultra-left errors of the Polish central committee, he pointed to the advances that had been made; there had been only 2 communist deputies in the National Assembly; there was now a workers' and peasants' bloc of 17. He warned the plenum of the danger of a radical-fascist putsch under Pilsudski; he urged the Comintern to deal seriously with the Polish-German territorial dispute if the Polish communists were not to be regarded as traitors by the Polish people when they acted together with the KPD against German fascist attacks on the Polish Corridor, Danzig, etc.

The American delegation was divided, but both sides again agreed to the resolution drafted by the commission which investigated thé situation in the American Workers' Party. It called for the immediate cessation of the fractional struggle, and for better trade union work, particularly in heavy industry. The party was to give greater attention to Negroes, and to the workers' movement and the national movement in Cuba, the Philippines, and South America. Resolutions were also passed on the French, Norwegian, and Czech parties.

The position of the Russian party in the Comintern was discussed at several points. In his opening speech Zinoviev, deploring the lack of initiative and independence in the sections, added that 'the influence of the CPSU, that is, of the party which has the greatest historical experience, must be maintained so long as the proletarian revolution has not triumphed in other countries'. Bordiga argued that Russia's internal problems could not be properly settled except within the framework of the Comintern. The Russian question should be on the agenda of every section. The CI could not determine its line correctly without analysing Russian State policy towards the classes in Russia, and in this the whole Comintern should collaborate with the CPSU. The Russian revolution could not be taken as the model for a revolutionary party in countries with capitalist, liberal, parliamentary institutions that were capable of defending themselves. Bukharin agreed that there were differences in the Russian and the West European situations. Lominadze attacked Bordiga, and those who had criticized Bukharin and Stalin (presumably in commission meetings). 'What is the meaning of these attacks if at the same time the attackers say they agree with the political theses? They are a petty attempt to exploit the Russian party discussion for fractional purposes.' Bordiga protested against the omission of the CPSU question from the agenda. His motion that a congress should be called in 1927 to discuss the relation between the revolutionary struggle of the world proletariat and the policy of the Russian State and the CPSU was referred to the presidium.

At the CPSU congress in the previous December Zinoviev reported that there were in all 55 communist parties, of which 25 were illegal and 5 semi-legal.]

EXTRACTS FROM A RESOLUTION OF THE SIXTH ECCI PLENUM PROTESTING AGAINST THE BLOCKADE OF CANTON

24 *February* 1926   *Inprekorr*, vi, 37, p. 516, 8 *March* 1926

[The boycott of British trade at Canton, imposed in the middle of 1925, led to a number of minor incidents. On 21 February 1926 the British Commissioner of Customs at Canton closed the ports of Canton and Whampoa, pending the return to the Customs authorities for examination of cargo removed by the

Canton strike committee from the custody of the Customs. The goods were returned on 25 February.]

The British Government has imposed a blockade of Canton, and through its mission in Peking has sent a note to the Chinese Foreign Minister containing threats against the revolutionary Government in Canton, and calling on the central Chinese Government to make Canton put an end to the strike of seamen and dockworkers.

This strike has been going on for eight months. This is due not only to the extraordinary stubbornness and solidarity of the workers themselves, but also to the support and deep sympathy of the democratic population throughout China. Of course the Kuomintang Government of Canton, which has the support of the popular masses of Kwantung province and the national-liberation movement of the entire country, cannot suppress the workers' movement at the command of British imperialists. . . .

To mislead public opinion at home and the working masses of other countries, British imperialism cites as pretext for the blockade the alleged seizure of foreign cargoes by the strikers and the violation of Anglo-Chinese agreements by the South Chinese Government.

These excuses will deceive nobody. The Canton Government cannot be forced to suppress a strike movement for the benefit of British capitalists, nor can that be done in virtue of any robber treaty forced on China by British imperialists. . . .

The revolutionary workers of the world, and above all the workers of Great Britain, must raise a loud protest against the imperialist attack. Canton must not be destroyed by the British colonizers. The liberation movement in China must be supported by all revolutionary workers and all honest adherents of the equality of nations.

EXTRACTS FROM THE THESES ON THE CURRENT QUESTIONS OF THE INTERNATIONAL COMMUNIST MOVEMENT PASSED BY THE SIXTH ECCI PLENUM

March 1926   *Inprekorr*, vi, 68, p. 1025, 5 *May* 1926

[For many sections, said Zinoviev, it had been a difficult year, in which the very existence of the party was at stake. United front tactics, he said, were not an episode, but valid for an entire period, until the proletarian majority had been won for communism in the most important countries. Parties should not, in their eagerness to expose reformism, put forward conditions which were unacceptable not only to the leaders, but to the rank and file of social-democracy. Klara Zetkin suggested that if the tactical line had been more carefully formulated, the crisis in the German, French, Norwegian, Polish, and Bulgarian parties might have been avoided. Bukharin thought there had been improvement in the sections, due to the trade union unity and united front campaigns, and to the repercussions of the many workers' delegations to the Soviet Union. Bela Kun dealt with the Pan-Europa movement, which he described as an attempt to restore the destroyed European market and prepare an offensive against the United States. The Comintern slogan of a 'United States of Socialist Europe' was intended to organize the workers against the effects in European politics and economy of American hegemony. America wanted class peace in Europe to guarantee the profits on its loans; this meant greater exploitation and mass unemployment; in the international field this policy was reflected in pacifism and the disarmament conference. The fight against this policy varied according to local circumstances, but it would peter out altogether if it were not focused on the central principle of fighting the influence of American capital in Europe. Pepper (USA) remarked that world events often put the USSR and the United States, negatively, on the same side. Locarno was directed against both, so was the League of Nations. In China and Mosul both were hostile to British policy, while European hostility to the United States pushed some countries, such as Germany and France, closer to the Soviet Union. He later reported for the political commission: it had rejected the French amendment which would have toned down the description of the French situation as critical, the British amendment which stated that British imperialism still had many favourable positive factors, and the American amendment arguing that real wages in the United States were falling and the working class becoming more revolutionary. The longest discussion had been provoked by Locarno; it had been agreed that this was the first attempt of the European debtor countries to organize against the United States.

   The theses, which had been drafted by Zinoviev and approved by the Russian politbureau, were put forward in the name of the CPSU delegation, and passed unanimously. Bordiga, who had said he would vote against them, was not present when the vote was taken. Although they referred to changes in the internal regime of the Comintern, he said, the plenum in its work had not taken even a first step towards making these changes a reality.]

I. CAPITALIST 'STABILIZATION' AND THE TACTICS OF WORLD REVOLUTION

   . . . In the past year it was hoped to conceal the true picture of the situation in the capitalist world, that immense complex of contradictions created by the war, behind a mask intended to mislead the working masses. That mask is the treaty of Locarno.

   The objective significance of this treaty is:

   1. American capitalism is consolidating its interests, as opposed to the interests of capitalist Europe ('pacification' of Europe as a guarantee that the debtors will 'work' and so be in a position to pay interest to America). At the same time Locarno represents the first, albeit weak, attempt on the part of the debtors to unite against America. . . .

   2. English imperialism, through this treaty, is defending its special interests as against France. . . .

3. The French bourgeoisie are protecting their special interests as against Germany. . . . At the same time Locarno registers the failure of the French attempt to establish hegemony over the European continent.

4. With the support of French imperialism, English imperialism is using Locarno to build up a front against the Soviet Union, to isolate it and to win Germany over to this policy.

These methods of 'ensuring peace' through the League of Nations . . . have turned out in practice to be methods of preparing new wars. Pacifist illusions, bound up with belief in the League of Nations, and particularly in Locarno, undoubtedly exist to a certain degree among the working masses. They are nourished by the social-democratic leaders, who take a hand in the deceitful policy of the League of Nations and are converting the Second International into an instrument of that policy. But the course of events has itself dispelled these illusions. . . . The idea is gaining ground among ever wider strata of the labouring people that new imperialist wars can be avoided only by a proletarian revolution, that the surest pledge against new wars is the strengthening of the Soviet Union, and that the only leader of the working masses against predatory wars is the Communist International. . . .

The Communist International rejects the premature conclusion that there can no longer be any kind of capitalist stabilization, but also emphatically rejects, now as before, the conclusion drawn by the social-democratic leaders that capitalism has already consolidated its position for the duration of an entire historical epoch. . . .

II. NEW PHENOMENA IN THE INTERNATIONAL LABOUR MOVEMENT AND UNITED FRONT TACTICS

The desire for unity has recently become very marked among the broad working masses of the different countries. . . . Today it means unity on the platform of class struggle. This is the result of a whole series of circumstances.

1. In a number of the biggest capitalist countries economic development is again making the position of the broad working strata worse. . . . In England unemployment is steadily mounting. The experience of the first 'Labour Government' dealt a serious blow to reformist illusions. The capitalist offensive, which is generating ever broader conflicts (the miners), awakens the consciousness of the need for organized mass action by the working class.

In Germany unemployment has attained gigantic proportions. The economic position of the working class is getting worse from day to day. The ruling classes intend to give the dethroned princes $2\frac{1}{2}$ milliard marks compensation. The government crisis is becoming a permanent one. The burden of taxation is growing heavier.

In France it is the working masses alone who will have to shoulder the consequences of the financial crisis. Events in Syria and Morocco are gradually bringing home to the workers that these are the prelude to new imperialist conflicts. The chronic parliamentary and cabinet crisis reveals the rottenness of the whole system of bourgeois democracy. . . .

2. In a number of the more important countries of Europe the coalition policy (i.e. the policy of social-democratic participation in bourgeois coalition governments, which will allegedly bring happiness to the workers by peaceful, reformist means) has suffered shipwreck. In the social-democratic parties of France, Germany, and Poland an open struggle is going on about future participation in coalition governments. The representatives of the 'left' wing, who are opposed to collaboration with the bourgeoisie, voice the misgivings of the social-democratic rank and file. . . . This does not mean that these social-democratic workers have finally given up their reformist illusions. Relapses are possible and to some degree inevitable. But, with correct tactics on our part, the period in which reformist illusions can again exert their effect can be shortened, until the social-democratic workers get rid of them once and for all.

3. A tremendous effect on the broad masses of the social-democratic working class is exercised by the economic progress of the Soviet Union. . . . The USSR will gradually become a magnet for them. The old calumnies spread by the leaders of international social-democracy about the Soviet Union are being visibly dispelled. The workers' delegations which have visited the Soviet Union have played and are playing an immense part in the struggle to liberate the social-democratic proletarian from reformist influence.

4. Recently in a number of European countries the social-democratic workers have begun instinctively to sense the approach of the danger of a new imperialist war. . . . All this generates a spontaneous mass pressure towards unity. . . .

The Communist International and its sections must be resolute and honest in meeting half-way this genuine desire for unity among social-democratic workers. . . .

Of course there can be no question of merging the communist parties with the social-democratic parties. This would be open treachery to the cause of the proletarian revolution, it would be the abandonment of the leading role in history which the proletariat is called on to play. Recognition of the necessity for the existence of an independent communist party is part of the ABC of Marxism–Leninism. The most valuable achievement of the working class in the recent past has been precisely the formation, despite tremendous obstacles, of independent communist parties in the individual countries, which openly castigate the treachery of the social-democratic leaders, openly propagate the idea of proletarian revolution, and work to prepare it. It is only under the banner of the communist party that the proletariat can—and, we are certain, will—come together in a closed front. . . .

The enlarged Executive of the Communist International calls imperatively on all its sections to act decisively, vigorously, and sincerely in meeting the wish of the social-democratic workers to establish a united front to fight the bourgeoisie, to unite with them in carrying through tactical actions, even under the most modest slogans, and to adopt towards them an attentive, comradely, and correct attitude, in order to make it possible for them to proceed jointly with us against the bourgeoisie.

Nevertheless the Communist International has no reason to revise its estimate of the objective role of social-democracy, and particularly of the social-democratic leaders, including the 'lefts' among them. . . . It does not doubt that, in the future as in the past, the majority of them will sabotage the united front. . . . It adheres to the point of view that in no circumstances does the united front mean a parliamentary bloc with the social-democratic leaders, or the amalgamation of the communist with the social-democratic party, the renunciation by the communist party of independent propaganda and agitation. Now as before the Communist International is of the opinion that the united front tactic is but a method of conducting revolutionary agitation among the masses, mobilizing them and winning the majority of the workers for the Communist International. . . . If in so doing our agitation is directed against the social-democratic leaders, that is solely because they stand in the way of bringing the workers together in the struggle for their elementary demands. . . .

III. THE CRISIS IN THE COMINTERN SECTIONS AND THE FIGHT AGAINST DEVIATIONS

. . . The ultra-left crisis in the Italian Communist Party (Bordiga), which lasted many years, was brought to an end at the last congress. . . . The correct political line of the Italian CP has already given it substantial successes among the masses and will no doubt yield even better results in the future. . . .

The crisis in the German Communist Party has not yet been completely overcome. After the defeat in the autumn of 1923 and the collapse of the Brandler *Zentrale*, the Communist International was compelled to give its consent to the 'lefts' taking over the leadership, although it knew that comrades Maslow, Ruth Fischer, and Scholem were capable of all kinds of marked ultra-left deviations. . . . Again and again the Communist International warned the party against the incorrect tendencies of these leaders. When at last it became obvious that this group was incapable of adhering to a correct line, and a group of the best workers from among the left had separated themselves from them, resolutely rejecting the Fischer–Maslow group and capable of taking over the leadership of the party, the Communist International supported the removal of the Maslow–Fischer group from the party leadership. For this purpose the International, together with the German delegation then in Moscow, addressed an open letter in August 1925 to all members and organizations of the KPD. Since then the correctness of the open-letter policy has been amply confirmed. . . . .

The state of affairs in France is of particular significance for the Communist International. Because of the situation in the country, the CPF will in the near future have a very great part to play. The objective situation is very favourable. The chief danger threatening this party comes from the right. . . . The present tasks of the CPF are: (1) by a comprehensive educational campaign based on the decisions of the conference of 1–2 December, as well as by democratizing the entire life of the party, to create a state of affairs which will promote differentiation among the right-wing opposition and win back the best among them to the party; (2) to restore discipline in the party, and not to shrink from expelling those elements which refuse to break off relations with Souvarine and Co. . . .

The enlarged Executive of the Communist International approves whole-heartedly the decision of the presidium of the ECCI not to carry over into the sections of the Comintern the discussion about the questions in dispute at the fourteenth congress of the CPSU.

IV. THE TASKS OF THE COMMUNIST INTERNATIONAL

1. Conditions favourable to the triumph of socialism in Europe are maturing steadily; therefore the subjective factors, that is, the determination of the working class, the internal cohesion of the communist parties, their bolshevik character, and the degree of their readiness to accomplish the great historical tasks awaiting them, have a growing importance. While bearing constantly in mind the possibility of delay in the development of the proletarian revolution, the communist parties must nevertheless continue their work of reinforcing their revolutionary character, in order to be equal at any time to the requirements of an accelerated revolutionary tempo. . . .

2. . . . In propagating the idea of establishing a United States of Socialist Europe as a means of liberating the proletariat and peoples of Europe from the dual yoke of national and North American capital, the following considerations must be kept in mind: (i) the slogan of a United States of Europe must be regarded as the political expression of relations between socialist Soviet republics arising as the result of a victorious proletarian revolution in the various countries; (ii) the victorious European proletarian revolution predicated by this slogan need not be the simultaneous

victory of the proletariat in the whole of Europe, but should be understood as an entire period of revolutionary upheavals in the course of which the proletarian revolution triumphs at first in a few countries, or even in only one, and gradually spreads to other countries. . . . A United States of Socialist Europe, in alliance with the Soviet Union, the oppressed peoples, and the socialist core of the American proletariat, would represent such a tremendous force that imperialist America would be powerless against it. . . .

5. The pressure for unity is the characteristic feature of the mood of the workers throughout the world. The desire for unity, the realization that unless working-class unity is restored the situation is bound to get worse, and the popularity of the unity slogan, particularly trade union unity, among the working masses are the most prominent features of the present phase of the labour movement.

6. On this foundation united front tactics must be applied with special vigour. Their comprehensive application is only just beginning. . . .

7. At present these tactics are concentrated on the trade union movement. The 'left wing' which is being formed in the labour movement of various countries is largely trade unionist; it follows that communist work in the unions is of growing importance. Support for the left elements in the unions and their efforts towards unity, the fight to re-establish trade union unity in every country and to form a unified International of unions standing on the platform of class struggle are the principal levers for operating united front tactics. The Communist International declares that in the interests of unity all communists will be prepared to see the Red International of Labour Unions cease to exist as a separate body, and amalgamate with the Amsterdam International on the basis of convening a joint world congress of the two Internationals, each retaining freedom of agitation. It is obvious that until such an amalgamation occurs every communist must support the RILU to the utmost. The Communist International is in complete agreement with the declaration made by the CC of the CPSU that the affiliation of the Soviet trade unions, which form part of the RILU, to the Amsterdam International is impossible, since in its present form Amsterdam is a tool of the imperialist League of Nations, does not conduct a proletarian class policy, sabotages working-class unity, etc. . . .

8. Two mistakes were frequently made in applying united front tactics: (a) In making proposals to social-democratic workers, our parties put forward demands, to be accepted before joint action was organized, which were from the outset unacceptable to workers still thinking along reformist lines. . . . (b) In their anxiety to reach agreement with the social-democrats, our organizations occasionally undertook not to agitate against the social-democratic party. In other words they renounced the right to conduct communist agitation. . . .

9. The organizational amalgamation of communist and social-democratic parties, or the fusion of the Second and Third Internationals (recently proposed by the Independent Labour Party in England) are wholly excluded. Impossible proposals of this kind are made by the social-democratic leaders in order to frustrate measures which are possible. . . . The re-establishment of international working-class unity, the creation of a single International covering all working-class forces is a task of epochal significance which will in time be accomplished by the Communist International. It was precisely to carry out this task that the proletarian vanguard, in severe struggles and faced by tremendous difficulties, created independent proletarian communist parties. . . . The foundation of independent communist parties, which are alone able to defend the interests of the proletariat as a class consistently and to the end, is an achievement which communists will never renounce.

10. As to the Independent Labour Party's proposal, the enlarged Executive recognizes that it was mainly the result of pressure from the proletarian section of the ILP, who were indignant at the ILP's rejection of the CPGB's proposal for a united front against the capitalist offensive. The enlarged Executive agrees with the CPGB in believing that readiness to establish a united front at home would be the best proof of the sincerity of the demand for an international united front.

11. United front tactics are of course intended primarily for working-class action. But this does not exhaust their possibilities. In favourable circumstances communists should put forward partial demands designed to attract semi-proletarian and petty-bourgeois strata. . . .

12. In a number of countries differentiation among the peasantry is visibly proceeding, and is having its effect on bourgeois (and Catholic) peasant associations, in which left wings are arising. . . . All CI sections must intensify their work in this field, and bring it into harmony with Comintern activities as a whole.

13. The rise of the national liberation movement and the gradual strengthening of the labour movement in the East are new factors of the utmost significance. It is one of the most urgent tasks today to direct the attention of the European and American workers to them, explaining their importance in the proletarian struggle for emancipation, and the necessity of supporting and collaborating with the struggle for freedom in the East.

It is the duty of the Communist International to give all support to workers' organizations in the East and to draw them into the international proletarian struggle. The Second International is suddenly beginning to take an interest in these questions. . . . It is trying to check the influence of the Comintern and the Soviet Union in the East. It wants to bring the labour movement of Japan, India, and China under reformist control.

The decision of the ILO to call an all-Asiatic workers' conference is a decisive step in this direction. Attempts are also being made to corrupt the young Indian labour movement by transplanting the reformist ideology of the British trade union leaders to India. The Communist International must bear this in mind and fight vigorously against such actions of the representatives of the labour aristocracy, designed to serve the imperialist bourgeoisie.

14. The plenum instructs the Executive to pay greater attention to the labour movement in Japan, where there are all the prerequisites for a proletarian mass movement. This is the more necessary as the reformists are already setting out to capture the newly-rising organizations of the Japanese labour movement. . . .

15. Awareness of the inevitability of a new world war . . . is growing among the proletarian vanguard throughout the world. The workers are realizing more and more that they can wage the fight against war only in closest co-operation with the Soviet Union. The fight against the war danger takes first place in the question of establishing an international united front. . . .

18. In view of the mass character of unemployment in some important European countries, the Comintern sections in the countries concerned must give the greatest attention to the unemployed. They must organize the unemployed and take over the leadership of this movement. . . .

19. In a few Comintern sections (Bulgaria, Poland) the danger has recently arisen of a terroristic deviation. Because of the regime established by hangman Tsankov, the Bulgarian workers have been seized by a certain enthusiasm for terroristic forms of defence, as seen for example in the Sofia Cathedral explosion, although the CC of the Bulgarian CP came out strongly against individual acts of terrorism. In Poland also a passing terroristic tendency is to be observed.

The Communist International decisively rejects individual terrorism. In rejecting this method of struggle it is guided exclusively by the principles of revolutionary expediency. This has nothing in common with the petty-bourgeois attitude to the revolutionary use of force. Every class-conscious proletarian knows that without the use of revolutionary terror the bourgeoisie cannot be overthrown . . . but that is precisely why communists reject the employment of individual terror, since individual acts which attempt to take the place of the mass struggle can only demoralize our movement, split our forces, and diminish our striking power.

20. The Communist International notes further that in a number of parties there is not even the elementary minimum of inner-party democracy. This has made many recent party crises more acute. . . . Democratic centralism means not only discipline, but discipline plus the genuine election of the leading committees, freedom of discussion within the party

on all questions of concern to the membership (except those on which, with the decision already taken, the party is proceeding to take action), and genuine individual initiative. . . .

21. The reconstruction of the party on a factory-cell basis has been completely justified. The objections of the French right and the Italian ultra-left are the outcome of their incorrect, anti-bolshevik line of thought.

EXTRACTS FROM THE THESES OF THE SIXTH ECCI PLENUM ON THE TASKS OF COMMUNISTS IN THE TRADE UNION MOVEMENT

March 1926   *Inprekorr*, vi, 68, p. 1038, 5 *May* 1926

[The meeting of the IFTU council in Amsterdam on 7 February 1925 rejected by 13 votes to 6 the British proposal for a conference between the Federation and the Russian unions, stating that the Russian unions were quite free to join the IFTU if they accepted its statutes; the Russian unions, it was said, wanted not to join but to capture the IFTU. Early in April representatives of the Russian and British unions met in London and set up a joint committee. The TUC meeting at Scarborough in September was attended by Tomsky and Lozovsky. Reporting to the fourteenth CPSU congress at the end of the year Zinoviev said that the joint committee was a phenomenon of immense importance, and a brilliant demonstration of the correctness of united front tactics.

Introducing the theses, Lozovsky listed twenty-two outstanding weaknesses in communist trade union work, and singled out the German CP for its hostile and provocative attitude to social-democratic workers in the factories. The programme of action suggested was limited to those points which would provide a basis for joint activities; it therefore omitted Dawes and Locarno, and fraternization in colonial wars. The RILU had drawn up a programme for union work in the Near, Middle, and Far East. In May 1925 Chinese unions with a million members had joined the RILU, and a Pacific trade union conference was to be held and a Pan-Asiatic trade union federation to be established

Klara Zetkin said it was not surprising if the workers sometimes doubted the honesty of their trade union campaigns, since in the factory they were called 'brothers' but in their socialist parties they were 'traitors and fascists'. She suggested that the use of such labels should be avoided.

The successful work of the CPGB in organizing the trade union left wing was contrasted with the failure of the KPD under Maslow–Fischer, when relations between communist and socialist workers had become much worse, and the party was saved from catastrophe only by a change of leaders. Bordiga was the only speaker against the theses. He approved of a trade union united front at the national level, but not internationally, and the theses were passed against his vote.]

I. NEW PHENOMENA IN THE INTERNATIONAL TRADE UNION MOVEMENT

Since the fifth world congress of the Comintern a number of events have occurred in the international trade union movement which require the most careful study if our future tactics are to be correct. These are: (1) the fall in the standard of living of the working masses; (2) new forms of class collaboration; (3) the growing influence of the American Federation of Labor on the reformist European trade union movement; (4) the rapid development of the trade union movement in colonial and semi-colonial countries; (5) the crystallization of a left wing in reformist unions; (6) the growing international influence of the Soviet trade unions and the desire of the workers to send delegations to the Soviet Union; (7) the establishment of the Anglo-Russian unity committee; (8) the sharpening of the struggle inside the Amsterdam International; (9) the growth among the masses of the desire for unity. . . .

IV. THE GROWING INFLUENCE OF THE AFL ON THE REFORMIST UNIONS IN EUROPE

The ideological and political influence of the American Federation of Labor has recently grown much stronger, not so much in America itself . . . as in Europe, where the right wing of the Amsterdam International has long been dreaming of finding American support in its struggle against the English trade union movement, which is becoming steadily more radical. The expansion of the reactionary influence of the AFL keeps pace with the rise of the international hegemony of American imperialism. . . .

V. RAPID TRADE UNION DEVELOPMENT IN THE COLONIAL AND SEMI-COLONIAL COUNTRIES

The trade union movement in colonial and semi-colonial countries is a post-war product; it is only in the last few years that it has become an organized force and has begun to play a large part in the national liberation struggle. The activities of the unions in China and India were particularly significant. The strikes in Shanghai, Hongkong, and Tientsin . . . introduced a consistent proletarian element into the Chinese struggle for national freedom, and the Chinese proletariat has become the axis and the chief power in the Chinese national freedom movement.

In these circumstances the affiliation of the Chinese unions to the Profintern is particularly significant; it shows that the unions in the countries enslaved by imperialism are seeking allies where they really can be found—in Moscow and not in Amsterdam. . . .

In relation to the union movement in the colonial and semi-colonial countries the communist parties have three tasks: (1) to establish a permanent link with the labour movement in all countries, in particular the link between the metropolitan country and the colony; (2) to give complete, unreserved, and all-round support to the labour movement in these doubly oppressed countries in its struggle for national and social emancipation;

(3) in those countries, such as France, where workers from the colonies come to work, to admit them to the unions and to conduct cultural and educational work among them in order to train them as militants in the fight for national and social emancipation.

VI. THE CRYSTALLIZATION OF A LEFT WING IN REFORMIST UNIONS

The growth of unemployment, the interminable economic crisis, the fall in living standards, and the growing financial and economic hegemony of the United States in the world market are accompanied by rising discontent among the proletarian masses, which is reflected in the reformist unions. . . . The practical question of closing their ranks for the fight confronts the workers, but that is impossible without a united front, without a working agreement between workers of different political beliefs, inside and outside the factory, on questions of practical interest to the working masses.

Thus the pressure of organized capital is driving the idea of unity deeper and deeper into the working masses, and the results are beginning to show in their daily struggle. There is practically not a single Amsterdam organization without its left tendency. . . .

The attitude of the Comintern and of communist parties to the growing opposition in the reformist unions is quite clear; it is the outcome of bolshevik tactical principles—to support every opposition in reformist organizations directed against their theory and practice. We cannot and should not wait while these left tendencies crystallize and take final shape. We must exert all our might to help the opposition movement, to support those workers who are beginning to throw off the influence of reformist ideology. . . . The communist parties must openly reach agreement with all opposition elements on the basis of a concrete programme of action, without for a single moment abandoning the struggle for the communist programme and communist demands. . . .

VIII. THE ANGLO-RUSSIAN UNITY COMMITTEE

The change in sentiment among the working masses and the majority of the organized working class in England is expressed organizationally in the creation of the Anglo-Russian unity committee. This did not happen without a struggle. The Amsterdam International made great efforts to prevent a rapprochement between the English and Russian unions, as did the reactionary wing of the trade union movement in England. Nevertheless the rapprochement took place and was consolidated by the establishment of the committee.

The Anglo-Russian committee, whose foundation was greeted joyfully by the masses, marks a new stage in the history of the international trade union movement. . . . It demonstrates the practical possibility of creating a unified International, and of a common struggle of workers of different political tendencies against reaction, fascism, and the capitalist offensive. . . .

All communist parties must support the Anglo-Russian committee in every way and wage a vigorous struggle against the social-democrats and right-wing Amsterdamers who are sabotaging the work of the committee and hope to break up the Anglo-Russian bloc. The Comintern welcomes most warmly the rapprochement between the English and Soviet trade unions, and for its part will do everything in its power to help the committee to carry out its tasks. . . .

X. THE CENTRAL COUNCIL OF THE SOVIET UNIONS AND AMSTERDAM

The slogan put forward by the fifth Comintern congress and the third Profintern congress of the merging of the Profintern and the Amsterdam International through an international unity congress, and the Anglo-Russian committee's slogan of a 'united, all-embracing international', encountered the sharpest opposition from international social-democracy and the Amsterdam right wing. This opposition took two forms; a campaign was started against the idea of an international unity congress as an 'impracticable and harmful fantasy', and at the same time the reformists attempted to reduce the entire problem to one of the relations between Amsterdam and the central council of the Soviet unions; then they began to sabotage the negotiations with the central council and even rejected the proposal for an unconditional conference. . . .

Social-democracy is trying to present the honest desire of the central council of the Soviet unions to do everything to establish real unity in the international trade union movement . . . as meaning that the central council is anxious to leave the Profintern, break the bonds that link it with the revolutionary trade union movement in other countries, join Amsterdam, throw off the influence of the CPSU, and so change the entire political orientation of the Soviet trade union movement. The central council of the Soviet unions is an integral part of the Profintern and will, like all member organizations of that body, carry out the policy laid down by the Profintern. . . .

XV. STRENGTHENING THE RILU

The struggle to establish a united international and the work of bringing communist and social-democratic workers closer together will be successful to the extent that we work at strengthening our own ranks nationally and internationally. While defending the unity of the trade union movement and submitting to trade union discipline, communists must vigorously defend their right to wage an ideological struggle within the unions, to defend their point of view and advance their own opinion. The fight to strengthen our own ranks in every country must be accompanied by a fight to strengthen the Profintern itself. It is essential to carry out planned and orderly work to strengthen all the organizations affiliated to the Profintern, and the revolutionary minorities in other unions, in conformity with united front tactics and the demand for trade union unity.

EXTRACTS FROM THE RESOLUTION OF THE SIXTH ECCI PLENUM ON
THE ENGLISH QUESTION

4 *March* 1926   *Thesen und Resolutionen*, VI Plenum, p. 104

[The ECCI report to the sixth plenum stated that the Executive had held many meetings about policy in Britain, and had approved the line taken by the party there. In his opening speech Zinoviev said that the best results over the past year had been gained in Britain and China; the policy of the CPGB showed how united front tactics should be used. Brown (CPGB) thought the resolution painted Britain's position in too gloomy colours; Britain still had immense resources and powers of resistance. Ferguson, claiming that there were no fractions within the CPGB, reported that it had 159 factory cells and seventy factory newspapers, which gave it powerful levers for mobilizing the masses. Trade union membership was obligatory for all party members; the Minority Movement was the party's biggest success; it had called a special conference in January 1925 to break the conspiracy of silence about the TUC report on its visit to Russia. Hardy said that party members worked hard in their union branches to get elected to office, and when they were there should be allowed a certain amount of freedom. If they merely put forward a straight communist programme they would lose their influence.

The foundation of the Minority Movement was decided on in 1924 at a meeting of the ECCI with representatives of the CPGB to discuss the slow growth of the British communist movement. It was intended at first to cover the left in both the Labour Party and the unions, but it soon restricted its activities to the unions. Its first conference was held in September 1924, with 270 (unofficial) delegates; the second, in January 1925, was attended by 630 delegates, who claimed to represent 750,000 trade unionists. The conference adopted a resolution on the dispatch of trade union organizers to India.

The CPGB had fifteen of its members among the 1,100 delegates attending the Labour Party conference at Liverpool in October 1925. Their attempt to bring up the question of CPGB affiliation had been ruled out of order, on the ground that it had been voted on the previous year and could not be brought up again for three years. After the Labour Party conference, which excluded communists as individual members of constituency parties, the CPGB started a 'national left-wing movement' with the *Sunday Worker* as its newspaper. The resolution (which some works of reference date 7 March) was passed unanimously.]

1. THE SITUATION IN GREAT BRITAIN

The most outstanding feature of the British situation is the continued decline of British imperialism. British finance-capital has been unable to maintain the position it held before the war. It has had to yield its place as the predominant imperialist Power to the United States of America.

This fact is reflected in the unfavourable trade balance, in chronic unemployment, in the decline of production in the basic industries below the pre-war level while the cost of living remains high—at least 75 per cent. higher than it was before the war.

Although the new policy of British imperialism towards its colonies—economic concessions to certain strata of the indigenous bourgeoisie and capital export, accompanied though they are by more severe political oppression—may for a time bring greater profits to some strata of British capitalists, this policy is bound in time to expose industry in the motherland to more acute competition and thus to weaken still further the British industrial system.

In the period of British imperial predominance British capitalists were in a position to secure the active support of the upper strata of the British working class for their imperialist policy by making concessions out of the super-profits squeezed out of the colonial peoples. Now British capitalists have lost their dominant position, they are trying to shift the burden of their losses, and of their losses in the war, on to the workers by reducing wages and lowering the standard of living.

2. THE REVOLUTIONIZING OF THE BRITISH WORKING CLASS

The methods used by the British capitalists to recapture their former position . . . are gradually making the British working class more revolutionary. The attempts to reduce wages and chronic unemployment are driving the workers to united resistance and to struggle against the capitalist system.

Another circumstance pushing the British workers to the left is the experience of the Labour Government. On the one hand it aroused broad masses of workers who had never before taken an active part in political life to political consciousness; while on the other the fiasco of the Mac-Donald Government, which brought no help to the working masses while openly supporting British imperialism, created among the active minority of the labour movement extreme disappointment with the reformist leadership. . . .

3. SYMPTOMS OF THE MOVEMENT TO THE LEFT

The movement among British workers to a more revolutionary position can be seen in:

1. The growth of a socialist ideology among the workers.

2. The development of a strong tendency to form a left wing in the British trade unions, most marked in the formation of the Minority Movement.

3. The resolutions passed at the Scarborough trade union congress (against imperialism, against the Dawes plan, and for factory committees).

4. The movement for trade union unity, as seen in the Anglo-Russian unity committee.

5. The support for the communist party's struggle against the decisions of the Liverpool conference of the Labour Party.

6. The beginnings of a left-wing organization within the Labour Party.

7. The mass movement of the unemployed.

8. The workers' campaign for the release of the twelve members of the CC of the CPGB (the petition was signed by 300,000 workers).

9. The mobilization of the workers to support the miners on 'Red Friday' (formation of action committees and the industrial alliance).

10. The pressure exercised by the rank and file of the Independent Labour Party on their leaders for a united front with the communists.

4. THE SUCCESSES OF THE COMMUNIST PARTY

. . . The success of the CPGB in extending its influence and in capturing the leadership of the working masses is of significance for all sections of the Comintern. The strength of the CP in this work is based on the following circumstances:

1. Since 1924 there has been no fractionalism in the British party. . . .

2. Experience has taught the British party the need to get a firm foothold in the unions. It insists on all its members being active members of the unions. . . .

3. The party realized that it was necessary to build bridges to the masses. It promoted the development of the Minority Movement in the unions, and is now engaged in giving shape to the left wing in the Labour Party. The systematic organization of fractions in the unions and the Labour Party was an important factor in this work. . . .

5. THE TASKS OF THE COMMUNIST PARTY

1. The party must continue to give the greatest attention to work in the unions and to support the Minority Movement to the utmost. . . .

2. The job, already begun, of giving form to the left wing in the Labour Party, is of great importance for the development of the British movement. . . .

3. The British party must continue its active support for international trade union unity. . . .

4. The British party must take an active part in the struggle of the oppressed colonial peoples and mobilize the British working masses to support every movement of revolt against British imperialism. . . .

7. Broad masses of the British working class still cherish illusions about parliamentarism and the traditions of liberalism. The party must wage an energetic struggle against the illusion that the British working class can win its freedom through a bourgeois parliament. . . .

8. Although the party has extended its ideological influence over the British working masses, it has not managed to translate this influence into new membership. . . . If the party sets about this job resolutely, it should be able to double its membership in 1926.

EXTRACTS FROM THE RESOLUTION OF THE SIXTH ECCI PLENUM ON THE DEVELOPMENT OF METHODS AND FORMS FOR CONSOLIDATING COMMUNIST PARTY INFLUENCE ON THE MASSES

8 *March* 1926   *Thesen und Resolutionen*, VI Plenum, p. 189

[An organization conference was held before the opening of the sixth plenum; there were 26 delegates, and representatives of 10 other countries, as well as representatives of the RILU, the Krestintern, and the departments of the ECCI. It was agreed that too much of the work of parties was being done at the centre, where there was 'an inflated apparatus'. More staff and more work should be delegated to the districts.

The conference passed a long and detailed resolution on the structure and work of factory and street cells, another on factory newspapers, and amended the May 1925 directives on the organizational structure of the party. Instructions were issued on the structure of central committees, their organization and trade union departments. The resolution passed by the conference on the results of its work claimed that reorganization on a factory basis had won new members and enlarged the sales of party literature; factory newspapers also increased the party's influence, and brought many workers into or back into the unions. Factory-cell committees were not yet working satisfactorily, but the work of party fractions in non-party organizations was going well. Low membership was attributed in part to the loss of 'unstable and alien elements', in part to the failure to treat new members with consideration, which drove them out; sometimes they were overburdened with work, sometimes given nothing at all to do.

The report of the organization department to the plenum found that the position in regard to factory cells and fractions was not altogether satisfactory; the orgbureau now had eleven responsible workers and five instructors attached to the CI sections. Dahlem, reporting on the conference to the plenum, stated that the factory-cell form of organization was particularly useful for illegal parties and promoted united front work.

At the plenum Bordiga said that bolshevization showed an unfavourable balance; the parties had not advanced as a result of these methods. Factory cells should not be the basic principle valid for all times and places, but a practical form to be used when and where suitable. The danger of a demagogic leadership existed in a territorial organization, but it could not be met by boycotting the intellectuals. Marx and Lenin had always emphasized the role in the revolution of deserters from the ruling class. Ex-workers had also played a treacherous role in the revolution. If all workers were organized in factory cells, which never discussed general political questions, they would have even less influence in the party than before, and less breadth of outlook; even more would be left to the intellectuals. What made a party proletarian was not its social composition measured by some mechanical criterion, but its revolutionary policy of class struggle. The party's political work should have a territorial basis.

Kuusinen, who reported on work in mass organizations, said the Comintern had to establish non-communist organizations of sympathizers for special purposes, a planetary system of organizations and committees revolving around the communist party and under its direct influence.

A great deal of attention was paid at this time to the organization of workers' delegations to the Soviet Union. The sections of the CI were asked to report fully on meetings at which the visitors spoke on their return, on the kind of questions asked, etc.

The proposals submitted by the organization conference were adopted unanimously by the ECCI. As a result of its recommendations one representative from each of the nine largest parties was sent to work in the organization department for six months. In its report to the sixth Comintern congress the department stated that in all there had been sixteen of them.]

1. Now that the work initiated by the third world congress to win the broad masses of the proletariat has already had considerable political success in many capitalist countries, thanks to the employment of united front tactics, the time has come to give the greatest attention to giving an organized character to and extending this influence on the masses. If our parties do not tackle this task, they will not be able in the present period to prevent the partial loss of the influence already won, and will have to make new efforts to win it back again. By the use and development of suitable organizational methods and forms, our parties must consolidate and extend their influence over the masses.

This work . . . has until now been carried on unsystematically and defectively. From now on it must be developed methodically and comprehensively in all fields, in accordance with Lenin's instructions on the organizational art, 'to make use of everyone and everything' in the proletarian class struggle, to organize not only the work of party members effectively, but as far as possible to draw in other forces of the proletariat as well, and even the most progressive elements within the peasantry and the middle classes, for sustained work of agitation and mobilizing the broadest masses.

2. The organization of mass campaigns . . . should be studied more

thoroughly. But this is not enough. In every such movement the communist party must learn how to single out the active non-party, syndicalist, and social-democratic elements among the masses drawn into the campaign, and incorporate them in the various agitation and action committees, or other united front bodies which may serve as organizational footholds for subsequent mass influence and mass movements. These united front committees, in the first place local (and formed in the factories), turn out to be in almost every sphere of work one of the most natural organizational forms for the activity of our party members outside the party itself. . . .

3. . . . Communist fractions and all party work must be organized in such a way that they lead not to the isolation of communists, but to constant contact with the greatest possible number of non-party, syndicalist, and social-democratic workers, exerting steady influence on them and making them more active. Special organizational methods and forms can be developed for each sphere of work, but the over-all aim is to organize a broad mass left movement, inseparably bound to the more or less invisible communist fraction. The same applies to work in factory committees, and in special circumstances also in so-called labour parties. . . .

4. A particularly important form of organizing communist influence over the masses is the sympathizing mass organization for specific purposes. These may be autonomous or independent. The form should be as flexible as possible; there may be collective as well as individual membership. In every country it must be agreed with the central committee which of these organizations should appeal to the trade unions to join collectively. . . . In several countries the new sympathizing mass organizations include peace leagues and associations against the imperialist oppression of Eastern peoples. In countries where the broad working and peasant masses are filled with a lively sympathy for Soviet Russia (particularly in connexion with a workers' delegation campaign) the channel might be societies of working friends of the new Russia. . . .

5. In many capitalist countries an appropriate and effective means of consolidating and expanding communist influence on the masses appears to be the development of non-party publishing activity on a wide basis. . . . But the publishers must really understand what should be published . . . in the way of popular scientific literature, popular illustrated workers' papers, calendars, belles-lettres, etc., in the interests of revolutionizing the masses. . . .

8. The entire work of communists among the masses is under the political guidance of the leading party bodies, on the basis of ECCI decisions and directives. . . . It must be indelibly impressed on every member of a party cell or a communist fraction that his work among non-party, social-democratic workers in the factory, the trade union, the co-operative, the sports league, the sympathizing mass organization, etc., as well as among

peasants, *is party work*, and is for the majority of members the most important part of their party work. In doing this work they must not lose themselves in the masses, but remain always revolutionary organizers of mass activity.

EXTRACTS FROM A RESOLUTION ON THE ORGANIZATION AND STRUCTURE OF COMMUNIST FRACTIONS IN TRADE UNIONS PASSED BY THE SECOND ORGANIZATION CONFERENCE AND ENDORSED BY THE SIXTH ECCI PLENUM

11 *March* 1926   *Inprekorr*, vi, 65, p. 986, 29 *April* 1926

The following instructions embody the principles on which the structure of communist fractions should be based. The varied structure of trade unions and the varying levels of development of communist parties make it necessary for the CI sections to determine their own methods by adapting these instructions to the particular conditions of their countries.

I

THE ROLE OF FRACTIONS

Communist members of a trade union and of its organizations (executive, conference, congress, etc.) are obliged to unite in a fraction and to perform active fraction work.

Communist fractions are to work energetically to bring the majority of the trade union members under their influence. They will be the more successful in this the more devotedly, intelligently, and vigorously they look after the interests of these members, the better they understand how to defend the proletarian class interests and to combine, in all spheres and on every occasion, the struggle for immediate demands with the struggle for the aims of the working class. Communist trade union work is carried on within the framework of the constitution and decisions of the union.

II

PARTY AND FRACTION

Party members must realize that fractions are not the foundation of the party and that they can therefore take decisions referring only to their special field of activity.

The success of fraction work depends on the unity, determination, and discipline of all fraction members. It is not the individual fraction member, often not even the fraction as a whole, but the communist party in its entirety which is held responsible by the broad working masses for the activity of communist fractions and every utterance of a communist fraction member.

The party committees determine the political and tactical line of communist fractions, give them instructions and directives, and supervise their work. Important fraction work must be discussed by the trade union department of the committee in the presence of representatives of the fraction. Serious differences of opinion between trade union department and fraction are to be resolved by the party committee in the presence of fraction representatives. Decisions of the committee are to be unconditionally carried out by the fraction. Failure to do so is a breach of discipline.

Candidates for all trade union congresses, conferences, and executives are to be nominated by the fraction leadership and require endorsement by the appropriate party committee. If necessary the party committee may itself nominate candidates.

The relevant party committee is at all times entitled to amend or annul decisions of the fraction, and to dismiss or appoint fraction committees or leaders. In such cases an explanation must be given to the fraction members.

Within the limits of general party instructions, the fraction decides internal questions and current work. Party committees should not interfere unnecessarily in the daily work of the fraction, but should grant it all possible freedom of action and initiative.

Fraction committees are obliged to report regularly to the relevant party committee or relevant department, and to the fraction committee next above it in rank.

III

THE STRUCTURE OF FRACTIONS

Communist trade union work is carried out in factories by the cells, and in trade union bodies by the fraction. Trade union fractions do not operate in the factory. . . .

The cell committee guides and supervises the activity of communist trade union officials in the factory. It must arrange for the nomination in factory trade union elections of comrades who carry out trade union work in the factory on the instructions of the cell. There is as a rule no direct contact between the fraction committee and the cell. Communication is carried on via the party committee. . . .

At the local level

1. All communist members of a trade union branch form a fraction in that branch. . . .

2. All communists in a trade union body (executive, union committee, etc.) form a fraction.

The communist fraction in the local administrative centre of a union acts as the committee for the communist fractions of the branches within that area. . . .

3. All fraction members shall be called together for a fraction meeting whenever necessary, but in any case before every trade union meeting, to discuss the execution of the instructions given by the appropriate party committee. If, for objective reasons, it is impossible to lay down the attitude of the fraction beforehand, the instructions of the fraction committee are binding on the entire fraction at the trade union meeting. Whatever the circumstances, comrades must always speak and vote as one.

4. If in any city the union branches are organized in a local council with communists among the committee, they shall form a fraction which shall act as the committee for all fractions in the branches represented in the council. . . .

At the District Level

1. Communist members of trade union district committees form a fraction. This fraction also acts as the committee for all fractions of the branches of that union in the district. . . .

2. If the district unions are organized into a district trade union council, communists on that council form a fraction which serves at the same time as the committee for all fractions in the area covered. It works under the direction and control of the corresponding district party committee (trade union department). The district party committee may also communicate direct with the district fraction committees of the individual unions. . . .

At the National Level

1. Communist members of the national executive committee of each union form a fraction, which is in charge of the work of all fractions in that union. . . .

2. Communist fractions in the national executive committees are subordinate to the communist fraction of the executive of the trade union federation. The latter works under the direct guidance of the central committee (trade union department). The CC may also treat directly with the fractions in the union national executives. . . .

Fractions in Unions of Different Tendencies

If in one industry there are unions of different tendencies (red, Amsterdam, syndicalist), fractions are to be formed in each of them, in accordance with their structure. Similarly, fractions should be organized in company trade unions of the Christian, Hirsch–Duncker, fascist, and other varieties.

To this end party organizations must try to recruit members of these unions to the party. In order that the fractions shall act in a planned and uniform fashion when the occasion arises, the relevant party committee (trade union department) shall when necessary call together the fractions or fraction committees in these different unions for joint consultation. . . .

V

FRACTIONS AT CONFERENCES AND CONGRESSES

Party committees, working through their trade union department and fraction committee, must make preparations (selection of delegates, draft resolutions, etc.) for trade union congresses, conferences, and delegate meetings. They must convene fraction meetings before these assemblies open, and guide and supervise communist work when they are in session. For the duration of these conferences and congresses, the fraction elects a bureau to deal with current work; the fraction bureau, working under the guidance of the relevant party committee, bears full political responsibility for its work to that committee.

A uniform attitude and the strictest discipline of all communists at these meetings is particularly necessary, since the broad working masses follow their course most attentively and hold the communist party responsible for the utterances of individual communists.

VI

FRACTIONS AND OPPOSITIONS

Every fraction must maintain contact with the non-communist oppositional elements in the trade unions. Meetings and discussions should be held with these sympathizers to enable a joint and united stand to be taken when the occasion arises. . . .

RESOLUTION OF THE SIXTH ECCI PLENUM ON THE REORGANIZATION OF ECCI WORK

11 *March* 1926   *Inprekorr*, vi, 68, p. 1071, 6 *May* 1926

[Eleven national secretariats were set up by the ECCI on 24 March 1926 to cover the following areas: (1) France and French possessions, Italy, Belgium, Switzerland; (2) Germany; (3) Czechoslovakia, Austria, Hungary; (4) Britain, Ireland, Holland, Australia, South Africa, India, Dutch East Indies; (5) United States, Canada, Japan; (6) Spain, Portugal, Latin America; (7) Norway, Sweden, Denmark, Iceland; (8) Poland, Finland, and the three Baltic States; (9) the Balkans; (10) the USSR; (11) China, Korea, Mongolia, Turkey, Persia, Egypt, Syria, Palestine. Each secretariat was to be led by a member of the

Executive, with a staff including representatives of the communist parties in the countries covered. A standing trade union commission was also established, consisting of Zinoviev, Bukharin, Piatnitsky, Ercoli, Treint, Ferguson, Smeral, Geschke, Tomsky, Lozovsky, and Nin.

The opening of the Lenin School, which was planned for October 1925, with Bukharin as the principal lecturer, had to be postponed because 'pedagogical demands (selection of suitable teachers, preparation of study material, etc.) present certain difficulties which it will take some time to overcome'. Among its personnel when it opened at the end of 1926 were Li Li-san, Chou En-lai, Thorez, Browder, and Ulbricht.

The resolution, adopted unanimously in commission, was drafted by the ECCI and passed unanimously by the plenum.]

1. The work of the Executive Committee of the CI must be put on a more systematic footing. The strongest sections of the CI must be drawn far more than hitherto into direct leadership of the CI. Reorganization of the Executive's work to this end, which is of great political as well as organizational importance, is essential for the following reasons.

The ECCI must be far more closely linked with the sections than hitherto. The sections must co-operate far more intensively in the solution of international problems, for only so can the communist parties develop more rapidly and normally. Greater participation by the sections in the leadership of the CI is essential if the parties are to acquire the training which will enable them to lead the revolutionary movement in their own countries.

More active collaboration of all sections in the work of the ECCI will also promote the selection of leaders both nationally and internationally. It will train parties and their leaders in the habit of initiative and give the rank-and-file membership a better understanding of the Comintern's problems. Finally, it will strengthen the communist parties' ability to recruit new members from among the non-party masses.

Progress in this direction is now both possible and necessary, for firmly based communist parties already exist in the most important countries, internally strong and with six or seven years experience behind them.

With these considerations in mind, the plenary session of the enlarged Executive approves the proposal of the fourteenth CPSU congress, which runs:

'Congress instructs the CPSU delegation to initiate moves to strengthen the apparatus of the CI and in doing so to follow a course which will give greater influence to foreign communist parties in the leadership of the CI.'

The enlarged Executive observes that this proposal is in complete accordance with the trend of earlier Comintern decisions.

Obviously, the CI must remain, now as before, a centralized world party; but the parties must more and more learn to rely on themselves.

This refers in particular to the selection of the leading bodies in the CI sections.

To effect this reorganization of ECCI work, the enlarged Executive instructs the larger CI sections, viz: the German, French, Italian, and Czech, each to appoint two representatives, and the other large parties (including the Eastern) one representative, to take part for at least six months in the work of the ECCI.

The enlarged Executive instructs the ECCI to carry these measures through unconditionally and without delay.

To facilitate reorganization, the plenary session of the enlarged Executive instructs the ECCI to reconstitute the presidium, the orgbureau, and the secretariat, as well as the ECCI budget commission, at its first meeting after the present meeting.

2. The plenary session of the enlarged Executive instructs the ECCI to conduct its work in future more methodically. With this in mind, the plenary session emphasizes the correctness of the principles of the scheme worked out by the ECCI secretariat for reorganizing ECCI work. The ECCI is to hold a regular monthly meeting attended by all members present in Moscow. To decide the most important questions of policy and principle, a plenary session of the ECCI is to be held every three months, attended by all ECCI members. Meetings of the ECCI presidium and orgbureau are also to be held regularly. The ECCI secretariat must be enlarged and reorganized on the basis of regional secretariats.

Working plans should be drawn up for the work of the CI. Every three months CI sections are to submit to the ECCI reports on their activities and future plans. The orgbureau of the ECCI must also examine regularly the plans of work of the subsidiary CI organizations and the ECCI departments. The ECCI orgbureau must regularly examine not only the structure of the parties, but also their entire organizational activity and distribution of newspapers and party literature. The action programmes of the sections must be carefully scrutinized by the ECCI.

In future, questions concerning the Eastern peoples are to occupy a far greater place than heretofore in the Executive's work, corresponding with their new and greater importance.

The enlarged Executive approves the steps taken by the ECCI to open the International Lenin School, and instructs the parties to adhere to the principles formulated by the presidium.

In drawing up the general plans of ECCI work, central place must be given to the next world congress of the CI. The plenary session of the enlarged Executive considers it desirable to convene the sixth congress for February–March 1927, if that is possible, and instructs the ECCI to determine the exact date. Careful preparations for the world congress must be made by the ECCI. The agenda obviously cannot yet be decided in detail, but the material dealing with the basic questions of our policy (trade union, peasant, nationality questions, etc.) can be collected and studied, and distributed to the sections for discussion in good time. The ECCI must make the necessary preparations for the discussion of the CI programme at the sixth congress. With this in mind, the plenary session of the enlarged Executive instructs the ECCI to set up an authoritative standing commission to take charge of the discussion in the sections of the draft CI programme.

3. When the Executive's machinery has been strengthened in this way, more careful supervision of the execution of CI decisions will be possible. The ECCI and the Comintern sections must take steps to organize reporting from the lowest cell up to the party committee and from the party committee to the ECCI. Only if the closest contacts are established will it be possible to put into effect the bolshevist principle of checking and supervising the execution of decisions. The plenary session of the enlarged Executive instructs the ECCI to check carefully and strictly the execution of world-congress decisions, particularly the last, fifth, world congress, as well as the decisions of the enlarged Executives. Examples of the questions to be checked in this way are the carrying out of international campaigns, bolshevist training of the membership, party reorganization, selection and training of new party functionaries, normalization of internal party life, entry of party membership into trade unions, application of united front tactics, etc.

At the congresses of the sections reports should be given on the work of the ECCI.

The ECCI is instructed to organize this supervision in a gradual but methodical manner.

RESOLUTION OF THE SIXTH ECCI PLENUM ON THE REPORT OF THE ECCI

13 *March* 1926   *Inprekorr*, vi, 52, p. 735, 6 *April* 1926

[The report of the ECCI for the period April 1925 to January 1926 reviewed the position in the chief sections. The Executive had met 3 times, the presidium 24 times, the orgbureau 12 times, and the secretariat 9 times. The agitprop department had concentrated on setting up central party schools; their chief difficulties were lack of money, of instruction material, and of trained instructors. The curriculum of party schools, it had been announced at the end of 1925, was to include economic geography, political economy, the history of the class struggle and the labour movement, and the theory and practice of Leninism. Earlier, Bela Kun had commended the French and British parties for their training work, France for its Leninist party school and Youth school, the CPGB because all its members took a course in elementary Marxism. The information department had decided that an information officer should be attached to each central committee to maintain contact with the department in Moscow. No party had yet done this, although several had established information departments, and reports and minutes were coming in more regularly. The department had created a 'central office for fighting the Second International', which had issued a number of pamphlets. The department also issued a bulletin, in four languages, for circulation to the central committees, dealing with the work of the ECCI and important events in the sections, and giving analyses of problems discussed by the ECCI. Too much of the department's work was directed to the ECCI instead of the sections: of the 5,600 pages of typescript put out by the department in the report period, 5,000 had gone to the ECCI and only 600 to the sections. The ECCI periodical *Communist International* appeared in an edition of 10,000 in Russian, 2,000 in German and English, and 1,000 in French. The French and English editions were abridged. The editors of the Russian edition decided which articles had to be included in the non-Russian editions; their editors were entitled to include articles on local problems, but so far none had done so. The resolution, put forward by the German, British, French, Czech, Italian, Chinese, and American delegations, was carried against the vote of Bordiga.]

The enlarged Executive takes note with satisfaction of the report of the ECCI and observes that in carrying out the decisions of the fifth congress and the enlarged Executive in 1925 it has great successes to record. First place must be given to its success in the struggle for the unity of the trade union movement.

Substantial progress was made in carrying out bolshevization. The communist parties of Great Britain and China have won great successes. The open letter of the Executive to the CP of Germany created the conditions for the consolidation of the KPD and for its first great successes among the masses. The right danger in Czechoslovakia and the left danger in Italy were overcome with the help of the Executive.

The enlarged Executive expresses its confidence in the Executive and calls on it to put into effect more strongly internal party democracy, nationally and internationally. The enlarged Executive calls on all sections of the CI to support the ECCI to the utmost in its work to create real mass parties which, even in the period of relative stabilization, will win and retain the confidence of the masses.

EXTRACTS FROM THE RESOLUTION OF THE SIXTH ECCI PLENUM ON THE
CHINESE QUESTION

13 *March* 1926   *Thesen und Resolutionen*, VI Plenum, p. 176

[The resolution was moved by Brown (CPGB) and passed unanimously. There was little discussion about China at the plenary meetings. The ECCI report stated that there were no party organizations in the rural areas of China, but the central committee had drafted a peasant programme and set up a peasant department; it had also opened a school to train peasant agitators (the school was run by Mao Tse-tung). Relations between the CCP and the KMT were 'not quite clear'. The CC of the CCP now defined them as a 'political bloc', whereas previously the term 'close alliance' had been used.

After Sun Yat-sen's death the right wing in the KMT had decided to take steps to check the influence of the Russian political and military advisers. In October 1925 the CCP secretary Chen warned the central committee to prepare for withdrawal from the KMT, but his suggestions were overruled by the Comintern delegate. At the second KMT congress in January 1926 7 CP members were elected to its Executive Committee, and 24 members as alternates. (At the seventh ECCI plenum in December 1926 Tan Ping-shan, the chief Chinese delegate, claimed that, of the total of 278 votes at the congress, the communists and the left controlled 168.) On 20 March 1926 Chiang Kai-shek had a number of Soviet advisers and communist political commissars in the KMT army arrested. The Canton branch of the CCP proposed a counter-attack and break with the KMT, but this was voted down by CCP headquarters at Shanghai, on the ground that their forces were not strong enough to defeat Chiang. Russian and Chinese CP support for Chiang's contemplated 'northern expedition' was promised in return for continued KMT–CP collaboration. The ECCI representatives in China had at first hesitated to give their support, believing that the expedition would give greater power and prestige to Chiang Kai-shek than to the communists. Stalin and Bukharin also hesitated, concerned about the Soviet position in Manchuria and fearing foreign intervention; other leading communists took the view that in its military activities the KMT acted as 'armed bandits and warlords'. A paper in the Trotsky archives records a comment by Stalin dated 25 March 1926: 'The Government of Canton should in the present period decisively reject the thought of military expeditions of an offensive character, and generally of any such actions as may provoke the imperialists to embark on military intervention.'

The expedition started from Canton in July 1926. Later the advance of the KMT armies was said to demonstrate the success of the ECCI's China policy. At the time no reference to the events of 20 March was made in the communist press, nor was it mentioned in the resolution on China passed by the seventh ECCI plenum at the end of the year. Chen did however propose to the ECCI that in future the CCP should co-operate with the KMT from outside, not inside that organization; the suggestion was rejected. The Russian advisers were soon reinstated by Chiang, who publicly dismissed the incident as a misunderstanding. On 15 May the Executive of the KMT voted that communists were henceforth to be excluded from senior posts in the KMT, and were to refrain from criticizing Sun Yat-sen's principles. In an 'open letter' Chen recognized Sun Yat-senism as the common belief of workers and bourgeoisie in the nationalist movement. Voitinsky, head of the Eastern department of the ECCI, was sent to China in May to correct the anti-KMT trend in the Chinese CP. While there he became convinced of the need for the CCP to withdraw from the KMT. On 26 June 1926 the CC of the CCP, the majority of whose members disapproved of Borodin's acquiescence in the KMT decisions of 15 May, again tried to break the 'bloc within', and suggested that some of the arms coming from Russia for the KMT armies should go to the peasants rather than to Chiang, but Borodin argued that this would only arouse Chiang's suspicions again. In *Pravda* Bukharin attacked the view that the CCP should withdraw from the KMT; this would be to lose contact with the masses and to yield the banner of revolution to the bourgeoisie. Chen's proposals were overruled by the politbureau of the Russian party and the ECCI. He was later denounced by the ECCI for his 'opportunist concessions' to the KMT, despite good advice from the ECCI.]

1. The political strikes of the Chinese workers in Shanghai and Hongkong (June–September 1925) were a turning-point in the Chinese people's fight for emancipation from foreign imperialists. They were the starting-point of a powerful national movement . . . in which the Chinese working class, organized in class trade unions and led by the communist party, appeared as the leading force in the movement of the democratic masses, as the most important protagonist of national independence and the establishment of a popular government. At the same time they led to a differentiation in the national liberation movement, in which certain sections of the Chinese large industrialists and commercial bourgeoisie broke away from the movement. . . .

2. The political action of the proletariat gave the movement a powerful impulse forward and strengthened all the revolutionary-democratic organizations in the country, in particular the revolutionary people's party of the Kuomintang and the revolutionary Government in Canton. The KMT, the core of whose members acted in alliance with the Chinese communists, is a revolutionary bloc of workers, peasants, intellectuals, and the urban democracy. . . . The revolutionary Government established in Canton by the Kuomintang party has already established contact with the broadest masses of workers, peasants, and urban democracy, and has, by relying on these classes, annihilated the counter-revolutionary bands supported by the imperialists, and radically democratized the entire political life of the Kwantung province. The Canton Government, which thus personifies the vanguard of the Chinese people in its struggle for independence, is a model for the future revolutionary-democratic structure of the country. . . .

Some sections of the Chinese big bourgeoisie who for a time attached themselves to the Kuomintang have in the last year left it; this has resulted in the formation of a small group on the right wing of the Kuomintang, which comes out openly against a close alliance with the working masses, advocates the exclusion of communists from the Kuomintang, and opposes the revolutionary policy of the Canton Government. The fact that the second Kuomintang congress in January 1926 condemned the behaviour of this right wing and emphasized the need for a fighting Kuomintang–communist alliance strengthens the revolutionary trend of Kuomintang and Canton Government activity and secures for the Kuomintang the revolutionary support of the proletariat. . . .

4. The growth of the revolutionary-democratic tendency in the Chinese national liberation movement and the increasing influence of the Chinese proletariat in this movement are closely connected with the powerful moral and political support received by the liberation movement from the international proletarian revolution in the shape of the Communist International and the working masses of the USSR. The fight of the Chinese people against the rule of the imperialists and the fight of the entire international proletariat against these imperialists are developing in the closest connexion with each other. It must be the task of all sections of the CI to explain clearly to the working masses in all imperialist countries the significance of the struggle of the Chinese working people against the imperialists; they must support this movement to the utmost and wage a vigorous struggle against all imperialist attempts to defeat it by military intervention or blockade. The watchwords of this struggle must be 'Hands off China', recognition of China's complete independence, abolition of all unequal treaties, and withdrawal from China of the troops of all imperialist States. At the same time the Chinese communists must explain to the working masses of China that only the Communist International, which leads the revolutionary struggle of the world proletariat, is the revolutionary ally of the Chinese working masses in their fight for national and social liberation. . . .

6. The Chinese Communist Party will be able to fulfil the historical tasks confronting it as leader of the struggle of the Chinese working masses against the imperialists only if, during the entire course of the struggle, it succeeds in strengthening its organization and its influence as the class party of the Chinese proletariat and section of the Communist International. . . . Not nearly enough has been done to give organizational structure to the party. The political independence of the Chinese communists will be developed in the fight against two harmful deviations— against right liquidationism, which fails to appreciate the independent class tasks of the Chinese proletariat and leads to a formless fusion with the national movement as a whole, and against the ultra-left sentiments expressed in the attempt to skip the revolutionary-democratic stage of the movement and to turn at once to the tasks of proletarian dictatorship and Soviet power, leaving entirely out of account the peasantry, which is the basic and decisive factor of the Chinese national liberation movement. Despite the peculiarities of the setting, the tactical problems of the Chinese national-revolutionary movement have a strong resemblance to those confronting the Russian proletariat during the 1905 revolution. Only if the Chinese Communist Party learns the lessons of that revolution . . . will it be able to avoid the deviations from the correct tactical line noted above, or, where they already exist, to eradicate them.

7. The most important question of the Chinese national liberation movement is the peasant question. The victory of the revolutionary-democratic tendency . . . depends on the degree to which the 400 million Chinese peasants take part in the decisive revolutionary struggle together with the Chinese workers and under their leadership. . . . The most important task of the Chinese Communist Party and the Kuomintang is to bring home to the peasant masses throughout China that only the creation of an independent revolutionary democratic regime based on an alliance between working class and peasantry can radically improve their material and political position, to win the peasant masses for active struggle on behalf of fighting slogans which link up political and economic demands comprehensible to and important for the peasantry with the general political tasks of the fight against militarists and imperialists. . . .

9. The Communist Party of China must keep special watch on the efforts of the international reformists who want to get a foothold among the Chinese proletariat and in the national liberation movement. . . . It must initiate a broad educational campaign against their propaganda, their pacifist and democratic slogans, which are designed to serve as cover for the offensive of American capitalists. . . .

10. The Chinese CP must become a mass organization of the Chinese proletariat. Given the existence of class trade unions with a membership of hundreds of thousands, its growth during the last year cannot be regarded as satisfactory. The Chinese CP must abandon as quickly as possible the old, narrow, sectarian conception of what makes a worker a member of the communist party, and remove every unnecessary formal obstacle to the entry of workers into the party. Only if the party grows and steadily consolidates its ranks will it ensure for itself leadership of the movement.

EXTRACTS FROM THE RESOLUTION OF THE SIXTH ECCI PLENUM ON THE FRENCH QUESTION

14 *March* 1926   *Thesen und Resolutionen*, VI Plenum, p. 112

[Loriot and Dunois, at the CPF congress at Clichy in January 1925, had criticized the resolutions of the fifth Comintern congress. (Reporting the congress in *Inprekorr*, Treint wrote that 'it was regrettable that Loriot, in a spirit of petty-bourgeois morality, asked how the party leadership had obtained the letter he sent to Dunois by Sadoul. The congress replied by giving the leadership a mandate to use all and every means to defend the party, the International, and the Russian revolution, and to expose their enemies.' Loriot, he added, could not, however, be classed with Souvarine and Rosmer.) The dispute within the French CP continued throughout the year, and in December 1925 a conference was called to discuss the situation. Loriot read out a 'letter from the 250' which had been sent to the ECCI, criticizing the party for having become 'a machine' and for its conduct of the Morocco campaign. Eleven of the twenty-six communist deputies had signed the letter. Doriot led the counter-attack; the 250 were 'counting on a right orientation in the Comintern as a result of Stalin's victory over Zinoviev'.

The ECCI presidium in January 1926 rejected Souvarine's request for re-admission, and prohibited members of the French party from having anything to do with him or his journal *La Révolution Prolétarienne* (a monthly periodical started in December 1924). An article published at the same time in *Inprekorr* said that the right wing (i.e. Trotsky's supporters) looked for leadership to Souvarine and his journal, and to the group of expelled members led by Rosmer and Monatte who published (since November 1925) the weekly *Bulletin Communiste*. Inside the party the right wing was led by Loriot and Dunois who, with their social-democratic and anarcho-syndicalist views, believed in 'the free play of ideas'. The central committee of the CPF, meeting at the end of January 1926, endorsed the condemnation of the right wing and expelled Loriot, Dunois, and others. Loriot, in the first number of his periodical *Contre le Courant*, anticipating the charges that were to be made against his group, wrote that 'to denounce an opportunist policy is never to play into the hands of the bourgeoisie'. 'The faction in power', he wrote on another occasion, 'have introduced into the [Russian] party the regime of the bludgeon, of secret diplomacy, of fear. . . . The sole nourishment offered to the party is the "official" literature, "official" theses, the "official" point of view. Whoever adopts it is a "bolshevik", whoever discusses it is a menshevik, a counter-revolutionary, a white guard.' The report of the ECCI to the sixth plenum noted that in the past year some of the best leaders of the CGTU had joined the party, and good work had been done in organizing the minority of the CGT. Lozovsky stated later in the proceedings that the attempt to amalgamate the CGTU and CGT in Alsace-Lorraine had failed because the programme of the proposed unity congress had included an item on the right of self-determination up to and including secession from France. In his opening speech, Zinoviev analysed the right danger in the CPF as coming from the syndicalists, who looked to Rosmer, the liquidationists, who looked to Souvarine, and the social-democrats, who looked to Loriot. These three had been expelled but they were the real leaders of the right wing in the CPF, who objected to factory cells as the basis of the party and to 'empty slogans' like 'clear out of Morocco' and 'fraternization' which, they alleged, had ruined the campaign for a united front against the war in Morocco. The spokesman for the right wing (Engler) denied that they were opposed to factory cells; they thought too exclusive an emphasis was placed on them. He protested against Zinoviev's and Bukharin's methods of treating the opposition as though they were anti-communist criminals. If the right were in the majority on a committee, the committee was enlarged to put them in a minority. Explusions were ordered quite mechanically, and if this went on many members would leave the party. He ended by asking the ECCI to state the terms on which Souvarine could be re-admitted.

Humbert-Droz reported for the French commission, in which Stalin had spoken of the right-wing danger, and looked forward to the emergence of a compact majority in the French central committee led by Semard, Thorez, and Monmousseau. The commission thought the CPF had been too crude in its management of the unions and too mechanical in its internal affairs. These errors stimulated but did not justify the right wing. The resolution, passed against Bordiga's vote, was an extremely long one. It urged the CPF and the CGTU to pay more attention to the unorganized workers and not to put forward impossible conditions in its united front proposals, but only those which the broad, unorganized masses could understand. The CPF had overestimated the fascist danger in France. 'It is impossible to keep the party in a state of continual tension when there is no revolutionary situation.' The resolution condemned Souvarine's and Rosmer's journals which aimed at 'sabotaging, denigrating, and disintegrating the French Communist Party'. The campaign and the twenty-four-hour strike against the wars in Morocco and Syria were in the best revolutionary tradition, but were not well prepared.]

I. THE ECONOMIC SITUATION

. . . The roots of the permanent parliamentary crisis lie in the disparity between the shrunken economic role of the petty bourgeoisie and their political influence. The masses who followed the left bloc and were demoralized by its impotence have begun to lose faith in its policy and are turning more to the left. It is the task of our party to take advantage of this leftward movement of the working masses in order to unite with them in the coming class struggles. . . .

The Role of the Proletariat and the Party

The changes which have taken place in the structure of the national economy and in France's political position raise in acute form the question of the role of the proletariat in the coming events. The proletariat cannot remain a passive observer of the struggle now being waged between large-scale capital and the petty bourgeoisie it has dispossessed. Already in the fight against the war in Morocco and Syria the proletariat showed that it is the only class which consistently resists the imperialist policy of the French bourgeoisie and seizes the initiative in this movement. . . .

Our party must realize that unless it wins the unions, and unless the overwhelming majority of the working class enters its ranks, the proletariat cannot wage its class struggle successfully. It must be frankly admitted that until now the CPF has had influence only over the vanguard of the labour movement. The socialist party follows in the wake of the petty bourgeoisie and the politically backward working strata. Out of this situation the right wing in the French party has constructed an entire theory, according to which the fight between the big and petty bourgeoisie about inflation, taxes, inter-allied debts is of no concern to the proletariat. . . .

In France we are faced with the following alternatives: Either the proletariat will succeed in winning the majority of the petty bourgeoisie and the peasants and solve the present crisis in a revolutionary way at the expense of large-scale capital, or, as in Italy, the petty bourgeoisie will follow large-scale capital, which will establish a reactionary regime resting on the intensified exploitation of the proletariat and the petty bourgeoisie and transferring the entire burden of the crisis on to them. . . .

II. THE SITUATION WITHIN THE PARTY AND THE TASKS OF THE PARTY

The dissensions in the French party go beyond the limits of the typical crises which have occurred in various sections of the CI in the last few years. We are faced with a wholly peculiar disorder in a party which has undoubtedly made a great advance in the last three years towards bolshevization but has not yet faced the test of civil war.

The Ideological Weaknesses of the Party

Three years ago the party went through a very severe crisis, in which it cleansed itself of opportunist elements of the Frossard type. In its social composition it has become a real workers' party. . . . But since it is composed mainly of the younger generation who came to communism after the war without serious Marxist training, and since this younger generation has not yet assimilated in the course of class struggles the necessary experience in the application of Leninist tactics, the ideological basis of the party is still insecure. . . .

The Lack of Experience in Revolutionary Struggle

In addition to this ideological weakness the French party lacks politically trained cadres, lacks the firmness which is won in the course of hard struggles. . . . It has known neither civil war nor defeats; it lives under a regime of legality; its political experience is extremely limited and its mass movements take the form of strikes and street demonstrations which at the most lead to collisions with the police. That is why bolshevization has not penetrated as deeply in France as in those parties which have conducted mass struggles.

Underestimating the Right

The right danger is not felt so acutely in France as in those countries which have gone through a period of civil war. The workers in France have not had the opportunity of judging the attitude of a Souvarine at the moment of armed struggle, as their German brothers could judge Paul Levi during the March action. The French communists still have only an abstract idea of Souvarine's treachery. Hence we are threatened by an underestimation of the right danger. Nevertheless this danger is knocking loudly on the party's door. It comes less from Souvarine's group of petty-bourgeois intellectuals than from certain syndicalists who are allied with the right and who have not yet given up their outdated ideas about the autonomy of the trade union movement. Their ideology is expressed in the organ published by Rosmer and Monatte. . . .

Ultra-left Mistakes

Lack of experience in class struggle has held up the development of the party and prevented it from fully grasping its ultra-left mistakes. . . . Since these ultra-left mistakes had no serious practical consequences for the mass of the party, it could not evaluate them correctly. . . .

Relations between Party and Trade Unions

The basic prerequisites for contact with the broad masses which will enable the party to play its leading part in the labour movement are good contacts between party and trade unions and a precise understanding of the role of trade unions. . . .

The active members of the party and the CGTU must understand that the normal development of the trade union movement and the party can be ensured only by co-operation based on a correct policy and on mutual confidence. Comrades working in the unions must realize that they remain party militants within the unions, carrying out the general directives of the party. . . .

Through Trade Unions to the Masses

. . . The absence of normal relations between the party and the unions is proof of a crisis in the attitude of the party and the CGTU to the masses. The failure of our party to increase in numbers, and the loss of members by many unions—and this at a time of severe financial crisis, of inflation, of impoverishment of the middle strata, of disintegration in the old parties, of a breakdown of parliamentarism, of two colonial wars and of increasing mass discontent—are extremely disquieting for the entire party and the CGTU, and must bring home to them that there is something that needs to be changed in their attitude to the masses. . . .

The Tactical Mistakes of the Party

. . . The party should not renounce partial demands, which may become the starting-point, within the capitalist framework, of a great mass movement, simply because they appear immediately realizable in the eyes of the masses. Such partial demands could include:

(a) cancellation of the internal debt at the expense of the banks and large-scale capital;

(b) the entire burden of taxation to be transferred to the rich;

(*c*) strict measures against the flight of capital abroad, etc. These slogans cannot be embodied in the programme of revolutionary measures to be taken by a workers' and peasants' government, for they would deprive it of its truly revolutionary character. Although in fact they cannot be put through by any bourgeois government, they seem to the masses to be capable of immediate realization, and they are therefore appropriate for mobilizing the masses, carrying them along, and convincing them of the need for a workers' and peasants' government and of the more radical revolutionary measures contained in its programme. . . .

The wars in Morocco and Syria give the party the opportunity of continuing its activities against war by intensifying its anti-militarist work. It must also utilize these convulsions in French imperialism to place its work in the French colonies, particularly those in the Mediterranean, on a broad footing. . . .

Within the Party

In this sphere the party must first of all liquidate what remains of the old group disputes within the leadership, by concentrating its attention on the dangers from the right. . . . Any attempt to place the leadership of the party in the hands of a single group would inevitably encounter active resistance from the party. The task of the leading group of the CPF requires that the basis of the party leadership be expanded. . . . It must also rally all the forces of the party on the platform laid down by the ECCI against the right-wing elements, which disorganize the party at the moment when it is preparing for immediately forthcoming struggles.

(*a*) Realization of democracy within the party; abandonment of exaggerated centralism in the party apparatus; more initiative in the local organizations, closer contact between these and the centre; appointment of a secretary at the centre to maintain contact with provincial organizations. . . .

(*c*) The party centre, as the organ of party leadership, must supervise the work of the political bureau more effectively.

(*d*) Establishment of normal relations between all party bodies and members of the trade union organizations on the basis of closest collaboration and the fundamental directives issued by the party. . . .

(*f*) Practical leadership of the parliamentary fraction by the centre, which must pay greater attention to the political work of the deputies. . . .

Resolution on the Right Wing

The party must come out emphatically against the ideological deviations of the right wing, against their disruptive activities, and against their lack of discipline. But in this struggle it must bear in mind that the right is by no means uniform.

The former policy of the party made a certain number of members discontented, and they attached themselves to the right, not because they agreed with its social-democratic or syndicalist programme, but because they were critical of the mechanization of the party's internal life, of its failure to adopt a correct attitude to the unions, of its left slogans and left policy. . . .

There is no doubt that the changes made by the conference of 2 December in the policy and the internal regime of the party, as well as in relations with the trade union movement, endorsed and expanded by the plenum, give all those who were justifiably dissatisfied, but who remained faithful to their party and the International, the possibility of working for their party. . . .

The right have raised the question of the readmission of those expelled. The International has never refused to readmit those who, when expelled, remained loyal and disciplined communists, or who recognized and condemned their errors and expressed the wish to return to the International. Certain conditions were made to Souvarine after the fifth world congress; he did not keep to them and the presidium has rejected his request for readmission; the enlarged Executive endorses the decision of the presidium. . . .

The enlarged Executive summons the right categorically to abandon all solidarity with these elements whose aim is to disintegrate the party from outside, to break with them finally, and to work loyally within the party on the basis of the political line laid down by the party and the International.

EXTRACTS FROM THE RESOLUTION OF THE SIXTH ECCI PLENUM ON
THE GERMAN QUESTION

15 *March* 1926   *Thesen und Resolutionen*, VI Plenum, p. 87

[The repercussions of the dispute within the CPSU in other parties, and particularly the KPD, was discussed at the fourteenth CPSU congress in December 1925. Zinoviev recapitulated the story of ECCI–KPD relations since 1923. Lominadze thought Zinoviev had dealt too lightly with the mistakes of the Maslow–Fischer group. The ultra-left crises in the German, Italian, and Polish parties were connected with the crisis in the CPSU. The Fischer group had hinted at 'kulak deviations' in the Russian central committee, as the opposition in Leningrad were now doing. The ECCI had saved these three parties from catastrophe, but if the discussion in the Russian party were carried over into the Comintern catastrophe could not be avoided. He therefore proposed that there should be no discussion of the CPSU crisis in other parties.

Riazanov (cheered by the Leningrad delegation, supporters of Zinoviev) said he was not going to take sides. 'The side which suffered defeat in 1923 made many mistakes, but the sudden change-over, or, as comrade Zinoviev incautiously put it, the transfer of power to another group, was a further aggravation of those mistakes. . . . We must say outright, and you know it perfectly well from experience, there are always rival groups in each communist party . . . and when they come into conflict, then, because of the attraction exerted by Moscow, some experienced tacticians . . . will eagerly seize on the changes which have occurred in Moscow . . . on the change of international magnitude which has occurred in the shape of the loss of authority by the chairman of the Comintern.' He added that the congress should endorse the actions of the ECCI presidium. Manuilsky, in charge of German affairs in the Comintern at the time, also said that they had been unwilling to hand over power in the KPD to Maslow and Fischer, but had yielded to the wishes of the Frankfurt congress. The arguments of the ultra left, he added, were that, whereas the Russian party was subject to peasant pressure, KPD policy was defined by proletarian interests. Russian party policy was a State policy, and the Comintern became an instrument of Russian State policy.

At a meeting of the presidium on 22 January 1926 Stalin said that the 'intermediate group' in the KPD—the Fischer–Maslow group—was 'diplomatically screening Scholem's "ultra-left" group', and hampering the efforts of the central committee to eliminate ultra-leftism in the KPD. The presidium noted that the German bourgeoisie had completed their turn to the West.

Zinoviev in his opening speech at the plenum suggested that there was an understanding or agreement between the ultra-lefts in Germany and Poland. Scholem denied this. He and his friends had opposed the open letter to the KPD, not because of its political line but because it treated them as an anti-Comintern fraction. They were not 'anti-communist, anti-bolshevik, corrupt elements bought by the bourgeoisie'; he asked that the attacks on them should cease. He supported the political line of the present KPD central committee, but was opposed to its policy of chopping off the left. This would lead to the formation of another KAPD. Braun, attacking Scholem, said there was a connexion between those who talked of 'red imperialism' and the turn of the German bourgeoisie to the West. Ruth Fischer admitted that ultra-left mistakes in the KPD had been glossed over by discipline instead of being fought out. This applied particularly to trade union and united front tactics, and the Hindenburg election. The KPD had had ten congresses, and at each one there had been a dispute about the party's leadership and its internal life. She had signed the open letter because its political line was right, but it had created mistrust and uneasiness among the left; only the left could lead the KPD, but it could not include the ultra-lefts. Rosenberg, who attributed Ruth Fischer's mis-statements to a bad memory, expressed his willingness to co-operate with the present KPD central committee. Thaelmann attacked both Fischer and the ultra-lefts (he made use of a letter sent by Maslow to Fischer, which she had not received. His explanation of how he obtained the letter was given in the commission, not the plenum.) The wall isolating the party from the masses had been broken down by the policy advocated in the open letter, which Fischer had approved in Moscow but sabotaged on her return to Germany. Bukharin questioned whether Fischer, Scholem, and their friends really approved of the line taken in the open letter, and the Comintern was right to be sceptical. Klara Zetkin made a bitter attack on Ruth Fischer, accusing her of dishonesty: she and Maslow had brought the KPD to the brink of catastrophe; politically and morally, they were unfit to lead the party. The KPD delegation put in a statement that, while not sharing Zetkin's views on October 1923, they endorsed her criticism of the Fischer–Maslow leadership.

In the German commission Stalin denied that the Comintern was moving to the right in the interests of the USSR. Such an assumption was insulting to the Russian party. He came out strongly in favour of the existing KPD *Zentrale*, and dismissed the charge that it was intellectually weak. 'What of it? If the policy is correct, theoretical knowledge will come in due course.' Of the Fischer–Maslow group he said it was 'the most undesirable and the most objectionable' group in the KPD.

On the last day of the plenum, Bukharin reported for the KPD commission, and the dispute flared up again. He said that ultra-leftism was the greatest obstacle to winning the masses. Bordiga, 'of course', had opposed the resolution drafted by the commission because of the 'ideological terror' used by the Comintern against the left in the KPD, and its method of arguing by quotations; he believed that the analysis and the tactical line were incompatible, an argument supported by Engel. Rosenberg agreed with the policy of the resolution, but not with its account of past history. Scholem, opposing the resolution because he 'could not vote against his past', said that in a period of stabilization the danger came from the right, not the left. Urbahns attacked Zetkin for her attempt to discredit the left, which she had been trying to do since the Levi crisis in 1921; her speech was a defence of Brandlerism. Hansen (Norway, but not on behalf of the Norwegian delegation) opposed the resolution not for what it said, but for what it failed to say against the right. It would encourage the right wing everywhere. The ultra-lefts in the KPD were split and defeated; the resolution should look ahead to a longer period and emphasize the right danger. Ruth Fischer said the resolution contradicted the open letter, which stood for the left kernel of the party; it would only make the strife in the party more acute. Remmele and Doriot said that the danger was not that the deviations were international in their character—that was to be expected—but that efforts were being made to organize them internationally. Lominadze, Manuilsky, Dimitrov, and Kuusinen repeated the charge. The ultra-lefts, said Lominadze, were trying to create the impression that there was a crisis in the Comintern, which was not true. Their object at the plenum was to unite on the platform of struggle against the CPSU and the CI. This threat to form an international left fraction, if not a new international, would fail because the ultra-lefts had no support in their parties. The fight against them had to take organizational as well as ideological forms. Manuilsky referred to the similarities between the German left and the French right—they shared a lack of belief in the Comintern and in the strength of the Russian revolution. The lack of belief in Russia was bound up with the idea of a 'west European' communism as opposed to the 'peasant communism' of Russia. This brought them into line with Locarno—an instrument of bourgeois policy, just as Souvarine was a tool of French capital. Bukharin concluded the discussion by saying that the CI would support the present leadership of the

CC of the KPD against both left and right. The resolution was passed against the votes of Hansen and Bordiga. (Urbahns, Fischer, Scholem, Maslowski, and Engel said they would have voted against it if they had had the right to vote; they had only a consultative voice.)

After the sixth ECCI plenum Fischer and Urbahns were accused of trying to create a crisis in the KPD and to start fractional struggles again. At a conference of political secretaries and editors of the KPD held on 16–17 April 1926 a resolution endorsing the plenum's decisions on the KPD was adopted by 65 votes to 2. The new central committee proposed by the ECCI in August 1925 consisted of Thaelmann and his followers, of whom Ulbricht, Neumann, and Remmele counted as the left, and Meyer and his group as the right. They were successful in putting an end to the movement for the creation of separate revolutionary unions.]

I. THE SITUATION IN GERMANY

The outstanding characteristic of the present situation in Germany is the acute economic crisis. . . . It has two aspects: one is the general crisis of the entire German economy provoked by Germany's international position, the Versailles peace treaty, and the Dawes plan. Germany has lost its colonies; export markets have been severely restricted by the tariff policy of many States, while Germany is compelled to expand production in order to provide the goods for the payment of reparations. . . .

The impossibility of reconciling the basic contradictions in the general situation, the complications introduced by the Locarno pact . . . and the effects of the economic crisis—all this has led to a permanent political crisis.

Against this background of crisis a process of regrouping within the working class is developing. Under the pressure of circumstances the great mass of workers are turning more and more to the platform of united class struggle. The trade union and social-democratic leaders, on the other hand, are trying to march in step with the ruling finance-capitalists, to split the working class, to corrupt a part of the labour aristocracy. . . . This open treachery to the interests of the German proletariat is accompanied by the most servile support for all important measures undertaken by the bourgeoisie. . . . The hopeless prospects for a bourgeois Germany dependent on the favour of foreign capital, the advance of Soviet economic development, the workers' delegations and the effect they have in Germany—all these work in the same direction. The idea of the unity of the working class in the fight against capital is becoming the centre of attention of the entire working class.

II. THE ROAD TO WINNING THE MASSES

This general situation determines the chief tasks of our party. The only real way out for the German proletariat is the way of its emancipation from the double yoke of native and foreign capital. The only way out of the blind alley of economic decline, falling living standards, permanent political crises, enslavement and a semi-colonial status for Germany is the way of a Soviet Germany.

A workers' and peasants' government as the embodiment of Soviet power is now the watchword of the proletarian vanguard. It is one which cannot be put into effect without the support of the great majority of the proletariat. The KPD must consider the winning of the masses as its chief task. . . .

III. ULTRA-LEFT TENDENCIES

Of late the greatest obstacle to winning the masses has been, and it still is, the ultra-left ideology of certain groups in the party. . . . They have completely forgotten the Marxist principle that tactics are determined by the given objective situation. Completely incapable of noticing what was new, still less of correctly analysing it, they have carried over the old methods quite mechanically to the completely new situation. During the Frankfurt congress they fought stubbornly against the CI on the trade union question; during the fifth world congress they were opposed to the international unity campaign, and justified their attitude by arguing that these tactics were allegedly in the interests of the Russian Government and meant giving aid to the MacDonald Government; they failed utterly to find the correct approach to the social-democratic workers. Thus the ultra-left turned out to be the most troublesome element in the process of winning the masses.

We must emphasize in particular the wholly rotten and almost social-democratic roots of this ideology, which has openly liquidationist features. They speak of Russian 'red imperialism', just as the bourgeois and social-democratic press does, of the possibility of a 4 August 1914 for the CI, about alleged alliances of the Soviet Union with Japanese imperialism, about 'Russian necessities of State' in regard to the Anglo-Russian unity committee. . . .

The bourgeois social-democratic origin of such trends of thought is obvious. The CI declares that all the healthy forces in the party must be mobilized against this liquidationist ideology in order to eradicate it completely. The Executive trusts that the ultra-left workers will understand what harm threatens the party if it does not eliminate root and branch these ultra-left tendencies.

IV. THE MASLOW–RUTH FISCHER GROUP

The Ruth Fischer group is the most vacillating, most unstable element in the KPD. The ideological basis of this group is lack of belief in the

communist party, in the workers' movement, and in the proletarian revolution. For these reasons Maslow contemplates a delay of decades in the
German revolution. . . . Such an attitude reflects the moods of a ruined
and decaying petty bourgeoisie, not the rising wave of the German labour
movement and the communist party.

With such an ideology it is utterly impossible to carry out a clear and
determined policy; this explains the continual unprincipled vacillations of
this group. On the most important questions at the Frankfurt congress the
Maslow–Ruth Fischer group swung between the Comintern line and the
ultra-left opponents of this line. . . . Finally the Ruth Fischer group allied
itself with the ultra-lefts, whom it had been opposing, for a joint attack on
the Comintern. The Executive replied with the open letter of August 1925
to the members of the KPD. Ruth Fischer signed this letter and thereby
condemned her own attitude. But immediately after the return of the
German delegation she organized an underground struggle against the
Comintern line and a fractional struggle against the new party leadership. . . .

The healthy development, the normalization, and the growth of the
KPD therefore require the immediate liquidation of the Ruth Fischer
fraction, with its double book-keeping in policy, its habit of saying one
thing and doing another, its lack of principle, its diplomacy which harms
the party and has shaken the confidence of the party membership in the
leadership, of the leading cadres towards each other, and of certain sections
of the party towards the Comintern. . . . The Ruth Fischer group has lost
the confidence both of the Communist International and of the left party
membership.

The enlarged Executive notes with indignation that Ruth Fischer has
broken the undertakings assumed by her signature of the open letter. The
Comintern Executive and the CC of the KPD gave her every opportunity
to correct her mistakes and to prove by deeds that she is ready to work in
the Communist International. Nevertheless she continued her disruptive
activities, her fight against Comintern policy. . . . The adherents of the
Maslow–Ruth Fischer group must choose between the policy of the CC
and the methods of unprincipled opposition. There is no middle road, no
middle group between these two.

V. OVERCOMING RIGHT TENDENCIES

The enlarged Executive points out that there is still a danger of right
deviations in the KPD, and a vigorous struggle must be waged against
them. The new KPD leadership has fought vigorously against any right
deviation that has made its appearance. . . .

The enlarged Executive declares that only a complete misinterpretation
of the new situation and the new tasks of the party could lead to the con-

clusion that the present course of the KPD signifies a return to the situation in the party before October 1923. The party is not going backwards; it is going forwards. The struggle which was conducted against the Brandler group was not annulled by the change in the KPD leadership; its results were made secure. . . .

VI. THE LEADERSHIP OF THE KPD

The present leadership of the KPD arose in the struggle against right errors and was strengthened in the struggle against ultra-left errors. The group of workers at the head of the KPD is the nucleus of a truly Leninist party leadership. . . .

VII. THE IMMEDIATE TASKS OF THE KPD

. . . At the present time the following demands are at the centre of the workers' struggle:

1. The fight against the employers' offensive—the fight for the unemployed. . . .
2. Transfer of the Dawes burden to the propertied classes. . . .
3. Strengthening the unions. . . .
4. Fight against monarchism and fascism. . . .
5. Fight for the needs of the working peasants. . . .
6. Organizing an active struggle for the demands of young workers, working women, public employees, and the impoverished sections of the petty bourgeoisie. . . .

The watchword which unites all these demands is the fight for an independent, socialist Germany, freely allied with the Soviet Union, with the class-conscious workers, and with all the oppressed peoples of the world.

EXTRACTS FROM A RESOLUTION ON FACTORY AND STREET CELLS PASSED BY THE SECOND ORGANIZATION CONFERENCE OF THE COMMUNIST INTERNATIONAL AND RATIFIED BY THE ORGBUREAU OF THE ECCI

26 *March* 1926   *Inprekorr*, vi, 65, p. 966, 29 *April* 1926

[The French were particularly critical of factory-cell organization, complaining that it had meant a severe loss of membership. Members who did not work in factories tended to drop out. The Clichy congress in January 1925 claimed 76,000 members; the Lille congress in June 1926 only 55,000. The decline was attributed to factory cells and to the loss of members in North Africa during the Moroccan war.]

I

THE MOST IMPORTANT RESULTS SINCE THE FIRST ORG-CONFERENCE

1. Since the first international organization conference (March 1925) the reorganization of communist parties on the basis of factory cells has made considerable progress. The ideological resistance which at that time could still be met in some parties has been almost completely overcome. In the most important parties . . . factory cells have been established which in essentials have already become the basic party unit. In some parties entire local and district party organizations have been reorganized into factory cells. . . .

2. In the light of these results it has been conclusively proved that:

(*a*) The factory cell is the appropriate basic unit for all parties in capitalist countries.

(*b*) Reorganization on a factory-cell basis improves the social composition of communist parties, strengthens the influence of the lower party bodies in the party committees, creates close relations between party committees and the membership, increases the activity of members, and thus provides guarantees for the operation of democratic centralism within the party.

(*c*) Factory cells have proved to be the most reliable supports in the struggle against ultra-left and right groups, and the best guarantee for the execution of the Comintern line.

(*d*) By their daily work in the factory, by defending the workers' interests, and by enlightening the workers, factory cells strengthen and consolidate the influence of the party over the non-party and social-democratic masses. They enable united front tactics to be applied fruitfully, and are an important preliminary for success in capturing non-party mass organizations, particularly trade unions. . . .

(*e*) The arguments of the opponents of reorganization that factory cells were suitable for factory work, but not for carrying out mass political campaigns, and that therefore the old form of organization according to place of residence should not be dissolved have been refuted by experience. . . .

(*f*) The publication of factory newspapers has turned out—where they are well edited and regularly issued—to be the most important instrument of factory-cell work. . . .

(*g*) To organize those members who do not work in factories (housewives, intellectuals, artisans, etc.), and to make proper use of them for party work, it is necessary to establish street cells. . . .

II

ERRORS AND DEFECTS

. . . The characteristic errors and defects are:

(*a*) In the establishment of cells:

Cells are still frequently set up either in an unplanned and unsystematic way, the initiative being left entirely to the comrades working in the factory . . . or in too minute and detailed a fashion, without any regard for the independent initiative of the party membership in the factories. . . . It is also no doubt due to mistakes in the work of reorganization that, as has happened in some cases, a large number of members are lost in the process. . . .

(*b*) In the structure of cells:

Too many members are attached to the cells who either work in other factories or who do not work in a factory at all. . . . Many cells still have no cell committee, but only a secretary, whose work is often only of a technical character. Where there is a committee, it is often inadequate. . . . Sometimes the committee only carries out technical jobs, such as collecting dues and distributing literature, and does not undertake and carry through the work of planning and guiding the activities of the cell. . . .

(*c*) In the work of the cells:

1. Inadequate political activity:

The decisive defect in the work of the cells is that the majority of them have not yet managed to engage in political activity. They are not sufficiently concerned with party questions, nor have they shown the capacity to combine their factory work with the political questions raised by the party. Most of them react only to the questions arising in the factory itself. . . .

2. Imprudent methods of work:

It is another serious defect that many factory cells still do not understand how to work invisibly, so that their members, while working steadily and energetically, do not fall victim to the terrorism of employers and governments. In practice this has often led to serious unheavals in cell work. . . . They also frequently neglect the job of creating a body of sympathizers around the cell and maintaining contact with them.

3. In the daily work of the cells:

The following defects are most obvious: the lack of systematic planned work, and of careful organization and distribution of work. . . . Cell meetings are too long, badly prepared, uninteresting, and are not held regularly. It is also clear from reports that many cells take no decisions on the questions discussed at their meetings.

4. Factory committee fraction and cell:

The attitude of communist fractions in factory committees to the factory cells is in many respects still unsatisfactory. . . . Many fractions refuse to carry out the decisions of the cell, while on the other hand the idea prevails in many cells that communist work in the factory committee can replace cell work. It is not clearly enough understood that the function of communist fractions in factory committees must be different from that of the cells, that the fraction is subordinate to the cell and works on its instructions.

5. Factory newspapers:

It must be recognized as a special defect that, although the great agitational and organizational value of factory newspapers has been clearly demonstrated, their number has fallen and their publication is more irregular. . . .

All the defects and errors noted here in the structure and work of the cells cannot however detract from the significant successes obtained in this field in the last few months. Few though they may be in number, and weak as many of them are, the fact that there are in existence in Germany, Italy, France, England, and other countries communist cells in large factories, which do good work, which extend the activities of party members, which lead the workers' struggle against the employers, which strengthen and deepen the power and influence of the party among the working masses in political struggles, has proved that the reorganization of the parties on the basis of factory cells is an important prerequisite for bolshevization.

EXTRACTS FROM THE DIRECTIVES ON THE STRUCTURE OF COMMUNIST PARTY CENTRAL COMMITTEES AND TRADE UNION DEPARTMENTS, ISSUED BY THE SECOND ORGANIZATION CONFERENCE AND RATIFIED BY THE ORGBUREAU OF THE ECCI

26 *March* 1926   *Inprekorr*, vi. 65, p. 983, 29 *April* 1926

I. RELATIO1 S BETWEEN CC DEPARTMENTS AND ITS LEADING ORGANS

1. The departments of the CC are those organs of the CC secretariat through which the secretariat accomplishes its tasks.

2. The departments are subordinate to the CC through the secretariat. Each department is under the direct control and constant supervision of one of the secretaries of the CC. . . .

II. DIRECTIVES FOR THE ORGDEPARTMENT OF THE CC

i. *Tasks of the Orgdepartment*

The orgdepartment has the following tasks:

1. To elaborate, to explain, and to supervise the execution of the organizational aspects of the decisions of party congresses and of the CC, as well as international decisions and directives. . . .

2. To guide, instruct, and supervise party reorganization on the basis of factory cells.

3. To keep the district party organization under constant and comprehensive organizational review. . . .

4. To examine the structure of the CC and the district committees of the party and work out concrete proposals for their improvement.

5. To draw up directives on the formation and structure of fractions in non-party mass organizations . . . in close collaboration with the relevant departments of the CC and to supervise the correct execution of these directives.

6. To draw up concrete assignments, directives, and instructions for all aspects of organizational work connected with the various tasks of the party, particularly in regard to the organization of national and international campaigns, elections, etc., on the basis of the directives and decisions of the ECCI, and . . . to supervise the execution of these measures.

7. To present and evaluate all the organizational experiences of party work . . . to keep an eye on the social composition of the party, party membership in trade unions and other mass organizations, length of membership in the party and former membership of other parties, composition of the leading organs, etc.

8. To establish a uniform system of information and statistics. . . .

9. To register and select cadres of leading party functionaries at the centre and in the districts. . . .

13. To maintain regular contact with the orgdepartment of the ECCI by sending in materials and reports.

14. To inform fraternal parties about org-work through the international press.

ii. *Methods of Work of the Orgdepartment*

The orgdepartment fulfils its tasks in the following way:

1. By sending CC instructors to instruct and supervise the work of district organizations and district party organs. . . .

2. By arranging organization conferences at national and district level.

3. By arranging periodic meetings with the leaders of the district orgdepartments. . . .

4. By maintaining continuous contact, written or personal, with district party committees.

5. By sending circulars and information material to the district committees. . . .

7. By publishing pamphlets and handbooks for party officials. . . .

iii. *Structure of the Orgdepartment*

1. The orgdepartment consists of a leader (if possible a CC member) and his deputy, a few responsible and technical workers, and one or several instructors. . . .

2. The current work of the department is divided among the full-time responsible workers. . . .

3. The collective character of the department's work is maintained by discussion among the responsible workers and regular meetings of the department. . . .

iv. *Orgdepartment and Orgbureau*

In many parties there is still uncertainty about the difference between the functions of the orgdepartment and the functions of the orgbureau. The bureau, which exists only in the central committee, consists exclusively of CC members, and is elected by the CC in plenary session to take charge of organization work generally, to establish the principles to be applied in organizational questions. . . . It is responsible for its work to the CC.

The orgdepartment, on the other hand, is a part of the machinery of the secretariat and the CC, and is responsible to the latter for its work. It is concerned with the carrying out of directives received from the orgbureau and with drafting resolutions for submission to the bureau for its approval. . . .

III. DIRECTIVES FOR THE TRADE UNION DEPARTMENT OF THE CC (FOR LARGE LEGAL PARTIES)

i. *Tasks of the Department*

The department has the following tasks:

1. To elaborate and to explain the decisions of party congresses and of the CC relating to the trade union movement, and to adapt them to the concrete circumstances of the country; to see to the execution of these decisions and to contribute to their formulation on the basis of its experience and the materials at its disposal.

2. To collect and work up material in the following fields, and to keep them under constant review, to suggest appropriate measures and to keep

party organs supplied with comprehensive information about them: (*a*) the economic life of the country . . . (*b*) the economic position of the working class . . . (*c*) the situation in the trade unions . . . (*d*) the movement for trade union unity; the development of left or right opposition movements in the unions and in the labour movement . . . (*e*) the industrial struggles of the working class. . . .

3. To work out instructions and directives on all the questions arising under this paragraph. . . .

4. To guide and supervise the work of party fractions in the national executive committees of the unions. . . .

5. To issue regular instructions to these fractions, and to the trade union departments of district party committees, on all questions of party policy concerned with the trade union movement. . . .

6. To see that a uniform party line is carried out in the unions. . . .

10. To take part in the work of the national fractions in preparation for trade union congresses and conferences. . . .

11. To select and to register members with experience in union work at the national and district level for employment in high posts in trade union bodies. . . .

ii. *Methods of Work of the Trade Union Department of the CC*

The department fulfils its tasks in the following way:

1. By receiving regular reports on the activities of the national trade union fractions. . . .

2. By organizing regular conferences with representatives of district and local trade union departments and fractions. . . .

4. By sending CC instructors to examine and improve the work of fractions. . . .

8. By publishing handbooks and pamphlets on trade union work for trade union officials.

iii. *Structure of the Trade Union Department of the CC*

1. The department consists of a leader, who should be a CC member, his deputy, and the requisite number of responsible workers and technical personnel. . . .

Meetings of the trade union department are attended by the leader and the responsible workers of the department, the representatives of the party fractions in the national and district trade union federations, CC instructors, representatives of the most important CC departments, of the org-department, the agitprop department, and the youth league.

EXTRACTS FROM AN ECCI MAY DAY MANIFESTO

April 1926   *Inprekorr*, vi, 61, p. 878, 20 *April* 1926

The background to May Day 1926 reveals new war dangers, new imperialist conflicts, the bankruptcy of the League of Nations. The imperialist Powers are themselves destroying the illusion that it is a League to preserve peace. Together with preparations for the fraudulent disarmament conference, we are witnessing the active struggle of the imperialists against the peoples of China, Syria, and Morocco. . . .

If the rule of the bourgeoisie is today still unbroken, if capitalist class society is still not destroyed, if the proletariat must still bear the yoke of oppression and exploitation, the responsibility rests on social-democracy, and *only* on social-democracy.

Comrades! Is it to be borne that today, eight years after the war, the most all-embracing organizations of the proletariat, the trade unions, should be split? Can we tolerate, after eight years of deprivation, a continuation of the old coalition policy? Is it possible to go on believing the agents of the League of Nations and the so-called disarmament conference, when the imperialists are enslaving the 70 million-strong German people and turning the small States of Europe into docile instruments to be used against the defeated nations and the Soviet Union? Shall not the proletarians in uniform be made aware of the growing war danger? Shall barracks-mentality and army drill separate them from the great proletarian army in the workshops? No, and again no. . . .

The demands of the proletariat can be met only by means of the revolutionary overthrow of the bourgeois dictatorship, only by the formation of a workers' and peasants' government in every country, and by the union of these governments in the United States of Socialist Europe, which will stretch out brotherly hands to the Soviet Union, the colonial peoples, and the American proletariat. . . .

Only in one country is there neither economic decline nor capitalist offensive. Only in one country are wages rising and the eight-hour day in force, has the land been wrested from the landlords and given to the peasants. . . . Only in one country are there neither fascist organizations nor white terror. That country is the Soviet Union.

EXTRACTS FROM AN ECCI MANIFESTO ON THE GENERAL STRIKE IN BRITAIN

5 *May* 1926   *Inprekorr*, vi, 70, p. 1111, 7 *May* 1926

[The ECCI had not waited for the beginning of the strike to issue appeals and manifestoes calling for support against 'the capitalists who were trying to destroy the British labour movement'. In a manifesto dated 25 April the ECCI wrote that 'victory or defeat for the miners means victory or defeat for the entire British working class. A strike by the miners would imply a general strike, and a general strike cannot remain an industrial struggle. It is bound to develop into a political struggle; the proletariat will be fighting the capitalists, that is to say, class will be fighting class. The British bourgeoisie and the British Government will mobilize the entire power of the State, because the basic question of capitalist society will be raised, the question of private property; the entire machinery of the capitalist State will be brought into action to defend private property. . . . The fight for wages and working conditions will raise before the working class the question of power.' It went on to warn 'the working masses who are ready for the fight' that their leaders were irresolute, and some were prepared to betray the fight before it had even begun. Even 'the left-wing leaders of the Labour Party and the unions are showing themselves unequal to the situation. . . . Only the Minority Movement and the CPGB have called on the workers to resist, have tried to organize the struggle, have advocated the militant unity of the trade union movement in Great Britain and throughout the world.' When the strike began on 3 May the ECCI and the RILU sent a number of messages to the IFTU proposing joint activities; the IFTU replied that it was already consulting with the TUC. Zinoviev wrote that nothing could now stop the revolutionary development of the British working class; whatever its origins, the strike was political in character, and there was a danger that the right-wing leaders had taken it over only in order to betray it at the first opportunity; Baldwin was less of a danger than Thomas. In a message to the CPGB dated 7 May the ECCI presidium urged the British communists to make clear to the masses that the strike was a class struggle—one side led by the TUC, the other by the Government. As the struggle developed, the party's slogans must be carried to a higher level, up to the slogan of the struggle for power. The Government no longer appeared as the mediator; the masks had fallen; it stood revealed as the executive organ of the employers. On 10 May Zinoviev published an article in which he wrote that if Lenin welcomed the Councils of Action in 1920 as equal in significance to February 1917 in Russia, 'what can we say of the incomparably greater events taking place in England today?' The Russian unions' offer of 2½ million rubles was rejected by the General Council, which decided not to accept any foreign financial help.]

To the workers of all countries

The events in Great Britain are of historic importance. The British capitalists are intent on the ruthless defeat and humiliation of the miners, the vanguard of the British proletariat, with the object of demoralizing the British labour movement and setting the British proletariat back for decades. The Conservative Government decided to wage 'preventive war' on the British working class, for it feared that the discontent, provoked by Conservative rule and growing steadily, would drive the wave of the labour movement still higher. For several months the Baldwin Government has been coldbloodedly preparing to destroy and suppress the British working class with the object of improving its own position in the country.

The great fight between capital and labour began as an industrial struggle but is developing into a political one. . . .

The army, the navy, the air force, and the police are being mobilized against the working class. A censorship has been established throughout the country and arrest warrants have been issued. The methods used in the world war against the 'external enemy' are now being used against the 'internal enemy', that is, the working class defending its rights.

The bourgeoisie have established a united front against the working class. . . . To this we must oppose the united front of the proletariat. The fight of the British proletariat is a fight of the entire world proletariat. The Communist International calls on all its members and adherents to do their utmost to support the great struggle of the British proletariat.

Miners of Germany, France, Czechoslovakia, Poland, Belgium, America, Japan, and other countries! To you the Communist International addresses its first word. The victory of your British brothers, which will be your victory too, depends on you. Not a single ton of coal or oil must be sent to British ports. . . .

Transport workers and railwaymen of the world, the eyes of the fighting British proletariat are on you. You must not allow a single train or ship to carry coal or oil to Britain so long as the fight is on. . . .

All sections of the Communist International are to propose to the social-democrats the immediate establishment of joint committees of action to support the struggle of the British workers. . . .

To the British workers the Communist International expresses its enthusiasm for the fight so heroically begun. . . . Since the days of the Chartists Britain has seen no movement so powerful as the present one. The British workers can be certain that all honest proletarians throughout the world will come enthusiastically to their aid.

The British workers will not forget the grave lessons of 1921. The heroes of Black Friday are deservedly suspect. The history of industrial disputes in Britain gives many examples of treacherous leaders placing themselves at the head of the movement in order to take the first opportunity of betraying it. Do not forget, comrades, that this is the greatest danger which threatens you. . . .

Whatever the immediate outcome of the fight now begun by the British workers . . . one thing is certain: this great struggle opens a new era in the class struggle not only in Britain but throughout the world.

EXTRACTS FROM THE ECCI THESES ON THE LESSONS OF THE GENERAL
STRIKE

8 *June* 1926   *Inprekorr*, vi, 84, p. 1339, 15 *June* 1926

[The failure of the general strike underlined two acute problems in Comintern
policy, the attitude of the CPGB to the trade union leaders, and the attitude of
the Russian unions to the Anglo-Russian trade union committee. The British
communist leaders were reprimanded for their failure to criticize the TUC
openly and sharply enough. The central council of the Russian unions had published a bitter attack on the General Council for its 'treachery', and several
members of the CC of the CPGB thought its tone too sharp. At a meeting in
Tiflis on 8 June Stalin referred to the leaders of the TUC and the Labour Party
as 'downright traitors or spineless fellow-travellers of these traitors'; one of the
reasons for the failure of the strike, he said, was that the CPGB enjoyed little
prestige among British workers, although its attitude throughout the strike was
absolutely correct.

The CC of the CPGB wrote to the CC of the CPSU protesting against the
Russian trade union declaration, made without prior consultation with the
CPGB. At the ECCI presidium on 7 August Stalin stated that the declaration
had been made with the knowledge and approval of the CI and the RILU.
Murphy objected to the interference of the Russian unions in the affairs of the
CPGB; any criticism should have come from the RILU. An attack on the
leaders, he said, was regarded by the British workers as an attack on their unions.
Stalin defended the action of the Russian unions, saying they could not give the
impression that they condoned the General Council's attitude. (Murphy was
won over to the Russian view on this matter.) The communist press continued
to issue manifestoes and appeals in support of the miners' strike, and reports on
the progress of fund-collecting, etc., became a regular feature of *Inprekorr*. A
'conference of revolutionary miners' was held in Essen on 16–17 June to discuss
ways and means of supporting the Miners' Federation of Great Britain (MFGB).
Representatives of the MFGB and the Russian miners' union met in Berlin on
7 July and advocated an early meeting of the Anglo-Russian committee. The
TUC agreed to the Russian request and the meeting was held in Paris at the end
of July. The British side wished the Russians to withdraw their charge of
'treachery', which was interference in internal TUC affairs; the Russian representatives refused, and wished to confine the agenda to the miners' strike. The
meeting was adjourned and resumed in Berlin in late August. In the meantime
the Comintern sections had issued statements repeating the charge of treachery
and urging British trade unionists to elect new leaders. On 17 August the ECCI
issued a statement attacking the General Council which wanted 'all its sins and
crimes against the English and the world proletariat to be forgiven'. It urged the
English unions to ensure the continued existence of the Anglo-Russian committee. In Berlin the Russians put forward a 14-point resolution attacking the
IFTU, proposing action in support of the miners, etc. This was rejected by the
British side, which argued that it would do more harm than good, and was in
any case irrelevant to the committee's purpose, which was to promote unity, and
would only arouse resentment.

THE COMMUNIST INTERNATIONAL

The policy of maintaining the Anglo-Russian committee in existence was one of the chief targets of the opposition in the Comintern. A few days after the termination of the strike Trotsky wrote (in a memorandum preserved in the Trotsky archives) that the refusal of the TUC to accept money from the Russian unions was bound to surprise the Russian people, who had so far not seen in the Soviet press any criticism of the General Council; the Soviet side of the committee had surrendered the right of criticism, which was an essential corollary of united front policy. The CPGB had followed their example. Later he wrote that once the General Council had betrayed the general strike the committee merely helped them to conceal their treachery from the masses. Stabilization in England rested on the support of the bourgeoisie by the TUC and the Labour Party, and it was disgraceful to act in concert with them. To Stalin's argument in favour of a bloc with reactionary trade unions as a defence against imperialist intervention he replied that if the TUC were really prepared for that it would not be reactionary. 'ECCI strategy . . . was based on unreal quantities and false calculations.'

At the meeting of the CC of the CPSU on 15 July Stalin defined the tasks of the committee as, *inter alia*, to 'widen the fissure between Amsterdam and the British trade union movement', to create conditions favourable to removing the reformist leadership of the unions, and replacing it by communist, to organize a movement against British intervention in the Soviet Union. Those who were trying to torpedo the committee were playing into the hands of the interventionists. At the ECCI presidium meeting on 7 August he suggested that the British side would be unwilling to break up the committee because of the financial help coming from the Russian unions to the MFGB.]

I. THE CRISIS OF ENGLISH CAPITALISM

(*a*) The position of the English economy within world economy, and England's situation as an imperialist State, can be said to be in irresistible decline. . . .

(*b*) One of the most important elements in the general decline of English capitalism is the chronic crisis in coal-mining, which is growing steadily more severe. This industry . . . was the basis of England's economic power. Its decline is a striking indication of the general decay of English capitalism. . . .

2. ENGLAND'S DECLINE AND THE LABOUR MOVEMENT

(*a*) . . . English capitalism in its classic period gave rise to the classic type of English trade unionism. Its socio-economic basis was the surplus profit which the English bourgeoisie received from all quarters of the globe, part of which entered into the wages of the English proletariat, which thus steadily raised its living standards and improved its skill.

Within the international labour army the English proletariat thus developed as a privileged group, occupying an exceptional position as a labour aristocracy, and to a certain extent bound economically by common interests to its employers.

(b) The beginning of the decline of English capitalism and the parallel decline in imperialist surplus profits have radically changed class relation-ships, both between the classes and within the working class. The growing acuteness of class contradictions has greatly diminished the political importance of traditional English liberalism. . . .

The strengthening of the Conservatives on the one side and the growth of the Labour Party on the other, the general move to the left of the workers . . . the formation of the communist party, the establishment of the so-called Minority Movement, the campaign for rapprochement with the Soviet Union, the creation under mass pressure of the Anglo-Russian committee—all these are links in one and the same chain of development.

(c) The process by which the English workers are shaking off the in-fluence of opportunism is not an even one. . . . The greatest obstacle is the hierarchy of trade union and Labour Party officials which grew up in the old conditions. The great majority of them are either conscious allies of the bourgeoisie and conscious enemies of the proletarian class movement, or 'leftists' (centrists) who, because of their timidity, their political cowardice, and their consequent inevitable inclination towards surrender, at critical moments go over to the enemy's side. . . .

4. THE COURSE OF THE GENERAL STRIKE AND ITS END

(a) The course of the general strike and its liquidation offer a vital lesson for the entire international proletariat. On 30 April the mine-owners presented the miners with an ultimatum. . . . When the miners rejected the terms offered the lockout began. Under mass pressure the General Council decided on the strike. . . . On 1 May the workers gave striking proof of their attitude in tremendous demonstrations.

In the meantime the Government was taking energetic measures to suppress the workers. On 1 May a state of emergency was declared over the whole country and troops were sent to Lancashire, Scotland, and Wales; all the forces of the counter-revolution were mobilized. At the same time Messrs. Thomas, MacDonald, and Co. took over the conduc-tor's baton in the General Council; the 'left' made a pitiful retreat to the background. . . .

The fear of what was happening and the preparations to liquidate the general strike were revealed above all in the statement that the strike was a 'purely industrial struggle'. . . .

(b) If the labour leaders acted as though they failed to understand the political character of the strike, the Government and the bourgeoisie understood it very well, and acted accordingly. . . .

(*c*) The 'left' leaders, who had a majority in the General Council, put up no resistance whatever to the deliberate traitors like Thomas, but marched all the time under right-wing orders. In fact Thomas and Co. ran the General Council throughout the course of the strike. . . . Thus the 'left' objectively played an even more shameful role, for they had a majority and bore direct responsibility for the conduct of the strike. . . .

(*e*) The Second International and Amsterdam in practice supported the policy of the right-wing leaders of the General Council, that is to say, they sabotaged the strike. . . . It was only under mass pressure that they took a few minimal steps in support of the strikers. From the point of view of the development of the movement, the policy of these associations was one of sabotage.

(*f*) The strike was called off because it was spreading, for the leaders feared nothing so much as its extension. . . . The strike could have moved forward and triumphed only if it developed further, that is, if the class struggle had become more acute. The decisive turning-point was already perfectly clear when the 'leaders' refused to accept financial aid from the Soviet trade unions, in collaboration with whom they had established the Anglo-Russian unity committee, and explained their refusal by saying that acceptance would have been wrongly interpreted. In trying to cover up this refusal by refusing all help from abroad, they isolated the English workers from the international proletariat. . . .

The tactics of the Government and the bourgeoisie were the tactics of vigorous and calculated offensive. The tactics of the trade union leaders were the tactics of betrayal and surrender. The refusal to shift the strike into political channels was at bottom a blow against the mobilization of internal forces. The refusal to accept international aid was a blow at the mobilization of the external forces of the proletariat. The order to end the strike put the finishing touch. The working class was demobilized by its leaders and lost the biggest battle in the history of the English labour movement. . . .

5. THE MINERS' STRIKE AND THE OUTLOOK FOR THE FUTURE

. . . The economic basis for reformism in England has disappeared once and for all. The shedding of parliamentary and constitutional illusions, the revelation of the role of the State as a class instrument, the inevitable disappointment in the old reformist leaders and their methods, the clarity with which the question of the seizure of power is now presented—all this must lead to a growth in the workers' class consciousness. The rapid decline of capitalism in England is bound to lead to further revolutionary struggles. . . .

6. THE LESSONS OF THE STRIKE

(*a*) The great English general strike completely confirmed the appraisal of the international political situation given by the Comintern as a period of relative and temporary capitalist stabilization. . . . Just as the colonial wars, the national revolution in China, the bankruptcy of Locarno, etc., reveal the baseness of social-democratic 'pacifism', so the civil war in Poland and the strike of millions of English proletarians reveal the pitiful reformist utopianism of social-democracy in the question of the class struggle. . . .

(*b*) The strike again brought up in pronounced form the question of the general strike as a method of struggle. It was on a scale, and had an impetus . . . previously unknown in the history of the labour movement. It proved, against all the assertions of the bourgeoisie and the labour renegades, that a general strike is possible, and can be victorious if it is correctly carried forward. . . . The reformist leaders surrendered because they were unable to break through the limits of their reformism, because they did not and could not dare to carry the strike forward and transform it from an industrial into a political struggle. Calling the strike off showed, not the bankruptcy of the strike as a method of struggle, but the bankruptcy of its reformist leaders.

(*c*) In this bankruptcy both wings of opportunism were involved, both the right, openly and insolently treacherous and consciously serving the bourgeoisie (Thomas, MacDonald, Clynes, and Co.), and the capitulators who conceal their opportunism (Purcell) and who, because of their petty-bourgeois political lack of character and cowardice, at the critical moment go over to the right wing. . . .

(*e*) The general strike demonstrated the correctness of the policy of the Comintern and the RILU on establishing international trade union unity. . . .

(*f*) In this connexion it would be wholly inexpedient for the Soviet trade unions to leave the Anglo-Russian unity committee. The Soviet workers did not send their representatives into the committee because they hoped thereby to substitute negotiations with opportunist leaders for the tasks of the revolutionary transformation of capitalist countries. . . . The English union leaders agreed to the committee under mass pressure. If they now make a turn to the right—which is not only possible, but highly probable—and draw closer to Amsterdam, if they themselves break up the committee or boycott it, that will only expose them and bring them into conflict with that part of the masses which still supports them.

Now particularly, when the English Government is opening the offensive against the workers, and inciting a campaign against the proletarian republic because of the support given by the Soviet trade unions . . . for the

English union leaders to break up the committee would be such a demonstratively anti-working-class act that it would greatly accelerate the leftward movement of the English working masses.

In these circumstances for the Soviet unions to take the initiative in leaving the committee . . . would deal a blow to the cause of international unity, a thoroughly 'heroic' gesture, but politically inexpedient and infantile.

(g) The experience of the struggle for international trade union unity, which was the prime object for which the Anglo-Russian committee was formed, has shown that this was a wholly correct step to take. The accusation that it was taken for national State reasons has been refuted by practice and repeatedly and emphatically rejected by the Communist International. . . .

(m) By and large the CPGB passed the test of its political maturity. The attempt to present it as a 'brake on the revolution' is beneath criticism. The ECCI was completely right when it unanimously approved the attitude of the CPGB. . . . The CPGB gave a correct appraisal of the liquidation of the strike as the 'greatest treachery', attacked the left sharply, and demanded the continuation of the strike despite the orders of the General Council, etc. . . .

7. OUR IMMEDIATE TASKS

A. *The Immediate Tasks of the British Communist Party*

1. Vigorous support for the striking miners.

2. Organization of fighting detachments against strike-breakers, and for self-defence.

3. Advocacy of the nationalization of mines without compensation and workers' control of the mines.

4. A campaign for new elections to all trade union bodies up to and including the General Council. Control of the leaders by the masses.

5. Exposure of the right-wing leaders of the unions and the Labour Party as deliberate traitors.

6. Exposure of the left as capitulators, who, although they had a majority, carried out the policy of the right wing and are therefore chiefly responsible for the defeat. . . .

17. Fight to rescind the decision to exclude communists from the Labour Party.

18. Strengthen and extend the Minority Movement, and concentration of all forces on capturing the most important industries (mining, railways, shipping, electricity). . . .

B. *The Tasks of the Comintern and its Sections*

1. Vigorous and unreserved support for the English miners' struggle under the slogan: 'The miners' cause is our cause'. . . .

3. Explaining to the masses the part played by Amsterdam, the Miners' International, and international social-democracy, which in fact sabotaged and broke the strike. . . .

5. A more intense fight for the unity of the trade union movement, nationally and internationally, and for the proletarian united front.

EXTRACTS FROM A MANIFESTO OF THE ECCI AGAINST INTERVENTION IN CHINA AND THE SOVIET UNION

13 *September* 1926   *Inprekorr*, vi, 116, p. 1967, 17 *September* 1926

[In January 1926 the Soviet manager of the Chinese Eastern Railway was arrested by Chang Tso-lin; his release in compliance with a Soviet ultimatum was followed in February by negotiations about the management and operation of the railway, which broke down in June. Chang Tso-lin demanded the recall of the Soviet Ambassador in Peking, Karakhan, and the Soviet government complied. Early in September Chang's forces seized the Soviet-owned CER river flotilla, and closed down a number of Soviet establishments in Manchuria. Notes of protest were sent by Chicherin on 31 August and 7 September 1926.

A paper preserved in the Trotsky archives gives the conclusion reached by a commission of the politbureau of the CPSU, consisting of Trotsky (chairman), Chicherin, Voroshilov, and Dzerzhinsky, to review Soviet policy in China; it is dated 25 March 1926. There was every reason to think that the mass movement in China would grow stronger, and it should be encouraged to the maximum; the imperialists were also preoccupied with China, and everything must be done to prevent an imperialist united front. Of the powers concerned, Japan was the most dangerous. The revolutionary movement, in need of a breathing space, must postpone the question of Manchuria's fate, that is, in practice agree that for the immediate future South Manchuria should remain in Japanese hands. This policy, which did not prejudice the general struggle against Japanese imperialism, must be agreed with the KMT and the Chinese CP, who would find it unpalatable because of the strength of anti-Japanese feeling. It was however essential, since the Chinese revolution could not withstand united imperialist pressure. A respite also suited Russian interests, but it must be made absolutely clear that Chinese interests were not being sacrificed to Russia's; the two coincided. Until China was unified, Russia would maintain loyal relations with all existing governments in China, central and provincial. They should make it clear to Chang Tso-lin that they recognized that good relations with Japan were necessary, and that if he cultivated good relations with Moscow this would give him a certain independence *vis-à-vis* Tokyo. Whatever concessions China was forced to make to Japan, they must make sure that these were not interpreted as Russian participation in sharing out spheres of influence. The purpose of concessions was to keep Japan from drawing closer to Britain, the chief and irreconcilable enemy of Chinese independence.]

The struggle of the Chinese people against the imperialist oppressors and their Chinese henchmen is developing at a gigantic pace. The advance of the army of the Canton Government, which represents the democratic, anti-imperialist interests of the peasants, workers, intellectuals, and merchants of the southern provinces, has dealt a severe blow to the militarists and their backers, the imperialist Great Powers. The enemies of Chinese freedom understand the scope of the defeat threatening them, and are preparing to meet it.

The danger of further armed imperialist intervention in China has become enormous. . . . Negotiations are already taking place in Tokyo between representatives of the English and Japanese Governments to coordinate their intervention plans. The other Great Powers will try to secure their share of the booty. English forces on the Yangtse and in Canton have already been in action, and reinforcements are on the way. Intervention is perhaps a matter only of days. . . .

Violating all treaties, the military overlord of the northern provinces, Chang Tso-lin, has committed a hostile act against the Soviet Union by seizing part of the property of the Chinese Eastern Railway, which . . . is the joint property of the Soviet Union and the Chinese Government. This is outright provocation, designed to involve the Soviet Union in military entanglements. There is no doubt that British imperialism is behind this action of Chang Tso-lin. The intervention plans elaborated under English leadership are thus directed not only against the Chinese people, but against the Soviet Union too. . . .

The Communist International directs the attention of the revolutionary workers and peasants of all countries to the great danger threatening the cause of world emancipation from these new Great Power machinations. . . . It calls on the workers and peasants and on all strata of the population of capitalist countries which sympathize with the Chinese people's struggle for freedom and with the Soviet Union's socialist construction to do all in their power to prevent this new intervention.

RESOLUTION OF THE PRESIDIUM OF THE ECCI DISMISSING ZINOVIEV FROM HIS POST AS PRESIDENT OF THE COMMUNIST INTERNATIONAL

25 *October* 1926   *Inprekorr*, vi, 128, p. 2208, 26 *October* 1926

[The two opposition groups in the CPSU, the 'old' led by Trotsky and the 'new' led by Zinoviev and Kamenev, joined forces at the April 1926 meeting of the CC of the CPSU. (In July Zinoviev stated that the greatest mistake he had ever made was his fight against the Trotskyist opposition.) The alliance of the two groups had its repercussions in the Comintern. On 23 July 1926 a resolution of the CC and CCC of the CPSU removed Zinoviev from the politbureau, the opposition being charged with trying to establish an illegal fractional organization. 'The threads of all these fractional steps of the opposition lead to the ECCI apparatus, at the head of which is politbureau member Zinoviev.' The opposition, it was said, showed tendencies to form international blocs with ultra-lefts like Korsch in Germany and ultra-rights like Souvarine in France, who had been expelled from the Comintern and were now attacking the CPSU. Through the ECCI apparatus the opposition was spreading views condemned by the CPSU among other parties and stirring them up against the CPSU.

In August and September the campaign in the Russian and Comintern press against Trotsky, Zinoviev, Kamenev, and their supporters grew more bitter. Trotsky wrote in September that despite the errors of the Polish and British communist party leaders not a hair of their head was harmed, because in the CPSU question they supported Stalin. Only a thoroughgoing discussion, including discussion of the CPSU, could free the Comintern sections from the mechanical pressure of the apparatus which had its main source in the regime prevailing in the CPSU; this prevented the correction of the party line by normal means. The resolution of the fourteenth CPSU congress on the need for a more democratic and more collective Comintern leadership was being changed in practice into its opposite. The most important decisions were taken by purely fractional methods and put into operation by secret emissaries dispatched by Stalin. A change in the Comintern, which was essential to the survival of the international revolutionary movement, could be brought about either parallel with a change in the CPSU regime, or in struggle against the dominant position of the CPSU in the Comintern. 'It is unnecessary to state that every effort must be made to ensure the first course. The struggle to change the regime in the CPSU is the struggle to heal the regime in the Comintern and to maintain the ideological leading role in it for our party.' Stalin's power lay in his apparatus. 'It has the party by the throat, and prevents it not only from speaking but from breathing.' The party had to win back its right over the machine.

The CC of the KPD sent a letter to the fifteenth conference of the CPSU, meeting in October 1926, drawing that party's attention to the effect of the opposition's policy on the internal life and the activities of the KPD. Its work was being hampered by the fractional connexions between the Russian and German oppositions, especially its work to win sympathy for the USSR among the German working class. The reply of the CPSU placed Urbahns, Scholem, and Weber (leaders of the 'ultra-left') in the same camp as the 'expelled renegades' Maslow and Fischer. The conference instructed the Russian representatives on the ECCI to continue the ideological struggle against deviations in the Comintern; it condemned the 'fractional and anti-Leninist' work of the CPSU opposition in the CI, and approved the decision of the CC on Zinoviev.

On 11 October 1926 the CC of the CPSU put to the opposition an ultimatum requiring its unconditional acceptance of party decisions, admission of its errors and its violation of discipline, dissolution of its fraction, and severance of all relations with opposition elements in the Comintern sections. On 16 October the opposition leaders admitted that they had violated party discipline, and condemned fractionalism. On the 23rd they were again warned, at a joint meeting of the CC and CCC of the CPSU attended by representatives of a number of other parties, against violations of discipline, and a resolution was passed stating that: 'Since Zinoviev does not represent the line of the CPSU in the CI . . . the CC and CCC do not find it possible for Zinoviev to continue his work in the Communist International.' At the same time Trotsky was dismissed from the politbureau, and Kamenev from his position as candidate member of that body. One of the charges against Zinoviev was that he had carried the struggle in the CPSU into the parties and policies of the Comintern. The ECCI presidium resolution was promptly endorsed by the central committees of all the major Comintern parties.

In a letter to the ECCI, dated 21 November, Zinoviev wrote: 'Following the decision taken by the leading organs of the largest Comintern sections, I ask to be released from my post as president of the ECCI, and in general from work in the Comintern at the present time.'

On the following day the ECCI unanimously adopted the following resolution:

'Taking into account the resolutions passed by the most important sections of the Comintern, the communist parties of the Soviet Union, Germany, France, England, Czechoslovakia, Poland, Italy, etc., as well as by the presidium of the ECCI, and having noted comrade Zinoviev's request of 21 November 1926, the plenum of the seventh enlarged Executive has decided to release comrade Zinoviev from his office as President of the ECCI and from his work in the Comintern.']

Considering the anti-Leninist line of the opposition bloc in the CPSU, considering the leading part which comrade Zinoviev, as President of the Comintern, played in carrying out this incorrect line, considering the opposition bloc's disruptive fraction work, unprecedented in the history of the bolshevik party, and considering the transference of these fractional machinations by comrade Zinoviev into the ranks of the Communist International, the ECCI delegation attending the joint plenum of the CC and the CCC of the CPSU, in accordance with the decisions of the most important sections of the Comintern, considers it impossible for comrade Zinoviev to remain and to continue to work at the head of the Comintern.

EXTRACTS FROM AN ECCI MANIFESTO ON THE REVOLT IN INDONESIA

20 *November* 1926   *Inprekorr*, vi, 143, p. 2506, 23 *November* 1926

[The Communist Party of Indonesia, which controlled most of the trade unions, had failed to 'capture' the only mass party in the country, Sarekat Islam, and had started a rival body, Sarekat Rakjat, around which to organize the national-ist movement. At a congress of Indonesian communists in June 1924 the pro-posal of the 'ultra-lefts' to dissolve Sarekat Rakjat was defeated. It was about this time that the leadership of the Indonesian CP was taken over by the Indonesians themselves, many Dutch communists having been deported by the Government. The events in China in 1925 had, it was claimed, brought three-quarters of a million Chinese in the country into the movement. Strikes and disturbances in the spring of 1925 were answered with repressive measures; in March the Dutch

CP protested against the 'police terror' in Indonesia, and the Eastern bureau of the ECCI followed with an appeal against the 'white terror' there. At the enlarged plenum in April 1925 the ECCI drew up a detailed programme for the Indonesian CP, urging it to advance nationalist rather than proletarian slogans. The absence of a native bourgeoisie in Indonesia meant that the nationalist movement there would be more consistently revolutionary than elsewhere. The programme of the revolutionary liberation movement, into which the CP was to draw all national-revolutionary parties, was to include independence, the withdrawal of foreign troops, universal suffrage, agrarian reforms, and the confiscation of large estates. At the sixth ECCI plenum in February–March 1926 it was reported that the Chinese workers in Indonesia had raised $50,000 for the Shanghai strikers. In the discussion Semaoen asked the Dutch party not to interfere in the work of the Indonesian CP. Seegers (Holland) admitted that there had been an 'imperialist' tendency in the Dutch party, but it had now been eliminated. In 1926 the CP of Indonesia claimed 3,000 members; Sarekat Rakjat 50,000. Plans for an insurrection were made early in the year; it started on 12 November in Java, and early in January 1927 in Sumatra, and was followed by wholesale arrests and sentences of imprisonment and exile. In the Dutch parliament, de Visser, who had taken over the leadership of the Dutch CP from Wijnkoop and Ravesteyn, asked for a labour and trade union committee of inquiry to be sent to Indonesia; the request was refused. De Visser, who had received the support of the social-democratic members of parliament, was criticized for this 'bourgeois' action by Smeral at the seventh ECCI plenum, but replied that the move had been made after consultation with the ECCI orgbureau. Affairs in Indonesia appear to have received little attention from the ECCI.

At the sixth Comintern congress in 1928 an Indonesian delegate appearing under the name of Samin (Semaoen?) stated that neither in Java in November, nor in West Sumatra in the following January, had the working masses been drawn into the struggle. The party apparatus was very weak, as were its contacts with the Comintern.]

The anti-imperialist revolt is spreading; from China it has reached Java, where the oppressed and exploited masses have risen against Dutch imperialism. An armed rebellion has broken out in western Java. . . . The Dutch Governor-General has declared that he intends to crush the revolt mercilessly.

The struggle for freedom in the Dutch colonies is not a new phenomenon. The population has never come to terms with imperialist rule. . . . Recently these struggles have assumed an organized form under communist party leadership. Under proletarian hegemony, a united front has been established to liberate the country from imperialist rule. This united revolutionary army includes the overwhelming majority of the population, proletariat, peasantry, intellectuals, and petty bourgeoisie.

Dutch imperialism has replied with measures of brutal repression. The communist party was the first victim; it was declared illegal, and its press forbidden; its leaders have been arrested or driven into exile. The revolutionary unions have been dissolved, meetings prohibited, newspapers shut down. The mass nationalist organization Sarekat Rajat has been declared illegal.

Nevertheless the rising wave of mass revolt has not been held back. The will to freedom cannot be defeated. . . . The Indonesian people are rising against inhuman and intolerable conditions. Dutch imperialism, armed to the teeth, will drown this freedom movement in rivers of blood if the Indonesian revolutionary movement is not supported by the workers and the oppressed peoples of the entire world. The Communist International greets the Indonesian revolutionary struggle and will support it to the utmost.

Workers of the world . . . organize mass demonstrations to show your sympathy for the Java revolt and to protest against imperialist terror. . . . Demonstrate outside the Dutch embassies and consulates and demand freedom for the Indonesian people and the withdrawal of imperialist armies from the colonies.

Oppressed peoples of the world! The Indonesian rebels are your vanguard . . . do everything you can to support them in their fight.

THE SEVENTH ENLARGED PLENUM OF THE ECCI

[The plenum, which met from 22 November to 16 December 1926, was attended by 191 delegates, of whom 100 had votes; 38 were members of the ECCI; Shao Li-tse attended as Kuomintang delegate.

At the opening session greetings were sent to the Miners' Federation of Great Britain and to the fighting Chinese masses, and an appeal to all workers on the misdeeds of Italian fascism. A message of greetings to the CPSU, moved by Thaelmann, and a protest against the continued imprisonment of Sacco and Vanzetti, moved by Duncan (USA), were passed unanimously. The first asserted that 'Every step taken by the USSR to expand its industrial production in the construction of socialism is of direct aid to the proletarian struggle in countries ruled by the capitalists. Recently a large number of workers' delegations have observed for themselves how the working class after its victory sets about building socialism in the land of proletarian dictatorship. . . . All their reports about the creative labour of the proletarian masses of the USSR in building socialism are received with enthusiasm in the capitalist countries, even by non-communist workers. They enhance the militancy, the revolutionary energy, and the determination of the armies in the fighting front of the social revolution. . . . It is the greatest good fortune for the world revolution that at the head of the proletariat of the USSR there is a party founded by Lenin, trained by Lenin, filled with his spirit, guiding the working class through all difficulties and dangers. . . . Just as all members of the CPSU rallied to the Central Committee after the upheavals of the recent discussion, so today all sections of the CI unite in an iron ring of mutual loyalty, devotion, and revolutionary solidarity around the CPSU.'

The Sacco and Vanzetti appeal was a summons 'to prevent the judicial murder threatening our working-class brothers Nicola Sacco and Bartolomeo Vanzetti. It is no longer possible to harbour illusions about the so-called constitutional guarantees which allegedly protect the rights of these persecuted comrades. . . . It is still possible to save them. The entire working class of the United States must be mobilized as one man. In all other countries where Wall Street dollar democracy . . . maintains embassies and consulates, whose job it is to report on public opinion about American affairs, it is possible for thousands and millions of workers to make their voice heard.'

The ECCI report to the plenum recalled that at the congress of the Dutch CP in 1925 Wijnkoop and his followers had a small majority, and rejected the ECCI proposal that the minority should receive representation in the central committee and the secretariat. On the initiative of the ECCI, a conference was called and elected a new central committee which 'carried out all the decisions of the ECCI'. Wijnkoop, Ravesteyn, and their followers boycotted the new CC, and in December 1925 and March 1926 were accused by the ECCI of fraction work, of 'appealing to the backward petty-bourgeois instincts of the Dutch proletariat', and of working to split the party. Wijnkoop had been invited to attend the sixth plenum earlier in the year, but had refused. At the congress of the Dutch CP in May 1926 Wijnkoop and Ravesteyn were expelled. They had started a 'committee to appeal to the world congress of the Comintern', and founded a fortnightly journal. Their expulsion was endorsed unanimously by the plenum.

Lozovsky, urging more trade union work in the colonies, reported that it was planned to hold a Pacific trade union conference in Canton in May 1927. The report of the trade union commission was given by Ercoli. A resolution on trustification, rationalization, and tasks in the trade unions was adopted.

A statement to the presidium of the plenum signed by Zinoviev, Kamenev, and Trotsky (there is a note by Trotsky in his archives saying it was most probably written by Zinoviev) denied that they favoured the views of the ultra-left; they asked for correct Leninist behaviour towards honest revolutionaries on the left; they disavowed anybody who denied the proletarian character of the Soviet party and State; they were not opposed to a united front policy, only to a united front with those who had betrayed the English miners. All their criticisms were directed against mistakes and deviations from the proletarian line. 'If the open exposition of one's views before the leading organ of the world communist party is fractionalism, what other ways exist to stand up for ideas within the framework of Comintern decisions?. . . If conferences and congresses are to be based on unanimity secured in advance, what need is there to convene them? . . . But we do not doubt that even if this mistaken resolution is adopted, the Comintern will remain as before the only organization capable of correcting its own errors and the errors of its sections.' They would, therefore, submit to any decisions taken and call on comrades who were of their mind to do the same.]

EXTRACTS FROM THE RESOLUTION OF THE SEVENTH ECCI PLENUM ON
THE SITUATION IN BRITAIN

December 1926   *Inprekorr*, vii, 16, p. 326, 5 *February* 1927

[There was a great deal about the British situation in the ECCI report. The
membership of the CPGB had risen from 6,000 to 12,000 in the course of the
year. Of the 304 reports issued by the information department, 39 had been
about Britain; the agitprop department had issued 13 bulletins and a great
many articles about the progress of the Russian relief campaign for the British
miners on strike. All CI sections had been given directives on their duty to help
the miners. Although the CPGB manifesto on 13 May had described the decision to call off the general strike as 'the greatest crime ever committed not only
against the strikers, but against the working class of Britain and the entire
world', the ECCI had criticized the party central committee for its tendency
to tone down its attacks on the General Council and its left wing. Bukharin
echoed this criticism in his opening speech: the CPGB was not consistent and
severe enough in its criticism of the 'left' leaders, which reflected an underestimation of the leftward swing of the masses.

Within the Comintern the continued existence of the Anglo-Russian trade
union unity committee was a matter of serious dispute. It had been discussed
at the fifteenth CPSU conference in October, where the opposition proposed
that the Russian side should take the initiative in breaking it up. Tomsky and
Bukharin spoke against them, and the conference decided that to do so would
be 'incorrect in principle and politically harmful', implicitly justifying the
opponents of trade union unity, particularly the Amsterdam leaders.

In theses drawn up for the conference dated 19 September 1926 (in the
Trotsky archives), Trotsky wrote that the tendency in the Comintern to substitute diplomacy for policy was most clearly illustrated in regard to the Anglo-
Russian committee. All arguments in favour of maintaining the committee
applied with double force in favour of entering the IFTU.

At the plenum Bukharin maintained that the Anglo-Russian committee was
an example to be followed throughout the International. Lozovsky admitted
that the miners' strike had created a crisis in the Anglo-Russian committee.
The English side were now doing everything to sabotage it and break it up.
Remmele agreed with this, and added that they were unable to do so because
of the pressure of mass sentiment. The KPD opposition had said that the
existence of the committee made it impossible for the CPGB to take over the
leadership of the strike; the CPSU opposition that the Russian unions should
have withdrawn after the betrayal of the strike. Murphy spoke on the lessons
of the general strike, and confessed that it was a mistake on the part of the
CPGB to criticize the Russian unions for attacking the General Council too
sharply. Vuyovich put the opposition case: the committee prevented the
Comintern from approaching the masses directly—that could be done only by
a united front from below. It hampered the British unionists who were trying
to get rid of their opportunist leaders if the Russian unions collaborated with
them. Implicitly the Russian trade unions were endorsing the TUC's treachery.

It was said that the committee would play its part in the event of intervention against Russia, but had not the entire attitude of the TUC shown that this was a delusion? Shatskin said that the British partner in the committee was not the TUC but the British proletariat.

The resolution, drafted by the CPGB, was passed unanimously.]

I. INTRODUCTION

1. The seven-months' struggle of the English miners which followed the general strike dealt heavy blows to English capitalism. In itself a reflection of the progressive decline of English capitalism, it substantially accelerated the rate of that decline.

2. England's position in the world economy is undermined, and its political position in the world has been weakened. England's foreign policy has suffered a number of setbacks; the Locarno plan for a bloc against the United States was frustrated at Geneva, and in addition there was the blow suffered in China by the Canton army's defeat of Wu Pei-fu and Sun Chuan-fang, England's agents. Its desperate attempt to construct an anti-Soviet bloc ended with such successes for Soviet policy as the Soviet agreement with Lithuania, etc. . . .

5. Within the country the miners' fight gave class contradictions an acuteness unknown in England before the general strike, and revealed to the working class the true character and beastliness of the capitalist dictatorship more clearly than years of propaganda could have done. . . .

8. The theses on the general strike adopted by the ECCI in June, and now confirmed by the seventh enlarged plenum, not only gave a correct analysis of the course of events but correctly indicated the general lines of development of the class struggle in England in the near future. . . .

III. THE POLITICAL SITUATION AFTER THE GENERAL STRIKE

14. The growing political and economic difficulties created by the prolongation of the miners' struggle forced the capitalist class to come out more and more openly and resolutely against the miners and the entire working class; it completely abandoned democratic externals and revealed all its institutions—government, monarchy, parliament, church, army, police, and press—as instruments of capitalist dictatorship. . . .

15. On the other hand the workers' class consciousness was intensified after the general strike. . . . This is shown in the marked growth of influence of the National Minority Movement in the trade unions. . . .

16. This growing class consciousness has also driven the trade union bureaucracy, from the General Council downwards, to close their ranks; having made up their minds to bring about the defeat of the miners, they are now driven to further treacheries to the working class. Most of these bureaucrats, right wing and former left, are working for an open alliance

with the capitalists; only a part of the lower ranks of the bureaucracy turned left with the workers. . . .

17. The complete and shameful surrender of the former 'left wing' in the General Council (Hicks, Purcell, Tillett, Bromley, etc.) during the general strike, their participation in the seven months' struggle of the General Council to defeat the miners . . . demonstrated the consolidation of the reformist ranks in face of the growing class consciousness of the workers.

18. The reformist Labour Party leaders were also forced by the sharpening of the class struggle to reveal their true features as agents of capitalism in the labour movement. . . .

21. Throughout the miners' struggle the Minority Movement issued clear and correct directives and conducted an energetic campaign to mobilize the masses in support of the miners. . . . The Minority Movement leaders showed some hesitation about criticizing the 'left' in the General Council, and made one or two mistakes which were later corrected. . . .

22. The miners' struggle aroused among the mineworkers a tremendous wave of sympathy for the communist party. . . . This can be seen in the doubling of the party's membership over the last six months and in the expansion of the party press, as well as in the applause which greeted party leaders when they spoke at miners' meetings. . . .

IV. THE COMMUNIST PARTY'S TACTICS

24. . . . The CPGB acted correctly when it did not shrink from telling the workers that the greatest responsibility for the miners' difficult position rested on the General Council and the Labour Party leaders. . . . Throughout the course of the miners' struggle the communist party correctly explained to the workers that the issue was not merely the miners' fight against the mine-owners, but a struggle of the entire working class against the entire capitalist class, including its executive committee, the Conservative Government. . . .

26. Since the general strike ended the communist party has unceasingly continued its campaign to expose the General Council . . . and emphasized the necessity of replacing the reformist leaders by revolutionaries who are true to the working class. . . . In this connexion it must be admitted that the party press was not always successful in placing responsibility for the betrayal of the miners where it belonged, as clearly as was required. A similar mistake was made by the party fraction in the Minority Movement executive; the CC immediately put this right. . . .

28. The communist party lost no opportunity of exposing and fighting the opportunist leadership of the political labour movement. . . .

30. Throughout the general strike and the miners' lock-out the CPGB on the whole pursued a correct political line; nevertheless a number of

mistakes were made, most of which were subsequently put right. In correcting these errors the party was supported by the comradely criticism and proposals of the ECCI. . . . Because of this help the CPGB was able to conduct a correct policy, despite all the difficulties arising from the present vigorous struggle of the workers against the attempts of the English bourgeoisie to stabilize their position at the expense of the workers.

V. SOME FUNDAMENTAL LESSONS OF THE STRUGGLE

31. The miners' struggle has given the working class of the world, and particularly of England, a number of important lessons which if studied will enable the workers to withstand the still more severe struggles that lie ahead. . . .

(c) For the English workers the most important lesson is that the separation of the class struggle into 'industrial' and 'political' is a misleading and dangerous swindle if applied to any big strike in England in the present period of capitalist decline. . . .

(d) The unconcealed capitulation of the right as well as of the left reformist leadership of the labour movement and their refusal to fight for the emancipation of the workers, or even to support the workers' demands to maintain their present living standard, are a practical demonstration of the complete bankruptcy of reformism. . . .

(f) The continued participation of the Soviet Russian unions, under CPSU leadership, in the Anglo-Russian unity committee, notwithstanding the criticism and exposure of the treachery and sabotage of the General Council and its delegates to the unity committee, the partially successful campaign for preventing the export of coal to England, the twenty-four-hour solidarity strike organized by the CGTU, and the local successes gained by the British party together with the ILP in the campaign to stop the transport of coal were a practical lesson to the communists in England and throughout the world of the importance of united front tactics in rallying the workers for the fight against capitalism and in forcing the reformist leaders to reveal their true features. . . .

VII. THE TASKS OF THE BRITISH PARTY

39. The enlarged Executive endorses the tasks of the CPGB as laid down by its eighth congress. . . .

Political Tasks

(i) The campaign to explain to the workers the political significance of the present period of capitalist decline, of the struggles which will culminate in the seizure of power by the working class . . . which must also demonstrate the necessity of making the maximum revolutionary use of parliament and of local-government bodies, while making clear the utter uselessness of these institutions for achieving working-class emancipation.

(ii) The campaign to mobilize the entire working class for the struggle for the dissolution of parliament, the overthrow of the Baldwin Government, and the formation of a real workers' government as a reply to the present and impending Conservative attacks on the living standards, the rights, and the liberties of the working class. . . .

(iv) The campaign to build a united trade union International as a guarantee against international economic and political reaction and the danger of a new world war; in particular the campaign to convene a world-unity congress by the RILU in association with the IFTU and to expose reformist sabotage of the Anglo-Russian unity committee. . . .

(v) The campaign for solidarity with the workers and peasants of the colonies . . . who, both in their struggle for complete independence and secession from the British Empire and in their fight against capitalist exploitation, are the most reliable allies of the British workers. . . .

Organizational Tasks

(i) The utmost organizational consolidation of the communist party, particularly recruiting, reconstruction on the basis of factory cells, fraction work, improvement of local and district organization, development of political training and the party press. . . .

(ii) Organizational consolidation and expansion of the Minority Movement as the cardinal prerequisite for reorganizing the trade union movement on industrial-union lines and replacing the reformist leaders by revolutionary workers. . . .

(iv) Organizational consolidation and expansion of the left-wing movement in the Labour Party as the most important prerequisite for a proletarian leadership of the Labour Party and the affiliation to it of the communist party.

(v) Preparing the workers for self-defence against fascism by building workers' defence corps under the supervision of the workers' mass organizations.

(vi) Organized fraction work in the co-operatives and co-operative guilds in order to lead their proletarian members in the fight against the middle-class influences prevailing in these bodies and give them a revolutionary proletarian policy. . . .

[VIII.] THE LESSONS FOR THE INTERNATIONAL WORKING CLASS

(1) The miners' strike shows that the attempt of the bourgeoisie to stabilize capitalism must lead to tremendous mass struggles, and that these struggles in their turn endanger capitalist stabilization. . . .

(5) The miners' strike has proved that under the old reformist leadership the working class cannot win any really big fight. Not only the right and left wing reformists in England, but international reformism as a whole, the Second International and Amsterdam and the Miners' International, failed shamefully. The workers can arrive at this truth only by their own experience, and the British miners' strike was the most important experience of the international proletariat in recent years. The necessity of revolutionary communist leadership not only in the final struggle of the proletariat, but also in its daily struggles to maintain living standards is the most fundamental and important lesson and achievement of the miners' fight.

RESOLUTION OF THE SEVENTH ECCI PLENUM ABOLISHING THE OFFICE OF PRESIDENT OF THE COMINTERN

December 1926   *Puti Mirovoi Revoliutsii*, ii, p. 468

[Ercoli reported on organizational changes. It was proposed to abolish the post of president, in order to establish a collective leadership into which it would be easier to draw the non-Russian parties. It was proposed that the ECCI should meet three times a year. Members of the presidium, increased in size to 18, plus 7 candidates, were to remain in Moscow and to meet fortnightly. The org-bureau was to be dissolved, to counteract the tendency to separate organizational from political work; in future organizational questions would be settled by the presidium. The political secretariat established after the plenum met twice a week. The report was adopted unanimously.]

The seventh enlarged plenum of the ECCI considers inexpedient the continued existence of the office of president of the CI, and taking into account the resolution already passed by the plenum releasing comrade Zinoviev from his duties as president of the CI, considers it necessary to abolish this post now.

This decision must, however, be submitted to the sixth world congress of the CI for ratification, in order that the relevant paragraphs 9 and 18 of the statutes of the Communist International shall be changed accordingly.

The seventh plenum instructs the ECCI to undertake the reconstruction of the central bodies of the ECCI (to create a political secretariat, determine its composition and functions, etc., to decide how it shall be chosen, etc.) arising from this decision.

EXTRACTS FROM THE THESES OF THE SEVENTH ECCI PLENUM ON THE
INTERNATIONAL SITUATION AND THE TASKS OF THE COMMUNIST
INTERNATIONAL

13 *December* 1926   *Puti Mirovoi Revoliutsii,* ii, p. 390

[Bukharin introduced the theses. One of the Comintern's tasks, he said, was to
expose the League of Nations as 'an organ of the imperialist bourgeoisie whose
primary purpose was to fight the proletarian revolution and the revolution in the
colonial and semi-colonial countries'. Some opposition members did not believe
in the possibility of building socialism in Russia, and for this they were praised
by the bourgeoisie and social democrats. He traced the course of economic re-
covery in Europe from the time of the Dawes plan to Locarno and the Franco-
German rapprochement; with every regrouping of forces, one factor remained
constant, the development of the anti-Soviet bloc.

Kuusinen spoke on the tasks of communist parties. In capitalist countries their
chief task was to liberate the masses from social-democracy, which was more
dangerous than fascism. They should cultivate methods of indirect leadership of
mass organizations. Social-democracy, which as a labour movement was bankrupt, had working-class support only in virtue of its traditions and the lies of its
leaders. It could be exposed by practical revolutionary work. The theses were
adopted with one abstention.]

I. CAPITALIST WORLD ECONOMY

1. The recent course of international relations confirms the appraisal
given by the last enlarged plenum of the ECCI. Notwithstanding certain
statements by opposition leaders (Zinoviev, Trotsky, and others) capitalist
stabilization is an indisputable fact (the growth of world production, of
international trade, currency stabilization, etc.). Equally indisputable,
however, is the partial and unstable character of this stabilization, as
shown in the feverish fluctuations of the market, in the extreme unevenness
of development, in the enormous contradiction between the capacity of
the productive apparatus and the actual volume of output, in the magnitude of chronic unemployment. Among the most important factors disturbing the process of capitalist stabilization are the growth of socialism
in the USSR, the decline of English capitalism, the unprecedented acuteness of the class struggle in England, and the great national revolution
in China. . . .

3. Despite this relative stabilization, capitalism is going through a
special crisis, which is far from being the 'normal' crisis of capitalist over-
production. . . . The present crisis of over-production, which results from
the expansion of productive capacity and the fall in mass purchasing
power, is to a large extent the continuation of the post-war hunger crisis,
for the present failure of demand is connected with the impoverishment

of the masses and the exhaustion of internal markets as a result of the world war.

4. This state of affairs pushes the problem of markets into the foreground. . . . The development and sharpening of imperialist conflicts is the inevitable consequence of the entire system of relations as formed. Thus the present phase may be defined as between revolutions, as a stage leading from one surge forward of the revolutionary wave to another, to which the course of historical development must lead, and for the approach of which—perhaps fairly soon—the communist parties should be prepared.

II. THE REGROUPING OF THE POWERS AND THE BASIC LINES OF INTERNATIONAL POLITICS

5. The characteristic feature of the present situation is the shift in the centres of economic power, and consequently the centres of political and military power also, to non-European countries, in the first place to the United States of America. . . .

Anglo-American rivalry to a large degree determines the regrouping of the imperialist Powers. England's attempt to reconquer, with the help of the Locarno pact, its position on the continent was frustrated by America. That cleared the way for Franco-German attempts at rapprochement, although America was an obstacle to the realization of close relations. . . .

Other important facts are the development of France into an industrial country and the economic renaissance of Germany, side by side with the economic decline of England and the advance of Italy. What we have witnessed, against this background, is the collapse of the treaty of Versailles, a radical regrouping of the Powers, the dissolution of the great Entente and the disintegration of the League of Nations as an instrument of 'Allied' policy.

6. The stages of this process of liquidation were as follows: (a) Versailles and later the occupation of the Ruhr. America stands aside. In Europe—hegemony of France. Politically, Germany is prostrate. (b) France cannot digest the occupation and suffers defeat. American and English intervention. Dawes plan. Germany begins to rise. (c) Locarno. Hegemony of England, exploiting the French failure. Political wooing of, and corresponding concessions to, Germany in exchange for its cooling off to the USSR. Promise to admit Germany to the League of Nations and beginning of Germany's 'westward orientation'. American capital flows into the German economy. (d) Geneva. America gently squeezes out England. Germany enters the League and receives a place on the League Council. Change in Franco-German relations. (e) Thoiry. Regrouping takes place in the League of Nations. By its 'peaceful' policy towards Germany France attracts to its side a number of small countries and gets a majority in both

the Assembly and the Council of the League. Radical regrouping of forces. At Thoiry—agreement and a number of important concessions on the part of France as the price for the purchase of the Saar and the mobilization of German railway bonds. America frustrates this agreement but the understanding remains. Collapse of Versailles combinations accelerated. Partly to counterbalance the German-French bloc, an Anglo-Italian bloc is formed. Italy tries to round off the anti-Soviet front by taking part in it. Italian differences with France grow more acute (Mediterranean, North Africa, Balkans, Asia Minor). Together with the regrouping of the Great Powers the Little Entente begins to disintegrate. Poland, having exchanged the French orientation for the English, again begins to incline towards France; French influence in the Balkans supplants English and Italian imperialism; conflicts between the Balkan States accumulate, and from this side too the danger of a new war is maturing.

7. The general tendency is the anti-Soviet tendency, making its way, under England's guidance, through all imperialist contradictions. Germany's westward orientation, the latest trends in Italian policy, Poland, the treaty system in the border States and Rumania, the Italo-Rumanian and Franco-Rumanian treaties, great English activity in the Baltic, the Balkans, Persia, Afghanistan, etc.—all this is an expression of the said general tendency. Nor is there any doubt at all of a tendency to occupy China,[1] with the object of directing its development along a national-capitalist road under the hegemony of foreign capital if the attempt altogether to suppress the national revolution fails. . . .

III. REGROUPING OF CLASS FORCES AND THE BASIC LINES OF INTERNAL POLICY

9. If attempts at stabilization by the bourgeoisie take the form, externally, of a struggle for foreign markets, internally these attempts mean, from the class point of view, intensified pressure on the working class and the broad working masses generally, a decrease in their share of the total national income, a heightened degree of exploitation. . . .

10. In Germany the starting-point of stabilization, of the strengthening of the economy and the State apparatus, was the defeat of the proletariat in the autumn of 1923, a defeat preceded by a number of other serious battles. . . . The resistance of the working class is here expressed in the movement to the left among broad masses; although it has not yet taken the form of active defensive struggle, the first beginnings of the rise of proletarian class struggle in Germany are already apparent. . . .

11. In England the attack on the working class evoked tremendous resistance, expressed in the general strike and the heroic strike of the English miners. From this point of view the miners' strike is of immense

[1] In the German version, encircle China.

importance in principle. England's crumbling position on the world market and the probability of its further decline, together with the collapse of the English world empire, give the struggle as a whole a more acute character, and so England has become the European country closest to a revolutionary situation. The polarization of class forces is proceeding rapidly. . . . The prospects of stabilization here too are becoming more and more questionable. . . .

15. On the basis of this attack and of the relative strengthening of the bourgeois State apparatus the social-democrats are being squeezed out of the governments, having played their part in saving the bourgeois regime at the most critical moment.

16. Thus in various forms is manifested one and the same regular tendency, arising from the post-war economics of capitalism. The socio-class limits to capitalist stabilization are set by the resistance of the working class, its ability to mobilize its forces and to withstand the attacks of capital. . . .

V. SOME CURRENT THEORETICAL QUESTIONS

22. One current theoretical question, in connexion with capitalist stabilization, is the question of super-imperialism. The impossibility, economically, of super-imperialism is shown by the unevenness of development and the intense contradictions of interest between the major imperialist States (this factor is underestimated by comrade Trotsky). Politically, it is expressed in the extreme instability of political agreements between States and blocs of States, as well as in the decline of the League of Nations, reflecting Anglo-French contradictions. The growth of militarism everywhere also refutes the theory of super-imperialism, whose purpose is: (1) to blunt the vigilance of the proletariat; (2) among German imperialists to preach the necessity of 'common' colonial possessions, that is, the return of the German colonies; (3) for propaganda against the USSR, which does not wish to enter the League of Nations; (4) for propaganda against colonial revolutions, disturbing the 'super-imperialist' peace. . . .

24. The Communist International considered and considers the USSR the most important fortress of the world revolution. The attempts of the social-democrats and their followers among the renegades from communism (and equally the insignificant groups of the right and 'left' opposition within the Comintern, encouraged by the speeches of the opposition in the CPSU) to represent the tempestuous economic development of the USSR as a process of 'kulak' degeneration, the CI rejects vigorously. Objectively such attempts only serve the class enemies of the proletariat. The enlarged plenum of the ECCI thinks that there is no place in the

ranks of the Communist International for people who regard the USSR as a land of capitalism and deny that it is a proletarian dictatorship.

25. The national liberation struggle in China confronts the Communist International with a question regarding the main perspective on which its Chinese section should, with the support of all other sections, be oriented. This is the road of the independent development of China, in alliance with the proletariat of the USSR and the entire world . . . in opposition to its capitalist development, which in the circumstances would infallibly occur under the tutelage of foreign capital. If the main task of the present moment is the united front of all national-revolutionary forces, including the anti-imperialist strata of the bourgeoisie, on the other hand it is already necessary to raise the question of satisfying the basic needs of the peasantry, of drawing them into alliance with the proletariat of China and preparing the Chinese proletariat for the role of leader of the Chinese revolution.

26. In capitalist countries the main question today is the attitude to capitalist rationalization. In contrast to the social-democrats, who regard it as their task to support and strengthen the capitalist regime, and who therefore favour capitalist rationalization, communists cannot and must not help capital to improve its economy. . . . It is their task to fight (1) against capitalist stabilization; (2) against any worsening in the position of the working class as a result of capitalist pseudo-rationalization; (3) for a higher standard of living for the working class; (4) for the dictatorship of the proletariat and the socialist organization of economy; (5) not for capitalist, but for socialist rationalization.

At the same time the communist party must fight against 'industrial democracy' based on class collaboration, and, by means of irreconcilable class struggle against the employers, to win an extension of the rights of factory committees up to workers' control of production and distribution. This militant task of class struggle is the communist party's answer to capitalist rationalization. . . .

VII. THE MAIN CURRENT TASKS OF THE COMINTERN

32. At the present moment one of the basic international tasks of the Comintern is to support the most important centres of the international revolutionary movement, that is, the USSR, the English workers, and the Chinese revolution. . . .

The enlarged plenum observes that almost all parties of the CI have failed to show enough energy in support of the English strikers and the Chinese revolution. What is necessary is a vigorous fight against the interventionist plans of imperialism, against English attempts at armed intervention in China, against the continued existence of unequal treaties, against anti-Soviet military treaties and secret agreements, etc. . . .

33. The fight against the danger of war should also be emphasized,

'pacifist', 'pan-European', and other social-democratic and bourgeois utopias must be pitilessly exposed. . . .

35. The social power of the bourgeoisie increases with the trustification of industry, and so does the need for stronger and stronger resistance and vigorous defensive action by the proletariat. Therefore a united working-class front is now more essential than ever before. On the agenda too is the struggle against the plans of the bourgeoisie to split the workers' movement, relying on the stratum of privileged workers to exert pressure on the rest of the masses and, intensifying the difference between the workers and the unemployed, by using unemployment as a threat to keep the employed section of the proletariat in a state of subjection and depression. . . .

38. It is essential to learn how to consolidate our achievements organizationally. The enlarged plenum observes that one of the most serious shortcomings common to practically all communist parties is the inability to exploit the positive results of campaigns organizationally. In a number of cases this leads to an insufficient growth of the party, even to stagnant membership, which is quite out of keeping with the growth of its political influence. . . .

Also on the agenda is the struggle against social-democracy. Social-democracy is finally and everywhere standing, despite its posture of 'opposition', on the side of the bourgeois governments. . . . Fighting to liberate the masses from the disintegrating influence of the Second International and Amsterdam, the communist parties demand: as against a policy of coalition, the most vigorous class struggle and the overthrow of capitalist governments; as against lying talk of a new and peaceful phase of capitalism, exposure of the terrible danger of war and preparation of the masses to turn such a war into a civil war; as against Pan-Europa, the Socialist United States of Europe; as against the League of Nations, a Union of Socialist Soviet Republics.

VIII. COMMUNIST PARTIES AND TRADE UNIONS

41. Industrial strikes and the economic struggle in general having a tendency, in conditions of trustification, to develop into political struggles, special importance attaches to communist work in the trade unions. . . .

43. Communists must not only advocate the entry of all employed workers into the unions, but also fight vigorously for retention of the unemployed in the unions and admission to the unions of organizations of unemployed proletarians, and for union support for the organizations, movement, and demands of the unemployed. . . .

44. The ECCI considers correct the concrete application of united front tactics practised by the Soviet communist trade unionists on the question of the Anglo-Russian committee. The combination of the greatest possible contact with the masses through the Anglo-Russian committee

with shattering condemnation of the treachery and capitulation of the right and so-called left leaders . . . can serve as an example of the correct and revolutionary application of united front tactics. The attempts made by the General Council, which helped the bourgeoisie to strangle the miners' strike, to liquidate the Anglo-Russian committee and its clearly hostile attitude to the Soviet trade unions (refusal to send a delegation to the All-Union trade union congress in Moscow, etc.) place the responsibility for what happens squarely on the shoulders of the leaders of the General Council and will help still further to expose them in the eyes of the English proletarian masses.

The struggle for international trade union unity, in which the leader was and is the Soviet unions, should gradually be internationalized, and communists everywhere must develop the work of the RILU and help to increase its influence and authority. . . .

IX. THE MAIN RESULTS OF THE WORK OF INDIVIDUAL COMMUNIST PARTIES, THEIR MISTAKES AND TASKS

45. The enlarged plenum observes that in the past year the most important section of the Communist International—the CPSU—has achieved great successes in socialist construction, strengthening the proletarian dictatorship in the USSR, strengthening the international position of the Union, giving fraternal help to the English miners and the Chinese people, and has closed its ranks by defeating the efforts of the opposition to provoke a severe internal crisis. . . .

47. The English Communist Party achieved a series of brilliant successes. . . . It greatly increased its membership, and still more its influence among the masses. It worked and is working energetically in the trade unions, and is on the road to becoming a mass revolutionary party of the proletariat. At the same time the ECCI observes that it made a number of mistakes (inadequate criticism of the 'left', incorrect formulation of the question of criticizing the General Council at the executive committee of the Minority Movement by some leading comrades, later corrected by the CC of the CPGB, incorrect appraisal of the tactics of the Soviet trade unions). The ECCI is convinced that these mistakes, in part recognized by the party and already corrected, will be fully and completely overcome. . . .

48. The Chinese Communist Party has grown in a short time into a first-class political factor in the country. While noting its successes and recognizing the general correctness of its position, the enlarged plenum points out a number of mistakes, the chief of which derive from an underestimation of the present movement, a failure to appreciate fully the necessity of the gradual introduction of agrarian reforms in those areas ruled by the Kuomintang, of satisfying other peasant demands, etc. . . .

The chief object of the Chinese Communist Party at the present moment is to rally all forces against the foreign imperialists and 'their' militarists. The subsequent tasks cannot be accomplished until this stage of the revolutionary struggle has been passed. . . .

50. The German Communist Party is becoming more and more a mass party. . . . The weak side of the party is its failure to consolidate its successes organizationally. Although it has had some success in trade union work, as a whole this is very weak. . . .

X. THE STRUGGLE FOR A LENINIST LINE AND THE PROBLEM OF LEADERSHIP

57. In assessing the 'criticism' of the CI line in the period from the beginning of the ebb of the revolutionary wave in Europe, a criticism directed against the CPSU (in the first place on the peasant question), against the 'insufferable regime' within the Comintern sections, the tactical line of the united front, etc., the enlarged plenum of the ECCI observes that these critics have either gone over completely to social-democracy (Höglund, Ström, Frossard, Paul Levi, etc.) or are on the way to doing so—either organizationally or as yet only ideologically—(Tranmael, Souvarine, Maslow, Ruth Fischer).

58. This departure from communism had its basic pivot in the world situation, the transition from a period of stormy development and triumphant advance of communism to the opening of capitalist stabilization.*

59. The struggle against these deviations as well as against right deviations . . . is an essential prerequisite for the success of the communist movement.

60. The enlarged plenum observes that the efforts of the opposition in the CPSU to create an international opposition fraction have suffered complete failure. The plenum, fully supporting the policy of the CC of the CPSU, observes that the opposition bloc, despite its declaration of 16 October, intends to continue its fractional struggle. Therefore the enlarged plenum of the ECCI considers it essential to continue the struggle against the views of the opposition, essentially anti-Leninist, and against any further attempts at fractional work. The enlarged plenum ratifies the resolution of the CC of the KPD expelling Maslow, Fischer, Urbahns, and others. The enlarged plenum is of the opinion that the Leninist teaching on the impermissibility of fractions in bolshevik parties should now be applied in full.

61. . . . The enlarged plenum resolves to take all steps necessary to establish closer connexions between the ECCI and the sections and to secure a united and firm collective international leadership.

* At the present time, stabilization, which is particularly clearly marked in Germany . . . has brought into being the so-called ultra-left deviation in Germany, turning in the case of Korsch, Schwarz, and others into outright and infamous counter-revolutionary renegacy.

EXTRACTS FROM THE RESOLUTION OF THE SEVENTH ECCI PLENUM ON
THE RUSSIAN QUESTION

15 *December* 1926   *Protokoll*, VII Plenum, p. 837

[It was the ultra-lefts in the KPD, said the ECCI report to the seventh plenum, who insisted that the Comintern should discuss the CPSU. In September 1926 they had circulated a 'declaration on the Russian question', signed by 700 KPD functionaries; on 16 September the CC of the KPD described it as an 'anti-bolshevik smear' and an attempt to split the party. The CPSU was the only item on the plenum agenda for which no commission was set up. Bukharin dealt with the question in his opening speech. 'It cannot be denied that the activity of fractional groups in the Comintern has been strongly animated by the cavalry attacks of the Russian opposition leaders on the CPSU leadership. The most diverse forces, inclined to take an anti-Comintern, indeed an anti-Soviet, position, rallied round the Russian opposition.' The attempt to form an international fraction had however failed because the opposition was defeated by the CPSU masses. Riese (KPD opposition) proposed that the plenum should invite the Russian opposition to state its views on the CPSU and the CPGB. In order to avoid the charge of a breach of discipline, this should be done through the CC of the CPSU. The Comintern was an international body, and differences of opinion should be thrashed out internationally. Thaelmann, in the chair, said that, as members and candidate members of the ECCI, Zinoviev, Kamenev, Trotsky, and Sokolnikov could appear at any time at the ECCI; Riese replied that, after what had happened, their appearance to explain their views, unless invited to do so, would be interpreted as a breach of discipline. Ercoli said that it would not be a breach of discipline for them to defend their views, but to invite them to do so would imply that the CI was split over the question of the Russian opposition. Thaelmann's proposal to pass on to the next question was agreed to unanimously. The KPD delegation disavowed Riese; his move had been a calculated political demonstration. The opposition would be defeated in the ECCI as it had been in the CPSU. On 22 November Zinoviev requested the permission of the CPSU delegation to speak at the plenum. The delegation replied that this would be tantamount to an appeal to the ECCI against the decision of the CPSU, and therefore another fractional step. Although his appearance was inexpedient, no member could be forbidden to appeal to the ECCI against his party.

The discussion on the CPSU was opened by Stalin in a three-hour speech. Disagreements in the party originated in the pressure of the bourgeoisie and bourgeois ideology on the proletariat, and the existence of various strata in the working class which provided the soil for opportunism. The various opposition trends in the CPSU were now united in one bloc because they were too weak to fight alone. The Trotskyist trend was in command because it was 'the most consummate opportunist trend of all' and was most successful in using left phrases to disguise its opportunism. After dealing with the disagreements on internal affairs, Stalin turned to the opposition in the Comintern. In the KPD and the French CP the anti-Soviet renegades based their arguments on the charges made by the CPSU opposition.

Zinoviev, speaking without CPSU permission, said that at the fifth congress the opposition had been reproached for not putting its case, although invited to do so. If he had not spoken, this would have been interpreted as reluctance on his part. He was not appealing to the ECCI against the CPSU, and he would avoid saying anything that could revive the fractional struggle. He wished to explain the questions of principle on which he disagreed with the central-committee majority. The chief one was the question of socialism in one country. Having dealt with this, he recalled that the thirteenth CPSU congress had declared that criticism should not be interpreted as the expression of fractionalism, for that in itself would force conscientious comrades into fractionalism. On many questions Lenin had formed a bloc with Trotsky on the central committee.

Pepper and Smeral attacked the opposition for disorganizing the Comintern and attempting to build a new party, and their complaints were echoed by delegates from other countries. Semard reported that one group in the French party, led by Suzanne Girault, disputed the CPSU's right to remove Zinoviev from his position in the Comintern, and protested against the decision not to allow the opposition to put its views before the next congress. Zinoviev, who spoke on 8 December, was attacked in *Pravda* the following day for having advanced an international platform to which all anti-CPSU elements could rally. Trotsky, who asked for unlimited speaking time, or at least two hours, was given one hour and interrupted when the hour was up. He too dealt with socialism in one country, and attacked Stalin for using 'biographical methods' to decide a question of principle. He too was censured by *Pravda* for continuing the fractional struggle, proving that 'an invisible anti-bolshevik, anti-Comintern bloc still exists on an international scale'. Bukharin accused the opposition of hypocritical strategy in presenting its platform, and explained that a 'Thermidor' was impossible in Russia because the proletariat, unlike the Jacobins, held the positions of economic power. Ercoli said that although the statutes gave Zinoviev and Trotsky the right to speak, they had abused it, and added: 'But there is something which is not in the statutes. That is the position of the Russian party in the International, its leading function. That goes beyond the framework of the statutes, and therefore I think the speeches of the leading opposition members must be condemned because they were an attempt to subvert the leading role of the Russian party in the International.' After Doriot, Manuilsky, Neumann, Kuusinen, Remmele, and others had spoken against the opposition, Vuyovich presented the opposition's criticism of the policy in regard to the Anglo-Russian trade union unity committee; his speech, too, was broken off by the chairman's ruling. Kamenev followed, with a speech that was constantly interrupted from the floor of the meeting. He attributed the right-wing deviation in the CPSU to Russia's position as a peasant country, to the delay in the world revolution, and to the pressure of NEP and the State apparatus. He regretted those in the KPD opposition who would not accept the severe conditions put forward by the CI, because 'a bolshevik can work and fight usefully for his class only inside the ranks of the CI, in one front with the first and still the only workers' State. He must submit even to the most severe demands of his party.' Otherwise they would be driven sooner or later into the ranks of the enemies of the Comintern and

Soviet Russia. The opposition did not deny that socialism was being built in Russia; the quarrel was about means and tempo, and about such questions as wages and housing. The statutes and programme of the CPSU and the CI would have to be rewritten if the theory of socialism in one country triumphed. NEP was strengthening the peasantry, whereas industrialization would strengthen the working class and reinforce the world revolution.

Kolarov reminded the plenum of Zinoviev's earlier opposition to Trotsky, and Zetkin marvelled at his sudden conversion to party democracy when he had been so zealous in ridding the CI of everyone who did not agree with him. She paid tribute to the past services of Trotsky, Zinoviev, and Kamenev, but said they had not justified their attitude. Several speakers, in attacking the opposition, argued that to accept the impossibility of building socialism in one country meant condemning the Russian working class to passivity.

Stalin replied to the discussion in a speech lasting three-and-a-half hours; he did not deal with the dispute as it directly affected the Comintern, except to reiterate that the opposition bloc was the kernel of a new party, which had parallel centres in other countries.]

Having examined the question of the opposition bloc in the CPSU, the seventh enlarged plenum of the ECCI resolves:

1. The opposition in the CPSU, in its ideological content, is essentially a right-wing danger to the party, frequently concealed behind left phrases.

2. The characteristic feature of the opposition is an underestimate of the internal forces of development in the Soviet Union, expressed in the denial of the possibility of socialist construction in the Soviet Union. The enlarged plenum believes that the land of the Soviets . . . has demonstrated its internationalism in deeds and has given most magnificent examples of its internationalism.

The enlarged plenum regards the accusation of national narrowness against the CPSU as a calumny. While orienting itself in all its work on the international revolution, while declaring that the final victory of socialism is possible only as the victory of the world revolution, and that only this revolution can guarantee the Soviet Union against war and intervention and still further accelerate the tempo of the Soviet Union's economic development, the CPSU is carrying through its policy of socialist construction quite correctly, in the firm conviction that the Soviet Union disposes within the country of everything that is 'necessary and sufficient' for the construction of a completely socialist society. The denial of this possibility by the opposition is nothing but a denial of the prerequisites for the socialist revolution in Russia, i.e. a social-democratic deviation.

3. From this denial follow . . . a false appraisal of the character of the State power ('far from a proletarian State'—comrade Trotsky, comrade Kamenev's statements, etc.), and finally utterances about the degeneration of the proletarian dictatorship in the CPSU into a Thermidor, which are outrageous and verge on counter-revolution.

By these wholly false and downright slanderous assertions the opposition in the CPSU is objectively supporting the enemies of the proletarian dictatorship and the renegades from communism (Korsch, Maslow, Ruth Fischer, Souvarine, the mensheviks and Social-Revolutionaries, as well as international social-democracy) in their efforts to create disbelief among the proletariat in regard to the proletarian revolution and the possibility of building socialism.

4. The enlarged plenum notes that in practice the attitude of a number of important opposition leaders concerning the most important questions of socialist construction would undermine the dictatorship and give effective support for the bourgeois elements in the country. . . .

6. . . . By taking up the struggle against the party, thereby violating the most elementary norms of party behaviour, the opposition shows that in its anti-party struggle it rejects the Leninist teaching on questions of organization, both in theory and in practice, as demonstrated by the attempt after [its utter defeat in the CPSU and even after its][1] capitulation (see the declaration of 16 October) to carry the struggle into other communist parties, and by the construction of a platform for all oppositional elements in the CI and even outside its ranks, thus doing a service to the enemies of communism.

7. For these reasons the enlarged plenum of the ECCI summons all sections of the CI to wage a resolute struggle against all attempts of the opposition in the CPSU and its adherents in other communist parties to destroy the ideological and organizational unity of the Communist International. . . . This struggle against the opposition is particularly necessary at the present moment when the imperialist States are trying to encircle the Soviet Union, when the social-democrats are supporting this movement under a cloak of pacifism, and the renegades from communism (Korsch, Schwann, and others) openly proclaim the harmfulness of defending the Soviet Union against the imperialist States. . . .

8. The enlarged plenum endorses the resolution of the fifteenth conference of the CPSU on the opposition bloc which condemned the platform and activities of the bloc as the expression of a social-democratic deviation and as endangering the unity of the CPSU.

[1] The words in brackets do not appear in the version from which this translation was made, but are to be found in the resolution as published in *Inprekorr* (vi, 157, p. 2849, 23 December 1926).

RESOLUTION OF THE SEVENTH ECCI PLENUM ON THE REPORT OF THE
ECCI

15 *December* 1926   *Protokoll*, VII Plenum, p. 839

[The ECCI report to the enlarged plenum said that the regional secretariats
had prepared 60 per cent. of the questions on the agenda at Executive and
presidium meetings, and the trade union commission 10 per cent. The secretariats were too absorbed in their own organizational work to cover general
questions such as international economic conferences, inter-allied debts, etc. A
special commission should be set up to deal with economic and political questions
international in their scope. The agitprop department had begun a systematic
study of social-democratic activities and of communist work in mass organizations, and was organizing propaganda about the construction of socialism in
the USSR. Parties which had sent workers' delegations to the Soviet Union had
been invited to list the questions asked by workers at meetings where reports
were given by members of the delegations. 'Information about the fifteenth
CPSU conference was very carefully organized.' International courses on
Leninism (the Lenin School) had been officially opened after the sixth plenum,
but most parties had not yet sent their students and regular tuition began only in
October. There were two German language groups, one English, one French,
and one Russian, with 86 students in all. For the orgdepartment it was reported
that the best material was received from countries to which an orgdepartment
instructor was attached, of which there were four. Four trainees had been sent by
the sections to the department, although the ECCI had agreed on eight. Party
organization had been discussed at 28 meetings of the orgbureau, and the
department had sent out 42 letters of instructions on these questions to different
parties. The information department had issued 304 reports on important
current questions in Russian, German, French, and English. The KPD, with a
membership of approximately 150,000, had too many street and not enough
factory cells. The French party had approximately 56,000 members, the
British 12,000—it had doubled during the past year, and each of its members
could be said to influence about 100 non-party sympathizers. The American
party had dropped, after reorganization, from 16,000 to 12,000. In Bulgaria the
party had been virtually wiped out after April 1925; a beginning had been made
to start it afresh on a factory-cell basis, but this could not be widely applied as it
was a country of small proprietors. The task of forming a capable party executive which would work in full contact and agreement with the ECCI was a
difficult one. As the party was illegal, democracy had to be sacrificed to discipline; deviations were encouraged by the white terror which isolated the rank and
file from the international movement, and by the loss of good party officials in
prison or by death. The most dangerous deviation in the Bulgarian party was
liquidationist in character. In France the chief dispute was whether the CGT
and the CGTU should merge. Some comrades alleged that the campaign for
unity was purely 'oratorical', not serious; others urged the liquidation of the
CGTU, whose members should join the CGT and strengthen its left wing, now
very weak. The party as a whole, and *L'Humanité*, did not give enough support

to the autonomy campaign in Alsace-Lorraine. Unanimity in the central committee was often bought at the price of mutual neutralization, so that no clear policy emerged. In Italy membership had declined because the party was illegal. The left wing, with a 10 per cent. representation at the last congress, had refused to accept responsible work in the party and had been suspended for one year. On 26 April 1926 the ICC considered Bordiga's request for a review of his case, and had decided that his complaints against the CC of the Italian CP were without foundation. The ECCI had endorsed this action. When factory committees were abolished by law, the party had started 'committees to defend the trade unions', in which communists constituted about half the membership. Some Italian comrades had objected that these committees would split the unions, but the ECCI had endorsed the move. In Japan the executive of the Workers' and Peasants' Party (Rodonominto), formed in March 1926, had decided to expel all communists, but the party was continuing its campaign for readmission. The Peace Preservation Law, passed in 1925, which made it an offence to conduct communist propaganda, was a severe handicap. Since the previous plenum a communist party had been founded in Korea.

The charge of opportunism against the Polish CP arose in connexion with Pilsudski's assumption of power. Pilsudski, with the support of part of the army, carried out a coup d'état on 11 May 1926, and there was fighting in Warsaw for the next two or three days. On 13 May the socialist and communist parties called a strike, but allowed the trains carrying Pilsudski's troops to run. On 15 May the Polish Government resigned, and some days later the communist deputies in the National Assembly voted for Pilsudski as President. The initial Comintern reaction was cautious. An article appeared in *Inprekorr* describing the events in Poland as the beginning of the revolutionary mass struggle against the large landowners and capitalists. The petty bourgeoisie supported Pilsudski because he embodied the idea of the national State, above classes. Many workers thought of him as a socialist because the capitalists were hostile to him. The Polish CP had called on the workers and peasants to support Pilsudski and push him further to the left, but caution was necessary because he refused to arm the workers without whom he could not have succeeded. It was not until June that the Polish CP attitude to Pilsudski changed, when Pilsudski's actions left them in no doubt about his future policy. In July the ECCI sent a long letter to the Polish CP criticizing its errors, to which the CC replied that, at the time, Pilsudski's coup appeared to have the backing of the masses and the radical intelligentsia, and to be directed against the capitalists and landlords. At the July meeting of the CC of the CPSU the opposition charged Stalin with responsibility for the Polish CP's mistake. The August meeting of the Polish CC condemned its earlier mistakes, and decided to make the campaign against Pilsudski's alleged preparations for war on the USSR the centre of its activities. The Polish Socialist Party was accused of treachery and of supporting the fascists. A minority of 4 (of a total central-committee membership of 16) wished greater emphasis to be placed on the right-wing danger in the Polish CP, and on 11 October issued a statement criticizing the August resolution.

In the National Assembly Pilsudski's candidate (Pilsudski had refused the office of President) received 292 votes against 193 with 63 abstentions (the CP voting against him); Pilsudski became War Minister, and later in the year Prime Minister.

In the ECCI report to the plenum the Polish party was said to have 'seen in Pilsudski's coup d'état a bourgeois-democratic revolution against the relics of feudalism'. Trotsky wrote that Pilsudski's movement and fascism had certain common features; one of the reasons why the Polish communist leaders (like the German) were unequal to their task was that they were constantly being changed, and sudden changes in the situation found them inexperienced and unprepared. (At the fourteenth CPSU congress Shumski said that in the Polish party they changed leaders as they changed gloves, even more frequently than in Germany.)

At the fourth Polish CP congress (held in Moscow) in September 1927 the debate on 'the May error' lasted three months. Warski was removed from the central committee and Manuilsky and Kuusinen put temporarily in charge. Bukharin at the sixth Comintern congress said: 'Had we not intervened there would now have been two Polish parties.']

The seventh enlarged plenum of the Executive takes cognizance of the report of the ECCI on its activities, approves the activities of the Executive, and expresses its confidence in it. The enlarged Executive confirms the correctness of the ECCI line in placing the great question of the international unity of the trade union movement in the foreground of its work.

The Executive has fulfilled the revolutionary duty of the Communist International in conducting international solidarity action for the general strike and the miners' strike in England.

The correctness of the Executive's tactics towards the Anglo-Russian committee has been proved by events. It would have been a great mistake to have shifted responsibility for sabotaging the international solidarity action and the British miners' strike from the shoulders of the reformist traitors on to the shoulders of the communists by breaking up the Anglo-Russian committee.

The Executive has quite rightly recognized the world-historical importance of the great Chinese revolution and has called on the proletariat to struggle against intervention by the imperialist Powers.

The enlarged Executive approves the measures taken by the Executive to prevent the fractional struggle being carried over by the opposition in the CPSU into other sections of the Communist International.

The enlarged Executive observes that the Executive correctly appraised the situation in Poland in connexion with the Pilsudski rising, and rectified the opportunist errors of the Polish party.

Energetic support for the German party in its struggle against the ultra-left fraction is also approved by the enlarged Executive, which at the same time notes that the Executive and the German party have succeeded in exposing the counter-revolutionary character of the ultra-left leadership and winning back many honest working-class elements for the Communist International.

The enlarged Executive notes with satisfaction that the Executive has made substantial progress in carrying out the decision of the sixth enlarged plenum on the collective leadership of the Communist International (permanent presence of the representatives of the most important parties in Moscow; active participation by the parties in the work of the Executive; steady growth in the politicalization of the ECCI's work; the weekly publication of the periodical *Communist International* as central organ of the ECCI). The seventh enlarged plenum calls on the Executive to give the greatest attention in its future work to eradicating fractionalism in the Communist International. The next practical step on the road to bolshevizing the Comintern sections must be the defeat of fractionalism, the creation of internally united Communist parties cut from a single block.

RESOLUTION OF THE SEVENTH ECCI PLENUM ON BRANDLER AND THALHEIMER

16 *December* 1926   *Protokoll*, VII Plenum, p. 871

[The resolution was put forward by the ICC and passed unanimously.]

Having examined the statement of comrades Brandler and Thalheimer of 20 October 1926, in which they request the annulment of the fifth enlarged Executive's decision condemning the political errors of comrades Brandler and Thalheimer and excluding them because of their fractional work from activity in the KPD and the Comintern, the International Control Commission proposes the following resolution to the seventh enlarged Executive of the CI:

'While adhering to the condemnation of the political errors of comrades Brandler and Thalheimer formulated by the fifth enlarged plenum of the ECCI, the seventh enlarged Executive observes that in the period since the fifth plenum comrades Brandler and Thalheimer have undertaken no fractional work, and have thus kept to the statement they made at the meeting of the ICC that they would refrain from any fractional activity.

'Consequently the enlarged Executive resolves to annul paras. 2 and 4 of the concluding section of the relevant resolution of the fifth enlarged Executive, in so far as it refers to comrades Brandler and Thalheimer, and to give them the opportunity of working in the Comintern. The question of using them for work in the German party is left to the discretion of the CC of the KPD.

'As to comrade Radek, this decision does not apply to him, since he has not ceased his fractional work since the fifth enlarged Executive.'

This resolution was accepted unanimously by the ICC.

EXTRACTS FROM THE RESOLUTION OF THE SEVENTH ECCI PLENUM ON
THE CHINESE SITUATION

16 *December* 1926   *Puti Mirovoi Revoliutsii*, ii, p. 435

[At the fifteenth CPSU conference in October 1926 Bukharin said that the central task in China was the fight against foreign imperialism, and therefore the
national-revolutionary united front had to be maintained. That included the
sections of the industrial and commercial bourgeoisie who did not collaborate
with imperialism. He underlined the importance of the Chinese revolution as an
example and attraction for China's colonial neighbours and for India.

The opposition in the CPSU was bitterly critical of Comintern policy in
China. In his theses for the fifteenth CPSU conference, dated 19 September
1926, Trotsky wrote that the policy towards the KMT was wholly opportunist.
Now was the time for the Chinese CP to act as an independent proletarian party,
fighting for proletarian hegemony in the struggle for national liberation. This
excluded its entry as an organization into the KMT, though it did not exclude a
long-term political bloc with that party. To the argument that the CP should
remain in the KMT because the KMT was fighting imperialism, Trotsky replied
that the criterion of its policy must be not the long-standing fact of national
oppression but the changing course of the class struggle both within Chinese
society and on the line where the Chinese classes and parties encountered foreign
imperialism. The masses were moving left, the bourgeoisie right; both competed
for influence over the petty bourgeoisie; this could not be won by manœuvres or
by good advice. The CP would gain influence as it gained in strength, and for
that it required an independent class policy. The communist struggle to lead the
national revolution to victory might not succeed, but success was unthinkable
without that independence. What class line, he wrote a few months later, could
the KMT be expected to follow when it was made up in part of the bourgeoisie
who feared and suffered from strikes, and in part of landlords who feared and
suffered from agrarian unrest? Why should a worker join the CP if it supported a
government which suppressed strikes?

The ECCI report, which gave a membership of 12,000 to the Chinese CP, of
whom 66 per cent. were said to be workers, and 5 per cent. peasants (the KMT
at this time claimed a membership of one million, the peasant unions 900,000,
and the trade unions half a million), stated that the right wing in the KMT had
accused the CCP of exploiting the national movement for its own purposes. The
CCP had made some concessions to Chiang Kai-shek in order to prevent his
alliance with the right wing. These had included an agreement that communists
should not occupy more than one-third of the offices in central and district
committees, nor the head post in any department of the KMT Executive. To
enable this agreement to be operated, the CCP had supplied the KMT with a
list of its members in the latter body. The KMT now had a 'centre' leadership,
collaborating with the left, which had isolated the right wing.

Answering the opposition at the plenum, Tan Ping-shan argued that the
KMT was not an ally of imperialism, nor had it lost the confidence of the
middle and petty bourgeoisie. It was only the right wing that had made a

common front with imperialism. The CCP and KMT must continue to work together so long as the CCP's freedom to agitate was not restricted. He referred to the difficulties created by the contradiction between the party's agrarian policy and its policy of alliance with the KMT. Bukharin thought that the CCP had paid insufficient attention to the peasants; it had not fought hard enough for agrarian reform in the areas controlled by the KMT. The imperialists might attempt to bribe the Chinese national bourgeoisie and so split the nationalist movement. Chinese communists must support the united national-revolutionary front; its success would depend on the peasantry, hence the importance of agrarian reforms and the necessity to support peasant demands. This policy, however, would repel the bourgeoisie, which made for serious difficulties. The question was discussed in commission; the right-wing tendency was represented by those who thought the peasant movement would endanger the united front, the left by Mif and others who urged the immediate formation of peasant Soviets. Mif, who worked in the Eastern department of the ECCI, had spent the greater part of 1926 in China organizing communist party schools.

In a long speech to the commission on 30 November Stalin criticized the slogan of village Soviets; this would be to outrun the movement in the cities, where Soviets were not on the agenda. He proposed instead the formation of peasant committees, under proletarian leadership, to agitate for agrarian reform. Before the plenum, in a telegram sent in October 1926, Stalin had urged the CCP to keep the peasant movement in check; Roy claims that it was his advocacy of support for the peasant movement, even though it would antagonize the bourgeoisie, which induced Stalin to modify his views. (At the end of 1927 Stalin admitted that the telegram had been a mistake.) To the proposal that the Chinese communists should withdraw from the KMT Stalin said: 'The withdrawal of the Chinese communists from the Kuomintang at the present time would be a profound mistake. The whole course, character, and prospects of the Chinese revolution undoubtedly testify in favour of the Chinese communists remaining in the Kuomintang and intensifying their work in it.' The advance of the Canton troops, he said, meant 'freedom of assembly, freedom to strike, freedom to organize for all the revolutionary elements in China in general, and for the workers in particular'. Thaelmann taunted Zinoviev for the similarity of his views to Chang Tso-lin's—both wanted the communists out of the Kuomintang. Doriot argued that for the CCP to leave the KMT would imply that the Chinese revolution was following a bourgeois and not a proletarian path. The American policy of 'winning China by kindness' would attract some bourgeois elements in the KMT. The commission agreed unanimously in favour of the CCP remaining in the KMT. When a member of the Chinese central committee, at its meeting on 13 December 1926, said: 'The KMT died on 20 March . . . why should we hold a decomposed corpse in our arms?', he was charged with left-wing deviations. Martynov wrote of the Canton committee, which was hostile to the KMT, that 'if this view were widely adopted in our party it would cause great rejoicing among the enemies of the Chinese revolution'. Roy, reporting later to the Eastern secretariat of the ECCI, said the Chinese central committee meeting which discussed the theses 'consisted of only three acting members'.

A number of press articles about this time presented elaborate analyses of the class composition of the KMT. The centre group, led by Chiang Kai-shek, was said to represent the bourgeoisie; the First People's Army, controlled by the centre, had expelled all communist officers and political commissars. The left, representing the petty-bourgeois, working class, and peasant masses, was led by Wang Ching-wei. Until May 1926 this left wing had included the CCP, but the communists now had their own separate fraction. The big bourgeoisie, wrote Tan Ping-shan, were trying to get control of the movement, reach agreement with the imperialists, and establish a bourgeois dictatorship. They feared the proletarian revolution, but 'the national revolution in China is part of the social world revolution, for victory in the national struggle to liberate China would weaken world imperialism'. Since China could only be free when its masses were free, the class struggle was a factor in the national revolution, which had to remain under proletarian leadership. Roy wrote that the future of the Chinese revolution depended on the class character of its leadership. If it were successful, China could avoid the capitalist stage of development because of the dominant role of the working class, the country's proximity to and alliance with Russia, and the decline of capitalism generally. The resolution, which Roy claims to have drafted in consultation with Bukharin and Bubnov (although he was opposed to collaboration with the bourgeoisie in China as in India), also outlined a programme for the CCP in areas controlled by the KMT; it was in fact collated from four drafts and two reports.

Trotsky wrote later that, unbelievable as it was, the resolution 'said not one word about the first counter-revolutionary coup d'état of Chiang Kai-shek in March 1926. Not one word about the shootings of workers and peasants and other repressive measures carried out by the Canton Government. . . . The troops of Chiang Kai-shek are described as a revolutionary army. . . . At approximately the same time the most responsible Russian comrades were giving advice to the effect that the development of a civil war in the country might weaken the fighting capacity of the Kuomintang. In other words, they officially forbade the development of an agrarian revolution.'

While the ECCI was in session, the National Government, in which the CCP held three posts, moved to Wuhan. When the session was over, Roy was sent to Wuhan with a number of other Comintern delegates and persuaded the Chinese communist leaders to accept the ECCI's policy.]

I. IMPERIALISM AND THE CHINESE REVOLUTION

1. The Chinese revolution is one of the most important and powerful factors disrupting capitalist stabilization. In the course of the last two years imperialism has suffered serious defeats in China, the results of which have made the world capitalist crisis far more acute. As a result of the victorious advance of the nationalist armies to north China the rule of the imperialists has been in fact broken over half the country's territory.

The further victories of the Canton revolutionary armies, supported by the broad masses of the Chinese people, will lead to victory over the imperialists, to the independence of China, and to its revolutionary unification, which will immensely enhance the forces of resistance to imperialist influence.

Sun Chuan-fang's inability to hold up the advance of the Canton armies has convinced the imperialist powers that the traditional method of using the native militarists as tools to defeat the national-revolutionary movement no longer meets the requirements of the situation. At the same time mutual rivalries prevent the imperialist powers from uniting for open military intervention. Imperialism is seeking new methods more in keeping with the new situation. The new policy shows an inclination to recognize the Canton Government; the initiative in this is being taken by American imperialism. Even England and Japan regard recognition of Canton as a permissible political step. But these are only diplomatic manœuvres hiding the hostile intentions of the imperialists towards the revolution.

2. Imperialism's basic strength in China is its virtual monopoly of the financial and industrial life of the country. . . . If it retains this base, it will find in China an important prop for stabilizing capitalism. Because of its colossal population, China offers a market with unlimited possibilities. With the necessary political guarantees, it can be a highly profitable field for investment. Its huge raw-material resources are practically untapped. Therefore imperialism will make the utmost efforts to defeat the Chinese revolution which threatens to overthrow it. . . . In the present situation imperialism prefers to intervene against the revolution by organizing civil war and financing the counter-revolutionary forces. At the moment it is trying to unite the forces of Chang Tso-lin, Wu Pei-fu, and Sun Chuan-fang to hold up the advancing national armies. . . .

3. Considered in its external aspect the Chinese revolution, because of its anti-imperialist character, forms an inseparable part of the world revolution. This state of affairs in China coincides with the following important factors favouring the further development and deepening of the Chinese revolution:

(*a*) Competition among the imperialist Powers in China, which weakens the position of world imperialism;

(*b*) the world capitalist crisis;

(*c*) the growth of the proletarian movement in Western Europe. Armed intervention in China would undoubtedly be resisted by the working class of the imperialist countries;

(*d*) the development of the national-revolutionary movement in the colonies, which will certainly become stronger as the Chinese revolution develops;

(*e*) the existence of the proletarian dictatorship in the USSR, which is geographically close to China, while the chief centres, economic, military, and political, of the imperialist Powers are geographically remote.

4. Parallel with the rapid development of the national-revolutionary movement, the social forces taking part in it are involved in a no less rapid process of regrouping.

The national revolution in China is developing in such peculiar conditions that it differs in substance both from the classic bourgeois revolutions of Western European countries in the last century, as well as from the 1905 revolution in Russia. The most significant of these peculiarities is China's semi-colonial status, its dependence on foreign imperialism. Another characteristic which distinguishes the Chinese revolution from earlier bourgeois-democratic revolutions is that it is taking place in the era of world revolution and is an inseparable part of the world movement to abolish the capitalist system. . . .

The most important peculiarity of China's economic situation today is the variety of forms existing side by side in the Chinese economy, beginning with finance-capital and ending with patriarchal survivals. . . . This determines both the weak class differentiation of the Chinese population and the low degree of organization of the basic social forces in the national revolution.

Added to this is the immense importance . . . of the disintegration of the central machinery of government and the establishment over large parts of the country of the rule of militarist organizations. . . . Their existence is conditioned by China's semi-colonial status, the dismemberment of the country, the backwardness of its economy, and the existence of vast agricultural over-population.

The development of the national-revolutionary movement in China at the present time depends on the agrarian revolution. . . . For objective reasons, the class struggle in the Chinese village has a tendency to develop in opposition to foreign imperialism and Chinese militarism, to what is left of large landownership, to the gentry and merchant money-lending capital, and in part to the kulak peasants.

5. Consequently the stage of development reached by the revolutionary movement in China is characterized by a significant regrouping of social forces. In its first stage the driving force of the movement was the national bourgeoisie and the bourgeois intelligentsia, who sought support among the proletariat and the petty bourgeoisie. In the second stage the character of the movement changed, and its social basis shifted to another class group. New and more revolutionary forms of struggle developed. The working class made its appearance on the Chinese stage as a political factor of the first order. . . . The proletariat formed a bloc with the peasants, who were taking militant action in their own interests, with the urban petty bourgeoisie, and with part of the capitalist bourgeoisie. This concentration of forces found its political expression in a corresponding grouping within the KMT and the Canton Government. At the present moment the movement

is on the road to the third stage, on the eve of a new class regrouping. At this stage of development the basic force of the movement is a bloc of a still more revolutionary character—the bloc of the proletariat, peasantry, and urban petty bourgeoisie, excluding the greater part of the big capitalist bourgeoisie. This does not mean that the entire bourgeoisie as a class stand aside from the national liberation struggle. Besides the petty and middle bourgeoisie, some forces of the big bourgeoisie may still go along with the revolution for a certain time. . . . In this period of transition the big bourgeoisie see that the [anti-]imperialist struggle, proceeding under proletarian leadership, is slipping from their control and objectively threatens their class interests. They are trying to win back their leading role with the object of crushing the revolution. They are trying to influence the revolutionary movement by using the ideology of bourgeois nationalism to counter the ideology of class struggle.

6. A parallel regrouping of the forces of the counter-revolution is taking place, closely connected with imperialist policy and under its influence, just as the development of the revolutionary forces is connected with the world revolution and is proceeding under its influence (the USSR and the world proletariat). . . . The big industrial bourgeoisie are hesitating more and more and inclining towards agreement with foreign capital, granting it the dominating role. Convinced that the militarists are no longer a wholly suitable instrument to crush the revolutionary movement, imperialism is seeking other allies within the national movement by adopting a policy of conciliation. It is trying to induce the national bourgeoisie to break with the revolutionary bloc. To strengthen the position of the imperialist agents within the ranks of the national movement, some strata of the big bourgeoisie, and even some militarists who have up to now stood aside from the national-revolutionary struggle and were even hostile to it, are beginning to go over to the side of the Canton Government. The object of this manœuvre is to wrest the leadership of the movement from the revolutionary bloc of the proletariat, peasantry, and urban petty bourgeoisie, and so arrest the development of the revolution. . . .

At this moment of transition, when the historically inevitable breakaway of the big bourgeoisie from the revolution is gradually taking place, the proletariat must clearly make as much use as possible of all those strata of the bourgeoisie which at the given moment are still in fact conducting a revolutionary struggle against imperialism and militarism.

On the other hand the proletariat and its party must tactically exploit all the contradictions among the bourgeois strata withdrawing from the revolution, and among the various imperialist groups, never losing sight of their basic aims and subordinating to them all their strategic manœuvres and tactical steps.

II. GENERAL PERSPECTIVES OF THE CHINESE REVOLUTION

7. The general perspectives of the Chinese revolution will become clear, if regarded in the light of the class groupings in both camps. Although, at this present stage of development, the Chinese revolution is historically bourgeois-democratic in nature, it is bound to acquire a broader social character. Its results will not necessarily create those socio-political conditions which lead to a capitalist development of the country. The Chinese revolution, occurring in the period of capitalist decline, is part of the universal struggle for overthrowing capitalism and establishing socialism. The structure of the revolutionary State will be determined by its class basis. It will not be merely a bourgeois-democratic State. It will represent the democratic dictatorship of the proletariat, the peasantry, and other exploited classes. It will be a revolutionary anti-imperialist government in the period of transition to non-capitalist (socialist) development.

The Chinese Communist Party should concentrate all its efforts on making a reality, in the long run, of this revolutionary perspective of transition into non-capitalist channels of development. . . .

8. The further development and prospects of the Chinese revolution depend primarily on the part played by the proletariat. The events of the last few years have shown that the fighting revolutionary national front can be organized only under proletarian leadership. . . . That is the basic principle determining the tactics of the Chinese revolution.

The feudal-militarist cliques, exercising political power in a large part of the country, represent the forces of reaction and are the agents of imperialism. The native bourgeoisie, as a class, are relatively ill-developed and weak. The economically stronger strata of the bourgeoisie (financial bourgeoisie and compradores) are so closely connected with foreign capitalism by commercial and financial ties that they have never taken any part at all in the anti-imperialist struggle. The industrial bourgeoisie went along with the national-revolutionary movement so long as it bore a purely bourgeois-democratic character, but at the first signs of revolution they either stood aside or tried to sabotage it. The petty bourgeoisie (petty-bourgeois intelligentsia, students, artisans, small traders, etc.) are in a country such as China a revolutionary factor. They played an important part in the past, and will play it in the future, but they are incapable of acting independently—they must go either with the bourgeoisie or with the proletariat. When the bourgeoisie desert the revolution or conspire against it, the exploited middle classes fall under the revolutionary influence of the proletariat. In these circumstances the moving force of the Chinese revolution at its present stage is the revolutionary bloc of the proletariat, the peasantry, and the petty bourgeoisie, the proletariat being the dominant factor in the bloc.

III. THE NATIONAL REVOLUTION AND THE PEASANTRY

9. At the present transitional stage the agrarian question begins to take on acute forms. It is the central problem of the present situation. The class which decisively tackles this basic question and is able to give a radical answer will become the leader of the revolution. In the given situation in China the proletariat is the only class able to pursue a radical agrarian policy. . . .

To overthrow the militarists for good, it is essential to develop, as part of the struggle against imperialism, the economic and political struggle of the peasantry, who form the overwhelming majority of the population. The fear that intensification of the class struggle in the village will weaken the united anti-imperialist front is unfounded. The defeat of the Second People's Army, brought about not by the forces of counter-revolution but by the rebellion of dissatisfied peasants, bears witness to the dangers inherent in this situation. If we fail to approach the agrarian question boldly, to give the required support to the practical economic and political demands of the peasant masses, the revolution is endangered. The refusal to place the question of the agrarian revolution in the foreground of the national liberation movement's programme, for fear of losing the indecisive and uncertain co-operation of one stratum of the capitalist class, is incorrect. . . . The communist party must not make such mistakes.

10. The specific peculiarity of the present situation is its transitional character, when the proletariat has to choose between a prospective bloc with large strata of the bourgeoisie and reinforcing its alliance with the peasantry. If the proletariat does not advance a radical agrarian programme it will not be able to draw the peasantry into the revolutionary struggle and will lose the hegemony of the national liberation movement. Under direct or indirect imperialist influence, the bourgeoisie will again begin to play a leading part. In the present situation this would strengthen the position of foreign capital in China, and promote capitalist stabilization.

The Canton National Government will not be able to retain power in the revolution, will not achieve complete victory over imperialism and native reaction, so long as the cause of national emancipation is not identified with the agrarian revolution. . . .

11. While recognizing . . . land nationalization as the basic demand of a proletarian agrarian programme, the Chinese Communist Party must at the present time differentiate its agrarian tactics and adapt them to the economic and political peculiarities in different parts of China. . . .

In territory under the Kuomintang National Government the programme of agrarian revolution should be given practical form. The Chinese Communist Party and the Kuomintang should immediately carry out the following measures to draw the peasantry over to the side of the revolution:

(a) maximum reduction of rents;

(b) abolition of the various forms of taxes weighing on the peasantry and their replacement by a single progressive agricultural tax. . . .

(d) confiscation of church and monastery lands, and of land belonging to reactionary militarists and compradores, and those landlords and gentry who are waging civil war against the Kuomintang National Government;

(e) securing to tenants the right to a perpetual lease on the plots of land they cultivate. . . .

(f) all-round support by the Canton Government of peasant interests; in particular, protection of the peasants against oppression and persecution by landlords, gentry, and usurers;

(g) disarming the Min Yuan and all other landlord forces;

(h) arming the poor and middle peasants and subordinating all armed forces in the village to the local agencies of the revolutionary Government;

(i) maximum support by the Government for all peasant organizations, including the Peasant Unions;

(j) provision of cheap government credits, fight against the usurers, support of peasant mutual-aid associations;

(k) government help for co-operatives and mutual-aid associations.

12. It is the task of the communist party to get these measures put into operation by the Canton Government as steps towards a more developed phase of the agrarian revolution. This highly important task will be carried out by creating peasant committees under communist leadership. As the revolution develops, the peasant committees will acquire the authority and strength required to fulfil the demands enumerated above and to reinforce the struggle, advancing more radical demands. . . .

In the parts of the country still controlled and ruled by reactionary militarists, the communist party must lead the peasants in the fight against feudalism, militarism, and imperialism. Work among the peasantry . . . is the surest way to distintegrate the reactionary armies. Communists should make use of every peasant organization that springs up spontaneously, such as the 'Red Lances', and strengthen communist influence in them.

13. The peasants' attitude to the revolution is determined largely by the conduct and actions of the national armies. . . . It is true that the peasantry everywhere welcomed the revolutionary army with enthusiasm, but it is equally true that this enthusiasm declined in the course of time. The demands of a prolonged and difficult military campaign mean new burdens for the peasants. The enthusiasm with which they greeted the

revolutionary armies will be made strong and firm if the communists and other revolutionary elements leading the movement realize that the peasantry must be compensated for their temporary burdens by a correct and bold agrarian policy. . . .

IV. THE COMMUNIST PARTY AND THE KUOMINTANG

14. The imperative necessity of gaining influence among the peasantry also determines the attitude of the communist party to the Kuomintang and the Canton Government. The machinery of the national-revolutionary Government provides an extremely effective channel for approaching the peasantry, and the communist party must make use of it. In the recently liberated provinces a State apparatus of the Canton type will be established. The task of communists and their revolutionary allies is to permeate the new government apparatus in order to give practical expression to the agrarian programme of the national revolution. This can be achieved by using the State machine to confiscate lands, lower taxes, and give real powers to the peasant committees, thus gradually introducing reforms based on a revolutionary programme.

15. For this and many other equally cogent reasons, the idea that the communist party should abandon the Kuomintang is mistaken. The entire process of development of the Chinese revolution, its character, and its prospects demand that the communists stay in the Kuomintang and reinforce their work in it. In order to intensify their activities in the ranks of the Kuomintang with the object of influencing the further development of the revolutionary movement, communists must enter the Canton Government. Since the establishment of the Canton Government, real power in it has been in the hands of the right-wing Kuomintang (of six commissars, five belong to the right wing). Although the Canton Government could not exist without the support of the working class, the workers' and peasants' movement even in Kwantung province has had to overcome various obstacles. The most recent events have shown that the communists ought to enter the Government in order to support the revolutionary left wing in its struggle against the feeble and hesitating policy of the right. The extension of the Canton Government's power to large areas gives this question of communist participation in the National Government greater urgency than ever.

16. The Communist Party of China should seek to make the Kuomintang a genuinely national party, a firm revolutionary bloc of the proletariat, the peasantry, the urban petty bourgeoisie, and other oppressed strata who are waging an energetic struggle against imperialism and its agents. To do this the communist party should take action in the following directions:

(*a*) Systematic and resolute struggle against the right wing in the Kuomintang . . . and their attempts to transform the Kuomintang into a bourgeois party;

(*b*) consolidate the left wing and establish close collaboration with it, without attempting to get the leading positions in it for communists;

(*c*) consistent criticism of the centre, wavering between the right and the left wing, between the further development of the revolution and compromise with imperialism.

V. THE TASKS OF THE CHINESE REVOLUTION AND THE CHARACTER OF THE REVOLUTIONARY GOVERNMENT

17. Lenin wrote: 'Before the epoch of world revolution, the movements for national liberation formed part of the general democratic movement; now, however, after the victory of the Soviet revolution in Russia and the opening of the era of world revolution, the movement for national liberation forms part of the world proletarian revolution.'

The programme of the Chinese revolution and the structure of the revolutionary State which it creates should be determined from this point of view. The process of class differentiation which accompanies the development of the revolutionary movement confirms this conception. The Canton Government, despite its bourgeois-democratic character, basically and objectively contains within itself the germ of a revolutionary petty-bourgeois State, of the democratic dictatorship of the revolutionary bloc of proletariat, peasantry, and urban petty bourgeoisie. The petty-bourgeois democratic movement is becoming revolutionary in China because it is an anti-imperialist movement. The Canton Government is a revolutionary one primarily in virtue of its anti-imperialist character. Being, above all, anti-imperialist, the Chinese revolution and the Government which it has created must strike at the very root of imperialist power in China. Rejection of unequal treaties and abolition of territorial concessions are not enough to shatter imperialism's position. The blow must be dealt at the economic foundations of imperialist power. This means that the revolutionary Government must gradually nationalize the railways, concessions, factories, mines, banks, and other undertakings owned by foreign capital. By these acts it will quickly extend the narrow limits of bourgeois democracy and enter the stage of transition towards revolutionary dictatorship. It would thus be a mistake to restrict the tasks of the Chinese revolution to (1) the defeat of imperialism, and (2) the liquidation of feudal survivals, on the ground that in its early stages this revolution has a petty-bourgeois character. The Chinese revolution cannot defeat imperialism without overstepping the limits of bourgeois democracy. In existing conditions the proletariat will lead the peasantry to revolutionary struggle. The movement to liquidate feudalism, proceeding under proletarian hegemony, must necessarily turn into an agrarian revolution.

Because of these peculiar circumstances, the tasks of the Chinese revolution are:

(*a*) To nationalize the railways and water transport;

(*b*) to confiscate all large undertakings, mines, and banks which fall into the category of foreign concessions; and

(*c*) to nationalize the land, by means of a series of radical reforms put into operation by the revolutionary State.

VI. THE COMMUNIST PARTY AND THE PROLETARIAT

18. To play the leading role in the revolution, the Chinese proletariat must strengthen its class organizations, political and industrial. The first task of the communist party is to organize and educate for this historical role. The small numbers and youth of the Chinese proletariat should be compensated by a high level of organization and the clarity of its ideology.

The trade union federation, embracing hundreds of thousands of industrial workers, as well as the national unions of railwaymen and seamen, are the basis for the communist party. The immediate task of the CP should be to strengthen these organizations by drawing the broad working masses into them. In the course of the national-revolutionary struggle in these last two years the working class has developed tremendous strength; it has won hegemony in the revolutionary movement. . . .

19. In order to draw the working-class masses into the movement and strengthen its position in the national revolution, the Chinese Communist Party should agitate for the following demands:

(*a*) complete liberty of action for revolutionary peasants' and workers' organizations, legalization of trade unions, introduction of advanced laws on trade unions, the right to strike;

(*b*) labour legislation: the eight-hour day, the six-day week, minimum wages;

(*c*) social legislation: inspection of health and labour conditions; the housing question; insurance for sickness, old age, invalidity, unemployment; protection of female and child labour; prohibition of night work for women; prohibition of labour in factories for children under fourteen;

(*d*) establishment of factory inspection;

(*e*) abolition of the system of fines and corporal punishment;

(*f*) removal of all kinds of military or police detachments from factory buildings;

(*g*) fight against unemployment: inclusion of the unemployed within the trade unions, organization of trade union employment exchanges. . . .

VII. ORGANIZATIONAL TASKS OF THE CHINESE COMMUNIST PARTY

21. The Communist Party of China is an organized force. It has leaders, is creating its cadres, and has mass support. The work of the CP has already assumed fairly substantial proportions and stable organizational forms. In the last six months it has made great advances in expanding its ranks, this growth being largely of working-class elements.

There are too few peasants in the party; nevertheless the party is already conducting work among the peasantry on an expanding scale.

One of the most important tasks now confronting the party is to extend and deepen, improve and strengthen its work of training the party membership. . . . One of the most important tasks of the party is the struggle for its open existence.

22. New members must be recruited, particularly in industrial areas. . . . The best working-class members of the party must be drawn into leading party work. Persistent work must be done to enlarge and strengthen party cadres. Special attention must be paid to training cell secretaries, fraction leaders in mass organizations, the leading personnel in district party committees. The CC and district committees should have permanent travelling instructors drawn from the best local party workers.

EXTRACTS FROM THE RESOLUTION OF THE SEVENTH ECCI PLENUM ON THE EXPULSION OF MASLOW, RUTH FISCHER, URBAHNS, SCHOLEM, AND SCHWANN FROM THE GERMAN COMMUNIST PARTY

16 *December* 1926   *Puti Mirovoi Revoliutsii*, ii, p. 465

[The affairs of the German party received much attention in the ECCI report. The organization department stated that of the 42 directives it had sent out, 15 were to the KPD. Maslow, who had been released from prison in Germany in July 1926, had refused several invitations to come to Moscow. Ruth Fischer had returned to Germany from Moscow without Comintern permission. The KPD central committee had therefore on 19 August expelled them (against the votes of Urbahns, Weber, and Schimansky) on charges of anti-party conspiracy with Korsch on a counter-revolutionary programme, and the expulsion had been endorsed on 26 August by 83 votes to 7 at a conference of political secretaries and editors of the KPD. They were now working with Korsch and Schwarz, whose expulsion from the KPD had been ratified by the ECCI on 22 June 1926, to split the KPD. Their expulsion was ratified by the ECCI on 28 August. In the subsequent discussion it was reported that a letter had been received from Maslow, Fischer, Scholem, Urbahns, and Schwann asking to be heard at the next congress. The terms of the telegram sent in reply were suggested by the KPD delegation:

'Message to be handed individually to each of the following: Maslow, Ruth Fischer, Urbahns, Scholem, Schwann: The presidium of the plenum has re-

ceived your communication of 16 November in which you appeal to the enlarged Executive against your expulsion. This communication, which is in full
accord with your practical political attitude in the last few months, contains the
strongest and most hostile anti-communist attacks on the Comintern and its
German section. Nevertheless the presidium of the enlarged Executive has
decided, at the suggestion of the German delegation, to give you the statutory
opportunity to appear before the seventh enlarged Executive to make your
appeal in person. The five signatories of the communication of 16 November
are hereby invited to appear immediately, without delay and without excuse,
before the Executive in Moscow. If you attach importance to the consideration
of your protest, you must begin the journey within twenty-four hours (at the
latest within forty-eight), otherwise the plenum will be compelled to discuss
and decide the question in your absence.' All accepted the invitation to appear
except Maslow, who was a Russian citizen. 'He has more confidence in the
German Embassy than in the proletarian State', said Remmele. On 31 July
1926 *Pravda* carried a Tass report from Berlin that the German authorities had
granted Maslow's request for the non-execution of the order deporting him
from Germany because he would be useful to them in building fractions within,
and so weakening, the KPD. Kuusinen, who reported on the meeting with the
expelled KPD members, referred to their 'contemptible hypocrisy and double
dealing'. Their request to be heard by the plenum was refused. They had defended Maslow's refusal to come to Moscow, since he might not be allowed to
return to Germany. The commission had answered that they had only moral,
not physical means at their disposal. When asked whether they were prepared
to recognize the validity and binding character of the ECCI decision on their
position, they had replied that they were prepared to carry out and support
every party decision, but not to change their views. On all Russian questions
they had agreed with the opposition in the CPSU, and said they could see
nothing wrong in trying to win back expelled members when the CI itself was
trying to win the social-democrats. The commission had come to the conclusion
that they were already on the other side of the barricades. Dengel said that after
the open letter (August 1925) it would have been easy to liquidate the KPD
opposition had it not been for the support it received from the Russian opposition. With no platform of its own, it had adopted the opposition platform;
objectively, it had forwarded the policy of German imperialism.]

In connexion with the written protest of 16 November 1926 of Maslow,
Ruth Fischer, Urbahns, Scholem, and Schwann against their expulsion
from the KPD, the seventh enlarged plenum appointed a commission to
investigate the case of these five persons. The commission, to whose
sessions the KPD delegation were invited, consisted of the following comrades: Kuusinen (chairman), Humbert-Droz (secretary), Birch (America),
Bell (England), Semard (France), Haken (Czechoslovakia), Furubotn
(Norway), Piatnitsky (USSR), Prukhniak (Poland), Ercoli (Italy),
Katayama (Japan), Stuchka (chairman of ICC). The commission took
verbal evidence from the appellants, with the exception of Maslow, and

reviewed the written material relating to their expulsion. After a thorough examination of the case the commission submits for ratification by the seventh plenum the following resolution:

1. The political group of appellants has been in conflict with the Communist International more than once. Not to mention earlier disputes, the present conflict was studied specially by an ECCI commission appointed in the autumn of 1925, and on its recommendation the ECCI sent an open letter to all members and organizations of the KPD. Representatives of the most important parties pointed out at the time that the Maslow–Ruth Fischer group had entered on the path of struggle against the Comintern. Even comrade Zinoviev at that time said of the leaders of this group that they were 'rabid elements, of whom some will tomorrow be found on the other side of the barricades'. The sixth enlarged plenum, meeting in March 1926, said in its resolution on the German question that the Maslow–Ruth Fischer group 'is a reflection of the moods of a ruined and decaying petty bourgeoisie' and that it was 'politically, organizationally, and morally bankrupt'.

2. The development of this group since the last enlarged plenum and in particular its statements in the commission of the seventh enlarged plenum have completely confirmed these assertions. On no single point did the appellants depart from their anti-communist views and their anti-party actions. The commission came to the conclusion that the appellants attempted by systematic fractional work to disorganize the party, to hamper its revolutionary work, and undermine its campaigns among the masses. . . . In their contacts, political and organizational, with the Korsch group their aim was to split the party. After their expulsion from the KPD they did not surrender their mandates as deputies, despite their undertaking, but usurped them from the communist party in order to join formally the parliamentary fraction of Korsch, Schwarz, and Katz under the false name of 'left communists'. Their speeches in the commission showed with the utmost clarity that they are not communists and not fighters in the workers' movement, but merely renegades of the proletarian revolution. . . . They made the outrageous statement in the commission that Maslow could not come to the USSR since neither he nor they had enough trust in the organs of the Soviet Government. Finally these renegades resorted in the commission of the enlarged plenum to insolent threats to compromise the KPD by means of certain 'revelations'.

3. The anti-communist development through which the Maslow–Ruth Fischer group has passed is far from being accidental, but is connected with the turn in the foreign policy of rising German imperialism and with the fact that since Germany's entry into the League of Nations and its acceptance of the clauses providing for the passage of troops in the event of intervention, the policy of the German bourgeoisie has become more

and more hostile to the Soviet Union. . . . Influenced by this bourgeois orientation, a basis was created among certain wavering strata of the proletariat for anti-Soviet and anti-Comintern groups, which—with the specific object of introducing confusion into the ranks of the revolutionary workers—are forced to cover their counter-revolutionary struggle against the communist movement by 'left' pseudo-communist phrases. . . .

5. The debates in the commission of the seventh enlarged plenum again showed that the appellants are altogether lost to the revolutionary movement and the workers' movement as a whole. The commission . . . unanimously concluded that the views and actions of the appellants are in conflict with the programme and principles of the Communist International (hostile attitude to the KPD, the Comintern, and the Soviet Union). The commission further observed that the conduct of the appellants violates the statutes of the CI . . . they did not deny that they have no intention of ceasing their fractional activity. They adhere to the view that a communist is not obliged to appear at the summons of the International Control Commission to answer grave accusations touching on his honour (of doing injury to the revolutionary movement—Maslow's unworthy conduct before a bourgeois court). By their conduct the appellants have shown that the reasons which made the ECCI presidium endorse their expulsion from the party by the CC of the KPD were well founded.

6. On the basis of these facts the commission resolves to propose that the seventh enlarged plenum

(a) ratifies the expulsion of Maslow, Ruth Fischer, Urbahns, Scholem, and Schwann from the KPD and the Comintern;

(b) calls on all conscious members of the party devoted to the cause of communism to sever all political and organizational bonds with these agents of the class enemy and to fight them as relentlessly as all other social-traitors.

RESOLUTION OF THE SEVENTH ECCI PLENUM ON BORIS SOUVARINE

16 *December* 1926   *Puti Mirovoi Revoliutsii*, ii, p. 470

[In the name of the CPGB, Murphy moved the final endorsement of Souvarine's expulsion for counter-revolutionary propaganda. He was supported by the French delegation, who said that they wished also to disavow Suzanne Girault, although she, like Trotsky, was a candidate member of the ECCI, and the French party could not change that until the next congress. The resolution was passed unanimously. Treint and Girault were known as Zinoviev's supporters, and had replaced Souvarine and Rosmer in the French CP when the latter were expelled for their support of Trotsky. Leadership in the French party was subsequently taken over by Doriot and Thorez.]

The seventh enlarged plenum resolves:

1. To exclude Boris Souvarine finally from the ranks of the Communist International for counter-revolutionary propaganda.

2. The paper of the Monatte–Rosmer group, *Révolution Prolétarienne*, for which Boris Souvarine writes, is to be regarded as counter-revolutionary.

3. To propose to the CC of the CPSU formally to forbid any member of the CPSU to have any dealings with Boris Souvarine in whatever capacity.

4. To forbid all communists to collaborate in any way, literary or otherwise, with the Monatte–Rosmer group or the journal *Révolution Prolétarienne*.

EXTRACTS FROM THE RESOLUTION OF THE SEVENTH ECCI PLENUM ON THE SITUATION IN THE COMMUNIST PARTY OF GERMANY*

7 January 1927   *Puti Mirovoi Revoliutsii*, ii, p. 46

[The KPD report to the seventh plenum stated that the anti-war campaign had been carried out in Germany in terms of opposition to German entry into the League of Nations, and that such events as sports matches between Russian and German teams were 'frequently converted, under the leadership of the party, into demonstrations for the Soviet Union'. At the plenum Bukharin said that the westward orientation in official German policy, which was basically anti-Soviet, was reflected in the 'anti-Muscovism' of the communist renegades.

The German opposition's strongest support came from Wedding, a working-class district of Berlin. There, as elsewhere in the KPD, there was uneasiness about Soviet military collaboration with the Reichswehr, a question raised in the Reichstag in December 1926.]

1. The unrelenting fractional struggle of the ultra-left leaders compelled the KPD in the last year to concentrate a great part of its attention and forces on defending party unity and a correct Leninist party line from encroachments of the ultra-left wing. In this internal struggle the German party, under the leadership of the present CC, has already had some success of a decisive character, to wit:

(*a*) The threat of a party split, which was the object of the hostile fractions, has been averted, and now the very idea of the formation of a new ultra-left party seems completely absurd.

(*b*) The worst disorganizers—such as Katz, Korsch, Schwarz, Ruth Fischer, Maslow, Scholem, etc., who tried to disrupt the party under cover of left phrases and by using openly anti-communist slanders—have been politically exposed, and after their expulsion from the party lost the confidence of all communist workers.

* Adopted by the presidium of the ECCI on 7 January 1927 on the instruction of the plenum.

(c) The overwhelming majority of the party has grasped the correctness of the line of the CC and the ECCI. Many honest revolutionary left workers, who formerly believed in the ultra-left leaders, have now been won over to the side of the party and the Comintern.

During the discussion within the party a broad explanatory campaign was carried on among all the members down to the smallest organization and the most insignificant factory group, in which such problems as the proletarian dictatorship in the USSR and the basic questions of the German revolution and the most important tasks of the KPD in the present period were put more clearly and sharply than ever before in any preceding discussion within the KPD.

2. Thus the most difficult part of the task of defeating the ultra-left opposition has been accomplished by the KPD. The final results are clear. It is now obvious to everybody that the ultra-left opposition within the KPD will be completely liquidated in the near future. But at the present moment, despite the weakness and fragmentation of the ultra-left opposition, an ultra-left mood and false views are found among some of the party's working-class members, though they are few. Although these workers have no confidence in the expelled fraction and have never wanted to break with the party, they have still not broken finally with some wavering oppositional groups. . . .

3. On the most important questions of principle the 'Wedding opposition' leaders are carrying on a fractional agitation which differs little in content from the anti-communist agitation of the expelled enemies of the party. For example they spread the lie about the degeneration of the proletarian dictatorship in the USSR and its 'appeasement' of the kulaks and Nepmen. They spread the slander that the Comintern is pursuing a 'liquidationist' policy, that it has betrayed the English strike and even the international revolution. . . . Last summer and autumn, under the influence of the blindly fractional attacks of the Russian opposition and the conscienceless anti-communist campaign of such anti-party elements as Korsch, Schwarz, Ruth Fischer, and Maslow, they inclined to the idea that in the fraction's war against the leadership of their own party and the Comintern, any slander is good, any weapon permissible. . . .

4. It is obvious however that the 'Wedding opposition' is different from the group of Fischer, Urbahns, Korsch, and Schwarz. The latter have simply become renegades and enemies of the party, deliberately aiming at the disruption of the KPD. The 'Wedding opposition' has recognized the limits of the party statutes and, at least in principle, observed a minimum of party discipline. . . .

5. At the same time all comrades in the 'Wedding opposition' are obliged to take note that a continuation of their fractional struggle can objectively only do harm to the communist movement, for all enemies of

the party, from the bourgeoisie and right-wing social-democrats to the expelled ultra-left leaders, are trying to use their fractional agitation to deal a blow at the KPD, just as the social-democratic leaders are trying to use the Trotskyist views of the Russian opposition (disseminated by the Wedding group too) as 'arguments' in their anti-Soviet and anti-communist campaign. The ultra-left 'expressions of solidarity' with Trotskyism can serve no one except the enemies of Soviet Russia and the Comintern....

6. Therefore the primary communist duty of the 'Wedding opposition' is to cease its fractional work and to adhere loyally to the united militant front of the KPD. . . . Its leaders must break their connexions once and for all with elements expelled from the party and hostile to it. . . . If they do not break with these disorganizers and do not submit to the decisions of the KPD and the Comintern, they will bear the entire responsibility for the consequences of their conduct.

EXTRACTS FROM AN ECCI PROTEST AGAINST UNITED STATES INTERVENTION IN LATIN AMERICA

29 *January* 1927   *Inprekorr*, vii, 13, p. 255, 1 *February* 1927

[A further ECCI manifesto, published early in February, protested against the occupation of Nicaragua by United States forces. This was described as an episode in the subjugation of the whole of Latin America, and in Anglo-American rivalry for control of the area. Mexico had set an example of resistance, and the Nicaraguan people had now risen against Diaz, the creature of the USA. At the fifth CI congress in 1924 it had been decided to set up a South American secretariat; this was done in the summer of 1925. Headquarters were at Buenos Aires, under Penelon, secretary of the Argentine CP and member of the ECCI. In December 1926 the Argentine party reported that it had 2,700 members, a full-time headquarters staff of 9, and 3 full-time regional organizers. The League against Imperialism (originally called the League of Oppressed Peoples) was organized in February 1926, and formally established at its first congress in Brussels a year later. Münzenberg reported that there were branches in Germany, France, Britain, and North, South, and Central America, and that one was being formed in India. It published a quarterly review in Berlin. The 174 delegates at the congress, who included Semaoen, Nehru, Fimmen, Lansbury, Hatta, Pollitt, claimed to represent 134 organizations. In the resolutions of the congress, all of which were passed unanimously, the working classes in imperialist countries were urged to support all movements for national independence, to demand the withdrawal of foreign troops from China, the abolition of unequal treaties, etc. The Comintern delegation was led by Lominadze.]

The United States army is occupying Nicaragua. North American imperialism is discarding its democratic mask, and openly and cynically proclaiming its intention of turning the countries of Latin America into colonies. It took possession long ago of the natural wealth, the industry, and the transport of Central and South America, and brought their governments into industrial and financial dependence. . . .

The workers and peasants of Mexico were the first to come out against United States oppression. Moved by steady mass pressure, the Mexican Government proclaimed its country's right to dispose of its own oil resources, in reply to which the Washington Government threatened military intervention.

The example of the Mexican people is drawing the other peoples of Central America into the struggle against North American imperialist exploitation. The people of Nicaragua rose against their 'President' Diaz, the creature of American capital. The United States fears a second Mexico. It intends to cut a canal through Nicaragua and wants therefore to bring the entire country into subjection. The occupation of Nicaragua on the pretext of protecting the lives of American citizens is also designed to intimidate Mexico.

To the protests from Latin America and from large sections in North America the Secretary of State, Kellogg, replied that intervention was necessary for the fight against bolshevism and the Third International, to save civilization. The whole world is laughing at the Philistine who conjures up the bolshevik spectre to conceal the robber plans of Yankee imperialism.

The Communist International has always fought imperialism, not excluding the strongest and most shameless of the imperialists, the United States. It calls on all anti-imperialist forces to support the small Nicaraguan nation. . . . The League of Nations reveals itself once more as defender of the interests of the big imperialist Powers, and is silent. The Second International is also silent.

The struggle of the peoples of Latin America for independence . . . is only a part of the universal struggle of the oppressed peoples against their imperialist oppressors, in which China, India, and Central America occupy the central positions. . . .

The proletariat of North America must protest against American imperialism. The workers and peasants of the entire world must demonstrate their solidarity with the small Nicaraguan people. Down with United States imperialism.

EXTRACTS FROM AN ECCI LETTER TO THE ELEVENTH CONGRESS OF
THE GERMAN COMMUNIST PARTY

February 1927   *Inprekorr*, vii, 25, p. 511, 4 *March* 1927

[The eleventh congress of the KPD was held in Essen from 1 to 7 March 1927. Kuusinen attended on behalf of the ECCI. The minority had 10 delegates out of a total of 186. Of these, three were Reichstag deputies; they were expelled, but did not surrender their parliamentary mandates. Jansen reported for the KPD delegation to the ECCI. He lumped Chamberlain, the SPD, and the party opposition together as enemies of the Soviet Union. Dengel and Ewert reported for the central committee; since the expulsion of Fischer, Maslow, and their followers, relations between the KPD and the Comintern and other CI parties had been good, and democracy within the party had been almost completely restored. At the previous congress, the ultra-left had tried to substitute 'West European communism' for Leninism, to split the KPD and the CI, and to start new organizations. 'We know that any attempt to establish a so-called West European communism leads to the reformist camp.' Stresemann's 'western orientation' put defence of the USSR in the forefront of KPD policy. 'Our entire policy must be built on the basis of our doing everything, to the end, for the Soviet Union.' As to Brandler and Thalheimer, the central committee had decided that, since they had not abandoned their views (though obeying the resolution against fractional activity), they could for the present be used only for literary work. They could resume political work once they had given up their erroneous views.

A letter to the congress was sent at the same time by the central committee of the CPSU, referring to the threat from Britain, and urging firmness and unity in eliminating the ultra-left sickness of the KPD, which kept the party from the masses and drove them into anti-Soviet social-democratic policies. In the 'platform of the opposition' submitted to the central committee of the CPSU in September 1927 Trotsky wrote that the left in the KPD were being forced by Stalin and his followers into forming a second party, their place being taken by 'downright adventurers' like Heinz Neumann.]

The eleventh congress of our German section coincides with an exceptional historical situation. Notwithstanding all the prattle of the social-democratic theoreticians and leaders about new and 'peaceful' forms of capitalism, the international situation has again become extremely acute. The United States, which is not a member of the League of Nations, is in fact waging an imperialist war against Nicaragua. . . . Countries which do belong to the League, in the first place England, whose ships are bombarding revolutionary Chinese cities with their long-range guns, are concentrating strong forces in China for a spring offensive against the fighting Chinese people. . . .

The Soviet Union, to which fighting China looks as an example of the liberation of the peoples from the yoke of native and alien imperialists, is again being attacked by His Majesty's Government. Chamberlain's aggressive note has created a tense situation throughout Europe. The Second International, which in this case too protests hypocritically against war, is in reality conducting an energetic campaign to prepare for intervention against the Soviet Union. . . .

The 'left' social-democratic leaders in Germany and a few trade union leaders are now trying to manœuvre. The Communist Party of Germany must understand the situation correctly. It must keep in its own hands the initiative in creating working-class unity. This is particularly important in the trade unions, whose activities will inevitably assume a political character. The KPD must everywhere expose the coalition policy of the social-democratic bosses, who have sold the German revolution to the bourgeois bloc. The KPD must really defend peace, and relentlessly expose and condemn the interventionist policy of the social-democratic leaders. . . .

The KPD can accomplish the immense tasks imposed on it only if it at last closes its ranks and adopts a correct Leninist platform, the platform of untiring and systematic struggle for the masses.

Now even the blind can grasp the part objectively played and still being played by the group of renegades from Katz to Maslow. Their attacks on the Soviet Union and the CPSU were merely part of that attempt to influence 'public opinion' which has now found its expression in Chamberlain's note. . . .

In the fight against right and ultra-left opportunist deviations the glorious German detachments of the international communist army will steel their ranks and become greater.

EXTRACTS FROM AN ECCI APPEAL AGAINST IMPERIALIST INTERVENTION IN CHINA

27 *March* 1927   *Inprekorr*, vii, 34, p. 725, 29 *March* 1927

[When the nationalist armies reached Nanking there was a good deal of looting in the city, and a number of foreign missionaries and consular officials were killed. The city was bombarded by British and United States gunboats on 24 March, and a number of Chinese civilians were killed. An article in *Inprekorr* explained this as a covering action to facilitate the retirement of the northern armies and the white guards. After Chiang's coup against the communists in April, Stalin wrote that 'the Nanking massacre served . . . as a signal for a new demarcation of the contending forces in China. In bombarding Nanking and presenting an ultimatum, the imperialists desired to make it known that they were seeking the support of the national bourgeoisie for a joint struggle against the Chinese revolution.' The United States was accused of encouraging England to intervene, this being presented as payment for the latter's benevolent neutrality in regard to American action in Nicaragua and Panama. An earlier ECCI appeal, dated 28 January, had called for action to stop the dispatch of forces to China and for the recognition of the Canton Government.]

A great and inhuman crime has been committed. 'Civilized' barbarians, with the English and American imperialists at their head, have by long-range bombardment destroyed and annihilated Nanking, one of the principal cities of the Chinese republic. The working-class districts have been flattened out, the corpses heaped mountain high. Some thousands of peaceful Nanking citizens have been shot . . . all because the latest victories of the Chinese revolution endangered imperialist rule in China. The Anglo-American command has sought to justify this monstrous crime organized by the imperialist marauders by the most barefaced lies. The executioners of the Chinese people who wear the uniform of so-called civilized Powers are circulating the contemptible and provocative story of attacks by the revolutionary troops on foreigners, the demolition of foreign consulates, etc. . . . . They know only too well that it was the retreating Shantung troops, the allies of foreign counter-revolution, China's native executioners, who lost their heads and fired the shots. But they need this dirty and bloody story to cover their own outrages and to justify in advance the outrages they intend to commit. . . .

The English Conservatives, who were negotiating with Canton, have at one stroke thrown off the mask of sham piety and hypocrisy and again exposed themselves to all workers, and particularly to the Chinese people, as ruthless robbers. . . . The United States, which was flirting with the national movement, making advances to the Chinese revolution, suddenly laid aside the rosy veil and demonstrated its military prowess by mass murder, by demolishing and plundering Chinese cities.

We must look the truth in the face. England and America have started a war against the Chinese people. . . . The hypocritical lies of the bourgeoisie and social-democrats that the imperialist troops were sent to China 'to protect women and children' are now exposed in all their repulsiveness. The imperialist troops were sent to China to protect the profits of the imperialists, to strangle the Chinese revolution. . . .

The Executive Committee of the Communist International calls on all workers, on all labouring people, all enemies of imperialist violence, all the oppressed to raise the banner of protest against this new executioners' war. . . . It calls on all the colonial and oppressed peoples of the world to make their decisive protest against imperialist violence in China. . . . It appeals to workers' organizations throughout the world to fight vigorously against this new war. . . .

Comrades, ten years ago the international bourgeoisie, led by England, tried to overthrow the workers' government in former Tsarist Russia. . . . Now, ten years later, the Chinese people have risen, and international capital, led by England and America, is out to crush them. These 'Christians' may slaughter thousands and ten of thousands, but they cannot strangle a people of 500 million who have raised the banner of freedom.

EXTRACTS FROM AN ECCI STATEMENT ON CHIANG KAI-SHEK'S
ANTI-COMMUNIST COUP

15 *April* 1927   *Inprekorr*, vii, 41, p. 859, 16 *April* 1927

[Chiang turned openly against his allies after his troops had taken over Shanghai in the course of the 'northern expedition'. Borodin and Blücher are said to have disapproved of the march on Shanghai, favouring a halt when the expedition reached the Yangtse.

A Comintern delegation consisting of Doriot, Tom Mann, and Browder, which had toured the areas through which Chiang's armies had passed and was informed of KMT attacks on local workers' organizations, apparently said nothing about this until after the break between the two parties.

Chiang's entry into Shanghai was facilitated by an insurrectionary strike in the city, which started on 19 February. Repressed with great brutality, it flared up again on 21 March, and the workers' organizations virtually took over the city as the northern armies retreated. Chiang arrived in Shanghai on 26 March. It was on the orders of the central committee of the Chinese CP that Shanghai was 'handed over' by the strikers to Chiang, who had threatened to dissolve any union that armed its members. Borodin had been instructed from Moscow to order them to hide their arms and not come into conflict with Chiang.

On 16 March *Pravda* had written that Chiang was being forced to bow to the will of the revolutionary masses. This referred to the meeting of the KMT Executive in March 1927 which attempted to limit Chiang Kai-shek's powers, and on paper did so. Two communists were nominated to the Government at Wuhan, to occupy the ministries of agriculture and labour. This apparent reconciliation did not conceal the widening rift, but was approved by the CI representatives, Borodin, Voitinsky, and Mandalyan.

At the beginning of April Wang Ching-wei, for the KMT, and Chen, the secretary of the Chinese CP, had signed a joint appeal to members of both parties calling for an alliance, alleging that counter-revolutionaries were spreading false rumours in order to split the two—some that the CP was going to eliminate the KMT, others that the KMT was about to break up the CP. Differences, if they existed, were not irreconcilable. The CP was anxious to maintain order in the liberated areas, and had approved the Government's policy of not taking the foreign concession areas by force. This joint statement was not criticized at the time, although later it was made one of the counts in the indictment of Chen as an opportunist.

On 3 April Chiang announced that he would act only on the orders of the KMT Executive (then in Wuhan). In a speech on 5 April (not reported but quoted by Vuyovich at the eighth ECCI plenum in May), Stalin said that Chiang was 'submitting to discipline' and there was no need 'to drive away the rights since we have a majority and the rights listen to us'. The communists needed the right wing. 'It has capable people who still direct the army, and lead it against imperialism.' Martynov wrote that the CCP had won a series of political victories, including the subordination of the generals to the KMT. (An article published at the end of May in *Communist International* said: 'The communists did not for one moment believe in the sincerity of this declaration.')

The *Communist International* (15 April 1927) referred to the danger of a split between the KMT and the CCP, and said the danger could be averted 'if the CP infused revolutionary workers' and peasants' blood into the veins' of the KMT—a phrase exploited by the opposition in its attacks on ECCI policy. An article by Trotsky, containing a warning against the 'Chinese Pilsudski' and arguing that to keep the CP a hostage within the KMT was tantamount to a betrayal, was refused publication. Chiang Kai-shek, he said, was not anti-imperialist, but only anti-British; he was willing to compromise with other Powers. For whom, he asked, had the revolutionary troops captured Shanghai?

On 12 April Chiang dissolved all communist and left-wing organizations in Shanghai, as well as in Nanking; their offices were raided and their members arrested; hundreds were executed. Three days later Chiang established his Government, in rivalry with Wuhan, at Nanking. In a statement to members of the KMT he said: 'The members of the KMT are firmly united but the communists try to alienate us from each other.' The communists had entered the KMT in order to extend their own influence and to become 'the dominating factor in Chinese politics'. Branches of the KMT which they could not control they tried to break up. 'They have stirred up mob violence and made it a powerful weapon in the political struggle. . . . The violence and disturbances conducted by the communists are liable to draw the Powers concerned into a united front against us.'

On 13 April Roy, on behalf of the ECCI delegation in China, protested to Chiang against the violation of the KMT–CP agreement, and urged him not 'to break the nationalist front'. The Comintern delegation at Wuhan declared that over the past year they had observed with growing dismay Chiang's acts of violence against the working class and the revolution. 'We watched all these violent actions of Chiang Kai-shek and his agents with great anxiety, but hoped that he would hesitate to turn a barefaced traitor to the nationalist movement. . . All the crimes of those who fight against imperialism can be temporarily over-looked. But . . . Chiang Kai-shek's crimes did not stop at the massacre of Kiangsi and Shanghai workers. They culminated in a revolt against the people's party and the people's government.'

The growing estrangement between Chiang Kai-shek and the Chinese communists appears to have been generally unknown among the Comintern rank and file; the issue of *Inprekorr* reproducing a *Pravda* leading article on the event also carried a brief statement signed by Humbert-Droz, Smeral, Kuusinen, and Murphy, of the Comintern secretariat, confirming the correctness of the news. Until a few days before, the communist press in Europe had been publishing friendly statements about Chiang. Victor Serge, an opposition supporter, wrote in his memoirs: 'We *know* that Chiang Kai-shek is preparing the open betrayal of the unions and his communist allies. We know that he is preparing a coup against the proletariat of Shanghai. . . . We are not permitted to speak. And Stalin takes the floor in Moscow before thousands of workers and solemnly assures them that we have nothing to fear from Chiang Kai-shek.' 'Chiang Kai-shek', Trotsky wrote, 'is now teaching the Chinese workers what we failed to teach them, what at the time we were forbidden to teach them.'

Bukharin wrote that Chiang's coup represented the revolt of the big bourgeoisie against the KMT and its left bloc. The nationalist camp had split into two, of which the bourgeois part tended to unite with the feudalist-militarist-imperialist counter-revolutionaries. Now that the KMT (by which he meant the KMT at Wuhan) was rid of its right-wing saboteurs and traitors, it must be made into a really mass organization; it would be wrong to surrender the KMT banner to the Chiang clique.

In his 'theses for propagandists' on the Chinese situation, approved by the CC of the CPSU and published in *Pravda* on 21 April, Stalin wrote that Chiang's coup 'marked the desertion of the national bourgeoisie from the revolution'. There were now two Governments and two camps in South China—the revolutionary centre at Wuhan and the counter-revolutionary centre at Nanking. The policy of preserving the unity of the KMT no longer accorded with the tasks of the revolution, whereas the policy of co-operation between the left KMT and the CP was particularly valuable and significant; without it the victory of the revolution would be impossible. To call for Soviets, as Radek and the opposition did, was to call for struggle against the revolutionary KMT Government at Wuhan, which included communists. For the communists to withdraw from the left KMT would be in line with the demand of the imperialists for their expulsion from the KMT. To carry out the policy of the opposition would therefore be to play into the hands of the enemies of the Chinese revolution.

According to the Moscow press, among the protests it received against Chiang's coup was one from his son, a student at the Sun Yat-sen University and member of the Komsomol; this was later published in *Inprekorr*. In it he 'rejected the bonds of kinship' with an enemy of the revolution. 'Down with the traitor and counter-revolutionary Chiang Kai-shek!'

After the expulsion of the opposition leaders in the CPSU the opposition in France and Germany published *The Shanghai Letter*. The introduction to the French edition was written by Treint, who arrived in Moscow early in 1927 as French member of the ECCI presidium. He had had no earlier connexion with the Trotsky opposition. He was disturbed, in Comintern headquarters, by the prevalent idea that the alliance with the Chinese national bourgeoisie had to be maintained at whatever cost. The letter, dated 17 March 1927 (it reached Moscow on 8 April), was sent by three CPSU members (their names are given as Nazonov, Fokine, and Albrecht) to the Russian delegation at the ECCI; it was not shown to the ECCI itself, whose place, according to Treint, was taken by the Stalin group, policy in China being directed by an almost daily exchange of telegrams between Stalin and Borodin. The letter itself is a report on the situation in the Chinese CP. It makes no direct attack on ECCI policy, but refers several times to the support given by the Comintern representatives to the central committee of the Chinese party in its mistaken course. They still thought the revolution in China was a bourgeois one, and that social peace would ensure its victory against the imperialists and militarists; they therefore tried to brake the leftward movement of the masses, which frightened the bourgeoisie and endangered the united front. The CC of the Chinese party had not reacted at all to the anti-communist moves of the KMT. The spontaneous strike of 300,000 Shanghai workers had petered out for lack of leadership, and the ECCI representatives continued to support the CC, which had not tackled the peasant question. The letter criticized the absence of any communist agrarian programme; the central committee had no trade union department, it had agreed to compulsory arbitration, and refrained from any independent work in the army.]

AGAINST IMPERIALIST WAR! AGAINST THE STRANGLING OF THE CHINESE REVOLUTION!

APPEAL OF THE EXECUTIVE OF THE COMMUNIST INTERNATIONAL TO THE PROLETARIAT OF THE WHOLE WORLD AND TO ALL OPPRESSED PEOPLES!

The Communist International summons all of you to open mass protest against imperialism, which is threatening the world with the vast misery of a new world war. Nearly thirteen years have passed since the first imperialist world war started, and mankind has not yet made good the destruction it wrought. . . .

Now the guns are again belching forth smoke. The clique of imperialists, still powerful, has begun a hangmen's war against the Chinese people. More than 170 warships are lying in Chinese harbours. Tens of thousands of infantry, Japanese, English, American . . . have been landed on the soil that is drenched in the blood and sweat of the sorely-tried Chinese masses. The most important Chinese cities are virtually occupied by the hordes of these 'civilized' hangmen. . . .

They have already begun to prepare war against the Soviet Union. The outrageous attack on the Soviet mission in China, the destruction of its premises, the plunderings, arrests, and ill-treatment, the siege of the Soviet Consulate in Shanghai by Tsarist white guards, the English, and the Americans—all this bears witness to a systematic plan being operated at the instigation of the imperialist pirates.

It is no accident that British imperialism is working to fetter the English labour movement and to deprive the trade unions of all their rights. It wants to ensure 'peace' while carrying out its 'heroic' military activities.

It is no accident that the French bankers' clique is putting through special laws which are turning the country into a military camp. . . .

It is no accident that all the forces of capital are uniting against the Chinese revolution and against the citadel of the workers' movement, the Soviet Union. A new blood-bath is being prepared, more criminal, more bloody, and more murderous than the one that began in 1914.

This is being covered up by the League of Nations, the most hypocritical institution of all times. . . . It is being covered up by the leaders of the Second International and Amsterdam, who yearn platonically for peace but use their best energies in the fight against the Soviet Union. . . .

In China the imperialists have not only blockaded the entire country. They have managed to destroy the unity of the Kuomintang and have bought over Chiang Kai-shek. This traitor to the Chinese revolution and the Chinese people has become the centre of the national counter-revolution. In agreement with the foreigners Chiang Kai-shek executed a coup in Shanghai and dissolved the Shanghai city council. His generals have disarmed the workers' corps and, on the orders of the foreign marauders, have shot down hundreds of proletarian men, women, and children. . . .

With the utmost indignation and the greatest hatred we declare Chiang Kai-shek a traitor to the revolution, an ally of the imperialist robbers, an enemy of the revolutionary Kuomintang, an enemy of the labour movement, and an enemy of the Communist International.

The working class of all countries, the oppressed people of all lands must realize that the Chinese bourgeoisie have withdrawn from the fight against imperialism in China, in fear of the tremendous rising wave of the workers' and peasants' movement. This movement is so vast that no imperialist forces will be able to crush the Chinese revolution. . . . The Chinese revolution, with its tremendous impetus and its immense influence on the colonial world and over the European proletariat, reflects the extreme intensification of the capitalist crisis. The depth of this crisis is drawing the imperialists together. . . . Their campaign against China, their criminal plans to provoke the Soviet Union are endangering the peace of the world.

EXTRACTS FROM A STATEMENT OF THE ECCI SECRETARIAT ON THE DOCUMENTS PUBLISHED BY CHANG TSO-LIN AFTER THE RAID ON THE SOVIET EMBASSY IN PEKING

29 *April* 1927   *Inprekorr*, vii, 47, p. 980, 3 *May* 1927

[Soviet diplomatic premises in Peking were raided by Chang Tso-lin's police on 6 April 1927. The Soviet chargé d'affaires protested on the same day, and on 9 April a protest was sent from Moscow. The papers published were said to have been taken from the office of the Soviet military attaché. They gave a great deal of information about relations between the Russians in China and the Chinese CP, especially on military and financial affairs; a number refer to the attitudes and policies of the Chinese communists, and their appraisals of the political situation. Their authenticity was (and to some extent remains) a matter of dispute. At the time Zinoviev wrote to Trotsky that they were partly genuine and partly forged; in the edition of a selection of the papers by C. M. Wilbur and J. L. How published in 1956, which examines the question of authenticity in great and careful detail, the editors note that in 1951 a professor in Tientsin had endorsed the authenticity of at least one of the documents.]

The Chinese press in the territory occupied by Chang Tso-lin is publishing a series of forged documents, allegedly found during the recent police raid on the Soviet Embassy in Peking. These 'materials' are now being reproduced by the entire bourgeois press as new revelations about the Comintern's work. They have been quoted in the English parliament and are being used to stir up bourgeois public opinion against the Soviet Union. The fuss being made in imperialist circles about these fantastic documents is in itself clear proof of the object of the police, who are in the service of foreign capital, in forcing their way into the Embassy. . . .

In these documents 'secret instructions from Moscow' are said to have been given, in which the Comintern recommends 'stirring up the popular masses against the conduct of foreigners in China, with the object of bringing about foreign intervention'. That is, the Comintern is credited with nothing less than support for the plans of the imperialist hangmen in China. . . .

All this humbug, which betrays the political ignorance of the experts in foreign pay who manufactured it, is so nonsensical that it makes refutation superfluous. It can be used only by hopelessly biased people or by conscious deceivers who try to justify the imperialist robbery of their governments in China by these unsavoury methods. . . . The workers of all countries will know what value to place on this attempt by Chang Tso-lin, inspired by foreign capitalists, to stifle the great movement of the working-class and peasant masses of China.

EXTRACTS FROM AN ECCI PROTEST AGAINST THE EXECUTION OF CHINESE COMMUNISTS

1 *May* 1927 *Inprekorr*, vii, 49, p. 1030, 10 *May* 1927

[During the raid on the Soviet Embassy in Peking, a number of Chinese communists were found on the premises. They were arrested, and executed by slow strangulation on 28 April.]

Chang Tso-lin, the hireling of world imperialism and bloody hangman of China, in obedience to the will of the imperialists, has had the twenty-five Chinese communists arrested in the diplomatic quarter of Peking put to death in a most horrible and agonizing way; among them was comrade Li Ta-chao, founder of the Chinese CP. . . .

It could only have been with the consent of the diplomatic corps that Chang Tso-lin's murderous scoundrels entered the foreign quarter, only with that consent could the Chinese communists have been handed over to their executioners to suffer such dreadful class revenge. The responsibility for their blood rests on the international gangs of murderers of the bourgeois-capitalist governments of all imperialist Powers. . . .

The extraterritoriality of the diplomatic quarter guarantees the right of asylum to all enemies of the Chinese revolution, monarchists, reactionary ministers, elements friendly to England and Japan, and all the other hirelings of foreign capital. . . . Only for communists, for revolutionary workers and the Kuomintang left, does the diplomatic quarter serve as a trap. The imperialist Powers have no hesitation in trampling on its diplomatic immunity when it comes to surrendering communists to Chang Tso-lin's executioners.

This is not the first time they have perpetrated such a villainy. On 24 November last year the Kuomintang district committee in Tientsin was destroyed by the English authorities, and fourteen of its members arrested and handed over to Chang Tso-lin . . . demonstrating the English Conservative Government's direct and open participation in the Chinese civil war on the side of reaction. . . .

After the blood-bath perpetrated by the English and American navies in Nanking, after the bombardment of Wanhsien by the English fleet last year, after the outrageous raid on the Soviet Russian Embassy, the only foreign Embassy to show friendship to the Chinese revolution, the world imperialist rabble have decided to do some blood-letting among the Chinese working class. . . .

The disarming and shooting down of workers organized by the latest hangman of the Chinese revolution, the treacherous general Chiang Kai-shek, and the executions of the communists in Peking are links in one chain, forged not in Peking and not in Shanghai, but by the imperialists of all countries in London.

THE EIGHTH PLENUM OF THE ECCI

[The proceedings of this meeting, held from 18 to 30 May 1927, were never published. There were 71 delegates, of whom 33 had voting powers. There were only two items on the agenda, China and the danger of war. The committee met, not as usually in one of the large halls, but in a small committee room where there was no place for visitors. The relevant documents, distributed only on the eve of opening, had to be returned at the end of the session. Stalin's speech on China was published, as well as a report made by Bukharin to the Moscow party organization. About a year later, after the supporters abroad of the Russian opposition had published Trotsky's speeches at the plenum, and Zinoviev's theses on China, a short report on the work of the plenum was published in Moscow by the ECCI political secretariat. The plenum had been called because 'the extreme complexity and gravity of the political situation required the Comintern to take new decisions and issue new directives'. The Second International and the IFTU were declared to be taking an active part in preparing war against the USSR; the danger of war had never been greater. The chief factors making for war were the situation in China and the rupture of diplomatic relations between Britain and the USSR. The new trade union law in Britain was meant to tie the hands of the working class in the event of war. This was the first question discussed by the Executive, and instructions were drafted for the sections. The Chinese revolution was thoroughly discussed, the report being made by Bukharin. While confirming the correctness of the previous Comintern line on a bloc with the national bourgeoisie, the Chinese communists were instructed to change their tactics radically and make the agrarian revolution the centre of their anti-imperialist struggle. The left Kuomintang was to be turned into a comprehensive mass organization, including trade unions, peasant unions, etc. The communists were to remain in the Kuomintang and turn the Wuhan Government into a revolutionary dictatorship of workers and peasants.

The situation in Britain and the tasks of the CPGB were also discussed, and 'some changes were made in the composition of the ECCI presidium'. It was decided to convene the sixth Comintern congress in the summer of 1928. The report continues: 'Despite the extreme gravity of the political situation the opposition in the CPSU thought it possible at the plenum to make an unprecedentedly blunt attack on the CPSU and the Comintern. Comrades Trotsky and Vuyovich (the opposition demand that comrade Zinoviev, who was removed by the seventh enlarged plenum of the ECCI both from his post as Comintern president and from any work in the Comintern, should take part in the work of the plenum was rejected against the vote of comrade Vuyovich) distributed their counter-theses on the main questions of the agenda, as well as a number of their fractional documents, spoke openly in the name of the opposition bloc, &c. All their documents contained numerous charges of "treachery" against the CC of the CPSU and the Comintern, etc.

'In appearing openly as a fraction, the opposition has broken the promise made in its declaration of 16 October to cease fractional struggle and not to support Maslow and his companions, expelled from the Communist ranks. When the break between Great Britain and the Soviet Union had already occurred, comrade Trotsky declared at the plenum that the greatest of all dangers now was the regime within the party, i.e., in reality, bolshevik discipline within the CPSU and the Comintern.

'All this proves that the opposition is on the brink of breaking with the Comintern. Consequently the plenum took a special decision sharply condemning the opposition and warning it that if it continued its fraction work the presidium of the ECCI together with the International Control Commission would be compelled to expel comrades Trotsky and Vuyovich formally from the Executive Committee. The plenum proposed that the CC of the CPSU take vigorous steps to put an end to the fraction work of the opposition in the CPSU.

'No delegation at the plenum supported the opposition. All resolutions were passed against the solitary vote of Comrade Vuyovich' (Vuyovich was a member of the ECCI, Trotsky a candidate member).

The resolutions as published had 'a number of insignificant omissions, made necessary because of the conditions created in a number of countries by bourgeois terrorist regimes'.

In his speech Trotsky made a vigorous attack on the regime within the CPSU. 'Every mistake of the leadership is "made good" by measures against the opposition, with more and more frequent expulsions as the party congress draws near.' They consoled themselves with the hope that once the opposition had been defeated, things would go well. On the contrary, along the road the CPSU was going, there could be only further difficulties and greater convulsions. The regime in the party weighed on the Comintern, where nobody dared to make open criticisms, on the fallacious pretext that to do so would injure the USSR.

In two letters to the ECCI presidium, dated 4 and 9 June 1927 (among the Trotsky papers at Harvard), Trotsky wrote that the ECCI report (the decision to suppress the report had apparently not yet been taken) omitted his speeches on the fictitious pretext that he had failed to correct the proofs in time. In fact the proofs had been sent to him after the report had gone to press. He recalled the resolution of the ECCI editorial commission of 21 May prohibiting publication of the report for the time being, and obliging speakers at the plenum not to make use of the speeches made there without the express permission of the editorial commission; Manuilsky had used distorted quotations from his, Trotsky's speeches. He asked the ECCI for permission to publish his speeches and the resolutions of the plenum as a separate pamphlet; permission was not given.

The preoccupation of the Russian leaders with internal affairs, and its repercussions on ECCI work, are reflected in Humbert-Droz's correspondence about this time. He worked in the Latin secretariat, and in February 1927 complained that it was impossible to work in an atmosphere so charged with intrigue. At the end of February 1927 he wrote to Ercoli that very few non-Russians were left at Comintern headquarters—most had been sent abroad on missions; Kuusinen was withdrawing more and more into his regional and editorial work, in the effort to evade responsibility for the general political work; there was in fact no effective political direction; Bukharin was very busy with Russian affairs; he wanted to avoid Russification, 'but so long as the methods of working here do not change, it will be fairly difficult to keep the best people of our parties here'. In April Humbert-Droz again wrote of the shortage of personnel at the ECCI; there were only four of them to do the work; he complained to Ercoli that Bukharin was too busy to give much time to Comintern affairs, and without him it was impossible to get serious decisions on political questions. Resolutions were contradictory and illogical, being drafted to give a little satisfaction to everybody. 'At the moment, I'd like to send the whole thing to the devil and get back to the workers in Switzerland. . . . Life in the *apparat* is more and more painful.']

EXTRACTS FROM A MANIFESTO OF THE EIGHTH ECCI PLENUM ON THE RUPTURE OF RELATIONS BETWEEN BRITAIN AND THE SOVIET UNION

May 1927   *Inprekorr*, vii, 57, p. 1219, 3 *June* 1927

[Diplomatic relations between Britain and the USSR were broken off in a note from Sir A. Chamberlain to the Soviet chargé d'affaires in London dated 26 May 1927. It had been preceded by a note dated 23 February 1927 charging the Soviet Government with violation of the 'no propaganda' clauses of the 1921 trade agreement, and by a raid on 12 May by British police on the premises of the Soviet trade delegation in London, from which a number of papers were removed. A selection from these papers was published shortly afterwards as a White Paper under the title *Documents Illustrating the Hostile Activities of the Soviet Government and Third International against Great Britain.*

In February Humbert-Droz had written to Ercoli, apparently in reply to a suggestion from the Italian CP that an anti-Italian boycott should be organized, that the Russians were against it because it might provoke the rupture of diplomatic relations with Italy and isolate the USSR, and divert attention from Russia and China. 'The interests of the USSR at the present hour, when England threatens a rupture, are certainly above everything else.' Two months later he wrote that England was doing everything to provoke war. 'We are very worried by the passivity of our parties in regard to China, and the connected danger of war on Russia.']

The heroic example of the workers and peasants of China is arousing the broad masses of the colonial peoples; the echo of their struggles and victories rings out in Indochina and Indonesia and the Indian Empire. The vampires of the imperialist capitals, the financial and commercial magnates, the potentates of heavy industry are trying to salvage the sources of their shameful profits. To the revolution of the colonial peoples demanding the right of self-determination they reply with war. Despite the contradictions of interest which divide them, the imperialist States are trying to forge a united front against the danger which threatens them all, the colonial revolt. . . .

The weight of anger of these stock-exchange sharks is, however, concentrated on the Soviet Union, which hovers before the oppressed nations as a shining example and remains the irreducible fortress of all the exploited and oppressed of the earth. In the night of their slavery the Soviet Union has lit the great torch of freedom. . . .

World imperialism, and British imperialism especially, can no longer tolerate the existence of the only workers' and peasants' Republic, whose example is a constant summons to the oppressed working masses and the enslaved peoples to follow the same road of emancipation. . . .

To defeat the Chinese revolution, to subject the colonies to still greater exploitation, to stifle the workers' movement, reduce wages, and lengthen the working day, in order to squeeze still greater profits out of all who labour, imperialism must destroy the fortress of the proletariat, the workers' State. The reactionary Baldwin Government is aiming for war against the Soviet Union. By a series of outrageous provocations . . . it is trying to involve the Soviet Union in war. The proletarian State contemptuously avoided the obvious trap . . . and has shown the whole world that it is pursuing a policy of peace. That forced British imperialism to throw off the mask and itself to assume responsibility for the rupture of diplomatic relations.

Comrades! This action by Great Britain reveals the great danger threatening the world working class; it requires it to mobilize all its forces against war and for the defence of the proletarian State. . . .

British imperialism will undoubtedly get from Hindenburg's Germany, in the name of the League of Nations, permission to send troops and arms through Germany to attack Russia. By persistent labours it has surrounded the Soviet Union with a ring of vassal States in which military dictatorship and terror against the workers and peasants prevail. Thanks to the coup d'état financed by London, Poland and Lithuania have governments which are obedient to Chamberlain, and Rumania has too, thanks to Mussolini's good services. . . .

But imperialism cannot arm for war without a fight against the working class and its organizations. War against the Soviet Union is a class war, a war against the proletariat. The great imperialist States know that the world proletariat stands guard over the Russian revolution, that it will fight against the war, that it will defend, not the fatherlands of its exploiters, but the fatherland of the working class and the exploited. Imperialism knows that it can count on the support of social-democracy, as it did in 1914. But today in every country there is a communist party to expose the treachery of the leaders of the Second International . . . a communist party which will do everything in its power to turn the imperialist war into a war against imperialism and into a social revolution. That is why the armaments drive is accompanied by a general offensive against the working class and its class organizations. . . .

The capitalist regime necessarily gives rise to war. . . . The fight for peace which is not at the same time a fight to lead the masses into revolutionary struggle against the capitalist regime is only a deceptive illusion and can lead only to a bloody morrow.

Workers, peasants, oppressed peoples! . . .

Rub the sleep from your eyes, get over your discouragement, turn on those who spread pessimism in your ranks and undermine your strength. War is near. Only by mass action, by huge protest meetings, by powerful demonstrations and protest strikes, by energetic mass battle will you be able to break the capitalist offensive and force the imperialist jackals to retreat.

Defend the Chinese revolution, prevent the transport of troops and munitions. Build of your millions an indestructible barricade to defend the threatened Russian revolution. . . .

Soldiers and sailors! Sons of workers and peasants, do not forget that you belong to the class of working people. Fraternize! If you are ordered to act as the hangmen and traitors of your class, remember that you have only one banner to defend, the red banner of the international working class.

EXTRACTS FROM THE RESOLUTION OF THE EIGHTH ECCI PLENUM ON
THE SITUATION IN ENGLAND

May 1927   *Inprekorr*, vii, 62, p. 1303, 14 *June* 1927

[Continued Soviet support for the Anglo-Russian trade union unity committee
was a primary target of attack by the CPSU opposition. At the seventh ECCI
plenum in December 1926 Vuyovich had said that since the committee did
nothing it did not in fact exist, while its English members continued to betray
the working class. The committee had met in Berlin at the end of March 1927,
the Russian side being led by Tomsky. On his return he reported that its decisions had been unanimous, and that the enemies of the working class who
hoped for its dissolution were disappointed. His report was approved by the
Russian trade union council. The principal decision had been one on non-
intervention in each other's affairs.

In a letter dated 2 April 1927 (in the Trotsky papers at Harvard; the addressee
is not named) Trotsky wrote that the Anglo-Russian committee had said
nothing about the exchange of notes between the British and Soviet Governments in February, or about the bombardment of Nanking. 'If the committee
exists, why is it silent? And if it does not exist, why is there silence about its
death?' In an attack on Tomsky's report of the Berlin meeting, Trotsky wrote
that it was impermissible to talk of 'unanimity' and 'cordial relations' with those
who had betrayed and would again betray the working class. If there was
unanimity with the General Council, what justified the existence of the Minority
Movement? It was argued that the committee served as a link between the
Russian unions and the British masses; on the contrary, it served to separate
them. The Russian press did not publish the statements of the General Council,
and the TUC did not publish the Russian statements. The argument that the
committee was a bond with the masses, he wrote later, was equivalent to saying
that strike-breakers serve as a bond with the strikers; nor did it strengthen the
Soviet position internationally—the agents of imperialism could never protect
the revolution from imperialism. Stalin had argued that it was useful to maintain
the committee until the British masses themselves rejected the TUC leaders;
on the contrary, it was in order to help the masses to overthrow those leaders
that the Russian unions should withdraw. In a document dated 16 May 1927,
prepared for the eighth plenum, Trotsky took up Bukharin's argument that the
committee served as a diplomatic instrument in the struggle to defend the
USSR. War was the supreme expression of imperialist policy; the fight against
it was the highest expression of the revolutionary policy of the international
proletariat. The international interests of the Soviet Union suffered severely
from the politbureau's attitude to the pseudo-lefts on the General Council.
'Nothing can do us more harm than lies and dishonesty in the revolutionary
proletarian camp.' This did not deceive their enemies, but only weakened their
friends. The Berlin resolution had put the authority of the workers' State behind
the pacifist lackeys of imperialism. If they had to make concessions to the class
enemy, they would do so to the boss himself, not to his menshevik henchmen,
and they would not gloss it over. 'When we yielded to Curzon's ultimatum, we

explained to the English workers that we were not yet strong enough to take up Curzon's challenge.' The concessions made in Berlin yielded nothing in return. They were one-sided and disguised. What could postpone a war was the danger for the bourgeoisie of its turning into a civil war; it was the war danger that demanded of them a firmer and more irreconcilably revolutionary policy.

At the plenary meetings Trotsky repeated the charge that the agreement reached at Berlin was treachery to the Minority Movement; it was a surrender to what was worst and most conservative in the labour movement. He proposed an addition to the resolution (it was rejected) to the effect that a break with the General Council would have the same significance in 1927 as the break with the Second International had had in 1914. The shaky structure of British imperialism now rested not on the right-wing social-democrats, but on the alleged left, without whom the right wing could not maintain its position in the labour movement. It had been right to set up the committee, but after the betrayal of the general strike the Soviet side should have withdrawn. The Berlin capitulation was a black stain on Comintern history. There was as much reason to break with Citrine as there had been to break with Chiang Kai-shek. Kamenev joined in the attack, arguing that the committee was a manifestation of the right deviation in the CPSU; to shout his speech down as 'Trotskyism' did not replace the need for analysis. Thaelmann, defending the committee's continued existence, said the reformists wanted it dissolved because it strengthened the Soviet Union's position and could play a part in future class struggles, national and international.

While the ECCI was meeting, the Russian unions were urging a further meeting of the committee on the General Council to discuss the war danger. After prolonged correspondence, the British side agreed to a 'preliminary' meeting in Berlin, which was held on 18–19 June. Reporting on 28 June to the Russian trade union council, Tomsky said that the Soviet side had urged the committee to widen its functions but the British had objected. Their efforts to put off the meeting amounted, at such a critical time, to sabotage. The Russians then published the correspondence between the two sides of the committee, without prior consultation with the TUC. Tomsky's charges were reproduced in the British press on 28 July, with the comment that it was difficult to understand the Russian trade union leaders' desire to continue to co-operate with traitors, saboteurs, and lackeys.]

1. The plenum of the CI Executive confirms the theses of the ECCI presidium adopted in June 1926 on the general strike, which described the fight of the English workers in the memorable days of May 1926 as a turning-point in the history of the English labour movement, and also confirms the resolution of the seventh enlarged Executive on the situation in England, put forward in connexion with the defeat of the miners. The enlarged Executive's prediction that the miners' defeat would give the signal for a reactionary offensive, both domestically and in English imperialism's foreign policy, has been completely confirmed. . . .

3. A series of provocations against the Soviet Union instigated by the English Government, particularly the raid on the Soviet trade delegation and the rupture of commercial and diplomatic relations, as well as incitement of the States bordering Russia to attack the Soviet Union, and the feverish effort to organize a Holy Alliance against the Soviet Union, reveal the true role of English imperialism, which is now the greatest danger to world peace. The danger is all the greater because English imperialism's war on China, as well as its ideological and technical preparations for world war, enjoy the open support of Labour Party leaders like Snowden and MacDonald, and General Council leaders like Thomas. . . .

5. The general strike and the miners' strike awakened the class consciousness of hundreds of thousands of workers and undermined their confidence in the political parties of capitalism. The inability of the Government to satisfy the needs of the petty bourgeoisie alienates many of their former supporters in this section of the population. . . .

6. The greater intensity of the class struggle in England is reflected in an accelerated differentiation within the labour movement. New groups of workers are coming into the movement, and the working masses are inclining unmistakably to the left. The Labour Party and trade union leaders, on the other hand, are moving openly towards the ruling class on all the burning questions of external and domestic policy. . . .

7. The January conference of trade union executives, which approved the General Council's report on the general strike and thereby condemned the miners' heroic struggle, was the first demonstration of the consolidation of the trade union bureaucracy on the platform of recognizing the necessity of wage reductions in order to stabilize English industry. . . .

9. The trade union bureaucrats and Labour Party leaders are calling for peace with the capitalists, while at the same time waging a furious struggle against communist workers and adherents of the Minority Movement and the left wing. Local Labour Party branches are being expelled for refusing to apply the Liverpool decisions directed against communists. . . .

13. On the one hand we see English imperialism incapable of solving the problems confronting it and so arresting its decline. . . . On the other we are witnessing the steady improvement and consolidation of the Soviet Union's position. This contrast increases British imperialism's enmity towards the Soviet Union, an enmity nourished by English capitalism's fear of the spread of a revolutionary spirit among the English workers and of the rising tide of revolt among the colonial peoples, particularly in China. This hostility has grown especially great because of the effective support given by the Russian workers to the English miners and because of the Soviet Union's open sympathy for the Chinese revolution. . . .

20. The Executive confirms the correctness of the political line of the CC of the CPGB laid down in its extraordinary session of 12 April. . . .

25. The plenum of the ECCI regards the General Council's circular of 25 March to the trades councils, in which they are presented with an ultimatum to sign a document undertaking to break off all relations with the Minority Movement, as an attempt to disrupt and demoralize the trades councils ... and as one aspect of the reformist bureaucracy's campaign to isolate the communists and their adherents in the Minority Movement. ...

26. The Executive Committee declares that at the present time all the English party's tasks must be subordinated to the fight against English imperialism's offensive policy, as shown in the trade union Bill, the war against China, and the preparation of a new war, as well as to fighting against the reformist leaders' support of that policy. ...

29. The communist party must continue to explain to the workers the importance of unity between the English workers and the Soviet proletariat, a unity which is essential in face of the English Government's militarist policy. The party must explain to the workers that the Anglo-Russian committee has not been able to accomplish its great task because of the sabotage of the entire General Council, from Hicks and Purcell to Thomas. On the question of unity with the Russian workers the General Council has played a double game. In words it came out for unity, but in practice it prevented the establishment of a real alliance between the workers of the two countries. ... The communist party must particularly make clear to the workers the real meaning of the last meeting of the committee in Berlin, at which the General Council, instead of extending the committee's functions, insisted on limiting them and pushed this policy through. ...

30. ... In connexion with the foregoing, the CPGB must carry out the following work:

(i) A thorough exposure of the campaign of forgery and provocation directed by the English Government against the Soviet Union. ...

(ii) Information about the Soviet Union's achievements in building socialism ... which enable the Soviet workers to support the workers of all countries in their fight against oppression.

(iii) Clear explanation of the fact that the Government's policy ... will damage English trade, and so create unemployment.

(iv) The party must link the campaign against the rupture of diplomatic relations and the war danger with the campaign against the anti-trade union Bill, and insist on a campaign against both by the Labour Party and Trade Union Congress.

(v) The party must emphasize the necessity of forming workers' committees of action everywhere to prepare the struggle against the Bill and the war danger, and must strengthen its agitation for a general strike to force the Government to resign.

EXTRACTS FROM THE RESOLUTION OF THE EIGHTH ECCI PLENUM ON
THE SPEECHES OF COMRADES TROTSKY AND VUYOVICH

May 1927   *VIII Plenum: Tezisy*, p. 197

[A statement made by Trotsky and Vuyovich (chairman of the Young Communist International) on this resolution (published by the opposition in Germany) said that it crowned the right-deviationist policy of the Comintern. That
deviation was to be attributed to the defeats suffered by the international
proletariat, to the temporary stabilization of capitalism, and to the slow progress
of socialist development in the USSR. The deviation aggravated the consequences of the defeats themselves. The plenum had ratified communist capitulation to the strike-breakers and traitors in the General Council of the TUC,
who had displayed a cowardly and contemptible attitude on the rupture of
Anglo-Soviet relations. On China it had endorsed the incorrect policy of the
past and prepared new defeats; Wang Ching-wei would ally himself with Chiang
Kai-shek to break the mass movement if he could not keep it in check. The
refusal to publish the opposition's statements disarmed the party. The proposal
to exclude it from the ECCI was a violation of Comintern statutes, as was the
refusal to admit Zinoviev to the ECCI meeting. It was evidence of ideological
weakness and bureaucratic and arbitrary behaviour. Together with the expulsion of opposition members of the CPSU, it was intended to silence any critical
voices at the fifteenth congress of that party. Sooner or later the line would have
to be corrected. The opposition represented the continuity of revolutionary
bolshevism.

After the conclusion of the ECCI meeting Kurella wrote in *Inprekorr* that the
opposition attack 'was sharper and more hostile than anything the opposition
bloc had done so far'. The fight against it represented the Comintern's fourth
front (the other three being China, Britain, and defence of the USSR), and the
battle had to be fought with as much energy by all CI sections. 'The opposition's attitude was one of irreconcilable struggle against the CI and the CPSU.']

The ECCI plenary session brings to the attention of the communist
workers of the world that, in the present extremely grave situation, under
enemy fire, some formerly leading members of the Comintern have taken
it upon themselves to make the most offensive and bitter attacks on the
communist world party. Everything that the opposition leaders do helps
to frustrate the important revolutionary tasks confronting us today. . . .
The fifth congress condemned Trotskyism as a petty-bourgeois deviation.
The seventh plenum condemned the opposition bloc as a social-democratic deviation. . . .

The policy advanced by comrades Trotsky and Vuyovich at the present
plenary ECCI session, and with which comrades Zinoviev and Radek are
in complete agreement, is in glaring, irreconcilable, and fundamental
contradiction to Comintern policy as laid down by Lenin. The basic
characteristic signs of their oppositional anti-communist line are:

1. Their hostility to and disparagement of the struggle of the Communist International against the war danger. The Trotskyists have turned their main forces not against the imperialist warmongers; according to comrade Trotsky, 'the greatest danger is the party regime'. With this slogan comrade Trotsky is in reality preaching reactionary defeatism, opposing his cause to the proletarian revolution. At the same time, despite repeated invitations to do so, he has not by a single word departed from his well known anti-Leninist position on basic questions of revolutionary tactics in the first world war. . . . He confined his demands, already rejected more than once by the Comintern, to breaking up the Anglo-Russian committee, which at the present time would only enable the reformists, who are no better than traitors to the English working class, to realize their intentions.

2. Their evaluation of the nature of the Chinese revolution is basically false, contradicting all Lenin's fundamental ideas on the tasks of communists in a bourgeois-democratic revolution in backward semi-colonial countries. Their defeatist use of individual and partial failures of the Chinese revolution, particularly Chiang Kai-shek's coup, to spread a petty-bourgeois, liquidationist, panicky mood; their slanderous analysis of the policy of the CPSU and the Comintern up to and after the Shanghai coup, with the object of charging them with betrayal of the Chinese revolution. . . .

3. Their complete political and organizational unity with expelled renegades from the KPD of the Maslow–Ruth Fischer group, whose immediate readmission to the Comintern comrade Trotsky proposed, and with the 'Information Bulletin' which the leaders of the opposition are constantly supplying with material. Thus not only the expelled ultra-left groups, but all other class enemies are being provided by the opposition leaders with a distorted account of the most secret affairs of the party which heads the proletarian dictatorship. The alliance of the Trotskyists with renegades of the Maslow type is particularly disruptive because the Maslow group are about to publish an anti-communist newspaper, are preparing to establish a separate party hostile to the Comintern and to create a counter-revolutionary 'fourth International'.

4. Their demand that the Comintern orient itself in the struggle against the war danger on anarcho-syndicalist elements . . . who are using the most despicable means to fight together with the worst white guards against the Comintern and the Soviet Union.

5. Their deliberate slandering and discrediting of the Communist International, which comrade Trotsky accuses of responsibility for the execution of Chinese proletarians; the Comintern leadership he defames as a body of bourgeois-liberals, 'spokesmen of the national bloc' against whose line he is fighting as against 'a shameful policy'. Deliberate slandering

and discrediting of the Soviet Union, whose policy comrade Trotsky reproaches as 'national-conservative narrowness'. . . . These attacks of comrade Trotsky are designed solely to shake the discipline of the bol-shevik organization of the revolutionary proletariat, undermine its unity, lower its prestige among the working class, and unnerve it in face of its imperialist social-traitor enemies.

Comrade Trotsky tried in vain to screen his menshevik attacks behind a veil of pseudo-radical left phrases, hypocritical assertions of his desire to submit to resolutions adopted, and dishonest proposals to 'regulate the conflict' in order to conceal his desertion from the communist workers. . . .

Comrades Trotsky and Vuyovich tried to disrupt the work of the plenary session of the ECCI, ceaselessly distributing fractional material hostile to the party, trying systematically to disrupt the work of the plenary session, and resorting to other disorganizing activities.

The plenary session of the ECCI is taking place at a moment of the utmost gravity, of a critical sharpening of the international situation. The present international situation is characterized not only by a sharpening of class struggles in general, but in the first place by the immediate danger of a predatory military attack by the English imperialists and their vassals on the Soviet Union . . . by imperialist intervention against the national liberation struggle in China, and by a joint and savage attack of all the forces of reaction on the Comintern. . . .

Precisely at this moment comrade Trotsky and his adherents begin an obdurate struggle against the Comintern, the sole leading organ of the world revolution, and against the Soviet Union, the sole state-organized form of the world revolution. Precisely at this moment the Trotskyists fling accusations of treachery against the world party of communism, and charge the State of the proletarian revolution with degeneration. Objec-tively this attack of the Trotskyist opposition follows the same line as the attack of the bourgeoisie and their agents, designed to annihilate the decisive power centres of the proletarian world revolution. . . .

The plenary session of the ECCI replies to these sorties of comrade Trotsky, which are nothing but the desperate struggle of a few political deserters against the communist front of the entire world, with the firm determination to put an end to these splitting intrigues. The policy of the leaders of the opposition, as well as the character of their attacks, is tanta-mount to outright sabotage of the communist struggle against imperialist war. The conduct of comrade Trotsky and his ideological comrades is permeated with the spirit of solidarity with the renegades, the spirit of menshevism, half-way between the camp of proletarian revolution and the camp of imperialist counter-revolution. This half-way position, charac-teristic of Trotskyism, is criminal at the present acute stage of the class struggle. The Comintern recognizes the obligation implacably and finally to liquidate this ultra-left social-democratic tendency and to put an end to the unceasing hostile attacks of this group of bankrupt leaders. . . .

In view of this the plenary session of the ECCI resolves:

1. The ECCI observes that both the principles and the conduct of comrades Trotsky and Vuyovich are incompatible with their position as member and candidate of the Executive Committee of the Communist International.

2. The ECCI categorically forbids comrades Trotsky and Vuyovich to continue their fractional struggle.

3. The plenary session of the ECCI empowers the presidium of the ECCI, in agreement with the ICC, formally to exclude comrades Trotsky and Vuyovich from the ECCI, if this struggle should not cease.

4. The ECCI proposes to the CC of the CPSU to take decisive steps to protect the CPSU from the fractional struggle of comrades Trotsky and Vuyovich.

EXTRACTS FROM THE THESES OF THE EIGHTH ECCI PLENUM ON WAR AND THE DANGER OF WAR

29 *May* 1927   *Inprekorr*, vii, 61, p. 1285, 10 *June* 1927

[The earlier sections of these theses elaborated the usual analysis of capitalist society as leading inevitably to war, of the dangers to that society represented by the existence of the Soviet Union, the Chinese and colonial revolts, the post-war economic crisis. If the Chinese revolution were defeated, the conflicts among the imperialist Powers would again advance to the foreground. Reaction and militarism were spreading and becoming more menacing. The chief function of the Second International and the IFTU was to undertake the ideological preparation for war; by their support of the League of Nations, of the Dawes plan, Locarno, etc., they were trying to persuade the workers that vigilance was uncalled for, the epoch of wars was over. At the same time they were actively helping in preparations for war against the Soviet Union and China by their propaganda against 'red imperialism' and 'Soviet terror', etc. The anarchist and syndicalist leaders were equally guilty because of their hostility to the dictatorship in the Soviet Union. In the event of a capitalist attack on the USSR, this would be held to justify their neutrality. The 'ultra-lefts' were also doing their part in demoralizing the proletariat, for if the social-democrats supported the bourgeoisie, the ultra-left supported the social-democrats. This made the united front with the non-communist *masses* even more urgent. Disarmament proposals were a sham so long as capitalism continued to exist. To support them was merely to spread illusions. Only the Soviet Union, which had abolished capitalism, was genuinely seeking peace. The hostility to war of the working masses, deceived by their reformist leaders, took the form of a cloudy pacifism. The communists must teach them that the way to peace lies through revolutionary action.

The chief speakers on this question were Kuusinen and Bell. Earlier in the year Radek had written of the possibility of Britain making war against Russia because of its anger about events in China, Soviet help for British miners, and the loss of the Russian market. The United States, however, was not interested in the Russian market, and the dependence of some European countries on America weakened the British position. In instructions to sections at the end of April 1927 the ECCI analysed the British position at the forthcoming world economic conference. The chief objects of the British would be to organize anti-Soviet measures and to build an imperialist united front against the Chinese revolution. With the blessing of the Second International, Britain would attack the Soviet foreign-trade monopoly and urge a financial boycott of Russia, and would attempt to win over Germany to this policy by offering the restoration of German colonies. (After the conference Varga wrote that it was due to United States support, Germany lacking the courage to take the same line, that Russia obtained recognition of its special position and its foreign trade monopoly.)

In his report of 4 June on the eighth plenum Bukharin explained that 'peace' could not be the chief Comintern slogan against the war danger because it did not apply to such circumstances as prevailed in China. Hence the universal anti-war slogans must be defence of the Russian and Chinese revolutions. He dealt once more with the question of the possibility of alliances with bourgeois States. If, as a result of unusual circumstances, a bourgeois State were on the side of the USSR and against the imperialists, communist parties would have to support that State; if such a State concluded an alliance with a proletarian State, communist parties would have to support that alliance. In a war between proletarian and imperialist armies, fraternization was not an appropriate slogan. Fraternization was a slogan intended to disorganize both sides in a war, and could therefore be used only in wars between imperialist States. If used in a civil war, national or international, it would undermine revolutionary discipline. In such a war the communist slogan must be 'come over to our side'. After the plenum the ECCI held a series of conferences on anti-militarist work with representatives of the Comintern sections.]

TACTICAL QUESTIONS OF THE STRUGGLE AGAINST IMPERIALIST WAR

26. Lenin's attitude to war determines communist party tactics for an entire historical epoch, the epoch of imperialist war. Slogans such as 'War on war', 'Turn imperialist war into civil war', or 'For the defeat of one's own bourgeois government in an imperialist war', are even today classic examples of genuine revolutionary internationalism. It is one of the merits of Leninism that it deals with questions of war in terms of their concrete historical conditioning. It defines three types of war: (a) wars fought between imperialist States; (b) national-revolutionary wars, and wars of colonial peoples against imperialism (China); (c) wars of the capitalist counter-revolution against the proletarian revolution and against the countries in which socialism is being built. It remains for the Comintern to translate the general treatment of the war question into concrete terms. . . .

27. (*a*) Bolshevism is utterly opposed to a superficial treatment of the war question. In his draft directives for the Russian delegation to the Hague conference Lenin expressly warned it against treating the question of the methods of fighting war thoughtlessly. He recommended all communist parties to study the real circumstances in which war arose. . . .

(*b*) Using the example of the 1914 war, bolshevism exposes the treachery of those who substitute empty phrases for serious and stubborn preparation of the struggle against war. . . . It also fights against both anarcho-syndicalism and the old Hervé school who admittedly advocated a 'general strike', a 'revolt', the 'sabotage of mobilization', but took no single practical step in preparation for the fight against war. . . .

29. . . . what conclusions are the communist parties to draw in the present situation?

(*a*) Bolshevism focuses the anti-war struggle on the mass movement and mass struggle. Activity among the masses in the factory, the unions, the countryside, the army—that is the task of communists before and during the war, that is the way to transform the war into a civil war.

(*b*) The extremely difficult conditions in which workers' organizations have to work in war-time . . . oblige the communist parties to be ready for war at any time. Communists must begin the fight against war . . . at the time when war is being prepared.

(*c*) Both before the outbreak of war and in war-time the communist parties must work persistently to set up an illegal apparatus for the fight against war; they should not however confine themselves to these underground activities, but by revolutionary action win freedom to agitate, and to lead the masses on to the streets in the fight to turn the imperialist war into a civil war, to capture power through the proletariat, to overthrow the bourgeoisie and establish the proletarian dictatorship.

(*d*) . . . The fight against war is not a single action; it requires great sacrifices from the working class, a series of mass actions (demonstrations, strikes in armament factories, etc.) which culminate in the victorious rising of the proletariat. Communist parties must do their utmost to extend these mass actions into a general strike. The Comintern realizes that in the case of a war between two imperialist Powers it is extremely difficult to bring off a general strike at the moment when war breaks out, but it is none the less absolutely essential for communist parties in all capitalist countries to conduct continuous propaganda and agitation for the general strike, both before and during the war.

It should be borne in mind that the moment for making the general strike slogan a slogan of action depends on the revolutionary development of the situation, i.e. when the general strike becomes practical. During its course communists must aim steadily at turning the general strike into an armed revolt.

30. War against China and the Soviet Union is not an ordinary war. It is imperialist war *par excellence*. . . .

(*a*) It is a special kind of war because it is openly a class war. . . . Every honest worker in the imperialist countries understands this.

(*b*) The 'fatherland defence' fetish is irrelevant for the peoples of the imperialist countries in the present war against China. Nobody in his senses believes that China threatens the British Isles. Therefore the bourgeoisie and their lackeys are forced to substitute for 'defence of the fatherland' such sophistries as 'defence of property', 'defence of interests', 'defence of prestige', 'defence of the flag', 'defence of civilization against bolshevism', etc. . . .

31. Consequently there are better possibilities for the fight against war now than there were in 1914–18. Communist parties are therefore required:

(*a*) In imperialist war *par excellence*, waged against China and (prospectively) against the Soviet Union; the workers in the capitalist countries waging this war must, as in all imperialist wars, be defeatists in regard to their own capitalist governments.

(*b*) In an ordinary imperialist war the workers must be in favour of the defeat of their own government; still more, in the imperialist and counter-revolutionary war against the Chinese revolution (represented today by Wuhan) or against the Soviet Union, they must fight actively for the victory of the working masses of China and the Soviet Union.

(*c*) The slogan of fraternization . . . remains one of the most important in anti-militarist work among the soldiers and sailors of imperialist armies and navies. . . . In imperialist war against China and the Soviet Union, this slogan must be linked with the demand to the soldiers in the imperialist armies to go over at a suitable moment to the side of the revolutionary troops. . . .

ERRORS AND DEFECTS IN COMMUNIST PARTY WORK

37. To be fully equal to the demands of the fight against war, both the Comintern as a whole and its sections must ruthlessly expose and correct their mistakes and failings.

(*a*) Practically all sections of the Comintern underestimate the war danger. All communist parties behave as if war were a matter of the more or less distant future, and not the bloody reality of today. . . .

(*b*) A number of Comintern sections fail to link questions of domestic policy with international problems. . . .

(*c*) One of the weaknesses of some comrades in our sections is their underestimation of the role of their own imperialism. . . . The error of the Dutch Communist Party was particularly marked; in the first stage of the

Indonesian revolt it confined itself to demanding the dispatch of a commission of inquiry, and quite forgot such elementary demands as the withdrawal of Dutch troops from Indonesia or recognition of the right of secession for Indonesia. Objectively such 'mistakes' are a capitulation to imperialism. . . .

COMMUNIST PARTY TASKS

38. What are the chief tasks of the Comintern and its sections in the struggle against the present war in China and against the danger of war on the Soviet Union?

(i) The central slogan must be 'Defence of the Chinese and Russian revolutions'. . . . The communist parties must explain to the masses that without revolutionary mass action no real fight against war is possible, that pacifism is merely deception, that the fight for a lasting peace and the prevention of war is tantamount to the overthrow of bourgeois government and the establishment of proletarian dictatorship.

(ii) Unceasing propaganda . . . against the imperialist war in China, denouncing its predatory character, the treachery of the social-democratic and reformist trade union leaders. . . .

(iv) Exposure of the international intrigues against the Soviet Union; mobilizing the masses in its defence under the slogan 'The international proletariat defends its fatherland'.

(v) Agitation for a general strike against war. . . .

(vi) Mass demonstrations before the embassies of those countries taking part in the punitive expedition against China. . . .

(x) Formation of action committees under the slogan 'hands off China and the Soviet Union', drawing in the trade unions. . . . More vigorous application of united front tactics. . . .

(xi) International struggle against fascism, as an armed force of the counter-revolution. . . .

(xv) The communist parties of all countries must give special attention to the formation of non-party organizations to bring together those who sympathize with the proletarian struggle for emancipation, with the working masses of the colonies, and who really hate the capitalist system with its oppression, wars, and exploitation (e.g. the League of Struggle against Colonial Oppression).

(xvi) More intense work in the army and navy.

(xvii) More intense activity in the colonies.

(xix) Greater internationalization of the Comintern sections. . . . Closer contact between the Comintern sections in the common struggle against war.

EXTRACTS FROM THE RESOLUTION OF THE EIGHTH ECCI PLENUM ON
THE CHINESE QUESTION

30 *May* 1927   *IKKI i VKP(b) po Kitaiskomu Voprosu*, p. 169

[The sub-committee of the Chinese commission of the plenum consisted of
Bukharin, Treint, and Togliatti. Treint and Togliatti disapproved of ECCI
policy on the Chinese peasant question, and Bukharin called on Stalin to
persuade them that a policy of 'unleashing the peasants' would invite certain
defeat. According to Treint, Stalin referred to Borodin's assertion that the KMT
would turn against the CP if there were an agrarian revolution, and urged that
time was necessary to enable them 'to manœuvre'. Treint asked whether the
CP would be expected to support Wuhan in the armed suppression of the
peasants, to which Bukharin is said to have replied 'Yes', while Stalin contended
that the CP had sufficient authority with the Chinese masses to make them
accept the policy of restraint.

Five plenary sessions were spent on the Chinese question. The secretariat's
abridged report stated that at these Trotsky exploited the difficulties in China
to attack the Comintern in preparation for his anti-Leninist struggle outside
the party to split the CPSU and the CI.

In addition to the resolution drafted by Bukharin and put forward in the
name of the CC of the CPSU, Zinoviev submitted theses (written before
Chiang's coup) although he was not allowed to attend the meeting. Five
hundred members of the CPSU, all pre-1917 bolsheviks, had sent in a statement
to the CC of the CPSU supporting the opposition line. Zinoviev argued that to
continue the alliance with the bourgeoisie while holding back the workers and
peasants would extinguish the revolutionary spirit of the masses; it meant
abandoning the possibility of the socialist revolution. The basic question was,
which class was to lead the peasants? The civil war, in the country as in the
town, was already a fact; in that war the Nationalist Government could not
remain neutral; it was in fact in the hands of the right wing, which had suppressed strikes and the peasant movement. The CCP was continuing to support
generals who oppressed the workers, and to remain in organizations which the
workers were deserting in disgust. If the KMT was a revolutionary parliament,
as Stalin had said, the parties in it were bound to engage in struggle, and the
communists should therefore be completely independent, organizationally and
politically. They now shared responsibility for all the anti-working-class actions
of the KMT. The right wing in the KMT were moving towards compromise
with imperialism, and the left were likely to be as reliable as the left in the TUC
General Council. Zinoviev enumerated a number of incidents in which the
KMT had acted against the working class, for although the majority of the
members of that party were on the left, it was led by the right-wing bourgeoisie
supported by the army command. He recalled that news of Chiang's action in
March 1926 had been suppressed in the Russian press for a year, although it
had led to the arrest of Soviet citizens. Similarly, the KMT decision of 13 March
1927, to which the Chinese CP had agreed, that communists were not to criticize
the KMT because this would disturb KMT–CP collaboration had not been

published. He drew a comparison between Chiang and Kemal Atatürk, who first used the communist party and then strangled it. Chiang would go the same way and compromise with Anglo-American imperialism, which would help to stabilize capitalism, free England's hands, and bring nearer an attack on the USSR. The Comintern should cease its diplomatic manœuvres among Chinese generals; this was a question of the class struggle, and it should rely on the masses.

Trotsky's theses, dated 7 May, which were refused publication, criticized Stalin's theses for their complete failure to draw the correct lessons from the events in China. The April defeat in China was the outcome not only of opportunist policy, but of bureaucratic leadership. Stalin's theses advocated arming the workers, but rejected the slogan of Soviets because they would be in conflict with a KMT Government. But against whom were the workers to be armed if not against that Government? The left KMT had no forces at its disposal; Soviets would create real organs of a new State power. The CP should appeal to the workers under its own name and banner, organize them, support every forward step of the KMT, oppose every step backward.

Trotsky also made two speeches at the plenary sessions. He defended Zinoviev's theses; Bukharin's contention that everything that had happened in China confirmed the ECCI's prediction would, he said, cause some surprise among the workers of Shanghai and Hankow. Bukharin had foreseen the desertion of the bourgeoisie, but what had been done to establish independent proletarian organizations which would carry the revolution forward? The workers and peasants should have been organized and armed independently, and taught to distrust the bourgeoisie, precisely because it was a bourgeois revolution in China. Bukharin's prediction that the bourgeoisie would desert the revolution was a commonplace, but that was not the same thing as waiting for the bourgeoisie to discard the proletariat, which Comintern policy had made it easy for them to do. To talk of a bloc of four classes was the rankest opportunism. Trotsky urged the Comintern not to assume responsibility for the Wuhan Government, which was bound to betray the revolution if it was a question of choosing between Chiang Kai-shek and the workers and peasants. The revolution could go forward either in the Soviet form or not at all. In a letter to the politbureau and CCC of the CPSU, dated 12 May 1927, Trotsky complained that all party meetings on China were open to non-party people; this made open criticism of the party leaders impossible; he asked for a closed meeting on China, without minutes. The request was refused.

Vuyovich also spoke against Bukharin's resolution. He recalled the occasions on which the central committee of the CCP had wished to adopt a more independent attitude to the KMT, and had been overruled by the ECCI representatives in China; and that Radek, as Rector of the Sun Yat-sen University, had, in July 1926 and subsequently, questioned the politbureau of the CC of the CPSU on these subjects, but received no reply.

Bukharin, introducing the resolution, said that since the seventh plenum the workers' and peasants' movement had made gigantic strides forward. Chiang's coup marked the end of the transitional stage of the regrouping of forces. The regrouping was now completed; the liberal bourgeoisie were a counter-revolutionary force. The party's task now was to create a mass basis for the KMT; he agreed that there was a strong bourgeois element in Wuhan who would sooner or later cross the barricades, but the KMT would come more and more to represent a bloc of the workers, peasants, and petty bourgeoisie. They must unleash the peasant revolution with the support of the CP and left KMT. In his report on the plenum Bukharin argued that the slogan of Soviets could not be used in China because there it was the KMT which embodied the revolutionary traditions uniting the workers, the peasants, and the petty bourgeoisie. The KMT was flexible and capable of adaptation and expansion.

The resolution of the plenum was rejected by the central committee of the Chinese Communist Party.]

I. THE MEANING OF THE CHINESE REVOLUTION

The ECCI observes that the immense international significance of the Chinese revolution is heightened by the fact that . . . it coincides with provocative attacks on the USSR and with the coming to a head of mighty conflicts among the imperialists, for the moment united in an anti-Chinese front.

Therefore only the abominable role of the social-democrats, taking an active part in the ideological preparation for war, only their bourgeois pacifism, which conceals their social imperialism, can explain the actual position of social-democrats and the Amsterdam leaders on the question of the Chinese revolution.

The CI believes that parties and other organizations which call themselves workers' associations and which do not wage a vigorous struggle against intervention in China . . . are not only helping the imperialists to strangle the Chinese workers and peasants, thus strengthening the imperialist system, but are rendering support to imperialism in its preparation of war against the USSR and of world wars in general. . . .

2. THE CRISIS IN THE NATIONAL-REVOLUTIONARY MOVEMENT IN CHINA AND THE NEW SITUATION

The ECCI observes that the course of the Chinese revolution has confirmed the evaluation of its moving forces given at the last (seventh) enlarged plenum. In particular the ECCI observes that the course of events has completely justified the seventh enlarged plenum's prediction that the bourgeoisie would desert the united national-revolutionary front and go over to the side of the counter-revolution.

This process was expressed in the counter-revolutionary coup of Chiang Kai-shek and a number of other generals, in the formation of the Nanking Government and the break-away of the right Kuomintang, who have created their own counter-revolutionary organization under Kuomintang colours.

Chiang Kai-shek's coup has created a new political situation in China and a new distribution of the main class forces in the country. It signifies a decisive regrouping of classes, and Comintern tactics must therefore proceed from this new situation. Any attempt to adopt tactics based on a compromise with Chiang Kai-shek or with the right Kuomintang would be nothing but direct surrender to Chiang Kai-shek and outright treachery to the interests of the Chinese revolution.

The principal reason for the treachery of the bourgeoisie and Chiang Kai-shek was the unfolding mass movement of the working class and peasantry and the successes of the Chinese Communist Party on the one hand, and the growing pressure of the united forces of world imperialism on the other. Fearing the development of the mass movement with its revolutionary class demands and slogans, the national bourgeoisie were bound to prefer—and did prefer—a deal with the imperialists and militarists. . . . Despite partial defeat and the counter-revolution of Chiang Kai-shek and Co., the revolution has moved to a higher stage; the bloc of bourgeoisie, petty bourgeoisie, peasantry, and proletariat has broken down and has begun to change into a bloc of proletariat, peasantry, and petty bourgeoisie, in which the leading role of the proletariat is steadily growing. . . .

The ECCI believes that the tactics of a bloc with the national bourgeoisie in the period of the revolution that has now closed were completely correct. . . . It also believes that the presidium acted correctly in issuing directives simultaneously about exposing Chiang Kai-shek, about getting control of important strategic positions in the machinery of the Kuomintang Government, about setting a course to isolate the right Kuomintang, orientation towards the masses, etc., etc.

Similarly the ECCI approves the attitude taken by the presidium immediately after Chiang Kai-shek's coup and first enunciated in the CI statement published immediately after the coup. The ECCI again emphasizes that Chiang Kai-shek's coup and the radical class regrouping that it expresses are the starting-point of all further tactics, excluding any unity, compromise, or conciliation with the bourgeoisie. . . .

With the right-wing social-democrats accusing the communists of splitting the Chinese national-revolutionary movement and the left falsely charging them with insufficient defence of the special interests of the Chinese proletariat, international menshevism is in fact becoming an open ally not only of foreign imperialism but also of its Chinese agents, the Nanking gang of executioners of the working class.

3. THE PARTIAL DEFEAT OF THE CHINESE REVOLUTION AND THE MAIN FORCES
OF COUNTER-REVOLUTION

The ECCI observes that the series of bourgeois counter-revolutionary coups (in Shanghai, Nanking, Canton, etc.) signifies a partial defeat of the

Chinese revolution and a definite growth in the forces of the counter-revolutionary bloc. But the ECCI does not believe that this defeat is decisive for the entire fate of the revolution. Such a view is false, if only because it sees the basic threat to the revolution in the Chinese bourgeoisie, disregarding their links with the forces of imperialism, and at the same time undervalues the powerful, spontaneous movement of the working masses. . . . It is the imperialist troops, who in fact occupied almost all the important industrial centres of China, which are the chief counter-revolutionary force in China. . . .

Against this partial defeat of the revolution there is to be set its move to a higher stage of development and the beginning of a more intensive mobilization of the masses. The growth of the peasant movement, the organization of armed forces into partisan detachments, the series of victories won by these spontaneously organized forces over the armies of the traitor generals, the maintenance, despite the raging terror of the counter-revolution, of the organizations of the working class, the steady growth of the communist party and the left Kuomintang—all these are important symptoms of the further development and deepening of the Chinese revolution.

The Wuhan Government and the left Kuomintang express in their basic tendencies the revolutionary bloc of the urban and rural petty-bourgeois masses with the proletariat. . . .

The ECCI therefore thinks profoundly incorrect the liquidationist view of the present crisis of the Chinese revolution as a decisive defeat, creating a new international situation. Being incorrect in substance, it can only serve to disorganize the proletarian ranks, a disorganization particularly harmful precisely now, when unity of will and unity of action are specially required of the Communist International and the revolutionary proletariat.

4. THE ORGANIZATION OF THE WORKING AND PEASANT MASSES AND THE BASIC TASKS OF THE CHINESE COMMUNIST PARTY

The tremendous difficulties in the way of the Chinese revolution . . . create conditions of struggle which make it imperative to draw the vast working masses into the struggle. . . . This can be done only on the basis of an agrarian revolution in the village and by satisfying the needs and political demands of the urban working class. . . .

Agrarian revolution, including confiscation and nationalization of the land—that is the fundamental internal socio-economic content of the new stage of the Chinese revolution . . . and the communist party should put itself at the head of this movement and lead it. At the same time, within the Government, the communist party should pursue a policy which will further the development of the agrarian revolution. At the present stage this can only be done by transforming the present Government into the political centre of the workers' and peasants' revolution and into an organ of the revolutionary, democratic dictatorship of the proletariat and peasantry. Only with such a policy, moreover, pursued at the base and at the top, will it be possible to create really promising armed detachments and reorganize the entire army on a sound, revolutionary basis.

In the towns it is necessary to aim at raising the material level of the working masses, at a decisive improvement of their status in the factory as well as in public life generally. . . . At the same time the policy of arming the working and peasant masses must be put through quickly, boldly, and vigorously. . . .

The ECCI believes that the Chinese CP should apply all its efforts, jointly with the left Kuomintang, to a vigorous campaign for the mobilization and organization of the masses. The most energetic recruiting of workers into the party, the most energetic recruiting, in town and village, of the labouring masses into the Kuomintang, which it is necessary to change as quickly as possible into the broadest mass organization—that is the chief task of the Chinese CP at the present moment. . . .

The ECCI decisively denies any opposition between the tasks of the national revolution and the tasks of the proletarian class struggle. It believes that such an attitude, held both by ultra-left European groups as well as by social-democrats, is nothing but a rejection of the hegemony of the proletariat in the democratic Chinese revolution, a rejection in favour of so-called labour unionism, which politically is one of the varieties of opportunism and turns the proletariat into an appendage of the democratic camp. . . .

5. THE COMMUNIST PARTY AND THE KUOMINTANG

The Chinese Communist Party can accomplish the tasks resting upon it to the extent that, as the vanguard of the working class, it maintains its own political personality, distinct from that of even the most left-wing petty-bourgeois revolutionaries.

Whatever the political situation, the communist party should never dissolve itself into any other political organization. It must be an independent force. Therefore it must never tie its hands in regard to the propaganda of its views and the mobilization of the masses under its banner; it should not renounce its right to criticize the vacillation and indecisiveness of the revolutionary petty-bourgeois democracy. On the contrary, only such criticism will push the petty-bourgeois revolutionaries to the left and ensure the hegemony of the working class in the revolutionary struggle.

But the independence of the communist party must not be interpreted as exclusiveness and isolation from the non-proletarian labouring strata, primarily the peasantry. With this in mind the ECCI decisively rejects the demand to leave the Kuomintang, and those views which in substance would inevitably have the same result. To issue the slogan 'It is not yet necessary to leave the Kuomintang' would be as foolish as to advance the slogan of leaving the Kuomintang, for what the present moment demands of the proletarian party is precisely the securing of the leading role of the proletariat within the Kuomintang. The Kuomintang in China is the specific Chinese form of the organization in which the proletariat works together with the petty bourgeoisie and the peasantry. In the given situation the proletariat cannot claim hegemony in the country without the communist party—the party of the working class—claiming hegemony within the Kuomintang.

The ECCI believes that the policy of underestimating the Kuomintang as a specific organizational form of the revolutionary movement would in fact lead to the capture of the Kuomintang colours by the right wing. Precisely because the Kuomintang banner is the most weighty political factor in the country, the bourgeois leaders led by Chiang Kai-shek are trying to appear under its colours. Communist party tactics should not provide a screen for this political manœuvre, which would be the case if the party left the Kuomintang, but should expose the bourgeois politicians as traitors to the cause of the national revolution, traitors to the Kuomintang, traitors to the anti-imperialist tradition of Sun Yat-senism, as deserters to the imperialist camp. The ECCI considers incorrect the view that the national-liberation (anti-imperialist) revolution 'is ended' and another, class revolution (peasant and worker) 'has begun'. After Chiang Kai-shek's coup it has become clear even to the broad masses that the national-liberation revolution can develop further only under working-class hegemony. And precisely for that reason the banner of the Kuomintang, the banner of the national-liberation struggle, cannot be yielded to the traitors to that struggle.

The ECCI believes . . . that the Chinese Communist Party must work to change the Kuomintang into a really mass organization embracing the labouring population of town and country. . . . Only such a policy . . . can create the prerequisites for the victorious development of the democratic revolution in China. Only such a policy will make it possible to institute the strongest counter-measures against the eventual and inevitable desertion of the vacillating groups among the left Kuomintang (as happened in Canton), and against the treachery of generals and other military leaders. . . .

The Chinese Communist Party, while maintaining and expanding its party organization, should in an increasing degree influence the work of the Kuomintang. It can do this only in so far as it acts with full consciousness of its class proletarian position, adhering to its own ideological and political line, strengthening its organization, bringing working-class communists into the party leadership, extending the party's influence, and increasing its authority among the working and peasant masses.

The ECCI notes that there has been in the Chinese CP a series of vacillations precisely on this point, that the party has not always shown sufficient firmness in criticizing the Kuomintang leaders, that within the party there has sometimes been a certain fear of the growth of the mass movement, in the first place the movement among the peasants to seize the land, turn out the gentry and landlords, etc.

These vacillations, particularly harmful at the present stage of the revolution, show that not all comrades in the Chinese CP have understood clearly enough the Comintern line in the Chinese revolution. Unless these mistakes and vacillations are clearly explained to the party, the ECCI considers that it will be impossible to avoid an increase in the danger of vacillation on certain fundamental questions of the Chinese revolution. The Chinese CP, as the party of the working class, must lead the peasants' agrarian movement and fight unrelentingly against all and every attempt to narrow the limits of this movement. . . .

6. THE WUHAN GOVERNMENT, THE QUESTION OF POWER, OF THE ARMY, AND THE TASKS OF THE CHINESE CP

The ECCI considers incorrect the view which underestimates the Wuhan Government and in practice denies its powerful revolutionary role. The Wuhan Government and the leaders of the left Kuomintang by their class composition represent not only the peasants, workers, and artisans, but also a part of the middle bourgeoisie. Therefore the left Kuomintang Wuhan Government is not a dictatorship of the proletariat and peasantry, but is on the road to such a dictatorship; and with the victory of the proletarian class struggle it will lose its bourgeois fellow travellers, surmount a number of betrayals, and inevitably develop in the direction of such a dictatorship.

The ECCI believes that the Chinese CP should take a most energetic part in the work of the Wuhan 'provisional revolutionary Government' . . . while criticizing the inadequate firmness even of its closest allies and ensuring a correct course for government policy. . . .

The ECCI does not consider it appropriate at the present time to advance the slogan of Soviets of workers' and peasants' deputies (in the territory of Wuhan) which is equivalent to the slogan of proclaiming Soviet power. To advance the slogan of the immediate formation of Soviets of workers', peasants', and soldiers' deputies at the given stage of development of the Chinese revolution would inevitably mean to work for dual power, for the overthrow of the Wuhan Government, jumping over the Kuomintang form of organizing the masses and the State power directly to a Soviet regime in China as the State form of the proletarian dictatorship. . . .

The ECCI also believes that at the present moment it is a matter of urgency to consider the question of reorganizing the army, of creating absolutely reliable revolutionary detachments, of the links between the army and workers' and peasants' organizations, of securing the cadres in the army, of turning the army from a mercenary into a regular army of the revolution, etc. Special attention should be paid to forming absolutely reliable detachments of revolutionary peasants and workers, to infiltrating communists and sound left Kuomintang people into the army, purging it of counter-revolutionary elements, creating a workers' guard. . . .

8. THE PARTIES OF THE COMINTERN AND THE CHINESE REVOLUTION

Proceeding from this general appraisal of the significance and role of the Chinese revolution, the ECCI observes that:

1. The majority of Comintern sections have shown insufficient awareness of this significance and have not been active enough in supporting the Chinese revolution.

2. The same inadequacy is to be observed in the work of communists inside the League against Imperialism. . . .

The ECCI directs attention to the need for the most serious preparations to hinder, not in words but in deeds, the dispatch of troops and arms to China. The ECCI imposes on all its sections the duty of working vigorously among imperialist troops and persuading them openly to go over to the side of the revolutionary troops of the Chinese people.

The ECCI instructs the CC of the various sections to work out a series of concrete measures directed to these ends.

The ECCI sends fraternal greetings to its Chinese section and promises it the warmest support in its great revolutionary struggle.

EXTRACTS FROM AN ECCI RESOLUTION ON THE PRESENT STAGE OF THE CHINESE REVOLUTION

14 *July* 1927   *IKKI i VKP(b) po Kitaiskomu Voprosu*, p. 204

[The fifth Chinese CP congress opened in Hankow at the end of April 1927. There were 94 voting delegates, and 30 with a consultative voice. A membership of over 50,000 was claimed. M. N. Roy attended on behalf of the ECCI. He described the KMT (i.e. Wuhan) as a revolutionary bloc of workers, peasants, and petty bourgeoisie. The debate on Chen's political report lasted four days; the resolutions passed attacked Nanking, but were conciliatory towards the Wuhan Government. The central committee refused to submit to the congress Mao Tse-tung's proposals for a land-reform programme, since this would have antagonized the landowning generals and officers of the Wuhan forces. It was the CP's task to broaden, not deepen, the revolution, by supporting the Wuhan forces' expedition against Chang Tso-lin. The political bureau elected at this congress included Chen, Chou En-lai, and Li Li-san.

In May, while the eighth plenum was meeting and asserting its faith in Wuhan, the garrison at Changsha attacked the local communists and executed their leaders. Chen again proposed a complete break with the KMT, but was overruled, and the CP continued to try to restrain the peasants in the areas under Wuhan (a policy of which Mao Tse-tung disapproved). The Wuhan Government, though asked to intervene, did nothing to check the severe repression by the troops of local strikes and disturbances. It declared that the success of the revolution depended on the co-operation of manufacturers and merchants, which in turn depended on their being treated as allies and obtaining government protection. The communist Minister for Agriculture was sent out in June 1927 to check peasant excesses. On 1 June Stalin sent a telegram to the Comintern delegates in China urging them to keep the agrarian revolution within the limits necessary to preserve the alliance with the KMT, while doing their best to get rid of the unreliable generals attached to Wuhan. Roy is said to have shown this telegram (never published) to Wang Ching-wei, the head of the Wuhan Government, believing he could secure Wang's support for Stalin's policy.

In June the Wuhan KMT conducted an open campaign against the CP, charging it with responsibility for industrial and peasant disturbances. The CC of the CCP met on 20 June and issued an appeal to workers' and peasants' organizations to accept KMT leadership and control. At the same time a letter sent to the KMT emphasized that the future of the revolution depended on its agrarian policy. The army consisted of peasants, who would welcome reform. The KMT was at the cross-roads; it could triumph with the peasants, or surrender to reaction. At the end of the month KMT forces raided and took over a number of trade union premises, and at the beginning of July the two communist members of the Government resigned. On 15 July the KMT political council expelled all communists from the KMT, and in the next few days arrested and executed a number of them. The central committee of the CP then declared the Wuhan KMT a counter-revolutionary organization. At Borodin's request, Roy was recalled to Moscow; Borodin himself left China at the end of July and was replaced as ECCI representative by Lominadze.

In July Bukharin wrote that after Wuhan's surrender to Chiang its revolutionary role was now ended, and the ECCI had instructed the communists to leave the Government. They were not, however, to leave the KMT; in its local and lower ranks communist influence could be decisive. It was the more necessary to stay in the KMT since the CP would probably be made illegal, and this would give the party a channel of access to the masses. The KMT masses should be urged to turn out its leaders.

The CC of the Chinese CP was accused of sabotaging ECCI decisions on the independence of the CP, the agrarian revolution, the arming of the workers and peasantry, etc. Instructions had been given it day by day, but these had been ignored. The Chinese politbureau had obstructed the agrarian revolution, and the most opportunist and defeatist, like Chen, had been in favour of leaving the KMT, which would have estranged them still more from the masses. It was therefore essential to have an extraordinary conference of the Chinese CP and elect new leaders. The present leaders advocated the Chinese version of Trotskyism. Chen, the obedient secretary who had on many occasions proposed withdrawal from the KMT, but had been overruled, was denounced for opportunism. The 'emergency conference', called by Lominadze and attended by twenty-two delegates, was held on 7 August; it dismissed Chen (who had already resigned) and adopted a more radical programme. The new politbureau, reduced to five, included Li Li-san and Chou En-lai, with Mao Tse-tung as candidate member. Chu Chiu-pai replaced Chen as secretary (Chen was expelled from the CCP in 1929).

The central committee of the CPSU then announced that the right deviation in the Chinese CP had been corrected. The Comintern line had been correct, but it had been misapplied in China. The resolution passed at the emergency conference stated that the Chinese revolution was now moving from the bourgeois-democratic to the socialist stage; unless the CCP won hegemony in the KMT, it would not win the leadership of the Chinese proletariat. The KMT had to be turned into a genuine mass-revolutionary organization; but the CP was to maintain its independence.

In the 'platform of the opposition' Trotsky wrote that to lay the blame on the Chinese communist leaders was 'superficial and contemptible'. In October 1927 he wrote that the Comintern, and even the majority of the presidium, had been left in such ignorance of the real course of events in China that they 'confused the hangman with the victim'. 'The cruel massacres of the Chinese proletariat . . . and the general weakening of the position of the Comintern and the Soviet Union, the party owes principally and above all to comrade Stalin.'

In the debate on the colonial question at the Comintern congress a year later, Neumann quoted as examples of the right-wing errors of the CCP the instructions of the Chinese central committee: 'We must keep firmly in our minds the fact that the party must in its peasant policy strictly pursue the line of suppressing excesses directed against the petty-bourgeois landowners and the military', and the central-committee decision that 'the workers' troops in Wuhan must be disbanded or attached to the army, in order to avoid any misunderstanding'. Strakhov (referred to also as Tsui Vito) in the same debate said: 'After it had become clear that a united front with Wang Ching-wei was no longer possible, we decided to withdraw from the Wuhan Government. But even then we still thought this to be a manœuvre, a move to improve our relations with Wang Ching-wei. The fact that the communists are in the Wuhan Government, we thought, gives the reactionaries an opportunity to say that the Wuhan Government is Red; therefore, we argued, we must withdraw so as to make it clear that the Wuhan Government is a national and not a communist Government. All these were disastrous mistakes committed in the Chinese revolution.']

The struggle of the Chinese workers and peasants is a struggle at the advanced outposts of the Communist International. The revolution in China continues to occupy the centre of the Comintern's attention.

Taking into account:

1. the feverish pace of events in China, the ever-changing political situation and relation of class forces within the country;

2. the exceptional difficulties now being met by the Chinese revolution in connexion with the treachery of generals and mercenary troops, with the consolidation of counter-revolutionary forces, and with a number of partial defeats which the Chinese revolution has recently suffered;

3. taking into account, finally, a number of serious mistakes made recently by the leadership of the Chinese Communist Party,

The Communist International considers it essential to turn to all comrades, members of communist parties, to the CC of the Chinese CP, and to all sections of the Comintern with the following directive, put forward in elaboration of the directives sent out earlier by the Executive of the Communist International:

1. The formulation of correct communist tactics imperatively demands the strictest and coolest consideration, in the light of Marxism–Leninism, of all the peculiarities of the given phase of a revolutionary situation, the correct identification of the stage through which the revolution is passing. . . .

2. The seventh enlarged plenum of the ECCI (December 1926) defined the Chinese revolution as both a bourgeois-democratic revolution—at the given stage of development—and one sharply directed against imperialist oppression. The ECCI pointed out that this bourgeois-democratic revolution has a tendency to grow into a socialist revolution. While determining the position and weight of the social forces fighting in China, the seventh enlarged plenum indicated at the same time that the class struggle would become more acute and class differentiation more marked; it pointed to the increasingly centrifugal tendencies in the single national-revolutionary front, and to the inevitability of the big bourgeoisie breaking away from that front. Proceeding from that, the ECCI issued directives concerned with preparing the workers and peasants for struggle against the bourgeoisie and their armed forces. This was a few months before Chiang Kai-shek's coup. Subsequent events, which reached their bloody apogee in the shooting of the Shanghai workers on 12 April of this year, confirmed the Comintern's predictions; a radical regrouping of classes occurred, the bourgeoisie committed treachery and deserted to the enemy camp; the revolution, having suffered a partial defeat, moved on to a new and higher stage.

3. The last ECCI plenum, meeting in May of this year, issued a detailed resolution on the Chinese question. The May plenum took the breakaway of the bourgeoisie as an accomplished fact. The plenum defined the concrete features of the situation . . . and indicated the appropriate line of conduct for the Chinese CP. . . .

4. In recent weeks events have developed extremely fast. What is most important and characteristic in these events is, in the opinion of the Comintern, as follows:

Class contradictions are becoming extremely acute. The mass movement of the Chinese proletariat and the mass agrarian-peasant movement have taken on much broader dimensions. For all political groups in the country without exception the question of their attitude to the agrarian revolution is one that cannot be evaded. The generals and the officers' corps are openly moving over into the counter-revolutionary camp and declaring themselves enemies of the peasants. . . . General Tang Sheng-chi, commanding the Wuhan armed forces, is shooting down peasants, executing communists, expelling them from the army. The generals, from Chiang Kai-shek to Tang Sheng-chi, are engaged in a counter-revolutionary conspiracy. At the same time the ruling elements of Wuhan are covering up the actions of the counter-revolutionary generals and helping them by disarming the workers, attacking proletarian organizations, braking the agrarian revolution, waging a struggle against the communists. The Kuomintang leaders are hastily preparing to exclude communists from the Kuomintang. Thus Wuhan has already become a counter-revolutionary force. . . .

5. Relying on Lenin's teachings, the Communist International considered and still considers that at certain stages it is legitimate, wholly admissible, and unavoidable, to conclude blocs and alliances with the national-colonial bourgeoisie, to the extent that they wage a revolutionary struggle against imperialism. . . . But blocs with bourgeois groups and support for their military forces are permissible only to the extent and so long as they do not hamper the independent activities of the Chinese Communist Party, only so long as the liberal bourgeoisie do not come out against the workers and peasants, so long as the bourgeoisie are still in a position to resolve the historical tasks of the bourgeois-democratic revolution. Support for the northern expedition was wholly correct so long as it gave an outlet to the mass revolutionary movement. Support for Wuhan was wholly correct so long as it opposed Chiang Kai-shek and Nanking. But these bloc tactics become radically false from the moment that the Wuhan Government capitulates to the enemies of the revolution. . . .

Obviously, there are certain difficulties for the party leadership in all this, particularly for the leadership of a young and inexperienced party. . . . In a tense revolutionary situation it is essential to grasp as rapidly as possible the peculiar features of the moment, to manœuvre promptly, to change slogans quickly, to redeploy the ranks of the proletarian vanguard, to react vigorously to a changing situation, to break up decisively blocs which from being a factor of revolutionary struggle have become fetters upon it.

6. If at a certain stage of the revolution communist support for the Wuhan Government was necessary, now it would be fatal for the Chinese CP, would throw it into the morass of opportunism. Despite the advice of the Comintern, the Kuomintang leaders not only in fact failed to support the agrarian revolution, but left its enemies full liberty of action. . . .

7. The present leadership of the Chinese Communist Party has recently made a number of profound political mistakes. The CCP should, in accordance with Comintern directives, have launched and proclaimed the agrarian revolution, openly criticized and exposed the half-hearted and timorous position of the 'radical' leaders of Wuhan and the Kuomintang Executive. . . . The CC and politbureau of the CC of the CCP did not obey these directives. Instead of proclaiming the agrarian revolution, the CC in a number of instances acted as a brake on it. . . . Matters went so far that the politbureau of the CC of the CCP 'agreed' to the disarming of the workers! . . . More than once the CI in secret directives sharply criticized the leadership of the CCP; the CI warned them that it would criticize the CC of the party openly if it did not correct its mistakes. Now, when the CC of the party has rejected the CI directives, the ECCI considers it its revolutionary duty to call openly on the members of the CCP to fight against the CC's opportunism.

8. The Comintern considers it essential to correct immediately these mistakes of the CCP leadership, which have now been demonstrated to all members of the CCP.

The Comintern considers it essential

1. that Chinese communists, without losing a minute, should demonstratively leave the Wuhan Government;

2. they should accompany this step with a declaration of political principle, explaining it by the hostility of the Wuhan Government to the agrarian revolution and the workers' movement. . . .

3. they should not leave the Kuomintang. They must remain in it, despite the campaign to expel communists being conducted by the Kuomintang leadership, and establish closer contacts with the Kuomintang rank and file . . . and prepare for the Kuomintang congress.

4. Every means must be used to intensify party work among the proletarian masses. . . .

5. To develop further the agrarian revolution. To continue the struggle to complete the bourgeois-democratic revolution by 'plebeian' means, i.e. by the revolutionary advance of the bloc of workers, peasants, and the urban poor under proletarian hegemony; systematically to arm the workers and peasants.

6. In view of repressions and sentences, to build a fighting illegal party apparatus.

7. . . . The ECCI calls on all members of the CCP to fight resolutely against the opportunist deviations of the party leadership. . . . The ECCI is confident that the CCP will find within itself adequate forces to change its own leadership and to disavow the leaders who have violated international Comintern discipline. It is essential that leaders of the workers' and peasants' organizations who are party members, who have grown up during the civil war, should get decisive influence in the CC. . . .

The ECCI believes that the course of the great Chinese revolution has awakened to political life and to political action such broad masses of workers and peasants that their movement cannot be suppressed by any force. With correct leadership the victory will go to the Chinese workers and peasants.

EXTRACTS FROM THE THESES OF THE ECCI PRESIDIUM ON JAPAN

15 *July* 1927   *Inprekorr*, viii, 1, p. 15, 3 *January* 1928; 2, p. 37, 6 *January* 1928

[The Japanese CP, dissolved in the spring of 1924 by a majority decision which the Comintern strongly disapproved, was revived as a small organizing group in August 1925. Tokuda attended the sixth ECCI plenum in the spring of 1926 and returned to Japan in June. The third congress of the party was held secretly in December 1926; it drew up a programme covering such measures as an eight-hour working day, defence of the Soviet Union, independence for Japanese colonies, abolition of the Imperial system. There was deep disagreement between those who believed in the need for a small and conspirative organization of professional revolutionaries, and those who wanted a 'mass proletarian party'. Seven leading Japanese communists were summoned to Moscow, where a special commission of the ECCI, under Bukharin, dealt with the question. The report of this commission was submitted to and approved by the ECCI presidium on 15 July 1927.]

I. JAPANESE IMPERIALISM AND THE WAR

The specific weight of the Far East in world economy and politics, which has grown enormously since the war, makes the problem of Japanese imperialism particularly urgent. The increasing strength of Japanese imperialism in recent decades, brought about by its greater aggressiveness, its penetration of China, and its moves in the direction of India, the Near East, the islands of the Pacific, and the territory of the Soviet Union, has made it a first-class Power. . . . Japanese imperialists are playing an extremely active part in preparing the coming war; and, in so far as Japanese intervention in China is an accomplished fact, it can be said that they are already waging this war.

It is impossible for Japanese capitalism to be neutral towards revolution in China, for its most vital and immediate interests are affected. For Japan, with its inadequate supplies of coal and iron, China is a primary source of raw materials. It is also the chief market for Japanese industry.... Capital investment by the Japanese bourgeoisie in China's industry, mines, and railways, particularly in Manchuria, amounts to 2·5 milliard yen. The development of the Chinese revolution is therefore a direct threat to these Japanese interests. . . .

Japanese imperialism's hostility to the Chinese revolution is made more intense because it endangers Japanese colonial rule and may spread to Japan's most important colonies, in the first place to Korea. The struggle against the Chinese revolution will therefore drive the Japanese imperialists into a bloc with the British imperialists, to joint action against the Chinese workers and peasants now, and to joint preparations for war against the Soviet Union in the more or less near future; to a considerable degree it has already driven them along this path.

This bloc, which Japanese imperialism has made with the Americans and the British to fight the Chinese revolution and the Soviet Union, does not however eliminate the decisive contradictions among them, which are growing more and more acute. Japanese and British imperialist interests are already in conflict in China. . . . Even more serious are the contradictions between Japan and the United States. The American Immigration Act was directed primarily against Japan. United States expansion in the Pacific, which runs counter to Japanese expansion, is bringing ever nearer a clash between the two. . . .

2. THE JAPANESE INTERNAL SITUATION

. . . In Japan there exist the objective prerequisites both for a bourgeois-democratic revolution (the survivals of feudalism in the political structure and the acuteness of the agrarian question) and for its transformation into a socialist revolution (the high level of capital concentration and trustification, the close interconnexions of State and industry, the comparatively close approximation to a State capitalist system, the alliance between bourgeoisie and feudal landowners).

But if Japan's economic situation offers a direct prospect of revolution, a tremendous obstacle and barrier is provided by its ideological backwardness. . . . Neither the Japanese proletariat nor the peasantry have revolutionary traditions or experience of struggle; the broad masses are only now awakening to political life, and only a very small proportion of them are involved in it; workers' and peasants' organizations are numerically small and have shown very little activity. Class instincts and recognition of the necessity for class struggle are still smothered by a stupefying patriotism or pacifist illusions. . . .

3. THE DRIVING FORCES OF THE JAPANESE REVOLUTION

As has been shown, Japan is today ruled by a bloc of capitalists and landowners, a bloc in which the capitalists predominate. Therefore any hope that the bourgeoisie can be used as a revolutionary factor, even to a limited extent and in only the first stage of the bourgeois-democratic revolution, must be abandoned. The analogy with China does not hold good. China was and is an object of imperialist policy, whereas the Japanese bourgeoisie are themselves an imperialist force of the first order. In China the 'national' bourgeoisie in the early stages of the revolution were themselves still striving for power, while the Japanese bourgeoisie are already in power and using the entire State machine, with all its feudal connexions and survivals, to the utmost to organize and maintain capitalist exploitation. Finally, the high level of capitalist development in Japan is of the greatest importance in this respect, for it means that the bourgeois-democratic revolution in Japan will immediately turn into a socialist revolution, a revolution against capitalism as such.

The driving forces of the Japanese revolution are the proletariat, the peasantry, and the urban petty bourgeoisie. . . . The Japanese proletariat must combine the struggle for the socialist revolution with hegemony in the struggle of all the working people of Japan for the bourgeois-democratic revolution. All the objective prerequisites are present in Japan for forming a revolutionary bloc of workers and peasants to counterbalance the reactionary bloc of landowners and capitalists. . . . But these must be made organizationally operative. The Japanese peasantry is vegetating in terrible poverty, oppressed by high taxes and rents. The revolutionary movement among the rural proletarians and semi-proletarians is growing extremely fast. About 12 per cent. of the peasants are already organized in peasant unions. The Japanese communists must make every effort to bring these unions, and the Workers' and Peasants' Party, under communist leadership.

4. THE COMMUNIST PARTY AND ITS ROLE

. . . Nowhere does the working class represent an absolutely uniform mass. It consists of a whole series of sub-strata, with different living standards and different levels of political and cultural development. Each of these sub-strata may have its own special interests—and does in fact have them—which may, in the eyes of politically backward and less class-conscious workers, obscure the general class interests of the proletariat, and very frequently do so. This occupational fragmentation can be overcome only by prolonged and persistent mass struggle. . . .

One of the chief failings of the Japanese Communist Party leaders was their misunderstanding and underestimation of the role of the communist party, and of its special function in the workers' movement. The idea that the communist party can be in any degree replaced by left-wing fractions in trade unions or by a broad workers' and peasants' party is basically wrong and opportunist. Without an independent, ideologically tested, disciplined, and centralized mass communist party there cannot be a victorious revolutionary movement.

The fight against any kind of liquidationist tendency, as expressed in fact in comrade Hoshi's policy, is therefore the most urgent task before Japanese communists. Just as the struggle of the entire working people must, in their interests as a whole, be led by the most advanced and revolutionary section, the working class, so the struggle of the working class must be led, in the interests of the whole class, by its revolutionary vanguard, the communist party. . . .

5. THE COMMUNIST PARTY AND THE SOCIAL-DEMOCRATS

In present conditions the communist party can develop only by fighting social-democracy. This applies in full to Japan. The social-democratic party there has 12,000 members, and about 150,000 trade unionists are affiliated to it. The social-democratic leaders are bribed agents of the bourgeoisie, trying on their behalf to infect the masses with the poison of conciliation, patriotism, and social-imperialism. . . .

The objective situation of Japanese imperialism and the historical course taken by the Japanese labour movement create extremely favourable conditions for the fight against social-democracy. There are no long-standing and deep-rooted social-democratic organizations or traditions in the Japanese working class. The 'upper stratum' of skilled workers, on whom reformism usually relies as its main support, is relatively small in Japan. Average wages are extremely low. The vast and unceasing stream of new labour from the proletarianized elements of the countryside, the tremendous pressure of agrarian over-population, intensified since the American escape valve was closed, make it highly unlikely that the Japanese worker's standard of living will rise under the capitalist regime. Of course Japanese capitalism has certain opportunities of bribing various sections of the labour-boss elements. But it can already be foreseen that reformist attempts to transplant to Japan the American model of trade unionism will be a wretched failure.

6. THE COMMUNIST PARTY AND THE TRADE UNIONS

. . . If it would be wrong and fatal to follow a line which leads to the merging of the communist party in the trade union left wing, it is no less wrong to follow a line which leads to the isolation of the party from the mass organizations of the proletariat. The 'theory of splits and unity' which comrade Kuroki advances, and which is in fact nothing but a justification for that line, is wholly and fundamentally incompatible with Leninism. Instead of analysing the concrete tasks confronting the party, and the historically determined methods of solving them, comrade Kuroki starts from artificially and arbitrarily constructed abstract images and logical categories. . . .

The mass organizations are the reservoir from which the communist party draws its reinforcements, and they are also the transmission belts linking the vanguard to the class and to the entire mass of working people. The bigger they are, the greater the potential reserves of the party, the wider the audience to which it can turn. A policy of splitting the mass organizations is therefore one which will diminish our reserves, narrow our own radius of action, weaken our ties with the masses, and isolate us from them. . . . Such a policy, moreover, is an abandonment of the struggle to win the social-democratic workers and the centrists, the struggle to expose right-wing reformism and reformism cloaked in revolutionary phrases. This would certainly be a service to the social-democrats, but it has nothing in common with Leninism. . . . It is no accident that comrade Kuroki's theory is bound up with an exaggerated and wholly disproportionate emphasis on the ideological factor, completely ignoring the economic, political, and organizational factors. That again leads to an impermissible overestimation of the intelligentsia, to isolation from the masses, to sectarianism, and to an idea of the party as a group of 'personalities with a Marxist outlook', mainly of course intellectuals, but not as a militant working-class organization. . . .

In applying united front tactics the communist party must on no account efface its own features, and in no case yield to the influence of those it is fighting; it must preserve complete independence, ideological and organizational. It is obvious that, in speaking of the united front, what we have in mind is not only and not so much the united front of the small and illegal communist party with the left-wing legal mass organizations . . . but also the united front of the mass organizations which are under communist influence (e.g. the Ronoto) with the social-democratic and centrist mass organizations. . . .

Proceeding from these considerations, the Japanese Communist Party must put forward the following programme of action and the following slogans:

1. Fight against the imperialist war danger.
2. Hands off the Chinese revolution.
3. Defence of the Soviet Union.
4. Complete independence for the colonies.
5. Dissolution of parliament.
6. Abolition of the monarchy.

7. Universal franchise from the age of eighteen.
8. Freedom of assembly, of association, of speech, and of the press, etc.
9. Eight-hour working day.
10. Unemployment insurance.
11. Repeal of all anti-labour laws.
12. Confiscation of the land of the Mikado, the landowners, the State, and the Church.
13. A progressive income tax.

These partial demands and slogans must be linked with the slogans of a workers' and peasants' government and the proletarian dictatorship. . . . The fight for these demands is the road to the dictatorship of the proletariat. But the fight will be successful only if there is an ideologically tempered mass communist party, Leninist, disciplined, and centralized, which leads the fight together with the world communist party and keeps in step with the entire Communist International.

The recognition of past mistakes by the Japanese delegation and their complete acceptance of all the instructions and decisions of the CI are a guarantee that the Japanese Communist Party will be able to eradicate the deviations in its ranks, will follow a correct political and organizational line, and will prove equal to the great tasks with which history confronts it.

ECCI APPEAL ON BEHALF OF SACCO AND VANZETTI

6 *August* 1927   *Inprekorr*, vii, 80, p. 1726, 9 *August* 1927

[There had been occasional references in the Comintern press to the Sacco and Vanzetti case in earlier years, the first article appearing in *Inprekorr* in October 1921. After their execution, the ECCI attacked 'the reformists' for sabotaging the movement to save the two men, which was part of the revolutionary struggle against the bourgeoisie and their social-democratic lackeys throughout the world. At the fifteenth CPSU congress in December 1927 Manuilsky said a number of mistakes had been made in the Sacco and Vanzetti campaign. In a number of sections, particularly in France, there had been a tendency to present the issue in sentimental terms, rather than as an instance of class justice. Nevertheless, it was a fine example of a united front campaign under communist leadership.]

Once again, at the twelfth hour, the Communist International appeals to the workers of the entire world. Once again it raises its voice to summon all workers to stay the arm of the executioners who are about to execute the sentence of American class justice. In tremendous demonstrations the workers of all countries have protested against the torture of the two revolutionaries, Sacco and Vanzetti, who for seven years have languished in gaol in constant danger of death. The sentence passed on them is a challenge to the world proletariat. It is an overture to, an announcement of new, ferocious reprisals, against not only the American but the international working class. The sentence shows that in 'civilized America' proletarian revolutionaries share the benefits of only one technical invention, the electric chair.

We appeal to all workers and to all revolutionary organizations:

Protest against the execution of the sentence; organize mass demonstrations against those responsible for this crime; organize protest strikes.

Only the united efforts of the world proletariat can save Sacco and Vanzetti from the electric chair.

Fight to the utmost against the bloodthirsty American bourgeoisie.

EXTRACTS FROM A STATEMENT OF THE ECCI PRESIDIUM ON THE MASLOW–RUTH FISCHER GROUP

17 *September* 1927   *Inprekorr*, vii, 96, p. 2073, 30 *September* 1927

[At the fifteenth CPSU congress Bukharin stated that the ultra-lefts who had been expelled from the KPD were beginning to form a new party, a branch of the Trotsky opposition; there was no depth of baseness to which the opposition would not sink in its attacks on Russia, the CPSU, and the Comintern. (This referred to the independent candidates put forward by the Urbahns–Maslow group in the Hamburg city parliament elections in September 1927.) At about the same time Trotsky wrote that the expulsion of the Urbahns group 'was dictated by this policy of getting rid of the entire left wing in the International. . . . The Stalin group are obstinately pushing the German left along the road of a second party.']

In reply to the statement of the Maslow–Ruth Fischer group addressed to the ECCI, signed by seventeen former members of the party including Maslow, Ruth Fischer, Scholem, and Urbahns, the presidium of the ECCI declares:

The said persons who now request their readmission to the Communist International cannot be accepted. The ECCI decisively rejects such proposals from renegades to the communist movement.

The Maslow group, who undertake in their statement to defend 'the USSR, the first country of proletarian dictatorship', are in fact doing everything to discredit the land of Soviets, the Soviet Government, and the communist party, and in doing so lend support to the furious attacks of world imperialism on the Soviet Union.

This group of splitters, who dissociated themselves from the party and for a time had direct organizational connexions with avowed counter-revolutionaries like Korsch, who have already organized their 'party' and their parliamentary fraction, make hypocritical statements about their struggle for unity and at the same time make game of communist workers by writing: 'The real point is that there is a struggle between two lines of policy, both inside Russia and internationally. Two lines which are incompatible and irreconcilable, whatever organizational compromises may for a time be reached' (*Fahne des Kommunismus*, 23, p. 90).

This is the manner in which this group of political bankrupts propose a 'compromise' between themselves and the Communist International, while maintaining at the same time that an ideological abyss lies between the two. The Communist International agrees that this last is true, for there can be nothing in common between the fight for the proletarian dictatorship and the attack on it, between organizing the Comintern and disorganizing it, between orientation to the revolution and orientation to ten years of 'peace and order', between the policy of fighting the international bourgeoisie who are advancing against the Soviet Union, and the policy of providing a cloak for the 'westward orientation' of the German bourgeoisie. . . .

The ECCI declares:

As early as 1925 in the open letter to the German Communist Party, Maslow's ideology was characterized as a cloak for the 'new orientation of the bourgeoisie' (towards the West, against the Soviet Union); the open letter stated outright that 'the so-called ultra-left tendency is often only a cover for social-democratic, reformist sentiments on the Levi pattern, which threatens to turn into direct treachery to the international working class. . . .'

This appraisal by the Communist International, which was then still under comrade Zinoviev's leadership, has been completely confirmed. If the Russian opposition now takes the Maslow group under its wing, that merely demonstrates the ideological depths to which the Russian opposition itself has sunk, but it is no argument for readmitting these moral and political bankrupts, these slanderers of the Soviet Union, the CPSU, and the CI, these people whom the seventh plenum of the ECCI described as 'agents of the class enemy', and against whom it called for a struggle 'as unrelenting as against all other social traitors'.

In virtue of these considerations, the ECCI resolves to reject the request of the seventeen renegades for readmission to the Comintern.

EXTRACTS FROM A DECISION OF THE ECCI PRESIDIUM AND THE ICC
EXPELLING TROTSKY AND VUYOVICH FROM THE ECCI

28 *September* 1927   *Inprekorr*, vii, 97, p. 2092, 4 *October* 1927

[On 24 June 1927 the central control commission of the CPSU stated that Trotsky and Zinoviev had exploited the difficulties encountered by the party in building socialism to undermine party unity, and had violated party discipline. It asked the central committee to deal with the question of their expulsion from that body. At a joint meeting of the central committee and the central control commission of the CPSU (held from 29 July to 9 August 1927) a KPD statement was considered which charged the CPSU opposition with supporting the ultra-left renegades of the KPD; it was only that support which kept the KPD opposition in existence. The *Fahne des Kommunismus* (edited by the expelled Urbahns) was a collection of calumnies against the Soviet Union and the Comintern, a part of imperialism's anti-Soviet arsenal.

The statement put in by the opposition (including Trotsky, Zinoviev, and Kamenev) came out for unconditional defence of the USSR against imperialism, and rejected any idea of a second party. It was true that a split threatened in the KPD; the opposition would continue to work for the readmission of those expelled, who included hundreds of old revolutionary workers. A new party in Germany would be a great danger. The opposition undertook to obey all CPSU decisions. Immediately after publication, this statement was attacked as being inadequate and evasive. In a speech to the presidium (the text is in the Trotsky papers at Harvard) Trotsky answered the charge of indiscipline. He did not doubt that the sentence had already been drawn up, and only required execution, since decisions were no longer made as a result of discussion. Fractional work now meant anything not expressly permitted by the CPSU secretariat, which itself violated the party statutes and so shook the foundations of discipline, suppressing what was the inalienable right and the supreme obligation of every party member. Discipline was important, but it could not take the place of a correct policy. Bureaucratic discipline on the basis of a false policy (transferred from the CPSU to the CI) did not unite but disorganized the party. The ECCI should observe Comintern statutes and party democracy. Vuyovich had been elected to the ECCI by the fifth CI congress, but the orgbureau of the CC of the CPSU had sent him to work in the provinces. Did the ECCI come to the defence of the rights of one of its own members? Now they were going to expel him from the ECCI. The ECCI, like the CPSU, violated its own constitution by failing to call a Comintern congress while the opposition was being crushed. 'The party regime is the greatest of all dangers, because it paralyses the chief force of resistance to the enemy—the proletarian vanguard. When a soldier's hands are bound, the greatest danger is not the enemy, but the rope binding the soldier's hands.' He and Vuyovich would no doubt be expelled from the ECCI, as Treint and Nin had been expelled from their parties. But what difference would that make to the real situation? His reply to the charge of moving towards a split was that Stalin's entire policy was directed to bringing about a split, or rather a series of splits. Only if the party reassumed its rights could unity be saved. The same applied to the Comintern. All the documents should be published and openly discussed, and a congress called to decide the issues. In an article published in November 1927 Zinoviev noted that, of the ECCI members and candidates elected at the fifth congress, twelve had been expelled by Stalin. To discredit the opposition, they were made responsible for the actions and speeches of people like Katz and Korsch in Germany, whom the opposition disowned.

The resolution was moved by Murphy (CPGB, who in his memoirs misdates the meeting). The session lasted, he says, from 9.30 p.m. to 5 a.m. Trotsky spoke for two hours. The resolution was passed against two votes.

The printing-press referred to below consisted of a duplicating machine used to reproduce opposition documents which the CPSU central committee declared to be 'anti-party' and therefore not fit for publication.

Writing shortly before his death, Trotsky recalled the CC meetings at which the opposition question was discussed: 'At sessions of the central committee at which I rose to read a declaration of the left opposition, I was constantly interrupted by whistling, shouts, threats, swear words. . . . By 1927 the official sessions of the central committee became truly disgusting spectacles. No question was discussed on its merits. Everything was decided behind the scenes at a private session with Stalin. . . . When the comedy was staged, each time it more closely resembled an obscene and rowdy bar-room burlesque.']

To all sections of the Comintern

At its meeting in May 1927 the eighth plenum of the ECCI 'categorically forbade comrades Trotsky and Vuyovich to continue their fractional struggle'. . . .

The facts show that in the intervening time this warning was not taken to heart. The opposition answered this categorical prohibition with an embittered attack on the CPSU and the Comintern, with further attempts to destroy the unity of the Leninist ranks both in the Soviet Union and throughout the world.

Called before the August plenum of the CC and the CCC of the CPSU, the opposition again promised, as it did in its statement of 16 October 1926, to cease its illegal fractional work against the party. This promise was given in the face of a direct threat to expel its leaders Trotsky and Zinoviev from the CC of the CPSU.

Nevertheless, a few days later, the undertaking given on 8 August met the same fate as that of 16 October. The opposition, in the most glaring fashion, broke the promise given to the party and the entire International, and thus finally made it impossible for comrades Trotsky and Vuyovich to remain on the ECCI.

Despite the undertaking given at the August plenum of the CC and the CCC, the opposition continued openly to form its own organization centres; this, in the objective nature of the case, is nothing but an attempt to create the kernel of a Trotskyist party alongside the Leninist CPSU.

At the same time it continued to maintain and extend its connexions with various foreign groups of renegades, such as the Maslow–Ruth Fischer group in Germany, Souvarine in France. . . . Besides the threat to create a second party outside and against the CPSU, it threatens to form a new 'fourth International' outside and against the Comintern.

At a time of the utmost gravity in the international position of the Soviet

Union, when the danger of imperialist intervention looms over the first proletarian State in the world, the opposition openly forms a bloc with groups representing the foulest scum of the international labour movement. . . .

The opposition, which uses the ultra-left and right apostates from communism abroad (Maslow and Souvarine) as its mouthpiece, continues within the Soviet Union, with increasing stubbornness and shamelessness, to spread deliberate lies about the leadership of the Comintern and the CPSU. . . .

The discovery a few days ago of a secret opposition printing-press shows particularly clearly how far the opposition has departed from the party and the Comintern. It transpired at the same time that in organizing this press the opposition did not shrink from using the services of non-party bourgeois intellectuals having connexions with politically suspect and openly anti-Soviet elements.

Whether it wants to or not, the opposition is thus becoming the centre, organizational as well as ideological, around which are crystallizing those strata hostile to us who cannot reconcile themselves to the proletarian dictatorship and work actively for its overthrow.

Called to task at the meeting of the ECCI presidium on 27 September, comrades Trotsky and Vuyovich made statements which in themselves indicate a further long step away from the Comintern and from Leninism towards Maslow and Souvarine. Replying to the charge of malicious violation of party discipline, comrade Trotsky openly declared that the discipline of the bolshevik party was not binding for him. In the speech which he read he said: 'Bureaucratic discipline on the basis of a false policy is not an instrument to close the ranks, but an instrument to disrupt and undermine the party.'

It is quite obvious that comrade Trotsky refused to submit to the proletarian discipline which he condemned in these words. He therefore considered it quite unnecessary to defend in any way comrades Serebriakov, Preobrazhensky, and Sharov, who on their own admission organized the anti-party press. Comrade Trotsky stated openly before the ECCI presidium that comrades Preobrazhensky, Serebriakov, and Sharov, as regards their policy, towered high over those who sought to cover their crimes by party discipline. People who with the help of bourgeois intellectuals organize a secret press against the party are said to tower politically over those who on behalf of the party keep guard over its unity, defend the basic principles of its discipline, without which the party and the Comintern could not exist at all as fighting organizations. . . .

The world organization of the revolutionary proletariat, the Comintern, and its leading section, the CPSU, are described, in sweet harmony with the yellow bourgeois press, as a crowd of people without minds or wills of their own, following behind their leaders, comrades Stalin and Bukharin. 'No single organization', says Trotsky, 'now discusses or makes decisions; they only carry them out. Even the ECCI presidium is no exception.'

The ECCI presidium considers it impossible for comrades Trotsky and Vuyovich to remain any longer on the ECCI, which they have accused of usurpation and against which they are conducting a bitter struggle, with the help of renegades abroad and secret printing-presses in the Soviet Union, organizing illegal centres, and uttering malicious slanders.

In order to maintain the unity of the Leninist ranks, to combat the undermining work of the opposition splitters, and in the belief that all the possible varieties of warning have already been exhausted, while to refrain any longer from organizational measures is beginning to be dangerous and intolerable, the presidium of the ECCI, at its joint meeting with the International Control Commission on 27 September 1927, unanimously resolves, in accordance with the resolution of the eighth plenum of the ECCI, to expel comrades Trotsky and Vuyovich from the ECCI.

EXTRACTS FROM AN ECCI MESSAGE TO THE NINTH CONGRESS OF THE BRITISH COMMUNIST PARTY

October 1927   *Inprekorr*, vii, 99, p. 2129, 11 *October* 1927

[The Soviet delegates invited to the Edinburgh trade union congress were not granted visas, and in their statement announcing this they reiterated their charges of treachery and sabotage against the General Council. At the congress the TUC withdrew from the Anglo-Russian committee. Andreyev, one of its Soviet members, accused them of making the break at the very moment when the committee was most needed. This, said Trotsky, was in itself a merciless exposure of the policy Andreyev had defended.

The Edinburgh congress also endorsed by a large majority the action of the TUC General Council in February 1927 ordering local trades councils to disaffiliate from the Minority Movement. The CPGB, after some initial opposition, instructed its supporters to obey the General Council, an action of which the ECCI strongly disapproved.

At its ninth congress the CPGB reaffirmed its support for a labour government, and again endorsed the policy of applying for affiliation to the Labour Party.]

The reactionary campaign of the Conservative Government and of the block of reactionary trade union and Labour Party leaders against the communist party and the revolutionary elements in the British labour movement has resulted in a growth of communist party influence accompanied by a certain decline in membership. The organizational consolidation of the growing influence of the CPGB, the further expansion of the party, and its transformation into a real mass party leading the struggle of the British workers, are possible only if the fight against the Conservative Government and its agents in the unions and in the Labour Party is waged still more vigorously.

The last trade union congress in Edinburgh, which in face of the danger of war broke up the Anglo-Russian committee and approved the hangmen's war on China, and the Labour Party conference in Blackpool have exposed the reformist leaders of the unions and the Labour Party as outright agents of British imperialism. Against them the most energetic and relentless struggle must be waged.

All the efforts of the agents of British imperialism in the labour movement, who are trying to establish peace in industry at the expense of the workers, in order to make things safe for the Conservative Government in its preparations for war on the Soviet Union, and to ensure its victory in the wars which it is now waging against the British proletariat, the Chinese people, and the colonial and semi-colonial peoples, will prove fruitless. The British labour movement is growing and developing despite the efforts of the lackeys and agents of imperialism. New labour struggles will soon break out.

It is the task of the congress to prepare the communist party for the leadership of these new struggles, fully aware that the leaders of the General Council and the Labour Party will play an even more openly treacherous part than they did in May 1926. . . . The young British Communist Party is called on to take the lead in these forthcoming battles not only against the ruling classes but also against their lackeys, and to ensure the victory of the proletariat.

EXTRACTS FROM AN ECCI MANIFESTO ON THE TENTH ANNIVERSARY OF
THE RUSSIAN REVOLUTION

November 1927   *Inprekorr*, vii, 108, p. 2337, 4 *November* 1927

The great experience of building socialism in the Soviet Union will make a deep mark on the consciousness of the world proletariat; it will help them after they have overthrown the power of capital to advance along already trodden paths which the revolutionary proletariat of the Soviet Union opened in the face of tremendous difficulties with the strength of their muscles and with their hearts' blood. But what is most instructive for the world proletariat is the glorious Leninist party of bolsheviks, the iron cohorts of the CPSU, under whose leadership the proletariat and the working masses of the Soviet Union won their victories in the civil war and on the economic front. It stood at the cradle of the Comintern in 1919. It lent its great experience and traditions to the revolutionary struggle. All sections of the Comintern use it as their ideological model. Without the CPSU and its rich experience the road of the world proletariat to victory would be more difficult and more painful.

The international working class can now sit in judgment on a decade of proletarian dictatorship and a decade of the bourgeoisie's efforts to stabilize capitalism.

When the ruling classes flung you, proletarians in the imperialist countries, into the trenches, when the vermin crawled in your bloody wounds, when you were hanging on the barbed wire or were convulsed by poison-gas attacks, you were told that that was the last war, to be followed by an age of peace and justice. Now you see that your sufferings and sacrifices were in vain. Never has mankind stood closer than it does today to frightful wars. . . .

Most threatening of all is the danger of a new counter-revolutionary war of the imperialist Powers on the Soviet Union. The capitalist world is drawing its sword against the country of proletarian victory, of socialist construction. It wants to destroy the strongest fortress of the world proletariat, whose existence ties its hands because it adds strength to the class struggle of the proletariat. The spectre of world bolshevism and the fear of proletarian revolution have so far held the ruling classes of all countries back from a new world war. Were it not for these fears all the destructive forces of capitalism would be unleashed.

The existence of the Soviet Union means that capitalism can no longer be securely stabilized. In no single country will the workers let themselves be curbed, as international capital would like to curb them. For the existence of the Soviet Union shifts the balance of forces between capital and labour throughout the world. The living embodiment of the great October revolution, the Soviet Union, stands on guard over the world proletariat's struggle against its oppressors. It is the most powerful instrument of liberation that history has ever placed in the hands of the oppressed and exploited classes. . . .

From the raid on the Soviet mission in China the threads of the counter-revolutionary conspiracy against the Soviet Union led from Peking to London, and to the raid on Arcos. The hand of the white guards who shot down Voikov was guided by the wire-pullers in London. The campaign to sever relations between France and the Soviet Union was and is one of the links in the chain of war being prepared against the Soviet Union.

If the capitalist world were to succeed in destroying this shield of the world proletariat in its fight for liberation, this proletarian fortress in the fight against the world capitalist offensive, mankind would witness a more frightful reaction than ever prevailed in even the bloodiest suppressions of rebellious workers. That is why the world proletariat, the oppressed and exploited of the whole world, must pledge their lives to the defence of the Soviet Union. . . . They must stand together and make a defensive wall

around the Chinese working masses. They must remember that the defence of the Chinese revolution and the Soviet Union is at the same time
self-defence of the proletariat against the capitalist offensive. . . .

Proletarians of all countries! Defend yourselves against the capitalist
offensive. Rise up in revolutionary struggle against your class enemy.
That is the best way you can defend the Soviet fortress of the world proletariat. . . .

Oppressed peoples of the colonies! The ten years of the October revolution have brought a practical solution of the national question on the
basis of the complete equality and fraternity of the peoples inhabiting the
Soviet Union. The Soviet Union is today the model of the future socialist
States of the whole world in which there will be no place either for economic
or national oppression. Hold fast in your mind that the October revolution
was, is, and will be the revolution of all the workers, all the oppressed, all
the exploited. Its ten years' existence is the greatest victory over world
imperialism. Rise in fraternal unity with the proletariat of the capitalist
countries against your exploiters. Break the chains and fetters in which
world imperialism has bound you.

Workers and peasants of revolutionary China! Hold high the banner
of revolt against the imperialist robbers. Make use of the experience of the
Russian October revolution to organize armed defence against the counter-
revolutionary forces of the Chinese bourgeoisie who are acting in alliance
with world capital. Strengthen your revolutionary peasant organizations.
Set up strong illegal communist party organizations everywhere, and your
victory is assured.

EXTRACTS FROM A RESOLUTION OF THE ECCI PRESIDIUM ON THE
OPPOSITION IN THE CPSU

23 *November* 1927   *Inprekorr*, vii, 117, p. 2633, 29 *November* 1927

[On 14 October *Pravda* accused the opposition of intending to form a new party.
Trotsky and Zinoviev were expelled from the central committee of the CPSU
on 23 October 1927, and from the CPSU itself on 14 November. The resolution
of 23 October stated that they had not merely broken their undertaking to
abandon fractionalism, but had in fact carried the struggle against the party
and its unity to a stage bordering on the formation of a new, anti-Leninist party,
in conjunction with the bourgeois intelligentsia. They also operated an illegal
press. Preobrazhensky, Serebriakov, and others who ran this press had been
expelled from the CPSU on 13 October. The case of Radek, Kamenev, Rakovsky, and other opposition members was referred to the fifteenth congress of the
CPSU. Approval of the resolution was immediately forthcoming from all the
major Comintern sections. In his speech at the central committee on 23 October
Trotsky charged the leaders of the CC majority with falsification of the evidence.
Whether they were aware of it or not, those who were expelling and arresting

the best old members of the party were the instruments of non-proletarian classes. In a letter to the CC secretariat on the following day Trotsky said that the minutes did not record the first part of his speech, or that he was interrupted from the platform, or that a book and a glass had been thrown at him. A few days later, when the CC made it known that no party meetings could be held in private dwellings, Trotsky wrote that the slogan of party unity was being used as an instrument of ideological terror against the overwhelming majority of the party.

A letter of Preobrazhensky and the others expelled for 'operating an illegal printing-press' to the fifteenth congress of the CPSU noted that the decision did not deal with the basic question 'why a group of old bolsheviks, each with more than twenty years' membership, who never ceased party work even in the most difficult years of Tsarist reaction—why these bolsheviks together with hundreds and thousands of younger party members were compelled at one stage of our revolution to organize the illegal printing of their documents, violate party discipline, etc.'. The question was, to what service was the printing-press put? The party press would not allow them to publish perfectly legal criticism, in which they were defending the agrarian programme of the CPSU.]

1. The ideology of the opposition in the CPSU reflects a complex of views which is totally incompatible with bolshevism. On the most essential matters it coincides with the ideas of the social-democrats as a whole, and of the Russian mensheviks in particular. To characterize the proletarian State, the Soviet Union, as 'Thermidorean', i.e. counter-revolutionary, as a 'degenerating' or 'degenerated' State, the analogous characterization of the CPSU and the entire regime of the proletarian dictatorship and its economic agencies, the charge of Bonapartism levelled against the leading circles of the CPSU and the Soviet Government—this entire ideology, copied from that of Martov, Kautsky, and Dan, shows that the opposition has broken its links with bolshevism. . . .

2. The opposition's menshevik theory is accompanied by corresponding tactics. It has methodically used the most despicable calumny to discredit leading comrades and leading bodies of the Comintern, the CPSU, and other Comintern sections. From fractional groups it has passed to the creation of a Trotskyist party, with an extensive network of committees, and to the establishment of a central committee. . . . It has passed from discussion within the party to appealing to the petty-bourgeois masses outside the party. By provoking and encouraging all the anti-Soviet counter-revolutionary forces, it is acting as pioneer of a bourgeois 'democratic' restoration. That is precisely why the opposition is supported by the openly counter-revolutionary parties, in the first place the social-revolutionaries and mensheviks.

3. The opposition is violating Comintern discipline as openly as it violates the discipline of the CPSU. It is not content with supporting the fractional work of its agents in the Comintern. It is gathering around itself

both the so-called ultra-left renegades as well as openly right-wing elements. . . .

4. These activities are open treachery to the revolutionary international movement of the proletariat. They are particularly criminal at a time when the work of socialist construction requires the co-operation of all forces and when the greatest imperialist States are advancing to an attack on the Soviet Union. . . .

5. The presidium of the ECCI notes with the greatest satisfaction that the Trotskyist party has suffered a shattering rejection by the party masses of the CPSU and the entire Soviet working class. . . . Notwithstanding the ultra-revolutionary phrases which it uses as concealment, the opposition has in fact joined the ranks of the social-democratic leaders against the social-democratic masses, who are becoming more radical, joined the ranks of all enemies of the Soviet State and the world proletarian revolution. This fact emphasizes its character as anti-revolutionary deserters, revealed in a situation when war threatens.

Consequently the ECCI presidium fully supports all the measures taken by the CC of the CPSU in fighting the Trotsky opposition and imposes on the CPSU the duty of taking further energetic steps to prevent any continuation of the criminal activities of the opposition disorganizers. . . .

The ECCI presidium is firmly convinced that the forthcoming fifteenth congress of the CPSU will preserve the strictest discipline and the complete organizational and ideological unity of the CPSU. . . . It will cleanse the party of all those who, like Maslow, Korsch, and Co., have gone or are going over to the side of the class enemies of the proletariat. The ECCI presidium states with satisfaction that all sections of the Comintern have declared against the opposition, and instructs the leading bodies of all sections to carry out continuous and energetic educational work on the anti-communist character of the opposition.

EXTRACTS FROM AN ECCI STATEMENT ON THE TASKS OF INDONESIAN COMMUNISTS

November 1927   *Inprekorr*, vii, 119, p. 2711, 2 *December* 1927

[After the risings of 1926–7 the Indonesian CP and left-wing trade unions were outlawed, and their members joined the National Party of Indonesia, a legal opposition party catering for all sections of the nationalist movement.]

Together with the revolutionary struggles in China, the rising in Indonesia at the end of 1926 and beginning of 1927 was one of the most important events proving that the oppressed masses of the East have already been drawn into the world-wide struggle between capital and labour. The ECCI has made a very thorough examination of the lessons of the Indonesian revolt.

The national-revolutionary movement in Indonesia differs from similar movements in other colonies because of the absence of any native bourgeoisie and the presence of concentrated proletarian masses in the large concerns owned by the imperialists; the working class began comparatively easily to take an active part in the movement.

The serious economic position of the masses, the impoverishment of the petty bourgeoisie and the intelligentsia, and the parallel growth of the communist party (which is the most important political organization among the Indonesian people) and the red trade unions are the characteristic features of Indonesian development in the last few years. . . .

The revolt broke out in November 1926, at first in Java and then in Sumatra. Both were bloodily suppressed, but their importance is tremendous, marking a culmination point in the history of the Indonesian national-revolutionary movement. They differed from the hunger revolts in which the history of this Indonesian colony is so rich in being a conscious and organized attempt to overthrow by armed force the rule of the Dutch occupiers.

The revolt took place under the leadership of the communist party. Hundreds of the best Indonesian communists were shot or thrown into jail. Even before the revolt the best leaders had been arrested. The party made great efforts to prepare itself for the revolt . . . but its entire course showed the lack of serious political and organizational preparation of the movement as a whole. It is highly characteristic that the revolt was conducted under the general slogan of fighting Dutch imperialism, without concrete political and economic slogans which might have mobilized the broad masses and brought the revolt to the final and decisive point of a general strike and a peasant uprising. . . .

During the revolt and in the period following its defeat the Dutch social-democrats, section of the Second International, consciously played the part of bodyguard to the Dutch slave-holders. They openly defended Dutch imperialism. . . .

What now are the tasks of the Indonesian Communist Party? Its first task is to rebuild the party as a completely independent organization, even at the cost of the greatest sacrifices.

The party must make every effort to rebuild the trade unions and to fight for their legalization. Using the trade unions as a basis, it must build up a mass workers' party.

While maintaining its illegal organization, the party must use every legal opening (such as elections, etc.). It must work actively in the national organizations, above all in those for young people. Connexions must be established with the left-wing labour movement in Australia, New Zealand,

and Japan, and above all with the national-revolutionary and workers' movement in China.

While preparing the masses for a new onslaught on Indonesian imperialism, and for the fight for an independent Indonesian republic, the communist party must train and organize them at the same time for the struggle for day-to-day demands, such as an amnesty for political prisoners, withdrawal of the occupation army, the right of association, the eight-hour day, abolition of Dutch as the official language, etc.

THE ECCI ON THE CANTON INSURRECTION

15 *December* 1927   *Strategiya i Taktika Kominterna*, p. 205

[Throughout the summer and autumn of 1927 there was a series of peasant risings, brutally suppressed, and occasional short-lived triumphs by the troops under communist control. In November 1927 the CC of the CCP, meeting in Shanghai, called for 'uprisings in the cities and villages' that would merge into a general insurrection for the establishment of Soviets. This policy was widely criticized, particularly by the deposed Chen and by the Russian opposition, on the ground that the revolutionary forces were defeated and demoralized and should not be led into putschist adventures, but withdrawn and reorganized; this was dismissed as opportunism. In September the politbureau of the Chinese CP decided to abandon the KMT banner, and at the end of that month *Pravda* wrote that 'Soviets' had passed from being a propaganda slogan to a slogan of action. The slogan was adopted by the Chinese CP in November. The ECCI had sent Heinz Neumann to China to assist Lominadze, and the two organized the insurrection in Canton which established the 'Canton Commune'. It lasted less than three days, and was suppressed with great brutality and very heavy loss of life. Five Russians arrested in the Soviet consulate were executed. It has been asserted that the insurrection was organized in obedience to a direct order from Stalin, who hoped for a victory in China that would redound to his credit at the fifteenth CPSU congress, which met in Moscow in December 1927. When the central committee of the Chinese CP met early in January 1928, it asserted that the Canton rising was not a putsch, but an inevitable stage in the development of the class struggle. The ECCI had been right in saying that the situation was revolutionary; the Canton failure was due to a series of mistakes and to lack of preparation. A year after the event, Lominadze admitted that they had exaggerated the strength of peasant revolts and the readiness of the workers and peasants to come to the aid of a revolutionary Canton; Neumann said that the troops in the city did not know the communist slogans; no preparatory work had been done among the enemy troops. Lozovsky reported that the workers of Canton continued at their jobs (including the transport of KMT troops), although in 1926 there had been 200,000 workers organized in the communist-controlled unions.

An anonymous article published in February 1928 attributed the failure to the military inexperience of the workers and the superiority of the reactionary armies which enjoyed imperialist support. Nothing had been done to win the support of the peasants around Canton, who remained indifferent, or to infiltrate into the armies outside the city. The decision to start the revolt had been taken by the Canton CP on 26 November, and the date decided at a meeting on 7 December. A Soviet of sixteen members was appointed beforehand. Its programme was to be the liberation of political prisoners, the arming of workers and peasants, nationalization of industry and banking, the land to be given to the peasants, the execution of all those responsible for the white terror. (The last was the only item on which there was time to take action; the article stated that more than 700 white guards had been shot.)

Lominadze wrote, immediately after the events, that there was no more reason to call it a putsch because it was heavily defeated than to call 1905 in Russia or 1923 in Hamburg a putsch. The revolt coincided with the highest point reached by the workers' and peasants' movement in the province, and was both justified and inevitable. At the sixth Comintern congress Pepper denied the charge of 'rejecting' Canton—he wished only to criticize Lominadze's and Neumann's organizational failure. Neumann attacked the right-wing errors of the Chinese CC during the revolution, their opposition to 'peasant excesses', and their acceptance of compulsory industrial arbitration; the left-wing CC which had taken its place made putschist errors. Lominadze also made a strong attack on Pepper, whom he accused of lack of principle, time-serving, and dishonesty. Strakhov defended the Canton insurrection; it had a genuine social basis and a mass character. The same defence was advanced by another Chinese delegate appearing under the name of Vorovsky.

The theses of the agitprop department of the ECCI on the first anniversary of the Canton events attributed the failure to CP weakness and lack of preparation, reformist treachery, imperialist aid for the Chinese bourgeoisie, the passivity of the proletariat weakened by bourgeois terror, the superiority of the opposing forces, etc. This, however, did not reduce the greatness of the events themselves; they were both a rearguard action and the opening of the Soviet phase of the Chinese revolution which would establish the revolutionary, democratic dictatorship of the workers and peasants.

After the insurrection Chiang ordered all Soviet consulates in KMT territory to be closed.]

To all workers, to all the oppressed, to all soldiers of capitalist armies!

In Canton, city of glorious revolutionary combat, the workers and peasants have seized power, and the banner of the Soviets, the red flag of revolution, has been raised over the capital of South China. The unparalleled courage of the Canton workers is of profound and universal significance.

All the forces of counter-revolution united against the workers and peasants—foreign imperialists, the bloody warlord-executioners, the counter-revolutionary bourgeoisie. These forces are waging a furious battle for Canton. They have surrounded it and cut it off from the rest of the world. The bourgeois press reports that red Canton has already fallen, that the mass execution of workers and communists has already begun, but that the workers' revolutionary detachments, the Chinese Red Army, have broken out. If this should turn out to be true, then the counter-revolutionary victory at Canton cannot be lasting. In Kwantung province the Soviet power is holding out strongly in five areas. New battles are inevitable. The movement is growing, despite partial defeats. The bourgeois counter-revolutionaries will be defeated. The imperialist robbers will be thrown out of Chinese territory. But at the moment the heroic Chinese revolution, the revolution of workers and peasants, stands beneath their axe.

Hasten to its help! Hasten to the help of the Chinese Soviets! Do not let a single soldier, a single sailor, a single gun or bullet be sent to strangle the Chinese revolution. Refuse to load ships with war supplies. Mobilize your forces. Demand the immediate withdrawal of imperialist troops from China.

Long live Soviet power in China!

Long live the international revolution!

EXTRACTS FROM THE THESES OF THE AGITPROP DEPARTMENT OF THE ECCI ON THE FIFTEENTH CONGRESS OF THE CPSU AND THE OPPOSITION

January 1928   *Inprekorr*, viii, 9, p. 165, 27 *January* 1928

[The fifteenth congress of the CPSU was held on 2–19 December 1927. Trotsky and Zinoviev were already expelled; Rakovsky and Kamenev were scarcely able to make themselves heard. A great many of their supporters had been sent out of Moscow, others expelled or imprisoned.

In a letter to the CPSU and the ECCI on 4 October, Trotsky, Zinoviev, Smilga, and others accused the central committee of violating party statutes in its efforts to pack the forthcoming congress. Moreover, rumours had been circulated by the GPU that the opposition was linked with a white-guard conspiracy. They asked for an open discussion of their platform; only the bankrupt resorted to lies and calumnies. The opposition platform (*The Real Situation in Russia*) had been drawn up by 200 old bolsheviks, of whom 13 were members of the CC or the CCC, and endorsed by several thousand CPSU members. The minutes of the joint meeting of the politbureau and CCC on 8 September at which it had been discussed were not published, although it had been agreed to do so.

In a letter to the congress dated 3 December 1927, on behalf of 121 named members of the CPSU, including Trotsky, Zinoviev, and Radek, Kamenev wrote that they could not renounce views they believed to be correct, but to preserve party unity they would cease all fractional work and dissolve all fractional organizations, and would ask like-minded comrades in the other Comintern parties to do the same. They categorically rejected the idea of a second party.

The resolution on Bukharin's report on the work of the CPSU representatives on the ECCI stated that the Comintern's most important task was to intensify the struggle against international reformism, which included the Trotskyist opposition. 'The Trotskyist opposition, which has broken completely with Leninism, with its menshevik-liquidationist platform, its slanders against the USSR which help the Soviet Union's worst enemies, openly carrying on splitting activities unprecedented in their insolence, rallying behind its banner the worst renegades and splitters—from Korsch and Ruth Fischer to Souvarine and Libers—such an opposition can no longer be tolerated in the Comintern's ranks.'

Manuilsky said that in Western Europe the State power was now at the service of the opposition; Humbert-Droz had been sent to France to open a discussion in the French central committee. Two days before it was to meet, he was arrested 'so that Treint, who had the opposition documents, should have the opportunity to slander the CPSU and the Comintern without encountering strong opposition'. In Germany, he said, Maslow enjoyed the support of the police.

The resolution on the opposition said that it had passed from ideological differences on tactical questions to differences of a programmatic character, and had become menshevik; it had become a tool of petty-bourgeois democracy within the USSR and of international social-democracy outside the country. It had violated not merely the party statutes but also Soviet law, and had taken up an open struggle against the proletarian dictatorship. Its actions had placed it among the avowed enemies of the Soviet Union. Its members had proceeded to the formation of their own Trotskyist party. The resolution endorsed the expulsion of Trotsky and Zinoviev. It also expelled seventy-five leading members of the joint opposition, including Drobnis, Evdokimov, Kamenev, Muralov, Piatakov, Radek, Rakovsky, Safarov, Smilga, I. N. Smirnov, and twenty-three members of the Sapronov opposition. The vote was unanimous. Sapronov and his group had detached themselves from the united opposition after the August meeting of the central committee. On 19 December, the day after the resolution on the opposition had been passed, Kamenev, Zinoviev, and twenty-one others applied for readmission; the congress referred the application to the central committee and central control commission with the recommendation that only individual applications should be considered, and a decision taken only after six months, during which time the applicants would have to demonstrate their adherence to the resolutions of the congress. Radek, Rakovsky, Smilga, and Muralov reaffirmed their submission to the congress decision on the dissolution of fractions, but stated that they could not renounce views which the course of events was demonstrating to be correct.

On 19 January 1928 it was announced that, the opposition having established illegal contacts with representatives of the foreign bourgeoisie in Russia in order to facilitate communications with its supporters outside the country, it was advisable to expel Trotsky, Rakovsky, Radek, Smilga, Serebriakov, and other 'traitors' from Moscow. Zinoviev and Kamenev were given party work in the provinces. This action was followed by further widespread arrests, deportations, and dismissals. In February and March Piatakov, Krestinsky, and Antonov-Ovseyenko dissociated themselves from the opposition.]

AN HISTORICAL TURNING-POINT

1. It would of course be quite incorrect to say that the importance of the fifteenth congress of the CPSU was limited to its decisions about the opposition. In every respect, the moment at which the congress was held was a most important turning-point in historical development.

The Soviet Republics have been in existence ten years. They have already entered the period of the real socialist reorganization of the economy and the culture inherited from the past. . . .

The first years of the 'stabilization process' in the capitalist world are also at an end, years which brought great dangers for the Soviet State and at the same time greater intensity in capitalist contradictions and the first signs of a new rise of the revolutionary wave in the West. . . .

THE LATEST OPPOSITION GROUP—A 'SOVIETIZED' INSTRUMENT OF INTERNATIONAL SOCIAL-DEMOCRACY

3. The characteristics of the most recent opposition are: the union of all former groups, which was not the case with earlier oppositions; such an accumulation of differences with the party that former theoretical differences became programmatic differences; the use of such methods of struggle against the party that the opposition transgressed the limits not merely of the party but of Soviet legality. The party was confronted with a solid united front of all elements discontented with its policy. . . .

On the eve of the congress the party was confronted with an opposition political platform which left no single question on which there were not profound differences between the opposition and the party. A platform had been elaborated, a programme for a new party, a platform of such a kind that it became objectively a manifesto for uniting all the counter-revolutionary strata of the population, a 'shattering document' for all those in the world who are fighting the Soviet Union. However freely the opposition uses 'left' phrases, it cannot be denied that the 'opposition platform' has become a counter-revolutionary programme of calumny against the proletarian dictatorship.

Finally, what confronted the party was not merely the programmatic but also the organizational crystallization of a new party. The opposition was creating its own illegal apparatus, its own illegal press, and had its own party discipline. It was proceeding to organize non-party elements and public actions and demonstrations against the party and the Soviet Government . . . thus turning itself into a 'Sovietized' instrument of international social-democracy. . . .

THE SHATTERING DEFEAT OF THE OPPOSITION—A RESULT OF THE IDEOLOGICAL
CONSOLIDATION OF THE CPSU

4. At the congress the opposition suffered a more complete defeat than any previous opposition in our party. What are the reasons for this? Firstly, the ideological growth of the CPSU. . . . It is no accident that, at the climax of its battle against the party, neo-menshevism, appearing in an openly anti-party and anti-Soviet form, had only roughly 4,000 people behind it in the entire party of a million members and did not receive a single mandate at the congress. . . .

The congress decisions leave only two paths open to the opposition: either complete submission to the party and ideological disarmament, or becoming an openly counter-revolutionary anti-Soviet party. Which will the opposition choose? The complete dead end which the opposition has reached has already led to its ordinary members leaving it in great numbers. A group of its leaders, with Zinoviev and Kamenev at their head, have also left it. We do not doubt that the serious, revolutionary part of the opposition will return to the party.

On the other hand it must be clearly recognized that the Trotskyist opposition . . . will continue the fight against the party. . . . The chief task of the party is to make this small handful of renegades from the party and the revolution, who represent a neo-menshevik party in process of formation, quite harmless. It may be taken for granted that the party and the proletarian dictatorship will execute this mission.

ALL COMINTERN SECTIONS MUST DRAW THE RELEVANT LESSONS FROM THESE
EVENTS

5. The history of the struggle with the opposition and its concluding episode are of the greatest political importance for the CPSU and the Comintern. All Comintern sections must draw the appropriate conclusions. The opposition 'episode' is by no means a 'national' or 'Russian' one. The origin, the development, and the collapse of the opposition in the CPSU . . . must be studied by the revolutionary proletariat of all countries, for the experience is instructive. . . . It shows the difficulties with which the working class in all countries will have to grapple after the seizure of power. . . .

The 'Russian' experiences with the opposition are tremendously important for all communist parties from another point of view too. The history of the Russian opposition is closely connected with the oppositions in the communist parties of various capitalist countries, and with the cases of individuals who turned away from communism when the first tremendous post-war wave of revolution had subsided. The fact that there has been a certain standstill, of course only relative, in the revolution, had essentially the same effect on the elements inclined to petty-bourgeois vacillation in both the CPSU and other communist parties. As a pendant, so to speak, of the opposition in the CPSU, the 'communist' opposition in West Europe crystallized. . . . This opposition, pitifully small in numbers and liquidationist in essence, has recently enjoyed a certain revival because of the extension of stabilization, the temporary defeat of the Chinese revolution, the greater imperialist pressure on the Soviet Union. But the strongest impulse to this 'revival' of the West European opposition came from the sharpening of the Russian opposition's struggle against the party. Hopes already extinguished flared up again.

The crushing defeat of the opposition at the congress, the capitulation of a number of its members, and the final transformation of the rest into a menshevik counter-revolutionary group, the undeniable beginning of a swing to the left, a revolutionizing of the West European working class, with its corollary of a more intense struggle between social-democracy and communism, all this is bound to deal the opposition a decisive blow. The communist parties must exert their utmost efforts to accelerate this natural process of decay to which the pitiful handful of renegades in all countries are condemned. . . .

THE MERGING OF THE INTERNATIONAL OPPOSITION WITH THE LEFT WING OF FASCISM AND OF INTERNATIONAL SOCIAL-DEMOCRACY

6. The 'communist' opposition in West European countries has recently displayed roughly the same features as the Russian opposition. Both have entered the 'decisive stage' of their struggle. All the decaying elements are coming together, in a strange international amalgam, openly bearing the Trotskyist standard. . . . What unites these variegated elements in the Trotsky fraction? A typically menshevik platform, in which the menshevik-liquidationist appraisal of the driving forces of the world revolution is allied with the despicable menshevik counter-revolutionary 'criticism' of the Soviet Union, the proletarian dictatorship, and the Comintern. . . .

The co-ordinated action of *Vorwärts* and Maslow's *Volkswille* in the campaign about the so-called 'banishment of the Russian oppositionists to Siberia' is in itself enough to show even the politically inexperienced worker that international capital has two faces but only one class content. . . . This unity of thought, of method, and of interests will become more and more pronounced. The communist parties must expose this merging of neo-menshevism with the left wing of fascism and of international social-democracy.

THE SIGNIFICANCE OF THE FIFTEENTH CONGRESS FOR THE CPSU AND THE COMINTERN

7. The international 'communist opposition' and the entire European social-democracy are trying to exploit the fifteenth congress decisions on the opposition as an argument against the proletarian dictatorship, the CPSU, and the Comintern. To answer this the communist parties must not only demonstrate the correctness of these decisions, but conduct agitation and propaganda on a broad scale to explain the great ideological and educational importance of the lessons to be drawn by all communist parties from the fifteenth congress decisions. The substance of these lessons is:

(a) The proletarian dictatorship is incompatible with the existence of two or more parties, or with the existence of fractions in the party of the working class. . . .

(b) The greatest danger for every communist party, even for those which are in power, lies in fractional disorders. . . . Only those who have a Trotskyist concept of the party can come to terms with or encourage a fractional struggle in the individual Comintern sections. The Comintern and its sections therefore have the duty of eradicating from their ranks, with the utmost energy, all elements of fractional struggle as an unhealthy Trotskyist legacy. . . .

(c) The firmness and boldness with which the CPSU, in the name of party unity, that most important pledge of victory for the revolutions, criticized its former leaders (Trotsky, Zinoviev, Kamenev) and engaged in general self-criticism, with which it examined its own policy (into the discussion of which the entire party was drawn), and the unity which the party membership displayed, show all West European communist parties the real advantages which bolshevik inner-party democracy has over that false 'freedom of thought, speech, and fraction', that freedom for the individual within the party, which allegedly exists in social-democratic parties, and from the survivals of which a few communist parties have still not liberated themselves.

EXTRACTS FROM AN ECCI RESOLUTION ON THE POLISH-LITHUANIAN CONFLICT

27 *January* 1928   *Inprekorr*, viii, 13, p. 260, 10 *February* 1928

[The long-standing frontier dispute between Poland and Lithuania was aggravated in the autumn of 1927 by complaints of the persecution of the Polish minority in Lithuania, and the arrest of a number of Lithuanians in Poland. Lithuania, denying the Polish charges, appealed to the League of Nations. The Russian press carried reports of Polish plans to attack Lithuania, and on

24 November the Soviet Government, in a note to Warsaw, argued that the preservation of peace depended on Poland. The League Council, with the concurrence of the two parties, adopted a conciliatory resolution recommending direct negotiations between them.

The sixth Comintern congress, on 19 August 1928, adopted a manifesto 'against the occupation of Lithuania by the Polish imperialists'. Pilsudski, it said, intended to march on Kovno, with the open or tacit approval of the Powers, particularly Britain. The offensive might start at any moment. He was assured of the support of the Socialist International and the socialist traitors in Poland and Lithuania, who regarded Pilsudski's plans as a step towards intervention in the USSR.]

1. The Polish-Lithuanian conflict has not become less acute. On the contrary, the danger that Poland will annex Lithuania has become still greater as a result of the League of Nations' hypocritical decision and the efforts of the Second International to lull the vigilance of the masses. The League of Nations resolution has not solved the Lithuanian question, but only postponed for a time the realization of Pilsudski's plans to annex Lithuania. It avoids the root of the question and does not eliminate the danger to Lithuania's independence. Lithuania gets a respite, to give it time to reach a peaceful understanding with Poland. That means it should submit 'voluntarily' to Poland and become its semi-colony. If Lithuania does not do this voluntarily, it will be forced to do so.

This is demanded by the interests of imperialist Britain and France, who are trying to build a united front against the Soviet Union from the Baltic to the Black Sea. It is demanded also by the interests of imperialist Poland. . . .

2. Lithuania's fascist Government, which represents the interests of the Lithuanian kulaks, landlords, and urban bourgeoisie, and sees its most dangerous enemy in the proletarian revolution, in the Soviet Union, is inclined, under imperialist pressure, to reach agreement with Poland. In order to deceive the vigilant masses, it greets the decision of the League of Nations as a great victory for Lithuania. . . . The prospects for the masses being successful in obstructing a Polish-Lithuanian agreement are this time much smaller than before, for the pressure of imperialist Britain, France, and Poland will certainly be stronger than before.

On the Lithuanian question all the bourgeois and petty-bourgeois parties in Poland are rallying round Pilsudski. Union between Lithuania and Poland is a very popular slogan among the bourgeois and even the petty-bourgeois Polish masses, and this makes Pilsudski's desire for annexation even greater. If he has not yet carried out his plans, it is only because the Soviet Union, which is always opposed to any annexation and enslavement of small nations, and Germany, which is interested in the maintenance of Lithuanian independence, have come out decisively against them.

3. It should be specially noted that the social-democratic leaders of all countries, who have long since turned themselves into despicable agents of imperialism, are zealously supporting Pilsudski's annexation plans. . . .

5. The ECCI calls on all CI sections, and on all those who are genuine opponents of imperialism and war, to display the utmost energy and initiative in exposing the plans of the imperialist robbers, Pilsudski's annexation projects, and the shameful part being played by the social-democratic leaders. . . .

The annexation of Lithuania is only the first step on the road of aggression by the imperialist robbers against the Soviet Union.

THE NINTH PLENUM OF THE ECCI

[The meetings were held from 9 to 25 February 1928, attended by 92 delegates, of whom 44 had voting powers, from 27 countries. It decided on the date for the sixth congress of the Comintern; the financial report for 1927 showed a total income of 1,375,000 rubles, derived from membership dues of 1,029,000 (on 1,707,769 members), publications 152,000, and collections 176,680. The two main items of expenditure were administration, 595,000 rubles, and grants for newspapers, clubs, education, etc., totalling 690,000 rubles.

An article in *Pravda* published shortly before the plenum argued that, with the masses turning more and more to the left, and the social-democratic leaders moving farther to the right, the Comintern must intensify its struggle against international social-democracy. The communist parties were to increase their efforts to expose Trotskyism as one of the main sources of the campaign of lies and slander against the Comintern. In the sections the opposition was weak, but in every country it was assured of the support of the bourgeoisie and social-democrats. Later in the year the ECCI agitprop department reported to the sixth congress that its resources had been taxed to the utmost by the ideological struggle against the opposition; its difficulties had been aggravated by constant changes of personnel in the department.

Second only to the opposition danger was the right-wing danger in the Comintern, as exemplified in the Austrian CP minority who 'did not even recognize' the rising of July 1927. This referred to a strike in Vienna called to protest against the acquittal of two members of a fascist organization charged with the murder of a socialist during an affray earlier in the year, which led on 15 July to collisions with the police; the Palace of Justice was burnt down and there were about 100 fatal casualties. The small Austrian communist party called for a general strike, but this was turned down by a conference of shop stewards. The ECCI immediately issued a manifesto on these events, which it attributed to working-class resistance to the fascist attack on their living standards, a sign of the weakness of capitalist stabilization. It would be suicidal for the Austrian workers not to push their struggle to the end. The social-democrats would certainly oppose their struggle, in collaboration with the police. It called for the formation of workers' Soviets in Vienna, the disarming of the police and of fascist organizations, and for a workers' and peasants' government. On

24 July the CC of the Austrian CP met and reached the conclusion that it had been organizationally unprepared for the events. It was too isolated from the masses to take over the movement, which had been betrayed by the social-democrats. In September 1927 the ECCI presidium passed a resolution on the 'opportunist error' of those Austrian communists who regarded the events of 15–16 July as a riot, not an insurrection. It was a general strike against the class rule of the bourgeoisie, a mass revolt which, with correct leadership, might have led to the proletarian dictatorship. The assertion of the ultra-lefts that 'the Austrian communists weren't even there' was a lie, but the party had failed to advance the slogan of Soviets and to organize mass discontent. It was a mistake to have convened the shop stewards, since these were dominated by the social-democrats. The July events did, however, demonstrate the bankruptcy of Austro-Marxism.

Right-wing tendencies were most clearly expressed, however, in the opposition to the new Comintern policy of 'class against class'. A minority of the French central committee wished to continue to give parliamentary support to the *bloc des gauches*, and in the central committee of the CPGB, as reported at the fifteenth CPSU congress, there had been strong opposition to work among the armed forces, and to the slogan of a general strike against the Trade Disputes and Trade Unions Act.

The new left policy summarized in the 'class against class' slogan, fore-shadowed by Bukharin at the fifteenth CPSU congress, implied the abandon-ment of united front tactics; the reversal was generally attributed to the change in Soviet domestic policies after the defeat of the opposition, to the failure of the policy of alliance with the Kuomintang, and to the dissolution of the Anglo-Russian committee, which had been represented as the triumph of united front tactics. The change, as Bukharin stated later in the year at the sixth Comintern congress, was made on ECCI initiative.

In a brief resolution, the presidium was instructed to establish a West European bureau of the ECCI 'in order to establish closer contact between the ECCI and the West European sections of the Comintern'.]

EXTRACTS FROM THE RESOLUTION OF THE NINTH ECCI PLENUM ON THE TROTSKY OPPOSITION

15 *February* 1928   *Resolutionen und Beschlüsse*, IX Plenum, p. 5

[The resolution was introduced by Thaelmann and passed unanimously. In his supporting speech Bukharin said that the question had to be considered in relation to the sharper attacks being made on communist parties, which had therefore to intensify their struggle against the social-democratic enemy. To make ideological or tactical concessions to social-democracy would diminish communist recruiting power. The opposition was an obstacle to winning the masses for communism, and hence a counter-revolutionary force. Opposition criticism of the CPSU and the Soviet Union was taken more seriously than the criticism of the right-wing social democrats who were avowed enemies. Either the Soviet Union was a proletarian State and the Comintern must on all questions of Soviet policy be on its side, or it was not a proletarian State. There was no third position. The opposition thought it was not a proletarian State and therefore there was no place for them in the Comintern; they were in fact its worst enemies. 'We have always held that, if there can be two parties in the USSR, then only in the sense that one rules, and the other is in prison.'

On 15 January *Pravda* published two letters, described as emanating from the 'Trotskyist centre', containing the following passage: 'We are against a second party and against a fourth International, irreconcilably against them, judging this question in the light of the interests of international bolshevism.... For the international working class as a whole, the opposition would get into the hopeless position of a sect if it allowed itself to be pushed into the position of a fourth International opposed to everything connected with the Soviet Union and the Comintern. What we must do is to win over the Comintern. The differences are deep enough to justify the existence of a left fraction. But in the present period this fraction is an instrument to exert influence over the communist party, that is, over its proletarian kernel.']

The ECCI plenum notes with satisfaction that the fifteenth congress of the CPSU has decisively put an end to the Trotskyist opposition by placing it outside the party. The plenum expresses its complete solidarity with the decisions of the CPSU and with the measures taken by the Soviet organs to stop the anti-Soviet activities of the opposition. The ECCI plenum believes that the decisions of the fifteenth congress are of the utmost importance for the further strengthening of the proletarian dictatorship and the construction of socialism in the Soviet Union. ...

The ECCI plenum agrees with the analysis of the international economic and political situation given by the CPSU congress and notes the following characteristic tendencies of the present historical phase:

1. The sharpening of contradictions among the capitalist groups in the struggle for the complete re-division of the world; sharpening of the struggle between imperialism and the oppressed colonial peoples, sharpening of the imperialist struggle against the Soviet Union, the emergence of the pre-conditions for new imperialist wars. ...

2. ... Social-democratic and reformist leadership is becoming more and more integrated with the economic and political system of imperialist organizations; the pressure of capital on the working class is becoming stronger.

3. The radicalization of the working masses as a result of the bourgeois offensive. ...

4. The anti-communist campaign opened jointly by the employers' organizations, the capitalist State, and social-democracy. ... The approaching phase of development will be marked by new collisions between the working class and the bourgeoisie, and by a bitter struggle between social-democracy and communism for influence over the working masses....

Social-democracy is putting into operation the whole machinery of lies and slander to stop the growth of sympathy among the international proletariat for the Soviet Union and communism, to misrepresent the real successes of socialist construction . . . to divert the workers from their struggle to overthrow capitalism. . . .

A particularly mendacious and pharisaical role in the fight against the Soviet Union and the CPSU is being played by the leaders of the so-called left wing of social-reformism, the Adlers and Bauers, Levis, Longuets, Lansburys, and Maxtons, who, aware that as the workers turn more to the left their sympathy for the Soviet Union grows, try to disguise their hostility to the proletarian dictatorship and to cover their fight against the Soviet Union with lying phrases of sympathy and 'conditional' support. . . . From the standpoint of the struggle for the masses now turning to the left, these so-called left leaders of opportunism are the most dangerous enemies of communism, of the CI, and the Soviet Union.

The danger of Trotskyism in the international workers' movement at the present time lies in this, that the Trotskyists directly support the ideology and policy of the left lackeys of reformism, that they strengthen the 'left' opportunist leaders in their struggle against communism and the Soviet Union and reinforce the methods of treachery and calumny which the reformists use in their struggle against Trotskyism [communism]. . . . On all basic questions the Trotskyist opposition has gone over to the platform of the 'left' lackeys of opportunism and has taken on an openly counter-revolutionary character. The Trotskyists, who, under cover of phrases about loyalty to the revolution and to the Soviet Union, slander the Communist International, the CPSU, and the proletarian dictatorship, whose external and internal policy they falsify and distort as much as the social democrats do, are, side by side with international social democracy, following a road leading to the overthrow of the Soviet power.

The Trotskyist opposition passed from fractional struggle within the CPSU to the creation of a second party, to street fighting, and to openly anti-Soviet actions, which . . . might have become a danger to the proletarian dictatorship because class elements hostile to the proletarian dictatorship gathered under the banner of the Trotskyist opposition. . . . The proletarian dictatorship cannot and should not tolerate counter-revolutionary attacks, from wherever they come and under whatever disguise they are made.

The Trotskyist opposition, which tried to break up the CPSU from within, was intellectually and organizationally defeated by the firmness of principle and the iron resolution of the CPSU and the working class of the Soviet Union. It has broken up into a number of groups, of which one (Kamenev and Zinoviev) is returning—not without vacillations—to the party platform and gradually turning away from Trotskyism, thus offering further proof of the correctness of the CPSU and Comintern line, while another is hesitating between the party and the Trotskyists. The remaining insignificant groups of Trotsky adherents are trying, after being defeated in the CPSU and the Soviet Union, to transfer the centre of their work to other sections of the Comintern.

The real opportunist face of the Trotskyist opposition can be seen most clearly in the platform which the Trotskyists have put forward to consolidate their related groups in other countries. They appeal in the first place to the openly opportunist and counter-revolutionary elements like Souvarine and Paz in France. They have formed a bloc with the anti-proletarian petty-bourgeois Maslow group in Germany, which is now talking of the turn to 'fascism' and 'tsarism' in the Soviet Union. Outside the Soviet Union, this group in Germany is the strongest support of the Trotskyist opposition. It is already linking up with the counter-revolutionary Korsch group . . . and at the same time sending out feelers to the left social-democrats. It is about to form itself into a separate party under the name of the 'Lenin League'. It is trying to become the international rallying point for all opposition groups in the struggle against the Comintern and the Soviet Union. It is trying to win over the renegades Rosmer and Monatte. . . .

The ECCI plenum is of the opinion that the development towards social-democracy of the Trotskyist opposition, its openly anti-Soviet position, its thoroughly hostile attitude to the proletarian dictatorship, its splitting methods in the communist parties have reached a point at which adherence to the Trotskyist opposition, solidarity with its views, is incompatible with membership of the Communist International.

The communist parties must wage an unrelenting struggle to liquidate Trotskyist groups, and above all fight their leaders. At the same time they must continue the ideological struggle to win those workers who are still hesitating but have not yet broken with the opposition.

EXTRACTS FROM THE RESOLUTION OF THE NINTH ECCI PLENUM ON THE ENGLISH QUESTION

18 *February* 1928   *Resolutionen und Beschlüsse*, IX Plenum, p. 26

[The resolution, passed unanimously, was introduced by J. R. Campbell, who had strongly opposed it in the commission. He warned the Executive against exaggerating the leftward movement of the masses, and ignoring the delays and zigzags in the movement.

The new line had been explained in an article by R. P. Dutt. It was intended to meet the change in the situation in Britain, where the bourgeois dictatorship was no longer liberal but reactionary, as shown in the break with Russia, the trade union law, etc. As a result, differentiation within the labour movement was becoming more marked—the upper ranks were in open coalition with capitalism, while the masses were becoming more revolutionary. The Labour Party was steadily losing the character which had made Lenin insist on communist affiliation, and losing its hold over the industrial workers.

The majority of the CPGB central committee were particularly dubious about the ECCI proposal of putting forward communist candidates at elections in opposition to Labour Party candidates. The ninth CPGB congress in October 1927 had adopted the slogan of a Labour Government under the control of the Labour Party Executive. Shortly before the plenum opened the CPGB central committee had by a majority endorsed its established policy towards the Labour Party. The resolution adopted argued that the Labour Party had not yet become a social-democratic party. As trade unionists, communists could state the CPGB point of view and 'lead all the genuine working-class elements in the [Labour] Party in the struggle against the bourgeois leadership'. It was a mistake to believe that Lenin's advice, given in 1920, was obsolete. 'The party in 1928, no less than in 1920, must help to push a Henderson–Snowden government into office.' It would put forward its own parliamentary candidates where they had run before, as candidates of disaffiliated local labour parties, and where, in heavily proletarian constituencies, a split vote would not let in the capitalist candidate. 'To contest the seats of reactionary leaders without having won the local workers to our support . . . would consolidate the rank-and-file workers against us throughout the country.'

Two days before the plenum opened, *Pravda* had written that the CPGB would have to reconsider its relations with the Labour Party, whose leaders were now openly on the side of the bourgeoisie. It could no longer allow its hands to be tied by formal adherence to such a party. The majority of the British delegation thought it wrong to depart from the advice given by Lenin in 1920, when the situation was more revolutionary. So long as the Labour Party was based on the trade unions, it would be a mistake to change communist policy. Arnot put the case for the minority; anything that concealed the CPGB's antagonism to the Labour Party was detrimental to its future. He was supported by Smeral and Pepper, who argued that the CPGB could win the leadership of the workers 'only over the dead body of the Labour Party'. Bukharin, putting the ECCI case, admitted that the Labour Party was not yet completely a social-democratic party, but a MacDonald government would be just as much an enemy as the Baldwin Government. Roy spoke in the same strain. Bennett (Petrovsky) reported for the commission to the plenary session, and Gallacher and Campbell announced that after the discussion in the commission they were thoroughly convinced of the correctness of the new line. (On 14 March the political bureau of the CPGB central committee unanimously endorsed the resolution, as did the central committee itself a few days later. This was followed by 'an energetic campaign to explain and popularize the new line'. In an article on the tenth anniversary of the foundation of the Comintern Bell wrote: 'Once more the Comintern came to the assistance of the British workers. The [British] Communist Party did not appreciate these deep and very far-reaching changes. . . . No better illustration can be formed of the advantages of an international party, as a corrective to national one-sidedness, than the story of the Ninth Plenum of the ECCI.')

The French CP had adopted the 'class against class' slogan before the ninth plenum, announcing it in an 'open letter' in November 1927; this followed instructions from the ECCI presidium, sent in April and September, that in the elections due to be held in 1928 there was to be no joint list with the socialists, and no standing down in favour of left candidates—electoral tactics earlier approved by the French politbureau. The 'open letter' presented 'class against class' electoral tactics as a special case of the united front; a joint list with the socialists would be permitted in the second electoral round on a programme (rejected by the socialist party congress in December 1927) which included the nationalization of banks, cancellation of war debts, defence of the USSR, etc. In the French central committee Renaud Jean described the new policy as catastrophic, and Doriot argued the case for some modifications. Since it was customary for the strongest left-wing candidates in the first electoral round to receive the support of the other left-wing candidates in the second round in order to defeat right-wing candidates, the new Comintern line made no distinction between the extreme right and the left-wing socialists. The boundary between 'reactionary' and 'left' had, according to the open letter, been eliminated by the national bloc. (An exception was made in Alsace, where the French CP made an electoral alliance with the German Catholic autonomists.) The plenum resolution on France, noting that old habits and traditions were obstructing the operation of the new policy, urged the French central committee to act more vigorously. Analysing the situation in France in similar terms to those used in the resolution on the CPGB, the resolution asserted that the class struggle in France was growing more acute, and the masses becoming more radical. The *bloc des gauches* had behaved treacherously, as had the socialist party and the CGT. The changed situation required changes in communist tactics; nevertheless the party had continued to repeat the old mistakes.

The resolution approved the expulsion of the 'Trotskyist fraction leaders' Treint, Girault, and others, by a decision of the central committee of the CPF on 11 January 1928. At the conference of the French Communist Party held at Saint-Denis at the end of June 1927, the opposition spokesmen complained that the documents of the CPSU opposition had not been published. Doriot was the principal speaker for the majority, and the resolution approving the action against the CPSU opposition was passed against two votes, one 'reserved' vote, and one abstention. Treint, justifying his opposition to ECCI policy, wrote at this time: 'There lies between the opportunist policy of the Stalin–Bukharin group in China and true Leninism the blood of the Chinese workers.' He accused them of concealing, even from the majority of the ECCI presidium, what was happening in China, and all the documents bearing on these events. A speech by Stalin at the Communist Academy 'was never published because the coup d'état of Chiang Kai-shek which occurred ten days later brutally and categorically refuted his words. But Radek, who spoke at the Communist Academy against Stalin and demonstrated that the treason of Chiang Kai-shek was then only a question of weeks and perhaps of days, was removed from his position as Rector of the Sun Yat-sen University. . . . In order to conceal these facts, it was necessary to create within the Russian party as well as the International, an organizational regime which becomes more and more intolerable—Stalinism is precisely this regime of bureaucratic strangulation and administrative terror applied in the Russian party and the International.'

In September Treint was expelled from the CC of his party, and the ECCI was requested to expel him from the Executive. He was charged with fractionalism, with having had dealings with Fischer and Maslow in Germany, and with Bordiga in Italy, and with having published opposition documents. At the CPF conference which met on 30 January–1 February 1928, the expelled members declared their readiness to cease opposition and dissolve their fraction provided the Comintern ended its policy of expulsions and readmitted those expelled, published the opposition documents, and opened a discussion on all questions in dispute. The conference voted 174 against 1, with 4 abstentions, to ratify the expulsion of Treint, Girault, and others. At the same conference the French party accused itself of having failed to understand the nature of the capitalist offensive, or to notice the radicalization of the masses; it had kept too rigidly within the bounds of bourgeois legality, and had failed to grasp France's leading role in the preparations for war. These errors had been pointed out in the open letter of 10 November 1927, but not enough had been done to apply the new line.]

1. The English bourgeoisie, who are facing more and more severe international competition, and chronic depression in the key industries, will certainly continue their policy of capitalist nationalization . . . of colonial repression and the suppression of national-revolutionary liberation movements. In foreign policy the preparation of war against the Soviet Union will continue as before to be their main preoccupation. The resistance of the working class to this policy of the ruling class will make the class struggle in Britain much more acute.

2. The policy of the British ruling classes is designed to draw the major workers' organizations—the Labour Party and the trade unions—into their sphere of influence, despite the resistance of the working class. The leaders of these organizations . . . are doing their best to transform them into subsidiary organizations of the bourgeois State and the employers' associations. . . .

4. This integration of capitalist bourgeoisie and reformism is accompanied by the development of the struggle between the right wing and the revolutionary workers. . . . From a federal type of organization based on the unions, the Labour Party is turning more and more into an ordinary social-democratic party and is beginning to exclude from its ranks even those communists and left-wing workers who represent the unions. The trade union leaders for their part are making stronger and stronger attacks on the Minority Movement and the communist party. . . .

5. On the other hand, these circumstances are aggravating and intensifying the discontent of the broad masses of the working class not only with the general situation in the country, but also with the reformist policy of the official leaders of the Labour Party and trade unions. . . . The perspective

of the workers' movement in England is one of class struggles of increasing sharpness. . . .

6. In these circumstances it is imperative for the communist party to take advantage of the leftward movement of the masses by adopting clearer and sharper tactics of opposition to the Labour Party and trade union leaders, to rouse the left-wing workers to struggle against the bureaucracy and so win the leadership of the working class in the class struggle against capitalism. . . .

7. Because of the special form of association between the unions and the Labour Party, the communist party, which is not affiliated to the Labour Party and has no rights within it, is frequently compelled to submit to Labour Party discipline (e.g. to accept the decisions of the Labour Party selection panels concerning parliamentary candidates). It is now necessary to wage an all-out fight against this discipline, which imposes on the workers' movement the will of the labour bureaucracy, which suppresses the will of the workers, and which hampers the communist party's freedom of action, by getting the local Labour Party organizations to call new conferences for the selection of parliamentary candidates on a basis which guarantees full rights to all workers in the Labour Party, including communists; and by calling unofficial conferences to select candidates if the local Labour Parties, dominated by the bureaucratic machine, should refuse to do so, or if they organize the conferences in a purely bureaucratic manner.

8. It is however not yet expedient to abandon the slogan of affiliation to the Labour Party, for it has not yet become entirely a social-democratic party. . . .

9. An energetic campaign must be conducted in the union branches for local control of the political levy, in order to make it possible to finance candidates favoured by the local rank and file.

10. The general political line must be based on the assumption that the communist party confronts not one enemy camp, but two, the Conservative Party . . . and an alliance of liberals, Labour Party, and union leaders, supported by part of the bourgeoisie, by the petty bourgeoisie, and by the labour aristocracy. . . .

11. . . . At the present time a labour government would from the start be objectively an instrument for attacking the workers. The experience of the MacDonald Government, the betrayal of the general strike and the miners' struggle, the changed attitude of the Labour Party and union leaders to the question of war, to relations with the Soviet Union, to China, India, and Egypt . . . make it essential for the English Communist Party to come out more boldly and clearly as an independent political party, to change its attitude to the Labour Party and Labour Government, and consequently to replace the slogan of a labour government by the slogan of a revolutionary workers' government.

12. This general change in the party's tactics determines its electoral tactics. During elections the communist party will come out as an independent organization, with its own platform, its own slogans, etc., different from and opposed to all other contending forces. It will put up as many of its own candidates as possible . . . and put up candidates in opposition to the official strike-breaking candidates of the Labour Party. . . .

13. It is absolutely essential to put up candidates against the leaders of the Labour Party and the TUC General Council. . . . Since large sections of the masses still support the reformist leaders, it is absolutely essential to propose a united front locally and nationally, in order once more to expose the Labour Party and trade union leaders who prefer unity with the capitalists to unity with the revolutionary workers. . . .

15. It is essential to start a mass campaign at once for a daily newspaper.

EXTRACTS FROM THE RESOLUTION OF THE NINTH ECCI PLENUM ON
THE TRADE UNION QUESTION

25 *February* 1928   *Resolutionen und Beschlüsse*, IX Plenum, p. 13

[This resolution, also passed unanimously, was introduced by Humbert-Droz. He argued that in the IFTU there was no longer a left wing prepared to co-operate with the communists and fight capitalism. Struggles within the IFTU reflected only the different national interests of the national bourgeoisie. That socialist parties were everywhere in opposition was itself a form of co-operation with the bourgeoisie, for they prevented the communist parties from assuming leadership of the discontented masses, who still followed their treacherous reformist leaders. The discussion in the commission, he said, showed that the parties had only weak links with the workers in large-scale industry; disputes often broke out without the CP being aware of what was happening, and they often intervened with ultra-left slogans such as the call for a general strike; this did not prevent them from also making reformist and opportunist errors. The commission had debated whether the tactical line should be changed, abandoning the united front and trade union unity slogans, ceasing work in reformist unions, and initiating splits to establish revolutionary unions, but had decided against this; the job of communists in the unions was still to get rid of the reformist leadership. The British delegates explained the changes introduced by the dissolution of the Anglo-Russian committee; for more than two years the CPGB had centred its trade union unity campaign on the committee, which had enabled it to strengthen its position in the unions and breach the wall erected by the social-democrats between the communist party and the masses. Unity would now have to be established at lower levels. Unity was not an end in itself, but a means of stirring the masses; it could not therefore be bought at the price of communist silence. The general line of argument put forward in the communist press was that, with capitalism in decline, the trade unions were no longer able to plead that they won reforms and improvements for the workers.

The unions were now working against the workers for capitalist rationalization and industrial peace, at the expense of the proletariat.]

I

THE INDUSTRIAL STRUGGLE AND THE TASKS OF COMMUNISTS

1. With the extremely rapid concentration of capital in the present period . . . and the amalgamation of capitalist organizations with the machinery of the bourgeois State, strikes quickly tend to assume a political character, and the forces of the proletariat come into collision with the forces of the bourgeois State. In these circumstances it is the task of communists to enlighten the masses about the perspectives of the struggle, to mobilize the broadest strata of workers, to demand as vigorously as possible their revolutionary unification, and to bring the entire struggle on to a higher plane.

2. Communists and revolutionary workers in general must make the basis of their tactics the resolute and relentless struggle against so-called 'industrial peace', which is nothing but the latest form of bringing the working class into subjection to the bourgeoisie. Therefore, in addition to putting forward concrete demands about wages and hours, the watchwords around which the masses must be mobilized are the freedom to strike, opposition to compulsory arbitration, opposition to social-democratic loyalty to collective agreements, and, as a rule, advocacy of short-term agreement only. . . .

4. The new forms of the bourgeois offensive against the working class are accompanied by a turn to the right among social-democratic politicians and trade union leaders, who actively support the tactics of industrial peace, put a brake on strikes, or betray them at the most critical moment. It is therefore the job of communists to pursue tactics which will enable them to seize strike leadership from the reformists. . . .

5. . . . Every strike must be made the arena of struggle for leadership between communists and reformists. The communist attitude must therefore be designed to secure leadership in strikes. It is necessary to mobilize the masses under communist slogans . . . to expose the treacherous attitude of the reformists and, when the opportunity is favourable, organize strikes against the will of the trade union bureaucracy. . . .

6. To be a good communist does not mean to propose strikes all the time, whatever the circumstances. This is particularly true of the general-strike slogan. The communist . . . should not limp behind the masses, nor should he run too far ahead: he should not play with strikes, but once a strike has been started, he must exploit every opportunity and prospect of struggle. . . .

7. To lead the masses in a strike, energetic work in advance of the strike

is essential. . . . Communists can win the leadership of a strike movement more easily if, before the strike, they launch a broad movement for the establishment of factory committees or win strong positions in them where they already exist. These factory committees are the best foundation for forming strike centres, elected and recognized by the broad working masses.

II

THE STRUGGLE AGAINST THE EXPULSION OF COMMUNISTS FROM TRADE UNIONS

Because of the radicalization of the labour movement, the Amsterdamers are opening a bitter campaign all along the line against communists in the trade unions. Expulsion from the unions, splitting the union organizations in which communists win predominant influence have become everyday events. . . . Among communists there has been a certain passivity on this question.

Communists must:

(a) Wage an open and vigorous struggle against expulsion under the slogan of trade union unity;

(b) Conduct this struggle primarily among the masses, by organizing protest meetings in favour of democracy within the unions. . . .

(d) The attempt to stay in the union must never lead a communist to renounce active revolutionary political work in the union.

III

ORGANIZATIONAL TASKS OF COMMUNISTS IN TRADE UNIONS

I

The ninth ECCI plenum considers it one of the most urgent tasks of the international revolutionary trade union movement to adopt an attitude based on clearly defined principles to the defects in the work of communist parties and revolutionary unions to win the masses for the revolutionary class struggle. Particular attention will have to be paid to the organizational tasks of the trade union movement in colonial countries. . . . Everywhere the political influence of communists in the trade unions is growing; but the organizational work of the communist parties is not keeping pace with this growth. . . .

2

Although organizational work must vary according to country and industry, there are nevertheless basic principles of organizational work applicable to all countries. Communists in trade unions in *all* countries must make it their task:

i. To capture the most important industries, industrial districts, large factories and plants.

ii. To get the greatest possible number of workers in every factory to do trade union work.

iii. To build up trade union bodies on a factory basis; to do this the local trade union branch machinery must be captured.

iv. To win the factory committees, where they exist, and to create them where they do not exist, and to make these committees the basic organizations of industrial unions.

v. To deal with all important trade union questions in the factory itself.

vi. Communists must take particular care that these committees . . . are not turned into instruments of capital–labour co-operation.

vii. To fight against bureaucratic centralism, to fight for broad trade union democracy, i.e. the greatest possible extension of local powers, proportional representation in trade union executives, annual elections, etc. . . .

xii. To strengthen the organization of the unemployed; to fight against the exclusion of unemployed from the unions. . . .

3

As regards revolutionary unions in countries where the unions are split . . . communists must:

i. Recruit new members. . . .

iii. Change the unions into industrial unions, without forcing mechanical fusion.

iv. Establish close links between the factory committees in all factories run by the same company or trust. . . .

v. Create every possible joint committee, action committee, and other united front bodies both with workers in reformist unions and with the unorganized. . . .

4

For those countries in which there is an organized trade union minority the most important organizational tasks are:

i. To win over as many trade unions and trades councils as possible to the opposition. . . .

iii. To carry out a constant campaign explaining recent defeats in the industrial struggle, pointing to the need to replace the leaders.

iv. To struggle unrelentingly against the slightest violation of trade union democracy, against expulsions, etc.

For those countries in which there is no organized opposition and in which work is carried out by fractions, communist efforts must be directed to

i. establishing fractions on the district, industry, and national level. . . .

iii. Fighting against bureaucratic centralism in the trade union movement and for the extension of the rights of local organizations.

EXTRACTS FROM THE RESOLUTION OF THE NINTH ECCI PLENUM ON THE CHINESE QUESTION

25 February 1928   *Resolutionen und Beschlüsse*, IX Plenum, p. 44

[At the CPSU congress in December 1927 Bukharin said that the Chinese revolution was far from dead; they might well be on the eve of a new revolutionary wave. There was no need for pessimism; Tan Ping-shan had been expelled for opportunism, and the party, now numbering between 20,000 and 25,000, was internally consolidated. Lominadze said the task of the Chinese party now was to organize for an armed insurrection under the slogan of Soviets, and to organize Soviets in certain areas, as had been done in some parts of Kwantung. (At the end of 1927, after an attack by the KMT army in Hunan, Mao Tse-tung withdrew the remnants of his forces to the remote mountain area of Chingkanshan, where he was joined by Chu Teh and his troops in the spring of 1928. His concentration on land reforms and the training of a peasant army did not at first meet with the approval of the Chinese central committee, which, in November 1927, rebuked him for regarding the industrial workers as 'auxiliaries of the peasants'.) The resolution on the work of the CPSU delegation to the ECCI stated that the Chinese nationalist bourgeoisie had exhausted their revolutionary possibilities, while the KMT had become the direct instrument of military cliques.

The meeting of the plenum appears to have been preceded by a 'Chinese conference'. At the sixth Comintern congress later in the year Pepper quoted Bukharin's statement there that to explain the Canton failure by military and technical reasons, as Neumann and Lominadze did, was incorrect. 'We did not have a sufficiently broad social basis for a victorious insurrection.' In the discussion of the Canton rising at the plenum it was agreed that preparations had been inadequate, both among the masses and among the enemy troops; the right danger had now given place to the danger that putschist tendencies would not be kept in check. The CCP was called on to reinforce its working-class core and to fight against the liquidators, as well as against those who did not understand the need for prolonged and detailed day-to-day work, but wanted immediate action against the counter-revolution. Immediately after the plenum *Pravda* wrote that the reactionary camp had consolidated its position, but the workers' and peasants' movement had reached a higher stage, under communist leadership and the banner of Soviets. Since the bourgeoisie had not solved the tasks of the bourgeois-democratic revolution, the CCP must concentrate all its forces on preparation for armed revolt. The opposition renegades said that the Chinese revolution had suffered a decisive defeat; this was liquidationism.

The resolution was put forward in the name of the CPSU and Chinese CP, and introduced by Bukharin and Stalin for the first, and Li (Li Li-san?) and Sian (Hsiang Chung-fa?) for the second. It was adopted unanimously. The ECCI representative referred to in the first paragraph was Lominadze.

Trotsky, in exile, wrote to an unnamed friend that, while the resolutions on the French and British parties represented an extreme and ill-considered switch to the left, the resolution on China was false from beginning to end, a continuation of the putschist Canton policy which would lead to the defeat of the third Chinese revolution (the letter is in the Trotsky archives). Referring to the resolution in his critique of the draft CI programme, Trotsky wrote that it was wrong to say that the KMT had gone over completely to the counter-revolution. That could only happen when the class needs of the bourgeoisie were satisfied, whereas China was still disunited, still subject to outside pressure, still unable to control its own market. 'Neither the workers nor the peasants would have followed the national bourgeoisie if we ourselves had not urged them to do so.' The resolution deleted the KMT, saying the revolution had taken place largely under communist leadership. It was precisely because this was not the case that the revolution had suffered defeat. What was now called a severe defeat was at the time described as 'the transition to a higher stage'. The important question, he added, was not whether China was ripe for socialism, but whether it was ripe for the proletarian dictatorship. The two were not identical because of the law of uneven capitalist development.]

1. The present period of the Chinese revolution is the period of the bourgeois-democratic revolution, which neither from the economic aspect (agrarian revolution and abolition of feudal relations), nor from the aspect of the national struggle against imperialism (China's unification as a single State and national independence), nor from the aspect of the class nature of the government (dictatorship of the proletariat and peasantry) has yet reached its conclusion. The characterization of the present stage of the Chinese revolution as one which is already a socialist revolution is false. Equally false is its characterization as a 'permanent' revolution (the attitude of the ECCI representative). To postulate a tendency in the revolution to jump over the bourgeois-democratic stage, while regarding it at the same time as a 'permanent' revolution, is a mistake similar to that made by Trotsky in 1905. This mistake is the more harmful in that it leaves out of account the outstanding national peculiarity of the Chinese revolution as a revolution in a semi-colonial country.

2. The first wave of the broad revolutionary movement of workers and peasants has subsided; by and large it moved under the slogans—and to a substantial degree under the leadership—of the communist party. In a number of centres of the revolutionary movement it has ended with most severe defeats for the workers and peasants, with the physical annihilation of part of the communist cadres and of the revolutionary cadres in general . . . with the complete exposure of the Kuomintang and the generals as counter-revolutionary . . . and, finally, with the transition of the entire revolutionary mass movement in China to a new stage, the stage of Soviets. . . .

3. At the present moment we are not confronted with a new and

powerful advance of the revolutionary mass movement throughout the country. Nevertheless there are a number of indications that the workers' and peasants' revolution is approaching such a stage. These signs include not only the heroic rising of the Canton workers, but primarily the unleashing of a peasant movement in some areas . . . as well as the increasingly frequent revolts among the troops of the warlords' armies. The catastrophic worsening of the economic conditions of the masses, the financial crisis and the ruin caused by the unending wars between the militarist groups, as well as extreme political oppression, will inevitably drive the masses on the road of further revolutionary struggle.

4. The course of the Chinese revolution has underlined one of its peculiar features, that is, its extremely unequal development. It is developing unequally in the different provinces. . . . It has also until now developed unequally as between town and country. While the peasant movement is developing in a number of provinces, the industrial workers' movement, drained of blood and gripped in the iron vice of the most extreme white terror, is in a number of industrial centres going through a stage of depression.

5. This situation dictates the basic tactical line of the party. The party must prepare itself for a violent surge forward of new revolutionary waves. This confronts the party with the immediate tactical task of organizing and carrying through armed mass risings, for the tasks of the revolution can only be solved by rebellion and by the overthrow of the present authorities. Precisely for that reason all party work must now be concentrated on winning over the worker and peasant millions, educating them politically, organizing them around the party and its slogans (confiscation of landlords' estates, eight-hour day, national unification of China, liberation from the imperialist yoke, overthrow of the existing Government, dictatorship of the proletariat and peasantry, establishment of Soviets). The greatest danger in the present situation would be for the vanguard of the workers' and peasants' movement, because of an incorrect appraisal of conditions, an underestimate of the power of the enemy, to break away from the masses, push forward too far, allow their forces to be split. . . . The communist party will certainly be defeated and disorganized if it does not apply itself on the broadest scale to win and to organize the masses. . . .

6. Consequently the ECCI directs special attention to the necessity of intensifying the party's mass work among the workers and peasants. At the same time an end must be put once and for all to terrorist practices in the trade union movement, for these are fatal to the party. The party must fight with the utmost energy against the use of violence to get strikes called. Only if the masses are convinced of the correctness of the path recommended by the party, only if it has their unreserved support and complete

confidence, can it lead the movement. It is equally necessary to intensify work to create and extend the network of peasant organizations . . . with a separate organization for the proletarian elements in the village. . . .

7. It is necessary to struggle resolutely against putschism in certain strata of the working class, against unprepared and unorganized actions in town and country, against playing with insurrection. Playing with revolts instead of preparing the mass rising of workers and peasants is the surest way to bring disaster to the revolution. In guiding the spontaneous guerrilla actions of peasants in the different provinces, the party must bear in mind that they can become the starting-point of the victorious rebellion of the entire people only if they are linked with the new surge forward of the revolutionary wave in the proletarian centres. . . . The ECCI is of the opinion that the chief task of the party in the sovietized peasant areas is to carry through the agrarian revolution and to organize Red Army detachments which can subsequently be united into a single national Chinese Red Army.

8. The most important prerequisite for the further development of the revolution is the consolidation of the Chinese Communist Party itself, its cadres, its provincial organizations, and its centre. The Chinese Communist Party has, it is true, by and large overcome its opportunist errors (the August 1927 conference), noted in earlier Comintern resolutions, but it has not yet completely adapted itself to the circumstances of the present situation, and is vacillating both in its tactics (underestimating the dangers of putschism, terrorist methods of struggle in the trade unions, enthusiasm for the rural guerrilla movement), as well as in matters of organization. . . .

9. The ECCI believes that the Chinese Communist Party must wage an unrelenting struggle against the attempts to organize a new, allegedly 'truly communist' workers' and peasants' party, really a bourgeois-reformist party, being made by a few former communists (Tan Ping-shan, etc.). Basically, this will be a menshevik, anti-worker, and anti-peasant party, a compliant tool of Chiang Kai-shek and other executioners of the working class and peasantry. . . .

10. The ECCI considers it indispensable to undertake a careful examination of the entire experience of the revolutionary movement in China. . . . In particular, it is necessary to study the experience of the Canton rising. This heroic attempt to organize Soviet power in China, which played a tremendous part in the development of the workers' and peasants' revolution, revealed several failings in the leadership; insufficient preparatory work among the workers and peasants as well as in the enemy's army . . . their completely inadequate knowledge of what was happening in Canton, the weakness of the political mobilization of the masses . . . for which the leaders on the spot have to bear their share of responsibility before the CI (Comrade N. among others). . . .

11. The ECCI imposes on all sections of the Comintern the duty of fighting against the calumny spread by the social-democrats and Trotskyists that the Chinese revolution is liquidated. These calumnies only lighten the work of the imperialists. . . . The Comintern sections in the imperialist countries must fight more vigorously than ever for the withdrawal of troops and warships from China, against all attempts to annex and partition Chinese territory, against all attempts to throttle the Chinese revolutionary movement. The ECCI calls on all workers, and in the first place on all communists, to fulfil their duty of proletarian solidarity and aid for the heroic Chinese proletariat.

EXTRACTS FROM THE APPEAL OF THE WEST EUROPEAN BUREAU OF THE ECCI ON EVENTS IN CHINA

May 1928   *Inprekorr*, viii, 47, p. 831, 18 *May* 1928

[When in the spring of 1928 the war between the Kuomintang forces and the northern warlords reached Shantung, Japan, fearing for its interests in the Chinese railways, dispatched troops to the area; they occupied two Chinese cities. On 3 May fighting broke out between the Japanese and KMT forces. Japanese warships in Chinese waters were reinforced. On 9 May the Japanese Government undertook to withdraw its naval and military forces when the emergency was over, but Japanese troops continued to occupy the railway zone. In an interview published in *Izvestiya* Chicherin, the Soviet Foreign Commissar, asserted that the United States, Britain, and France approved the steps taken by Japan.]

The military partition of China has begun. Predatory Japanese imperialism has occupied Shantung. The world bourgeoisie, who smothered the national-revolutionary movement of the Chinese workers and peasants in blood, are turning from intervention to the open conquest of the country. Japan is hurrying to exploit the advantages of its strategical position to tear off the first morsels. . . . The war begun by Japan can turn into a world conflagration, a war of the imperialists for the general partition of the world, a re-division of colonies, a bloody campaign against all the oppressed peoples. Only the prompt and courageous solidarity of the international proletariat and the oppressed peoples can prevent or postpone the catastrophe.

The Mikado's Government is not waging war against Chiang Kai-shek, who has offered his services more than once to the various imperialist gangs and is now being bribed by American imperialism. In Shantung as in Manchuria Japanese imperialism is waging a predatory war against the Chinese people. It is the first to start on the partition of China because in Japan itself the government of bourgeois-feudal reaction can only keep in power by open war against the entire people. Japanese fascism, which brutally suppresses the workers' movement, shoots down peasants, and throws not hundreds but thousands of militants into prison, is no longer even in a position to continue to use parliamentary deception to conceal its dictatorship. The recent parliamentary elections were held in an atmosphere of raging terror; but this did not prevent the workers and peasants appearing in a united revolutionary front at the elections, or the communist party from taking part in them at the head of the workers and the village poor. . . .

Tanaka's Government which, notwithstanding its bribery of deputies, has half of parliament against it, stays in power only by the force of bayonets, but even these are beginning to become unreliable, and bourgeois-feudal reaction is intensifying its terrorist regime to maintain discipline in the army. To strengthen the military dictatorship inside the country and distract the workers' attention from the political and economic crisis, the Mikado's Government is looking for an easy and brilliant victory in Shantung.

Workers, peasants, and soldiers of Japan!

It is your first revolutionary duty to stop those who have raised the sword against the Chinese people. Answer the occupation of Shantung by organized and selfless struggle against the Government, above all in Japan itself. . . .

The counter-revolutionary Kuomintang has veiled its agreement with the foreign imperialists by the provocative lie that the 'eradication of bolshevism' in China will provide guarantees against imperialist intervention. The occupation of Shantung by the Japanese deals an annihilating blow at this provocative falsehood.

Only under proletarian leadership will the Chinese working masses defeat the counter-revolution inside the country and win independence for revolutionary China. Only the power of the workers and peasants organized in Soviets, by destroying imperialism's positions and eliminating its economic and political agents inside China, will with the help of the world proletariat lead the national revolution to victory and open a broad road to socialism. . . .

To conquer the country in order to partition it—that is the imperialists' policy in China. The first part of this criminal plan they have carried out by joint military intervention against the national revolution. Japan's capture of new war booty in Shantung is the beginning of the second stage. Japan will be followed by the other imperialist robbers, in the first place England and the United States, who will demand their share in the plunder.

England, which is inciting Japan and approves the Japanese robbery, is out to get a free hand for itself for military conquest. . . . American military activity has become more marked and more intense as a result of the occupation of Shantung. The Washington Government is frankly out for a new division of colonies, the winning of new markets and raw material sources. The protection offered to Nanking and the 'indignation' about the occupation of Shantung only mean that American imperialism will stop at nothing to secure for itself unrestricted opportunities for plunder.

More than once the Communist International has given warning that the attack on the Chinese people is the prelude to a gigantic monstrous world war. The partition of China started by Japan is a further step towards war. The world catastrophe is approaching with increasing rapidity.

The more intense attacks on the Soviet Union are only part of the general plan of the international robbers to re-divide the world. The existence of the Soviet Union, as the citadel and lighthouse of the proletarian world revolution, as the instrument for relentlessly exposing the secret war plans of the bourgeoisie, represents an immense danger for all the incendiarists of war.

RESOLUTION OF THE ECCI PRESIDIUM ON THE LENINBUND

4 *May* 1928   *Inprekorr*, viii, 44, p. 791, 8 *May* 1928

[The Leninbund was formed by expelled members of the KPD in the spring of 1928, to put up its own candidates. Ruth Fischer, Maslow, and Scholem resigned very shortly after its formation, considering it too sectarian. The 'letter of instructions from the Trotskyist centre' published by *Pravda* on 15 January 1928 noted that Maslow and Fischer appeared to think that the CPSU opposition was opposed to a second party because of special conditions in the USSR. That was not so; it was irreconcilably opposed to a second party in general and on principle. The CPSU and the Comintern had to be captured from within; the KPD opposition should not put up separate candidates—to do so would justify the attitude of the capitulators Kamenev and Zinoviev (who, with others, were readmitted to the CPSU in June 1928).

Radek, in exile in Tobolsk, had sent a telegram to *Pravda* and to the *Rote Fahne* protesting against separate candidates of the Leninbund. Every revolutionary German worker must be urged to vote for the KPD candidates against the German bourgeoisie and social-democracy. Trotsky, in a letter to his fellow-exile Beloborodov (in the Trotsky archives), criticized the use of the name Leninbund. 'Opposition' was good enough, and was international. The use of the name Leninbund might be taken as the first steps in establishing a new party. He, like Radek, opposed separate candidatures.

In the May 1928 elections the KPD polled 3·2 million votes and won 54 seats (compared with 2·7 million votes and 45 seats in 1924); the SPD vote rose from 7·8 to 9·1 million, and its seats from 131 to 152; the Nazis polled 800,000 votes and won 12 seats; the left communists 80,000 votes, but no seats.]

On 15 April the *Fahne des Kommunismus* published an open letter to the Comintern and to the CC of the KPD, the ostensible purpose of which was to request the admission of the so-called Leninbund to the Comintern or its recognition as a sympathizing organization.

The presidium of the ECCI declares that this 'request' is nothing but a manœuvre by which Maslow, Ruth Fischer, Urbahns, and Co. are trying to use for their own counter-revolutionary political activities the workers who are discontented with their policy and whom they have misled. In their request there is no word of condemnation of the counter-revolutionary splitting activity of the Maslow–Urbahns group; it is even expressly stated that they do not submit to the resolutions of Comintern congresses. The passage refers to their acceptance of the fifth Comintern congress resolutions on questions 'of principle'; that is, they do not accept the resolutions which condemned Trotskyism.

In this request they resort to political pressure (the threat to put forward their own candidates), a method which has evoked a protest even from some prominent Trotskyists (e.g. Radek).

The foundation of a separate party and the decision to put forward separate candidates, at a moment when all the bourgeois forces in Germany, from the nationalists to the social-democrats, are coming out against the communist party, and the bourgeois coalition Government is preparing to dissolve the League of Red Front Fighters, amount to a repetition of malevolent treachery by the Maslow–Fischer–Urbahns League, that group of renegades who do not shrink from covering their counter-revolutionary activity with Lenin's name.

In view of the fact that a number of workers were misled by the false information given out by the leaders of the Maslow–Fischer–Urbahns League, the ECCI presidium resolves:

To readmit to the KPD and the Comintern, after an interval of six months for testing and verification, all those members of the Maslow–Fischer–Urbahns group who

(1) immediately condemn the activities of this group as anti-proletarian and counter-revolutionary;

(2) promptly leave the Bund and demand its immediate dissolution;

(3) publicly undertake to obey the decisions of the CC of the KPD, and the leading bodies of the Comintern.

EXTRACTS FROM THE RESOLUTION OF THE POLITICAL SECRETARIAT
OF THE ECCI ON THE IMMEDIATE TASKS OF THE JAPANESE COMMUNIST
PARTY

4 *May* 1928   *Inprekorr*, viii, 55, p. 1005, 8 *June* 1928; 56, p. 1022, 12 *June* 1928

[Government proceedings against the Japanese Communist Party became more marked towards the end of 1927, as the JCP extended its activities, particularly in preparation for the elections to the Diet which were to be held, for the first time under a universal male franchise, in February 1928. Itself illegal, it worked through the Rodonominto, or Workers' and Peasants' Party, whose list of candidates included ten communists, none of whom was elected; the Workers' and Peasants' Party received nearly 200,000 votes. In March the police rounded up a number of suspects, raided union offices, etc. The leading communists escaped arrest. The Workers' and Peasants' Party and a number of other labour organizations were dissolved by government order, as well as radical students' bodies.]

1. The growth of the broad mass movement of the Japanese workers and peasants, as shown in the recent elections and in the increasing resistance to attacks by the Government, opens a new page in the history of the class struggle in Japan. . . .

The greatest success of the Japanese communists was the re-establishment of the communist party itself. The party succeeded in taking an active, indeed a leading, part in mobilizing and organizing the vanguard of the awakening masses. Despite threats and brutal suppression the party is continuing this activity and thus giving the most effective answer to the reactionary imperialist Government of Japan.

2. Everything that happened before and after the election campaign completely confirmed the basic ideas of the Comintern resolution of 15 July 1927, namely, that in Japan as elsewhere, notwithstanding the special circumstances of the class struggle in that country, a communist party can develop only by fighting social-democracy. . . .

3. In the light of recent events it is clear that the communist party committed a serious mistake is not opposing the proposals for an unconditional amalgamation of the Rodonominto, the Nichiroto, and the Sakai Minsuto (social-democrats). An amalgamation plan of that kind should not have been regarded as a form of united front tactics at all. The purpose of united front tactics is to mobilize for the struggle against capitalism and reformism and thus to strengthen the revolutionary organizations of the working class. . . .

4. In order to be able to accomplish its new, great, and responsible tasks, the young communist party must strain every nerve to strengthen itself numerically and ideologically. Particular efforts must be made to strengthen and improve the illegal apparatus, in order to counter govern-

ment action through the police and the judiciary to annihilate the communist party and all other revolutionary organizations. The party must take steps to improve its machinery, and at the same time let no legal opportunity slip for establishing contact with the masses as a means of extending and utilizing its ideological and organizational influence among the workers and poor peasants.

5. The creation of an illegal party journal, appearing regularly, is urgently necessary, to enable the party to expand and strengthen its organization. . . .

6. The communist party is called on to lead the struggle for the reestablishment of the revolutionary mass organizations—the Rodonominto, the Hyogikai (left-wing trade union organization), and the Seinen Domei (youth league) dissolved by the Government. . . .

7. The party must fight vigorously against any move, open or concealed, to abandon the struggle for these organizations, and against the mood of retreat in general.

Particular attention must be paid to defending the Hyogikai. To leave the left-wing unions and enter the centrist unions would mean more than open surrender by the working class; it would encourage the Government in its terrorist policy and the reformist leaders in their treachery. Special measures must be taken to prevent members of the Hyogikai from transferring to the centrist unions. . . . At the same time our party must retain the initiative in the struggle to re-establish the unity of the unions, split by force and intrigue by the reformists. . . .

11. The communist party must conduct agitation among the workers to induce them to influence the Rodonominto to pursue the following parliamentary tactics: The small Rodonominto party should not merge with the general bloc of so-called workers' organizations, which includes the social-democrats. . . . It is the imperative duty of the Rodonominto deputies to take an active part in the workers' and peasants' struggle and to use the parliamentary tribune for this purpose. This does not exclude the possibility and necessity, in certain circumstances, of maintaining contact by means of joint conferences with deputies representing social-democratic and centrist organizations, in order to influence their parliamentary tactics. . . .

12. The communist party must make it clear to the workers that the Rodonominto group in parliament, because of their extreme numerical weakness, will be able to play an independent part only if they conduct an energetic struggle (supported by the communist party and the masses) against imperialism, for the demands of the workers and peasants, for strengthening the revolutionary organizations. Regardless of the difficulties they will encounter, the Rodonominto deputies must speak out against the robber war being waged by Japanese imperialism in China,

and must force the reformist deputies to join in the campaign or reveal themselves as avowed allies of the government's robber policy.

THE SIXTH CONGRESS OF THE COMMUNIST INTERNATIONAL

[The sixth congress was held in Moscow from 17 July to 1 September 1928. It was attended, according to one source, by 532 delegates of whom 387 had voting powers; according to another, by 575 delegates of whom 372 had voting powers. Piatnitsky, for the mandates commission, reported that invitations had been sent to 66 parties and organizations with a total membership of 4 million, of whom 1·8 million were in parties and 2·2 million in youth organizations. The increase of rather more than a half million compared with the fifth congress was accounted for by the CPSU. Fifty-eight parties were represented, six without voting powers. The representatives of Outer Mongolia and Korea were given guest tickets only, since their status was not settled.

A questionnaire completed by the delegates showed that 50 per cent. were of working-class origin (compared with 58 per cent. at the previous congress), 25 per cent. were from the free professions, 17 per cent. were non-manual workers, and 4 per cent. from the countryside. According to present occupations, 62·2 per cent. of the delegates were party officials, and 21 per cent. in industrial occupations; 278 delegates had never before attended a Comintern congress; 4 had attended all six.

The congress was opened by Bukharin, who reported for the ECCI. He gave a long analysis of the world economic situation: structural changes had aggravated capitalist contradictions and altered the balance of forces. This was again raising the question of a re-division of the world, i.e. of war. The focus of these contradictions was Anglo-American rivalry. Social-democracy was already bankrupt, but continued to exist on the basis of capitalist stabilization. It was no longer sufficient to explain the strength of social-democracy as being due to the super-profits of colonial exploitation; such an explanation did not apply to the United States and Germany, where colonial profits were replaced by the differential profits arising from superior technical development. Social democracy, which in 1914 had merely defended the capitalist fatherland, now embodied the aggressive aspirations of that fatherland; its chief task now was ideological preparation for war against the USSR. The response to that from the Comintern was the new tactical line adopted at the ninth plenum and embodied in the resolutions on the British and French communist parties. 'As to the English party, we have broken with all the old traditions of the English labour movement.' The strongest tradition was that of a united organized working class. This unity was the reformists' trump card; they used it to fight revolutionary ideas and the revolutionary party; it was the greatest obstacle to the liberation of the proletariat from reformist influence. There had been a great deal of opposition from some French and British communist leaders, but the ECCI had convinced them that the new line was correct. To believe that this move was an attempt to answer the opposition's criticism was childish; it was called forth by the change in the objective situation.

On China Bukharin argued that failure had been due not to a mistaken policy, but to the faulty application of a correct policy, for which the Chinese central committee and some of the Comintern's representatives in China were responsible. They had failed to note the changes in the objective situation which made the KMT an enemy instead of an ally, and had held back the agrarian revolution and the development of the workers' mass movement. The reaction to the other extreme, of insufficiently prepared and putschist risings, had now been corrected.

There was, Bukharin said, too much provincialism and not enough internationalism in the CI sections, as shown by the failure of many of them to support the miners in England and the revolution in China. Symptoms of a bureaucratic attitude were increasing, not only in the CPSU. Without more local initiative, it was difficult to promote the selection of cadres, who were very weak in theoretical matters. Leadership in the parties was over-centralized; it was true of many of them that at times only a small circle of officials had any real party life. The discussion of party questions was too often reduced to an exchange of catchwords. 'We have learnt well how to conduct operations against every kind of deviation; we do it brilliantly. But as for a real study of the problems, genuine argumentation and not a mechanical fight against opponents—that we have still to learn.' In the unions there was a tendency for communists to dictate to, rather than persuade, non-communist unionists; while many were good unionists, they did their union work in a social-democratic and not a communist spirit.

The greater danger of war gave added importance to the illegal work of the sections. The creation of illegal organizations, particularly among the armed forces, was an urgent matter, because even before war came, special legislation against communist parties would be introduced.

For the Comintern as a whole, Bukharin said at the end of his report, the right-wing danger was the greatest; it was revealed by the failure to criticize sharply enough the left social-democratic leaders, and by an exaggerated respect for bourgeois legality. The bitter fractional struggles in some parties had to be settled. In Yugoslavia the fractional struggle had gone on for seven years and had weakened the party, already suffering from police terror; extraordinary measures had had to be taken and a new leadership had now been appointed; in Poland the party congress had dragged on for three months because every item had been stubbornly disputed, although actual political differences were negligible; the party as a whole had been responsible for the mistakes made at the time of the Pilsudski coup. The ECCI had had to intervene to prevent a split. The Polish party was of crucial importance because of its position in time of war.

In the discussion on Bukharin's report de Visser (Holland) complained that, though he agreed with what Bukharin had said, the report had in fact told them virtually nothing about the work of the ECCI. On a number of important questions the Executive had either given no lead at all, or given one too late. Bodemann, a Swiss delegate, thought a good deal of ECCI material sent out to the sections was irrelevant, or it came too late. They did not want editorials for reproduction, but facts. If they had the facts, they could write the articles themselves. On trade union questions they had had contradictory advice from the ECCI and its departments.

Lozovsky said that the opposition to the resolutions of the fourth RILU congress, which had been passed unanimously, had an organized character in Germany and the United States. The KPD critics objected to such phrases as 'Amsterdam is the tool of capitalism'. The IFTU, he said, was not an erring brother, but an enemy of the working class. Opposition to RILU policy was used to conceal an anti-Comintern line. The CC of the KPD had a correct attitude on this, but the CC of the American party had at first opposed the fourth RILU congress resolutions, although they had now changed their minds.

As at previous congresses, the United States delegation was bitterly divided. The minority (whose spokesmen were Bittelman, Foster, and Cannon) argued that insufficient weight was given to the growing contradictions of American imperialism and the radicalization of the masses. But the right-wing majority (Pepper, Wicks, Lovestone, Winestone) were protected by the CI, despite their errors and their passivity on the Negro question. Wicks accused Cannon of taking his arguments from 'former comrade Trotsky', and Lovestone asked for the dissolution of the Foster–Cannon fraction. He admitted their past errors, and incidentally attacked Lozovsky (who supported the Foster faction). 'It is the tragedy of the RILU that comrade Lozovsky creates confusion on any question he touches.' Lozovsky disagreed with the American proposals for revising the statutes of the Trade Union Educational League, the American equivalent of the British Minority Movement, which made membership conditional on recognition of the proletarian dictatorship. (At the end of the year Bittelman and Foster denounced Cannon and Schachtman to the CC of the American CP as Trotskyists, and they were expelled.)

Delegates from South American countries appeared for the first time in large numbers at a Comintern congress. Lacerda (Brazil) said there had been communist parties in a number of Latin American countries since 1920, but the Comintern had only recently begun to take an interest in them. The RILU had set up a Latin American trade union secretariat in Montevideo. After the congress the Latin secretariat of the ECCI was divided into two—one section for Latin Europe, one for Latin America.

Koplenig, an Austrian delegate, raised the question of the July 1927 events. The episode needed clearer theoretical analysis. The ECCI had linked it to capitalist stabilization, the Austrian social-democrats described it as the last flicker of the post-war crisis. Some Austrian communists denied altogether that it was a rising, and disagreed with the ECCI criticism of the Austrian CP's failure to put forward the slogan of Soviets.

Stuchka reported for the International Control Commission. When the ICC was set up at the fifth congress, he said, it had been intended to review expulsions, in a deliberative capacity. This would have involved them in thousands of cases, particularly for the CPSU, and their function had changed gradually to 'passing sentences' to be ratified by the ECCI or the presidium. In April 1925 the ICC had decided that it would examine complaints by individuals against sections only if the cases were politically important, or were referred to it by the ECCI presidium or secretariat. It had dealt with roughly 200 complaints, 74 from the CPSU, 38 from the KPD, and 36 from Polish members. It was necessary for a proportion of the ICC members to be permanently in Moscow, to deal with such cases. The KPD had used expulsion too freely in dealing with the right opposition. There had been a large number of cases concerning comrades in emigration, where the absence of practical daily work exaggerated personal differences. As an audit commission the ICC needed a technical staff. Up to now it had used the staff of the CPSU.

The ECCI organization department was not in favour of having central control commissions in the Comintern sections, most of which were not strong enough to risk the dangers of dual power. The CCC of the Czech party, for example, had found itself in opposition to the Czech central committee as well as the ECCI. The ECCI endorsed the department's attitude, but in its report stated that in practice some sections still retained central control commissions.

The admission of the communist parties of Cuba, Korea, New Zealand, and Paraguay to the Comintern was formally ratified, as well as that of the Irish Workers' League, the Socialist Party of Ecuador, and the Revolutionary Socialist Party of Colombia.

Replying to the discussion on the ECCI report, Bukharin said that 'directly revolutionary situations, let us say in Europe, are possible and even probable, even without war. In the event of war they are absolutely inevitable. Wars will inevitably be accompanied by revolutions.'

The congress adopted on 29 August immensely long theses (seventy-six in all) on 'the fight against imperialist war and the tasks of communists', which started off by denouncing the disarmament conference at Geneva and the proposal for a pact for the renunciation of war (the Kellogg Pact) as despicable attempts to deceive the working class (the Soviet Union adhered to the Kellogg Pact in 1929). Hostility to the Soviet Union and the Chinese revolution were the chief forces driving towards war. The League of Nations had now become merely an instrument to serve the needs of war. Policies making for war were possible only because of the active support of the social-democrats and their allies, the Trotskyists. The customary analysis of the origin of wars and the impossibility of eliminating them otherwise than by the armed insurrection of the proletariat against the bourgeoisie was followed by an explanation of which wars were just, and which unjust—wars fought by proletarian States against intervention, or by colonial countries against their oppressors, fell into the first category. In wars among imperialists, i.e. unjust wars, it was the duty of the proletariat to work for the defeat of its own government and for the transformation of the war into civil war. In the other cases it was to support and defend the proletarian State or the oppressed country, and again work for the defeat of its own imperialist government. The concept of 'the aggressor' was irrelevant, as it was in 1914. In anti-revolutionary and anti-colonial wars aggression was determined not by military action, but by historical and political criteria. An unjust war was one fought by reaction, counter-revolution, imperialism, however hostilities opened.

Before the outbreak of war, communists should conduct a political and propagandist battle against pacifism. Communist trade union and factory work should concentrate on those industries most vital in war-time, engineering, chemicals, transport. Anti-militarist work among the armed forces was also of the utmost importance. An illegal party organization had to be set up before the outbreak of war, to enable the transition to illegality to be made smoothly, since on the outbreak of war imperialist governments would declare communist parties illegal. Since a democratic or just peace was impossible under capitalism, the central slogan in war-time should be not peace but the proletarian revolution. The slogan of a general strike against war was illusory unless interpreted as a stage in the development of revolution; the refusal to bear arms was in all cases a mistake. Communists were needed in the army, to do their revolutionary work there, but they were to oppose conscription. At the front they were to organize fraternization, to unite the troops on both sides against their officers, leading to disintegration of the armies and civil war. The events in Germany in October 1923, in Vienna in July 1927, and in Canton in December 1927, are given as examples of civil war that did not arise out of an imperialist war. In the event of an imperialist war on the USSR the proletariat in the imperialist countries must fight not only for the defeat of their own countries, but for the victory of the Soviet Union. It must regard the Red Army not as 'the enemy' but as the army of the international proletariat, to which it owes its support. Wars between the proletarian and the bourgeois States were both unavoidable and necessary; the Soviet Union's peace policy was merely a more advantageous way of fighting capitalism. Similarly, in any war between colonial countries and their oppressors, the communists were to support the oppressed peoples, while continuing the class struggle within the colonies. In the national armies of the colonial countries, their policy must be that of the 'bourgeois revolution', i.e. democratization in order to make them revolutionary. The CP must organize cells in these armies and turn them into anti-imperialist armies.

The theses went on to explain that capitalist disarmament proposals were a farce that could not be played without social-democratic support. Two schools of thought concentrated on disarmament. The first believed that there were objective tendencies at work making for the elimination of war, and that these forces should be supported by armaments limitation and international agreements; the tendencies were summarized in the theory of 'organized capitalism' and of 'super-imperialism'. Far from leading to the elimination of war, they were symptoms of the preparation for war on the largest scale. Under capitalism a pan-European or world league of States was Utopian or, if realized, reactionary. The second school of thought urged total disarmament, i.e. disarmament of the proletariat as well as the bourgeoisie. But since it was essential for the proletariat to be armed, the slogan of total disarmament was counter-revolutionary. The Soviet proposals for total disarmament at the League of Nations conference were quite different in character, being sincere and designed to prove that disarmament and the elimination of war were possible only after the overthrow of capitalism.

All Comintern sections underestimated the war danger and the inevitability of war, as shown in their failure to carry out the decisions of the eighth plenum; e.g. the parties in the Baltic countries failed to realize that the negotiations for a customs union between Estonia and Latvia were a step in the preparation of war against the USSR. Very little was being done in regard to the armed forces, munitions industries, national minorities, etc., or to organize mass action at home in support of colonial revolutionary movements. Mass organizations should be used and new ones set up to concentrate on the fight against imperialist war.

Bell (CPGB) opened the debate on the theses, which was long drawn out but tepid. Many speakers said war was imminent because of the sharpening conflict between Britain and America, and general capitalist hostility to the USSR. Dimitrov said that lasting and peaceful coexistence of the two systems was impossible. Some States, because of special circumstances, might prefer not to join in an anti-Soviet war, and with these the USSR should make military alliances. In replying to the discussion Vasiliev, for the ECCI, and Bell commented on the lack of interest shown by the delegates, and their failure to report on what their parties were actually doing, or to engage in self-criticism. The theses were adopted unanimously.

On 1 September the congress passed a resolution instructing all sections, in view of the preparations for war on the USSR, to organize an international day of struggle against imperialist war and for the defence of the Soviet Union.

The reports of the ECCI, the ICC, and the YCI were adopted on 29 August in a one-line resolution: 'Congress approves the activities of the ECCI, the ICC, and the YCI.'

In moving the congress manifesto (submitted by the presidium and adopted unanimously) Bukharin referred to its proceedings as the Comintern's 'Long Parliament'. The adoption of the CI programme marked the end of a historical phase. They had achieved a unanimous appraisal of the nature of the epoch in which they were living. Reporting after the congress to the Moscow party organization, he mentioned that Bordiga's group in Italy had sent a statement proposing that Trotsky be made chairman of the congress and that all those who had endorsed the resolutions of the fifteenth CPSU congress should be expelled. The statement had not been discussed either at the congress itself or in its commissions.

Molotov reported to the Leningrad CPSU organization; one of the outstanding characteristics of the congress, he said, had been the unanimity of its decisions. 'The Comintern has achieved unity on the basis of overcoming Trotskyism.'

The theses of the agitprop department of the ECCI on the sixth congress issued shortly after its conclusion stated that it marked the dividing line between the period of relatively peaceful coexistence among the imperialist Powers and between the capitalist and Soviet worlds, in which class struggles were only partial in character, and of the first wave of the colonial revolution, and the period of growing imperialist contradictions, of sharper struggles between capitalism and the Soviet Union, of preparation for war against the USSR, of sharper class struggles, of the growing identity of reformism with the bourgeois State, of collaboration between reformism and fascism, of deeper contradictions between the colonies and the metropolitan Powers, of a new and more powerful wave of colonial revolutions. The deliberations of the congress had armed the Comintern to meet this situation.

Bukharin, who took such a prominent part in the proceedings of the congress, was already aware at this time that his position was seriously threatened. Stalin and his supporters in the politbureau of the CPSU had by now decided on the policy of industrialization and of an offensive against the richer peasants (kulaks), to which Bukharin and the right-wing group were opposed. (Nin called the changes in policy 'epileptic zigzags'.) A document in the Trotsky archives dated 11 July 1928 records a conversation between Bukharin and Kamenev on that day, in which Bukharin said: 'I haven't spoken to Stalin for several weeks. He is an unprincipled intriguer who subordinates everything to his maintaining power. . . . He has yielded now in order to cut our throats. We know this, but he manœuvres in a way that makes us appear the splitters.' The middle ranks of the central committee did not grasp the depths of the differences, and feared a split. Having yielded to Stalin before, they found it difficult to oppose him now. Bukharin had the support of Tomsky, Rykov, and Uglanov; Peters was with them, but frightened. Yagoda and Trelisser were with them, but Voroshilov and Kalinin had changed sides at the last moment. 'Sometimes at night I ask myself, have we the right to be silent? Do we lack courage? But calculation dictates prudence.' Bukharin thought that Stalin would seek Kamenev's support, and asked him not to help Stalin to crush them. He also asked him not to telephone, as his line was tapped. Only Rykov and Tomsky knew of his visit. Stalin, he said finally, longed to be recognized as a theoretician—'only that is missing'—and had made a number of damaging changes in the Comintern programme.

It was highly probable, Trotsky wrote to Rakovsky on 14 July, that the centre-right bloc [i.e. Bukharin–Stalin] would maintain a semblance of unity at the congress in order to lay a gravestone on the opposition, but what would happen next? There might be an ultra-left zigzag, but it was impossible to predict. One could predict what a Marxist would do, but not what a centrist would do. In October he wrote that the number of hours Bukharin had spoken at the congress was in inverse proportion to his influence. Stalin, though not at the congress, had won over most of Bukharin's supporters; he had no need to speak. 'The impersonal mechanism of power acted for him.' 'Externally', Trotsky wrote in 'Who Leads the Comintern' (in the Trotsky archives), 'the leadership of the sixth congress seemed Bukharin's. He gave the report, put out the strategic line, put forward and carried through the programme . . . and opened and closed the congress. . . . And yet everybody knows that in fact Bukharin's influence on the congress was virtually nil.' For meanwhile groups were breaking up and re-forming, and fractions consolidating. 'This monstrous dualism' revealed what a 'secondary, subordinate, purely decorative part is played by so-called "ideology" in a regime run by the bureaucrats of the machine.' The publication of Bukharin's collected works, Trotsky said at another time, would mean his end. They used to laugh at Zinoviev's 'two perspectives', but Bukharin had none. Politically, he had never taken anything seriously, not even himself.

In an unaddressed letter (in the Trotsky archives), from an unnamed correspondent who clearly held some kind of position in the Comintern and attended the congress, it is stated that the ECCI had not discussed the reports from the sections or the items on the agenda. With the exception of the CPSU no party or even central committee had discussed the draft programme. The theses on the war danger and the colonies were not ready when the congress opened. All the delegates had been appointed by the respective politbureaux; not one had been elected. They were all aware of the deep differences in the CPSU, and were drawn into fractional alliances without any understanding of the real causes of disagreement and their seriousness. He had found not a single convinced defender of the programme or the colonial theses; all were dissatisfied, but hoped that the programme would give the parties something to think about besides the disagreements in the CPSU. He was appalled by their ignorance of theory. 'Unfortunately, since the work of the congress proceeded without leadership, even the most crass and crude incoherences were accepted as the revelations of the highest political sagacity.' Relations were so strained that the only question which really engaged the attention of the delegation bureaux was how to patch up an external compromise between the hostile fractions in almost all parties. There was a crisis of leadership in the French, German, Polish, Czech, Yugoslav, and other parties. During the congress Rykov's supporters in the CPSU held meetings with Ewert's supporters in the KPD 'out of town', while the Stalinists met Thaelmann's group. In the French party several groups were at loggerheads, and outside the party there were at least eight opposition groups. In the American party relations between the Foster group and the Pepper group were very strained—the members did not speak to each other. The differences derived from different views of the world situation, the policy of the CPSU, etc. Pepper's group exaggerated the development of American capitalism and saw immense difficulties in the way of a revolutionary movement; Ewert held an analogous position about Germany. The opposition's documents were not discussed—the opposition itself scarcely mentioned; the Chinese revolution was glossed over—they preferred to speak of India. Trotsky's critique of the draft programme was not discussed in the delegations, but those who had seen it found it extremely interesting.

In a second letter the same correspondent reported a conversation with Ercoli (Togliatti), who had the impression that the Russians considered the congress a heavy burden they were unable to shake off, but they were not in a position to enliven it so that it could do useful work. Togliatti is quoted as saying: 'The tragedy of the thing is that it is impossible to speak the truth about the most important, most vital current problems. We cannot speak. In this atmosphere, to tell the real truth would have the effect of an exploding bomb. Not that it would be a bad thing if a large part of those taking part in the congress were to be wiped off the face of the earth. I'm terribly worried. I don't really know what to do, what to say, how to act to change the situation. It's a pity that Bordiga is not here. He would have played a great historical part. He would have told all of us the truth.' Togliatti was further reported as finding Trotsky's documents of great interest, and complaining bitterly of congress documents not being distributed beforehand. He was a co-rapporteur on the colonial question, but had been informed only two weeks earlier, and had still been unable to arrange a meeting with Kuusinen, who was the chief rapporteur. ' I haven't an idea what he's going to talk about. I haven't seen his theses.'

Thorez is reported to have said, in a conversation with the same correspondent, that the French delegation were uneasy and sceptical. Bukharin had spoken of inter-imperialist contradictions, of the war danger and the USSR. But where were the proletariat and the communist parties? The implication was that the USSR was the basis of the world revolution. Thorez did not agree. It was a platform, an example, a moral and material help to the world revolution, but not its basis or its centre. He wondered how they had been forced to swallow the theory of socialism in one country. The fight against Trotskyism was necessary, but not with such a theory. They knew nothing of what was really happening. The situation was delicate, almost unbearable.

In his letter to Rakovsky Trotsky wrote that he had sent four documents to the congress. A statement, a commentary entitled 'What Now?', a critique of the draft programme, and a statement 'on the origin of the legend of Trotskyism'. The signatures of 191 oppositionists in exile in the USSR were added, whose agreement Trotsky had received by telegraph. They included Rakovsky, Smilga, I. N. Smirnov, Muralov, and Serebriakov. These documents were published some years later in English, German, and French by Trotsky's supporters abroad. To the charge that the Comintern's enemies would use his words he asked, what was of more use to the enemy, an incorrect policy or its exposure? Social-democracy was a parasitical body living on the mistakes of the communist party—its capitulations and its putsches. In the four years since the fifth congress (there had been no objective obstacle to convening the sixth congress earlier) the Comintern's leaders and policy had been changed; there had been innumerable meetings of the League against Imperialism, the Friends of Soviet Russia, the Anglo-Russian trade union unity committee; but the Comintern had not met. 'Formally all questions in these more than four years have been decided by the ECCI or the presidium; in fact by the politbureau of the CPSU, more precisely by its secretariat.' The same was true of the CPSU —this had been true neither of the Russian party nor of the Comintern in the worst days of the Civil War and intervention. The greater the divergence between the policy of the leaders and the historical line of the proletariat, the less willing were the leaders to submit their actions to criticism; their policy had to be imposed from above, by measures of the apparatus and even of the State. The basic cause of the crisis was the delay in the world revolution caused by the series of serious proletarian defeats. Up to 1923 these were defeats of the post-war movement, when the communist parties were non-existent or inexperienced and weak. After 1923 they were defeats of Comintern policy. To say that the defeats were inevitable, whatever the policy, was paralysing fatalism and a denial of the bolshevik conception of the role and importance of revolutionary leadership. Capitalism had been able to stabilize because the Comintern leadership was not equal to its job, incapable of exploiting revolutionary situations. Instead they sought for revolutionary forces outside the proletariat, idealized the peasant parties, made supra-class alliances, etc. 'The object of their strategy was to accomplish by manœuvre what can only be achieved by revolutionary class forces.' They were not strategists, but bureaucrats, of every size except large, and for them 'bolshevik flexibility' referred to the elasticity of their own backbones. To lead, Trotsky wrote, means to foresee, and it was necessary to 'stop flattering Thaelmann solely because he grubs in the gutter for the vilest epithets to fling at the opposition, as Tan Ping-shan was petted at the seventh plenum because he translated Thaelmann's insults into Chinese. . . . It is necessary to stop replacing party leaders in order to punish them for mistakes committed by the ECCI or because they do not approve of the GPU when it punishes proletarian revolutionists. . . . It is necessary to stop "appointing" leaders simply on the basis of their certificate of good behaviour, i.e. if they are against the opposition.' The opposition was the conscious expression of the proletariat's anxiety about the fate of the dictatorship.

In their appeal to the Comintern against their expulsion and banishment, sent to the ECCI presidium on the eve of their deportation from Moscow, Trotsky, Rakovsky, Radek, Smilga, Preobrazhensky and a 'number of other old Bolsheviks' wrote: 'The struggle in the Russian Communist Party is going on, to all intents and purposes, behind the back of the International, without its participation, and even without its knowledge. . . . On every critical occasion the communist parties are placed before a *fait accompli*. They put their signature to decisions already made.']

EXTRACTS FROM THE THESES OF THE SIXTH COMINTERN CONGRESS ON THE INTERNATIONAL SITUATION AND THE TASKS OF THE COMMUNIST INTERNATIONAL

29 *August* 1928   *Protokoll*, vi, 4, p. 13

[The theses were presented in connexion with Bukharin's report. In the debate a number of delegates complained that they could see no difference between the second and the third period—both were marked by stabilization and technical progress after the ebbing of the revolutionary wave. Bukharin replied that the fifth congress had referred to an era of democratic pacifism, not stabilization. (Introducing the theses on bolshevization early in 1925, Zinoviev had given his own scheme of periodization, with its own third period.) Later ECCI reports show that in the commission and at delegation meetings there was a good deal of opposition to the new line, although this was reflected only rarely in the plenary sessions. From subsequent statements it appears that the Russian delegation were dissatisfied with Bukharin's draft theses, and amended them to emphasize the international significance of the Soviet economic plan and the contradictions of capitalist stabilization, and to sharpen the attack on the left social-democrats.]

I. INTRODUCTION

After the first imperialist world war, the international labour movement passed through a series of phases of development, reflecting the various phases of the general crisis of the capitalist system.

The first was the period of extremely acute crisis of the capitalist system, and of direct revolutionary action on the part of the proletariat. This period reached its highest point in 1921, culminating on the one hand in the victory of the USSR over the forces of intervention and internal counter-revolution, and in the consolidation of the proletarian dictatorship and the establishment of the Communist International; and on the other, in a series of severe defeats for the Western European proletariat and the beginning of the general capitalist offensive. This period ended with the defeat of the German proletariat in 1923.

This defeat marked the starting-point of the second period, a period of gradual and partial stabilization of the capitalist system, of the 'restoration' of capitalist economy, of the development and expansion of the capitalist offensive, and of the continuation of the defensive battles fought by the proletarian army weakened by severe defeats. On the other hand, this period was a period of rapid restoration in the Soviet Union, of important successes in the work of building socialism, and also of the growth of the political influence of the communist parties over the broad masses of the proletariat.

Finally came the third period, the period in which capitalist economy and the economy of the USSR began almost simultaneously to exceed their pre-war levels (the beginning of the so-called 'reconstruction period' in the Soviet Union, the further growth of socialist forms of economy on a new technological basis).

For the capitalist world, this is a period of rapid technical development, and of the accelerated growth of cartels and trusts, one in which a trend towards State capitalism can be observed. At the same time it is a period of intense development of the contradictions in the world economy, operating in forms determined by the entire prior course of the general crisis of capitalism (contraction of markets, the USSR, colonial movements, growth of the inherent contradictions of imperialism). This third period, in which the contradiction between the growth of the productive forces and the contraction of markets becomes particularly accentuated, will inevitably give rise to a fresh era of imperialist wars among the imperialist States themselves; wars of the imperialist States against the USSR; wars of national liberation against imperialism; wars of imperialist intervention and gigantic class battles. This period, in which all imperialist antagonisms grow sharper (antagonisms between the capitalist States and the Soviet Union, the military occupation of North China as the beginning of the partition of China, the mutual struggles between the imperialists, etc.), and the contradictions in capitalist countries become more acute (the swing to the left of the masses of the working class, growing acuteness of the class struggle), and colonial movements of revolt are launched (China, Egypt, and Syria)—this period will, through the further development of the contradictions of capitalist stabilization, increasingly shake that stability and lead inevitably to the most severe intensification of the general capitalist crisis. . . .

II. RELATIONS BETWEEN STATES AND QUESTIONS OF SO-CALLED FOREIGN POLICY

7. Relations between the capitalist States and the Soviet Union, between imperialism and China, between Europe (primarily England) and the United States are at the basis of all international relations today. Germany's development and the consequent regrouping of powers are one of the main factors in the change in the relations between European States.

8. The most important factor in capitalist development as a whole today is the shift of the economic centre of gravity to the United States, with the resulting increase in its imperialist aggressiveness. . . .

9. The rapid expansion of the United States inevitably brings its interests into conflict with those of declining but still immensely strong English imperialism. The antagonism between the dollar republic, with its rapid rate of development and comparatively few colonial possessions, and the British colonial empire, declining but with a gigantic colonial monopoly, is the axis of international contradictions in the present period. It is precisely here that the focal point of the coming struggle for a re-division of the colonial world is to be found (and not only of the colonial). Anglo-American 'co-operation' has turned into the fiercest rivalry, opening prospects of an immense collision between the two.

10. The influence of American capital in Europe is most marked in Germany's economic advance. With the help of United States credits, Germany, which was completely ruined economically, has reached a new high level of development which gives it greater political importance. The expansion of monopolist capitalism in Germany leads on the one hand to an ever more rapid breakdown of the Versailles system, and on the other to an ever more decisive 'Western' orientation (that is, imperialist and anti-Soviet). If, in the days of its economic decline and its political and national humiliation, Germany sought agreement with the proletarian State, the only State which opposed the imperialist enslavement of Germany, the neo-imperialist tendencies now coming to a head are driving the German bourgeoisie more and more into an anti-Soviet attitude.

11. This, in its turn, is bound to change the alignment of the European Powers. The existence of a whole series of inter-European contradictions (above all those between Italy and France, in the Balkans and North Africa) leads, with the general instability of relations, to a constant re-grouping of States. But amidst all this variety and change one chief tendency clearly emerges, the anti-Soviet tendency. . . . The change in Germany's position is to some extent the culmination of a certain stage in

this process of preparing a counter-revolutionary imperialist bloc for war against the Soviet Union.

12. The fight for markets and spheres of investment not only contains the seed of wars against the Soviet Union and among the imperialists: it has already led to a large-scale war of intervention to divide up the vast Chinese market. Where the imperialists see both an object of exploitation and a revolutionary movement which undermines the dominance of capitalist principles, the most likely outcome is the formation of an imperialist bloc. . . .

III. BOURGEOIS STATE POWER AND THE REGROUPING OF CLASS FORCES

13. In the great majority of capitalist countries the policy of the bourgeoisie is at present determined by two main tasks: to improve 'competitive capacity', i.e. to further capitalist rationalization; and to prepare for war. From the social, class point of view, this policy means greater pressure on the working class, and a rise in the rate of exploitation, accompanied by 'compensating methods' of economic and political corruption, consciously operated to an ever increasing extent by social-democracy.

14. The centralization of capital, the incorporation of large land-ownership via the banks into the general system of finance-capital, leads to an ever stronger consolidation of the forces of the united exploiters, whose organizations merge with the agencies of State power. . . .

15. This evolution in the relations between the State power and the employers' organizations, the concentration of all the forces of the bourgeoisie in the bourgeois State, gives rise in all capitalist countries to a reactionary reshaping of the so-called bourgeois State order. This change, which is a characteristic reflection of the present capitalist crisis, is expressed politically in the general crisis of bourgeois democracy and bourgeois parliamentarism, and is given particular emphasis by the sharpness which it imparts to all economic struggles between capital and labour. In every big industrial strike the workers come into collision with the giant capitalist trusts which are integrated with the forces of the imperialist State. Such a strike immediately assumes a political character . . . and this forces the bourgeoisie and the State to resort to the economic and political corruption of certain sections of the working class and their political and trade union organizations. The close bonds between the reformist trade union and party leaders, the employers' organizations, and the bourgeois State . . . the theory and practice of 'industrial democracy' and industrial peace—all these are means to prevent the unfolding of the class struggle. . . .

17. At the same time the resistance of the workers is growing in many ways; they have already recovered from the severe defeats of the preceding period. . . .

IV. THE CLASS STRUGGLE, SOCIAL-DEMOCRACY, AND FASCISM

18. Despite the sharpening of the class struggle, reformism in the European and American labour movement still shows signs of life and of political tenacity. The socio-economic reason for this is the slow rate of development of the capitalist crisis. . . .

19. The process by which the leaders of the labour bureaucracy are becoming bourgeois in character is consciously promoted by social-democracy. From a shamefaced defence of capitalism, social-democracy has turned into its active supporter. . . .

20. Corresponding to this ideological attitude is the practical activity of social-democracy and the reformist trade union leaders, as shown in their campaign for the adoption of 'American' methods to corrupt and disrupt the working class. . . .

22. In foreign affairs the social-democratic and reformist trade union leaders in the imperialist countries are the most consistent representatives of bourgeois State interests. They support this State, its armed forces, its police, its expansionist aspirations, and its unprincipled hostility to the Soviet Union; they support its robber treaties and agreements, its colonial policy, its occupations, annexations, protectorates, and mandates. . . .

24. In addition to drawing in the social-democrats, the bourgeoisie at critical moments and in certain circumstances turn to projects for a fascist regime.

The characteristic feature of fascism is this, that the bourgeoisie, faced by the breakdown of capitalist economy and by particular subjective and objective circumstances, exploit the discontent of the small and medium urban and rural bourgeoisie, and even of certain strata of declassed proletarians, to form a reactionary mass movement to bar the road to revolution. Fascism resorts to the direct use of force to break up the workers' and poor peasants' organizations and to win power. . . .

More or less developed tendencies and seeds of the fascist movement are to be found today almost everywhere. The ideology of class collaboration, which is the official social-democratic ideology, has many points of contact with the ideology of fascism. . . .

In the international field fascism pursues a violent and provocative policy. The fascist dictatorships in Poland and Hungary are displaying more and more aggressive tendencies and are a constant threat to peace. They threaten the working class of all countries with military gambles and wars.

V. THE COLONIAL COUNTRIES AND THE CHINESE REVOLUTION

25. The general crisis of the international capitalist system is most clearly expressed today in the revolts and revolutions of the colonial and semi-colonial countries. . . .

26. The most important of these, an event of epochal importance, is the Chinese revolution. In its immediate scope it covers tens of millions, and indirectly hundreds of millions, a gigantic mass which for the first time is taking up in such strength the battle against imperialism. China's close links with Indochina and India immensely increase the significance of the revolution there. The entire course of this revolution, its democratic character, its inevitable transformation into a proletarian revolution, are bound to make clear to the entire world proletariat its international importance in all its immensity.

27. As an anti-imperialist movement for national liberation, the Chinese revolution is at the present stage, according to its objective content, a bourgeois-democratic revolution which will inevitably become a proletarian revolution. As it developed . . . the national bourgeoisie (the Kuomintang) in a series of upheavals at last landed in the counter-revolutionary camp, and made an alliance with the feudalists and an agreement with the imperialists. Therefore the struggle against imperialism is inseparably bound up with the struggle for the land and the fight against the counter-revolutionary bourgeoisie. . . .

These tasks can be accomplished only if the broad peasant masses, under the leadership and hegemony of the Chinese proletariat, carry through a successful insurrection. The main features of the Chinese revolution at its present stage are that the bloc of imperialists, feudalists, and bourgeoisie has, despite its internal contradictions, inflicted severe defeats on the proletariat and the peasantry and physically destroyed a large part of the communist party cadres. The labour movement has not yet fully recovered from its defeats. On the other hand the peasant movement is advancing in a number of areas. Where peasant insurrections were victorious, organs of peasant power have been set up, in some cases peasant Soviets. The communist party is growing and consolidating; its authority and influence among the masses are growing. . . .

VI. THE TACTICAL LINE AND PRINCIPAL TASKS OF THE COMMUNIST INTERNATIONAL

30. The struggle against the approaching imperialist war, defence o the Soviet Union, the fight against intervention in China and against the partition of China, defence of the Chinese revolution and colonial revolts— these are now the main international tasks of the communist movement. . . .

32. A victory for imperialism in its struggle against the Soviet Union would be a defeat not only for the proletariat of the Soviet Union; it would be the most serious defeat the international proletariat had ever suffered. The labour movement would be set back for decades. . . .

35. In the 'advanced' capitalist countries, in which the decisive battles for the proletarian dictatorship and for socialism will be fought out, the

communist parties . . . must tirelessly explain to the working masses the direct connexion between propaganda for 'industrial peace' and for arbitration, and reprisals against the revolutionary vanguard of the proletarian movement and preparation for imperialist war.

36. With the growth of industrial trustification and of the tendencies making for State capitalism, with the merging of State organizations and trusts with the reformist trade union machine, with the new ideology of social-democracy, thoroughly bourgeois and actively imperialist, the fight against bourgeois labour parties must be intensified. This policy follows from the changed constellation of forces and the changed attitudes of social-democracy, which has entered a stage that is, from the imperialist point of view, 'more mature'. The congress therefore fully approves the tactics laid down by the ninth ECCI plenum. Their unconditional correctness has been completely confirmed by the results of the French elections and the experience of the English movement.

37. These tactics, while changing the form of the united front, do not change its essential content. To sharpen the struggle against social-democracy shifts the emphasis decisively to the united front from below. . . .

VII. INDIVIDUAL SECTIONS: THE RESULTS OF THEIR WORK, THEIR ACHIEVEMENTS, ERRORS, AND TASKS

43. The congress notes that there have been a number of great successes in the work of the Comintern. These include the expansion of communist influence, which for the first time has reached the countries of South America, Africa, and Australia, and has grown stronger in a number of Asian countries. . . . finally, the continuing bolshevization of the parties, the acquiring of experience, internal consolidation, elimination of the internal struggle, elimination of the Trotskyist opposition in the Comintern. At the same time attention must be called to a number of defects in the CI sections: the slow growth of a militant international outlook, a certain provincialism manifested in the underestimation of the importance of questions of particularly wide bearing, the weakness of work in the unions, the incapacity to exploit organizationally the growing political influence of the parties, stagnation in membership figures, the inadequate attention paid by a number of parties to work among peasants and oppressed national minorities, a certain bureaucratic development of the party machine and of working methods, . . . a relatively low theoretical level among the party cadres, weak contacts with large factories, the far from complete party reorganization on a factory-cell basis, etc.

44. The English Communist Party, whose activities were appraised by the seventh enlarged plenum of the Executive, is confronted by new tasks. The marked shift of the leaders of the General Council and the Labour

Party to the right . . . confronts the CP with tasks which require a much clearer class standpoint and a more decisive struggle against the Labour Party. . . . The English CP did not immediately grasp the new situation and made a serious error at its last congress when it advanced as its central slogan the fight for a labour government under the control of the Labour Party Executive. The ninth plenum of the ECCI adopted a tactical resolution on the changed situation in England which implies a decisive reshaping of all party work. . . .

46. The Italian Communist Party has managed, in spite of the extreme terror employed against it, to maintain its illegal organization and continue its agitation and propaganda work. . . . In its internal life the party has overcome 'Bordigism', which was once the prevailing ideology among the membership, and achieved a substantial degree of unity in ideological and political views. This makes it possible for the party to conduct the struggle against right deviations (renunciation of the struggle for the leading role of the proletariat) with greater vigour than before, for in the present situation these deviations are the greatest danger to the party. . . .

47. The $3\frac{1}{4}$ million votes given to the German Communist Party in the last elections demonstrate the immense growth of communist influence among the working masses, and at the same time reveal the great discrepancy between the party's political influence and its organizational strength (membership is stagnating at 125,000). . . .

The Red Front Fighters' League, which is becoming a mass organization, is a tremendous achievement. The complete defeat of the ultra-left deviation, the collapse of the so-called Leninbund and the self-exposure of its social-democratic nature are also great victories for the KPD. The KPD, one of the best detachments of the international proletarian army, is confronted by the best organized social-democracy, which still has extraordinarily strong roots in the country; this creates a favourable soil for right deviations in the party. The party must therefore fight systematically against such deviations. . . .

49. The Polish Communist Party (which is illegal) has not only maintained its position in conditions of fascist terror but also increased its membership, while its political influence has grown even more, so that it is becoming a political factor of weight in the country, particularly in the industrial centres. The party, which has corrected the gross opportunist errors it made at the time of the Pilsudski coup, now has a correct political line. The greatest danger is the internal struggle, which is not justified by the existence of any really serious political differences. In view of the special importance of the Polish party and the great responsibility resting on it in the event of war, the sixth congress categorically demands the cessation of the fractional struggle and instructs the ECCI to take on its behalf all the necessary measures. . . .

52. The Workers' (Communist) Party of America has become more active and is making good use of a certain crisis in American industry. . . .

As to the formation of a labour party, the congress decides to shift the emphasis to work in the trade unions and to the organization in unions of the unorganized, thus laying the real foundations for the practical carrying out of the slogan of a comprehensive labour party, organized from below up. Mistakes in this field cannot, however, be attributed solely to the majority in the party membership.

The most important task for the party is to put an end to the fractional struggle, which has no foundation in serious differences of principle, to improve party recruiting among the workers, and to take decisive steps to draw workers into leading party posts.

53. The Japanese Communist Party entered the electoral struggle for the first time with its illegal organization. Despite the terror it is conducting agitation among the masses, has an illegal paper. . . . The chief task of the party, which has overcome its internal ideological vacillations, is to become a mass party. . . . Notwithstanding the extreme difficulty of party work (the law on the death penalty for 'dangerous thinking') and numerical weakness, the party must make every effort to defend the Chinese revolution and to combat the predatory policy of Japanese imperialism.

54. The Chinese Communist Party has suffered a number of severe defeats, which are to be attributed to a series of grave opportunist errors in the past, to the lack of independence and freedom to criticize *vis-à-vis* the Kuomintang, to the failure to understand the transition from one stage of the revolution to the next and the need for prompt preparations for defence, and, finally, to the braking of the agrarian revolution. Under the blows of defeat the heroic party corrected these mistakes and declared a relentless war on opportunism. Its leaders, however, fell into another error and did not put up enough resistance to openly putschist, adventurist sentiments which led to abortive revolts in Hunan, Hupeh, &c. . . .

57. The sixth world congress notes with particular satisfaction that in the Soviet Union, the country of proletarian dictatorship, the CPSU, the party of the proletariat, having overcome the social-democratic deviation of Trotskyism in its ranks, and having surmounted a number of the objective economic difficulties of the reconstruction period, has made substantial progress in socialist construction and has proceeded directly to the socialist transformation of peasant farming. Further work in socialist construction must be based on industrialization. . . .

The congress observes that the CPSU noted in good time the elements of bureaucratic petrifaction in certain agencies of the apparatus of the State, the economy, the trade unions, and even the party, and has begun a vigorous struggle against them. . . .

VIII. THE STRUGGLE FOR THE LENINIST LINE AND THE UNITY OF THE COMINTERN

58. The immense difficulties of the period of stabilization in capitalist countries and of reconstruction in the Soviet Union resulted in the formation within the Comintern of oppositional groups, which tried to organize themselves on an international scale. Their various wings and trends (from extreme right to extreme left) found their most complete outlet in criticism of the dictatorship in the Soviet Union, to which they libellously ascribed a more or less petty-bourgeois character, accusing it of undermining the international proletariat's ability to act. . . . All these trends, inspired and held together by Trotskyism, formed a single bloc, but, after the defeat of the Trotskyist opposition in the CPSU, began to fall apart. . . .

59. Within the communist parties . . . the main deviation is to the right of the correct political line. This is shown in the survivals of 'legalism', in an exaggerated respect for the law, in 'tailism', in passivity during strikes, in an incorrect attitude to social-democracy (e.g. the resistance in France to the decisions of the ninth ECCI plenum). . . .

60. The sixth world congress imposes on all parties the obligation to fight against these deviations, above all to fight against them by means of persuasion. The congress observes that the decisions of the seventh enlarged session of the ECCI on raising the theoretical level of party cadres, training new officials, etc., have not been carried out in a number of the most important countries. . . .

61. The congress imposes on the ECCI the duty of continuing to guard the unity of the CI and its sections by every means. . . . The most significant failings apparent in the internal life of our parties today (bureaucratic tendencies, declining membership in many countries, political inactivity of the primary party organizations, etc.) can only be eliminated if the level of their political life is raised, on the basis of broad internal democracy. This does not by any means exclude, but rather presupposes, the all-round strengthening of iron party discipline, the unconditional subjection of the minority to the majority . . . and of all Comintern sections to the Executive.

STATUTES OF THE COMMUNIST INTERNATIONAL ADOPTED AT ITS SIXTH CONGRESS

29 *August* 1928   *Protokoll*, vi, 4, p. 101

[At the fifteenth congress of the CPSU in December 1927 Bukharin stated that the resolution of the previous congress on collective Comintern leadership had not been put into operation. Permanent and adequate representation of the parties in Moscow was essential. The CPSU should assign more members for work in the ECCI, which had been drained of some of its staff by the establishment of the West European secretariat; others were working on the programme, which could not be postponed a third time.

Piatnitsky reported to the congress for the statutes commission. The preamble to the earlier statutes, he said, was no longer necessary now that the programme had been adopted. The paragraphs on fractions and non-party mass organizations were new, as were the provisions dealing with ECCI bureaux abroad; other paragraphs had been changed to agree with current CI practice and plenum decisions. In listing the attendance at the plenary sessions of the ECCI since the fifth congress (from 281 at the fifth plenum to 72 at the ninth), he said they had found that business was settled more quickly at the smaller meetings, and these would in future be the rule. The changes were adopted unanimously without discussion.

In the debate on Bukharin's report, Münzenberg complained of the general neglect of work in non-party organizations, which it was feared would lead to opportunism. The objects of such work, he said, were to awaken the apathetic, to build bridges to non-party people, to provide organizations for sympathizers with the USSR who could not always be brought into the CP, to counteract social-democratic influence, and to find recruits for communism. They had themselves started several organizations which were under communist influence, but the older mass organizations, such as trade unions and co-operatives, had still to be conquered. Their most promising organizations were the League against Imperialism, the Friends of Soviet Russia, and the Red Front Fighters in Germany. Some delegates complained that the abundance of such subsidiary organizations was a heavy burden on small parties.]

I. GENERAL RULES

1. The Communist International—the International Working Men's Association—is the union of communist parties in various countries into a single world communist party. As the leader and organizer of the world revolutionary movement of the proletariat and the embodiment of the principles and aims of communism, the Communist International strives to win over the majority of the working class and the broad strata of the poor peasantry; it fights for the principles and aims of communism, for the establishment of the world dictatorship of the proletariat, for the establishment of a World Union of Socialist Soviet Republics, for the complete abolition of classes, and for the achievement of socialism—the first stage of communist society.

2. The individual parties which are members of the Communist International are called the Communist Party of . . . name of country (Section of the Communist International). In any given country there can be only one communist party affiliated to the Communist International as its section.

3. Membership of the communist party and of the Communist

International is open to all those who accept the programme and rules of the given communist party and of the Communist International, who belong to one of the primary units of a party, actively work in it, abide by all the decisions of the party and of the Communist International, and regularly pay party dues.

4. The basic unit of the communist party organization is the nucleus in the place of employment (factory, workshop, mine, office, store, farm, etc.) which embraces all the party members employed in the given enterprise.

5. The Communist International and its sections are built up on the basis of democratic centralism, the fundamental principles of which are: (*a*) election of all the committees of the party, subordinate and superior, at general meetings of party members, conferences, congresses and international congresses; (*b*) periodical reports by party committees to their constituents; (*c*) decisions of superior party committees to be binding on subordinate committees, strict party discipline and prompt and precise execution of the decisions of the Communist International, of its agencies, and of the leading party committees.

Party questions may be discussed by the members of the party and by party organizations until such time as a decision is taken upon them by the competent party committee. Once decisions have been taken by the congress of the Communist International, by the congress of the respective section, or by leading committees of the Comintern or of the section, these decisions must be unconditionally carried out even if part of the party membership or of the local party organizations is in disagreement with it.

Where a party exists illegally, the superior party committees may appoint the subordinate committees and co-opt members to their own committees, subject to subsequent endorsement by the relevant superior party committee.

6. In all non-party workers' and peasants' mass organizations (trade unions, co-operative societies, sports organizations, ex-service men's organizations), and in their leading committees and at their conferences and congresses, as well as in municipal and parliamentary bodies and their committees, communist fractions must be formed, even if there are no more than two party members, for the purpose of strengthening the party's influence and for carrying out its policy in these organizations and bodies.

7. The communist fractions are subordinate to the competent party bodies.

Note:

i. Communist fractions in international organizations (Red International of Labour Unions, International Class War Prisoners' Aid

Society, International Workers' Relief, etc.) are subordinate to the Executive Committee of the Communist International.

ii. The organizational structure of the communist fractions and the manner in which their work is conducted are determined by special instructions from the Executive Committee of the Communist International and from the central committees of its sections.

II. THE WORLD CONGRESS OF THE COMMUNIST INTERNATIONAL

8. The supreme body of the Communist International is the world congress of representatives of all parties (sections) and organizations affiliated to the Communist International.

The world congress discusses and decides programmatic, tactical, and organizational questions connected with the activities of the Communist International and of its individual sections. Power to alter the programme and rules of the Communist International lies exclusively with the world congress of the Communist International.

The world congress shall be convened once every two years. The date of the congress and the number of delegates from each section to the congress shall be determined by the Executive Committee of the Communist International.

The number of votes to be allocated to each section at the world congress shall be determined by a special decision of the congress itself, in accordance with the membership of the given party and the political importance of the given country. No binding mandate can be recognized.

9. Special congresses of the Communist International shall be convened on the demand of parties which, at the preceding world congress, had an aggregate of not less than one half of the votes.

10. The world congress elects the Executive Committee of the Communist International (ECCI) and the International Control Commission (ICC).

11. The headquarters of the Executive Committee is decided on by the world congress.

III. THE EXECUTIVE COMMITTEE OF THE COMMUNIST INTERNATIONAL AND ITS MACHINERY

12. The leading body of the Communist International in the period between congresses is the Executive Committee, which gives instructions to all the sections of the Communist International and supervises their activity.

The ECCI publishes the central organ of the Communist International in not fewer than four languages.

13. Decisions of the ECCI are binding on all sections of the Communist International and must be promptly carried out. The sections have the right to appeal against decisions of the ECCI to the world congress, but must continue to carry out such decisions pending the decision of the world congress.

14. The central committees of the various sections of the Communist International are responsible to their respective party congress and to the ECCI. The latter has the right to annul or amend decisions of party congresses and of central committees of parties and also to make decisions which are obligatory for them (cf. para. 13).

15. The ECCI has the right to expel from the Communist International entire sections, groups, or individual members who violate the programme and rules of the Communist International or the decisions of the world congress and of the ECCI. Persons and bodies expelled have the right of appeal to the world congress.

16. The programmes of the sections of the Communist International must be endorsed by the ECCI. Should the ECCI refuse to endorse a programme, the section concerned has the right to appeal to the world congress.

17. The central press organs of the individual sections must publish all the decisions and official documents of the ECCI. These decisions must, whenever possible, be published also in the other organs of the party press.

18. The ECCI has the right to accept affiliation to the Communist International of organizations and parties sympathetic to communism, such organizations to have a consultative voice.

19. The ECCI elects a presidium responsible to the ECCI, which acts as the permanent body conducting all the business of the ECCI in the intervals between its meetings.

20. The ECCI and its presidium have the right to establish permanent bureaux (Western European, South American, Eastern and other bureaux of the ECCI)[1] for the purpose of establishing closer contact with the various sections of the Communist International and for the better guidance of their work.

Note:

The competence of the permanent bureaux of the ECCI shall be determined by the ECCI or by its presidium. The sections of the Communist International falling within the scope of activities of the permanent bureaux of the ECCI must be informed of the powers conferred on them.

21. The sections must carry out the instructions of the permanent bureaux of the ECCI. Sections may appeal against these instructions to

---

[1] The remainder of this paragraph does not appear in the German edition from which this translation was made, but is in the Russian and the English versions.

the ECCI or to its Presidium, but must continue to carry them out pending the decision of the ECCI or of its presidium.

22. The ECCI and its presidium have the right to send representatives to the various sections of the Communist International. Such representatives receive their instructions from the ECCI and are responsible to it for their activities. The plenipotentiaries of the ECCI have the right to participate in meetings of the central party bodies as well as of the local organizations of the sections to which they are sent. They must carry out their commission in close contact with the central committee of the section to which they are sent. They may, however, act in opposition to the central committee of the given section at congresses and conferences of that section, if the policy of the central committee in question diverges from the instructions of the ECCI. Representatives of the ECCI are obliged in particular to supervise the execution of the decisions of the world congresses and of the Executive Committee of the Communist International.

The ECCI and its presidium also have the right to send instructors to the sections of the Communist International. The powers and duties of instructors are determined by the ECCI, to whom the instructors are responsible.

23. Meetings of the ECCI must take place not less than once every six months. A quorum consists of not less than half the membership of the ECCI.

24. Meetings of the presidium of the ECCI must be held not less than once a fortnight. A quorum consists of not less than one-half the membership of the presidium.

25. The presidium elects the political secretariat, which is empowered to take decisions, and which also prepares questions for the meetings of the ECCI and of its presidium, and acts as their executive organ.

26. The presidium appoints the editorial committees of the periodical and other publications of the ECCI.

27. The presidium of the ECCI sets up a department for work among women, standing commissions for groups of sections of the Communist International (regional secretariats), and other departments necessary for its work.

IV. THE INTERNATIONAL CONTROL COMMISSION

28. The International Control Commission investigates matters concerning the unity and cohesion of the sections of the Communist International and also matters connected with the conduct of individual members of the various sections.

For this purpose the ICC:

(a) examines complaints against the actions of central committees of

communist parties lodged by party members who have been subjected to disciplinary measures for political differences;

(b) examines analogous matters concerning members of central bodies
of communist parties and of individual party members which, in its
opinion, require its intervention, or which are submitted to it for
examination by the responsible agencies of the ECCI;

(c) audits the accounts of the Communist International.

The International Control Commission must not intervene in political
differences or in organizational and administrative conflicts in the communist parties.

The headquarters of the ICC are fixed by the ICC in agreement with
the ECCI.

V. RELATIONS BETWEEN THE SECTIONS OF THE COMMUNIST INTERNATIONAL AND THE ECCI

29. The central committees of all sections of the Communist International and of all affiliated sympathizing organizations must send to the
ECCI the minutes of their meetings and reports of their work.

30. Resignation from office by individual members or groups of members
of central committees of the sections is regarded as disruption of the communist movement. Leading posts in the party do not belong to the occu-
pant of that post, but to the Communist International as a whole. Elected
members of the central leading bodies of the various sections may resign
before their time of office expires only with the consent of the ECCI.
Resignations accepted by central committees of sections without the
consent of the ECCI are invalid.

31. The sections of the Communist International must maintain close
organizational and information contact with each other, arrange for
mutual representation at each other's conferences and congresses, and,
with the consent of the ECCI, exchange leading comrades. This applies
particularly to the sections in imperialist countries and their colonies, and
to the sections in countries adjacent to each other.

32. Two or more sections of the Communist International which (like
the sections in the Scandinavian countries and in the Balkans) are politically connected with each other by common conditions of struggle, may,
with the consent of the ECCI, form federations for the purpose of co-
ordinating their activities, such federations to work under the guidance
and supervision of the ECCI.

33. The sections of the Comintern must regularly pay affiliation dues
to the ECCI, the amount of such dues to be determined by the ECCI.

34. Congresses of the various sections, ordinary and special, may be
convened only with the consent of the ECCI.

Should a section fail to convene a party congress prior to a world congress, that section, before electing delegates to the world congress, must convene a party conference, or plenum of its central committee, for the purpose of preparing the questions for the world congress.

35. The Young Communist International is a section of the Communist International with full rights, and is subordinate to the ECCI.

36. The communist parties must be prepared to carry on their work in illegal conditions. The ECCI must assist the parties in their preparations for transition to illegal activities.

37. Individual members of sections of the Communist International may move from one country to another only with the consent of the central committee of the section of which they are members. Communists changing their domicile must join the section in the country of their new domicile. Communists leaving their country without the consent of the central committee of their section must not be accepted into other sections of the Communist International.

PROGRAMME OF THE COMMUNIST INTERNATIONAL ADOPTED AT ITS SIXTH CONGRESS

1 *September* 1928   *Protokoll*, vi, 4, p. 45

[The draft of the programme was published in June by the programme commission of the ECCI, with an explanation that, though it was based on the principles embodied in the draft adopted by the fifth congress four years earlier, there were a number of differences due to the changed form of the capitalist crisis, the revolution in China, the building of socialism in the USSR, the rise of fascism, the imperialist degeneration of social-democracy, the lessons of the struggle against the opposition, and the advance of communism.

It was discussed at great length in the plenary sessions, and at eleven sessions of the programme commission, and then referred section by section to a smaller revision commission. Bukharin reported for the commission, and the programme was then adopted unanimously by the congress without further debate. It was, he explained, the first attempt to formulate in concrete terms the task of establishing the world proletarian dictatorship, unlike the *Communist Manifesto*, which was primarily of a propagandist character. The programme, which analysed the basic trends in historical development which would bring capitalist society to its end, was the first attempt to elaborate the international strategy and tactics of the proletariat. The variety of conditions was so great, their interaction so complex, that the document was bound to be a long one, and this had been criticized in the commission; but a briefer and more abstract analysis would not have enabled them to deal with such questions as fascism, the role of social-democracy, colonial insurrections, the agrarian revolution. There had been no differences on theoretical principles. One member had said that it would be incomprehensible to the colonial masses; Bukharin had agreed, and added that European workers would not understand it either without further explanation and commentary, but the programme did its job of analysing an extremely complex and difficult situation. Reimann would have liked more attention paid to the national question in non-colonial countries, to the question of religion, and to internal party problems such as deviations. Some had wanted the programme to be restricted to the statement of basic principles; others had objected that this would provide no key or guide to action. Narayan objected to the inclusion of India among the 'rural countries' and to the suggestion that the bourgeoisie could be allies in the anti-imperialist struggle. An Indonesian delegate appearing under the name of Alfonso (Tan Malaka) criticized the programme for failing to draw the lessons of the Chinese revolution. In so far as the draft dealt with it, the programme was opportunist, and meant 'waiting until the bourgeoisie have killed our revolutionary comrades and torn our proletarian party to pieces, as happened in China'. He was attacked at the congress as a Trotskyist, but denied the charge. In reporting after the congress to the Moscow CPSU organization, Bukharin said that the 'Trotskyist group' had sent in an alternative programme—'We found nothing pertinent or serious in it'—which was merely a repetition of previous criticisms of CI policy in China and Britain, and of socialism in one country. Trotsky's criticism of the programme (published later outside the USSR as a book) was not made available to the congress delegates as a whole, though an abridged version was distributed to a number of them.]

INTRODUCTION

The epoch of imperialism is the epoch of dying capitalism. The world war of 1914–18 and the general crisis of capitalism which it unleashed, being the direct outcome of the profound contradiction between the growing productive forces of world economy and national barriers, prove that the material prerequisites for socialism have already matured in the womb of capitalist society; they prove that the capitalist shell has become an intolerable restraint on the further development of mankind, and that history has put on the order of the day the revolutionary overthrow of the capitalist yoke.

From the centres of capitalist power to the most remote corners of the colonial world, imperialism subjects the great mass of proletarians in all countries to the dictatorship of the finance-capitalist plutocracy. With elemental force it exposes and deepens all the contradictions of capitalist society, intensifies to the utmost the oppression of the exploited classes, and brings to a head the struggle between capitalist States. In so doing it gives rise to inexorable world-wide imperialist wars which shake the entire prevailing regime to its foundations, and leads with iron necessity to the proletarian world revolution.

Imperialism binds the whole world in the chains of finance capitalism, forces its yoke on the proletarians of all countries, peoples, and races by starvation, blood, and iron, and intensifies in an immeasurable degree the exploitation, oppression, and enslavement of the proletariat. In so doing, imperialism directly confronts the proletariat with the task of seizing power, and compels the workers to unite closely in a single international army of the proletariat of all countries, irrespective of frontiers and of all differences of nationality, culture, language, race, sex, or occupation. Thus, while developing and completing the process of creating the material prerequisites of socialism, imperialism at the same time mobilizes the army of its own gravediggers by compelling the proletariat to organize in a militant international workers' association.

On the other hand, imperialism detaches from the great mass of the working class that section whose material circumstances are the most secure. This upper stratum of the working class, bribed and corrupted by imperialism, which constitutes the leading cadres of the social-democratic parties, has an interest in the imperialist exploitation of the colonies, is loyal to 'its' bourgeoisie and 'its' imperialist State, and at decisive moments in the class struggle is to be found in the camp of the class enemies of the proletariat. The split in the socialist movement in 1914 caused by this treachery, and the subsequent treachery of the social-democratic parties, which became bourgeois labour parties, demonstrated clearly that the international proletariat can accomplish its historical mission of smashing the imperialist yoke and establishing the proletarian dictatorship only in relentless struggle against social-democracy. Hence it is only on the communist platform that the forces of world revolution can be organized. In opposition to the opportunist Second International of social-democracy, which had become an agency of imperialism within the working class, there arose inevitably the Third, Communist International, the international organization of the working class, the embodiment of the true unity of the revolutionary workers of the entire world.

The war of 1914–18 gave rise to the first attempts to found a new, revolutionary international as a counterpoise to the Second, social-chauvinist International, and as a weapon of resistance to belligerent imperialism (Zimmerwald, Kienthal). The triumph of the proletarian revolution in Russia provided the impetus to the formation of communist parties in capitalist centres and in the colonies. In 1919 the Communist International was founded, which, for the first time in history, closely unites in the practical revolutionary struggle the vanguard of the European and American proletariat with the proletarians of China and India and the coloured labour slaves of Africa and America.

The Communist International, the united and centralized international party of the proletariat, is the only organization which upholds the principles of the First International in the new context of the revolutionary proletarian mass movement. The lessons of the first imperialist war and of the subsequent period of the revolutionary crisis of capitalism—the series of revolutions in Europe and the colonial countries, the lessons of the proletarian dictatorship and the construction of socialism in the Soviet Union, the lessons of all sections of the Communist International as recorded in the resolutions of its congresses, and finally the increasingly international character assumed by the struggle between the imperialist bourgeoisie and the proletariat—all this makes it essential to have a single programme of the Communist International that is common to all its sections. As the most comprehensive critical generalization of the entire historical experience of the international revolutionary movement of the proletariat, the programme of the Communist International is the programme of the fight for the world proletarian dictatorship, the programme of the struggle for world communism.

Assembling under its banner the revolutionary workers who lead the millions of the enslaved and the exploited against the bourgeoisie and their 'socialist' agents, the Communist International considers itself the executor of the historical legacy of the Communist League and the First International, both led directly by Marx, and as the inheritor of the traditions of the pre-war Second International. The First International established the intellectual premisses of the international proletarian struggle for socialism. In its best days the Second International prepared the ground for the broad expansion of the labour movement among the masses. The Third, the Communist International, is continuing the work of the First, it is gathering the fruits of the work of the Second, while resolutely discarding its opportunism and social-chauvinism and its bourgeois distortion of socialism; it has begun to make a reality of the proletarian dictatorship. The Communist International carries on all the glorious and heroic traditions of the international labour movement: the traditions of the English Chartists and the French insurgents of 1831; of the revolutionary workers of Germany and France in 1848; of the immortal fighters and martyrs of the Paris Commune; of the valiant soldiers of the German, Hungarian, and Finnish revolutions, of the workers of the former Tsarist autocracy, the victorious bearers of the proletarian dictatorship; of the traditions of the Chinese proletarians, the heroes of Canton and Shanghai.

In its theoretical and practical work the Communist International, relying on the historical experience of the revolutionary labour movement in all continents and among all peoples, stands unreservedly on the platform of revolutionary Marxism and of the form it took later, Leninism, which is nothing but the Marxism of the epoch of imperialism and the proletarian revolution.

The Communist International champions and propagates the dialectical materialism of Marx and Engels, and employs it as a revolutionary method of perceiving reality, in order to accomplish the revolutionary transformation of that reality; it fights actively against every variety of bourgeois philosophy, and against opportunism in theory and practice. With its platform of consistent proletarian class struggle, it subordinates the temporary, sectional, national, and partial interests of the proletariat to its enduring, general, international interests. It mercilessly exposes the doctrine, borrowed by the reformists from the bourgeoisie, of 'class peace', in all its forms. In meeting the historical demand for an international organization of revolutionary proletarians, the gravedigger of the capitalist system, the Communist International is the only international force that has as its programme the dictatorship of the proletariat and communism, and that comes out openly as the organizer of the international proletarian revolution.

I. THE CAPITALIST WORLD SYSTEM, ITS DEVELOPMENT, AND ITS INEVITABLE DESTRUCTION

1. *The Laws of Capitalist Dynamics and the Epoch of Industrial Capital*

Capitalist society, which arose on the basis of commodity production, is distinguished by the monopoly held by the class of capitalists and large landowners in the most important and decisive means of production, by the exploitation of the wage-labour of the class of proletarians who, deprived of the means of production, are compelled to sell their labour power; it is distinguished by commodity production for profit; and by the planlessness and anarchy of the production process as a whole which this involves. The exploitation relationship and the economic domination of the bourgeoisie are expressed politically in the State, the capitalist organization serving as instrument for the suppression of the proletariat.

The history of capitalism has completely confirmed the Marxist theory of the laws of development of capitalist society and of its contradictions, leading to the destruction of the entire capitalist system.

In their search for profits the bourgeoisie were compelled to expand productive forces on an ever-increasing scale, and to consolidate and extend the dominion of capitalist relations of production. Thus as capitalism developed it constantly reproduced at a higher level all the inherent contradictions of the capitalist system, above all the fundamental contradiction between the social character of labour and the private character of appropriation, between the growth of productive forces and property relations under capitalism. The rule of private property in the means of production and the anarchic course of production combined with the development of the contradiction between the tendency towards the unlimited expansion of production and the restricted consumption of the proletarian masses (general over-production) to disturb the economic equilibrium between the different branches of production; this brought in its train periodically recurring and devastating crises and mass unemployment. The rule of private property was expressed also in competition within each capitalist country and on the steadily expanding world market. This form of capitalist rivalry resulted in a series of wars, the inseparable corollaries of capitalist development.

In the competitive struggle, large-scale production, because of its technical and economic superiority, supplanted and destroyed pre-capitalist economic forms; capital became more and more concentrated and centralized. In industry the law of concentration and centralization was manifested primarily in the outright ruin of small enterprises, and partly in their degradation to the position of auxiliary units of large enterprises. In agriculture, which, because of the monopoly in land and of absolute rent, necessarily lagged behind the rate of general development, this law of concentration and centralization was manifested not only in the differentiation of the peasantry and the proletarianization of broad peasant strata, but also and above all in the subordination, open and concealed, of small peasant farms to the dictatorship of large capital. The small farm could maintain an appearance of independence only at the price of the most extreme exertion of labour and of systematic under-consumption.

The increasing use of machines, steady technical improvement, and the consequent uninterrupted rise in the organic composition of capital were accompanied by a further division of labour, and by an increase in its productivity and intensity. This resulted in the wider employment of the labour of women and children, and in the creation of enormous industrial reserve armies which were constantly replenished by proletarianized peasants forced out of their villages and by the impoverished petty and middle bourgeoisie of the towns. The division of society into two camps, with a small handful of capitalist magnates at one pole and vast masses of proletarians at the other; the steady rise in the rate of exploitation of the working class; the reproduction on a higher scale of the fundamental contradictions of capitalism and their consequences (crises, wars, etc.); the uninterrupted growth of social inequality; the rising discontent of the proletariat, drawn together and schooled by the process of capitalist production itself—all this undermined the foundations of capitalism and brought the hour of its collapse nearer.

At the same time a profound change occurred in the social and cultural life of capitalist society: the parasitic degeneration of the bourgeois rentier; the general decay of the family as a result of the growing contradictions between the widespread employment of women in social production and the forms of domestic and family life inherited in large part from earlier economic epochs; the growing shallowness and degeneration of intellectual and cultural life as a result of the minute specialization of labour, of the distortions of urban life and the narrowness of rural life; the inability of the bourgeoisie, notwithstanding immense progress in the natural sciences, to achieve the synthesis of a scientific philosophy; the growth of idealistic, mystical, and religious superstitions—all these phenomena proclaimed the approaching historical end of the capitalist system.

2. *The Epoch of Finance Capital (Imperialism)*

The period when industrial capital was dominant was in the main one of 'free competition', of the relatively steady development and expansion of capitalism over the whole earth, as the colonies that were still free were divided up and occupied by arms. As this happened the inherent contradictions of capitalism grew steadily; their weight bore most heavily on the colonial periphery which was methodically plundered, intimidated, and enslaved.

At the beginning of the twentieth century this period gave place to the period of imperialism, one in which capitalism developed in a series of conflict-ridden leaps and free competition began rapidly to give way to monopoly. In this period, when all formerly 'free' colonies were already appropriated, the disputes concerning a redistribution of colonies and spheres of influence assumed more and more the character of armed struggle.

Thus capitalist contradictions, embracing the whole world, were manifested most clearly in the epoch of imperialism (of finance-capital). Imperialism is a historically new form of capitalism, a new relationship between the various parts of capitalist world economy, a changed form of relations between the primary classes of capitalist society.

This new historical period was the outcome of the operation of the most important laws of motion of capitalist society. It arose out of the development of industrial capitalism and as its historical sequel. In imperialism the basic trends and laws of motion of capitalism, all its fundamental contradictions and antagonisms, stand out more clearly. The law of capital concentration and centralization led to the formation of powerful monopolist associations (cartels, syndicates, trusts) and to a new form of giant undertaking combining several enterprises linked together by the banks. The fusion of industrial and banking capital, the absorption of large landownership into the general system of capitalist organization, and the monopolistic character of this form of capitalism transformed the epoch of industrial capitalism into the epoch of finance-capital. The 'free competition' of the earlier period which had replaced feudal monopoly and the monopoly of trading capital, was now changed into the monopoly of finance-capital. Capitalist monopolies, however, do not eliminate the free competition from which they arose, but exist above and alongside it; this produces a series of exceptionally grave and profound contradictions, frictions, and conflicts.

The growing use of complicated machinery, chemical processes, and electrical power, the higher organic composition of capital on this basis, and the consequent fall in the rate of profit, which can be only temporarily halted by a policy of higher cartel prices favouring the largest monopolist associations, stimulate the quest for colonial super-profits and make the struggle for a new division of the world more acute. Standardized mass production requires new external markets. A feverish search is set on foot for new sources of raw materials and fuel to meet the growing demand. A further impulse is given to the export of capital by the system of high protective tariffs, which makes the export of goods more difficult and ensures super-profits for exported capital. In this way the export of capital becomes the essential and specific form of economic association linking the various parts of capitalist world economy. Lastly, the monopolistic domination of colonial markets, of raw material sources, and of spheres for capitalist investment accentuates the general unevenness of capitalist development to an extreme degree and brings to a head the conflicts among the 'Great Powers' of finance-capital for a redivision of colonies and spheres of influence.

Thus the growth of the productive forces of world economy leads both to a further internationalization of economic life and to a struggle for the re-division of a world already divided up among the most powerful finance-capitalist States. The methods used in this struggle change and grow sharper, price-cutting being replaced more and more by coercive pressure (boycotts, high tariffs, tariff wars, wars in the real meaning of the word, etc.). Thus the monopolistic form of capitalism is necessarily accompanied by imperialist wars, which in their scope and the destructive power of their technique are without parallel in history.

3. *The Forces of Imperialism and the Forces of Revolution*

The imperialist form of capitalism has a tendency to unite the various fractions of the ruling class and to bring the broad mass of the proletariat into opposition, not to the individual employer, but more and more to the entire class of capitalists and their State. This form of capitalism breaks down the barriers of the national State, which have become too cramping, and expands the domain where the ruling nation among the large capitalist States exercises power. It brings the millions suffering national oppression, the so-called small nations, and the colonial peoples into opposition to this State. Finally, it accentuates to the utmost the contradictions among the imperialist States.

This being the case the State power, as it becomes the dictatorship of the finance-capitalist oligarchy and the expression of its concentrated strength, acquires special importance for the bourgeoisie. The functions of this multi-national imperialist State expand in all directions; it develops agencies which facilitate both the struggle for external markets (mobilization of the economy for war) and the struggle against the working class; militarism (land, sea, and air forces, chemical and bacteriological weapons) grows to gigantic proportions; the pressure of the imperialist State on the working class (greater exploitation and outright suppression coupled with a systematic policy of bribing the bureaucratic-reformist upper strata) is heightened. These developments reflect the tremendous growth of the specific weight of State power. In these conditions every more or less important action by the proletariat becomes an action against the power of the State, i.e. it becomes a political act.

In this fashion capitalist development, particularly in its imperialist phase, reproduces the fundamental contradictions of capitalism on an ever-widening scale. Competition among small capitalists ceases only to give way to competition among large capitalists; where this dies down, competition flares up between powerful associations of capitalist magnates and their States; from being local and national, crises spread over several countries and finally become world crises; local wars are succeeded by wars between coalitions of powers and then by world wars; the class struggle loses its character of isolated actions by small groups of workers and takes on national dimensions, turning finally into the international struggle of the world proletariat against the world bourgeoisie. Lastly, the two main revolutionary forces gather in opposition to the powerful con-centrated forces of finance-capital—the workers of the capitalist countries and the popular masses of the colonies, held under by foreign capital, who are advancing under the leadership and hegemony of the international revolutionary proletarian movement.

This basic revolutionary tendency is, however, temporarily crippled by the bribery of certain sections of the European, North American, and Japanese proletariat by the imperialist bourgeoisie, and by the treachery of the national bourgeoisie in the colonial and semi-colonial countries who are frightened by the revolutionary movement. Because of their position on the world market (greater technical development, the export of capital to countries with a higher rate of profit, etc.) and their plundering of the colonies and semi-colonies, the bourgeoisie of the imperialist Powers secure additional profits; these they use to raise the wages of a section of 'their' workers, who thus have an interest in the development of capitalism in 'their' fatherland, in the plunder of the colonies, and in loyalty to the imperialist State. This systematic bribery was and is practised in the strongest imperialist countries on an extremely wide scale; it is reflected most strikingly in the ideology and practice of the labour aristocracy and the bureaucratic strata of the working class, that is, the leading cadres of social-democracy and the trades unions, who have shown themselves to be the direct channels for bourgeois influence in the proletariat and the most stalwart pillars of the capitalist system.

While imperialism stimulates the growth of a corrupt upper stratum in the working class, in the long run it undermines their influence in the working class. For the heightening of imperialist contradictions, the worsening of the position of large masses of workers and mass unemployment, the enormous costs of military conflicts, the loss by certain Powers of their monopoly position on world markets, and finally the loss of colonies, etc., undermine the foundations of social-imperialism among the masses. Similarly, the systematic bribery of various strata of the bourgeoisie in the colonies and semi-colonies, their treachery to the national-revolutionary movement, their rapprochement with the imperialist Powers, can only for a time halt the development of the revolutionary crisis. In the long run this brings about more intense imperialist oppression, a decline in the influence of the national bourgeoisie over the popular masses, a more acute revolutionary crisis, the unleashing of a mass peasant agrarian revolution, creating the prerequisites for proletarian hegemony in the struggle of the masses in the colonies and dependent countries for independence and complete national emancipation.

4. *Imperialism and the Downfall of Capitalism*

Imperialism has developed the productive forces of world capitalism to a very high degree. It has completed the creation of all the material prerequisites for the socialist organization of society. Imperialist wars show that the productive forces of world economy have outgrown the limits of the imperialist State and require the economy to be organized on an international scale embracing the whole world. Imperialism seeks to resolve this contradiction by paving the way with fire and sword for a single state-capitalist world trust which will organize the entire world economy. The social-democratic ideologues extol this bloody utopia as a peaceful method of the new, 'organized' capitalism. In reality, however, this utopia comes up against such great and insuperable objective obstacles that capitalism must with iron necessity break down under the weight of its own contradictions. The law of the unequal development of capitalism, which operates still more powerfully in the imperialist epoch, makes lasting and firm international combinations of imperialist Powers impossible. Imperialist wars, on the other hand, growing into world wars and marking the road by which capital centralization strives to reach its limit in the single world trust, are accompanied by such devastation, impose such burdens on the working class and on the millions of proletarians and peasants in the colonies, that capitalism must collapse under the blows of the proletarian revolution long before that goal is reached.

Imperialism, the highest phase of capitalist development, immensely increases the productive forces of world economy, shapes the entire world in its own image, and drags all colonies, all races, all peoples into the sphere of finance-capitalist exploitation. At the same time the monopolist form of capital increasingly develops elements of parasitic degeneration and decay, of the decline of capitalism. To a certain extent monopoly capital eliminates the driving force of competition, pursues a policy of high cartel prices and obtains unrestricted control of markets, and thus tends to obstruct the further expansion of productive forces. Imperialism piles up untold wealth from the immense super-profits it squeezes out of the millions of colonial workers and peasants. In this process imperialism creates the type of the decaying, parasitically degenerating rentier State and entire strata of parasites who live by coupon-clipping. The epoch of imperialism, which completes the process of creating the material pre-requisites of socialism (concentration of the means of production, socialization of labour on a gigantic scale, the strengthening of workers' organizations) at the same time makes the contradictions between the 'Great Powers' sharper, and provokes wars which result in the breakdown of the single world economy. Thus imperialism is decaying, dying, capitalism. It is the last stage of capitalist development as a whole; it is the onset of the socialist world revolution.

Thus the international proletarian revolution arises from the conditions of capitalist development generally, and specifically from its imperialist phase. The capitalist system as a whole is approaching its final collapse. The dictatorship of finance-capital breaks down and yields to the dictatorship of the proletariat.

II. THE GENERAL CRISIS OF CAPITALISM AND THE FIRST PHASE OF WORLD REVOLUTION

1. *The World War and the Course of the Revolutionary Crisis*

The imperialist struggle of the biggest capitalist states to re-divide the world led to the first imperialist world war (1914–18). This war shook the entire system of world capitalism and so opened the period of its general crisis. The war forced the entire national economy of the belligerent countries into its service, created the mailed fist of State capitalism, drove unproductive expenditure to dizzy heights, destroyed immense quantities of the means of production and of living labour power, ruined broad strata of the population and laid incalculable burdens on the industrial workers, peasants, and colonial peoples. It sharpened the class struggle, which grew into open revolutionary mass action and civil war. The imperialist front was breached at its weakest point—Tsarist Russia. The February revolution of 1917 overthrew feudal absolutism; the October revolution overthrew the bourgeoisie. This victorious proletarian revolution expropriated the expropriators, wrested the means of production from the bourgeoisie and the landowners, and for the first time in human history established and consolidated the proletarian dictatorship in an immense country, created a new type of State, the Soviet State, and thus marked the first stage in the international proletarian revolution.

The violent shock suffered by world capitalism, the greater acuteness of the class struggle, the immediate impact of the October proletarian revolution gave rise to a series of revolutions and revolutionary actions both in Europe and in the colonial and semi-colonial countries: January 1918, workers' revolution in Finland; August 1918, 'rice riots' in Japan; November 1918, revolutions in Austria and Germany which overthrew the semi-feudal monarchies; March 1919, proletarian revolution in Hungary, insurrection in Korea; April 1919, Soviet government in Bavaria; January 1920, bourgeois-national revolution in Turkey; September 1920, occupation of the factories by the workers in Italy; March 1921, insurrection of the proletarian vanguard in Germany; September 1923, rising in Bulgaria; autumn 1923, revolutionary crisis in Germany; December 1924, insurrection in Estonia; April 1925, rebellion in Morocco; August 1925, rebellion in Syria; May 1926, general strike in England; July 1927, workers' revolt in Vienna. All this, together with such events as the rebellion in Indonesia, the profound ferment in India, the powerful Chinese revolution which has shaken the whole of Asia, are links in the chain of international revolution, constituent parts of the profound general crisis of capitalism. This international revolutionary process comprehends both the struggle for the proletarian dictatorship and the national liberation wars and colonial revolts against imperialism, which in their turn are inseparably connected with the agrarian revolution of the peasant millions. Thus immense masses of people have been swept into the current of revolution. World history has entered a new stage of its development, the stage of the long-drawn general crisis of the capitalist system. The unity of world economy is reflected in the international character of the revolution, the unevenness of the development of the different parts of that economy in the variation in the time at which revolution occurs in different countries.

The first attempts at a revolutionary overthrow which grew out of the acute capitalist crisis of 1918-21 ended with the victory and consolidation of the proletarian dictatorship in the Soviet Union, but with defeats for the proletariat in a number of other countries. These defeats were primarily the result of the treacherous tactics of the social-democratic leaders and the reformist bosses of the trade union movement; they were also due in part to the fact that the majority of the working class did not yet support the communists, and that in a number of the most important States there was no communist party at all. These defeats enabled the bourgeoisie to achieve a partial stabilization of capitalism by increasing the exploitation of the proletarian masses and the colonial peoples and by steeply reducing their standard of living.

2. *The Revolutionary Crisis and Counter-Revolutionary Social-Democracy*

In the course of the international revolution the leading cadres of the social-democratic parties and the reformist trade unions, as well as the capitalist para-military detachments of a fascist character, proved themselves to be, by their hostility to the revolution and by their promotion of partial capitalist stabilization, the strongest counter-revolutionary force.

The war crisis of 1914 to 1918 was accompanied by the shameful collapse of the social-democratic Second International. In direct opposition to the thesis of Marx and Engels in the *Communist Manifesto*, that under capitalism the proletariat has no fatherland, in direct opposition to the anti-war resolutions of the Stuttgart and Basel congresses, the leaders of the social-democratic parties, with but a few exceptions, voted the war credits and came out decisively for the defence of the imperialist 'fatherlands' (i.e. the State organizations of the imperialist bourgeoisie); instead of fighting against imperialist war, they became its loyal warriors and protagonists, and sang its praises (social-patriotism turned into social-imperialism). In the subsequent stage social-democracy supported the predatory peace treaties (Brest, Versailles); standing shoulder to shoulder with the generals, it was an active force in the bloody suppression of proletarian risings (Noske); it engaged in armed struggle against the first proletarian republic (Soviet Russia); it betrayed the proletariat which had seized power and surrendered it to the enemy (Hungary); it entered the imperialist League of Nations (Thomas, Paul-Boncour, Vandervelde); it placed itself openly on the side of the imperialist slave-owners against the colonial slaves (the English Labour Party); it actively supported the most reactionary executioners of the working class (Bulgaria, Poland); it took the initiative in promulgating imperialist defence legislation (France); it helped to strangle the strike of the English miners; it helped and is still helping to keep China and India down (the MacDonald Government); it is the propagandist for the imperialist League of Nations, the spokesman for capital, and the organizing force in the fight against the proletarian dictatorship in the Soviet Union (Kautsky, Hilferding).

In systematically carrying out this counter-revolutionary policy, social-democracy makes use of its two wings: the right, overtly counter-revolutionary wing is indispensable for negotiations and direct contacts with the bourgeoisie, while the 'left' is used to execute particularly subtle manœuvres for deceiving the working class. While playing with pacifist and sometimes even with revolutionary phrases, 'left' social-democracy turns against the workers, particularly at critical moments (the English Independent Labour Party and the 'left' leaders of the General Council of the English unions during the 1926 general strike, Otto Bauer and Co., during the Vienna rising, etc.); it is therefore the most dangerous fraction in the social-democratic parties. Although social-democracy, in serving bourgeois interests within the working class, is entirely in favour of class collaboration and of co-operation with the bourgeoisie, it is at certain times forced to assume the position of an opposition party, and ostensibly to defend the class interests of the proletariat in its industrial struggles; by this trick it gains the confidence of part of the working class and then the more disgracefully betrays the workers' permanent interests, above all when decisive class struggles are being fought.

The principal function of social-democracy today is to undermine proletarian unity, which is essential for the struggle against imperialism. By splitting and destroying the united front of proletarian struggle against capital, social-democracy is becoming the chief pillar of imperialism within the working class. International social-democracy of all shades, the Second International, and its trade union branch the Amsterdam International Federation of Trade Unions, have thus become the reserves of bourgeois society, its most reliable mainstays.

3. *The Capitalist Crisis and Fascism*

Alongside social-democracy, which helps the bourgeoisie to oppress the working class and blunt its proletarian vigilance, stands fascism.

In the imperialist epoch the intensification of the class struggle, the expansion of the elements of class war—particularly after the imperialist world war—led to the bankruptcy of parliamentarism. Hence the 'new' methods and forms of governing (e.g. the system of 'inner Cabinets', the operations of oligarchic groups behind the scenes, the deterioration of 'representative assemblies' and distortion of their function, the restriction and elimination of 'democratic freedoms', etc.). In certain historical conditions this process in which bourgeois-imperialist reaction conducts its offensive assumes the form of fascism. The relevant conditions are: instability of capitalist relationships; the presence in large numbers of socially declassed elements; the impoverishment of broad strata of the urban petty bourgeoisie and the intelligentsia; discontent among the rural petty bourgeoisie; finally the constant threat of proletarian mass action. To secure greater durability, solidity, and stability for their power, the bourgeoisie are to an increasing degree compelled to abandon the parliamentary system in favour of fascist methods of rule, which are independent of party relationships and combinations. Fascism is a method of directly exercising the bourgeois dictatorship, ideologically disguised under ideas of 'the national community' and representation according to occupation (i.e. in fact representation of the various groups of the ruling classes). It is a method which uses its own peculiar brand of social demagogy (anti-semitism, occasional attacks on usury-capital, impatience with the parliamentary 'talking-shop') to exploit the discontent of the petty-bourgeois masses, the intellectuals, etc.; and which corrupts by creating a compact and paid hierarchy of fascist fighting squads, a fascist party machine, and a fascist bureaucracy. Fascism also seeks to penetrate the ranks of the working class by winning over its most backward strata by exploiting their discontent, the passivity of social-democracy, etc. Fascism's chief function is to annihilate the revolutionary vanguard of the working class, i.e. the communist strata of the proletariat and their leading cadres. The combination of social demagogy, corruption, and active white terror, and the most extreme imperialist aggressiveness in foreign policy are characteristic features of fascism. When the position is particularly critical for the bourgeoisie fascism resorts to anti-capitalist phraseology, but once it is certain of its power it is revealed more and more openly as the terroristic dictatorship of large capital, and discards its anti-capitalist lumber.

According to changing political circumstances, the bourgeoisie resort either to fascist methods or to coalitions with social-democracy, while social-democracy itself, particularly at critical moments for capitalism, not infrequently plays a fascist part. In its development social-democracy displays fascist tendencies, which does not, however, prevent it, when the political situation changes, from coming out against the bourgeois government as an opposition party. For normal capitalism both fascism and coalition with social-democracy are extraordinary methods. They indicate the existence of a general capitalist crisis and are used by the bourgeoisie to halt the advance of the revolution.

4. *The Contradictions of Capitalist Stabilization and the Inevitability of the Revolutionary Collapse of Capitalism*

Experience since the war shows that the stabilization of capitalism, which was achieved by the defeat of the working class and the systematic depression of its living standards, can only be partial, temporary, and rotten.

The rapid and feverish development of technology, verging in some countries on a new technical revolution, the acceleration of capital concentration and centralization, the formation of giant trusts, of 'national' and 'international' monopolies, the merging of the trusts and the State, the growth of capitalist world economy—all this cannot overcome the general crisis of the capitalist system. The breakdown of world economy into a capitalist section and a socialist section, the shrinking of markets, and the anti-imperialist movement in the colonies intensify to the utmost all capitalist contradictions, developing on new, post-war foundations. The reverse side of technical progress and of the rationalization of industry is the closing down and liquidation of a series of enterprises, the restriction of output, the ruthless exploitation of labour power, all leading to vast and unprecedented chronic unemployment. In a number of highly developed capitalist countries the position of the workers has deteriorated absolutely. Greater competition between imperialist States and the constant danger of war, the ever heightening tension of class conflicts are creating conditions in which the general capitalist crisis and the proletarian world revolution will reach a new and higher stage of development.

As a result of the first in the series of imperialist wars (the world war of 1914–18) and the October victory of the workers in the former Tsarist empire, the world was split into two irreconcilably hostile camps: the camp of the imperialist States and the camp of proletarian dictatorship in the Soviet Union. The differences in the class structure and class character of the State power, the fundamental difference in the aims of their policy, domestic, external, economic, and cultural, the basically different trend of development—all these bring the capitalist world into acute hostility towards the State of the victorious proletariat. Now two antagonistic systems are in conflict in what was once a single world economy—capitalism and socialism. The class struggle, which previously assumed forms determined by the absence of any State in which the proletariat held power, is now reproduced on an enormous and truly universal scale, for the working class of the whole world now has its own State, the only fatherland of the international proletariat. The existence of the Soviet Union, with its influence on the working and oppressed masses of the entire world, is in itself the clearest expression of the profound crisis of the world capitalist system and an unparalleled extension and heightening of the class struggle.

Incapable of overcoming its inherent contradictions, the capitalist world seeks a way out by founding an international association (the League of Nations) whose main purpose it is to put a stop to the irresistible growth of the revolutionary crisis and to strangle the union of proletarian republics by blockade or war. Nevertheless all the forces of the revolutionary proletariat and the oppressed colonial masses are rallying round the Soviet Union; the unstable world capitalist coalition, rotten at the core but armed to the teeth, is confronted by a united and resolute world coalition of labour. Thus a new basic contradiction emerged from the first round of imperialist wars, epochal in its scope and significance—the contradiction between the Soviet Union and the capitalist world.

Moreover, the internal contradictions of the capitalist section of world economy have themselves become more acute. The shifting of the world economic centre to the United States and the transformation of the 'dollar republic' into a universal exploiter have heightened the tension between that country and European capitalism, above all English capitalism; the conflict between England, the most powerful of the old conservative imperialist Powers, and the United States, the strongest of the younger imperialisms, which has already attained world hegemony, is becoming the axis of the world-wide conflict among finance-capitalist States. Germany, which has recovered economically from its spoliation under the Versailles peace treaty and is once more pursuing an imperialist policy, is becoming a serious competitor in the world market. Contradictions in the Pacific, centring on the conflict between the United States and Japan, are becoming more involved. In addition to these principal contradictions, antagonism is growing between the interests of the shifting and unstable groupings of Powers, in which those of the second rank are used as instruments by the imperialist giants and their coalitions.

Because the European home markets have shrunk as a result of the war, and the Soviet Union has dropped out of the purely capitalist economic sphere, while the most important sources of raw materials and fuel have been completely monopolized, the increase in the productive capacity of world capitalist industry means that conflicts develop among the capitalist States. The 'peaceful' struggle for oil, rubber, cotton, coal, iron, for the redistribution of markets and of spheres for capital investment, is driving inexorably to a new world war, which will be the more devastating the greater the progress made in the present feverish development of military technology.

Contradictions are growing also between the metropolitan and the colonial and semi-colonial countries. Insurrectionary outbreaks have been stimulated by the weakening of European imperialism as a result of the war, by capitalist development in the colonies, the influence of the Russian revolution, the centrifugal tendencies in the premier maritime and colonial power in the world, the British Empire (Canada, Australia, South Africa). The great Chinese revolution, which has stirred up hundreds of millions of the Chinese people, is making a tremendous hole in the entire edifice of imperialism. The continuing revolutionary ferment among the millions of Indian workers and peasants threatens to destroy the domination of England, the citadel of world imperialism. In Latin America the growth of tendencies hostile to the powerful imperialism of the United States is a force which is undermining the extension of North American capital. Thus the revolutionary process in the colonies, which is drawing the overwhelming majority of the world's population, held in subjection to the finance-capitalist oligarchy of a few 'great Powers', into the struggle against imperialism, also reflects the profound general crisis of capitalism. Even in Europe, where imperialism has bent under its oppressive yoke a whole series of small nations, the national question intensifies the internal contradictions of capitalism.

Finally, the revolutionary crisis is coming inexorably to a head in the very centres of imperialism. The bourgeois offensive against the working class, against its living standards, its organizations, and its political rights, and the increasing use of white terror are arousing the proletarian masses to greater resistance and sharpening the class struggle between the workers and the trusts. The vast conflicts between capital and labour, the increasing radicalization of the masses, the greater influence of the communist parties and the respect they enjoy, the immense increase in the sympathy of the broadest proletarian masses for the country of proletarian dictatorship— all these are unmistakable symptoms of the approach of a new revolutionary tide in the centres of imperialism.

Thus the edifice of world imperialism is being undermined from a number of directions, and the partial stabilization of capitalism shaken, by the contradictions and conflicts among the imperialist powers, the rising of the colonial millions, the struggle of the revolutionary proletariat in the mother countries, and finally, by the leading force of the world revolutionary movement, the proletarian dictatorship in the Soviet Union. The international revolution is advancing.

Against this revolution imperialism is mobilizing all its forces: expeditions against the colonies, a new world war, and the campaign against the Soviet Union are now on imperialism's order of the day. This is bound to release all the forces of the international revolution, leading inexorably to the downfall of capitalism.

III. THE ULTIMATE AIM OF THE COMMUNIST INTERNATIONAL—WORLD COMMUNISM

The ultimate aim of the Communist International is to replace capitalist world economy by a world communist system. Communist society, towards which the entire course of historical development is leading, is the only hope for mankind, for it alone can eliminate the fundamental contradictions of the capitalist system which threaten mankind with degeneration and ruin.

The communist regime will eliminate the division of society into classes; that is to say, by abolishing the anarchy of production it will abolish every kind and form of oppression and of man's exploitation of man. Warring classes will be replaced by a single world commonwealth of labour. For the first time in history mankind will take its fate into its own hands. Instead of destroying countless lives and untold wealth in class wars and national wars, mankind will use all its energies in the struggle with the forces of nature, in developing and raising its own collective strength.

Once having abolished private property in the means of production and made them public property, world communism will replace the spontaneous forces of the world market, the planless sway of competition, the blind operation of social production, by the socially planned regulation of production in accordance with the rapidly growing needs of society. With the anarchy of production and competition abolished, devastating crises and still more devastating wars will disappear. The immense waste of productive forces, the convulsive development of society will be replaced by the ordered disposition of all material wealth and the economy will develop without friction through the unrestricted, harmonious, and rapid development of productive forces.

The abolition of private property, the withering away of classes will put an end to the exploitation of man by man. To work will no longer mean to work for the class enemy. From being nothing more than making a living, it will become the first necessity of life. Poverty will vanish, economic inequality among men will vanish, along with the poverty of the oppressed classes and the wretchedness of material life in general; the hierarchy established by the division of labour will disappear and with it the antagonism between mental and manual labour; lastly, all traces of social inequality between the sexes will disappear. Together with all these, the agencies of class rule will disappear, above all the State. As the embodiment of class rule, it will wither away as classes themselves disappear. Gradually every kind of coercion will die out.

The disappearance of classes will do away with every kind of monopoly in education. Culture will become a common good for all and the class ideologies of the past will be replaced by the scientific-materialist world outlook. This will make the domination of man by man, in whatever form, impossible; undreamed of possibilities of social selection and of the harmonious development of all the capacities dormant in mankind will be opened up.

The expansion of productive forces will not be hampered by any social restrictions. In communist society there will be no place for private property in the means of production, no selfish striving for profit; the masses will not be kept in the poverty and artificial ignorance which obstruct technical progress in capitalist society; the enormous unproductive expenditure characteristic of capitalism will cease. The maximum productivity of social labour will be secured, and incalculable human energies set free for a tremendous development of art and science, by the most expedient utilization of natural forces and natural conditions of production in the different parts of the world, by eliminating the contradiction between town and country which results from the backwardness of agriculture and its low technical level; by the most comprehensive collaboration between science and technology and research, the results being applied for the benefit of society; by the planned organization of scientific work, the introduction of the most up-to-date methods for the statistical analysis and planned regulation of the economy, and, finally, by the rapid growth of social needs, which is the most powerful driving force in the whole system.

By developing the forces of production, communist world society will make it possible to raise the well-being of all mankind and to cut down to the minimum the amount of time devoted to material production; a golden age of culture unparalleled in history will open. In contrast to capitalism, this new culture, of a humanity united for the first time in history, between whom all State frontiers have fallen, will rest upon clear and transparent human relationships. It will bury for ever mysticism and religion, prejudices and superstitions, and so give a powerful impulse to the development of triumphant scientific knowledge.

This highest stage of communism, when communist society has already developed on its own foundations, when, together with the all-round development of man, the social forces of production have made a mighty advance, and society has inscribed on its banner: 'From each according to his abilities, to each according to his needs', presupposes a lower historical stage of development, the socialist stage. At this stage communist society is only beginning to cast off the capitalist shell; it still bears, economically, morally, and intellectually, the birthmarks of the old society from whose womb it emerged. Under socialism productive forces are not developed far enough to enable the products of labour to be distributed according to need. Distribution proceeds rather in accordance with performance. The division of labour, that is, the allocation of certain labour functions to certain groups of people, has not yet been eliminated; in particular, the contradiction between mental and manual labour still persists. Despite the abolition of classes, traces of the old class division of society still survive, and consequently survivals of proletarian State power, of coercion, of law. Some remnants of inequality therefore still exist. The contradiction between town and country remains. But none of these survivals of the old society is any longer protected and defended by any social force. Since they are linked with a definite stage in the development of productive forces, they will disappear as mankind, liberated from the shackles of the capitalist system, rapidly gains control over the forces of nature, educates itself anew in the spirit of communism, and advances from socialism to complete communism.

IV. THE PERIOD OF TRANSITION FROM CAPITALISM TO SOCIALISM AND THE PROLETARIAN DICTATORSHIP

1. *The Transition Period and the Conquest of Power by the Proletariat*

Between capitalist and communist society lies the period of the revolutionary transformation of the one into the other. To it there corresponds a period of political transition, in which the State can be nothing but the revolutionary dictatorship of the proletariat. The transition from the world dictatorship of imperialism to the world dictatorship of the proletariat covers a long period of proletarian struggles, defeats, and victories, a period of the continuing general crisis of capitalism and the maturing of socialist revolutions, that is, of civil wars of the proletariat against the bourgeoisie, a period of national wars and colonial revolts which, while not in themselves socialist movements of the revolutionary proletariat, objectively become a consistent part of the proletarian world revolution to the extent that they shake imperialist rule; a period when capitalist and socialist socio-economic systems exist side by side within world economy, in 'peaceful' relationships as well as in armed conflict; a period of the formation of a union of Socialist Soviet States, a period of the wars of imperialist States against them, a period when the union between these States and the colonial peoples becomes closer and closer, etc.

Unevenness of economic and political development is an absolute law of capitalism, and is even more marked in the imperialist epoch. Hence the international proletarian revolution cannot be conceived as a single act taking place everywhere simultaneously. The victory of socialism is therefore possible at first only in a few capitalist countries, or even in one, but every such victory enlarges the basis of world revolution and makes the general capitalist crisis still more acute. In this way the capitalist system approaches its final breakdown. The dictatorship of finance-capital collapses and yields to the proletarian dictatorship.

While bourgeois revolutions signify no more than the political emancipation of a system of production relationships that is already established and economically dominant, and the transfer of power from the hands of one exploiting class to another, the proletarian revolution signifies the violent irruption of the proletariat into the property relations of bourgeois society, the expropriation of the exploiting classes, and the transfer of power into the hands of that class whose mission it is to reshape radically the economic basis of society and to abolish all exploitation of man by man. While bourgeois revolutions took centuries to put an end throughout the world to the political domination of the feudal nobility, which could be destroyed only by a series of separate revolutions, the international proletarian revolution can accomplish its task in a shorter time, because of the closer interdependence of countries, although it is by no means a single event, but extends over an entire epoch. Only with the complete victory of the proletariat throughout the world and the consolidation of its power will the prolonged epoch of the intensive construction of a socialist world economy open.

The conquest of power by the proletariat is the necessary prerequisite for the development of socialist forms of economy and the cultural growth of the proletariat, which will reshape its own nature, become mature enough to guide society in all spheres of human activity, draw the other classes into this process of transformation, and thus create the basis for the abolition of classes altogether.

In the course of the struggle for the proletarian dictatorship and the subsequent refashioning of society, the basis for that dictatorship is created by the alliance of workers and peasants, under the intellectual and political hegemony of the working class, in opposition to the bloc of landowners and capitalists.

The transition period as a whole is characterized by the relentless suppression of the resistance of the exploiters, the organization of socialist construction, the mass retraining of the people in the spirit of socialism, and the gradual elimination of class divisions. Only to the degree in which the society of the transition period fulfils these great historical tasks will it change into communist society.

The dictatorship of the world proletariat is thus the most essential and decisive prerequisite for the transition from capitalist to socialist world economy. This dictatorship can, however, be established only by the victory of socialism in individual countries or groups of countries. The newly arisen proletarian republics will ally themselves with those already in existence, and these federations, drawing in the colonies as they throw off the imperialist yoke, will increase steadily in number and will finally become the World Union of Socialist Soviet Republics, uniting the whole of mankind under the hegemony of the international proletariat organized as a State.

The conquest of power by the proletariat does not mean the peaceful 'capture' of the ready-made bourgeois State machine by means of a parliamentary majority. The bourgeoisie make use of every kind of force and terror to maintain their stolen property and strengthen their political mastery. Like the feudal nobility before them, the bourgeoisie will not give up their place in history to the new class without the most bitter and desperate struggle. The violence of the bourgeoisie can be broken only by the most resolute use of violence by the proletariat. The conquest of power by the proletariat means the violent annihilation of bourgeois power, the destruction of the capitalist State machine (the bourgeois army, police, civil-service hierarchy, courts, parliament, etc.) and its replacement by new agencies of proletarian power, which serve primarily as instruments for the suppression of the exploiters.

2. *The Proletarian Dictatorship and its Soviet Form*

The October revolution of 1917 and the Hungarian revolution, which immensely enlarged the experience gained in the Paris Commune of 1871, have shown that the most appropriate form of proletarian State power is a new type of State, the Soviet State, differing in principle from the bourgeois State not only in its class content but in its internal structure. This is precisely the form of State power which, originating directly in the broadest mass movement of the working people, ensures the maximum activity of the masses and so offers the surest pledge of their final victory.

The Soviet State, as the highest form of democracy, the embodiment of proletarian democracy, is the very opposite of bourgeois democracy, which is a masked form of bourgeois dictatorship. The Soviet State is the dictatorship of the proletariat, the rule of a single class. In contrast to bourgeois democracy, the Soviet State openly avows its class character and proclaims its task of suppressing the exploiters in the interests of the over-whelming majority of the population. It deprives its class enemies of political rights and, in certain historical circumstances, may grant to the proletariat, with the object of strengthening its leading position, a number of temporary privileges as against the scattered petty-bourgeois peasantry. While disarming and suppressing its class enemies, the proletarian State regards this deprivation of political rights and certain restrictions on liberty as temporary measures dictated by the struggle against the efforts of the exploiters to defend or restore their privileges. It inscribes on its banner the pledge that the proletariat does not hold power in order to perpetuate it, that it does not act in its craft or professional interests, but aims at uniting the backward and scattered masses of the rural prole-tarians, the semi-proletarians, and the working peasants more and more closely with the advanced strata of the workers, and so gradually and methodically eliminating class divisions altogether. As the all-embracing expression of the unity and organization of the masses under proletarian leadership, the Soviets in fact mobilize the broadest strata of workers, peasants, and labouring people for the struggle and for socialist construc-tion, and draw them into the practical administration of the State. In all their activities they rely on the mass organizations of the working class, put into practice among the working people the most far-reaching demo-cracy, and are infinitely more closely linked with the masses than any other form of State. The right of electing and recalling representatives, the fusion of executive and legislative power, the substitution of elections at the place of work (factory, shop, etc.) for territorial elections—all these measures ensure that the working class and the broad masses of the labour-ing people under its hegemony will take a regular, constant, and active part in all public affairs, economic, political, military, and cultural. This sharply distinguishes the Soviet proletarian dictatorship from bourgeois parliamentary republics.

Bourgeois democracy, with its formal equality of citizens before the law, is built on the glaring economic inequality of classes. Bourgeois democracy does not tamper with the monopoly of the capitalist class and the largest landowners in the decisive means of production. On the contrary, it strengthens that monopoly and so converts, for the exploited classes and above all for the proletariat, formal equality before the law, democratic rights and liberties—which in any case are in practice systematically curtailed—into a legal fiction, a means of deceiving and enslaving the masses. So-called bourgeois democracy is capitalist democracy, reflecting the political domination of the bourgeoisie. The Soviet State, on the other hand, by depriving the exploiting classes of the means of production, which then become the monopoly of the proletariat, the ruling class, secures for the working class and for working people generally the material basis for exercising their rights by placing at their disposal public buildings, printing presses, means of transport, etc.

As regards political rights, the Soviet State, while denying these to the exploiters and enemies of the people, abolishes, for the first time in history, all inequalities of citizenship based, under the rule of the exploiters, on differences of sex, religion, or nationality. In this respect it secures a degree of equality unknown in the bourgeois world. At the same time the proletarian dictatorship creates the material conditions which make this equality real in practice; these include measures for the emancipation of women, the industrialization of former colonies, etc.

Thus Soviet democracy is proletarian democracy, the democracy of the labouring masses, democracy directed against the exploiters.

The Soviet State completely disarms the bourgeoisie and concentrates all arms in the hands of the proletariat. It is the State of the proletariat in arms. The armed forces, like the proletarian dictatorship as a whole, are built on class principles, which secure to the industrial proletariat the leading role. While maintaining revolutionary discipline, this system ensures close and continuous contact between the warriors of the Red Army and Navy and the working masses, and their participation in the administration of the country and the construction of socialism.

3. *The Proletarian Dictatorship and the Expropriation of the Expropriators*

The victorious proletariat uses the power it has seized as a lever of economic revolution, i.e. for the revolutionary transformation of capitalist property relations into relations of the socialist mode of production. The starting-point for this tremendous economic revolution is the expropriation of the large landowners and capitalists, i.e. the conversion of the monopolist property of the bourgeoisie into the property of the proletarian State.

In this sphere the Communist International postulates as the most important tasks of the proletarian dictatorship the following:

A. *Industry, Transport, and Communications*

(a) The confiscation (expropriation without compensation) and proletarian nationalization of all large private capitalist industrial undertakings (factories, mines, power stations) and the transfer of all national and municipal undertakings to the Soviets.

(b) The confiscation and proletarian nationalization of private capitalist transport services by rail, road, water, and air (commercial and passenger air services), and the transfer to the Soviets of every kind of State and municipal property in the means of transport.

(c) The confiscation and proletarian nationalization of private capitalist enterprises in the transmission of communications (telegraph, telephone, and wireless) and the transfer to the Soviets of State and municipal communication services.

(d) The organization of workers' management of industry; the creation of State management organs with strong trade union participation. Factory councils to be guaranteed their appropriate functions.

(e) The reorganization of industry to meet the needs of the broadest masses; reorganization of those industries which served the needs of the former ruling classes (luxury trades, etc.); strengthening of those industries which promote the development of agriculture, in order to reinforce the ties with peasant farming; ensuring the development of State economic enterprises and accelerating the rate of development of the entire national economy.

B. *Agriculture*

(a) The confiscation and proletarian nationalization of all large landholdings in town and country (belonging to individuals, churches, monasteries, etc.) and the transfer of all State and municipal property in land, including forests, minerals, waters, etc., to the Soviets, all land to be subsequently nationalized.

(b) The confiscation of all production equipment on large landholdings, such as buildings, machinery, and other equipment, cattle, installations for processing agricultural products (mills, dairies, kilns, etc.).

(c) The transfer of large farms, particularly model farms and those of considerable economic importance, to the organs of the proletarian dictatorship, to be organized and run as Soviet farms.

(d) The transfer of part of the confiscated land of the large landowners and other landowners to the peasants (to the poor peasants and partly also to the middle peasants), particularly where these lands were formerly cultivated by tenant farmers and served to hold them in economic bondage. The size of the part to be handed over to the peasants to be determined by economic expediency and by the need to neutralize the peasants and win them over to the proletarian cause. It will therefore vary according to different local conditions.

(e) Prohibition on the sale and purchase of land, which is to be retained by the peasants and not transferred to capitalists, speculators, etc. Any infraction of this prohibition to be vigorously combated.

(f) In the fight against usury all usurious debt agreements and all debts owed by the exploited strata of the peasantry to be annulled; poor peasants to be exempt from taxation, etc.

(*g*) Large-scale measures to be initiated by the State to improve agricultural productive forces, such as electrification, manufacture of tractors, production of chemical fertilizers, the raising of good seed and pedigree cattle on Soviet farms, large-scale provision of credits for agricultural improvements.

(*h*) The encouragement and financing of agricultural co-operatives and all forms of collective production in the village (producers' co-operatives, communes, etc.). Systematic propaganda for co-operative peasant association (co-operative marketing, purchase, and credits) based on the independent activities of the peasant masses themselves; propaganda in favour of large-scale agricultural production, which because of its indisputable technical and economic superiority will be of great and immediate advantage and the most likely method of enabling the broad mass of working peasants to make the transition to socialism.

C. *Trade and Credit*

(*a*) The proletarian nationalization of private banks (the entire gold reserve, all securities, deposits, etc., to be transferred to the State) and the transfer of central, municipal, and similar banks to the proletarian State.

(*b*) Centralization of the entire banking system; all nationalized large banks to be subordinated to one central State bank.

(*c*) Nationalization of wholesale trade and of large retail trade concerns (warehouses, grain elevators, large stores, stocks of goods, etc.) and their transfer to organs of the Soviet State.

(*d*) Every encouragement to be given to consumers' co-operatives as the most important part of the machinery of distribution; their work to be co-ordinated and the masses to be ensured independent participation in their establishment.

(*e*) Monopoly of foreign trade.

(*f*) Cancellation of public debts to capitalists, domestic and foreign.

D. *Protection of Labour, Social Legislation, etc.*

(*a*) Reduction of the working day to seven hours, and to six hours in occupations particularly injurious to health. The working day to be still shorter, and a five-day week to be introduced, in countries with highly developed productive forces. The working day to be determined in accordance with increases in labour productivity.

(*b*) Prohibition as a general rule of night work, and of work in occupations particularly injurious to health, for all females; prohibition of child labour, prohibition of overtime.

(*c*) The working day for juveniles to be shortened (six-hour maximum for those under eighteen). Socialist reorganization of juvenile labour by combining material production with general and political education.

(d) Social insurance of every kind (health, old age, accident, unemployment, etc.) at State expense (at the cost of the private employer where private enterprise still exists), to be administered by the insured persons themselves.

(e) A comprehensive public-health system and the establishment of free medical services; war to be waged on the social diseases (alcoholism, venereal disease, tuberculosis).

(f) Social equality of the sexes before the law and in social life, with a radical reform of marriage and family law. Recognition of maternity as a social function; protection of mothers and infants; initiation of measures for the care and upbringing of children and juveniles by society (crèches, kindergartens, children's homes, etc.). Establishment of institutions which will gradually reduce domestic burdens (public kitchens and laundries); planned cultural struggle against the ideologies and traditions of female bondage.

E. *Housing*

(a) Confiscation of properties of large landlords.

(b) Transfer of the confiscated houses to the local Soviets.

(c) Bourgeois districts to be settled by workers.

(d) Palaces and large public and private buildings to be handed over to workers' organizations.

(e) Large-scale house-building programmes to be carried out.

F. *The National and Colonial Question*

(a) Recognition of the right of all nations, regardless of race, to complete self-determination, i.e. going as far as political secession.

(b) Voluntary union and centralization of the military and economic forces of all peoples liberated from capitalism for the fight against imperialism and the construction of socialist economy.

(c) Vigorous and resolute struggle against any limitations or restrictions directed against any people, nation, or race. Complete equality of all nations and races.

(d) The Soviet State secures and promotes the development of the national cultures of the nations liberated from capitalism with all the means at its disposal, consistently seeking to give the content of these cultures a proletarian character.

(e) Every encouragement to be given to the economic, political, and cultural advance of the formerly oppressed 'areas', 'border areas', and 'colonies' with the object of creating a firm foundation for genuine and complete national equality.

(f) Fight against all survivals of chauvinism, of national hatred, of race prejudice, and other ideological relics of feudal and capitalist barbarism.

G. *Means for Exerting Ideological Influence*

(*a*) Nationalization of printing works.

(*b*) Monopoly of newspapers and publishing.

(*c*) Nationalization of large cinema and theatre concerns.

(*d*) Utilization of the nationalized means of producing goods for intellectual purposes for an extensive programme of political and general education of the working people and for building a new socialist culture on proletarian class foundations.

4. *The Cardinal Features of the Proletarian Dictatorship's Economic Policy*

In implementing all these measures the proletarian dictatorship must be guided by the following principles:

1. The complete abolition of private property in land and the nationalization of all land cannot be accomplished at one stroke in the most highly developed capitalist States, where the principle of private property is deeply rooted among broad strata of the peasantry. In these countries land nationalization can be undertaken only gradually, in a series of transitional measures.

2. As a rule the nationalization of production should not extend to small and medium-sized businesses (peasants, artisans, self-employed craftsmen, small and medium traders, small-scale manufacturers, etc.), for the following reasons:

First, because the proletariat must distinguish clearly between the property resulting from the labour of the small producer, who can and must gradually be drawn into socialist construction, and the property capitalists derive from exploitation, which must be abolished as an essential prerequisite for the construction of socialism. Secondly, because, having achieved power, the proletariat, particularly in the early stages of the dictatorship, will not have at its command enough organizational ability not merely to abolish capitalism, but also to organize immediately on a socialist basis medium-sized and small productive units. These small units (particularly the peasant farms) will be drawn into the general socialist organization of production and distribution only gradually, and with comprehensive and systematic support from the proletarian State for every form of their collectivization. Any attempt to destroy their economic operations by violence, and any compulsory collectivization would only yield negative results.

3. The existence of a substantial number of small production units (primarily farms, artisans, small traders, etc.), not only in the colonies, semi-colonies, and economically backward countries, in which the petty-bourgeois masses represent the great majority of the population, but also in the centres of capitalist economy (United States, Germany, and to some

extent even England), requires in a greater or less degree, in the early stages of development, the maintenance of market relations, the money system, etc. The multiplicity of these economic forms (from large-scale socialized industry to small peasants and craftsmen), which is necessarily accompanied by a struggle among them; the corresponding multiplicity of classes and class groups with their different economic incentives; the struggle between different economic interests, and finally the prevalence of customs and traditions in every sphere of economic life, the legacy of a bourgeois social order which cannot be eradicated at one stroke—all this requires the proletariat, in its conduct of the economy, to establish the correct combination between large-scale socialist industry and the small concerns of small commodity producers; such a combination, based on market relations, will secure the leading role of socialist industry and at the same time ensure the most rapid progress for the great mass of peasant farms. Therefore, the greater the specific weight of scattered small peasant labour in the economy of a country, the more widespread are market relations, the smaller the importance of direct planned management, and the more will the general economic plan have to depend on estimates of spontaneous economic relations. The reverse also holds true: The smaller the specific weight of small-scale enterprises, the greater the share of socialized labour, the greater the total of concentrated and socialized means of production in the economy as a whole, the more restricted will be the scope of market relations, the greater the importance of controlled economic development as compared with economic anarchy, the greater and more comprehensive the planned management of production and distribution.

The technical and economic superiority of large-scale socialized industry, the concentration of all the decisive economic 'commanding heights' (industry, transport, banking, large-scale agriculture, etc.) in the hands of the proletarian State, the planned conduct of the economy, the power of the State machine as a whole (budget, taxation, administrative legislation, and legislation generally) will, provided the proletarian dictatorship has a correct class policy, i.e. correctly estimates class relations, steadily and methodically squeeze out both what remains of private capital and any new seeds of capitalism that take root in town or country (large peasants and kulaks) with the expansion of the economy of small commodity producers in conditions of more or less free trade and market relations. At the same time the organization of the peasantry in co-operatives, and the expansion of collective forms of economy, will draw the bulk of peasant farms (i.e. the small and medium holdings) into the developing system of socialism. The outwardly capitalist forms and methods of economic activity associated with market relations (price calculations, money wages, purchase and sale, credit and banks) will serve as levers of socialist change in so far as they encourage to an increasing extent the development of enterprises of a consistently socialist type, i.e. in so far as they serve the socialist sector of the economy.

Thus, provided the Soviet State pursues the correct policy, market relations in a proletarian dictatorship carry within themselves the seeds of their own destruction. In helping to squeeze out private capital and transform peasant economy, in contributing to the centralization and concentration of the means of production in the hands of the proletarian State, they promote the process of eliminating market relations altogether.

In the likely event of armed capitalist intervention, or of a prolonged counter-revolutionary war against the proletarian dictatorship, those in control of the economy must be guided primarily by the need to defend the proletarian dictatorship; it may become necessary to introduce 'war communism' as the economic policy. This is nothing but the organization of rational consumption in the interests of military defence, combined with a system of reinforced pressure on the capitalist groups (confiscations, requisitions, etc.). Free trade and market relations will be more or less liquidated, and the individualist economic incentives of the small producers in large measure destroyed, such action being accompanied by a diminution in the forces of production. A policy of 'war communism' is historically justified because it undermines the material basis of the strata within the country hostile to the working class, secures a rational distribution of supplies, and facilitates the armed struggle of the proletarian dictatorship. None the less it should not be taken as a 'normal' economic policy for the proletarian dictatorship.

5. *The Proletarian Dictatorship and the Classes*

The dictatorship of the proletariat is the continuation of its class struggle in new conditions. The proletarian dictatorship is a stubborn struggle, bloody and bloodless, violent and peaceful, military and economic, educational and administrative, against the forces and traditions of the old society, against the capitalist enemy outside the country and the remnants of the exploiting classes within the country, and against the seeds of a new bourgeoisie taking root in an environment from which commodity production has not been eradicated.

After the end of the civil war this stubborn class struggle assumes new forms; prominent among them is the struggle of socialist forms of economy against survivals of the old economic methods and new manifestations of these methods. The forms assumed by this struggle necessarily change at the different stages of socialist development; in certain circumstances the struggle may become more acute in the first stage.

In the initial stage of the proletarian dictatorship the policy of the proletariat towards other classes and social groups is determined by the following principles:

1. The big bourgeoisie and large landowners, the section of the officers' corps devoted to their interests, the army staff and the higher ranks of the civil service are consistent enemies of the working class who must be pitilessly crushed. It is, however, possible to use the organizational skills of a certain section of these elements, but as a rule only after the consolidation of the dictatorship and the decisive defeat of all revolts and conspiracies by the exploiters.

2. In regard to the technical intelligentsia, brought up in the bourgeois tradition and closely associated, in its higher ranks, with the commanding apparatus of capital, the proletariat, while vigorously suppressing all counter-revolutionary activities on the part of the hostile strata of the intelligentsia, must bear in mind the need to draw this skilled social force into the work of socialist construction, and to encourage in every way the groups among them that are neutral, and especially the groups that are well disposed towards the workers' revolution. In opening up to view the full panorama of economic, technical, and cultural construction under socialism in all its social significance, the proletariat must systematically bring over to its side the technical intelligentsia, subject it to its ideological influence, and secure its active co-operation in the work of transformation.

3. It is the task of the communist parties, supported by the rural proletariat, to win over to their side all the exploited and labouring strata of the village. The victorious proletariat must distinguish clearly between the various groupings within the peasantry, carefully weigh their relative importance, and support in every way the propertyless, semi-proletarian strata of the peasantry by transferring to them a part of the landowners' estates, helping them in their struggle against the usurers, etc. The medium strata of the peasantry must be neutralized, and all resistance by the rural bourgeoisie allied with the large landowners ruthlessly suppressed. As it strengthens its dictatorship and progresses with the building of socialism, the proletariat must pass from the policy of neutralizing the middle peasants to a policy of a firm alliance with them, without, however, allowing even the idea of sharing power with them to emerge. For the proletarian dictatorship reflects the fact that only the industrial working class is able to lead the entire mass of the working people. But, while being the rule of the proletariat alone, it is also a special form of class alliance between the proletariat as the vanguard of the working people and the numerous non-proletarian strata among them, or the majority of them; it is an alliance for the final overthrow of capital, for completely crushing the resistance of the bourgeoisie and their attempts to restore the old order, for the final establishment and consolidation of socialism.

4. The urban petty bourgeoisie, who constantly vacillate between extreme reaction and sympathy with the proletariat, must also be neutralized and as far as possible won over to the proletarian cause. This can be done by leaving them their small property, retaining a certain degree of freedom in trade, eliminating usurious loans, and by the proletariat helping them in every way to fight against every form of capitalist oppression.

6. *Mass Organizations in the System of Proletarian Dictatorship*

While these tasks of the proletarian dictatorship are being accomplished, radical changes occur in the tasks and functions of mass organizations, particularly labour organizations. Under capitalism the trade unions, the first mass labour organizations in which the broad proletarian strata united and received their training, are the principal weapons in the industrial and mass struggles against concentrated capital and its State. Under the proletarian dictatorship they become its most powerful lever, a school of communism drawing the great mass of the proletariat into the socialist management of production. The unions become an organization directly linked with all parts of the State apparatus, influencing all branches of its work, safeguarding the long-term as well as the day-to-day interests of the working class and combating bureaucratic distortions in the organs of the Soviet State. Thus the trade unions become the backbone of the economic and political organizations of the proletariat, for they provide from their own ranks the leading cadres for constructive work, draw broad masses of the proletariat into this work, and make it their special task to fight against the bureaucratic excrescences which are bound to develop as a result of the low cultural level of the masses and of the influence of classes hostile to the proletariat.

Under capitalism working-class co-operative organizations are condemned—in defiance of reformist utopias—to play an extremely modest part. Frequently, because of conditions under capitalism generally, and of the reformist policy of their leaders, they degenerate and turn into appendages of the capitalist system. Under the proletarian dictatorship the co-operatives can and must become the most important units in the machinery of distribution.

Lastly, the peasant agricultural co-operatives (marketing, purchasing, credit, and producers' co-operatives) can and must become one of the basic forms of organization linking the countryside with the town, provided they are under appropriate management and conduct a systematic struggle against capitalist elements, while ensuring the active participation of the broad masses of rural working people who follow the proletariat. Under capitalism co-operative associations of peasant farmers, in so far as they show any vitality at all, usually turn into capitalist undertakings, for they are completely dependent on capitalist industry, capitalist banks, and the capitalist environment as a whole, and are managed by reformists, by the village bourgeoisie, and often even by the landlords. Under the proletarian dictatorship they develop into a different system with different relationships, and are dependent on proletarian industry, proletarian banks, etc. In this way, and provided that the proletariat pursues a correct class policy, i.e. conducts a systematic class struggle against capitalist elements inside and outside the co-operatives, agricultural co-operatives, under the guidance of socialist industry, become one of the most important levers for the socialist transformation of the countryside, for its collectivization. This, however, does not exclude the possibility that in some countries the consumers' co-operatives, and agricultural co-operatives in particular, will at first, under the leadership of the bourgeoisie and their social-democratic agents, serve as counter-revolutionary strongholds and sabotage the economic activities of the workers' revolution.

The proletariat wages all these battles and accomplishes its work of construction through a great variety of organizations, which must become the real driving forces of the Soviet State and the links which connect it with the broadest masses of all strata of the working class; it secures unity of will and action through the leading role of the communist party in the system of the proletarian dictatorship.

The party of the proletariat relies directly on the trade unions, and on a series of other organizations covering the working masses and, through them, the peasants (Soviets, co-operatives, Young Communist League, etc.), and in this way it guides the Soviet system as a whole. Only the devoted support of all mass organizations for the Soviet Government, the unshakeable unity of class will, and the leadership of the party enable the proletariat to fulfil its tasks as organizer of the new society.

7. *The Proletarian Dictatorship and the Cultural Revolution*

This role of organizer of a new human society presupposes that the proletariat will become culturally mature, refashion its own nature, and steadily promote from its ranks new proletarian cadres able to assimilate all the achievements of technology, science, and administration, with the object of constructing socialism and the new socialist culture.

While the bourgeois revolution against feudalism presupposes that a new class has grown within the womb of the feudal social order, superior to the ruling class in virtue of its greater cultural maturity, and dominant in economic life even under feudalism, the proletarian revolution develops in entirely different conditions. In capitalist society the working class is exploited economically, oppressed politically, and downtrodden culturally, and therefore it is only in the transition period, only after it has seized State power, that it can break the bourgeois monopoly of education, master all knowledge, and transform its own nature in the light of its experiences in the tremendous work of construction. Such a transformation, on a mass scale, is essential to the development of a communist consciousness among the masses, to the cause of socialism itself. This can take place only in the course of practical activities, in the revolution. Thus the revolution is necessary not only because there is no other way of overthrowing the ruling class, but because only in revolution can the class which overthrows it cleanse itself of all the filth of the old society and become capable of founding a new society.

While destroying capitalist monopoly in the means of production, the working class must also get rid of the bourgeoisie's monopoly of education, i.e. it must take over the entire educational system, up to and including the universities. It is a matter of great urgency for the proletariat to train its own specialists from among the working class, for production (engineers, technicians, organizers, etc.) as well as for military affairs, art, and science. Furthermore, it is necessary to raise the general cultural level of the broad proletarian masses, further their political training, improve their knowledge and technical qualifications, familiarize them with the routine of public work and administration, combat the survivals of bourgeois and petty-bourgeois prejudices, etc.

Only to the extent that the proletariat appoints its own most advanced elements to all 'key positions' in socialist construction and culture, only to the extent that these elements continue to expand steadily by drawing more and more members of the proletarian class into the process of cultural transformation, until at last the division of the proletariat into 'advanced' and 'backward' strata is obliterated, only to that extent will the proletariat ensure the victorious construction of socialism and build a barrier against bureaucratic decay and class degeneration.

In the course of the revolution the proletariat reshapes not only its own nature, but also the nature of the other classes, especially the numerous petty-bourgeois strata of town and country, and in particular the labouring strata of the peasantry. The working class gives the broadest masses an opportunity to share in the cultural revolution, draws them into the work of building socialism, organizes them and trains them in the spirit of communism by every available means, and fights vigorously against all anti-proletarian and craft ideologies. The proletariat works methodically and with special emphasis to get rid of the general and cultural backwardness of the village, and so, with the development of collective forms of economy, creates the prerequisites for eliminating class divisions in society.

The fight against religion, 'the opium of the people', occupies a special place among the tasks of the cultural transformation of the broad masses. This fight must be waged stubbornly and systematically. The proletarian government must deprive the church, as an agency of the former ruling classes, of all State support, prohibit any interference by the church in the public educational system, and ruthlessly suppress the counter-revolutionary activities of ecclesiastical organizations. The proletarian government permits freedom of belief, but at the same time uses all the means at its disposal to promote anti-religious propaganda, abolishes the privileged status of the former established church, and refashions the entire educational system on the basis of the philosophy of scientific materialism.

8. *The Struggle for the World Proletarian Dictatorship and the Principal Types of Revolution*

The international proletarian revolution consists of a series of processes, differing in character and in time: purely proletarian revolutions; revolutions of a bourgeois-democratic type which turn into proletarian revolutions; wars of national liberation, or colonial revolutions. It is only when this development reaches its conclusion that the revolutionary process emerges as the world proletarian dictatorship.

The unequal development of capitalism, accentuated in the epoch of imperialism, has given rise to a great variety of types of capitalism with differing degrees of maturity in different countries, and to a great variety of conditions of the revolutionary process peculiar to each. It follows with historical inevitability that the proletariat will seize power in a variety of ways and with varying degrees of rapidity, and that in a number of countries it will be necessary to pass through a transitional stage to the proletarian dictatorship. It follows further from this that the construction of socialism will assume different forms in different countries.

The varied conditions and roads of the transition to the proletarian dictatorship in different countries may be reduced schematically to the following three types: in highly developed capitalist countries (the United States, Germany, England, etc.), with powerful productive forces, a high degree of centralization of production, relatively insignificant small-scale enterprise, and an old and well-established bourgeois-democratic political regime, the principal political demand of the programme is the direct transition to the proletarian dictatorship. In the economic domain the essential demands are the expropriation of all large concerns, the establishment of a substantial number of Soviet State farms, the transfer of only a relatively small proportion of the land to the peasants, comparatively small scope for the operation of spontaneous market relationships, rapid socialist development in general and very rapid collectivization of peasant farms.

Countries at a medium level of capitalist development (Spain, Portugal, Poland, Hungary, the Balkans, etc.), where semi-feudal relationships largely survive in agriculture, although the material prerequisites for the construction of socialism are present in some degree, the bourgeois-democratic revolution not having been completed: in some of these countries it is possible that the bourgeois-democratic revolution will develop more or less rapidly into the socialist revolution, while in others there may be types of proletarian revolution which will have many tasks of the bourgeois-democratic revolution to accomplish. In the first case it is possible that the proletarian dictatorship will be established not immediately, but only in the course of the transition from the democratic dictatorship of the proletariat and peasantry to the socialist dictatorship of the proletariat, while the second, where the revolution develops as a directly proletarian one, presupposes a broad agrarian and peasant movement led by the proletariat; the agrarian revolution plays a tremendous, sometimes a decisive part. With the expropriation of large estates, a considerable part of the confiscated land is handed over to the peasantry; after the victory of the proletariat market relations prevail over a large area; the task of organizing the peasantry into co-operatives and into large production units is one of the most important of the many tasks of socialist construction. The rate of that construction is relatively slow.

Colonial and semi-colonial countries (China, India, etc.) and independent countries (Argentina, Brazil, etc.): in some of these countries industry is only rudimentary, in others it is fairly well developed, but for the most part insufficient to provide a basis for independent socialist construction; both in the economy as in the political superstructure, medieval feudal relationships prevail, or the 'Asiatic mode of production'; the key industries, the dominant trading, banking, and transportation concerns, as well as plantations, etc., are concentrated in the hands of foreign imperialist groups. In these countries the struggle against feudalism, against pre-capitalist forms of exploitation, the consistent pursuit of the peasant agrarian revolution, and the struggle against foreign imperialism and for national independence are of decisive importance. Here the transition to the proletarian dictatorship is as a rule possible only through a series of preparatory stages, only as the outcome of an entire period of transformation of the bourgeois-democratic into the socialist revolution. In most of these countries the successful construction of socialism is possible only with the direct help of the countries where the proletarian dictatorship is already established.

In still more backward countries (for example in parts of Africa) where there are virtually no industrial wage earners, where the majority of the population live in tribal conditions and traces of the old clan society still survive, where there is practically no national bourgeoisie and foreign imperialism appears primarily as armed conquest and seizure of the land— in these countries the struggle for national liberation is the central task. Here victorious national uprisings may open the road to socialism while by-passing the capitalist stage, if sufficiently powerful help is given by the countries with a proletarian dictatorship.

At a time when, in the advanced capitalist countries, the seizure of power by the proletariat is on the order of the day, while in the Soviet Union the proletarian dictatorship already exists and is a factor of world importance, the liberation movements provoked by the penetration of world capital into the colonial and semi-colonial countries can lead— despite the immaturity of social conditions there if they are regarded in isolation—to socialist development, provided they receive the help and support of the proletarian dictatorship and the international proletarian movement generally.

9. *The Struggle for the World Proletarian Dictatorship and Colonial Revolutions*

The peculiar conditions of the revolutionary struggle in colonial and semi-colonial countries, the inevitability of a prolonged period of struggle for the democratic dictatorship of the proletariat and peasantry and for its development into a proletarian dictatorship, and the decisive importance of the national factor in this contest impose a number of special tasks on the communist parties of these countries; the general tasks of the proletarian dictatorship cannot be mastered before these special tasks are accomplished. The Communist International considers that the most important among them are the following:

1. The overthrow of foreign imperialism, of feudalism, and of the landlord bureaucracy.

2. Establishment of the democratic dictatorship of the proletariat and peasantry on the basis of Soviets.

3. Complete national independence and political unification.

4. Cancellation of State debts.

5. Nationalization of large undertakings (in industry, transport, banking, etc.) belonging to the imperialists.

6. Expropriation of large landowners, of church and monastery estates, nationalization of all land.

7. Introduction of the eight-hour day.

8. Establishment of a revolutionary workers' and peasants' army.

As the struggle continues to develop and to become more acute (sabotage by the bourgeoisie, confiscation of enterprises belonging to the sabotaging sections of the bourgeoisie, which is bound to develop into the nationalization of large-scale industry), the bourgeois-democratic revolution, consistently pursued, will be transformed into the proletarian revolution in those colonies and semi-colonies where the proletariat acts as leader and exercises hegemony over the movement. In colonies without a proletariat the overthrow of imperialist power must be accompanied by the organization of a popular (peasant) Soviet regime, the confiscation of businesses and land owned by foreigners, and the transfer of this property to the State,

Colonial revolutions and national liberation movements play an extremely important part in the struggle against imperialism and the conquest of power by the working class. In the transition period colonies and semi-colonies are also important because they represent the village on a world scale *vis-à-vis* the industrial countries, which represent the town in the context of world economy. Hence the problem of organizing a socialist world economy, of the correct combination of industry and agriculture, resolves itself to a large extent into the question of relations with the former colonies of imperialism. To establish a fraternal militant alliance with the working masses of the colonies is therefore one of the principal tasks of the industrial world proletariat as leader and hegemon in the fight against imperialism.

The course of the world revolution drives the workers of the imperialist States into the fight for the proletarian dictatorship, and at the same time rouses hundreds of millions of colonial workers and peasants to the struggle against foreign imperialism. Once centres of socialism exist, in the form of socialist Soviet republics with steadily growing economic power, the colonies which have broken away from imperialism draw nearer, economically, to the industrial centres of world socialism and gradually unite with them. Drawn in this way into the path of socialist construction, and by-passing the stages of development when capitalism is the dominant system, they can make rapid economic and cultural progress. Peasant Soviets in the backward ex-colonies, and workers' and peasants' Soviets in the more advanced, will gravitate politically towards the centres of proletarian dictatorship and will in this way be drawn into the general system of the ever-expanding federation of Soviet republics and the world dictatorship of the proletariat.

Socialism, as the new mode of production, will thus develop on a world scale.

V. THE PROLETARIAN DICTATORSHIP IN THE SOVIET UNION AND THE INTERNATIONAL SOCIALIST REVOLUTION

1. *The Construction of Socialism in the Soviet Union and the Class Struggle*

The most striking manifestation of the profound crisis of the capitalist system is the division of the world economy into capitalist countries and countries building socialism. Hence the internal consolidation of the proletarian dictatorship in the Soviet Union, the successes of socialist construction, the growing influence and authority of the Soviet Union among the proletarian masses and the oppressed colonial peoples signify the continuation, the strengthening, and the spread of the international socialist revolution.

In their countries the workers of the Soviet Republics have at their disposal the necessary and sufficient material prerequisites both for the overthrow of the large landowners and the bourgeoisie and for the establishment of complete socialism. With the help of the international proletariat they heroically repelled the attack by the armed forces of the counter-revolution, internal and external. They have reinforced their alliance with the bulk of the peasant masses and achieved great successes in socialist construction.

The links established between proletarian socialist industry and small peasant farming which ensure the development of agricultural productive forces while guaranteeing the leading role of socialist industry; the combination of industry and agriculture which has replaced capitalist production for the satisfaction of the unproductive consumption of parasitic classes; production not for the sake of capitalist profits but to satisfy the rapidly growing needs of the masses—a development which in the long run greatly stimulates the expansion of the entire production process; finally, the concentration of key economic positions in the hands of the proletarian State, the extension of the sphere of economic planning, resulting in a more economic use and in the most expedient distribution of the forces of production—all this enables the proletariat to advance rapidly along the road of socialist construction.

By improving the productive forces of the entire national economy, by steadily pursuing a policy of industrialization—the rapid rate of which is dictated by both the international and the domestic situation—the Soviet proletariat, notwithstanding the attempts at financial and economic boycott regularly and deliberately made by the capitalist powers, is increasing the relative share of the socialized (socialist) sector of the national economy in the means of production, in total output, and in trade turnover. Because the land is nationalized and industrialization is going ahead, socialist State industry, State transport and banking, operating through State trading and the rapidly growing co-operative system, are coming more and more to serve as guides for small and very small peasant farming.

In agriculture the improvement in productive forces is occurring in conditions which impose limits on the process of differentiation among the peasantry (land nationalization and the prohibition on the sale and purchase of land, steeply progressive taxes, financial aid for co-operatives and producers' associations established by the poor and middle peasants, legal regulation of the employment of hired labour, restrictions on the political and social rights of the large peasants, special organizations for the village poor, etc.). But since the productive forces of socialist industry have not yet reached that level of development which would make it possible to reorganize agriculture thoroughly on the basis of new agricultural techniques and so facilitate the rapid concentration of peasant farms into large communes (collective farms), the large peasants are also making some progress and uniting with the so-called 'new bourgeoisie', economically and, in a more gradual way, politically as well.

The proletariat of the Soviet Union controls all the decisive key economic positions; it is methodically squeezing out what remains of private capital in the towns, whose share in the total economy declined very steeply in the last phase of the New Economic Policy; the proletariat is obstructing in every way the expansion of the exploiting strata in the countryside which grow out of the development of a commodity and money economy; it is supporting the existing Soviet farms and promoting the foundation of new ones; it is incorporating the bulk of simple commodity producers among the peasantry into the proletarian system of economy, and so into socialist construction, by means of rapidly developing co-operative organization, which, in a proletarian dictatorship where socialist industry plays the leading part in the economy, is identical with the development of socialism. With the transition from reconstruction to the expanded reproduction of the entire technical basis of the country's production, the proletariat of the Soviet Union faces new tasks, which it has already begun to tackle: the creation of new capital resources (the production of means of production in general, expansion of heavy industry, electrification) and, in addition to the further encouragement of marketing, purchasing, and credit co-operatives, the direct organization of the peasants, on a steadily expanding scale, into collective producers' co-operatives, a task which calls for large-scale material assistance from the proletarian State.

Already established as the decisive economic force in the Soviet Union, which puts its stamp on the development of the entire economy, socialism is advancing nearer and nearer to its completion by systematically overcoming the difficulties which arise from the petty-bourgeois character of the country and are natural in periods when class contradictions become for a time more acute.

The need to re-equip industry and to make large new capital investments gives rise to a number of grave difficulties on the path of socialist development which, in the final analysis, are due to the technical and economic backwardness of the country, and to the destruction caused by the world war and civil war. Nevertheless the standard of living of the working class and the broad masses of the working population continues to improve. *Pari passu* with the continuing socialist rationalization and scientific organization of industry, the seven-hour day is gradually being introduced, opening new prospects for improvements in the working and living conditions of the proletariat.

Backed by the growing economic strength of the Soviet Union and by the steady expansion of the socialist sector of the economy, the working class, under the leadership of the communist party steeled in revolutionary battle, is drawing more and more millions of the labouring people into the work of building socialism. In the countryside it relies on the village poor and forges strong links with the middle peasantry, while never halting for a moment its struggle against the large peasants. To accomplish these ends it develops broad mass organizations (the party as the guiding force, the trade unions as the backbone of the entire system of proletarian dictatorship, the Young Communist League, co-operatives of every kind, associations of housewives, working women, and peasant women, various other associations, worker and peasant press correspondents, sports organizations, scientific societies, educational and cultural organizations) and encourages the initiative of the masses; it selects and promotes workers to leading posts in all branches of the economy and the administration. The constant attraction of the masses into the work of socialist construction, the steady renovation of the entire machinery of the State, the economy, the trade unions by recruitment from the ranks of the proletariat, the systematic training of fresh socialist cadres from the ranks of the working class, particularly young workers, in high schools and special courses, etc., for all branches of construction—these provide the best guarantees against bureaucratic petrifaction and social degeneration of the leading proletarian cadres.

2. *The Soviet Union and its Obligations to the International Revolution*

The proletarian dictatorship in the Soviet Union overthrew Russian imperialism, liberated all the former colonies and oppressed peoples of the Tsarist empire, and laid a firm foundation for their cultural and political development by industrializing these territories; it secured the juridical position of the autonomous regions, autonomous republics, and union republics in the constitution of the Union, and granted full rights of national self-determination, thus ensuring to the various nationalities of the Union not merely formal, but real equality.

As the country of proletarian dictatorship and socialist construction, of tremendous working-class achievements, of the alliance of proletariat and peasantry, as the country of a new civilization advancing under the banner of Marxism, the Soviet Union was bound to become the base of the international movement of all oppressed classes, the centre of the international revolution, the most significant factor in world history. In the Soviet Union, for the first time in history, the proletariat is fighting for its own fatherland. The Soviet Union is the most powerful centre of attraction for the colonial peoples fighting for their liberation.

Thus the Soviet Union is becoming a significant factor in the general capitalist crisis, not only because it has laid the foundations of a new socialist economic system and so dropped out of the capitalist world system, but also because it has a revolutionary part to play without parallel in history, the part of a driving force of the international proletarian revolution spurring the proletariat of all countries on to the conquest of power; it acts as a living example of the fact that the working class is capable not only of destroying capitalism, but also of building socialism as well; as a Union of Socialist Soviet Republics, it serves as a model of fraternal relations between all peoples of the earth, of the economic unity of the working people of all countries in the single world socialist economy which the proletariat of the world must establish after it has captured State power.

The existence side by side of two economic systems—socialist in the Soviet Union and capitalist in other countries—imposes on the workers' State the task of warding off the attacks of the capitalist world (boycott, blockade, etc.). At the same time it has to manœuvre in the economic field and to make use of its economic connexions with capitalist countries (with the aid of the foreign-trade monopoly, one of the basic prerequisites for successful socialist construction, and by means of credits, loans, concessions, etc.). The guiding line to be followed must be that of establishing as wide contacts as possible with foreign countries, but only in so far as they prove useful to the Soviet Union, i.e. help to strengthen Soviet industry by creating a basis for heavy industry, electrification, and finally for a socialist machine-building industry. Only in so far as its economic independence of the capitalist environment is made secure, can the Soviet Union withstand the danger that its socialist achievements will be destroyed and the country transformed into an appendage of the capitalist world system.

Despite the importance of the Soviet market, the capitalist States constantly vacillate between their commercial interests and the fear that the Soviet Union will grow stronger, implying a further development of the world revolution. The dominating tendency in the policy of the imperialist States is, however, the effort to encircle the Soviet Union and instigate a counter-revolutionary war against it, with the object of destroying the Soviet Union and establishing a terrorist bourgeois regime throughout the world.

However, neither the persistent imperialist attempts to encircle the Soviet Union politically nor the growing danger of a military attack prevent the Communist Party of the Soviet Union, as that section of the Communist International which stands at the head of the proletarian dictatorship, from fulfilling its international duties and rendering support to all the oppressed—to the labour movement in capitalist countries as well as to the colonial peoples in their struggle against imperialism and against every form of national oppression.

3. *The Duties of the International Proletariat to the Soviet Union*

The Soviet Union is the true fatherland of the proletariat, the strongest pillar of its achievements, and the principal factor in its emancipation throughout the world. This obliges the international proletariat to forward the success of socialist construction in the Soviet Union and to defend the country of proletarian dictatorship by every means against the attacks of the capitalist powers.

The world political situation has now put the proletarian dictatorship on the order of the day, and inevitably all events in world politics concentrate on the one central point—the struggle of the world bourgeoisie against the Russian Soviet Republic, which is bound to rally to itself all Soviet movements among the advanced workers of all countries and all movements for national freedom among the colonies and oppressed peoples (Lenin).

In the event of an attack by the imperialist States on the Soviet Union, and of a war against it, the international proletariat must answer by bold and resolute mass action and by fighting to overthrow the imperialist governments, its slogan the proletarian dictatorship and alliance with the Soviet Union.

In the colonies, above all the colonies of an imperialist State which is attacking the Soviet Union, the strongest effort must be made to take advantage of the preoccupation elsewhere of the armed forces of imperialism to unleash the anti-imperialist struggle, to organize revolutionary action, and so to overthrow imperialist rule and win complete independence.

The advance of socialism in the Soviet Union and the growth of its international influence not only provoke the hatred of the imperialist Powers and their social-democratic agents; they also arouse the greatest sympathies of broad masses of working people throughout the world, and the readiness of the oppressed classes of all countries to fight in every way for the country of proletarian dictatorship if it is attacked by imperialism.

Thus the development of the contradictions within world economy today, the accentuation of the general capitalist crisis, and the armed attack of imperialism on the Soviet Union lead with iron necessity to a tremendous revolutionary explosion. This explosion will bury capitalism under its ruins in a number of so-called civilized countries; in the colonies it will unleash the victorious revolution, immensely expanding the base of the proletarian dictatorship, and so mark a gigantic step forward to the final victory of socialism throughout the world.

VI. THE STRATEGY AND TACTICS OF THE COMMUNIST INTERNATIONAL IN THE STRUGGLE FOR THE PROLETARIAN DICTATORSHIP

1. *Ideologies in the Working Class Hostile to Communism*

In its fight against capitalism for the proletarian dictatorship, revolutionary communism comes up against numerous tendencies among the working class: some express in greater or less degree ideological subjection to the imperialist bourgeoisie, while others reflect the ideological pressure of the petty bourgeoisie, who from time to time rebel against the chains of finance-capital, but are incapable of pursuing in their struggle a consistent and scientific strategy and tactics, and waging this struggle in the organized fashion based on strict discipline which is characteristic of the proletariat.

The immense social power of the imperialist State, with all its subsidiary machinery—schools, the press, the theatre, the church—is revealed most clearly in the existence of denominational and reformist tendencies within the working class, which represent the greatest obstacle on the road to the socialist revolution of the proletariat.

Denominational tendencies, tinged by religion, are shown primarily in the existence of denominational trade unions, most of which are directly connected with corresponding bourgeois political organizations and with an ecclesiastical organization of the ruling class (Catholic unions, Young Men's Christian Association, Zionist organizations, etc.). These tendencies most clearly reflect the ideological captivity of many proletarian strata and most of them have a romantic feudal appearance; their leaders, who sanctify the infamy of the capitalist regime with holy water and terrorize their flock with the spectre of damnation, are the most reactionary detachments of the class enemy in the proletarian camp.

Subjection to the ideological influence of the bourgeoisie in a cynically commercial form, secular and imperialist in character, is represented by contemporary 'socialist' reformism. It borrows all its principal theories from the code of imperialist politics and now takes as its model the consciously anti-socialist and openly counter-revolutionary American Federation of Labor. The 'intellectual' dictatorship of the American trade union bosses, those lackeys of the bourgeoisie, merely reflects the 'intellectual' dictatorship of the dollar; assisted by English reformism and His Majesty's socialists in the 'Labour' Party, American reformism has become the chief element in the theory and practice of international social-democracy as a whole and of the leaders of the Amsterdam International. The German and Austrian social-democratic leaders cover this theory with a surface of Marxist phraseology and so conceal their base betrayal of Marxism. 'Socialist' reformism, the chief enemy of revolutionary communism in the labour movement, with its broad organizational basis in the social-democratic parties and, through them, in the reformist trade unions, is a force that, in all its practice and theory, works against the proletarian revolution.

As regards foreign policy, the social-democratic parties actively encouraged the imperialist war under the banner of 'defence of the fatherland'. They give their whole-hearted support to imperialist expansion and 'colonial policy'; the main features of the foreign policy of reformism are a leaning towards the counter-revolutionary 'Holy Alliance' of the imperialist States ('League of Nations'), advocacy of 'ultra-imperialism', mobilization of the masses under pseudo-pacifist slogans while at the same time actively supporting imperialism in its attacks on the Soviet Union and its preparations for war against the Soviet Union.

As regards domestic policy, social-democracy has set itself the task of giving direct encouragement and support to the capitalist regime. The policy of reformism at home is to give unreserved support to capitalist rationalization and the stabilization of capitalism, to guarantee class peace, 'industrial peace', to merge the workers' organizations with the organizations of the employers and of the imperialist robber State, to practise so-called 'economic democracy', which in reality is tantamount to complete subjection to trust capital, to toady to the imperialist State and especially its pseudo-democratic façade, to take an active part in building up the organs of this State—police, army, gendarmerie—and its class justice, to defend this State against the attacks of the revolutionary communist proletariat and to act as executioner in times of revolutionary crisis. Ostensibly, reformism wages a trade union struggle against the bourgeoisie, but in this too it considers its chief task to be to conduct this struggle in such a way as to protect the capitalist class from every kind of shock and to preserve intact the foundations of capitalist property.

In the theoretical field, social-democracy has completely abandoned Marxism. Having traversed the stage of revisionism, it has reached that of bourgeois liberal social reform and overt social imperialism. It has replaced Marx's theory of capitalist contradictions by the bourgeois theory of harmonious capitalist development; his theory of crises and of the impoverishment of the proletariat has been pigeonholed; the formidable, burning theory of the class struggle transformed into the insipid advocacy of class peace; the theory of the intensification of class contradictions has been exchanged for philistine fairy tales of the 'democratization' of capitalism; to the theory of the inevitability of war under capitalism it has opposed the bourgeois lie of pacifism and the deception of 'ultra-imperialism'; it has exchanged the theory of the revolutionary collapse of capitalism for the counterfeit coinage of a 'healthy' capitalism leading by peaceful paths to socialism; it has substituted evolution for revolution, active collaboration with the bourgeois State for its destruction, the theory of coalition with the bourgeoisie for the theory of proletarian dictatorship, the gospel of defence of the imperialist fatherland for a theory of international proletarian solidarity, idealist philosophy and an inclination to feed on the religious crumbs falling from the bourgeoisie's table for Marx's dialectical materialism.

A number of trends can be distinguished within this social-democratic reformism which are particularly characteristic of its bourgeois degeneration.

Constructive socialism (MacDonald and Co.)—the very name of which suggests hostility to the proletarian revolution and a positive attitude to the capitalist order—carries on the liberal, philanthropic, anti-revolutionary, bourgeois traditions of the Fabian Society (S. and B. Webb, Bernard Shaw, Lord Olivier, etc.). By rejecting on principle the proletarian dictatorship and the use of force in the struggle against the bourgeoisie, it lends support to the use of violence in the struggle against the proletariat and the colonial peoples. As apologist of the capitalist State it conceals behind a socialist mask its admiration for State capitalism, and is at one with the most vulgar ideologues of imperialism in both hemispheres in condemning the theory of the class struggle as 'pre-scientific'. As a means to eliminate capitalism, 'constructive socialism' advances a moderate programme of nationalization with compensation, the taxation of land-rents, inheritance, and profits. As a resolute opponent of the proletarian dictatorship in the Soviet Union, 'constructive socialism', in close alliance with the bourgeoisie, is an active enemy of the communist movement of the proletariat and of the colonial revolutions.

'Co-operativism', or 'co-operative socialism', is a special variety of 'constructive socialism' (Charles Gide, Totomianz, and Co.). It too repudiates the class struggle, and advocates consumers' co-operatives as the peaceful method of eliminating capitalism, though in reality it promotes the consolidation of capitalism with all its strength. 'Co-operative socialism', which has at its command, in the mass organizations of consumers' co-operatives, an extensive propaganda machine for systematically exerting influence on the broad masses, wages a bitter struggle against the revolutionary labour movement. It obstructs the realization of its aims and is one of the most active elements in the camp of reformist counter-revolution.

So-called 'guild socialism' (Penty, Orage, Hobson, etc.) is an eclectic attempt to combine 'revolutionary' syndicalism with bourgeois-liberal fabianism, anarchist decentralization ('national industrial guilds') with State capitalist centralization, the medieval restrictions of craft guilds with modern capitalism. In starting from the demand for the abolition of the 'wage system' as an 'immoral' institution, to be eliminated by workers' control of industry, guild socialism completely ignores the most important question, the question of power. By advocating the organization of workers, intellectuals, and technicians in a federation of national 'industrial guilds', and the transformation of these guilds by peaceful means ('control from within') into organs of industrial administration within the framework of the bourgeois State, guild socialism is in reality defending that State and obscuring its imperialist anti-proletarian class character. It assigns to the State the part of representative of the interests of 'consumers', standing 'above classes', *vis-à-vis* the 'producers' organized in the guilds. By preaching 'functional democracy' (i.e. a system of representation for the classes in capitalist society considered as professions, each with its respective function in social production), guild socialism paves the way for the fascist 'corporate State'. The majority of guild socialists reject both parliamentarism and 'direct action', and so condemn the working class to complete inactivity and to passive subjection to the bourgeoisie. Guild socialism is thus a peculiar form of trade-unionist, utopian opportunism, and cannot possibly play anything but an anti-revolutionary part.

Finally, there is the Austro-Marxist form of social-democratic reformism. As part of the ideological 'left wing' of social-democracy, Austro-Marxism engages in a peculiarly subtle deception of the working masses. It prostitutes Marxist terminology while breaking away from the principles of revolutionary Marxism (by following Kant, Mach, etc., in the philosophical field), toys with religion, borrows the theory of 'functional democracy' from the English reformists, and advocates 'building up the republic', i.e. building up the bourgeois State. Austro-Marxism recommends 'class collaboration' when 'class forces are at an equilibrium', i.e. precisely when a revolutionary crisis is maturing. This theory is designed to justify coalition with the bourgeoisie to destroy the proletarian revolution on the pretext of defending 'democracy' against the attacks of reaction. Objectively and in practice, the violence which Austro-Marxism considers permissible in the event of a reactionary offensive turns out to be reactionary violence against the proletarian revolution. The 'functional role' of Austro-Marxism is to deceive the workers who are already turning towards communism; hence it is a particularly dangerous enemy of the proletariat, more dangerous than the avowed adherents of predatory social imperialism.

All these tendencies, as component parts of 'socialist' reformism, are agencies of the imperialist bourgeoisie in the working-class camp; but communism also comes up against a number of petty-bourgeois tendencies which reflect the waverings of unstable social strata (the urban petty bourgeoisie suffering disintegration, the lumpen-proletariat, declassed intellectuals and bohemian riff-raff, impoverished craftsmen, certain strata of the peasantry, etc.). These tendencies are distinguished by their extreme political instability; they frequently coat their right-wing policy with left-wing phrases, or fall prey to adventurism, substituting swaggering political gestures for an objective appraisal of class forces. Their empty revolutionary boasting often turns into profound pessimism, and into complete capitulation to the enemy. In certain circumstances—particularly when the political situation changes sharply, or when it is necessary to make a temporary retreat—these tendencies can most dangerously disorganize the proletarian ranks and obstruct the revolutionary proletarian movement.

Anarchism, whose most prominent representatives (Kropotkin, Jean Grave, etc.) treacherously went over to the imperialist camp of the bourgeoisie in the 1914–18 war, denies the need for comprehensive, centralized, and disciplined proletarian organizations, and so leaves the proletariat defenceless against the powerful capitalist organizations. By advocating individual terrorism, it deflects the proletariat from the methods of mass organization and mass struggle. By rejecting the proletarian dictatorship for the sake of an abstract concept of 'liberty', anarchism deprives the proletariat of its strongest and sharpest weapon against the bourgeoisie, against their armies and all their agencies of oppression. Far from being a mass movement in the centres of the proletarian struggle, anarchism is more and more becoming a sect which in all its tactics and all its activities—including its opposition to the working-class dictatorship in the Soviet Union—is objectively enrolling in the united front of the anti-revolutionary forces.

'Revolutionary' syndicalism, not a few of whose ideologues went over, in the critical period of the war, to the camp of 'anti-parliamentary' counter-revolution of a fascist type, or became peaceful reformists on the social-democratic model, obstructs the development of the masses towards a revolutionary position wherever it can exert influence; like anarchism, it repudiates the political struggle (particularly revolutionary parliamentarism) and the revolutionary dictatorship of the proletariat. It preaches occupational decentralization of the labour movement, and especially of the trade union movement; it rejects the party of the proletariat, denies that insurrection is necessary, and exaggerates the importance of the general strike ('folded-arm tactics'). Its attacks on the Soviet Union, a corollary of its repudiation of the proletarian dictatorship, place it in this respect in one camp with social-democracy.

All these trends and tendencies are at one with social-democracy, the chief enemy of the proletarian revolution in the labour movement, on the basic political issue of their attitude to the proletarian dictatorship. Hence they all take their stand, more or less decisively, together with social-democracy against the Soviet Union. Social-democracy, which has completely betrayed Marxism, relies to an ever increasing extent on the ideology of the Fabians, the constructive socialists, and the guild socialists. These trends are becoming the official liberal-reformist ideology of the bourgeois 'socialism' of the Second International.

In the colonial countries, as among the oppressed peoples and races as a whole, communism comes into collision with the influence of certain peculiar tendencies in the labour movement, which had some positive part to play at a certain stage of development, but have become reactionary in the new stage.

Sun Yat-senism in China was the ideology of petty-bourgeois national 'socialism'. In the 'three principles' (nationalism, democracy, socialism) the concept of the people obscured the concept of class; socialism was presented not as a particular mode of production brought into being by a particular class, the proletariat, but as a vague picture of social welfare; the fight against imperialism was not linked to the prospects of the class struggle in China. Hence Sun Yat-senism, which played a great and positive part in the first stage of the Chinese revolution, became transformed, with the progress of class differentiation in the course of the revolution, from one ideological form of its development into fetters on its development. His successors have exaggerated precisely those features of his ideology which have become objectively reactionary, and have made it the official ideology of the Kuomintang after its transformation into an openly counter-revolutionary force. The ideological development of the Chinese proletarian masses and the working peasantry must therefore be accompanied by a resolute struggle against the treachery of the Kuomintang and the elimination of what has remained of the ideology of Sun Yat-senism.

Trends such as Gandhism in India, which, permeated through and through with religious conceptions, idealize the most backward and economically reactionary ways of living, and see salvation not in proletarian socialism but in the return to these backward forms, which preach patience and reject the class struggle, turn in the course of the development of the revolution into openly reactionary forces. More and more, Gandhism is becoming an ideology directed against the revolution of the popular masses. Communism must fight against it relentlessly.

Similarly, Garveyism, at one time the ideology of the American Negro petty bourgeoisie and workers, and still with a certain influence over the Negro masses, today impedes the movement of these masses towards a revolutionary position. While at first advocating complete social equality for Negroes, it turned into a kind of 'Negro Zionism' which instead of fighting American imperialism advanced the slogan 'Back to Africa'. This dangerous ideology, without a single genuinely democratic feature, which toys with the aristocratic attributes of a non-existent 'Negro kingdom', must be vigorously resisted, for it does not promote but hampers the struggle of the Negro masses for liberation from American imperialism.

Opposed to all these tendencies is proletarian communism. As the powerful ideology of the revolutionary working class of the world, it is distinguished from them, and above all from social-democracy, in that it wages the revolutionary struggle for the proletarian dictatorship in complete harmony with the tenets of Marx and Engels, in theory and practice, and to this end employs all forms of proletarian mass action.

2. *The Chief Tasks of Communist Strategy and Tactics*

The victorious struggle of the Communist International for the proletarian dictatorship presupposes the existence in every country of a united, steeled, disciplined, and centralized communist party closely linked with the masses.

The party is the vanguard of the working class, composed of the best, most conscious, most active and bravest among them. It embodies the essential experiences of the entire proletarian struggle. Based on the revolutionary theory of Marxism, and representing day by day the permanent, general interests of the entire class, the party personifies the unity of proletarian principles, proletarian will, and revolutionary proletarian action. It is a revolutionary organization held together by iron discipline and the strictest revolutionary rules of democratic centralism; it achieves this position by the class consciousness of the proletarian vanguard, by its devotion to the revolution, by its capacity to maintain unbroken contact with the proletarian masses, and by the correctness of its political leadership, which is constantly verified and clarified by the experiences of the masses themselves.

In order to accomplish its historic mission of bringing about the proletarian dictatorship, the communist party must advance and achieve the following strategic aims:

To win over to its side the majority of its own class, including proletarian women and young workers. To do this, it is essential for the communist party to secure dominant influence in the large proletarian mass organizations (Soviets, trade unions, factory committees, co-operatives, cultural and sports associations, etc.). Of the utmost importance in winning the majority of the proletariat is systematic work to capture the trade unions, those comprehensive mass organizations of the proletariat which are so closely linked with its day-by-day struggles. One of the most important tasks of the preparatory period of the revolution is to work in the reactionary unions, to capture them skilfully, to gain the confidence of the broad masses organized in unions, to depose the reformist leaders and squeeze them out of their positions.

A further prerequisite for achieving the proletarian dictatorship is the establishment of proletarian hegemony over the broad strata of the labouring masses. To attain this, the communist party must bring under its influence the masses of the poor in town and country, the lower strata among the intellectuals and the so-called 'little men', i.e. the petty-bourgeois strata in general. Party influence over the peasantry is a question of particular importance. The communist party must secure the whole-hearted support of those strata of the rural population which are closest to the proletariat, that is, first of all, agricultural labourers and the village poor. This requires special organizations for agricultural workers, all possible support for them in their struggle against the rural bourgeoisie, and strenuous work among smallholders. As to the middle strata of the peasantry in developed capitalist countries, the communist party should endeavour to neutralize them. The fulfilment of all these tasks by the proletariat, which represents the interests of the entire people and acts as leader of the broadest masses in the struggle to throw off the yoke of finance-capital, is an essential preliminary to the triumph of the communist revolution.

At the world level, the most important strategic tasks of the Communist International in the proletarian struggle are concerned with the revolutionary battle in the colonies, semi-colonies, and dependent countries. Here the broadest masses of the working class and peasantry must be mobilized around the revolutionary banner, and this can only be done if there is the closest fraternal co-operation between the proletariat of the oppressing countries and the working masses of the oppressed nations.

While organizing the revolution against imperialism under the banner of proletarian dictatorship in the so-called 'civilized States', the Communist International supports every movement against imperialist violence in the colonies, semi-colonies, and dependent countries (e.g. in Latin America); it carries on vigorous propaganda against every kind of chauvinism and imperialist ill-treatment of enslaved peoples and races, large and small (the attitude towards Negroes and workers of the 'yellow races', anti-semitism, etc.), and supports their struggle against the bourgeoisie of the oppressing nation. The Communist International fights particularly vigorously against chauvinism among the Great Power nations, which is fostered by the imperialist bourgeoisie and their social-democratic agent, the Second International, and contrasts their practice with the practice of the Soviet Union, which has established relations of fraternity and equality among the peoples inhabiting its territory.

The communist parties of the imperialist countries must give systematic help to the revolutionary liberation movements of the colonies, and to movements of oppressed nations in general. The duty of giving active support to such movements rests in the first place on the workers of that country on which the oppressed nation is financially, economically, or politically dependent. Communist parties must openly acknowledge the colonies' right to secede, and conduct propaganda to that end, that is, in favour of colonial independence of the imperialist State. They must recognize the right of the colonies to armed defence against imperialism (i.e. the right to rebellion and revolutionary war), conduct propaganda for this defence, and support it with all the means at their disposal. Communist parties must pursue this policy in regard to all oppressed peoples.

In the colonial and semi-colonial countries themselves the communist parties must wage a bold and persistent struggle against foreign imperialism, and untiringly advocate close relations and alliance with the proletariat of the imperialist countries; they must advance the slogan of agrarian revolution, conduct propaganda for it, and put it into practice, rousing the broad peasant masses to throw off the landlords' yoke, and waging war on the reactionary, medieval influence of the priests, missionaries, etc.

In these countries the main task is to organize the workers and peasants independently (in the communist class party of the proletariat, trade unions, peasant leagues, peasant committees, and, when the situation is revolutionary, in Soviets), and emancipate them from the influence of the national bourgeoisie. Temporary compromises with the national bourgeoisie are permissible only if they do not hamper the revolutionary organization of the workers and peasants and if they serve the struggle against imperialism.

In determining its tactical line, every communist party must take into its calculations the given internal and external situation, the relation of class forces, the degree of stability and strength among the bourgeoisie, the level of militancy and preparedness among the proletariat, the attitude of the middle strata, etc. The party determines its slogans and methods of struggle in accordance with these conditions, starting from the need to mobilize and organize the masses as widely as possible at the highest possible level of that struggle. When a revolutionary situation is developing, the party advances a series of transitional slogans and partial demands corresponding to the given circumstances; these must be subordinated to the principal revolutionary aim, which is the seizure of power and the overthrow of the bourgeois capitalist order. To neglect the every-day demands and every-day struggles of the proletariat is as mistaken as to restrict the party's activities to them exclusively. The task of the party is to use these every-day needs of the working class as a starting-point to lead the workers on to the revolutionary struggle for power.

When the revolutionary tide is rising, when the ruling classes are disorganized and the masses in a state of revolutionary ferment, when the middle strata are inclined to turn towards the proletariat and the masses display their readiness for battle and for sacrifice, it is the task of the proletarian party to lead the masses to a frontal assault on the bourgeois State. This can be achieved by propaganda in favour of transitional slogans on a rising scale (workers' councils, workers' control of production, peasant committees for the forcible confiscation of landowners' estates, disarming of the bourgeoisie and arming of the proletariat, etc.), and by organizing mass actions, to which all branches of the party's agitation and propaganda must be subordinated, including parliamentary activities: among such actions are strikes, strikes combined with demonstrations, strikes combined with armed demonstrations, and finally the general strike, combined with armed insurrection against the State power of the bourgeoisie. This highest form of struggle follows the rules of the art of war and presupposes a plan of campaign, offensive fighting operations, and boundless devotion and heroism on the part of the proletariat. An absolutely essential preliminary to actions of this kind is the organization of the broad masses in militant bodies which, by their very form (councils of workers, peasants, and soldiers, etc.), must embrace and set in motion the largest possible number of working people, and more intense revolutionary work in the army and navy.

When making the transition to new and more radical slogans, the following basic rule of Leninist political tactics must be observed: the party must guide the masses to a revolutionary position in such a way that they are convinced by their own experience of the correctness of the party's policy. If this rule is not observed, the party will inevitably be cut off from the masses and fall into putschism; communism will degenerate ideologically into 'left' dogmatism, petty-bourgeois 'revolutionary' adventurism. Equally ruinous is it if the party fails to act at the height of the revolutionary movement, when a bold and resolute attack on the enemy is called for. To allow such an opportunity to pass without going over to insurrection is to leave the initiative to the enemy and to condemn the revolution to defeat.

When the revolutionary tide is not rising the communist parties, taking as their starting-point the workers' daily needs, must put forward partial slogans and demands and link them with the chief aims of the Communist International. They must not advance transitional slogans which presuppose the existence of a revolutionary situation, and which, used at an inappropriate time, might become slogans in favour of merging with the system of capitalist organizations (e.g. the slogan of control of production). Partial demands and slogans are absolutely essential to correct tactics, while a series of transitional demands is inseparably linked with the existence of a revolutionary situation. To reject the use of partial demands and slogans 'on principle', is, however, equally incompatible with communist principles, for such tactics virtually condemn the party to passivity and isolate it from the masses. Hence united front tactics, as a method of fighting successfully against capital, of mobilizing the masses on class lines, and of exposing and isolating the reformist leaders, are an essential part of the Communist International's tactics throughout the entire prerevolutionary period.

Systematic and persistent work in the trade unions and in other proletarian mass organizations is essential to the correct use of united front tactics and in general to winning over the masses. Every communist must belong to a trade union, even to an extremely reactionary one if it has a mass character. Leadership of the workers' struggle can be captured, and the working masses organized in unions won for the party, only by steadfast and sustained work in the union and the factory for the untiring and vigorous defence of the workers' interests and by unrelenting struggle against the reformist bureaucracy.

In contrast to the reformists' attempts to split the unions, communists stand for the unity of the trade unions in each country and throughout the world, on the basis of the class struggle, and give whole-hearted support to the Red International of Labour Unions. While supporting everywhere the day-to-day demands of the working masses and of all working people generally, using the forum of bourgeois parliaments for purposes of revolutionary propaganda and agitation, and subordinating all partial tasks to the primary goal of the struggle for the proletarian dictatorship, the parties of the Communist International advance partial demands and slogans in the following main spheres:

In defence of the workers' interests in the narrower sense, that is, questions connected with the industrial struggle (defence against the attacks of trust capital, questions of hours and wages, compulsory arbitration, unemployment) which turn into political questions (large-scale industrial disputes, trade union law, the right to strike, etc.); questions of a directly political character (taxation, price rises, fascism, the persecution of revolutionary parties, white terror, government policy generally); finally, questions of foreign policy—the attitude to the Soviet Union and to colonial revolutions, the fight for international trade union unity, the fight against imperialism and the war danger, systematic preparation for the struggle against imperialist war.

As regards the peasantry, partial demands are concerned with fiscal policy, peasant indebtedness on mortgages, the fight against usury capital, the land requirements of the village poor, rent, share-cropping, etc. Starting from these partial demands, the communist party must gradually heighten its slogans until they converge in the slogans of confiscation of large estates and of a workers' and peasants' government (which is synonymous in developed capitalist countries with the proletarian dictatorship, and in backward countries and a number of colonies with the democratic dictatorship of the proletariat and peasantry).

Systematic work must also be carried on among young workers and peasants (first and foremost by the Young Communist International and its sections) and among proletarian and peasant women. Such work, starting from the special circumstances of the life and struggle of these strata, must link their demands with the general demands and fighting slogans of the proletariat.

In the struggle against colonial oppression the communist parties in the colonies themselves must put forward partial demands in accordance with the circumstances of the country, such as complete equality for all nationalities and races, abolition of all privileges for foreigners, the right of association for workers and peasants, a shorter working day, prohibition of child labour, cancellation of usurious loan agreements, reduction or abolition of rents, lower taxes, etc. These partial demands must be subordinated to the following basic demands of the communist party: complete political independence for the country and the expulsion of the imperialists, a workers' and peasants' government, the land for the people, an eight-hour day, etc. In the imperialist countries the communist parties must conduct a campaign for the withdrawal of the imperialist troops from the colonies, carry on active propaganda in the army and navy in support of the oppressed peoples' struggle for independence, mobilize the masses to prevent the shipment of troops and munitions, organize strikes and other forms of mass protest, etc.

The Communist International must pay particularly great attention to methodical preparation of the struggle against the danger of imperialist war. Ruthless exposure of social-chauvinism, social-imperialism, and pacifist verbiage which merely veil the imperialist plans of the bourgeoisie; propaganda for the Communist International's principal slogans; untiring organizational work to accomplish these tasks, for which the combination of legal and illegal methods of work is absolutely essential; systematic work in the army and navy—these must be the communist parties' activities in connexion with the war danger. The principal slogans of the Communist International in the fight against the war danger are: turn the imperialist war into civil war, defeat of one's 'own' imperialist government, defence of the Soviet Union and of the colonies, should imperialist war be made on them, with every possible means. To carry on propaganda for these slogans, to expose 'socialist' sophisms and 'socialist' camouflage of the League of Nations, to keep always in mind the memory of the lessons of the 1914 world war—all this is the imperative duty of every section and every member of the Communist International.

In order that revolutionary work and activities may be co-ordinated and given appropriate guidance, the international proletariat requires international class discipline, for which the most important prerequisite is the strictest discipline in the communist parties. International communist discipline must be expressed in the subordination of local and particular interests to the common and enduring interests of the movement, and in the execution without reservation of all decisions made by the leading bodies of the Communist International.

In contrast to the social-democratic Second International, whose parties submit only to the discipline of 'their' national bourgeoisie and their 'fatherland', the sections of the Communist International recognize only one discipline: the discipline of the world proletariat, which ensures victory in the struggle of the workers of all countries for the world proletarian dictatorship. In contrast to the Second International, which splits the trade union movement, fights against the colonial peoples, and practises unity with the bourgeoisie, the Communist International is an organization that stands guard over the unity of proletarians in all countries, the working people of every nation and race, in the fight to throw off the imperialist yoke.

Resolute and unafraid, the communists are waging this struggle on every sector of the international class front, defying the bloody terror of the bourgeoisie, confident of the inevitable triumph of the proletariat.

'Communists disdain to conceal their views and aims. They openly declare that their aims can be attained only by the forcible overthrow of all the existing social conditions.

'Let the ruling class tremble at a communist revolution. The proletariat has nothing to lose but its chains. It has a world to win.

'Proletarians of all countries, unite!'

EXTRACTS FROM THE THESES ON THE REVOLUTIONARY MOVEMENT IN COLONIAL AND SEMI-COLONIAL COUNTRIES ADOPTED BY THE SIXTH COMINTERN CONGRESS

1 *September* 1928   *Protokoll*, vi, 4, p. 154

[The theses were drafted and introduced by Kuusinen. Colonial work as a whole, he said, was one of the weakest sides of Comintern activity; in most colonial and semi-colonial countries they did not have real communist parties. The ECCI and the West European parties were largely to blame for this. Vasiliev echoed the same complaint; the communist parties in the countries which had sent troops to intervene in China had done nothing to establish contact with the troops; the ECCI had had to undertake this work in China itself, which was extremely difficult. Most of the communist parties in colonial countries were leaders with no rank and file behind them. They had no trade union fractions and were ideologically very weak. If the Indian CP were properly organized it would have its fractions in the four provincial workers' and peasants' parties, which were about to amalgamate, and gain control of the united party. Sikandar (S. Usmani), an Indian delegate, said that the numerous communist groups in India had still to be brought together into a single disciplined party. A plea for more help from the Comintern and CPGB to organize the Indian CP was also made by another Indian delegate, Razur. Katayama criticized the CPGB for its 'criminal neglect' of Ireland and India, and the Dutch and American parties for their neglect of Indonesia, the Philippines, and the Negroes. The ECCI report praised the French CP campaign against the war in Morocco; it was the first time that members of the armed forces had been drawn into a mass movement.

In the discussion it emerged that there was a good deal of tension between the communist parties of the metropolitan countries and those in the colonies. The CPGB, Kuusinen said, must advise and train the Indian party, but the two should not be one, as this would arouse Indian mistrust. It was wrong for the

Tunisian and Algerian parties to be sections of the French party; they had to be completely independent; this would eliminate any ground for suspicion and mistrust. One of the first tasks of the new ECCI would be to build up the parties in the colonies.

The report on Indochina was given by a delegate appearing as An; Indochina had a strong and concentrated proletariat; and a revolutionary mass organization would have to be created to take the lead; the Comintern must give its attention to founding a CP and trade unions in Indochina, as well as peasant organizations. Padi-Animin, for Indonesia, asked for greater activity from the Dutch party. During the rebellion it had done what it could, whereas the Comintern and other parties had done nothing; this was a sad experience.

On Latin America Vasiliev said that there was great sympathy there for communism and the Soviet Union, even though most of these sympathizers had no clear idea of what communism meant and what the Soviet Union was like. These feelings had to be given an organizational frame; there was no need for workers' and peasants' parties in South America—the Comintern must give all possible help in establishing communist parties. Shargi (Persia) objected to the passage in the theses on Persia; Reza Shah represented reaction, not nationalism and progress.

Kato reported that the Japanese party had been handicapped by legalism, liquidationism, and ultra-left sectarianism, but it had now become the rallying centre for the revolutionary masses. In the Far East Korea occupied roughly the same place as Poland in Europe; the fractional struggle there had prevented the emergence of a real party (a Korean Communist Party had been founded in 1925 and admitted provisionally to the Comintern by the presidium in March 1926).

In the debate China received comparatively little attention; the chief point in dispute was whether the colonies were being 'decolonized', i.e. whether the metropolitan country was promoting or retarding the industrialization of its colonies; India served as the focus of this discussion. With the exception of Murphy, the members of the British delegation believed that Britain was industrializing India, to take advantage of cheap labour there. Bukharin in his opening speech came out against the decolonization theory; the Indians themselves (none of whom, strictly speaking, was a delegate) were divided. Roy, in Berlin, had pleaded ill-health and did not attend the congress, but had written that decolonization was proceeding, and contained the seeds of the dissolution of the British Empire. He is said to have advanced the decolonization theory at the end of 1927. The bourgeoisie were not only withdrawing from the national revolution, but were moving towards an agreement with the imperialists to crush it. S. Tagore (appearing at the congress as Narayan) claims that when, in April 1927, he went as a representative of the Bengal Workers' and Peasants' Party to Moscow, he and Bukharin agreed that some kind of decolonization was proceeding in India. 'If it were true', Kuusinen said, 'that British imperialism had really turned to the industrialization of India, we should have to revise our entire conception of the nature of imperialist colonial policy'. Usmani agreed with Kuusinen and added that this nonsensical theory could only have been thought up by those who had lost direct contact with India. Investment was not industrialization. Britain, he said, had learnt from the Russian revolution and was determined to destroy industry in India and thrust the proletariat back into the villages; it had found its agent in Gandhi. The Comintern should work up an anti-British movement in Persia and Afghanistan. Bennett (Petrovsky), the ECCI representative in Britain, said the word decolonization was used merely to emphasize the progress of industrialization, and Rothstein (CPGB) argued that the theses tended to underestimate the degree of industrialization, while at the same time speaking of the proletariat acting independently. If the theses were correct, the proletariat in India would be getting weaker; the draft referred to deviations in imperialist policy to meet the needs of finance-capital, but finance-capital was part of imperialism, and to explain its operations as a deviation from imperialism was nonsensical. Murphy attacked Bennett and Rothstein; the logical conclusion of their theory would take them into the Second International. Martynov (CPSU) argued that while capital export developed the colonies, imperialism as such hampered their development—the process was dialectical. Remmele said those who believed in decolonization were revising Lenin, and Wolfe (USA) said that both tendencies were in operation, but decolonization was the weaker of the two; the contradiction was a feature of imperialism. Arnot (CPGB) denied that the British delegation upheld the decolonization theory, but the theory embodied in the draft theses was wrong; it led to a misleading selection of data and hence to a false interpretation. Imperialism by its own contradictions fostered in the colonies the industry that was going to compete with it, thus transferring domestic contradictions to the world scene. Rothstein, in a statement on behalf of the British delegation majority, took the same line; it was fundamentally erroneous to describe as 'rural continents' and 'agrarian hinterlands' countries where large numbers of industrial workers organized strikes. 'All the charges made against us, which unfortunately are becoming more and more a kind of automatic reaction against those who dare to criticize any theses put forward in the name of the ECCI— that we are social-democrats, Amsterdamers . . . have no effect on us.' The charge that the British delegation, which had submitted alternative theses, had advanced the theory of decolonization was an attempt to conceal the un-Leninist character of the theory of agrarianization. If these polemical methods were retained, they would stifle healthy discussion; communists should be encouraged to give their opinions openly and fearlessly; sticking labels on them would merely crush independent thought, and Comintern discussions would lose their value. Lozovsky, who contended that changes in the form of exploitation did not imply changes in the imperialist-colonial relationship, said that if decolonization followed automatically on industrial development there would be no basis for the national-revolutionary movement. He thought the attempt to classify colonies in categories was misleading, and the delegate from Ecuador pointed out that the classification in the theses did not correspond with that adopted in the programme. He thought the theses overemphasized the agrarian character of Latin America.

On China, Kuusinen defended Comintern policy towards the Kuomintang, although the inevitable break should have been foreseen earlier; ECCI directives had been correct, but badly executed. The Chinese party had 100,000 members, of whom 80 per cent. were peasants. Lominadze rejected the 'libellous Trotskyist charge' that the Canton revolt was a putsch organized by the Comintern. But he, Lominadze, had at the time mistaken this rearguard action in the closing stage of the revolutionary wave that had reached its highest point in mid-1927 for the onset of a new revolutionary wave. At the present time the slogan of armed revolt was purely propagandist except in the case of spontaneous peasant movements, where the communists should take the lead. Strakhov, who gave a long account of events in China, admitted that it was a mistake, after March 1926, to continue the common struggle with the nationalist bourgeoisie at the cost of weakening the peasant movement and industrial strikes. Mistakes had also been made in policy towards Wuhan. Only a correct policy towards the peasants could now save the situation and eliminate unorganized putschism. The agrarian revolution could triumph only against the national bourgeoisie.

After Canton, said Strakhov, the banner of the Chinese revolution could only be the banner of the Soviets. They already had 131 rural Soviets where the gentry had been expelled and their land confiscated. There was a tendency in the party which would identify the revolution completely with peasant demands. Others underestimated the role of the peasantry. He agreed that the proportion of peasants in the CCP was too high; the remedy was not to stop admitting peasants, but to recruit more industrial workers. (A number of other Chinese speakers insisted on the inadequacy of a purely peasant movement to accomplish the revolution; this had to be organized and led by the working class.) Vasiliev said that the ECCI had asked the Chinese CP whether the industrial workers were leaving that party because of government persecution, or because of its mistakes, and had been told that the loss was due primarily to the mistakes of the CCP and to its organizational and political weakness. On the other hand a great many peasants had joined, sometimes entire villages, rich and poor, and there was occasionally a class struggle within the CP on questions of agrarian policy. Neumann urged the Indians to learn the lesson of China: 'The national bourgeoisie will betray you even at the beginning of the revolutionary movement.'

In replying to the discussion Kuusinen remarked that the guiding thread of their policy must be the leading role of the proletariat in colonial revolutionary movements; imperialism could not be overthrown unless the bourgeois-democratic revolution passed over into the socialist revolution; this was not an automatic process but needed the intervention of the working class organized in communist parties. Participation of the national bourgeoisie in the revolutionary movement was unlikely, but not impossible. It would occur when the class situation did not threaten them, or when they could use the masses to get concessions from imperialism. The political implications of the decolonization theory raised the question whether the communist parties could make alliances with the national bourgeoisie. The Swaraj party in India, he said, was not 'an ordinary counter-revolutionary party', and a real Indian communist party could have exploited the mass movement stirred up by the Swaraj party which, he added, was affiliated to the League against Imperialism. Whether the colonial revolution was an adjunct to, or a part of, the world socialist revolution was a theoretical question; the important practical thing was that it was an ally.

Kuusinen rejected the decolonization theory. The theses were accepted against 12 British votes and one abstention.

The sixth congress of the Chinese CP was held in Moscow at the same time as the Comintern congress; it was attended, among others, by Chou En-lai and Li Li-san. The congress agreed that after Canton the CCP should have turned from insurrection to organization. (A circular letter from the CC dated 8 November 1928 said that trade union organizations had shrunk to almost nothing, and the party organizations in the cities were scattered and shattered.) 'In the whole country there is not one healthy nucleus of industrial workers.' The CCP, wrote Chan Fu-yun, a delegate to the congress, had called for strikes and risings too often. This had weakened the party and isolated it from the masses. The congress endorsed the resolutions of the seventh, eighth, and ninth ECCI plenums on China, and called attention to the incorrect use of the phrase 'permanent revolution' in the Chinese central committee's resolution of November 1927, 'which might have led to incorrect tactics'. Chu Chiu-pai, who had succeeded Chen (condemned for opportunism) as secretary, was condemned as a putschist left-deviationist, and was succeeded by Hsiang Chung-fa. Mao Tse-tung, whose independent policy towards the peasants had led to his demotion in 1927, was elected to the central committee (he was not present at the congress). The programme adopted called for an extension of the Soviet areas, for the formation of a regular Red Army, for co-ordination of the work among peasants with the urban workers' movement. The CCP was to work for the overthrow of the Kuomintang Government; a cautious and moderate programme was outlined for communist policy in the Soviet areas. The delegates to the sixth Comintern congress were instructed to emphasize the inadequacy of the help given by fraternal parties. The CCP was to work with the Japanese CP on questions connected with Japanese troops in China, and permanent connexions were to be established with the CP in Indonesia and Indochina.]

I. INTRODUCTION

1. The sixth congress of the Communist International declares that the theses on the national and colonial question drawn up by Lenin and adopted at the second congress still have full validity, and should serve as a guiding line for the further work of the communist parties. Since the time of the second congress the significance of the colonies and semi-colonies, as factors of crisis in the imperialist world system, has become much more topical. . . .

2. . . . The insurrection in Shanghai in April 1927 raised the question of the hegemony of the proletariat in the national-revolutionary movement, and finally pushed the native bourgeoisie into the camp of reaction, provoking the counter-revolutionary coup d'état of Chiang Kai-shek.

The independent activity of the workers in the struggle for power, and above all the growth of the peasant movement into agrarian revolution, also impelled the Wuhan Government, which had been established under the leadership of the petty-bourgeois wing of the Kuomintang, to go over to the camp of counter-revolution. The revolutionary wave, however, was already beginning to ebb. . . . Its last powerful onslaught was the insurrection of the heroic Canton proletariat which under the slogan of Soviets attempted to link up the agrarian revolution with the overthrow of the Kuomintang and the establishment of the dictatorship of the workers and peasants.

3. In India, the policy of British imperialism, which retarded the development of native industry, evoked great dissatisfaction among the Indian bourgeoisie. Their class consolidation, replacing the former division into religious sects and castes . . . confronted British imperialism with a national united front. Fear of the revolutionary movement during the war compelled British imperialism to make concessions to the native bourgeoisie, as shown, in the economic sphere, in higher duties on imported goods, and, in the political sphere, in insignificant parliamentary reforms introduced in 1919.

Nevertheless a strong ferment, expressed in a series of revolutionary outbreaks against British imperialism, was produced among the Indian masses as a result of the ruinous consequences of the imperialist war (famine and epidemics, 1918), the catastrophic deterioration of the position of wide sections of the working population, the influence of the Russian October revolution and of a series of insurrections in other colonial countries (as for example the struggle of the Turkish people for independence).

This first great anti-imperialist movement in India (1919–22) ended with the betrayal by the Indian bourgeoisie of the cause of national revolution. The chief reason for this was the fear of the growing wave of peasant risings, and of the strikes against native employers.

The collapse of the national-revolutionary movement and the gradual decline of bourgeois nationalism enabled British imperialism once more to revert to its policy of hindering India's industrial development. Recent British measures in India show that the objective contradictions between British colonial monopoly and the tendencies towards independent Indian economic development are becoming more accentuated from year to year and are leading to a new deep revolutionary crisis. . . .

5. In North Africa in 1925 there began a series of rebellions of the Rif Kabyle tribes against French and Spanish imperialism, followed by the rebellion of the Druze tribes in the 'mandated' territory of Syria against French imperialism. In Morocco, the imperialists only succeeded in dealing with these rebellions after a prolonged war. The greater penetration of foreign capital into these countries is already calling into life new social forces. The rise and growth of the urban proletariat is manifested in a wave of mass strikes which is sweeping for the first time over Palestine, Syria, Tunis, and Algeria. Gradually, but very slowly, the peasantry in these countries is also being drawn into the struggle.

6. The growing economic and military expansion of North American imperialism in the countries of Latin America is transforming this continent into one of the most important focal points of antagonism within the colonial system. The influence of Great Britain, which before the war was decisive in these countries, and reduced many of them to the position of semi-colonies, is, since the war, being replaced by their still closer dependence on the United States. By increased capital exports, North American imperialism is capturing the commanding positions in the economy of these countries, subordinating their governments to its own financial control, and, at the same time, inciting one against the other. . . .

7. In the majority of cases imperialism has up to now succeeded in suppressing the revolutionary movement in the colonial countries. But all the fundamental questions raised by these movements remain unsolved.

The objective contradiction between the colonial policy of world imperialism and the independent development of the colonial peoples has not been eliminated, either in China, or in India, or in any other of the colonial and semi-colonial countries; on the contrary, the contradiction is becoming more acute; it can be overcome only by the victorious revolutionary struggle of the colonial labouring masses. Until then it will continue to operate in every colony and semi-colony as one of the most powerful objective factors making for revolution.

At the same time, the colonial policy of the imperialist Powers acts as a powerful stimulant to antagonisms and wars between these Powers. These antagonisms are becoming more acute, especially in the semi-colonies, where in spite of the alliances frequently established between the imperialists, they play an important part. Of greatest significance, however, for the development of the revolutionary movement in the colonies, is the contradiction between the imperialist world on the one hand and the Union of Soviet Socialist Republics and the revolutionary labour movement in the capitalist countries on the other.

8. The establishment of a fighting front between the active forces of the socialist world revolution (the Soviet Union and the revolutionary labour movement in the capitalist countries) on the one side, and between the forces of imperialism on the other, is of decisive importance in the present epoch of world history. The labouring masses of the colonies, struggling against imperialist slavery, represent a most powerful auxiliary force of the socialist world revolution. The colonial countries are the most dangerous sector of the imperialist front. The revolutionary liberation movements of the colonies and semi-colonies are rallying to the banner of the Soviet Union, convinced by bitter experience that there is no salvation for them except in alliance with the revolutionary proletariat. . . .

The proletariat of the USSR and the workers' movement in the capitalist countries, headed by the Communist International, are in their turn supporting and will more and more effectively support in action the liberation struggle of all colonial and other dependent peoples; they are the only sure bulwark of the colonial peoples in their struggle for freedom from the imperialist yoke. Furthermore, alliance with the USSR and the revolutionary proletariat opens for the masses of China, India, and all other colonial and semi-colonial countries the prospect of independent economic and cultural development, avoiding the stage of capitalist domination, perhaps even the development of capitalist relations in general. . . .

There is thus an objective possibility of a non-capitalist path of development for the backward colonies, the possibility that the bourgeois-democratic revolution in the more advanced colonies will be transformed, with the aid of the victorious proletarian dictatorship in other countries, into the proletarian socialist revolution. In favourable objective conditions, this possibility will be converted into a reality, and the path of development determined by struggle and by struggle alone. Consequently, the theoretical and practical advocacy of this path and the most self-sacrificing struggle for it are the duty of all communists. . . .

Thus, all the basic questions of the revolutionary movement in the colonies and semi-colonies are most closely connected with the great epoch-making struggle between the capitalist and socialist systems, a struggle now being conducted on a world scale by imperialism against the USSR, and within each capitalist country between capitalist class rule and the communist movement. . . .

II. THE CHARACTERISTIC FEATURES OF COLONIAL ECONOMY AND OF IMPERIALIST COLONIAL POLICY

9. The recent history of the colonies can only be understood if it is looked upon as an organic part of the development of capitalist world economy as a whole. . . .

Where the ruling imperialism is in need of a social support in the colonies it first allies itself with the ruling strata of the previous social structure, the feudal lords and the trading and money-lending bourgeoisie, against the majority of the people. Everywhere imperialism attempts to preserve and to perpetuate all those pre-capitalist forms of exploitation (especially in the villages) which serve as the basis for the existence of its reactionary allies. . . .

The growth of famines and epidemics, particularly among the pauperized peasantry; the mass expropriation of the land of the native population, the inhuman conditions of labour (on the plantations and mines of the white capitalists, and so on), which at times are worse than open slavery—all this exerts its devastating effect on the colonial population and not infrequently leads to the dying out of whole nationalities. The 'civilizing mission' of the imperialist States in the colonies is in reality that of an executioner.

10. It is necessary to distinguish between those colonies which have served the capitalist countries as colonizing regions for their surplus population, and which in this way have become extensions of the capitalist system (Australia, Canada, etc.), and those which are exploited by the imperialists primarily as markets for their commodities, as sources of raw material, and as spheres for capital investment. . . .

Colonies of the first type became Dominions, that is, members of the given imperialist system with equal or nearly equal rights. . . .

11. . . . In its function as colonial exploiter, the ruling imperialism is related to the colonial country primarily as a parasite, sucking the blood from its economic organisms. The fact that this parasite, in comparison to its victim, represents a highly developed civilization makes it a so much more powerful and dangerous exploiter, but this does not alter the parasitic character of its functions.

Capitalist exploitation in every imperialist country has proceeded by developing productive forces. The specific colonial forms of capitalist exploitation, however, whether operated by the British, French, or any other bourgeoisie, in the final analysis hinder the development of the productive forces of the colonies. The only construction undertaken (railways, harbours, etc.) is what is indispensable for military control of the country, for guaranteeing the uninterrupted operation of the taxation machine, and for the commercial needs of the imperialist country. . . .

12. Since, however, colonial exploitation presupposes some encouragement of colonial production, this is directed on such lines and promoted only in such a degree as correspond to the interests of the metropolis, and, in particular, to the interests of the preservation of its colonial monopoly. Part of the peasantry, for example, may be encouraged to turn from grain cultivation to the production of cotton, sugar, or rubber (Sudan, Cuba, Java, Egypt), but this is done in such a way that it not only does not promote the independent economic development of the colonial country, but, on the contrary, reinforces its dependence on the imperialist metropolis. . . .

Real industrialization of the colonial country, in particular the building up of a flourishing engineering industry which would promote the independent development of its productive forces, is not encouraged but, on the contrary, is hindered by the metropolis. This is the essence of its function of colonial enslavement: the colonial country is compelled to sacrifice the interests of its independent development and to play the part of an economic (agrarian raw material) appendage to foreign capitalism. . . .

13. Since the overwhelming mass of the colonial population is connected with the land and lives in the countryside, the plundering character of the

exploitation of the peasantry by imperialism and its allies (the class of landowners, merchants, and money-lenders) acquires special significance. Because of imperialist intervention (imposition of taxes, import of industrial products from the metropolis, etc.), the drawing of the village into a money and commodity economy is accompanied by the pauperization of the peasantry, the destruction of village handicraft industry, etc., and proceeds much more rapidly than was the case in the leading capitalist countries. On the other hand, the retarded industrial development puts narrow limits to the process of proletarianization.

This enormous disproportion between the rapid rate of destruction of the old forms of economy and the slow development of the new has given rise in China, India, Indonesia, Egypt, etc., to an extreme 'land hunger', to agrarian over-population, rack-renting, and extreme fragmentation of the land cultivated by the peasantry. . . .

The pitiful attempts to introduce agrarian reforms without damaging the colonial regime are intended to facilitate the gradual conversion of the semi-feudal landowner into a capitalist landlord, and in certain cases to create a thin stratum of kulak peasants. In practice, this only leads to greater pauperization of the overwhelming majority of the peasants, which in its turn paralyses the development of the home market. It is on the basis of these contradictory economic processes that the most important social forces of the colonial movements are developing.

14. In the period of imperialism, the part played by finance-capital in gaining an economic and political monopoly in the colonies is particularly prominent. This is shown most clearly in the economic results of the export of capital to the colonies. The capital is used primarily in trade; it functions mainly as usurious loan capital and is directed to the task of preserving and strengthening the imperialist machinery of suppression in the colonial country (by means of State loans, etc.), or of gaining full control over the allegedly independent State organs of the native bourgeoisie in semi-colonial countries.

The export of capital to the colonies accelerates the development of capitalist relations there. The part which is invested in production does to some extent accelerate industrial development; but this is not done in ways which promote independence; the intention is rather to strengthen the dependence of the colonial economy on the finance-capital of the imperialist country. . . .

The favourite form of investment in agriculture is in large plantations, with the object of producing cheap food and monopolizing vast sources of raw material. The transference to the metropolis of the greater part of the surplus value extorted from the cheap labour power of the colonial slaves retards the growth of the colonial economy and the development of its productive forces, and is an obstacle to its economic and political emancipation. . . .

15. The entire economic policy of imperialism towards the colonies is determined by its anxiety to preserve and increase their dependence, to intensify their exploitation and, as far as possible, to impede their independent development. Only under the pressure of special circumstances may the bourgeoisie of the imperialist States find themselves compelled to encourage the development of large-scale industry in the colonies. . . .

All the twaddle of the imperialists and their lackeys about the policy of decolonization being pursued by the imperialist Powers, about encouraging the 'free development of the colonies', is nothing but an imperialist lie. It is of the utmost importance for communists in the imperialist and the colonial countries to expose these lies.

III. ON COMMUNIST STRATEGY AND TACTICS IN CHINA, INDIA, AND SIMILAR COLONIAL COUNTRIES

16. As in all colonies and semi-colonies, so also in China and India the development of productive forces and the socialization of labour stand at a comparatively low level. This circumstance, together with foreign domination and the presence of strong survivals of feudalism and pre-capitalist relations, determine the character of the next stage of the revolution in these countries. The revolutionary movement there is at the stage of the bourgeois-democratic revolution, i.e. the stage when the prerequisites for proletarian dictatorship and socialist revolution are being prepared. Corresponding to this, the general basic tasks of the bourgeois-democratic revolution in the colonies and semi-colonies may be laid down as follows:

(*a*) A shifting in the relationship of forces in favour of the proletariat; emancipation of the country from the yoke of imperialism (nationalization of foreign concessions, railways, banks, etc.) and the establishment of national unity where this has not yet been attained; overthrow of the power of the exploiting classes at whose back imperialism stands; organization of Soviets of workers and peasants and of a Red Army; establishment of the dictatorship of the proletariat and peasantry; consolidation of the hegemony of the proletariat;

(*b*) The carrying through of the agrarian revolution; freeing the peasants from all pre-capitalist and colonial forms of exploitation and bondage; nationalization of the land; radical measures for alleviating the position of the peasantry with the object of establishing the closest possible economic and political union between town and country;

(*c*) Parallel with the further development of industry, transport, etc., and with the corresponding growth of the proletariat, the extension of trade unions, strengthening of the communist party and its conquest of a solid leading position among the working masses, the eight-hour working day. . . .

How far the bourgeois-democratic revolution will be able in practice to accomplish all its basic tasks, and how far these tasks will be achieved only by the socialist revolution, will depend on the course of the revolutionary movement of the workers and peasants, its successes or defeats in the struggle against the imperialists, feudal lords, and the bourgeoisie. In particular, colonial emancipation from the imperialist yoke will be facilitated by the development of the socialist revolution in the capitalist world and can only be completely guaranteed by the victory of the proletariat in the leading capitalist countries.

The transition of the revolution to the socialist phase demands the presence of certain minimum prerequisites, as, for example, a certain level of industrial development, of trade union organization, and a strong communist party. The most important is the development of a strong communist party with mass influence; this would be an extremely slow and difficult process were it not accelerated by the bourgeois-democratic revolution, which is already developing as a result of the objective conditions in these countries.

17. The bourgeois-democratic revolution in the colonies is distinguished from the bourgeois-democratic revolution in an independent country chiefly in that it is organically linked with the national liberation struggle against imperialist domination. The national factor exerts considerable influence on the revolutionary process in all colonies, as well as in those semi-colonies where imperialist enslavement already appears in its naked form and drives the masses to revolt. On the one hand, national oppression hastens the ripening of the revolutionary crisis, intensifies the dissatisfaction of the masses of workers and peasants, facilitates their mobilization, and endows their revolutionary outbursts with the elemental character of a genuine popular revolution. On the other hand, the national factor not only influences the movement of the working class and peasantry, but can also modify the attitude of all other classes in the course of the revolution. Above all, the poor urban petty bourgeoisie and the petty-bourgeois intelligentsia are during the early stages brought largely under the influence of the active revolutionary forces; secondly, the position of the colonial bourgeoisie in the bourgeois-democratic revolution is for the most part ambiguous, and their vacillations, corresponding to the course of the revolution, are even greater than in an independent country. . . .

Together with the national liberation struggle, the agrarian revolution constitutes the axis of the bourgeois-democratic revolution in the more advanced colonial countries. That is why communists must follow with the greatest attention the development of the agrarian crisis and the intensification of class contradictions on the land; they must from the outset give a consciously revolutionary direction to the discontent of the workers and to the incipient peasant movement, turning it against imperialist exploitation and bondage and against the yoke of the various pre-capitalist (feudal and semi-feudal) conditions under which peasant economy is suffering, declining, and perishing. . . .

18. The national bourgeoisie in these colonial countries do not adopt a uniform attitude to imperialism. One part, more especially the commercial bourgeoisie, directly serves the interests of imperialist capital (the so-called compradore bourgeoisie). In general, they maintain, more or less consistently, an anti-national, imperialist point of view, directed against the whole nationalist movement, as do the feudal allies of imperialism and the more highly paid native officials. The other parts of the native bourgeoisie, especially those representing the interests of native industry, support the national movement; this tendency, vacillating and inclined to compromise, may be called national reformism. . . .

In order to strengthen its position in relation to imperialism, bourgeois nationalism in these colonies tries to win the support of the petty bourgeoisie, of the peasantry, and in part also of the working class. Since it has little prospect of success among the workers (once they have become politically awake), it becomes the more important for it to obtain support from the peasantry.

Here precisely is the weakest point of the colonial bourgeoisie. The unbearable exploitation of the colonial peasantry can only be ended by the agrarian revolution. The bourgeoisie of China, India, and Egypt are by their immediate interests so closely bound up with landlordism, usury capital, and the exploitation of the peasant masses in general, that they oppose not only the agrarian revolution but also every decisive agrarian reform. They fear, and not without reason, that even the open formulation of the agrarian question will stimulate and accelerate the revolutionary ferment in the peasant masses. Thus, the reformist bourgeoisie cannot bring themselves to approach practically this urgent question. . . . In every conflict with imperialism they attempt, on the one hand, to make a great show of their nationalist 'firmness' of principle, and, on the other, to spread illusions about the possibility of a peaceful compromise with imperialism. In both respects the masses are doomed to disappointment, and in this way they gradually outlive their reformist illusions.

19. An incorrect appraisal of the national-reformist tendency of the bourgeoisie in these colonial countries may give rise to serious errors in the strategy and tactics of the communist parties concerned. . . .

20. The petty bourgeoisie in the colonial and semi-colonial countries play a very important role. They consist of various strata, which in different stages of the national-revolutionary movement play very diverse roles. . . .

The petty-bourgeois intelligentsia, the students, and others are very frequently the most determined representatives not only of the specific interests of the petty bourgeoisie, but also of the general objective interests of the entire national bourgeoisie. In the early stages of the national movement they often appear as spokesmen of the nationalist struggle. Their role on the surface of the movement is comparatively important. In general, they cannot represent peasant interests, for the social strata from which they come are connected with landlordism. The advance of the revolutionary wave may drive them into the labour movement, into which they carry their hesitating and irresolute petty-bourgeois ideology. Only a few of them in the course of the struggle are able to break with their own class and rise to an understanding of the tasks of the class struggle of the proletariat, and to become active defenders of proletarian interests. Frequently the petty-bourgeois intellectuals give to their ideology a socialist or even communist colour. In the struggle against imperialism they have played, and in such countries as India and Egypt still play, a revolutionary role. The mass movement may draw them in, but may also push them into the camp of extreme reaction, or encourage the spread of utopian reactionary tendencies in their ranks. . . .

The peasantry, as well as the proletariat and as its ally, is a driving force of the revolution. The immense many-millioned peasant mass constitutes the overwhelming majority of the population even in the most developed colonies (in many it is 90 per cent. of the population). . . . The peasantry can only achieve its emancipation under the leadership of the proletariat, while the proletariat can only lead the bourgeois-democratic revolution to victory in union with the peasantry.

The process of class differentiation among the peasants in the colonies and semi-colonies where feudal and pre-capitalist survivals are widespread proceeds at a comparatively slow rate. Nevertheless, market relationships in these countries have developed to such a degree that the peasants are no longer a homogeneous mass as to their class. In the villages of China and India, particularly in certain parts of these countries, it is already possible to find exploiting elements, originally peasants, who exploit the peasants and village labourers through usury, trade, employment of hired labour, the sale or leasing of land, the lending of cattle or agricultural implements, etc., etc.

In general it is possible that, in the early stages of the peasantry's fight against the landlords, the proletariat may be able to win leadership of the entire peasantry. But, as the struggle develops, some of the upper strata of the peasantry may pass into the camp of counter-revolution. The proletariat can win leadership of the peasantry only if it fights for its partial demands, for the complete carrying through of the agrarian revolution, only if it takes the lead in the struggle of the peasant masses for a revolutionary solution of the agrarian question.

21. The working class in the colonies and semi-colonies has characteristic features which are important in the formation of an independent working-class movement and proletarian class ideology in these countries. The greater part of the colonial proletariat comes from the pauperized village, with which the worker retains his connexion even when engaged in industry. In the majority of colonies (with the exception of some large industrial towns such as Shanghai, Bombay, Calcutta, etc.) we find, as a general rule, only the first generation of a proletariat engaged in large-scale production. The rest is made up of ruined artisans driven from the decaying handicrafts, which are widespread even in the most advanced colonies. The ruined artisan, the small property-owner, carries with him into the working class the narrow craft sentiments and ideology through which national-reformist influence can penetrate the colonial labour movement . . . .

22. . . . At first the interests of the struggle for their class rule compel the most important bourgeois parties in India and Egypt (Swarajists, Wafdists) to demonstrate their opposition to the ruling imperialist-feudal bloc. Although this opposition is not revolutionary, but reformist and opportunist, this does not mean that it has no special significance. The national bourgeoisie are not significant as a force in the struggle against imperialism. Nevertheless, this bourgeois-reformist opposition has a real and specific significance for the development of the revolutionary movement—and this in both a negative and a positive sense—in so far as it has any mass influence at all.

What is important about it is that it obstructs and retards the development of the revolutionary movement, in so far as it secures a following among the working masses and holds them back from the revolutionary struggle. On the other hand, bourgeois opposition to the ruling imperialist-feudal bloc, even if it does not go very far, can accelerate the political awakening of the broad working masses; open conflicts between the national-reformist bourgeoisie and imperialism, although of little significance in themselves, may, under certain conditions, indirectly serve as the starting-point of great revolutionary mass actions.

It is true the reformist bourgeoisie try to check any such outcome to their oppositional activities, and in one way or another to prevent it in advance. But wherever the objective conditions exist for a deep political crisis, the activities of the national-reformist opposition, even their insignificant conflicts with imperialism which have virtually no connexion with revolution, may acquire serious importance.

Communists must learn how to utilize each and every conflict, to expand such conflicts and to broaden their significance, to link them with the agitation for revolutionary slogans, to spread the news of these conflicts among the masses, to arouse these masses to independent, open manifestations in support of their own demands, etc.

23. The correct tactics in the struggle against such parties as the Swarajists and Wafdists during this stage consist in the successful exposure of their real national-reformist character. These parties have more than once betrayed the national-liberation struggle, but they have not yet finally passed over, like the Kuomintang, to the counter-revolutionary camp. There is no doubt that they will do this later on, but at present they are particularly dangerous precisely because their real physiognomy has not yet been exposed in the eyes of the masses. . . . If the communists do not succeed at this stage in shaking the faith of the masses in the bourgeois national-reformist leadership of the national movement, then in the next advance of the revolutionary wave this leadership will represent an enormous danger for the revolution. . . . It is necessary to expose the half-heartedness and vacillation of these leaders in the national struggle, their bargainings and attempts to reach a compromise with British imperialism, their previous capitulations and counter-revolutionary advances, their reactionary resistance to the class demands of the proletariat and peasantry, their empty nationalist phraseology, their dissemination of harmful illusions about the peaceful decolonization of the country and their sabotage of the application of revolutionary methods in the national struggle for liberation.

The formation of any kind of bloc between the communist party and the national-reformist opposition must be rejected; this does not exclude temporary agreements and the co-ordination of activities in particular anti-imperialist actions, provided that the activities of the bourgeois opposition can be utilized to develop the mass movement, and that these agreements do not in any way restrict communist freedom of agitation among the masses and their organizations. Of course, in this work the communists must at the same time carry on the most relentless ideological and political struggle against bourgeois nationalism and against the slightest signs of its influence inside the labour movement. . . .

24. An incorrect understanding of the basic character of the party of the big national bourgeoisie gives rise to the danger of an incorrect appraisal of the character and role of the petty-bourgeois parties. The development of these parties, as a general rule, follows a course from the national-revolutionary to the national-reformist position. Even such movements as Sun Yat-senism in China, Gandhism in India, Sarekat Islam in Indonesia, were originally in their ideology radical petty-bourgeois movements which, however, were later converted by service to the big bourgeoisie into bourgeois national-reformist movements. Since then, in India, Egypt, and Indonesia, a radical wing has again arisen among the petty-bourgeois groups (e.g. the Republican Party, Watanists, Sarekat Rakjat), which stand for a more or less consistent national-revolutionary point of view. In such a country as India, the rise of some such radical petty-bourgeois parties and groups is possible. . . .

It is absolutely essential that the communist parties in these countries should from the very outset demarcate themselves in the most clear-cut fashion, both politically and organizationally, from all petty-bourgeois groups and parties. In so far as the needs of the revolutionary struggle demand it, temporary co-operation is permissible, and in certain circumstances even a temporary alliance between the communist party and the national-revolutionary movement, provided that the latter is a genuine revolutionary movement, that it genuinely struggles against the ruling power, and that its representatives do not hamper the communists in their work of revolutionary education among the peasants and the working masses. In all such co-operation, however, it is essential to take the most careful precautions against its degenerating into a fusion of the communist movement with the petty-bourgeois revolutionary movement. . . .

IV. THE IMMEDIATE TASKS OF THE COMMUNISTS

28. The building up and development of the communist parties in the colonies and semi-colonies, the elimination of the excessive discrepancy between the objective revolutionary situation and the weakness of the subjective factor, is one of the most important and urgent tasks of the Communist International. In this task it encounters a whole host of objective difficulties, determined by the historical development and social structure of these countries. . . .

The communist parties in the colonial and semi-colonial countries must make every effort to create a cadre of party functionaries from the ranks of the working class itself, utilizing intellectuals in the party as directors and lecturers for propagandist circles and legal and illegal party schools, to train the advanced workers as agitators, propagandists, organizers, and leaders permeated by the spirit of Leninism. The communist parties in the colonial countries must also become genuinely communist parties in their social composition. While drawing into their ranks the best elements of the revolutionary intelligentsia, becoming steeled in the daily struggle and in great revolutionary battles, the communist parties must give their chief attention to strengthening the party organization in the factories and mines, among transport workers, and among the semi-slaves in the plantations. . . .

29. Together with developing the communist party itself, the most important of the immediate general tasks in the colonies and semi-colonies is that of work in the trade unions. . . .

Communists must conduct revolutionary propaganda in reactionary trade unions with mass working-class membership. In those countries where circumstances dictate the need to establish separate revolutionary trade unions (because the reactionary trade union leadership hinders the organization of the unorganized workers, acts in opposition to the most elementary demands of trade union democracy, and converts the trade unions into strike-breaking organizations), the leadership of the RILU must be consulted. Special attention needs to be given to the intrigues of the Amsterdam International in the colonial countries (China, India, North Africa) and to the exposure of its reactionary character before the masses. It is obligatory for the communist party in the metropolis concerned to afford active help to the revolutionary trade union movement of the colony by advice and by the dispatch of permanent instructors. Up to now too little has been done in this connexion.

30. Wherever peasant organizations exist—regardless of their character, as long as they are real mass organizations—the communist party must take steps to penetrate into these organizations. One of the most urgent tasks of the party is to present the agrarian question correctly to the working class, explaining the importance and decisive role of the agrarian revolution, and making members of the party familiar with methods of agitation, propaganda, and organizational work among the peasantry. . . . Communists must everywhere attempt to give a revolutionary character to the existing peasant movement. They must also organize new revolutionary peasant unions and peasant committees, and maintain regular contact with them. Both in the peasant masses and in the ranks of the proletariat, it is essential to carry on energetic propaganda in favour of a fighting bloc of the proletariat and peasantry.

Special workers' and peasants' parties, however revolutionary their character may be at particular periods, may all too easily change into ordinary petty-bourgeois parties; hence it is not advisable to organize such parties. The communist party should never build its organization on the basis of a fusion of two classes; as little should it make use of this basis, characteristic of petty-bourgeois groups, in its task of organizing other parties. . . .

33. In China, the rising wave of the revolution will once more confront the party with the immediate practical task of preparing for and carrying through armed insurrection as the only way to complete the bourgeois-democratic revolution and overthrow the power of the imperialists, landlords, and national bourgeoisie—the power of the Kuomintang.

In existing circumstances, characterized primarily by the absence of a revolutionary impulse among the broad masses of the Chinese people, the party's chief task is the struggle for the masses. . . . At the same time, the party must explain to the masses the impossibility of a radical improvement in their position, the impossibility of the overthrow of imperialist rule and of accomplishing the tasks of the agrarian revolution, unless the power of the Kuomintang and militarists is destroyed and a Soviet regime established.

The party must utilize every conflict, however insignificant, between the workers and the capitalists in the factories, between the peasants and landlords in the villages, between the soldiers and officers in the army, deepening and sharpening these class clashes in order to mobilize the broadest masses of workers and peasants and to win them to its side. The party must utilize every act of violence by international imperialism against the Chinese people, which at present takes the form of the military conquest of different regions, as well as all the bloody exploits of infuriated reaction, to widen the popular protest of the masses against the ruling classes.

Within the party, attention must be concentrated on restoring the cells and local party committees destroyed by the reaction, on improving the social composition of the party, and establishing cells in the most important industries, the largest factories and railway workshops. The most serious attention must be given by the CCP to the social composition of village party organizations, to ensure that they consist of the proletarian, semi-proletarian, and poor rural strata. . . .

34. The basic tasks of the Indian communists consist in the struggle against British imperialism for the emancipation of the country, the destruction of all survivals of feudalism, the agrarian revolution, and the establishment of the dictatorship of the proletariat and peasantry in the form of a Soviet republic. These tasks can be successfully carried out only if a powerful communist party is created, able to place itself at the head of the broad masses of the working class, the peasantry, and all the toilers, and to lead them in armed insurrection against the feudal-imperialist bloc. . . .

The union of all communist groups and individual communists scattered throughout the country into a single, illegal, independent and centralized party is the first task of Indian communists. While rejecting the principle of building the party on a two-class basis, communists must utilize the connexions of the existing workers' and peasants' parties with the labouring masses to strengthen their own party, bearing in mind that the hegemony of the proletariat cannot be realized without the existence of a consolidated steadfast communist party, armed with the theory of Marxism. . . .

The communists must unmask the national-reformism of the Indian National Congress and, in opposition to all the talk of the Swarajists, Gandhists, etc., about passive resistance, advance the irreconcilable slogan of armed struggle for the emancipation of the country and the expulsion of the imperialists.

In relation to the peasantry and peasant organizations the Indian communists are faced first and foremost with the task of informing the peasant masses about the general demands of the party on the agrarian question, for which purpose the party must work out an agrarian programme of action. Through workers connected with the village, as well as directly, the communists must stimulate the struggle of the peasantry for partial demands, and in the process of the struggle organize peasant unions. It is essential to make sure that the newly created peasant organizations do not fall under the influence of exploiting strata in the village. . . .

It must be remembered that in no circumstances can communists relinquish their right to open criticism of the opportunist and reformist tactics of the leadership of those mass organizations in which they work.

35. In Indonesia the suppression of the rising of 1926, the arrest and exile of thousands of members of the communist party, seriously disorganized its ranks. The need to rebuild the destroyed party organizations demands from the party new methods of work, corresponding to the illegal conditions created by the police regime of Dutch imperialism. The concentration of party activities on the places where the town and village proletariat is concentrated, the factories and plantations; restoration of the dissolved trade unions and the struggle for their legalization; special attention to the practical partial demands of the peasantry; development and strengthening of peasant organizational work within all the mass nationalist organizations, in which the communist party must establish fractions and rally to itself the national-revolutionary elements; resolute struggle against the Dutch social-democrats who, supported by the Government, are attempting to secure a foothold for themselves among the native proletariat; winning over the numerous Chinese workers for the class struggle and national-revolutionary struggle, and the establishment of connexions with the communist movement in China and India— these are some of the most important tasks of the Indonesian Communist Party. . . .

37. In Egypt the communist party will be able to play an important part in the national movement only if it is based on the organized proletariat. The organization of trade unions among the Egyptian workers, the intensification of the class struggle, and leadership in that struggle are, consequently, the first and most important tasks of the communist party. The greatest danger to the trade union movement in Egypt at the present time lies in the bourgeois nationalists getting control of the unions. Without a decisive struggle against their influence, a genuine class organization of the workers is impossible. One of the most marked failings of the Egyptian communists in the past has been their exclusive concentration on the urban workers. The correct formulation of the agrarian question, the gradual drawing into the revolutionary struggle of the broad masses of agricultural workers and peasants, and the organization of these masses are some of the most important tasks for the party. Special attention should be devoted to the building up of the party itself, which is still very weak.

38. In the French colonies of North Africa the communists must work in all existing national-revolutionary mass organizations in order to bring

together the genuinely revolutionary elements, on a consistent and clear platform, into a fighting bloc of workers and peasants. As far as the organization *Étoile Nord Africaine* is concerned, the communists must work to ensure its development, not into a party, but into a fighting bloc of the different revolutionary organizations, to which the trade unions of industrial and agricultural workers, peasant unions, etc. are collectively affiliated; the leading part must be secured for the revolutionary proletariat, and for this purpose it is necessary, above all, to develop the trade union movement as the most important organizational channel for communist influence over the masses. It must be our constant task to establish ever closer co-operation between the revolutionary sections of the white proletariat and the native working class. . . .

The communist organizations in each individual country must attract into their ranks in the first place the native workers, fighting against any negligent attitude towards them. The communist parties, genuinely based on the native proletariat, must formally and in fact become independent sections of the Communist International.

39. In connexion with the colonial question, the sixth congress draws the special attention of the communist parties to the Negro question. The position of the Negroes varies in different countries, and accordingly requires concrete investigation and analysis. The territories in which compact Negro masses are to be found can be divided into the following groups: (1) the United States and some South American countries, in which the compact Negro masses constitute a minority in relation to the white population; (2) the Union of South Africa, where the Negroes are the majority in relation to the white colonists; (3) the Negro States which are actually colonies or semi-colonies of imperialism (Liberia, Haiti, Santo Domingo); the whole of Central Africa, divided into the colonies and mandated territories of various imperialist powers (Great Britain, France, Portugal, etc.). The tasks of the communist parties have to be defined according to the concrete situation. . . .

In the Union of South Africa, the Negro masses, who constitute the majority of the population and whose land is being expropriated by the white colonists and by the State, are deprived of political rights and of freedom of movement, are exposed to the worst kinds of racial and class oppression, and suffer simultaneously from pre-capitalist and capitalist methods of exploitation and oppression.

The communist party, which has already had some successes among the Negro proletariat, has the duty of continuing still more energetically the struggle for complete equality of rights for the Negroes, for the abolition of all special regulations and laws directed against Negroes, and for confiscation of the estates of the landlords. In drawing into its ranks Negro workers, organizing them in trade unions, fighting for their admission into the trade unions of white workers, the communist party is obliged to struggle by every means against racial prejudice among white workers and to eradicate such prejudices entirely from its own ranks. The party must vigorously and consistently advance the slogan of the creation of an independent Native Republic, with guarantees for the rights of the white minority, and translate this fight into action. . . .

41. The tasks of the communist parties of the imperialist countries in the colonial question bear a threefold character. First, the establishment of lively connexions between the communist parties and the revolutionary trade union organizations of the metropolitan countries and the corresponding organizations of the colonies. The connexions hitherto established cannot, with a few exceptions, be regarded as adequate. This fact can only in part be explained by objective difficulties. It must be admitted that, up to now, not all the parties in the Communist International have fully grasped the decisive importance which the establishment of close, regular, and unbroken relations with the revolutionary movements in the colonies has in affording these movements active and direct practical help. Only in so far as the communist parties of the imperialist countries really support the revolutionary movement in the colonies, in so far as their help actually widens the struggle of the colonial countries against imperialism, can their position on the colonial question be recognized as a genuinely bolshevik one. This is the criterion for their revolutionary activity in general.

The second category of tasks consists in practical support of the struggle of the colonial peoples against imperialism through the organization of effective mass actions by the proletariat. In this respect, too, the activity of the communist parties of the big capitalist countries has been insufficient. The preparation and organization of such demonstrations of solidarity must without fail become one of the basic elements of communist agitation among the working masses of the capitalist countries. . . . A special task in this category is the struggle against missionary organizations, which act as one of the most effective levers of imperialist expansion and of the enslavement of the colonial peoples.

While striving for the immediate recall of the armed forces of imperialism from the oppressed countries, the communist parties must work unceasingly to organize mass actions to prevent the transport of troops and munitions to the colonies. Systematic agitational and organizational work among the troops for fraternization with the rebellious masses in the colonies must serve as preparation for the desertion of the occupation armies to the side of the workers and peasants and their armed forces.

The struggle against the colonial policy of social-democracy must be looked upon by the communist party as an organic part of its struggle against imperialism. The Second International, by the position it adopted on the colonial question at its last congress in Brussels, has finally sanctioned what the practical activity of the different socialist [parties of the imperialist] countries during the post-war years had already made quite clear: the colonial policy of social-democracy is a policy of active support of imperialism in the exploitation and oppression of the colonial peoples. It has officially adopted the point of view which lies at the basis of the 'League of Nations', according to which the ruling classes of the developed capitalist countries have the 'right' to rule over the majority of the peoples of the globe and to subject these peoples to a frightful regime of exploitation and enslavement.

In order to deceive a part of the working class and to secure its co-operation in maintaining the robber colonial regime, social-democracy defends the most shameful and repulsive exploits of imperialism in the colonies. It conceals the real nature of the capitalist colonial system, it keeps silent about the connexion between colonial policy and the danger of a new imperialist war which is threatening the proletariat and labouring masses of the whole world. Wherever the indignation of the colonial peoples finds an outlet in the struggle against imperialism, social-democracy, for all its lying phrases, in fact always stands on the side of the imperialist executioners of the revolution.

RESOLUTION OF THE SIXTH COMINTERN CONGRESS ON THE APPEAL OF TROTSKY, SAPRONOV, AND OTHERS

1 *September* 1928   *Protokoll*, vi, 4, p. 210

[Kolarov reported for the appeals commission; the resolutions on Trotsky, Sapronov, and others, on Maslow and Ruth Fischer, and two further resolutions on similar lines relating to Suzanne Girault and her group in France, and Wijnkoop in Holland were passed unanimously without discussion. From the chair Thaelmann announced that a number of delegations had put their views before the congress in written statements. On behalf of the German, Czech, Polish, Austrian, and a number of other parties, he moved a resolution 'completely approving the political and organizational line of the CPSU and its Leninist central committee', and all the decisions of the ECCI since the fifth congress on this question. Other delegations, in groups, put in the same resolution, which was carried unanimously without discussion.

At the end of the proceedings Bukharin, in moving the congress manifesto, expressed the hope that they had said the last word 'on that page of our internal history which may be described as the Trotskyist crisis within the Communist International. . . . If the international workers' movement and the revolution in the colonial countries find their most powerful bulwark here in the USSR, it is completely understandable that cracks and tremors here should shake the entire structure of our movement, shake and unsettle the entire international communist army. Our party has come through this crisis not without internal convulsions, not without pain or friction.' The healthy working-class instinct for unity had dealt a crushing blow at the Trotskyist opposition and in all other parties its pitiful fragments had crumbled away. 'The congress has drawn the last line on this page. We have lost a whole series of our former comrades . . . and the vote taken here on this question signifies their political death.']

Having examined the petitions from Trotsky, Sapronov, and other oppositionists expelled from the CPSU to be readmitted to the party, the sixth world congress of the CI resolves:

1. The world congress fully approves the decision of the fifteenth congress of the CPSU and the resolution of the ninth ECCI plenum on the incompatibility of membership of the Trotskyist opposition and propaganda of its views with membership of the bolshevik party. In its programmatic, political, and organizational views, the Trotskyist group has fallen to the level of menshevism, and objectively has become an organ of struggle against the Soviet regime. Its expulsion from the CPSU was therefore correct and unavoidable.

2. The petition of those excluded to the world congress is a further proof that Trotsky and the small handful of his adherents who have not submitted to the conditions put forward by the fifteenth congress, as the great majority of the former opposition have done, are continuing their struggle, their splitting work, their campaign of calumny against the CPSU and against the proletarian dictatorship. The congress considers it unnecessary to debate with the enemies of the CI the counter-revolutionary political content of the Trotskyist platform, since the entire membership of all communist parties have more than once most decisively rejected the views of the opposition.

3. The sixth world congress ratifies the decision of the fifteenth congress of the CPSU on the expulsion of Trotskyists, and recognizes that the measures subsequently taken against the opposition leaders arose entirely from revolutionary necessity; it rejects the request of Trotsky, Radek, Sapronov, and the others expelled for readmission to the party.

RESOLUTION OF THE SIXTH COMINTERN CONGRESS ON THE APPEAL OF MASLOW AND RUTH FISCHER

1 *September* 1928   *Protokoll*, vi, 4, p. 211

Having examined the letter of 23 August 1928 from Maslow and Ruth Fischer, the sixth world congress resolves:

1. The world congress ratifies all the decisions against the Trotskyist Maslow–Fischer group taken by the plenary sessions of the ECCI and the presidium and by the KPD.

2. The entire counter-revolutionary splitting activity of the leaders of

this group makes it impossible to place any confidence in the sincerity of their statements, and shows that they are neither able nor willing to become bolshevik fighters in the ranks of the KPD.

3. The world congress therefore resolves to reject their request for re-admission and to proceed with the next item on the agenda.

4. At the same time the world congress approves the statement of the CC of the KPD that the way back to the KPD is open to all those workers expelled for adherence to the Trotskyist group who break with Maslow, Ruth Fischer, and the other renegades from communism, and obey without reservation all decisions of the Communist International.

EXTRACTS FROM A DECISION OF THE ECCI PRESIDIUM ON THE CIRCUMSTANCES CONNECTED WITH THE EMBEZZLEMENT OF PARTY FUNDS IN HAMBURG

6 *October* 1928　　　　　　　　　　　*Inprekorr*, viii, 115, p. 2263, 9 *October* 1928

[The right wing and moderates, who feared the sharp left turn in the Comin-tern, seized on the Wittorf case in the hope that it would help them to change the composition of the KPD *Zentrale*.

Wittorf, Thaelmann's brother-in-law, had misappropriated his district party funds to the extent of 1,850 marks, and Thaelmann had tried to hush the scandal up. The deficit was discovered, and at the meeting of the CC of the KPD on 25–26 September the centrist group, known as conciliators, carried a resolution sharply condemning as a political error Thaelmann's attempt to keep the matter a secret from his colleagues on the central committee. At Thaelmann's request, the question was referred to the ECCI. The ECCI presidium rehabilitated Thaelmann.

In a letter to Codovilla in Buenos Aires, Humbert-Droz wrote of the 'mechan-ical discipline' being applied in the KPD by the Thaelmann–Remmele–Neumann leadership. The right wing was being excluded without discussion or serious ideological analysis. On the resolution about Thaelmann he wrote that it amounted to a revision of the sixth congress decision on the KPD, discredited the KPD *Zentrale* in the eyes of the masses for the questionable advantage of re-establishing Thaelmann's personal authority, and would make the internal regime of the KPD worse.]

1. The CC of the KPD acted correctly in proceeding vigorously against the embezzlement of party funds by Wittorf and expelling him from the party for this crime.

2. Comrade Thaelmann, who is unreservedly in favour of the strong measures taken by the CC in the Hamburg organization, made a serious mistake in not immediately informing the CC of this theft by Wittorf as soon as he learnt of it. The presidium observes, however, that this omission on Thaelmann's part did not originate in a desire to protect Wittorf, but

arose solely from the wish to choose such a time and manner for disciplining Wittorf that the public settlement of the entire affair would do as little harm as possible to the party, and not be exploited by the bourgeoisie and the social-democracy to make it more difficult for the party and the Comintern to carry out their most important campaign against the class enemies of the proletariat.

3. Unfortunately, the ECCI presidium must at the same time observe that the CC of the KPD published the resolution condemning comrade Thaelmann at a moment when the party's political position was extremely difficult (for it was in the middle of a campaign against armoured-cruiser social-democracy), without any attempt beforehand to bring it to the notice of the ECCI and the active party functionaries, and without any thought for the reaction of the party membership to such a step. The ECCI presidium believes that the CC of the KPD made a mistake that was extremely dangerous for the party, giving the class enemies of the proletariat an opportunity to undermine by a filthy campaign against comrade Thaelmann, the KPD, and the Comintern the party's campaign against social-democracy in connexion with the building of armoured cruisers, and to weaken the proletariat's position in its fight against imperialism. . . .

Such a crass mistake was possible only because the majority of the members, who were not fully informed, allowed themselves to be misled by political opponents within the CC. Instead of acting in the spirit of the sixth world congress decisions and concentrating on the fight against the right danger and against the tendency towards conciliation in regard to right deviations, these comrades proceeded to exploit the Wittorf affair in their fractional group interests against comrade Thaelmann as one of the chief representatives of the sixth world congress line. This was an attempt to change the party leadership and so to obstruct the execution of the political line adopted by the sixth world congress. . . .

The ECCI presidium proposes that the CC of the KPD shall: take steps to liquidate all fractional groups in the party, and draw into responsible party work the best party forces which stand by the decisions of the Comintern and the Essen congress; make certain changes in the composition of the leading CC bodies (politbureau, secretariat, *Rote Fahne* editorial board). . . .

The ECCI presidium observes that the CC of the KPD with comrade Thaelmann at the head pursued a correct political and organizational line both before and after the Essen congress, as, *inter alia*, the May elections showed. . . . The presidium is convinced that the CC of the KPD will continue to carry out this correct Leninist policy.

The presidium expresses its complete political confidence in comrade Thaelmann, and believes that it is his duty to continue to discharge all the functions in the party and the ECCI imposed on him by the Essen party congress and the sixth Comintern congress.

EXTRACTS FROM AN ECCI RESOLUTION ON THE NEGRO QUESTION

26 *October* 1928   *The Negro Question*, p. 56

[At the sixth Comintern congress Ford (USA) reported that the struggle within the American party had handicapped work among Negroes very severely; they had no more than fifty Negro members, and had not organized a single Negro union. The few Negroes in the party who raised these questions were driven out. There were strong traces of white chauvinism in the party; of the nineteen resolutions and documents sent by the ECCI in recent years to the CPUSA none had been discussed or acted upon. Later in the proceedings Jones, another Negro delegate, also referred to the party's inactivity, chauvinism, and race prejudice. The Negro commission of the congress had discussed the slogan of 'a Negro republic in America'; at present the Negroes were a national but non-territorial minority. Bunting (South Africa) said the majority of the South African delegation were opposed to the proposal made in the commission for an independent South African native republic, because it would arouse the intense hostility of the white workers, urban and rural. Pepper defined the Negroes as 'a colony within the USA', and hence falling within the Comintern policy of national self-determination for oppressed colonial peoples. The Negro nation could be developed out of the 'compact mass of farmers on a contiguous territory'. He advocated the slogan of a Negro Soviet Republic. The Negro question was a national and not a racial one.

Negro delegates to the sixth congress held a conference on 31 July 1928 with representatives of the RILU, the CGTU, and the Trade Union Unity League (USA) on organizing the Negro proletariat. A committee was set up, to bring the Negro workers of the world together, organize them in unions, and get them admitted to existing unions. After the debate on the colonial theses a sub-committee on the Negro question was set up; it drafted a resolution endorsed by the political secretariat and published on 26 October 1928.

On 19 October 1928 the political secretariat of the ECCI discussed the attitude of the South African CP, in which the majority of the CC objected to the slogan of an independent South African Native Republic. It came to the conclusion that the weakness of the CP in South Africa, despite objectively favourable conditions, might be explained by this attitude. The party must lead the national agrarian revolutionary movement of the native masses; opposition to a native republic betrayed a defective understanding of the party's tasks.

The resolution adopted stated that 'the united front of the British and South African white bourgeoisie against the toiling negro population, backed by the white and negro reformists, creates for the CP in South Africa an exceptionally complicated but favourable position of being the only political party in the country which unites the white and black proletariat and the landless black peasantry. . . . Unfortunately, the CP of South Africa did not give evidence of sufficient understanding of the revolutionary importance of the mass movements of the native workers and peasants. . . . The CP of South Africa found itself in stubborn opposition to the correct slogan proposed by the Comintern calling for an independent native South African republic.' The CP was advised to participate in such bodies as the African National Congress with the object of transforming them into revolutionary organizations, and to organize the Negroes in trade unions and peasant unions. It was stated that the membership of the CP in South Africa numbered 1,750, 'predominantly black in composition'.

The Comintern's decisions on propaganda among Negroes marked a departure from its earlier policy. In the American party platform adopted in 1925 the Negro question had been treated on orthodox capitalist–labour lines, the Negro bourgeoisie being placed in the same category as white capitalists. After the sixth congress Negroes were re-defined as an oppressed nation; American CP propaganda treated the 'black belt' as a nation requiring its own national-revolutionary movement. Negro leaders were to be trained for work not only in the United States, but in colonies with Negro populations elsewhere, and a number of them were sent to Moscow for training. Some members of the American CP objected to the application of the national and colonial theses to Negroes and Jews, but met with little support as the earlier policy had been markedly unsuccessful in winning Negro recruits.]

1. The industrialization of the South, the concentration of a new Negro working class population in the big cities of the East and North and the entrance of the Negroes into the basic industries on a mass scale, create the possibility for the Negro workers, under the leadership of the Communist Party, to assume the hegemony of all Negro liberation movements, and to increase their importance and role in the revolutionary struggle of the American proletariat.

The Negro working class has reached a stage of development which enables it, if properly organized and well led, to fulfill successfully its double historical mission: (a) to play a considerable role in the class struggle against American imperialism as an important part of the American working class; and (b) to lead the movement of the oppressed masses of the Negro population.

2. The bulk of the Negro population (86 per cent) live in the southern states; of this number 74 per cent live in the rural districts and are dependent almost exclusively upon agriculture for a livelihood. Approximately one-half of these rural dwellers live in the so-called 'Black Belt', in which area they constitute more than 50 per cent of the entire population. The great mass of the Negro agrarian population are subject to the most ruthless exploitation and persecution of a semi-slave character. In addition to the ordinary forms of capitalist exploitation, American imperialism utilizes every possible form of slave exploitation (peonage, share-cropping, land-lord supervision of crops and marketing, etc.) for the purpose of extracting super-profits. On the basis of these slave remnants,

there has grown up a super-structure of social and political inequality that expresses itself in lynching, segregation, Jim-Crowism, etc.

NECESSARY CONDITIONS FOR NATIONAL REVOLUTIONARY MOVEMENT

3. The various forms of oppression of the Negro masses, who are concentrated mainly in the so-called 'Black Belt', provide the necessary conditions for a national revolutionary movement among the Negroes. The Negro agricultural laborers and the tenant farmers feel the pressure of white persecution and exploitation. Thus, the agrarian problem lies at the root of the Negro national movement. The great majority of Negroes in the rural districts of the South are not 'reserves of capitalist reaction', but potential allies of the revolutionary proletariat. Their objective position facilitates their transformation into a revolutionary force, which, under the leadership of the proletariat, will be able to participate in the joint struggle with all other workers against capitalist exploitation.

4. It is the duty of the Negro workers to organize through the mobilization of the broad masses of the Negro population the struggle of the agricultural laborers and tenant farmers against all forms of semi-feudal oppression. On the other hand, it is the duty of the Communist Party of the U.S.A. to mobilize and rally the broad masses of the white workers for active participation in this struggle. For that reason the Party must consider the beginning of systematic work in the south as one of its main tasks. . . .

FOR COMPLETE EMANCIPATION OF OPPRESSED NEGRO RACE

5. To accomplish this task, the Communist Party must come out as the champion of the right of the oppressed Negro race for full emancipation. While continuing and intensifying the struggle under the slogan of full social and political equality for the Negroes, which must remain the central slogan of our Party for work among the masses, the Party must come out openly and unreservedly for the right of Negroes to national self-determination in the southern states, where the Negroes form a majority of the population. The struggle for equal rights and the propaganda for the slogan of self-determination must be linked up with the economic demands of the Negro masses, especially those directed against the slave remnants and all forms of national and racial oppression. Special stress must be laid upon organizing active resistance against lynching, Jim-Crowism, segregation and all other forms of oppression of the Negro population.

6. . . . The existence of a Negro industrial proletariat of almost two million workers makes it imperative that the main emphasis should be placed on these new proletarian forces. The Negro workers must be organized under the leadership of the Communist Party, and thrown into joint struggle together with the white workers. The Party must learn to

combine all demands of the Negroes with the economic and political struggle of the workers and the poor farmers.

AMERICAN NEGRO QUESTION PART OF WORLD PROBLEM

7. The Negro question in the United States must be treated in its relation to the Negro questions and struggles in other parts of the world. The Negro race everywhere is an oppressed race. Whether it is a minority (U.S.A., etc.), majority (South Africa) or inhabits a so-called independent state (Liberia, etc.), the Negroes are oppressed by imperialism. Thus, a common tie of interest is established for the revolutionary struggle of race and national liberation from imperialist domination of the Negroes in various parts of the world. A strong Negro revolutionary movement in the U.S.A. will be able to influence and direct the revolutionary movement in all those parts of the world where the Negroes are oppressed by imperialism.

8. The proletarianization of the Negro masses makes the trade unions the principal form of mass organization. It is the primary task of the Party to play an active part and lead in the work of organizing the Negro workers and agricultural laborers in trade unions. Owing to the refusal of the majority of the white unions in the U.S.A., led by the reactionary leaders, to admit Negroes to membership, steps must be immediately taken to set up special unions for those Negro workers who are not allowed to join the white unions. At the same time, however, the struggles for the inclusion of Negro workers in the existing unions must be intensified and concentrated upon, special attention must be given to those unions in which the statutes and rules set up special limitations against the admission of Negro workers. The primary duty of the Communist Party in this connection is to wage a merciless struggle against the A. F. of L. bureaucracy, which prevents the Negro workers from joining the white workers' unions. . . . Every effort must be made to see that all the new unions organized by the left wing and the Communist Party should embrace the workers of all nationalities and of all races. The principle of one union for all workers in each industry, white and black, should cease to be a mere slogan of propaganda, and must become a slogan of action.

PARTY TRADE UNION WORK AMONG NEGROES

9. While organizing the Negroes into unions and conducting an aggressive struggle against the anti-Negro trade union policy of the A. F. of L., the Party must pay more attention than it has hitherto done to the work in the Negro workers' organizations, such as the Brotherhood of Sleeping Car Porters, Chicago Asphalt Workers Union, and so on. The existence of two million Negro workers and the further industrialization of the Negroes demand a radical change in the work of the Party among the Negroes.

The creation of working class organizations and the extension of our influence in the existing working-class Negro organizations, are of much greater importance than the work in bourgeois and petty-bourgeois organizations, such as the National Association for the Advancement of Colored People, the Pan-African Congress, etc.

10. The American Negro Labor Congress continues to exist only nominally. Every effort should be made to strengthen this organization as a medium through which we can extend the work of the Party among the Negro masses and mobilize the Negro workers under our leadership.

11. The importance of trade union work imposes special tasks upon the Trade Union Unity League. The T.U.U.L. has completely neglected the work among the Negro workers, notwithstanding the fact that these workers are objectively in a position to play a very great part in carrying through the program of organizing the unorganized. . . .

WHITE CHAUVINISM EVIDENCED IN THE AMERICAN PARTY

The C. E. C. of the American Communist Party itself stated in its resolution of April 30, 1928, that 'the Party as a whole has not sufficiently realized the significance of work among the Negroes'. Such an attitude toward the Party work among the Negroes is, however, not satisfactory. The time is ripe to begin within the Party a courageous campaign of self-criticism concerning the work among the Negroes. Penetrating self-criticism is the necessary preliminary condition for directing the Negro work along new lines.

13. The Party must bear in mind that white chauvinism, which is the expression of the ideological influence of American imperialism among the workers, not only prevails among the different strata of the white workers in the U.S.A., but is even reflected in various forms in the Party itself. White chauvinism has manifested itself even in open antagonism of some comrades to the Negro comrades. In some instances where Communists were called upon to champion and lead in the most vigorous manner the fight against white chauvinism, they instead yielded to it. In Gary, white members of the Workers Party protested against Negroes eating in the restaurant controlled by the Party. In Detroit, Party members, yielding to pressure, drove the Negro comrades from a social given in aid of the miners' strike. . . .

16. The Party must seriously take up the task of training a cadre of Negro comrades as leaders, bring them into the Party schools in the U.S.A. and abroad, and make every effort to draw Negro proletarians into active and leading work in the Party, not confining the activities of the Negro comrades exclusively to the work among Negroes. Simultaneously, white workers must specially be trained for work among the Negroes. . . .

22. In the work among the Negroes, special attention should be paid

to the role played by the churches and preachers who are acting on behalf of American imperialism. The Party must conduct a continuous and carefully worked out campaign among the Negro masses, sharpened primarily against the preachers and the churchmen, who are the agents of the oppressors of the Negro race.

PARTY WORK AMONG NEGRO PROLETARIAT AND PEASANTRY

23. The Party must apply united front tactics for specific demands to the existing Negro petty bourgeois organizations. The purpose of these united front tactics should be the mobilizing of the Negro masses under the leadership of the Party, and to expose the treacherous petty bourgeois leadership of those organizations. . . .

25. In order to reach the bulk of the Negro masses, special attention should be paid to the work among the Negroes in the South. For that purpose, the Party should establish a district organization in the most suitable locality in the South. Whilst continuing trade union work among the Negro workers and the agricultural laborers, special organizations of tenant farmers must be set up. Special efforts must also be made to secure the support of the share croppers in the creation of such organizations. The Party must undertake the task of working out a definite program of immediate demands, directed against all slave remnants, which will serve as the rallying slogans for the formation of such peasant organizations.

EXTRACTS FROM A LETTER FROM THE ECCI TO THE ALL-INDIA CONFERENCE OF WORKERS' AND PEASANTS' PARTIES

2 *December* 1928   *Meerut Trial*, Exhibit P 334

[Until 1929 the communist movement in India consisted of scattered groups rather than an organized party. (An official Comintern handbook lists the Indian CP as founded in 1926, though not recognized as a CI section.) It has been suggested that Roy, who was unpopular with a number of his Indian colleagues (one of whom later charged him with misapplication of Comintern funds), was sent to China at the end of 1926 by the ECCI in order to leave the CPGB a free hand to organize a party in India. Communist propaganda, printed in Britain and Germany, was directed mainly to the trade unions. The Profintern assiduously courted the All-India Trade Union Congress, acting on many occasions through its Pan-Pacific Trade Union secretariat in Shanghai, and providing propaganda material, pamphlets, etc. through the British Minority Movement. The League against Imperialism also interested itself in the unions, and sent a representative by the name of J. W. Johnstone to India to promote its work among them. Ryan, an Australian member of the Pan-Pacific secretariat, attended the 1928 meeting of the All-India TUC, at which it was decided to affiliate to the League against Imperialism. In a letter to the secretary of the All-India Trade Union Congress a Bengal trade union secretary wrote: 'I have now begun to realize why there is such a strong feeling of hostility created against the so-called communists everywhere. . . . Right or wrong they try to dictate their terms to other trade unionists, who in most cases have to yield to them because they have no solidarity but are rent asunder.'

The fifth plenum of the ECCI in March 1925 recommended Indian communists to work in the Indian National Congress and its Swaraj (Home Rule) organizations. In July 1925 the CPGB arranged a conference in Amsterdam (Roy was not allowed entry into England) attended by Roy representing the ECCI and Upadhyaya, and presided over by Sneevliet. Glading (CPGB), who had just returned from India, said he had found no communists there. It is clear from the report on this conference that there was a good deal of ill-feeling and mistrust between the CPGB and its Indian associates, and rivalry for control over the work done in India and among Indians abroad. In November 1925 a 'Labour Swaraj' party was formed within the Indian National Congress, and in the following year merged with the Bengal Workers' and Peasants' Party which had been established in Calcutta in February 1926; the second conference of the WPP held at the end of the year was attended by Saklatvala, the London communist M.P. Its membership at the beginning of 1928 is given as 125, with an affiliated membership of 10,000. Two of its members were on the executive committee of the Indian TUC, and three on the committee of the Indian National Congress.

At the meeting of the Indian National Congress in Madras in December 1927 the communists present met and adopted a constitution, and decided to affiliate to the CI. (Nothing seems to have come of this attempt.) The meeting was attended by B. Bradley and P. Spratt, sent from the CPGB as organizers. Spratt had arrived at the end of 1926, Bradley shortly afterwards, with instructions to form a workers' and peasants' party in which the communists would exercise control. The Bombay WPP was set up in February 1927, and in May a number of Indian communists met in that city to elect an executive committee; it made no formal request to Moscow for affiliation, but stated that it looked to the Comintern for guidance. It is clear from the speeches at the sixth CI congress in the following year that this attempt to form an Indian communist party also petered out. In a letter to Indian communists at the end of 1927 Roy wrote that the WPP was too openly identified with the communists. 'It is publicly known that practically all the members of the CC of the CP are the leaders of the WPP. Of course, it should in fact be so, but the cat has been unnecessarily let out of the bag by publishing the list of the CC of the CP.'

At the sixth Comintern congress the Soviet delegation were in favour of withdrawing support from the WPP, the British delegation in favour of continuing support, and the Indian delegation divided. (The British, like Roy, were in favour of a mass legal party controlled by an illegal CP.) It was decided that support should be withdrawn, but the Indian communists did in fact continue with their preparations for an all-India conference of workers' and peasants' parties (of which there were four), which was held in Calcutta on 21–23 December 1928. It is suggested that the decisions arrived at in Moscow reached India too late for a change to be made, and the local communists were linked more directly with the CPGB than with the CI. Bradley attended the conference as representative of the CPGB. Invitations had also been sent to the Comintern, Profintern, and Krestintern, the League against Imperialism, the Pan-Pacific trade union secretariat, the Minority Movement, Labour Research Department, and Indian Seamen's Union (London, which existed only on paper). The political resolution adopted by the conference was drafted by Spratt. The conference voted for collaboration with the Independence League (the more radical section of the Indian National Congress), although it was said to have a 'fundamentally bourgeois, even fascist, and ultimately counter-revolutionary' character. After the conference the communist leaders of the WPP reconstituted themselves as the Communist Party of India, elected a central committee, and applied for admission to the Comintern. The present ECCI letter was accompanied by a long extract from the colonial theses of the sixth Comintern congress. After the conference Roy wrote that the communists, who were its driving force, hoped to make the WPP the centre for all revolutionary national forces; the WPP would have fractions in other organizations, but not accept office in them. Shubin, who at the tenth ECCI plenum made a vigorous attack on Roy for his attitude to the Independence League and questioned whether he had any support among Indian communists, wrote that Roy's articles were spreading the illusion that real progress could be made through Congress. (At the end of 1930 R. P. Dutt wrote that there was still no Communist Party in India.)]

The Communist International supporting everywhere the revolutionary movement of the toilers and the oppressed, through your organisation, albeit not part of our international body, sends its greetings to the workers and peasants of India now waging a heroic struggle against imperialist oppression and feudal reaction upon one of the most important sections of the world front. The victorious progress of this struggle demands in our opinion, above all, the creation of an independent class party of the proletariat, the uniting and raising of the isolated actions of the peasants to the highest political level, and the formation of a real revolutionary bloc of workers and peasants, under the leadership of the proletariat not in the form of a united workers' and peasants' party, but on the basis of co-operation in deeds between the mass organisations of the proletariat on the one hand, and peasant leagues and committees on the other, for the overthrow of the imperialists and the destruction of the political and economic basis of colonial exploitation and slavery. The growing influence of the workers' and peasants' parties, and particularly the attendance of thousands of peasants at your provincial conferences, proved that the understanding of the necessity for this militant bloc is penetrating among ever larger masses of toilers.

Your conference is taking place at a moment which may become the turning point in the history of the national revolution. The furious preparations of the British bourgeoisie for a new imperialistic slaughter, and the intensification of all forms of colonial plunder and terror, place the peoples of India in a position from which there is no other way out, but open and determined fight for the overthrow of the alien yoke. The revolutionary crisis in the country is maturing. In the strike movements various detachments of the working class (particularly the textile workers of Bombay) begin to come out as an independent force, conscious of the irreconcilability of its interests with imperialism and the chaffering bourgeoisie, and of its historic role as the champion of the national revolution. More painfully, and slowly, but with equal certainty, the oppressed, ruined and disunited peasantry is entering the path of organised struggle. Growing unemployment, ruin and hopelessness stir also the town petty bourgeoisie to revolutionary activity. The pent-up discontent of the masses, the despair, and the sublime hatred for the oppressors, is already breaking forth to transform these isolated and defensive actions into an aggressive fight against British imperialism and its native allies; that is the fundamental task before your Conference.

The main obstacle to the victorious organised struggle against British imperialism and its feudal allies in the period of increasing terrorism and bloody repression is the influence of opportunist bourgeois nationalism. Each day brings and will bring fresh proof of the treachery of the bourgeoisie, of its cringing before imperialism, of its intention to bargain and to come to terms with the latter behind the backs of the toilers of India and at their expense. Lately this treachery has assumed the character of the most cynical toying with the slogan of 'independence' which the Swarajists now throw out to deceive the masses, now tuck away in their pocket (the Motilal Nehru Report), in order to penetrate into the Simon Commission through the back stairs, and now raise again in a distorted shape, simultaneously with the 'dominion status' slogan. However crude and downright dishonest this game may be, the penal regime and bloody repression of any exposing criticism, particularly Communist criticism, create a state of things under which the fraud of bourgeois nationalism still keeps its hold on a considerable section of the toilers. The struggle against this fraud compels you not only to determined and relentless exposure of the bourgeois treachery, but also through systematic everyday activity to bring home this exposure, to the masses of the workers and peasants. The experience of the last movement in Bardoli showed how great the danger is still that not only the bourgeoisie, but even the usurers who buy out the peasants' lands, find themselves able to subordinate the movement of the peasants and to utilise it for their own ends. No declarations of readiness to combat opportunism have any revolutionary worth if there is no practical and actual proof of the waging of this struggle among the masses, and of the overcoming of the bourgeois influence in persistent every day work.

The greatest danger to the organisation of the masses, to the creation of a revolutionary bloc of the proletariat and the peasantry and to the proletarian leadership in this bloc, consists not only in bourgeois nationalism as such, but comes from the organisations and groups of 'prominent' petty-bourgeois intellectuals actually influenced by the former 'Independence League'. The wavering and oscillating petty-bourgeois intellectuals of India are either tied up with the system of landlordism and usury and preach a return to obsolete forms of pre-capitalist exploitation idealised by them, or they reflect the interest of capitalist exploitation being the agents of the bourgeoisie within the national movement. In either case they deny the importance of the class struggle, and whilst claiming to be 'at the head' of the workers' and peasants' movement, they are fit in reality only to behead it. The better elements alone of the petty-bourgeoisie intellectuals with a revolutionary frame of mind may rise to the proletarian class viewpoint, and become a positive factor in the national revolutionary struggle.

The 'Independence League' at least in its present shape in fact assists official Swarajism in its nefarious play with the slogans of 'independence' and 'dominion status'. Duly appreciating the very fact of the organisation of this League as proof that at the present time one cannot approach the masses without demanding independence and the overthrow of imperialism, your Conference at the same time cannot fail to disassociate itself from the confusion and twaddle which characterises the advertised League platform with its lavish promises.

The masses must realise that all the talk of the organisers of the League in their platform about 'nationalisation' and 'socialisation' is an empty sound if in the same breath they recommend FOR THE PRESENT 'impartial board for arbitration with a view to making strikes and lockouts unnecessary' (platform of the Bengal Independence League). . . .

The masses want from the political leaders of the petty-bourgeoisie not words but revolutionary deeds. The more determined and outspoken your criticism, the sooner the League will either expose itself as the Left-wing of bourgeois nationalism, or having shaken off the politicians at the head, will join, for a certain period and within certain limits, the national-revolutionary camp (retaining, however, even in this case their incorrigible half-heartedness, chronic wavering, and inevitable confusion in the whole of their politics and tactics).

The experience of all revolutions shows that the peasantry is inevitably deceived and defeated if it acts without the alliance and the leadership of the proletariat. In explaining to the peasantry the need for the workers' and peasants' bloc it is not difficult at the same time to explain to them, upon the grounds of the severe experience of the Indian revolution, the need for the leadership of the proletariat in this bloc. The Indian proletariat has demonstrated to all the toilers that it represents the most revolutionary force in the country; it has shown that it will stop at nothing in this struggle neither in the town nor in the village, that it marches and will march, in the front rank of the fight against British imperialism, feudalism, and the reformist bourgeoisie. The proletariat is helping and will help the peasantry which has been thrust by imperialism into a singular condition of humiliation, disunion and barbaric exploitation, shrouded in the falsehoods of religion, caste and nationalism, to organise its force and to break the shackles of slavery, bondage, land hunger, and imperialist and feudal oppression. The leadership of the proletariat, as the more concentrated, united, enlightened and hardened section of the toilers in this struggle, will secure the victory to the workers' and peasants' bloc. It is extremely important to demonstrate to the peasants in deeds and practice the significance of a fighting alliance with the proletariat in their everyday struggle, already now.

The organisation of the workers' and peasants' bloc is based upon the common interest of the workers, peasants, and the town poor, in the fight against imperialism and feudal reaction. Nevertheless, it does not eliminate the class differences, and therefore, it does not imply by any means the fusion of the workers and peasants into one PARTY. In the Great October Revolution the proletariat gained the following of the peasantry of all the nations which inhabited the former tzarist Russia just because it was organised into the independent Bolshevik Party, into a Party armed with the Marxian–Leninist theory, irreconcilable to petty-bourgeois waverings, disciplined, self-sacrificing, capable of screening itself underground from the blows of the tzarist terror, at the same time never ceasing to take advantage of all the legal possibilities. The Indian proletariat, we feel sure, will follow this path.

The Indian proletariat will be the champion of the national revolutionary fight and lead to victory the peasantry, the town poor, and all the toilers, if it organises and consolidates its vanguard—the Communist Party, which will educate the working masses in the spirit of a clear and unmistakable class policy, in the realisation of the need for tremendous sacrifices in order to overthrow imperialism and bourgeoisie. The existing (only on paper) Communist Party of India, since it does not show any signs of revolutionary life, has no grounds to consider and even call itself Communist, although there are individual Communists among its members. Under the conditions of imperialist terror, by the feeble organisation of the Indian workers and the bullying of the reformist trade union bureaucrats, the task of building a genuine Communist Party will be considerably facilitated if at the same time broad revolutionary organisations of the workers are formed with the active participation of Communists, or a broad Left wing created in the trade union movement upon the platform of consistent class struggle. . . .

In the work among the peasants the task is to pass from general slogans and to draw in the peasants to the real revolutionary struggle in the defence of the everyday interests of the masses. Your organisations cannot afford to wave aside even seemingly backward manifestations of the anger of the peasantry. You must endeavour in every manifestation of this kind to discover its revolutionary substance and to transfer it to a higher level of class-consciousness. In view of the tremendous variety of forms of land tenure in India, and the multitude of forms of pre-capitalist and semi-feudal bondage, the best way to embrace the peasant movement in the various districts and localities is to organise from below peasant leagues led wherever possible by agricultural labourers and poor peasantry proved in the fight. It is necessary, not only in words, but in deeds, to endeavour to raise the isolated actions of the peasants to the level of an agrarian revolution. Under the slogans of abolition of every form and vestige of feudalism and semi-feudalism, of confiscation of the land of Zemindars, usurers, priests and its transfer to the use of the toiling peasantry while securing in the first place the interest of the poor peasants, the agrarian revolution has been and remains the pivot of the national-revolutionary struggle in India. . . .

Concerning organisational forms, your Conference will have to discuss the question of separating the workers' organisations from the peasants' organisations, so that the former be ensured a clear-cut and consistent class development, and the latter the full embracing of the struggling peasantry. Provincial workers' and peasants' parties, after an appropriate distribution of their branches and members upon this class basis, are bound to develop in the future into revolutionary mass organisations of the workers on the one hand, into peasants' leagues and committees on the other, which in turn will strive to gain the leadership inside existing peasant bodies or will build new peasants' organisations. The periodical conferences and meetings of these mass organisations, called from time to time, should constitute one of the forms expressing the militant bloc of the worker and peasant masses. If your conference accepts this point of view, it will put before itself the question of forming a Committee for the coordination of the activities of the local workers' and peasants' organisations, having in mind chiefly their independent revolutionary development upon the class basis.

The Indian toilers, in their hard struggle, are nearing the fulfilment of their great historic task. The proletariat now organising its forces can rely on the support of the peasantry, of the poor of the towns, and of all the oppressed and exploited of India for whom there is no salvation except as the result of the triumphant revolution. It can rely upon the support of the proletarians of all lands and of the oppressed peoples throughout all the world. We appeal to your Conference to wage a determined fight against waverings and backslidings, to criticise grave opportunistic blunders, to work out the revolutionary tactics for the forthcoming fights, to pass to such forms of organisation which, as international revolutionary experience has proved, open the possibility for winning the masses to the cause of the Revolution.

EXTRACTS FROM AN OPEN LETTER FROM THE ECCI PRESIDIUM TO THE GERMAN COMMUNIST PARTY ON THE RIGHT-WING DANGER IN THAT PARTY

19 *December* 1928   *Inprekorr*, viii, 142, p. 2829, 21 *December* 1928

[The new Comintern line of fighting *à outrance* against the socialist parties met with a good deal of opposition in the KPD. Those who disagreed were attacked as 'liquidators'. They were accused of organizing a fractional struggle, failing to grasp that the class struggle in Germany was becoming more acute, adopting a passive and pessimistic attitude; supporting them was a group of 'conciliators', who did not want the KPD to take up the fight against the right danger as such, but only against errors committed by the right; they also objected to disciplinary action against the right, urging that methods of persuasion only should be used; their crowning offence was the proposal that Brandler and Thalheimer should be put forward as Reichstag candidates. After the ninth plenum of the ECCI in February 1928 the CPSU and KPD delegations had considered and rejected the proposal put forward by the 'conciliator' group in the KPD that Brandler and Thalheimer should be readmitted without qualification to the KPD.

A letter from Lozovsky to Humbert-Droz dated 16 February 1928 suggested that the Brandler question would not be settled in a hurry. Brandler wished to go to Germany but for the time being that was out of the question; he would probably have to wait a year or two. If the CPSU delegation at the ECCI refused permission for him to return, Lozovsky would apply for him to work in the Profintern.

At the sixth CI congress in August, Bukharin said the Comintern would give no support to those members of the KPD who wanted to change its leaders. This would lead to another struggle within the party and make a bad impression on the working class. The ECCI supported the Thaelmann *Zentrale*. Thaelmann said the Trotskyist renegades of the KPD had been thoroughly routed, but there were serious dangers from the right. Ewert spoke of the February discussion, when those who advocated 'tolerance and patience' were threatened with expulsion. Stalin had said that if Ewert continued on his present line, he would become the rallying point for all the discontented and right-wing elements in the KPD. This, said Ewert, meant that the normal differences which were inevitable in any party could be exploited in a fight for power within the party. Even a CC majority could degenerate into a faction. Ulbricht and Lominadze joined in the attack on Ewert and the 'conciliators' who were, they said, trying to get the views of the right adopted.

At a meeting of the KPD central committee on 19 October 1928 the CC candidate members Hausen and Galen opened their attack with the explanation that 'the revolution comes before the party'. They demanded a radical reform of the KPD and the CI; the decisions of the sixth congress, which meant the abandonment of united front tactics, were a new and worse edition of the disastrous Fischer-Maslow policy, and the attack on the right wing would have catastrophic results for the KPD. Ulbricht replied that unless they fought against the right, they would find themselves drawing nearer the social-democrats, and that would be the end of the KPD.

Between the central committee meeting, and the national conference of KPD officials which met on 3–4 November, 28 district party committees had discussed the dispute, and 2 had shown a majority against the central committee.

At the November conference a resolution endorsing the decisions of the sixth congress, which had been passed by 30 votes to 9 at the meeting of the central committee on 2 November, was carried by 221 votes against 4; the 19 'conciliators' voted for the resolution with reservations. A resolution asking the central committee of the CPSU to take action against Brandler for breach of discipline (he had returned to Germany from Russia without permission) was carried against 19 votes and 2 abstentions. He was accused of having 'slipped from liquidationism into renegacy'.

The CC of the KPD referred the Hausen–Galen case to the ECCI; their attitude was tantamount to an appeal for an organized struggle against the CI and the KPD; they had distributed copies of Brandler's programme, which had already been rejected; the collection of signatures in its support was the first step in the registration of members for an anti-party organization.

The ECCI commission set up to deal with the question held four meetings. Hausen, a member of the KPD since 1919 who had served a two-year prison sentence, said the group was formed after the Essen congress of the KPD; it had views but no discipline of its own. The reply of the KPD politbureau to Brandler's proposals for the KPD programme of action violated the Essen congress decision on 'party concentration', created artificial differences within the party, and split it. Their opinions had been reinforced by the ninth plenum agreement between the CPSU and the KPD, and they had made this clear at the time. They thought the emphasis in KPD policy should be on the united front in the factories, not on the fight against the social-democrats, and that the KPD paid relatively too much attention to the unorganized workers in comparison with the organized. He personally had agreed with the ECCI resolution of January 1924 on the October retreat, but not with the resolution of the fifth Comintern congress which had altered the analysis of the October defeat under the influence of Fischer and Maslow. He had approved and defended the action taken by the CPSU against Trotsky. (In reply to Kuusinen's question whether he thought the measures against Trotsky right and just, Hausen replied: 'It is not good that Trotsky is in exile, but I think it is politically necessary.')

The CC of the KPD on 14 December, having decided that the activities of Brandler and Thalheimer were incompatible with membership of a Comintern section, asked the CC of the CPSU (of which party the two were members) to take action. There was no point in expelling the right-wingers in the KPD unless Brandler and Thalheimer were also expelled. They had 'developed their false conceptions into a platform and . . . must be fought against as an opportunist group'.

Two commissions were set up by the presidium, one to draft the 'open letter', the other to draft a confidential communication to the German central committee. Gusev (CPSU) reported Brandler as saying that the party had become a barracks. Kuusinen's opinion was that Brandler and Thalheimer had always been social-democrats, and objectively were already outside the party. He, Ulbricht, Molotov, and Stalin made vigorous attacks on Humbert-Droz and Serra (an Italian representative in the political secretariat) for their support of the right wing (they were supporters of Bukharin). Molotov, for the CPSU delegation, said Brandler and Thalheimer had already taken up positions of irreconcilable struggle against the party, its policy, and its discipline. Klara Zetkin wanted the decision to be postponed, as the question was so serious. Stalin concluded his speech, which distinguished between the right wing in the KPD, who were already an anti-party faction, and the right wing in the CPSU, who 'had not yet crystallized', by saying that the presence of such people as Brandler and Thalheimer in the Comintern could no longer be tolerated.

An article published in the Comintern press immediately after the open letter, concluded with the words: 'Brandler, Thalheimer, and the other leaders of the right fraction . . . will play their part, subjectively as well as objectively, outside the Communist ranks, hand in hand and shoulder to shoulder with all the renegades who begin by attacking the Comintern and end with an insane hatred for the USSR.'

On 21 December the politbureau of the KPD accepted the open letter without reservation. On 24–25 January 1929 the central committee of the KPD also gave its unconditional approval; the right wing were, not only objectively but subjectively, agents of reformism. No KPD member was to attend any meeting of the 'liquidators' (who had held a conference on 30 December) or to work with them in any capacity. The central committee approved the expulsion from the KPD of Paul Frölich, J. Walcher, Böttcher, and seven others who had all refused to accept the conditions laid down in the open letter, and welcomed the expulsion by the ECCI of Hausen and Galen, and by the CC of the CPSU of Brandler and Thalheimer. More than a hundred members were expelled by subsidiary committees of the KPD. One of the charges against the conciliators was that they underestimated the importance of the reparations question as a means of obtaining German help for intervention against the USSR; another that they made a false and opportunist distinction between the bourgeois democratic State and dictatorial fascist rule.

In a letter to Trotsky (in the Trotsky archives) in November 1928 Andrés Nin wrote from Moscow: 'Here, in the Comintern, there is complete disarray. Nothing at all is done. Everybody is awaiting the outcome of the fight between Stalin and the right. Demoralization is complete. The majority of the presidium is, of course, with Stalin, because it's certain that he will come out on top. Only Tasca and Humbert-Droz are unconditionally with Bukharin. Tasca has the support of the CC of his [Italian] party. Humbert-Droz is quite alone, because he has no contact with his [Swiss] party. Piatnitsky is hesitating. In fact he's asking himself what the Comintern will come to if, after having removed Trotsky, Radek, Zinoviev, and so many others, Bukharin too is removed. Who will then guide the Comintern, he wonders. Manuilsky and Neumann?' The members of the right with whom he had spoken were prepared to give battle but had little confidence in Bukharin's decisions. In Germany the situation was catastrophic; the almost certain expulsion of Brandler and Thalheimer would split the party. The situation in France made him weep. In the United States the fractional war had gone to extraordinary lengths. Divergences among the opposition groups made it impossible for them to take advantage of the situation. At the same time Humbert-Droz wrote to Codovilla in Buenos Aires that he wanted to go to South America to help the young parties there 'and at last to be directly useful instead of mouldering away into a bureaucrat in a machine'.]

Since the German revolution of 1923 the openly opportunist right-wing elements in the German Communist Party, particularly the adherents of Brandler, have never entirely ceased their fractional activities. Brandler's false policy takes the form of a tendency to capitulate to the bourgeoisie and to form a bloc with the social-democrats. The right wing have never given up the hope of again assuming the leadership of the party and changing its policy; their fractional activity has at times been relaxed, at other times it has been very intense.

In its resolution on the fractional activity of Radek, Brandler, and Thalheimer, the fifth ECCI plenum observed that 'an organized fraction exists in the KPD, to which a few groups within the party as well as a group of members of the CPSU (Brandler, Thalheimer, Radek, and others) belong, and which carries on fractional work on the basis of a political platform formulated in a series of articles and documents'. The plenum severely reprimanded Brandler, Thalheimer, Radek, and others, and stated that 'if they continue their fraction work they will inevitably place themselves outside the ranks of the party'.

Before the Essen party congress in 1927 the fractional activities of Brandler's adherents revived again. At the congress they tried to push through Brandler's ideas, which he had set out in an article on the 'action programme' written before the congress but published only early in 1928. The opportunist interpretation of the slogan of 'production control' advanced by the right wing was rejected by the congress; it also condemned the Brandler group's opportunist errors on the question of the workers' government, which made this a transitional form between bourgeois democracy and proletarian dictatorship, and on united front tactics, which they interpreted as a bloc with social-democracy; this might have led to impermissible obligations towards the left social-democrats and to the renunciation of an independent communist policy.

The next stage of the right-wing fraction's work was connected with the ninth plenum and the fourth RILU congress. The right-wing elements in the KPD, including Brandler's adherents, declared open war on the decisions of the fourth RILU congress and on this basis drew together more closely than before. They began to expand their fractional work, attacked the entire policy of the CC of the KPD, and started to work out their own political platform, the first drafts being embodied in various fractional documents.

The Wittorf case provided them with the desired opportunity to attempt to put their fractional designs into effect and seize leadership of the party in order to change its political line as laid down by the sixth Comintern congress. . . .

To the ECCI presidium's resolution of 6 October the right wing replied with sharp fractional attacks. According to them this decision threatened ruin not only to the German party but to the Comintern. . . . This was the starting-point of their quite open steps to organize their fraction.

The principal leaders of the fraction are Brandler and Thalheimer, formerly members of the KPD and now members of the CPSU. Brandler and Thalheimer, as is known, committed a number of grave errors in 1923. After the events of 1923 the indignation of the KPD masses was so great that Brandler and Thalheimer were very near to expulsion from the party. But the ECCI and the CC of the CPSU, assuming that they would over-come their opportunist tendencies, gave them a last chance to improve and admitted them to the CPSU.

As the latest events in the KPD show, Brandler and Thalheimer have proved themselves to be politically incorrigible. Throughout 1926–7 they systematically refused to admit unreservedly their chief mistakes, and quite recently publicly reiterated their refusal. . . . Their adherent, the CC candidate Galen, turned the *Volksrecht*, a party organ appearing in Offenbach, into a fraction newspaper; another adherent, the CC candidate Hausen, published an open letter to the members of the Breslau district party consisting entirely of fractional attacks on the CC and the Comintern. Shortly thereafter the same Hausen began to publish, as responsible editor, the fraction's paper *Gegen den Strom* (information bulletin of the opposition). This paper, as well as other material put out by the fraction, was sent to all party organizations and publicly distributed.

In the commission set up by the ECCI presidium to deal with this matter, Hausen (on 27 November 1928) frankly admitted the existence of a right-wing fraction in the KPD. He admitted that it has its own political platform, not yet formulated in a single document, stated that recently, and particularly before CC meetings, he had conversations with Thal-heimer, and that before leaving for Moscow he met Brandler to discuss with him the need for a definitive formulation of the fraction's political platform for the forthcoming party congress.

At the same commission Galen tried to deny the existence of a right-wing fraction and his participation in its work. But he could not deny, firstly, the fractional character of the work in the Offenbach party organiza-tion, of which he is leader, where at Galen's invitation Brandler made two fractional speeches, or, secondly, the fractional character of the paper which he edits, *Das Volksrecht*, which published Brandler's speeches and statements and waged a fractional struggle against the KPD.

It is therefore indisputably proven that there exists in the German Communist Party a regular right-wing fraction which has a central leadership and a political platform and applies discipline within the fraction. According to Hausen its platform is given in Brandler's action programme, and in articles in the first issue of *Gegen den Strom*, and in *Das Volksrecht*. . . .

The natural consequence which the members of the right-wing fraction draw from the basic theses of their platform is non-recognition of the decisions of the fourth RILU congress and the sixth Comintern congress, and the fight against these decisions. This road leads to an open and outright break with the RILU and the Comintern.

On the other hand it becomes clearer every day that the right-wing fraction's political platform is drawing closer to that of the social-democrats. . . . Thus Brandler, Thalheimer, and other leaders of the right-wing fraction, both in their platform and in their fractional work, have turned out to be genuine left social-democratic politicians. Objectively they are becoming instruments of the reformists, agents of reformism in the communist party. Not only do they reject the decisions of the fourth RILU congress and the sixth Comintern congress, not only do they refuse to obey these decisions, they are beginning to work actively against their practical execution, attempting to sabotage and counteract the political actions of the party taken to put these decisions into effect. During the armoured cruiser campaign they did the greatest damage by using the Wittorf case to intensify their fractional struggle against the CC of the KPD. . . .

The right wing's political platform, as well as their actions, show the direction in which they are moving. The formation of a new opportunist party within the communist party, the splitting of the communist party, the alliance of this right wing with the left social-democrats, and a bloc between this opportunist concentration and the social-democratic party—these are the three main stages on the road from the Comintern to the Second International, a road which has now been reached by the straying leaders of the right-wing fraction. . . .

Such a deep gulf has opened between the right-wing fraction and the party that there can no longer be any talk of 'conciliation' between them. There is no longer any place in the KPD for the conciliators. The time has come when a choice must be made between the party and the right fraction—either the party or the fraction. At the present moment a conciliatory attitude towards the right implies not only abandonment of the struggle against the right wing and their splitting work, but actual support for the right against the party. . . .

P p

In the last two months the conciliators have shown ever greater patience towards the right, and ever greater impatience towards the party. There is no concrete criticism of the ideas and actions of the right fraction, while the attacks on the party have grown sharper, and approximate more and more to the criticisms made by the right itself. Typical in this connexion is the political platform submitted by the conciliators to the politbureau of the KPD, signed by Ewert, Dietrich, Schumann, and others, in which the sixth Comintern congress slogan: 'Fight on two fronts, against the right and the "left" ', is replaced by a new slogan: 'Fight on two fronts, both against the right and against the inner-party line of the CC of the KPD.' For the line proclaimed by the sixth congress of concentration against both right and left deviations from Leninism, the conciliators thus substitute concentration against the right (in words) and against the Leninist KPD (in deeds).

It is clear that the KPD can no longer tolerate the splitting activities of the right wing, and that it must demand of the conciliators a complete break with the right as well as consistent struggle against them, under the leadership of the CC of the KPD. Proceeding from these considerations, the ECCI presidium endorses the decision of the CC of the KPD of 14 December on the conditions to be put to the right, namely:

a. That, without reservation or limitation, they recognize and adhere to party discipline as laid down in the theses and statutes of the Comintern and the KPD;

b. That they declare their unreserved agreement with the programme of the Communist International, in all its parts. . . .

c. That they recognize as binding all decisions of the sixth Comintern congress and the fourth RILU congress, as well as those of the CC and the district committees of the KPD, and undertake to carry them through without reservation;

d. That they condemn their activities, their formation of a fraction, their convening of special meetings and conferences, their speeches against the sixth congress decisions as injurious and disruptive, incompatible with discipline and the principles of the Comintern, and that they explicitly declare their intention to refrain in future from such and similar actions;

e. That they admit that the publication of their own papers and bulletins, and the distribution of leaflets and writings abusing the party and the Comintern, by the fraction and by some comrades linked with the fraction, are incompatible with party discipline, and that they therefore explicitly declare that they will immediately cease to do so. . . .

The rejection of these conditions will be followed by the immediate expulsion from the Comintern of all the leading members of the right.

The ECCI presidium entrusts the CC of the KPD with the practical execution of all measures necessary for the fulfilment of these decisions.

Brandler and Thalheimer, who are members of the CPSU, will be invited to appear before its central control commission. It is obvious that if these comrades refuse to appear on the given date before the CCC of the CPSU, they will be immediately expelled from the CPSU.

At the meeting of the commission of the ECCI presidium on 8 December 1928 Hausen and Galen, candidate members of the CC of the KPD, were asked to cease their fraction work, to stop publishing *Gegen den Strom* and *Das Volksrecht*, to stop distributing the fraction's documents, and no longer to defend the right wing's political platform. Both Hausen and Galen evaded a direct answer, and in fact refused to meet these demands by saying 'No' to the question whether they would cease publishing the two papers mentioned. To the further question whether they were ready to obey unconditionally the decisions to be taken in their presence by the ECCI presidium, they again answered 'No'.

Consequently the ECCI presidium decided to expel Hausen and Galen from the German Communist Party and from the Communist International.

The ECCI presidium is firmly convinced that those workers who are still under the influence of the right-wing leaders will not allow themselves to be led out of the communist party into social-democracy, and that they will decide to break with the leaders of the right-wing fraction.

APPENDIX

THE EXECUTIVE COMMITTEE OF THE COMMUNIST INTERNATIONAL

THE presidium elected by the third enlarged plenary session of the ECCI in June 1923 and announced at the time consisted of: Zinoviev, Zetkin, Bukharin, Radek, Terracini, Kolarov, Katayama, Kuusinen, Neurath, Souvarine, MacManus, Shatskin, and one representative of the Scandinavian countries. The secretariat consisted of Kolarov, Piatnitsky, and Neurath, with Kuusinen, Rakosi, and Brand as deputies. *Desiat Let Kominterna* gives Smeral instead of Neurath, Bordiga instead of Terracini, and Schüller instead of Shatskin, and adds Neurath, Terracini, and Stewart as deputies. The secretariat is given as Kolarov, Kuusinen, Piatnitsky, and Rakosi, and the first three of these, together with MacManus, Terracini, Schüller, and Souvarine, formed the orgbureau.

At the fifth Comintern congress the election commission appointed by the presidium agreed on a list of 44 members of the ECCI and 26 candidate members. Their election and the election of Zinoviev as president, was unanimously endorsed by the congress.

Austria: Fiala
United States: Foster, Ruthenberg; candidate, Dunne
Britain: Pollitt, MacManus; candidates, Stewart, Gallacher
Belgium: Jacquemotte
Bulgaria: Kolarov; candidate, Dimitrov
Germany: Geschke, Schlecht, Rosenberg; candidates, Robert, Fischer, Thaelmann
Holland: Wijnkoop
Yugoslavia: Boskovic, Marinovic; candidate, Simic
India: Roy
Ireland: candidate, Larkin
Italy: Bordiga, Ercoli; candidates, Marco, Rienzi, Maffi
China: Chen Tu-hsiu
Norway: Schefflo; candidate, Hansen
Poland: Grzegorzewski; candidates, Bogutski, Nedobitny
Russia: Zinoviev, Bukharin, Stalin, Kamenev, Rykov; candidates, Sokolnikov, Trotsky, Lozovsky, Piatnitsky
Rumania: Christescu
Ukraine: Manuilsky, Frunze
Finland and Baltic States: Kuusinen; candidate, Mitskiewicz
France: Semard, Treint, Sellier; candidates, Guye, Jeramme, Girault, Doriot
Czechoslovakia: Neurath, Smeral, Muna; candidates, Vercik, Dobrovolny, Zapotocky
Sweden: Höglund, Kilbom; candidate, Samuelson
Java: Semaoen

Japan: Katayama
Latin America: Penelon
Spain: Perez Solis (also given as Oscar Persolis)
Klara Zetkin was elected as an individual member, Bela Kun as an individual
candidate member.

This list, reproduced from the report of the congress proceedings, gives 41
members and 29 candidates; *Desiat Let Kominterna* gives a slightly different list;
Boscovic and Marinovic do not appear as members, but Vuyovich, Schüller,
Hessen, Filipovic, and Katslerovich do; it omits the names of Robert (alias
for Volk), Simic, Sokolnikov, Guye (probably a misprint for Guy Jeramme)
and Marco from the candidates, and adds Maslow, Scoccimarro, Petrov, and
Markovic, making 44 members and 28 candidates.

The International Control Commission, also put forward by the presidium
and endorsed unanimously, consisted of Murphy, Browder, Astrogilado (Brazil),
König, Lauersen (Denmark), Gennari, Stuchka, Angareitis, Prukhniak, Solts,
Felix Kon, Cachin, Kreibich, Kabakchiev, Pogelman, Stirner (Mexico), and
Mejid (Turkey); in *Desiat Let Kominterna* the Turkish member's name is given
as Shafik.

The presidium elected by the ECCI after the congress consisted of: Zinoviev,
Bukharin, Stalin, MacManus, Pollitt, Thaelmann, Geschke, Ercoli, Manuilsky,
Smeral, Semard, Schefflo, Kuusinen, Kolarov, Katayama, Vuyovich; the
candidate members were Kamenev, Rykov, Sokolnikov, Fischer, Schlecht,
Rienzi, Frunze, Neurath, Muna, Treint, Hansen, Zetkin, Roy, Hessen, and one
representative of the American Workers' Party. The names of Roy and Hessen
are omitted from the list published in *Desiat Let Kominterna*, where Pollitt is given
as a candidate member.

The secretariat consisted of Kuusinen, Geschke, Piatnitsky, Treint, Humbert-
Droz, with MacManus and Neurath as candidates; the orgbureau of the five
secretariat members plus Schüller, Bogutski, Dunne, Mitskiewicz, MacManus,
Kun, Petrov, and one representative each from the Czech and Italian parties.

The fifth ECCI plenum, meeting in March 1925, does not appear to have
published the list of members appointed to the presidium; the twelve members
of the orgbureau are given as: Kuusinen, Geschke, Piatnitsky, Humbert-Droz,
Treint, Schüller, Bogutski, Dunne, Matskewicz, MacManus, Kun, and Petrov.
The secretariat consisted of Kuusinen, Piatnitsky, Treint, Katz, Humbert-Droz,
Neurath, and Kornblum.

At the sixth ECCI plenum a year later the following were elected to the
presidium: Zinoviev, Bukharin, Stalin, Manuilsky, Thaelmann, Remmele,
Semard, Treint, Ercoli, Ferguson, Kuusinen, Katayama, Chen Ho-sian (given
elsewhere as Su-Fan), Roy, Kilbom, Kolarov, Ruthenberg, Zetkin, Lozovsky;
the candidates were Dimitrov, Boskovic, Bogutski, and Bedacht; the record
published at the time of the plenum gives, in addition to these names, Smeral
and Lominadze as members, and Vuyovich as candidate member.

There is agreement about the composition of the secretariat and the orgbureau. The first consisted of Geschke, Jacob, Ercoli, Ferguson, Smeral, Kuusinen, Humbert-Droz, Roy, Piatnitsky, Kornblum, and Petrov, with Dimitrov

and Pepper as candidates; the second of the secretariat members with the exception of Jacob and Kornblum and the addition of Manuilsky, Treint, and Dimitrov.

The seventh plenum elected to the presidium: Bukharin, Gallacher, Haken, Duncan, Katayama, Cremet, Kolarov, Kuusinen, Lozovsky, Manuilsky, Murphy, Prukhniak, Remmele, Roy, Ruthenberg, Semard, Semaoen, Sillen, Stalin, Tan Ping-shan, Thaelmann, Zetkin, Shatskin, Smeral, and Ercoli; the candidate members were Bogutski, Geschke, Codovilla, Kun, Maggi, Molotov, Piatnitsky, Treint, Schüller, and Humbert-Droz; *Desiat Let Kominterna* gives Gennari instead of Maggi. The secretariat consisted of Bukharin, Cremet, Kuusinen, Manuilsky, Piatnitsky, Remmele, Roy, Smeral, and Ercoli, with Lozovsky, Molotov, Murphy, and Humbert-Droz as candidate members.

After the eighth ECCI plenum Bernard replaced Cremet on the presidium, and Maggi replaced Ercoli, who became a candidate member. On the secretariat Barbé, Gallacher, and Maggi replaced Bernard, Murphy, and Ercoli.

The 27 presidium members appointed by the ninth plenum were: Foster, Engdahl, Thaelmann, Remmele, Gallacher, Murphy, Kolarov, Hsiang, Roy, Katayama, Semaoen, Kuusinen, Semard, Barbé, Humbert-Droz, Ercoli, Maggi, Prukhniak, Kilbom, Bukharin, Stalin, Jilek, Smeral, Manuilsky, Zetkin, Shatskin, Lozovsky; the candidates were: Weinstein, Perman, Piatnitsky, Molotov, Kun, Schüller, Bennett (Petrovsky), Arnot, Geschke.

The sixth Comintern congress elected an Executive Committee of 59 members and 43 candidate members. The names marked with an asterisk were elected to the presidium, those with a dagger as presidium candidates.

Brazil: Amerigo Ledo
France: Barbé,* Semard,* Thorez; candidates, Doriot, Monmousseau, Frachon
Britain: Bell,* Campbell; candidates, Pollitt,† Horner
Yugoslavia: Boskovic; candidate, Boznic
USSR: Bukharin,* Lozovsky,* Manuilsky,* Molotov,* Piatnitsky,* Rykov, Skrypnik, Stalin;* candidates, Gopner, Gusev, Moirova, Yaroslavsky
Switzerland: Wieser
Argentine: Ghioldi
Uruguay: Gomez
Czechoslovakia: Gottwald, Jilek,* Smeral;* candidates, Vercik, Zapotocky, Reimann
Germany: Dengel, Pieck, Remmele,* Thaelmann;* candidates, Heckert,† Ulbricht, Schneller, Ewert
Holland: candidate, de Visser
Belgium: Jacquemotte
Mexico: Carillo
Japan: Kato;* candidate, Asano (Watanabe)
Bulgaria: Kolarov;* candidate, Dimitrov
Hungary: Kun*
Austria: Koplenig
Poland: Lenski,† Prukhniak;* candidates, Lovitski, Purmann,† Sokolik

China: Li Kwang, Hsiang, Tsiu Vito;* candidates, Chang Piao,† Chen Kwang
U.S.A.: Lovestone, Foster;† candidates, Gitlow,* Huiswood
Finland: Manner
Baltic: Mitskiewicz
Indonesia: Musso;* candidate, Darsono
Rumania: Popescu
Sweden: Samuelson, Kilbom;* candidate, Sillen
Italy: Serra,* Ercoli;* candidates, Garlandi, Turni
Greece: Syphneios
Canada: Spector
Turkey: Ferdi
Chile: Fermín-Araja
Norway: Furubotn; candidate, Hansen†
India: Chatterji; candidate, Maoroji
Australia: candidate, Kavanagh
Cuba: candidate, Lopez
S. Africa: candidate, Maloka
Spain: candidate, Pascal
Colombia ⎫
Ecuador ⎭ : candidate, Riasco Giulio
Denmark: candidate, Thogersen
Egypt ⎫
Palestine ⎬ : candidate, Shauki
Syria ⎭
Y.C.I.: Blenkle, Rust,† Khitarov;* candidates, Billoux, Hwan Li
Personal: Katayama,* Kuusinen,* Zetkin,* Humbert-Droz;* candidate, Varga

One source also gives Rosso and Milkovic as candidate members of the presidium, although their names are not given among the Executive.

The International Control Commission consisted of: Angareitis, Anwelt, Cachin, Codovilla, Eberlein, Flieg, Gorkic, Hsiu Yen, Iskrov, Kon, Maggi, Mondok, Murphy, Shargi, Sirola, Solts, Stefanescu, Stuchka, Cheng Chen, Weiss, Weinstone, Tskhakaya.

The presidium, meeting on 5 September 1928, appointed to the political secretariat: Barbé, Bell, Bukharin, Kuusinen, Molotov, Piatnitsky, Remmele, Serra, Tsiu Vito, Smeral, and Humbert-Droz; the candidates were Manuilsky, Lozovsky, and Khitarov.

SOURCES

Full title   *Abbreviated title*

Bell, T., *The British Communist Party*. London, 1937

Bericht der Exekutive der Kommunistischen Internationale: 15. Dezember   Bericht der Exekutive
1922–15. Mai 1923. Moscow, 1923

Bericht über die Tätigkeit der Exekutive der Kommunistischen Internationale vom IV. bis V. Weltkongress. Hamburg, 1924

Bericht über die Verhandlungen des IX. Parteitages der KPD. Berlin, 1924

Bericht über die Verhandlungen des 10. Parteitages der KPD. Berlin, 1926

Beschlüsse und Resolutionen angenommen von der 2. Orgkonferenz der Erw. Exekutive und bestätigt vom Orgbüro des EKKI am 26. März 1926. Hamburg, 1926

Blumberger, J. T. P., *Le Communisme aux Indes Néerlandaises*. Paris, 1929

Borkenau, F., *The Communist International*. London, 1938

Brandt, C., *Stalin's Failure in China 1924–1927*. Harvard, 1958

Brandt, C., Schwartz, B., Fairbank, J. K., *A Documentary History of Chinese Communism*. London, 1952

Bukharin, N., *Itogi Plenuma IKKI: Doklad 4 iuna 1927*. Moscow, 1927

Carr, E. H., *The Interregnum 1923/1924*. London, 1954

XIV S'ezd Vsesoyuznoi Kommunisticheskoi Partii. Moscow, 1926

Chiang Kai-shek, *Declaration to Kuomintang Members April 1927*. Shanghai, 1927

Die chinesische Frage auf dem 8. Plenum der Exekutive der Kommunistischen Internationale, Mai 1927. Hamburg, 1928

Communist Papers. Documents selected from those obtained on the arrest of   Cmd. 2682
the communist leaders on the 14th and 21st October 1925. Cmd. 2682. London, 1926

Communist Policy in Great Britain: The Report of the British Commission of the Ninth Plenum of the Comintern. London, 1928

The Communist Position on the Negro Question. New York, n.d. [1929]   The Negro Question

Desiat Let Kominterna v Resheniyakh i Tsifrakh, ed. by A. Tivel and M. Kheimo. Moscow, 1929

Deutscher, I., *The Prophet Unarmed*. London, 1959

Draper, T., *The Roots of American Communism*. New York, 1957

Ein Jahr Arbeit und Kampf. Tätigkeitsbericht der Exekutive der KI 1925–26. Hamburg, 1926

Erweiterte Exekutive (Februar–März 1926): Thesen und Resolutionen.   Thesen und Resolutionen, VI. Plenum
Hamburg, n.d. [1926]

Eudin, X. J., and Fisher, H. H., *Soviet Russia and the West 1920–1927*. Stanford, 1957

Eudin, X. J., and North, R. C., *Soviet Russia and the East 1920–1927*. Stanford, 1957

Fischer, R., *Stalin and German Communism*. Harvard, 1948

Flechtheim, O. K., *Die KPD in der Weimarer Republik*. Offenbach a.M., 1948

Hu Chiao-mu, *Thirty Years of the CP of China*. Peking, 1951

IKKI i VKP(b) po kitaiskomu voprosu (osnovnye resheniya). Moscow,   IKKI i VKP(b) po
1927   Kitaiskomu Voprosu

Full title	Abbreviated title
Internationale Presse-Korrespondenz (September 1921–). German edition of ECCI periodical, Berlin	*Inprekorr*
Isaacs, H. R., *The Tragedy of the Chinese Revolution*. London, 1938	
Der Kampf um die Kommunistische Internationale: Dokumente der russischen Opposition nicht veröffentlicht vom Stalin'schen ZK. Berlin [1928]	
Kara-Murza, T., *Strategiya i Taktika Kominterna v Natsionalno-Kolonialnoi Revoliutsii na primere kitaya*. Ed. by P. Mif. Moscow, 1934	*Strategiya i Taktika Kominterna*
K.I. pered shestym vsemirnym kongressom. Moscow, 1928	
Die Komintern vor dem 6. Weltkongress. Tätigkeitsbericht der Exekutive der Kommunistischen Internationale für die Zeit vom 5. bis zum 6. Weltkongress. Hamburg, 1928	
Kommunisticheskii Internatsional (May 1919–). Periodical publication of the ECCI. Moscow	
Kommunisticheskii Internatsional v Dokumentakh, ed. B. Kun. Moscow, 1933	*K. I. v Dokumentakh*
KPSS v rezoliutsiyakh i resheniyakh s'ezdov, konferentsii, i plenumov TsK. 2 vols. Moscow, 1953	
Laqueur, W. Z., *Communism and Nationalism in the Middle East*. London, 1956	
Die Lehren der deutschen Ereignisse: Das Präsidium des Exekutivkomitees der Kommunistischen Internationale zur deutschen Frage Januar 1924. Hamburg 1924	*Die Lehren der deutschen Ereignisse*
Mandalian, T., *Rabochee dvizhenie kitaya*. Moscow, 1928	
Mif, P., *Heroic China. Fifteen Years of the Communist Party of China*. New York, 1937	
Murphy, J. T., *New Horizons*. London, 1941	
Neuntes Plenum des EKKI (Februar 1928). Resolutionen und Beschlüsse. Hamburg, 1928	*Resolutionen und Beschlüsse, IX. Plenum*
North, R. C., *Moscow and Chinese Communists*. Stanford, 1953	
Overstreet, G. D., and Windmiller, M., *Communism in India*. University of California Press, 1959	
Pelling, H., *The British Communist Party*. London, 1958	
Proceedings of the Meerut Conspiracy Case: In the Court of R. Milner White, 19 July 1929. Meerut, 1929	*Meerut Trial*
Programmnye Dokumenty Kommunisticheskikh Partii Vostoka. Ed. by L. Magyar, P. Mif, M. Orakhelashvili, G. Safarov. Moscow, 1934	
Protokoll der Konferenz der Erweiterten Exekutive der Kommunistischen Internationale, Moskau, 12–23. Juni, 1923. Hamburg, 1923	
Protokoll: Erweiterte Exekutive der Kommunistischen Internationale, Moskau, 21. März–6. April 1925. Hamburg, 1925	
Protokoll: Erweiterte Exekutive der Kommunistischen Internationale, Moskau, 17. Februar bis 15. März 1926. Hamburg, n.d. [1926]	
Protokoll der Erweiterten Exekutive der Kommunistischen Internationale, 22. November–13. Dezember 1926. Hamburg, 1927	*Protokoll, VII. Plenum*
Protokoll: Fünfter Kongress der Kommunistischen Internationale. 2 vols. Hamburg, n.d. [1924]	*Protokoll, v.*
Protokoll des 6. Weltkongresses der Kommunistischen Internationale, Juli–September 1928. 4 vols. Hamburg, 1928	*Protokoll, vi.*
Puti Mirovoi Revoliutsii. Sedmoi Rasshirenny Plenum Ispolnitelnovo Komiteta Kommunisticheskovo Internatsionala 22 Noyabrya—16 Dekabrya 1926. Stenograficheskii Otchet. 2 vols. Moscow, 1927	*Puti Mirovoi Revoliutsii*

Full title	Abbreviated title

Record, W., *The Negro and the Communist Party*. University of North Carolina Press, 1951

Rothschild, Joseph, *The Communist Party of Bulgaria*. New York, 1959

Schevenels, Walther, *Forty-five Years: International Federation of Trade Unions 1901–1945*. Brussels, [1957]

Schwartz, B. I., *Chinese Communism and the Rise of Mao*. Harvard, 1951

Serge, V., *From Lenin to Stalin*. London, 1937

Spratt, P., *Blowing up India*. Calcutta, 1955

Stalin, J., *Works*. Moscow, 1952–

Swearingen, R., and Langer, P., *Red Flag in Japan*. Harvard, 1952

Tätigkeitsbericht der Exekutive der Kommunistischen Internationale, Februar bis November 1926. Hamburg, 1926

Thalheimer, A., *1923: Eine verpasste Revolution?* Berlin, 1931

Thesen und Resolutionen des V. Weltkongresses der Kommunistischen Internationale, Moskau, vom 17 Juni bis 8 Juli 1924. Hamburg, 1924   *Thesen und Resolutionen, v.*

Trotsky, L., *The Lessons of October 1917*. London, 1925

— *The Real Situation in Russia*. London, 1928

— *Problems of the Chinese Revolution*. New York, 1932

— *The Revolution Betrayed*. London, 1936

— *The Third International after Lenin*. New York, 1936

— *Stalin*. New York, 1941

— *Die internationale Revolution und die Kommunistische Internationale*. Berlin, 1929

Trinadtsaty s'ezd rossiiskoi Kommunisticheskoi Partii. Moscow, 1924

Über die Bolschewisierung der Parteien der Kommunistischen Internationale. Thesen, einstimmig angenommen von der Erweiterten Exekutive der Komintern. Moskau, März/April 1925. Berlin, 1925

La Verité sur la Chine. La Lettre de Shanghai: Document inédit caché par Staline. Paris, [1928?]

Voprosy kitaiskoi revoliutsii. Moscow, 1927

VIII Plenum ispolnitelnovo komiteta Kommunisticheskovo Internatsionala 18–30 Maya 1927. Tezisy, rezoliutsii i vozzvaniya. Moscow, 1927   *VIII Plenum: Tezisy*

Walter, G., *Histoire du Parti Communiste Français*. Paris, 1948

Whiting, A. S., *Soviet Policies in China 1917–1924*. Columbia University Press, 1954

Wilbur, C. M., and How, J. L., *Documents on Communism, Nationalism, and Soviet Advisers in China 1918–1927*. Columbia University Press, 1957

INDEX